T0202947

Communications
in Computer and Information Science 1537

Emmanouel Garoufallou ·
María-Antonia Ovalle-Perandones ·
Andreas Vlachidis (Eds.)

Metadata and Semantic Research

15th International Conference, MTSR 2021
Virtual Event, November 29 – December 3, 2021
Revised Selected Papers

Editors
Emmanouel Garoufallou (iD)
International Hellenic University
Thessaloniki, Greece

María-Antonia Ovalle-Perandones (iD)
Complutense University of Madrid
Madrid, Spain

Andreas Vlachidis (iD)
University College London
London, UK

ISSN 1865-0929   ISSN 1865-0937 (electronic)
Communications in Computer and Information Science
ISBN 978-3-030-98875-3   ISBN 978-3-030-98876-0 (eBook)
https://doi.org/10.1007/978-3-030-98876-0

This Springer imprint is published by the registered company Springer Nature Switzerland AG
The registered company address is: Gewerbestrasse 11, 6330 Cham, Switzerland

Preface

Metadata and semantics are integral to any information system and important to the sphere of Web of Data, Semantic Web, and Linked Data. Research and development addressing metadata and semantics is crucial to advancing how we effectively discover, use, archive, and repurpose information. In response to this need, researchers are actively examining methods for generating, reusing, and interchanging metadata. Integrated with these developments is research on the application of computational methods, linked data, and data analytics. A growing body of literature also targets conceptual and theoretical designs providing foundational frameworks for metadata, knowledge organization, and semantic applications. There is no doubt that metadata weaves its way through nearly every aspect of our information ecosystem, and there is great motivation for advancing the current state of understanding in the fields of metadata and semantics. To this end, it is vital that scholars and practitioners convene and share their work and research findings.

Since 2005, the International Metadata and Semantics Research Conference (MTSR) has served as a significant venue for the dissemination and sharing of metadata and semantic-driven research and practices. This year marked the 15th edition of MTSR, drawing scholars, researchers, and practitioners who are investigating and advancing our knowledge on a wide range of metadata and semantic-driven topics. The 15th International Conference on Metadata and Semantics Research (MTSR 2021) was organized by the Complutense University of Madrid, Spain, taking place between November 29 and December 3, 2021. Due to the COVID-19 pandemic, and taking into account all the available information and ongoing uncertainties and our concerns about the health and wellbeing of our community, the MTSR 2021 Organizing Committees decided to organize MTSR 2021 as an online conference. The MTSR 2021 Chairs, Organizing Committees, and Steering Committee adapted to an unprecedented situation and worked together to adjust the organizational structure of the conference to the current pandemic circumstances.

The MTSR conference series has grown in terms of the number of participants and paper submission rates over the past decade, marking it as a leading international research conference. Continuing the successful legacy of previous MTSR conferences, MTSR 2021 brought together scholars and practitioners who share a common interest in the interdisciplinary field of metadata, linked data, and ontologies. In total, 147 professionals from 41 countries registered for the MTSR 2021 online conference.

The MTSR 2021 program and the proceedings show a rich diversity of research and practices from metadata and semantically focused tools and technologies to linked data, cross-language semantics, ontologies, metadata models, semantic systems, and meta-data standards. The general session of the conference included 13 papers covering a broad spectrum of topics, proving the interdisciplinary view of metadata. The benefits and challenges of making data findable, accessible, interoperable, and reusable (FAIR) across domains and disciplines have been recognized and the opportunities for reuse, repurpose, and redeployment of data using semantic technologies have been verified. Recent advances on neural networks, natural language processing, and knowledge graphs have been presented, promoting innovations and methods for topic modeling, semantic annotation, and automatic metadata generation.

Metadata as a research topic is maturing, and the conference supported the following eight tracks: Digital Libraries, Information Retrieval, Big, Linked, Social, and Open Data; Agriculture, Food, and Environment; Open Repositories, Research Information Systems, and Data Infrastructures; Digital Humanities and Digital Curation; Cultural Collections and Applications; European and National Projects; Knowledge IT Artifacts in Professional Communities and Aggregations; and Metadata, Identifiers, and Semantics in Decentralized Applications, Blockchains, and P2P Systems.

Each of these tracks had a rich selection of short and full research papers, in total 21, giving broader diversity to MTSR, and enabling deeper exploration of significant topics. MTSR 2021 also brought together researchers, scholars, practitioners, educators, and information professionals coming from libraries, archives, museums, cultural heritage institutions, and organizations from the educational sector (DOAbLE).

All the papers underwent a thorough and rigorous peer-review process, with two to five reviewers assigned to each paper. The review and selection for this year was highly competitive, and only papers containing significant research results, innovative methods, or novel and best practices were accepted for publication. From the general session, only 12 submissions were accepted as full research papers, representing 25% of the total number of submissions, and one submission was accepted as a short paper. An additional 15 contributions from tracks covering noteworthy and important results were accepted as full research papers, representing 44.1% of the total number of submissions, and six were accepted as short papers, bringing the total of MTSR 2021 accepted contributions to 34. The acceptance rate of full research papers for both the general session and tracks was 32.9% of the total number of submissions.

The Complutense University of Madrid was founded by Cardinal Cisneros because of the "Inter cetera" Papal Bull granted by Pope Alexander VI on April 13, 1499. Nowadays the Complutense University of Madrid has three main objectives: to educate professionals who will be useful for society, to foster scientific research, and to disseminate knowledge and the intrinsic values of the university. A wide range of degrees is offered to meet the expectations of intellectual, economic, and scientific demands. The Department of Library and Information Science at the Faculty of Documentation Sciences, which was the School of Library and Information Science before 2006, has the following research lines: society and library; information policies, information and communication technologies (ICT), and scientific communication; management, assessment, and administration in information science units; and photo documentation.

MTSR 2021 was pleased to host a remarkable keynote presentation by Marcia Lei Zeng, a Professor of Information Science at Kent State University, USA. In her presentation "Semantic Enrichment of LAM Data to Support Digital Humanities", Marcia addressed the field of digital humanities (DH) and the impact on libraries, archives, and museums (LAMs): "The field of digital humanities (DH) has advanced tremendously over the last decade and continues to expand. The demands for smarter and bigger historical and cultural heritage data, which usually cannot be obtained through web crawling or scraping, have directed attention toward the data provided by libraries, archives, and museums (LAMs). In order to enhance LAM data's quality and discover-ability while enabling a self-sustaining ecosystem, "semantic enrichment" has become an increasingly used strategy for LAMs during recent years, representing a major step in enhancing existing LAM data through semantic technologies." Marcia presented a framework for approaches used in semantic enrichment that can be applied to LAM data at various levels. She focused on structured and semi-structured data, with additional discussions on turning unstructured data into structured data, with the aim of maximizing LAM data's discoverability, use- and reuse-ability, and their value in the mainstream of DH and Semantic Web.

We conclude this preface by thanking the many people who contributed their time and efforts to MTSR 2021 and made this year's conference possible despite the unforeseen obstacles caused by COVID-19. We also thank all the organizations that supported this conference. We thank all the institutions and universities that co-organized MTSR 2021. We extend our sincere gratitude to the members of the Program Committees (both main and special tracks), the Steering Committee, and the Organizing Committees (both general and local), to all the special track chairs, and to the conference reviewers who invested their time generously to ensure the timely review of the submitted manuscripts. A special thanks to keynote speaker Marcia Lei Zeng. Also a special thank you to Anxhela Dani, Vasiliki Georgiadi, Chrysanthi Chatzopoulou, Chrysanthi Theodoridou, and Ilias Nitsos for supporting us throughout this event, to Anxhela Dani and Vasiliki Georgiadi who assisted us with the preparation of this proceedings and the Book of Abstracts, and to Vasiliki, Nikoleta, and Stavroula for their endless support and patience. Our thanks go to our best paper and best student paper sponsor euroCRIS. Finally, our deepest thanks go to all the authors and participants of MTSR 2021 for making the event a great success.

December 2021   Emmanouel Garoufallou
                                              María-Antonia Ovalle-Perandones
                                                        Andreas Vlachidis

Organization

General Chair

Emmanouel Garoufallou   International Hellenic University, Greece

Chair for MTSR 2021

María-Antonia Ovalle-Perandones   Complutense University of Madrid, Spain

Program Chair

Andreas Vlachidis   University College London, UK

Special Track Chairs

Miguel-Ángel Sicilia	University of Alcalá, Spain
Francesca Fallucchi	Guglielmo Marconi University, Italy
Riem Spielhaus	Georg Eckert Institute – Leibniz Institute for Educational Media, Germany
Ernesto William De Luca	Georg Eckert Institute – Leibniz Institute for Educational Media, Germany
Armando Stellato	University of Rome Tor Vergata, Italy
Nikos Houssos	IRI, Greece
Michalis Sfakakis	Ionian University, Greece
Lina Bountouri	Publications Office of the European Union, Luxembourg
Emmanouel Garoufallou	International Hellenic University, Greece
Jane Greenberg	Drexel University, USA
R. J. Hartley	Manchester Metropolitan University, UK
Stavroula Antonopoulou	Perrotis College, American Farm School, Greece
Rob Davies	Cyprus University of Technology, Cyprus
Fabio Sartori	University of Milano-Bicocca, Italy
Angela Locoro	Università Carlo Cattaneo - LIUC, Italy
Arlindo Flavio da Conceição	Federal University of São Paulo, Brazil
Rania Siatri	International Hellenic University, Greece

Steering Committee

Juan Manuel Dodero	University of Cádiz, Spain
Emmanouel Garoufallou	International Hellenic University, Greece

Nikos Manouselis	AgroKnow, Greece
Fabio Santori	Università degli Studi di Milano-Bicocca, Italy
Miguel-Ángel Sicilia	University of Alcalá, Spain

Local Organizing Committee

Michela Montesi	Complutense University of Madrid, Spain
Isabel Villaseñor-Rodríguez	Complutense University of Madrid, Spain
Patricia-Gema Acevedo-Zarco	Complutense University of Madrid, Spain

Organizing Committee

Chrysanthi Chatzopoulou	European Publishing, Greece
Anxhela Dani	Hellenic Foundation for Culture, Greece
Vasiliki Georgiadi	International Hellenic University, Greece
Iro Sotiriadou	Perrotis College, American Farm School, Greece
Chrysanthi Theodoridou	International Hellenic University, Greece

Technical Support Staff

| Ilias Nitsos | International Hellenic University, Greece |

Program Committee

Trond Aalberg	Norwegian University of Science and Technology, Norway
Rajendra Akerkar	Western Norway Research Institute, Norway
Getaneh Alemu	Southampton Solent University, UK
Arif Altun	Hacettepe University, Turkey
Stavroula Antonopoulou	Perrotis College, American Farm School, Greece
Ioannis N. Athanasiadis	Wageningen University, The Netherlands
Sophie Aubin	Institut National de la Recherche Agronomique, France
Thomas Baker	Sungkyunkwan University, South Korea
Panos Balatsoukas	King's College London, UK
Wolf-Tilo Balke	TU Braunschweig, Germany
Tomaz Bartol	University of Ljubljana, Slovenia
José Alberto Benítez	University of León, Spain
Ina Bluemel	German National Library of Science and Technology, Germany
Lina Bountouri	Publications Office of the European Union, Luxembourg
Derek Bousfield	Manchester Metropolitan University, UK

María Poveda-Villalón   Universidad Politécnica de Madrid, Spain
Marios Poulos   Ionian University, Greece
T. V. Prabhakar   Indian Institute of Technology, Kanpur, India
Aurelio Ravarini   Università Carlo Cattaneo – LIUC, Italy
Maria Cláudia Reis Cavalcanti   Military Institute of Engineering, Brazil
Cristina Ribeiro   INESC TEC, University of Porto, Portugal
Eva Mendez Rodriguez   Universidad Carlos III of Madrid, Spain
Dimitris Rousidis   International Hellenic University, Greece
Athena Salaba   Kent State University, USA
Salvador Sánchez-Alonso   University of Alcalá, Spain
Ricardo Santos-Muñoz   Spanish National Library, Spain
Fabio Sartori   University of Milano-Bicocca, Italy
Noemi Scarpato   San Raffaele Roma Open University, Italy
Christian Scheel   Georg Eckert Institute – Leibniz Institute for
        Educational Media, Germany
Jochen Schirrwagen   University of Bielefeld, Germany
Birgit Schmidt   University of Göttingen, Germany
Joachim Schöpfel   University of Lille, France
Michalis Sfakakis   Ionian University, Greece
Cleo Sgouropoulou   University of West Attica, Greece
Kathleen Shearer   Confederation of Open Access Repositories,
        Germany
Rania Siatri   International Hellenic University, Greece
Miguel-Ángel Sicilia   University of Alcalá, Spain
Carla Simone   University of Siegen, Germany
Flávio Soares Corrêa da Silva   University of São Paulo, Brazil
Ahmet Soylu   Norwegian University of Science and Technology,
        Norway
Riem Spielhaus   Georg Eckert Institute – Leibniz Institute for
        Educational Media, Germany
Lena-Luise Stahn   CeDiS - Freie Universität Berlin, Germany
Armando Stellato   University of Rome Tor Vergata, Italy
Imma Subirats   Food and Agriculture Organization (FAO) of the
        United Nations, Italy
Shigeo Sugimoto   University of Tsukuba, Japan
Maguelonne Teisseire   Irstea Montpellier, France
Jan Top   Wageningen Food & Biobased Research,
        The Netherlands
Robert Trypuz   John Paul II Catholic University of Lublin, Poland
Giannis Tsakonas   University of Patras, Greece
Chrisa Tsinaraki   Joint Research Centre, European Commission,
        Italy
Andrea Turbati   University of Rome Tor Vergata, Italy

Yannis Tzitzikas	University of Crete and ICS-FORTH, Greece
Christine Urquhart	Aberystwyth University, UK
Evgenia Vassilakaki	National Library of Greece, Greece
Sirje Virkus	Tallinn University, Estonia
Andreas Vlachidis	University College London, UK
Zhong Wang	Sun Yat-sen University, China
Katherine Wisser	Graduate School of Library and Information Science, Simmons College, USA
Georgia Zafeiriou	University of Macedonia, Greece
Cecilia Zanni-Merk	INSA Rouen Normandie, France
Fabio Massimo Zanzotto	University of Rome Tor Vergata, Italy
Marcia Zeng	Kent State University, USA
Marios Zervas	Cyprus University of Technology, Cyprus
Thomas Zschocke	World Agroforestry Centre (ICRAF), Kenya
Maja Žumer	University of Ljubljana, Slovenia

Track on Metadata and Semantics for Digital Libraries, Information Retrieval, Big, Linked, Social, and Open Data

Track Chairs

Emmanouel Garoufallou	International Hellenic University, Greece
Jane Greenberg	Drexel University, USA
Rania Siatri	International Hellenic University, Greece

Program Committee

Panos Balatsoukas	Loughborough University, UK
Ozgu Can	Ege University, Turkey
Sissi Closs	Karlsruhe University of Applied Sciences, Germany
Mike Conway	University of North Carolina at Chapel Hill, USA
Phil Couch	University of Manchester, UK
Milena Dobreva	University of Malta, Malta
Ali Emrouznejad	Aston University, UK
Panorea Gaitanou	Ionian University, Greece
Jane Greenberg	Drexel University, USA
R. J. Hartley	Manchester Metropolitan University, UK
Nikos Korfiatis	University of East Anglia, UK
Rebecca Koskela	University of New Mexico, USA
Dimitris Rousidis	International Hellenic University, Greece
Athena Salaba	Kent State University, USA
Miguel-Angel Sicilia	University of Alcala, Spain

Christine Urquhart	Aberystwyth University, UK
Evgenia Vassilakaki	National Library of Greece, Greece
Sirje Virkus	Tallinn University, Estonia
Georgia Zafeiriou	University of Macedonia, Greece
Marios Zervas	Cyprus University of Technology, Cyprus

Track on Metadata and Semantics for Agriculture, Food, and Environment (AgroSEM 2021)

Track Chair

Miguel-Angel Sicilia	University of Alcala, Spain

Program Committee

Ioannis Athanasiadis	Wageningen University, The Netherlands
Patrice Buche	INRAE, France
Caterina Caracciolo	Food and Agriculture Organization (FAO) of the United Nations, Italy
Stasinos Konstantopoulos	NCSR "Demokritos", Greece
Claire Nédellec	INRAE, France
Ivo Pierozzi	Embrapa, Brazil
Armando Stellato	University of Rome Tor Vergata, Italy
Maguelonne Teisseire	Irstea Montpellier, France
Jan Top	Wageningen Food & Biobased Research, The Netherlands
Robert Trypuz	John Paul II Catholic University of Lublin, Poland

Track on Metadata and Semantics for Open Repositories, Research Information Systems, and Data Infrastructures

Track Chairs

Nikos Houssos	RedLink, Greece
Armando Stellato	University of Rome Tor Vergata, Italy

Honorary Track Chair

Imma Subirats	Food and Agriculture Organization of the United Nations, Italy

Program Committee

Sophie Aubin	Institut National de la Recherche Agronomique, France
Gordon Dunshire	University of Strathclyde, UK

Jan Dvorak	Charles University of Prague, Czech Republic
Jane Greenberg	Drexel University, USA
Siddeswara Guru	University of Queensland, Australia
Keith Jeffery	Keith G Jeffery Consultants, UK
Nikolaos Konstantinou	University of Manchester, UK
Rebecca Koskela	University of New Mexico, USA
Jessica Lindholm	Malmö University, Sweden
Paolo Manghi	Institute of Information Science and Technologies, National Research Council (ISTI-CNR), Italy
Brian Matthews	Science and Technology Facilities Council, UK
Eva Mendez Rodriguez	University Carlos III of Madrid, Spain
Joachim Schöpfel	University of Lille, France
Kathleen Shearer	Confederation of Open Access Repositories, Germany
Jochen Schirrwagen	University of Bielefeld, Germany
Birgit Schmidt	University of Göttingen, Germany
Chrisa Tsinaraki	European Commission, Joint Research Centre, Italy
Yannis Tzitzikas	University of Crete and ICS-FORTH, Greece
Zhong Wang	Sun Yat-sen University, China
Marcia Zeng	Kent State University, USA

Track on Metadata and Semantics for Digital Humanities and Digital Curation (DHC 2021)

Track Chairs

Ernesto William De Luca	Georg Eckert Institute – Leibniz Institute for Educational Media, Germany
Francesca Fallucchi	Guglielmo Marconi University, Italy
Riem Spielhaus	Georg Eckert Institute – Leibniz Institute for Educational Media, Germany

Program Committee

Maret Nieländer	Georg Eckert Institute – Leibniz Institute for Educational Media, Germany
Elena Gonzalez-Blanco	Universidad Nacional de Educación a Distancia, Spain
Steffen Hennicke	Georg Eckert Institute – Leibniz-Institute for Educational Media, Germany
Ana Garcia-Serrano	ETSI Informatica - UNED, Spain
Philipp Mayr	GESIS, Germany

Noemi Scarpato	San Raffaele Roma Open University, Italy
Andrea Turbati	University of Rome Tor Vergata, Italy
Christian Scheel	Georg Eckert Institute – Leibniz Institute for Educational Media, Germany
Armando Stellato	University of Rome Tor Vergata, Italy
Wolf-Tilo Balke	TU Braunschweig, Germany
Andreas Lommatzsch	TU Berlin, Germany
Ivo Keller	TH Brandenburg, Germany
Gabriela Ossenbach	UNED, Spain
Francesca Fallucchi	Guglielmo Marconi University, Italy

Track on Metadata and Semantics for Cultural Collections and Applications

Track Chairs

Michalis Sfakakis	Ionian University, Greece
Lina Bountouri	Publications Office of the European Union, Luxembourg

Program Committee

Trond Aalberg	Oslo Metropolitan University, Norway
Enrico Francesconi	Publications Office of the European Union, Luxembourg, and National Research Council, Italy
Manolis Gergatsoulis	Ionian University, Greece
Antoine Isaac	Vrije Universiteit Amsterdam, The Netherlands
Sarantos Kapidakis	University of West Attica, Greece
Christos Papatheodorou	National and Kapodistrian University of Athens and Athena Research Centre, Greece
Chrisa Tsinaraki	Joint Research Centre, European Commission, Italy
Andreas Vlachidis	University College London, UK
Maja Žumer	University of Ljubljana, Slovenia

Track on Metadata and Semantics for European and National Projects

Track Chairs

R. J. Hartley	Manchester Metropolitan University, UK
Stavroula Antonopoulou	Perrotis College, American Farm School, Greece
Robert Davis	Cyprus University of Technology, Cyprus

Program Committee

Panos Balatsoukas	Loughborough University, UK
Mike Conway	University of North Carolina at Chapel Hill, USA
Emmanouel Garoufallou	International Hellenic University, Greece
Jane Greenberg	Drexel University, USA
Nikos Houssos	RedLink, Greece
Nikos Korfiatis	University of East Anglia, UK
Damiana Koutsomiha	Perrotis College, American Farm School, Greece
Paolo Manghi	Institute of Information Science and Technologies, National Research Council (ISTI-CNR), Italy
Dimitris Rousidis	International Hellenic University, Greece
Rania Siatri	International Hellenic University, Greece
Miguel-Angel Sicilia	University of Alcalá, Spain
Armando Stellato	University of Rome Tor Vergata, Italy
Sirje Virkus	Tallinn University, Estonia

Track on Knowledge IT Artifacts in Professional Communities and Aggregations (KITA 2021)

Track Chairs

Fabio Sartori	University of Milano-Bicocca, Italy
Angela Locoro	Università Carlo Cattaneo - LIUC, Italy
Arlindo Flavio da Conceição	Federal University of São Paulo, Brazil

Program Committee

Federico Cabitza	University of Milano-Bicocca, Italy
Riccardo Melen	University of Milano-Bicocca, Italy
Aurelio Ravarini	Università Carlo Cattaneo - LIUC, Italy
Carla Simone	University of Siegen, Germany
Flávio Soares Corrêa da Silva	University of São Paulo, Brazil
Cecilia Zanni-Merk	INSA Rouen Normandie, France

Track on Metadata, Identifiers, and Semantics in Decentralized Applications, Blockchains, and P2P systems

Track Chair

Miguel-Angel Sicilia	University of Alcalá, Spain

Program Committee

Sissi Closs	Karlsruhe University of Applied Sciences, Germany
Ernesto William De Luca	Georg Eckert Institute – Leibniz Institute for Educational Media, Germany
Juan Manuel Dodero	University of Cádiz, Spain
Francesca Fallucchi	Guglielmo Marconi University, Italy
Jane Greenberg	Drexel University, USA
Nikos Houssos	Sentio Solutions, Greece
Nikos Korfiatis	University of East Anglia, UK
Dimitris Rousidis	International Hellenic University, Greece
Salvador Sánchez-Alonso	University of Alcalá, Spain
Michalis Sfakakis	Ionian University, Greece
Rania Siatri	International Hellenic University, Greece
Armando Stellato	University of Rome Tor Vergata, Italy
Robert Trypuz	John Paul II Catholic University of Lublin, Poland
Sirje Virkus	Tallinn University, Estonia

Co-organized by

UNIVERSIDAD
COMPLUTENSE
MADRID

INFORMATION STUDIES

Celebrating 100 years

School of Information

LEIBNIZ INSTITUTE
FOR EDUCATIONAL MEDIA
|Georg Eckert Institute

DIPARTIMENTO DI
INFORMATICA, SISTEMISTICA E
COMUNICAZIONE

INTERNATIONAL
HELLENIC
UNIVERSITY

International Hellenic University

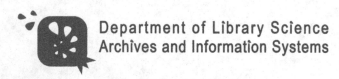

Department of Library Science
Archives and Information Systems

Department of Library Science Archives and Information Systems

Cyprus
University of
Technology

Awards Sponsored by

Contents

**Track on Knowledge IT Artifacts (KITA) and Decentralized
Applications, Blockchains and P2P Systems, and General Session**

Track on Digital Humanities and Digital Curation, and General Session

**Track on Digital Libraries, Information Retrieval, Big, Linked, Social
and Open Data**

Metadata, Linked Data, Semantics and Ontologies - General Session, and Track on Agriculture, Food and Environment

A Process Reverse Engineering Approach Using Process and Observation Ontology and Probabilistic Relational Models: Application to Processing of Bio-composites for Food Packaging

Mélanie Münch[1]([✉])[iD], Patrice Buche[1,2][iD], Cristina Manfredotti[3][iD], Pierre-Henri Wuillemin[4][iD], and Hélène Angellier-Coussy[1][iD]

[1] IATE, U. Montpellier, INRAE, CIRAD, Montpellier SupAgro, Montpellier, France
melanie.munch@gmail.com, patrice.buche@inrae.fr
[2] LIRMM, U. Montpellier, CNRS, INRIA GraphIK, Montpellier, France
[3] UMR MIA-Paris, AgroParisTech, INRAE, U. Paris-Saclay, Paris, France
cristina.manfredotti@agroparistech.fr
[4] Sorbonne Universites, UPMC, U. Paris 06, CNRS UMR, Paris LIP6, France
pierre-henri.wuillemin@lip6.fr

Abstract. Designing new processes for bio-based and biodegradable food packaging is an environmental and economic challenge. Due to the multiplicity of the parameters, such an issue requires an approach that proposes both (1) to integrate heterogeneous data sources and (2) to allow causal reasoning. In this article, we present POND (Process and observation ONtology Discovery), a workflow dedicated to answering expert queries on domains modeled by the Process and Observation Ontology (PO^2). The presentation is illustrated with a real-world application on bio-composites for food packaging to solve a reverse engineering problem, using a novel dataset composed of data from different projects.

Keywords: Ontology · Probabilistic model · Causality · Food packaging

1 Introduction

The massive amount of plastics used each year results in a constant accumulation of wastes in our environment, with harmful effects on our eco-systems and human health. Faced to the depletion of fossil resources and the increasing production of unrecovered organic residues (agricultural, urban, forestry and from agro-food industries), innovative technologies are developed for the production of bio-sourced, biodegradable and recyclable materials in order to increase the circularity of plastics. Among bio-polymers, poly(3-hydroxybutyrate-co-3-hydroxyvalerate), called PHBV, is a promising bacterial bio-polymer that is

E. Garoufallou et al. (Eds.): MTSR 2021, CCIS 1537, pp. 3–15, 2022.
https://doi.org/10.1007/978-3-030-98876-0_1

biodegradable in soil and ocean and that can be synthesized from all kinds of carbon residues. The development of PHBV bio-composites loaded with lignocellulosic fillers is largely motivated by a decrease in PHBV's cost, an improvement of the carbon footprint and a reduction of the global warming [6]. However, the augmentation of added lignocellulosic fibers has a negative impact over the bio-composite's brittleness and its process-ability. When developing bio-composites, a compromise must then be found between the maximum acceptable filler content, the filler size and the resulting properties. Yet, finding causal explanations for this compromise from data alone can be a challenging task. If previous works have suggested the use of interventions (i.e. changing a variable while keeping all other constant) to build causal models [23], in the case of bio-based food packaging, such interventions can become really time and money consuming. In this article, we present POND (PO² ONtology Discovery), a workflow dedicated to answering expert queries for domains modelled by the Process and Observation Ontology (PO²) [17]. The main idea is to study Knowledge Bases (KBs) [11] using PO² to integrate expert knowledge into the learning of an extension of the Bayesian Networks (BNs), the Probabilistic Relational Model (PRM) [14]. While POND is able to answer a wide range of questions (qualitative and quantitative), in this article we focus on causal questions and illustrate the workflow with a real-world application on bio-based food packaging. Our original contributions are (1) the complete integration of PO² in a pipeline to answer expert queries, (2) a tool for answering causal assumptions that allows reverse engineering approaches and (3) a meta-analysis over multiple sources on bio-based packaging. Section 2 presents the background necessary for POND. It covers the PO² ontology, PRMs, as well as the combination of the two and causal discovery from data. Section 3 introduces our workflow and emphasizes its contributions to the state of the art on combining ontologies and probabilistic models and causal questions answering. Section 4 illustrates this workflow with a real-world application on bio-based packaging. This work has been defined in the framework of a regional (MALICE Languedoc-Roussillon) and two European (H2020 RESURBIS and NOAW) interdisciplinary projects involving computer scientists, data scientists and biomass processing experts for food and bio-based material production. MALICE project was the first to study several itineraries to produce composites using different biomass. It has been followed by RESURBIS (resp. NOAW) projects dedicated to urban (resp. agricultural) waste valorization.

2   Background

2.1   The Process and Observation Ontology

PO² is a generic process and observation ontology initially dedicated to food science [17], developed using the Scenario 6 of the NeON methodology [26], by re-engineering a first ontology for the eco-design of transformation processes [9]. It represents transformation processes by a set of experimental observations taken at different scales and links them on a detailed timeline. It has been recently used for bio-based products transformation process, especially food packaging design. Figure 1 presents an overview of its different parts, it is described by 67 concepts and 79 relations. A **transformation process** is defined by a succession of **steps** inscribed in a **temporal entity**. To each step, multiple **components** (which represent features of interest) can be added, themselves associated with different **results** and their corresponding units of measurements. PO^2 ontology version 2.0, implemented in OWL 2[1], is published on the AgroPortal ontology library[2], and is Creative Commons Attribution International (CC BY 4.0)[3].

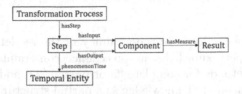

Fig. 1. Main parts of the PO^2 ontology.

2.2 Probabilistic Models: BN and PRM

A BN is the representation of a joint probability over a set of random variables that uses a directed acyclic graph (DAG) to encode probabilistic relations between variables. In our case, learning is done under causal constraints, which can be used to deduce causal knowledge through the essential graph (EG) [18], a semi-directed graph associated to the BN. Both the BN and its associated EG share the same skeleton, but the EG's edges' orientation depends on the BN's Markov equivalence class. A same edge's orientation for all equivalent BNs means that this orientation is necessary to keep the underlying probabilistic relations encoded in the graph: in this case, the edge is also oriented in the EG and is called an **essential arc**. Otherwise, it stays unoriented in the EG, meaning that its orientation does not modify the probabilistic relations encoded in the BN. In order to integrate expert knowledge under the form of causal constraints in the learning, we rely on PRMs, that extend BNs' representation with the oriented-object notion of classes and instantiations. PRMs [14] are defined by two parts: the **relational schema** RS (Fig. 2 (a)), that gives a qualitative description of the structure of the domain defining the classes and their attributes; and the **relational model** RM (Fig. 2 (b)), that contains the quantitative information given by the probability distribution over the different attributes. Classes in the RS are linked together by so-called **relational slots**, that indicates the direction of probabilistic links. Using these structural constraints, each class can then be learned like a BN[4], meaning they can be associated to an EG once instantiated.

Using constraints while learning BNs brings more accurate results, for parameters [7] or structure [8] learning. In case of smaller databases, constraining the

---

[1] https://www.w3.org/TR/owl2-overview/.
[2] http://agroportal.lirmm.fr/ontologies/PO2.
[3] https://creativecommons.org/licenses/by/4.0/.
[4] We use the classical statistical method Greedy Hill Climbing with a BIC Score.

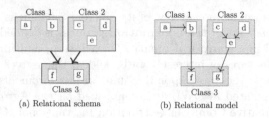

Fig. 2. The high (a) and low (b) level structures of a PRM

learning can also greatly improve the accuracy of the model [21]. In this article we integrate expert knowledge as precedence constraints. Previous works already proposed methods for complete [5] or partial [22] node ordering. In our case we transcribe incomplete knowledge as a partial structural organization for the PRM's *RS* in order to discover new causal relations, as presented in [20].

2.3 Knowledge Discovery

Numerous works have proposed to use ontological knowledge in order to build probabilistic models and discover relations. For instance, different ontologies' expansions integrate probabilistic reasoning (such as BayesOWL [10,28] or HyProb-Ontology [19]). These however do not allow the learning of relations. Other works directly uses the ontology's structure to build a BN, as for the objects properties that can be considered as probabilistic dependencies [13] or causal relations [1], which cannot however be applied with PO^2. Finally, some methods are tied down to specific cases, such as [2] that uses predefined templates to support medical diagnosis, which cannot be extended to other medical applications. While POND uses only PO^2, its complexity allows to deal with various tasks which gives it wider applications than a simple domain ontology.

For causal discovery, since correlation is not causation, the data set has to verify some conditions: no external factor (the **causal sufficiency** [25]); no missing or erroneous data, selection bias or deterministic cases [15]. In short, if not all possible events are present in the learning set, or if their proportion is altered and does not represent reality, then it is impossible to draw good causal discoveries. Discovering causality from verified dataset can be done through independence tests between the variables [25,27], but does not allow to introduce external constraints during the learning. Other works also proposed EGs to learn causal models: [16] presents two optimal strategies for suggesting interventions to learn causal models; [24] and [4] use an EG to build a causal BN (CBN) while maintaining a limited number of intervention recommendations. These approaches do not require any external knowledge about the domain. In our case however, the data is encompassed in an ontology and a BN cannot be learned directly. Our goal is to use this knowledge to be as close as possible of a CBN, which is a BN whose relations' orientation translate a causal implication.

3   POND: PO² ONtology Discovery

We now present the POND workflow, whose aim is to integrate expert knowledge in order to query it. We focus here on how different sources can be studied in order to answer complex probabilistic and causal questions. A particular focus is cast on causal discovery and how it allows reverse engineering.

3.1   Knowledge Integration

Expert knowledge comes from: (1) experimental data, gathered from different sources (such as publications, books or data produced in different projects); and (2) direct interviews, where experts of a domain are solicited. This information is then structured under the PO² ontology. In our case, the interesting point is that all the data is now easily accessible thanks to its semantization. Once the data gathered and structured, the expert can express expert queries. Some can be answered through a simple query over the data described in the ontology (Competency Questions); others require a more in-depth analysis (Knowledge Questions, KQs). In this article, we will focus on **causal KQs** (cKQs), which can be formalized in two different ways. Given X_i and X_j groups of the domain's attributes:

cKQ_1 *Does X_i have a causal influence over X_j?*
cKQ_2 *What is the impact of X_j over X_i?*

    Both illustrate the double reading offered by a CBN: while cKQ_1 focuses on the descriptive aspect, cKQ_2 allows to interrogate the nature of the relations between different variables. Once a cKQ expressed, we then build the probabilistic model. As seen in Sect. 2.3, we focus here on expressing the expert knowledge as a RS in order to guide the learning of the model. The originality of our approach is that this expression is done through two means:

1. **A mapping of the ontology's attributes in the RS.** Thanks to the common vocabulary defined by the PO² ontology, the expert can easily extract these attributes, even if they are measured in different contexts and depend on different sources of knowledge. For instance, a temperature might be measured at Step A with one source and at Step B with another. In this case, only the expert can tell whether these attributes are similar (i.e., if they can be compared) or not. With PO²'s semantic, the expert can thus select the attributes that are interesting to study, by specifying the process, step and component that lead to the interesting result (i.e., the datatype property which owns the value). This combination of results composes the BN's learning database.
2. **A definition of the precedence constraints.** Precedence constraints are possible orientations between the attributes encoded in the RS: if a relation is learned between two attributes linked by such an orientation, the learnt relation has to be oriented following it. These precedence constraints can

either be deduced from the temporal information of PO^2 (a change of an attribute at time t may have an influence over an attribute at time $t+n$, but not at time $t-n$), or given by the expert according to their own knowledge ("I know that X_1 may have an influence over X_2").

Our contribution in this section is the automation of this knowledge integration in a workflow: thanks to PO^2, any transformation process can be easily integrated into a RS, using only a vocabulary specific of the studied domain.

3.2   Causal Discovery

Once the RS defined, a PRM can be learned and then instantiated as a BN. Since this is done under causal constraints, we can use the EG to deduce causality [20]. Indeed, the resulting model can be seen as the intersection of all the models constrained by the dataset used for the learning (expressed in the EG) and all the models constrained by the expert knowledge (expressed in the RS). Although it is not usually enough to learn a CBN, the EG's essential arcs can be used to complement expert knowledge. The causal validation is done as follows:

- If a relation is learned between two variables with an expert precedence constraint, then the causality is validated by the expert's knowledge.
- If a learned relation is an essential arc on the EG, then the causality is validated by the EG. This is the case even if no precedence constraint has been placed between those attributes.
- If a relation is learned, but is neither an essential arc nor part of a precedence constraint, then it is impossible to deduce causality.

Even if a complete CBN is not learned, this causal discovery has two goals:

- **Helping the expert criticize.** Since we aim to learn a real-world model, the evaluation of its performances cannot be done directly. However, by presenting the learned causal relations to the expert, we give them a tool to criticize and question it. An example of this critic is given in Sect. 4.3.
- **Answering the cKQs.** cKQs depend on causal discovery to be answered: cKQ_1 directly requires the presence (or absence) of causal relations and in order to express the interactions questioned by cKQ_2, we need first to define the causality between the studied variables.

3.3   Causal Inferences

While what was explained in the previous section is enough to answer cKQ_1, answering cKQ_2 requires a more in-depth analysis. To illustrate this, we consider the CBN presented in Fig. 3 as the result of a causal validation, and the following cKQ_{ex}: *"Which intervention should I do on the accessible variables to maximize the variable E?"*, which is a sequence of the cKQ_1 (*"Which variables have a impact over E?"*) and the cKQ_2 (*"What is the influence of these variables?"*).

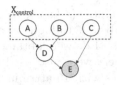

Fig. 3. Example of a CBN. The set $X_{control}$ represents the control variables, meaning the ones on which the expert can intervene; E is the target variable.

In order to answer cKQ_{ex}, we first need to assess which variables in $X_{control}$ (the set of variables on which the expert can intervene) are necessary. In our case, we see that the direct parents of E are D and C. However, D is not in $X_{control}$, so we need to look at its own parents, which are A and B. Since they both belong to $X_{control}$, then in order to answer cKQ_{ex}, we define $X_{inter} = \{A, B, C\}$. Because we consider a CBN, then intervening on X_{inter} will have an effect over the target E. In practice, for each possible combination of values of X_{inter}, we can predict the values of E and their associated probability, which constitute a base of possible scenarios. In order to sort these, the expert expresses their own criteria of acceptability, as "which values are better for the target variable", or "which conditions should apply on X_{inter}". These criteria can be of two kinds:

- **Hard Criteria.** Some values or combinations of values are impossible to obtain: these scenarios are automatically discarded. For instance, the expert might wish that the sum of the values from X_{inter} does not exceed a certain value; or they might want to exclude some values for E (in our case, the goal is to maximize E: thus, it is not interesting to consider the lowest values).
- **Soft Criteria.** In this case, the expert needs to sort their preferences regarding the context. Maybe having a high value for E is not interesting if A also needs to be high; or a lower value for E with a higher probability might be more interesting than a better scenario with less chances of happening.

Defining these criteria helps the expert to select an answer corresponding to their need. As seen in Sect. 4.3, this can be used to do reverse engineering, whose goal is to understand how a system works through deductive reasoning. Section 4.3 shows an example where we formulate the composition of an optimal biomass.

4 Application to Bio-composites Packaging Materials

Given the context of bio-packaging, we define cKQ_{bio}: *"Which filler allows to optimise the packaging's tensile properties?"*.

4.1 Knowledge Base Presentation

Data was collected from four projects focused on the development of PHBV-based bio-composites using lignocellulosic fillers (LFs) stemming from organic waste streams, e.g. crop residues (*Chercheur d'avenir region Languedoc-Roussillon MALICE* and *NoAW*), agro-food by-products (*FP7 EcoBioCAP*) or urban waste (*H2020 Resurbis*). LFs were obtained by dry fractionation of the raw biomass. Pure cellulose fibers were also used as reference, representing in the end a database of 85 samples with 15 attributes.

4.2 Expert Integration

Integrating expert knowledge requires the expert to map from the knowledge base to the RS the attributes relevant for the cKQ, and to organize their potential precedence constraints. In this section, we present the main results used to learn our final model, as well as an example of the integration of some expert critics.

Attributes Selection.[5] The expert describes LFs by three main categories: biochemical composition with the plants' main organic (**cellulose, hemicellulose, lignin**) and inorganic (**ash**) compounds; apparent median diameter (**D50**); **filler content**. Tensile parameters were determined from stress-strain curves obtained by tensile tests performed until the break of materials. The **Young's modulus** (slope of the initial section of the curve), **stress at break** (stress value at moment of material fracture) and **strain at break** (elongation value at moment of material fracture) respectively characterize the stiffness, the resistance and the ductility of the material. While these are enough to consider cKQ_{bio}, the expert helped us determine three other categories, in order to offer a better overview for the expert feedback: **permeability** (to water vapour), thermal properties (**crystallization** and **melting** temperatures) and thermal degradation (**onset** and **peak** temperature). Discretization is important, as it can influence the learning of the different relations and may be subject to change depending on the feedback from the expert. Table 1 presents an excerpt of it, where control variables are evenly distributed, while others follow a distribution chosen by the expert.

Table 1. Example of the discretization used for some variables *(number of examples)*.

Lignin	]0;19.4] *(32)*	]19.4;26.4] *(30)*	]26.4;49[*(23)*	
Filler content	]2;4] *(10)*	]4;11] *(34)*	]11;21] *(22)*	]21;50[*(19)*
Strain at break	]0.2;0.5] *(19)*	]0.5;0.8] *(44)*	]0.8;1] *(15)*	]1;1.07[*(3)*

Precedence Constraints Definition. The expert defines two precedence constraints that may be refined after each iteration.

- Between the filler variables and the package's characteristics. We consider the first as control variables, whose values may have an impact over the final result. We create two classes in the RS, with a relational slot from the control variable's class towards the package's characteristic's class.

---

[5] For the rest of the article, all attributes represented in the model are **bolded**.

- Between the different package's characteristics. They cannot influence each other (e.g. the tensile attributes have no influence over the thermodynamic ones). As a consequence, we compartmentalise the RS characteristic's class into different separated sub-classes, such that they have no relational slot except the one from the control variable class.

Expert Feedback. Once a model is learned, discussion with an expert is required to criticize both (1) the learned relations and (2) the probabilistic dependencies. For example, in Fig. 4, the expert mentioned that the **crystallization** temperature could not be explained by the **melting** parameter, and that the learned relation translates a correlation, not a causation. As a consequence, we create a constraint that prevents the learning of this link. Finally, **strain at break** was not expected to not be explained by any parameter, which suggested to try a new discretization to better represent the variable. The expert is also useful to explain the lacks of knowledge. Regarding the **melting** temperature, this model highlights (through near-zero probabilities) that if **content** $\in$]21;50[, then **melting** $\notin$]1;1.02[. This was fully expected since the melting temperature is not supposed to increase when adding LFs.

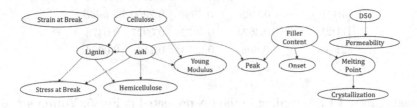

Fig. 4. Model learned after one iteration.

4.3   Knowledge Question Answering

We now consider the CBN accepted by the expert, presented in Fig. 5. For the sake of the example, we present a simplified version where all non-relevant variables were removed. cKQ_{bio} addresses two possible interventions for improving the three considered tensile properties: (1) **filler content** and (2) **LF**.

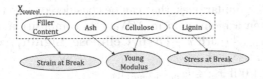

Fig. 5. Extract of the BN selected for Biomass Discovery. Since all relations are influenced by precedence constraints, we consider this as a CBN validated by the expert.

Finding Optimal Content. According to Fig. 5, **Filler Content** has a causal influence only on **Strain at Break**. Depending on the expert's criteria, multiple readings of the conditional probability table (Table 2) are possible:

– When aiming for the highest value possible for **Strain at Break** (]1;1.07]), the probabilities are almost zero. Thus, it cannot realistically be satisfied.
– With a hard criteria aiming for the second highest value of **Strain at Break**, a **content** of]2;4] could be considered, as it guarantees a probability of 0.3963 to obtain the second best value (]0.8;1]).
– In the case of an industrial process, however, the expert might want to place a hard criteria for a reasonable probability of success. In this case, a **content** of]4:11] should be applied, since it guaranties a probability of success of 0.7.

Table 2. Conditional probabilities of Strain at Break (*maximum likelihood*).

Filler content	Strain at break			
	]0.24;0.5]	]0.5;0.8]	]0.8;1]	]1;1.07]
]2;4]	0.0061	0.5915	*0.3963*	0.0061
]4;11]	0.002	*0.7060*	0.2260	*0.0660*
]11;21]	0.3623	0.4972	0.0927	0.0478
]21:50]	*0.6062*	0.2774	0.113	0.0034

Proposing new LF. According to the BN presented in Fig. 5, **Young's Modulus** and **Stress at Break** depend on components of the biomass. We first define some criteria of acceptability:

– **Hard criteria** HC_1. The sum of the **ash, cellulose,** and **lignin** must not exceed 100 (i.e. the biomass must be possible). We fix HC_1 such that, given $x \in \{$**Ash, Cellulose, Lignin**$\}$ and its interval $[x_{min}; x_{max}]$, we have $\sum_x x_{min} < 100$.
– **Hard criteria** HC_2. We want the target variables within interesting range of values, and fix **Stress At Break** $> 0.8 \cap$ **Young Modulus** > 0.8.
– **Hard criteria** HC_3. The probability of success must be higher than 0.25.
– **Soft criteria** SC_1. When no corresponding biomass is found, we allow the system to look for similar ones, that can be considered close to the one we are looking for. Given a biomass m in AtWeb, its composition x_m and a target interval $[x_{min}; x_{max}]$ (with $x \in \{$**Ash, Cellulose, Lignin**$\}$), we define a score $S_m = \sum_x \sigma(m, x)$
with $\sigma(m, x) = \begin{cases} 0 \text{ if } x_m \in [x_{min}; x_{max}]; \\ min(abs(x_m - x_{min}), abs(x_m - x_{max})) \text{ otherwise.} \end{cases}$
The lower S_m is, the closer the biomass is to our recommendation.

In order to suggest new biomasses for packaging composite making, @Web RDF database [3] including experimental data about biomass deconstruction [12] has been queried using these criteria, which returned five solutions (Table 3 presents the first three). Each of these scenarios assesses the probability of obtaining a value over 0.8 for the tensile properties. The most probable one ($p = 0.41$) is not an exact match; however, the closest match, the rice husk, has an S-score of 0.73, meaning it is really similar to the scenario's recommendations. This corroborates with the second scenario, which also recommends the rice husk with a slightly lower probability of outcome. The last scenario, finally, proposes the pine bark, with a S-score of 5.24 (due to the pine bark's **ash** value of 1.44). It is important to note that a limit of this model is tied to the discretization required by BN learning. When dealing with values close to the border of the interval, predicting the result is more difficult. Moreover, Table 1 shows that some categories are underrepresented compared to the others (e.g. **Strain at Break** $\in$]1;1.07]). If this choice of discretization bears a meaning for the domain, it however introduces bias: some categories may artificially have a bigger weight than the others during the learning only because they do not have enough samples. That is why the database used for the learning must be really representative, to allow a smoother discretization which would prevent this edge effect.

Table 3. Results of Biomass Querying with respect to HC_1, HC_2, HC_3 and SC_1. When no exact result, a S-score was calculated to find the closest match.

p	0.41	p	0.40	p	0.28
Ash	[6.7;24.7]	Ash	[6.7;24.7]	Ash	[6.7;24.7]
Cellulose	[25.6;33]	Cellulose	[10.9;25.6]	Cellulose	[10.86;25.59]
Lignin	[26.4; 49]	Lignin	[19.4; 26.4]	Lignin	[19.4; 26.4]
Exact match	$\emptyset$	Exact match	Rice Husk	Exact match	$\emptyset$
Close match	Rice husk	Close match	$\emptyset$	Close match	Pine Bark
$S_{RiceHusk}$	0.73	S	$\emptyset$	$S_{PineBark}$	5.24

4.4 Conclusion

In this paper we have presented POND, a complete workflow dedicated to answer EQs over processes represented by the PO^2 ontology. We focused on causal discovery aspects and illustrated it with a real-world example, the bio-packaging transformation process. Thanks to the use of the ontology, this workflow allows the expert to easily handle the knowledge integration part and to add more knowledge under the form of precedence constraints. During the answering, they can also express criteria of acceptability to elect the best answer for their needs. As in all causal discovery contexts, multiple conditions must be verified in order to be accepted, as described in Sect. 2.3. This also requires the expert to be trustworthy, both for the constraints' definition and the model verification. Finally, as presented in the example, a database too sparse for the learning could lead to questionable discretization that could be difficult to interpret. Future works will look into the use of the answers to assess the quality of the current KB and see how it can be used either to suggest correction for the current base, or generation of new data to fulfill knowledge holes. Another interesting task would be to address the dedication of POND to the PO^2 ontology, which represents a limit; while the method should work in theory with any other semantic structuration of the data, it needs to be reworked to be adapted.

Acknowledgement. We would like to thank Claire Mayer (PhyProDiv Team, INRAE IATE) who provided data for the biomass discovery aspect. Our work has been partially financed by the French national research agency ANR in the framework of D2KAB (ANR-18-CE23-0017) and DataSusFood (ANR-19-DATA-0016) projects.

References

1. Ben Messaoud, M., Leray, P., Ben Amor, N.: Semcado: a serendipitous strategy for learning causal bayesian networks using ontologies. Symbolic and Quantitative Approaches to Reasoning with Uncertainty, pp. 182–193 (2011)
2. Bucci, G., Sandrucci, V., Vicario, E.: Ontologies and bayesian networks in medical diagnosis. HICSS, pp. 1–8 (2011)
3. Buche, P., Dibie-Barthelemy, J., Ibanescu, L.L., Soler, L.: Fuzzy web data tables integration guided by a termino-ontological resource. IEEE Trans. Knowl. Data Eng. **25**(4), 805–819 (2013)
4. Castelletti, F., Consonni, G.: Discovering causal structures in bayesian gaussian directed acyclic graph models. J. Royal Stat. Soc. Series A Royal Stat. Soc. **183**, 1727–1745 (2020)
5. Cooper, G.F., Herskovits, E.: A bayesian method for the induction of probabilistic networks from data. Mach. Learn. **9**(4), 309–347 (1992)
6. David, G., et al.: Using life cycle assessment to quantify the environmental benefit of upcycling vine shoots as fillers in biocomposite packaging materials. Int. J. Life Cycle Assess. **26**(4), 738–752 (2020). https://doi.org/10.1007/s11367-020-01824-7
7. De Campos, C.P., Ji, Q.: Improving bayesian network parameter learning using constraints. In: ICPR, pp. 1–4 (2008)
8. De Campos, C., Zhi, Z., Ji, Q.: Structure learning of bayesian networks using constraints. In: ICML, pp. 113–120 (2009)
9. Dibie, J., Dervaux, S., Doriot, E., Ibanescu, L., Pénicaud, C.: $[MS]^2O$ - A multiscale and multi-step ontology for transformation processes: application to microorganisms. In: ICSS, pp. 163–176 (2016)
10. Ding, Z., Peng, Y., Pan, R.: BayesOWL: uncertainty modeling in semantic web ontologies. In: Ma, Z. (eds.) Soft Computing in Ontologies and Semantic Web. Studies in Fuzziness and Soft Computing, vol. 204. Springer, Heidelberg (2006). https://doi.org/10.1007/978-3-540-33473-6_1
11. Ehrlinger, L., Wöß, W.: Towards a definition of knowledge graphs. In: SEMANTiCS (Posters, Demos, SuCCESS) (2016)
12. Fabre, C., Buche, P., Rouau, X., Mayer-Laigle, C.: Milling itineraries dataset for a collection of crop and wood by-products and granulometric properties of the resulting powders. Data in Brief **33** (2020)

13. Fenz, S.: Exploiting experts' knowledge for structure learning of bayesian networks. Data Knowl. Eng. **73**, 73–88 (2012)
14. Friedman, N., Getoor, L., Koller, D., Pfeffer, A.: Learning probabilistic relational models. In: IJCAI, p. 1300–1307. Morgan Kaufmann Publishers Inc. (1999)
15. Glymour, C., Zhang, K., Spirtes, P.: Review of causal discovery methods based on graphical models. Front. Gene. **10**, 524 (2019)
16. Hauser, A., Bühlmann, P.: Two optimal strategies for active learning of causal models from interventional data. Int. J. Approximate Reason, pp. 926–939 (2014)
17. Ibanescu, L., Dibie, J., Dervaux, S., Guichard, E., Raad, J.: Po2- a process and observation ontology in food science. application to dairy gels. Metadata Seman. Res., 155–165 (2016)
18. Madigan, D., Andersson, S.A., Perlman, M.D., Volinsky, C.T.: Bayesian model averaging and model selection for markov equivalence classes of acyclic digraphs. Commun. Stat. Theory Methods **25**(11), 2493–2519 (1996)
19. Mohammed, A.-W., Xu, Y., Liu, M.: Knowledge-oriented semantics modelling towards uncertainty reasoning. SpringerPlus **5**(1), 1–27 (2016). https://doi.org/ 10.1186/s40064-016-2331-1
20. Munch, M., Dibie, J., Wuillemin, P., Manfredotti, C.E.: Towards interactive causal relation discovery driven by an ontology. In: FLAIRS, pp. 504–508 (2019)
21. Munch, M., Wuillemin, P.-H., Manfredotti, C., Dibie, J., Dervaux, S.: Learning probabilistic relational models using an ontology of transformation processes. In: Panetto, H., Debruyne, C., Gaaloul, W., Papazoglou, M., Paschke, A., Ardagna, C.A., Meersman, R. (eds.) OTM 2017. LNCS, vol. 10574, pp. 198–215. Springer, Cham (2017). https://doi.org/10.1007/978-3-319-69459-7_14
22. Parviainen, P., Koivisto, M.: Finding optimal bayesian networks using precedence constraints. J. Mach. Learn. Res. **14**, 1387–1415 (2013)
23. Pearl, J.: Causality: Models, 2nd edn. Reasoning and Inference. Cambridge University Press, USA (2009)
24. Shanmugam, K., Kocaoglu, M., Dimakis, A.G., Vishwanath, S.: Learning causal graphs with small interventions. In: Cortes, C., Lawrence, N., Lee, D., Sugiyama, M., Garnett, R. (eds.) Advances in Neural Information Processing Systems. vol. 28. Curran Associates, Inc. (2015)
25. Spirtes, P., Glymour, C., Scheines, R.: Causation, Prediction, and Search. MIT press, 2nd edn. (2000)
26. Suárez-Figueroa, M.C., Gómez-Pérez, A., Fernández-López, M.: The neon methodology for ontology engineering. In: Suárez-Figueroa, M.C., Gómez-Pérez, A., Motta, E., Gangemi, A. (eds.) Ontology Engineering in a Networked World, pp. 9–34. Springer (2012) https://doi.org/10.1007/978-3-642-24794-1_2
27. Verny, L., Sella, N., Affeldt, S., Singh, P., Isambert, H.: Learning causal networks with latent variables from multivariate information in genomic data. PLOS Comput. Biol. **13** (2017)
28. Zhang, S., Sun, Y., Peng, Y., Wang, X.: Bayesowl: a prototype system for uncertainty in semantic web. ICAI **2**, 678–684 (2009)

A UML-Style Visual Query Environment Over DBPedia

Kārlis Čerāns(✉) [iD], Lelde Lāce [iD], Mikus Grasmanis [iD], and Jūlija Ovčiņņikova [iD]

Institute of Mathematics and Computer Science, University of Latvia, Riga, Latvia
{karlis.cerans,lelde.lace,mikus.grasmanis,
julija.ovcinnikova}@lumii.lv

Abstract. We describe and demonstrate a prototype of a UML-style visual query environment over DBPedia that allows query seeding with any class or property present in the data endpoint and provides for context-sensitive query growing based on class-to-property and property-to-property mappings. To handle mappings that connect more than 480 thousand classes and more than 50 thousand properties, a hybrid approach of mapping pre-computation and storage is proposed, where the property information for "large" classes is stored in a database, while for "small" classes and for individuals the matching property information is retrieved from the data endpoint on-the-fly. The created schema information is used to back the query seeding and growing in the ViziQuer tool. The schema server and the schema database contents can be re-used also in other applications that require DBPedia class and property linking information.

Keywords: DBPedia · SPARQL · Visual queries · ViziQuer · RDF data schema

1 Introduction

DBPedia [1, 2] is one of the central Linked Data resources and is of fundamental importance to the entire Linked Data ecosystem. DBPedia extracts structured information from Wikipedia[1]-the most popular collaboratively maintained encyclopedia on the web. A public DBPedia SPARQL endpoint[2], representing its "core" data, is a large and heterogeneous resource with over 480 thousand classes and over 50 thousand properties, making it difficult to find and extract the relevant information. The existing means for DBPedia data querying and exploration involve textual SPARQL query formulation and some research prototypes that offer assisted query composition options, as e.g., RDF Explorer [3], that do not reach the ability to use effectively the actual DBPedia schema information to support the query creation by end-users.

There is a DBPedia ontology that consists of 769 classes and 1431 properties (as of July 2021); it can be fully or partially loaded into generic query environments, as SPARKLIS [4] (based on natural language snippets), or Optique VQs [5, 6] or ViziQuer

---

[1] https://www.wikipedia.org/.
[2] http://dbpedia.org/sparql.

© Springer Nature Switzerland AG 2022
E. Garoufallou et al. (Eds.): MTSR 2021, CCIS 1537, pp. 16–27, 2022.
https://doi.org/10.1007/978-3-030-98876-0_2

[7] (based on visual diagrammatic query presentation). The DBPedia ontology alone would, however, be rather insufficient in supporting the query building process, as it covers just a tiny fraction of actual DBPedia data classes and there are quite prominent classes and properties in the data set (e.g., the class *foaf:Document*, or any class from *yago:* namespace, or the property *foaf:name*) that are not present in the ontology.

We describe here services for the DBPedia data retrieval query composition assistance, running in real time, based on the full DBPedia data schema involving all its classes, all properties, and their relations (e.g., what properties are relevant for instances of what classes; both class-to-property and property-to-property relevance connections are considered). We apply the developed services to seeding and growing visual queries within the visual ViziQuer environment (cf. [7, 8]), however, the services can be made available also for schema-based query code completion in different environments, including the ones for textual SPARQL query composition, as e.g., YASGUI [9].

Due to the size of the data endpoint we pre-compute the class-to-property and property-to-property relevance mappings, using then the stored information to support the query creation. We limit pre-computation of the class-to-property mapping just for sufficiently large classes as most classes would have way less instances than the connected properties (for smaller classes the on-the-fly completion approach is used).

The principal novelty of the paper is:

– A *method for auto-completing queries*, based on the class-to-property and property-to-property connections, working over the actual DBPedia data schema in real time, and
– A *visual query environment* for exploration and querying of a very large and heterogeneous dataset, as DBPedia is.

The papers' supporting material including a live server environment for visual queries over DBPedia can be accessed from its support site http://viziquer.lumii.lv/dss/.

In what follows, Sect. 2 outlines the query completion task. The query completion solution architecture is described in Sect. 3. Section 4 describes the DBPedia schema extraction process to build up the data schema necessary for query completion. The visual query creation is described in Sect. 5. Section 6 concludes the paper.

2 Query Completion Task

A *diagrammatic presentation* of a query over RDF data is typically based on nodes and edges, where a node corresponds to a query variable or a resource (or a literal) and an edge, labelled by a property path, describes a link between the nodes. A *UML-style query diagram* (as in ViziQuer [7], Optique VQs [5] or LinDA [10]) would also provide an option (in some notations, a request) to specify the class information for a variable or a resource represented by the node. Furthermore, some links of the abstract query graph can be presented in the UML-style query notation as node attributes.

The presence of a class information for a variable or a resource in a query, facilitated by the UML style query presentation, could facilitate the query readability. Still, this would not preclude queries that have nodes with empty class specification (cf. [8]).

18   K. Čerāns et al.

Figure 1 shows example visual queries corresponding to some of QALD-4 tasks[3,4], suitable for execution over DBPedia SPARQL endpoint, in the ViziQuer notation (cf. [8] and [11] for the notation and tool explanation).

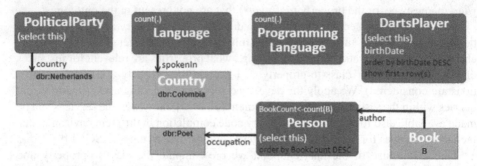

Fig. 1. Example visual queries. Each query is a connected graph with a main query node (orange round rectangle) and possibly linked connection classes. Each node corresponds to a variable (usually left implicit) or a resource and an optional class name. There can be selection and aggregation attributes in a node. The edges correspond to properties (paths) linking the node variables/resources. [8] Also describes more advanced query constructs.

From the auto-completion viewpoint a query can be viewed as a graph with nodes allowing entity specifications in the positions of classes and individuals and edges able to hold property names[5].

The process of the visual query creation by an end-user starts with query initialization or *query seeding* and is followed by query expanding, or *query growing*[6]. Within each of these stages the query environment is expected to assist the end-user by offering the names from the entity vocabulary (involving classes, properties, possibly also individuals) that would make sense in the query position to be filled.

The simplest or *context-free* approach for the entity name suggestion would provide the entities for positions in a query just by their type–a class, a data property, or an object property (or an individual). This approach can provide reasonable results, if the user is ready to type in textual fragments of the entity name. The "most typical" names that can be offered to the user without any name fragment typing still can be significantly dependent on the context information where the entity is to be placed.

Another approach, followed e.g., by SPARKLIS [4] or RDF Explorer [3] would be presenting only those extensions of a query that would lead to a *query with non-empty solutions* (if taken together with the already existing query part). In the case of a large data endpoint, as DBPedia is, this would not be feasible, as even the simple queries to the endpoint asking for all properties that are available for instances of a large class typically do time-out or have running times not suitable for on-the-fly execution.

---

[3] http://qald.aksw.org/index.php?x=task1&q=4.

[4] cf. also http://www.irisa.fr/LIS/ferre/sparklis/examples.html.

[5] Even if the query has a more complicated structure, the completion suggestions are computed on the basis of the described simple node-edge model.

[6] The same applies also to query building in other (e.g.textual) notations.

We propose to use an in-between path by suggesting to the end-user the entity names that are ***compatible with some local fragment*** of the existing query (these are the entity names that make sense in their immediate context). We shall follow a ***complete*** approach in a sense that all names leading to an existing solution of the extended query need to be included into the suggestion set (possibly after the name fragment entry), however the names not leading to a solution can sometimes be admitted, as well.

In a schema-based query environment the main context element for a property name suggestion would be a class name, however, suggestion of a class name in the context of a property and suggestion of a connected property in the context of an existing property would be important to support the property-centered modeling style, and to enable efficient auto-completion within a textual property path expression entry[7] (after a property name within an expression, only its "follower" properties are to be suggested, along with inverses of those properties whose triples can have common object with the last property from the already entered part of the property path).

3   Query Completion Principles

In what follows, we describe the principles of the query completion that can be shown to efficiently serve both the query seeding and context-aware query growing tasks for a SPARQL endpoint, as DBPedia core, with more than 480 thousand classes and more than 50 thousand properties, offering the text-search, filtering and prioritization options over the target linked entity sets. The query completion method has been implemented within a data shape server[8] (also called schema server), featuring the example environments over the DBPedia core and other data sets.

3.1   Entity Mapping Types

The query completion on the data schema level is based on class-to-property and property-to-property relations, observing separately the outgoing and incoming properties for a class[9], and "following", "common subject" and "common object" modes for the property-property relations. The relations shall be navigable in both directions, so:

- The class-to-property (outgoing) relation can be used to compute the outgoing properties for a class, and source classes for a property,
- The class-to-property (incoming) relation can be used to compute the incoming properties for a class, and target classes for a property,
- The "following" property-property relation can be used for computing "followers" and "precursors" of a property.

---

[7] For DBPedia core the direct property-property relation is much smaller than the property-property relation derived from the property-class-property mappings. For endpoints with less subclassing and the class structure more fully representing the property availability, the property-property mapping derived from the property-class-property relation may be sufficient.

[8] https://github.com/LUMII-Syslab/data-shape-server.

[9] A property p is outgoing (resp., incoming) for a class c, if there is a c instance that is subject (resp., object) for some triple having p as its property.

For each of the mappings it is important to have the list of suggested entities ordered so that the "most relevant" entities can be suggested first. To implement a context-aware relevance measure, we compute the triple pattern counts for each pair in the class-to-property and property-to-property relations; for the class-to-property (outgoing) relation also the counts of "data triple" patterns and "object triple" patterns are computed separately. An entity X is higher in the list of entities corresponding to Y, if the triple pattern count for the pair (X, Y) is higher[10].

For query fragments involving an individual, the means shall be available for retrieving all classes the individual belongs to, all properties for which the individual is the subject (the properties "outgoing" from an individual) and for which the individual is the object (the properties "incoming" into the individual). We expect that the data SPARQL endpoint shall be able to answer queries of this type efficiently.

A further query completion task is to compute the individuals belonging to a class or available in the context of a given property (the class-to-individual, property-to-individual (subject) and property-to-individual (object) mappings). Since these mappings may return large sets of results for an argument class or property (e.g., around 1.7 million instances of *dbo:Person* class in DBPedia core), a text search with entity name fragment within the results is necessary. Such a search can be reasonably run over the SPARQL endpoint for classes with less than 100000 instances. For larger classes the suggested approach in query creation would be to start by filling the individual position first (using some index for the individual lookup as e.g., DBPedia Lookup[11]).

The solution that we propose can also provide linked entity (property, class, individual) suggestion from several initial entities; this is achieved (logically) by computing the linked entity lists independently for each initial entity and then intersecting[12].

3.2 Partial Class-to-Property Mapping Storage

The modern database technologies would allow storing and serving to the query environment the full class-to-property and property-to-property relations[13]. Still, this may be considered not effective for a heterogeneous data endpoint, as DBPedia is, where for about 95% of classes the number of class instances is lower than the number of properties that characterize these instances. Out of 483 748 classes in the DBPedia core there have been 93 321 classes (around 19%) with just a single instance; in this case only a single link from the class to an instance is available in data. To record the relation of such a singleton class to the properties, all properties that the class instance exhibits, would need to be recorded. Since an instance may belong to several classes, such full storage of the class-to-property mapping is considered superfluous.

---

[10] In the case of a heterogeneous endpoint, as DBPedia core is, the computation of local frequency of target instances in a context can give substantially different results from looking at the global "size" of the target entity.

[11] https://lookup.dbpedia.org/

[12] if a class c corresponds to both a property p and a property q, it is going to be suggested in a context of both p and q, although there may be no instance of c with values for both p and q.

[13] There are about 35 million rows in the class-to-property (outgoing) relation in DBPedia core; the class-to-property (incoming) relation is much smaller.

Therefore, we propose to pre-compute and store the class-to-property relation just *for a fraction of classes* (we call them "large" classes), and to rely on the information retrieval from the data endpoint itself, if the class size falls below a certain threshold[14] (regarding the property-property relation, our current proposal is to store it in full).

The partial storing of the class-to-property relation does not impede the possibility to compute the linked property lists for a given class, since for the classes that are not "large", these lists can be efficiently served by the data SPARQL endpoint[15].

The property-to-class direction of such a "partially stored" class-to-property relation becomes trickier, as, given a property, only the large classes are those that can be directly retrieved from the data schema. In order not to lose any relevant class name suggestions, we assign (and pre-compute) to any "small" class its representing superclass from the "large" classes set (we take the smallest of the large superclasses for the class). There turn out to be 154 small classes without a large superclass in the DBPedia endpoint (in accordance with the identified superclass information); the property links are to be pre-computed for these classes, to achieve complete class name suggestion lists.

The effect of suggested extra small classes in the context of a property can be analyzed. We note that in the DBPedia core out of top 5000 largest properties just 50 would have more small classes than the large ones within the source top 30 class UI window; in the case of target classes the number would be 190; so, the potentially non-exact class name suggestions are not going to have a major impact on the user interface (lowering the large class threshold would lower also the extra suggestion ratio even further).

3.3 Schema Server Implementation and Experiments

The schema server is implemented as REST API, responding to GET inquiries for (i) the list of known ontologies, (ii) the list of namespaces, (iii) the list of classes (possibly with text filter) and (iv) the list of properties (possibly with text filter), and POST inquiries for computing a list of classes, properties, and individuals in a context. The POST inquiries can specify query limit, text filter, lists of allowed or excluded namespaces, result ordering expression and the data endpoint URL; Further on there is a query context element, involving a class name (except for class name completion), individual URI (except for individual completion) and two lists of properties–the incoming and the outgoing ones; in the case of property completion, the context information sets can be created for both their subject and object positions.

The parameters of the schema server operations allow tuning the entity suggestion list selection and presentation to the end user. They are used in the visual tool user interface customization, in applying specific namespace conditions, or featuring basic and Full lists of properties in a context, as illustrated in Sect. 5.

A preliminary check of the schema server efficiency has found that the operations for suggesting classes and properties in a context perform reasonably, as shown in Table 1. For each of the link computation positions at least 10 source instances that can be

---

[14] Within our initial prototype version, the class-to-property mapping is pre-computed for top 3000 largest classes; these classes contain at least about 1000 instances each.

[15] In the case of the DBPedia core endpoint the size of such a list for classes with less than 1000 instances typically do not exceed a few hundred.

expected to have the highest running times (e.g., the largest entities) are considered and the maximum of the found running times is listed.

The experiments with the schema server have been performed on a single-laptop (32 GB RAM) installation of the visual tool, with the PostgreSQL database over the local network and remote access to the public DBPedia endpoint[16] as the data set; the query time is measured by the printouts from the schema server JavaScript code.

Table 1. Entity list suggestion timing estimates

	Time upper estimate
Top 30 classes (all classes, dbo: namespace only, all except yago:), with possible text filter	259 ms
Top 30 properties (all properties, object properties, data properties), with possible text filter	412 ms
c → p links (data and object out properties), from a large class	882 ms
c → p extended links (in/out object properties, with other end range/domain class, if available), from a large class	2141 ms
c → p links (data and object out properties), from a small class	2438 ms
c → p extended links (out and in object properties, with other end range/domain class, if available), from a small class	1148 ms
p → p links (data and object out properties), from incoming and outgoing properties	577 ms
p → p extended links (in/out object properties, with other end range/domain class, if available), from incoming and outgoing properties	2760 ms
p → c links, from an in and an out property (including the large classes only and both the large and small classes suggestion cases)	269 ms

We note that the queries for computing the entities in a multiple context, do not tend to blow up the execution time, if compared to the single-context inquiries.

4 Data Schema Retrieval

Some of the data endpoints may have an ontology that describes its data structure; however, it may well be the case that the ontology does not describe the actual data structure fully (e.g., including all classes, all properties and all their connections present in the data set)[17], therefore we consider retrieving the data from the SPARQL endpoint itself[18].

---

[16] http://dbpedia.org/sparql.

[17] The DBPedia ontology covers just a tiny fraction of the actual DBPedia core data structure.

[18] The data owner or a person having access to the data dump can also have other options of producing the data schema.

The extraction of small and medium-sized schemas can be performed by methods described in e.g., [12] and [13]. We outline here retrieving the DBPedia schema.

The DBPedia core schema retrieval has been done from a local copy, installed from DBPedia Databus site[19] (the copy of December 2020).

The basic data retrieval involves the following generic steps that can be followed on other endpoints, as well:

1) Retrieve all classes (entities that have some instance), together with their instance count[20].

2) Retrieve all properties, together with their triple count, their object triple count (triples, where the object is an URI) and the literal triple count.

3) For classes deemed to be "large"[21], compute the sets of its incoming and outgoing properties, with respective triple counts, including also object triple count and literal triple count for outgoing properties. For the classes, where direct computation of properties does not give results (e.g. due to the query timeout), check the instance counts for all *(class,property)* pairs separately[22].

4) Retrieve the property-property relations, recording the situations, when one property can follow the other (a), or both properties can have a common subject (b), or a common object (c), together with the triple pattern counts.

5) Pre-compute the property domain and range information, where possible (by checking, if the source/target class for a property with largest property triple count is its domain/range).

6) Create the list of namespaces and link the classes and properties to them.

   The following additional schema enrichment and tuning operations are performed, using the specifics of the DBPedia endpoint organization.

7) Compute the display names for classes and properties to coincide with the entity local name, with some DBPedia-specific adjustments:

   a. If the local name ends in a long number (as some yago: namespace classes do), replace the number part by '..', followed by the last 2–4 digits of the number allowing to disambiguate the display names),

   b. If the local name contains '/', surround it by [[and]],

   c. For the *wikidata:* namespace, fetch the class labels from wikidata[23] and use the labels (enclosed in [[and]]) as display names.

8) Note the sub-class relation[24] (to be used in the class tree presentation, and in determining the "representative" large classes for small classes).

---

[19] https://databus.dbpedia.org/dbpedia/collections/latest-core.

[20] this requires setting up a local DBPedia instance to enable queries with 500K result set, split e.g., in chunks of 100K, we order the classes by their instance count descending.

[21] currently, the 3000 largest classes; the class count, or size threshold is introduced by the user; the optimal level of the threshold can be discussed.

[22] we did the detailed computations automatically for classes larger than 500K instances.

[23] http://query.wikidata.org/.

[24] From the explicitly stated ontology and the sub-class-of assertions in the main data graph.

9) Note the class equivalence relation, to allow the non-local classes to be "represent-ed" by the local ones in the initial class list.

10) For each "small" class, compute its smallest "large" super-class (for use in the property-to-class mapping to suggest also the "small" class names). Perform the step (3) for "small" classes that do not have any "large" superclass.

The schema extraction process currently is semi-automated. It can be expected that after a full automation and some optimizations it would be able to complete within a couple of days. The process can be repeated for new DBPedia configurations and data releases. The database size on the PostgreSQL server (including the tables and indices) amounts to about 20 GB. The dump of the database for the currently analyzed DBPedia endpoint can be accessed from the paper's supporting website.

5   Visual Query Creation

To enable the creation of visual queries over DBPedia (cf. Fig. 1 in Sect. 2), the ViziQuer tool [7] has been connected to the data schema server and enriched by new features involving: (i) new shape of the class tree, (ii) means for query seeding by properties and individuals, and (iii) search-boxes for names in attribute and link dialogues and for classes in the node property pane.

The implementation of the tool allows also for endpoint-specific extensions to customize the tool appearance while working on specific data endpoints.

The created ViziQuer/DSS tool can be accessed from the paper's supporting website.

We briefly explain the visual environment elements that enable the schema-supported query creation experience, relying on the schema server API, (cf. Section 3).

For the query seeding there are tabs with class, property and individual selection, the class tab can show either the full list of classes, or the full list of classes without the dominating *yago:* namespace, or just the *dbo:* namespace classes (the top classes of the first two choices are in Fig. 2); the properties in their tab can be listed either in the basic (moving down the *dbp:* namespace properties and a few more "housekeeping" properties), or in the full mode (ordering just by the triple count descending). The property search can be restricted to either data or object properties only (a property of "dual nature" would be present in both lists). Both the class and property lists are efficiently searchable. There is also an option to obtain a list of subclasses for a class. Double click on an item in any of the tabs, initiates a new query from this element.

The main tools for query growing are the attribute and link addition dialogues, illustrated in Fig. 3, in the context of the *dbo:Language* class (cf. Figure 1); both basic and full lists of attributes and links are illustrated. In the link list the principal (range or domain) class is added, if available in the data schema for the property; the lists are efficiently searchable, as well.

If a query has been started by a property or an individual, there is an option to fill in the class name (in the element's property pane to the right of the diagram) from the class name suggestions created in the context of the selected node and its environment in the diagram. Figure 4 illustrates the class name suggestion in the context of an outgoing property *dbo:spokenIn*.

Classes	Properties	Individuals	Classes	Properties	Individuals	Classes	Properties	Individu

		Pers			All properties

Use filter ☐ Only from dbo: ✔ Exclud   Use filter ☐ Only from dbo: ☐ Exclud   Use filter ✔ Basic list

foaf:Document (15.5M)	+ Person (1.74M)	rdfs:label (31.2M)
+ owl:Thing (4.94M)	+ foaf:Person (1.62M)	rdfs:comment (18.5M)
+ CareerStation (2.48M)	+ schema:Person (1.62M)	abstract (18.5M)
skos:Concept (2.02M)	wikidata:[[person]] (1.62M)	foaf:primaryTopic (15.5M)
+ Agent (1.97M)	+ dul:NaturalPerson (1.62M)	foaf:isPrimaryTopicOf (15.5M)
+ TimePeriod (1.92M)	+ yago:Person.. (1.22M)	dc:language (15.5M)
+ dul:TimeInterval (1.77M)	+ PersonFunction (515K)	skos:broader (4.07M)
+ Person (1.74M)	+ dul:SocialPerson (336K)	gold:hypernym (4.01M)
+ foaf:Person (1.62M)	MilitaryPerson (42.5K)	foaf:name (3.85M)
geo:SpatialThing (1.20M)	+ yago:GoodPerson.. (12.0K)	team (2.75M)
+ Place (979K)	+ yago:BadPerson.. (10.9K)	skos:prefLabel (2.02M)
+ Location (975K)	+ yago:EnlistedPerson.. (9.25K)	careerStation (1.49M)
+ Work (585K)	+ yago:Businessperson.. (8.93K)	birthPlace (1.35M)
+ schema:CreativeWork (583K)	umbel-rc:PersonWithOccupation (8.36K)	years (1.28M)
+ PopulatedPlace (578K)	+ yago:ReligiousPerson.. (8.26K)	

Fig. 2. Schema tree examples in the visual query tool: top classes except from *yago:* namespace, filtered classes, top properties

☐ rdfs:label	☐ rdfs:label	○ languageFamily =>	● owl:sameAs =>
☐ rdfs:comment	☐ rdfs:comment	○ spokenIn =>	○ rdf:type =>
☐ abstract	☐ abstract	○ foaf:isPrimaryTopicOf =>	○ dbp:wikiPageUsesTemplate ›
☐ foaf:name	☐ foaf:name	○ owl:differentFrom =>	○ dct:subject =>
☐ iso6393Code	☐ wikiPageLength	○ rdfs:seeAlso =>	○ wikiPageExternalLink =>
☐ iso6392Code	☐ wikiPageRevisionID	○ foaf:homepage =>	○ dbp:fam =>
☐ geo:geometry	☐ wikiPageID	○ languageRegulator =>	○ languageFamily =>
☐ geo:lat	☐ dbp:name	○ is language of <=	○ spokenIn =>
☐ geo:long	☐ dbp:glotto	○ is foaf:primaryTopic of <=	○ foaf:isPrimaryTopicOf =>
☐ georss:point	☐ dbp:familycolor	○ is gold:hypernym of <=	○ prov:wasDerivedFrom =>
☐ iso6391Code	☐ dbp:iso	● is languageFamily of <= Language	○ dbp:states =>
☐ totalPopulation	☐ dbp:glottorefname	○ is programmingLanguage of <= Softw	○ dbp:region =>

Fig. 3. Top attribute and link suggestions in the context of *dbo:Language* class and outgoing property *spokenIn*: top of basic and full attribute lists, top of basic and full link lists

The created visual environment can be used both for *Exploration* and *Querying* of the data endpoint (DBPedia).

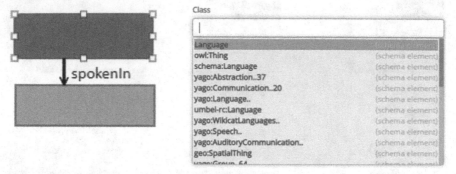

Fig. 4. Visual diagram after selection of *dbo:spokenIn* property from the initial property list, and following class name suggestion for its source class

The exploration would allow obtaining the overview of the classes and properties in the textual pane, together with their size, the subclass relation in the class tree is supported based on the subclass data retrieved from the data endpoint. The class and property lists can be filtered, so allowing to reach any of the 480 K classes and 50 K properties. For each class and property its surrounding context is available (starting from most important classes/properties), as well as the queries over the data can be made from any point reached during the exploration phase (the exploration can be used to determine the entities for further query seeding).

Within the data querying options, the environment provides the visual querying benefits (demonstrated e.g., in [5] and [11]) in the work with the data endpoint of principal importance and substantial size. The environment would allow creating all queries from e.g., the QALD-4 dataset, however, the end user experience with query creation would need to be evaluated within a future work.

6   Conclusions

We have described a method enabling auto-completion of queries based on actual class-to-property and property-to-property mappings for the DBPedia data endpoint with more than 480 thousand classes and more than 50 thousand properties by using hybrid method for accessing the stored data schema and the data endpoint itself.

The created data schema extraction process can be repeated over different versions of the DBPedia, as well as over other data endpoints, so creating query environments over the datasets that need to be explored or analyzed. The open-source code of the visual tool and the data schema server allows adding custom elements to the environment that are important for quality user interface creation over user-supplied data.

An interesting future task would be also moving the schema data (currently stored on PostgreSQL server) into an RDF triple store to enable easier sharing of endpoint data schemas as resources themselves and processing the schema data themselves by means of visual queries and integrating them with other Linked Data resources. An issue to be addressed would be the efficiency of the schema-level queries over the data store, however, it can be conjectured that a reasonable efficiency could be achieved. The technical replacement of the PostgreSQL server by an RDF triple store (and generating SPARQL queries instead of SQL ones) is not expected to be a major challenge since the schema server architecture singles out the schema database querying module.

Acknowledgements. This work has been partially supported by a Latvian Science Council Grant lzp-2020/2-0188 "Visual Ontology-Based Queries".

References

1. Bizer, C., et al.: "DBpedia-a crystallization point for the Web of Data" (PDF). Web Semant. Sci. Services Agents World Wide Web **7**(3), 154–165 (2009)
2. Lehmann, J., et al.: DBpedia-a large-scale, multilingual knowledge base extracted from Wikipedia. Semant. Web **6**(2), 167–195 (2015)
3. Vargas, H., Buil-Aranda, C., Hogan, A., López, C.: RDF Explorer: A Visual SPARQL Query Builder. In: Ghidini, C., et al. (eds.) ISWC 2019. LNCS, vol. 11778, pp. 647–663. Springer, Cham (2019). https://doi.org/10.1007/978-3-030-30793-6_37
4. Ferré, S.: Sparklis: an expressive query builder for SPARQL endpoints with guidance in natural language. Semant. Web **8**, 405–418 (2017)
5. Soylu, A., Giese, M., Jimenez-Ruiz, E., Vega-Gorgojo, G., Horrocks, I.: Experiencing OptiqueVQS: a Multi-paradigm and ontology-based visual query system for end users. Univ. Access Inf. Soc. **15**(1), 129–152 (2016)
6. Klungre, V.N., Soylu, A., Jimenez-Ruiz, E., Kharlamov, E., Giese, M.: Query extension suggestions for visual query systems through ontology projection and indexing. N. Gener. Comput. **37**(4), 361–392 (2019). https://doi.org/10.1007/s00354-019-00071-1
7. Čerāns, K., et al.: ViziQuer: A Web-Based Tool for Visual Diagrammatic Queries Over RDF Data. In: Gangemi, A., et al. (eds.) ESWC 2018. LNCS, vol. 11155, pp. 158–163. Springer, Cham (2018). https://doi.org/10.1007/978-3-319-98192-5_30
8. Čerāns, K., et al.: Extended UML class diagram constructs for visual SPARQL queries in ViziQuer/web In Voila!2017. CEUR Workshop Proceed. **1947**, 87–98 (2017)
9. YASGUI. https://yasgui.triply.cc/
10. Kapourani, B., Fotopoulou, E., Papaspyros, D., Zafeiropoulos, A., Mouzakitis, S., Koussouris, S.: Propelling SMEs Business Intelligence Through Linked Data Production and Consumption. In: Ciuciu, I., et al. (eds.) OTM 2015. LNCS, vol. 9416, pp. 107–116. Springer, Cham (2015). https://doi.org/10.1007/978-3-319-26138-6_14
11. Čerāns, K., et al.: ViziQuer: a Visual notation for RDF data analysis queries. In: Garoufallou, E., Sartori, F., Siatri, R., Zervas, M. (eds.) Metadata and Semantic Research. CCIS, vol. 846. Springer, Cham (2019). https://doi.org/10.1007/978-3-030-14401-2_5
12. Dudáš, M., Svátek, V., Mynarz, J.: Dataset summary visualization with LODSight. In: The 12th Extended Semantic Web Conference (ESWC2015)
13. Čerāns, K., Ovčiņņikova, J., Bojārs, U., Grasmanis, M., Lāce, L., Romāne, A.: Schema-Backed Visual Queries over Europeana and Other Linked Data Resources. In: Verborgh, R., et al. (eds.) ESWC 2021. LNCS, vol. 12739, pp. 82–87. Springer, Cham (2021). https://doi.org/10.1007/978-3-030-80418-3_15

Generating Answerable Questions
from Ontologies for Educational Exercises

Toky Raboanary⑩, Steve Wang, and C. Maria Keet(✉)⑩

Department of Computer Science, University of Cape Town, Cape Town, South Africa
{traboanary,mkeet}@cs.uct.ac.za, WNGSHU003@myuct.ac.za

Abstract. Proposals for automating the creation of teaching materials across the sciences and humanities include question generation from ontologies. Those efforts have focused on multiple-choice questions, whereas learners also need to be exposed to other types of questions, such as yes/no and short answer questions. Initial results showed it is possible to create ontology-based questions. It is unknown how that can be done automatically and whether it would work beyond that use case in biology. We investigated this for ten types of educationally useful questions with additional sentence formulation variants. Each type of questions has a set of template specifications, axiom prerequisites on the ontology, and an algorithm to generate the questions from the ontology. Three approaches were designed: template variables using foundational ontology categories, using main classes from the domain ontology, and sentences mostly driven by natural language generation techniques. The user evaluation showed that the second approach resulted in slightly better quality questions than the first, and the linguistic-driven templates far outperformed both on syntactic and semantic adequacy of the questions.

Keywords: Ontology-based question generation · Ontologies for education · Natural Language generation

1 Introduction

Ontologies and knowledge graphs are used in an increasing variety of ontology-driven information systems. Our focus is generating questions from ontologies for educational purposes. If there is an annotated textbook in cultural heritage, one can link it to an ontology and develop an educational game by generating educational questions to foster active learning in the same spirit as alluded to in [6]. Question generation from an ontology or linked data has been investigated mainly for multiple-choice questions (MCQs) using tailor-made algorithms or SPARQL queries [2,20,23], knowledge graph construction for it [21], and architectures more broadly [22]. There are multiple types of questions beyond MCQ, such as similarity, yes/no, and short answers that may be automatically marked as well [6,21]. Here, we focus on the two latter types of questions. For instance, from the axiom Collection ⊑ ∀hasMember.(Collection ⊔ CulturalHeritageObject) in

© Springer Nature Switzerland AG 2022
E. Garoufallou et al. (Eds.): MTSR 2021, CCIS 1537, pp. 28–40, 2022.
https://doi.org/10.1007/978-3-030-98876-0_3

Cultural-On [11], one could generate a question "Does a collection have a member that is only a cultural heritage object?". This opens up many possibilities for question construction for multiple axiom types, as well as combinations thereof; e.g., given CulturalInstituteOrSite ⊑ ∀isSubjectOf.CreativeWork and CulturalInstituteOrSite ⊑ CulturalEntity, to generate "Which cultural entity is a subject of only a creative work?". It is unclear what the prerequisites of the ontology are, i.e., which axiom(s) type(s) is (are) needed for which type of educational questions, and which type of questions one possibly could generate from an ontology. Questions can be generated from instance or type-level information (ABox or TBox), where we zoom in on the TBox since it is relevant for learning generic knowledge. In this paper, we aim to answer the following questions:

1. Which of the types of questions that are educationally relevant can be generated from the TBox of an ontology? Or, from the ontology viewpoint: What are the axiom prerequisites, i.e. types of axioms that must be in the ontology, to be able to generate a particular type of educational question?
2. Can the outcome be generalised to any combination of ontology (+ textbook) with question templates whilst maintaining good quality questions?

We aim to answer these questions in this paper. Taking the principal types of questions as identified by education research, we systematically assess what the axiom prerequisites are and devise templates for the questions with linguistic variants. A template is a linguistic structure containing gaps that are intended to be filled in to create a sentence. We examined 10 educational types of questions and their axiom prerequisites, represented in the description logic $\mathcal{ALC}$. Three different approaches were developed and implemented to automatically generate the questions from the ontology: 'basic' templates with DOLCE [15] categories for key variables, templates that use a top-level vocabulary of the domain ontology to tailor the basic templates, and natural language generation (NLG)-based tailoring of the basic templates, where the first two approaches informed the third one. The generated questions were evaluated by humans on perceived syntactic and semantic correctness. The first two approaches resulted in poor performance (26% and 34% of good quality), whereas the domain-independent but NLG-enhanced templates reach over 80% very good syntactic and 73.7% as good or very good semantic quality. The algorithms, source code, templates, generated questions, ontologies and data used in the experiment are available at https://github.com/mkeet/AQuestGO.

The remainder of the paper is structured as follows. We present the related work in Sect. 2, the question generation in Sect. 3, and the evaluation with discussion in Sect. 4. We conclude in Sect. 5.

2 Related Work

Questions can be generated from ontologies [2,6,7,19,22,23], using either generic systems [2,7,19,23] or tailor-made for a specific domain, such as biology [6,24] and mathematics [14]. They may have a new purposely-built [6] or existing [7,23] ontology as input. Most research focuses on MCQ generation [2,7,19,23], which mainly deal with distractor generation and difficulty control.

Concerning the verbalisation, i.e., generating the natural language sentences, only [5,24] evaluated the linguistic quality of the generated questions. Bühmann et al. [5] considered their syntax (fluency) and their semantics (adequacy), but the sentences are over the ABox rather than the TBox. Zhang and VanLehn [24] evaluated the fluency and ambiguity of their questions, but their approach is designed for one knowledge base. Vinu et al. [23] consider the surface structure of generated questions with regex, yet they did not evaluate their verbalisation approach. Also, the generalisability of approaches is found wanting: most of them used only one ontology in their experiment, except those which used three [1,7] and four [23] ontologies.

Chaudhri et al.'s idea for non-MCQ educational question generation with their "intelligent textbook" [6] is appealing for fostering active learning. However, they did not make their question templates or the construction process available, nor is it clear how this could be reused for other ontologies beyond their "Inquire Biology" use case for one hand-crafted ontology and one particular textbook.

Question generation is also used for other tasks; notably, ontology validation [1]. Abacha et al. [1] evaluated their questions, but covered only a subset of possible sentence constructions, such as omitting quantifiers explicitly. Further afield, there are statement generation verbalisation systems [4], and frameworks [17] for verbalising RDF, OWL and SPARQL, whose experiences may be of use, but they do not generate (educational) questions.

3 Question Generation

The design choices are described before we proceed to the question specifications and algorithms.

3.1 Design Choices

There are core choices for the template design within the context of ontology-based question generation in anticipation of their quality. For the templates themselves, there are four core options:

Type A: Fixed template structure where one fills in the slots with the relevant variable (class, object property (OP), quantifier) fetched from the ontology, at that level of specification; e.g., Is a [owl:thing] [owl:objectproperty] [quantifier] [owl:thing]? as template which could have an instantiation resulting in, e.g., "Is a cultural heritage object a member of some collection?".

Type B: As Type A, but specify the category at least, especially for the OWL class; e.g., that it has to be a dolce:process, or a bfo:continuant (cf. owl:thing), so that for the template instantiation, it will pick that or any of its subclasses so as to broadly constrain the filler type. This is likely to increase the quality of the syntax and semantics of the generated questions. A foundational ontology is well-suited for this.

Type C: As Type B, but tailor the template with the domain ontology vocabulary to some degree; e.g., select a high-level class from the domain ontology, e.g., CulturalEntity from Cultural-On, so that the considered slot of the template will only be instantiated with a subclass of culturalon:CulturalEntity. One may expect better semantics of the questions, but it comes at the cost of reduced generalisability across domain ontologies.

Type D: Contextualise the templates based on the ontology vocabulary using NLG techniques, but do not perform tailoring of slots with any ontology vocabulary. This assumes that the question quality is more dependent on the linguistic realisation module of the NLG process than on the representation of the domain knowledge.

3.2 Types of Questions and Their Prerequisites

The types of questions considered in this paper are adjusted from [6] and extended with questions from the Webclopedia QA typology [10] that is based on actual educational questions. They are also included in [9] and are shown to be suitable for education [18]. We chose this typology because its question templates are abstract (not domain-specific), which is appropriate for the generalisability purpose, and it is based on 17,384 questions and their answers.

Templates of different question types are specified, and each slot in the template is replaced by the appropriate class or object property (OP) or quantifier in an ontology. We selected DOLCE [15] for the Type B templates, but one could take another foundational ontology. For the Type C examples below, terms in Cultural-On are used. Each question template is mapped to Description Logic (DL) queries to check that the generated question is answerable by the ontology. For Type D, we devised several templates (e.g., templates in active/passive voice and hasX OP naming format) for each type of questions.

The aggregate number of variants of templates designed for the three approaches are presented in Table 1. The different numbers of variants are due to peculiarities of the approaches, such as more tailoring with domain ontology vocabulary (hence |Type A/B| ≤ |Type C|), and accommodating active/passive voice or not. Due to space limitations, we present all types of questions with their prerequisites only briefly and more details can be found online.

Yes/No and True/False Questions. These questions expect yes/no or true/false as an answer. Since the ontology operates under Open World Assumption , the answer to a question is no only if the ontology explicitly states so. For instance, using Thing or any of its subclasses, a template "*Does a X OP a Y?*" (for numbers i,iv in Table 1) can be generated if $X \sqsubseteq \exists OP.Y$ or $X \sqsubseteq \forall OP.Y$ (Answer: Yes) or if $X \sqsubseteq \neg \forall OP.Y$ (Answer: No). Template examples of this type are:

Type A template: *Does a* [Thing] [OP] *a* [Thing]?
Type B template: *Does a* [Endurant] [OP] *a* [Thing]?
Type C template: *Does a* [CulturalEntity] [OP] *a* [Thing]?
Type D templates: *Does a* [T_Noun] [OP_Verb] *a* [T_Noun]?
　　　　　　　　 Does a [T_Noun] [OP_Verb_Prep] *a* [T_Noun]?

Table 1. Numbers of variants of templates by type of template.

Group of TQ	No.	Type of Questions (TQ)	A/B	C	D
Yes/No	i	Two classes and one property	4	6	6
	ii	Two classes, one property, and a quantifier	4	4	10
	iii	One Endurant and one Perdurant	4	4	1
True/False	iv	Two classes and one property	4	6	10
	v	Two classes, one property, and a quantifier	4	6	20
Equivalence	vi	Equivalence	2	5	3
Subclass	vii	Two classes and one property	1	4	5
	viii	Additional quantifier	1	1	10
	ix	One class and one property	4	4	4
Narrative	x	Narrative	2	2	6
		Total	30	42	75

where for Type D, T_Noun states that the class name Thing is a noun, OP_Verb means that the OP name is a verb and OP_Verb_Prep indicates it also has a preposition. Then, "*A X OP some Y. True or false?*" *(ii,v)* and "*A X OP only a Y. True or false?*" *(ii,v)* can be generated if $X \sqsubseteq \exists OP.Y$ (Answer: Yes) or if $X \sqsubseteq \neg\exists OP.Y$ (Answer: No), and if $X \sqsubseteq \forall OP.Y$ (Answer: Yes) or if $X \sqsubseteq \neg\forall OP.Y$ (Answer: No), respectively. Finally, "*Does a X Y?*" *(iii)* can be generated if $X \sqsubseteq \exists$participates-in.Y (Answer: Yes), or if $X \sqsubseteq \neg\exists$participates-in.Y (Answer: No).

Equivalence Questions. This is possible to generate provided the two classes are asserted or inferred to be equivalent. The template "*Are there any differences between a X and a Y?*" (*vi* in Table 1) can be generated and results in "Yes" if $X \equiv \neg Y$, and "No" if $X \equiv Y$ is asserted or inferred in the ontology.

Subclass Identification Questions. These questions can be casted as "Which" questions. The template "*Which X OP Y?*" *(vii)* can be generated if there is a class Z that satisfies the axiom pattern $Z \sqsubseteq X \sqcap \exists OP.Y$ or $Z \sqsubseteq X \sqcap \forall OP.Y$. Then, the template "*Which X OP some Y?*" *(viii)* can be generated if there is a class Z that satisfies the axiom pattern $Z \sqsubseteq X \sqcap \exists OP.Y$. The template "*Which X OP only a Y?*" *(viii)* can be generated if there is a class Z that satisfies the axiom pattern $Z \sqsubseteq X \sqcap \forall OP.Y$. Finally, "*What does a X OP?*" *(ix)* can be generated if there is a class Y such that $X \sqsubseteq \exists OP.Y$ or $X \sqsubseteq \forall OP.Y$.

Narrative Questions. A class X in an ontology can be "defined" if it satisfies one of the following criteria: 1) it is annotated with a definition; 2) it has at least one equivalent class; 3) it has at least one superclass, at least one subclass or a combination of both; for instance, "*Define X.*" (number *x* in Table 1).

The 10 types of educational questions with their specific axiom prerequisites presented as a summary here answer our first research question. The full specifications can be found in the supplementary material online.

3.3   Dynamic Question Generation: The Algorithms

This section presents an overview of the three approaches we have designed for the dynamic question generation: template variables using foundational ontology categories (Appr 1), using main classes from the domain ontology (Appr 2), and sentences mostly driven by natural language generation techniques (Appr 3). Appr 1 and Appr 2 adopt 'Algorithm 1', with the difference that the former takes Type A and Type B templates as input and the latter takes Type C templates as input. Appr 3 uses 'Algorithm 2' and takes Type D templates as input. All details about the algorithms can be found in the supplementary material.

Algorithm 1: Ontology Element-Based Templates. Algorithm 1 is composed of some variant sub-algorithms depending on the type of questions, but several steps are the same. There are 3 different types of tokens that are going to replace the slots in templates: quantifier tokens (denoted with [quantifier]), OWLObjectProperty tokens, and OWLClass tokens. A [quantifier] in the template is replaced with either 'some' ($\exists$) or 'only' ($\forall$). When the token appears as an [ObjectProperty] then it can be replaced with any of its object subproperties in the ontology that satisfies the axiom prerequisites of the question type. If [X], indicating an OWLClass, appears in the template, then it can be replaced with any subclass of X.

Overall, the algorithm picks a template and tries to fill it with contents from the ontology, taking into account the vocabulary, axiom prerequisites, hyphen checking (e.g., 'Bumble-Bee' is converted to 'bumble bee') and article checking (e.g., 'a elephant' is converted to 'an elephant'). For example, with the template *"Does a [Thing] [ObjectProperty] a [Thing]?"*, the algorithm can generate a question like "Does a catalogue describe a collection?" from the axiom Catalogue $\sqsubseteq$ $\exists$describes.Collection.

Algorithm 2: Natural Language-Driven Templates. Algorithm 2 not only fills in the question templates, but also fetches all axioms satisfying the axiom prerequisites from a selected type of questions. Then, it processes the contents of the ontology by fetching the vocabulary elements of a selected axiom, picks an appropriate variant of a template that the vocabulary can be used in, and makes some linguistic adaptation before generating the whole question.

The improvements incorporated were partially informed by the analysis of the 'bad' sentences generated by Algorithm 1. There are three major changes:

- *using class expressions to generate questions, rather than only the declared domain and range of OPs,* so using only asserted and inferred knowledge.
- *improving common grammar issues, availing of SimpleNLG [8] and Word-Net [16], for subject and verb agreement, gerund form generation, and article checking.* Also, a basic part of speech (POS) tagging for the classes and OPs was added to get the appropriate form, by using WordNet [16].
- *choosing the appropriate template for a given axiom by considering the POS of classes and OPs, and classifying the OP.* We designed an algorithm based

on an FSM that classifies the name given to an OP to find the appropriate template for an axiom and provides the appropriate equivalent text. It considers 6 linguistic variants. An OP name may: 1) have a verb, 2) start with a verb followed by a preposition, 3) start with 'has' and followed by nouns, 4) be composed of 'is', nouns and a preposition, 5) start with 'is', followed by a verb in a past participle form and ends with a preposition, or 6) start with 'is', followed by a verb in a past participle form and ends with 'by' (i.e., passive voice variants for 4–6). The FSM strategy is a sequence detector to determine the category of an OP and chunks it. For instance, the OP *is-eatenBy*, which is an instance of OP_ Is_ Past_ Part_ By (the 6th variant), is transformed into a list of words (is, eaten, by). Then, it detects each component, and from that, the POS of each token is obtained, and, finally, it generates the appropriate group of words: "is eaten by", which will be used in the question.

So, for the axiom Leaf ⊑ ∃eaten-by.Giraffe, the appropriate template is *"Is a* [T_Noun][OP_Is_Past_Part_By] *a* [T_Noun]*?"* and a correct generated question would be "Is a leaf eaten by a giraffe?" rather than "Does a leaf eaten by a giraffe?". Finally, the mapping between the vocabulary elements of the axiom and the tokens of the selected template is done sequentially.

4 Evaluation

The evaluation aims to gain insight into the quality of the algorithms with respect to 1) the syntax, 2) the semantics of the sentences, and 3) the generalisability of the approach to multiple ontologies. To this end, we have conducted three evaluation sessions. The first two evaluation sessions with Appr 1 and Appr 2, using Algorithm 1 were of a preliminary nature, in that we focused only on the first two aims of the evaluation and used only one ontology. The third evaluation also considered the potential for generalisability using Appr 3 with Algorithm 2. Ethics approval was obtained before the evaluation sessions.

4.1 Materials and Methods

Materials. Three ontologies were used in our evaluation: an extended version of African Wildlife Ontology (AWO) [13], where we added 19 classes (a.o., BumbleBee, Land, Fly) and 4 OPs (a.o., participate-in, live-on) so that the question generator can generate all specified types of questions; the Stuff Ontology [12], developed by the same author as AWO, which is a core ontology about categories of 'stuff', such as pure and mixed stuff, colloids (e.g., foam, emulsion) and solutions; and the BioTop [3] top-domain ontology that provides definitions for the foundational entities of biomedicine. For the first 2 experiments, we only used the extended version of AWO, while all three were used for the third experiment.

Methods. The methods of the three evaluations are as follows. *First experiment:* Each participant ($n = 5$) evaluated 30 questions generated by Appr 1 using AWO and the templates with DOLCE categories (Type B). Students from the University of Cape Town (UCT) were recruited to complete the evaluation. All participants have at least a secondary school pass of English and can speak English fluently. *Second experiment:* Each participant ($n = 6$) evaluated 40 questions generated by Appr 2, using AWO and the subject domain-tailored templates (Type C). The requirements for each participant are the same as for the first experiment. Each evaluator could participate in either the first or second experiment or in both. We used a pass/fail mechanism for both evaluations to determine whether a sentence conforms to English syntax and semantics. All evaluators were allowed to comment on each sentence and encouraged to do so if the answer was negative. *Third experiment:* 95 questions were generated from the three ontologies using Appr 3. From an ontology, for each type of questions, axioms satisfying the axiom prerequisites are randomly selected for the question generation using the Type D templates. We generated 39, 12 and 44 questions from AWO, Stuff Ontology and Biotop Ontology, respectively. The difference is due to having more or less content satisfying the prerequisites. The 12 questions from the Stuff Ontology still do cover all groups of questions. Seven students and one staff member at UCT ($n = 8$) who have English as their first language or speak English fluently (self-declaration) participated in the evaluation. Only two of them participated in the first two experiments. Each participant evaluated all 95 generated questions and had to answer whether each question is syntactically and semantically correct, choosing between A: Very Good, B: Good, C: Average, D: Bad, and E: Very Bad. Their differences were explained to the participants during the meeting before evaluating the generated questions. All evaluators were allowed to comment on each sentence. We use the central tendency (the median for ordinal values) to determine the quality of the questions.

4.2   Results

Appr 1 with Type A and B templates generated some correct questions, such as "Does a herbivore walk?", but the majority failed semantically or syntactically, such as "Is the fly eaten by the walk?". Overall, 26% of the generated questions were considered as quality questions.

Appr 2 with subject domain-specific (Type C) templates generated some correct questions such as: "Does a carnivore eat a terrestrial?" and "True or False: A warthog eats some omnivore.", but also semantically nonsensical ones, such as "Did the terrestrial participate in all the hibernate?". Overall, 34% of the generated questions were considered as quality questions.

For the third experiment, with Appr 3, some of the good generated questions are: "Does a bumble bee fly?" and "True or false: A collective process has a granular part that is a process.". Of the ones classified as 'bad' by the participants, some indeed are, yet others as not (discussed below); questions include "Does a mixed stuff have a part stuff that is a stuff?". In analysing the data, it was evident that one of the eight participants did not perform a proper assessment but randomly selected answers since some good questions were evaluated as bad and vv.; e.g., "Does a carnivorous plant eat an animal?" was labelled with 'Very Bad' and "A condition is a condition of only a situation. True or

false?" as 'Good', which is not the case. Therefore, we chose not to consider this
participant in further analysis.

The seven participants gave feedback on a total of 665 sentences for syntactic
and semantic evaluation; hence, we have 1330 data points. Figure 1a shows the
percentage of answers from the evaluators for each answer option (Very Good,
$\cdots$, Very Bad), and Fig. 1b presents, in percentage, the quality of the generated
questions, which refers to the median of the set of evaluations of each question.
For the syntax (Fig. 1b), 81.05% of the generated questions were classified 'Very
Good' (77 out of 95 questions); hence, given the ordinal values ordering and the
number of participants, at least four evaluators judged the syntax of the question
as 'Very Good'. Regarding semantics (Fig. 1b), 53.68% and 20% of the questions
were 'Very Good' and 'Good', respectively, based on their central tendency.
Disaggregating by ontology, the results are as shown in Fig. 1c, from which it
can be noted that the results for AWO are better than those from the others.
We confirmed with a statistical hypothesis test (Fisher's exact) that the results
are statistically significantly different (p-value $= 0.003887$ for the syntax and p-
value $= 3.733e-08$ for the semantics). Regarding the inter-rater agreement, the
Fleiss Kappa coefficients computed with R language are $k = 0.0856 > 0$ and $k =
0.11 > 0$ for the syntax and the semantics, respectively, which both mean 'slight
agreement'. Then, overall, 4 out of 7 evaluators agreed on a single assessment on
85.26% and 60% of the questions generated for their syntax and their semantics,
respectively.

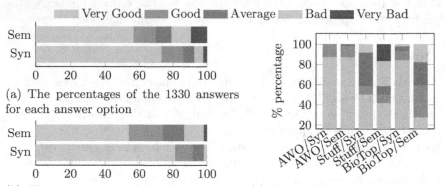

(a) The percentages of the 1330 answers
for each answer option

(b) The percentages of the 95 questions
that were classified as V Good, $\cdots$, V Bad

(c) Syn and Sem quality of the generated questions for each ontology

Fig. 1. Aggregate results of the human evaluation; Syn: syntax; Sem: Semantics.

4.3 Discussion

From the first two experiments, one can see that specifying the template to a
lower level class token helps improve the quality of the generated questions. However, the need for tailoring the generic templates to a specific domain ontology

increases the manual effort and decreases the generalisability of question generation across domains. Analysis of the feedback provided by the participants from the first two experiments gave insights as to why the quality rate of generated questions was so low, which amount to two major issues causing the low quality:

- the use of domain and range of OPs to generate questions since it could select unconnected classes, and
- slots that do not adapt to the names of the ontology elements inserted, or: there is a large variation in naming elements within and across ontologies that a fixed template cannot cater for. Since the approach would ideally work for a range of ontologies, it suggested that a reverse order—find the right template for a given axiom—may be a better strategy.

The analysis of the first two approaches assisted in designing Appr 3 and to focus on linguistic aspects instead. This had a much larger improvement in question quality compared to tailoring a generic template to a domain ontology.

The 'slight agreement' between evaluators may come from their different levels of strictness, the disagreement on the place of the word "only" in the questions and the difficulty to understand difficult questions from specific domains, especially for those from Stuff and BioTop Ontology. Understandability of educational questions also straddles into educational research and language proficiency, which is beyond the current scope.

Challenges for Generating and Evaluating Questions. There are three main persistent challenges, which affect either the quality of the questions or the user's perception thereof. First, there are words with more than one POS category that are hard to disambiguate in the ontology cf. within-sentence disambiguation for POS tagging; e.g., 'stuff' that can be a noun or a verb.

Second, there is the 'hasX' naming issue of OPs, such as hasTopping, that have already the name of the range in its name. This then results in generated questions such as "Which condition has a life that is some life?", but that ideally would end up as "Which condition has a life?". Furthermore, the question "Does a mixed stuff have a part stuff that is a stuff?" is correct but not 'nice', because the word 'stuff' is repeated 3 times due to the ontology elements MixedStuff, Stuff, and hasStuffPart. Ideally, it would recognise such corner cases and render the question as "Does a mixed stuff have a part that is also a stuff?". Refinement could be made to Algorithm 2 to accommodate for this style of naming OPs after determining several possible OP naming variants, though the algorithm likely always will run behind a modeller's varied naming practice.

Third, there are misunderstood questions, which is an issue that is also unlikely ever to be resolved. The AWO contains general knowledge and is easy for most people to understand. However, since the Stuff and BioTop ontologies are in a specialised domain, we obtained 'Bad' evaluations for some generated questions. For instance, "A mixed stuff has a part stuff that is a stuff. True or false?" is syntactically and semantically correct but was misunderstood by most participants. Also, words with a specific ontological meaning, such as inhere in, were not appropriately assessed; e.g., "True or false: A process quality inheres in a process." is correct but was misunderstood.

Generalisability of Education Question Generation. As can be observed in Fig. 1, the questions generated from the AWO were evaluated as better than those from Stuff and BioTop. There are three possible reasons for this: either template overfitting, or the AWO additions for coverage testing, or because it was common-sense knowledge, cf. specialised domain knowledge. As stated above, some questions from Stuff and BioTop were misunderstood during the evaluation. In addition, AWO does not have OPs with the "hasX" naming scheme, while the two other ontologies do. Finally, for Stuff Ontology, the word "stuff" has several POS tags, and this affects the quality of the generated questions.

Even though BioTop was not developed by the same developer as the AWO and Stuff ontologies, one can see that the results from BioTop are better than those from the Stuff Ontology. So, this may suggest that Appr 3 with Type D templates and Algorithm 2 has not been overfitted to the modelling style of the AWO developer, therewith indicating potential for generalisability.

Furthermore, we commenced with assessing potential usefulness of our approach for preserving cultural heritage. As a first step in this direction, we generated 3632 questions by using Appr 3 with Algorithm 2 from 3 DH ontologies: Cultural-ON [11] (306 questions), Copyright Ontology (280) and Latin Dance Ontology (3046). For instance, if one can link a dance textbook annotated with the Latin Dance Ontology, one can reuse those generated questions to develop an educational game. Those details and generated questions are available from the supplementary material for further analysis and use. A cursory evaluation indicates that, although our algorithm does not yet cover all corner cases of the myriad of vocabulary naming practices used in ontologies and similar artifacts, there are relevant and good educational questions, such as "What is cross body lead a part of?" and "Does a catalogue describe a collection?".

Overall, it can be concluded that Appr 3 with Type D templates and Algorithm 2 results in good quality questions and generalisability, answering Question 2 from the Introduction (Sect. 1) in the positive.

5 Conclusions

Three approaches to answerable question generation from ontologies were proposed, involving the specification of axiom prerequisites, a foundational ontology, NLP techniques, template design, and the design and implementation of their respective algorithms. The human evaluation showed that the NLP-based approach (Appr 3 with Type D templates and Algorithm 2) outperformed the others by a large margin. The generated questions from 3 ontologies in different domains were deemed for 80% to have very good syntactic quality and 73.7% very good or good semantic quality. The results also indicated good prospects of generalisability of the proposed solution to ontologies in other subject domains.

Current and future work involves various extensions, including improving on the questions generated from the DH ontologies, more combinations of prerequisites to generate educationally more advanced questions, and link them to annotated textbook text.

Acknowledgements. TR acknowledges support from the Hasso Plattner Institute for Digital Engineering through the HPI Research School at UCT.

References

1. Abacha, A.B., Dos Reis, J.C., Mrabet, Y., Pruski, C., Da Silveira, M.: Towards natural language question generation for the validation of ontologies and mappings. J. Biomed. Semant. **7**(1), 1–15 (2016)
2. Alsubait, T., Parsia, B., Sattler, U.: Ontology-based multiple choice question generation. KI - Künstliche Intelligenz **30**(2), 183–188 (2016)
3. Beisswanger, E., Schulz, S., Stenzhorn, H., Hahn, U.: BioTop: an upper domain ontology for the life sciences. Appl. Ontol. **3**(4), 205–212 (2008)
4. Bouayad-Agha, N., Casamayor, G., Wanner, L.: Natural language generation in the context of the semantic web. Semant. Web **5**(6), 493–513 (2014)
5. Bühmann, L., Usbeck, R., Ngonga Ngomo, A.-C.: ASSESS—automatic self-assessment using linked data. In: Arenas, M., et al. (eds.) The Semantic Web - ISWC 2015: 14th International Semantic Web Conference, Bethlehem, PA, USA, October 11–15, 2015, Proceedings, Part II, pp. 76–89. Springer, Cham (2015). https://doi.org/10.1007/978-3-319-25010-6_5
6. Chaudhri, V.K., Clark, P.E., Overholtzer, A., Spaulding, A.: Question generation from a knowledge base. In: Janowicz, K., Schlobach, S., Lambrix, P., Hyvönen, E. (eds.) Knowledge Engineering and Knowledge Management: 19th International Conference, EKAW 2014, Linköping, Sweden, November 24–28, 2014. Proceedings, pp. 54–65. Springer, Cham (2014). https://doi.org/10.1007/978-3-319-13704-9_5
7. EV, V., Kumar, P.S.: Automated generation of assessment tests from domain ontologies. Semant. Web **8**(6), 1023–1047 (2017)
8. Gatt, A., Reiter, E.: SimpleNLG: a realisation engine for practical applications. In: Proceedings of the ENLG 2009, pp. 90–93 (2009)
9. Graesser, A.C., Person, N., Huber, J.: Mechanisms that generate questions. Quest. Inf. Syst. **2**, 167–187 (1992)
10. Hovy, E., Gerber, L., Hermjakob, U., Junk, M., Lin, C.Y.: Question answering in Webclopedia. In: Proceedings of the 9th Text retrieval conference (TREC-9) (2001)
11. Italian Ministry of Cultural Heritage and Activities: Italian institute of cognitive sciences and technologies, cultural-on (cultural ontology): cultural institute/site and cultural event ontology (2016). http://dati.beniculturali.it/cis/3.2
12. Keet, C.M.: A core ontology of macroscopic stuff. In: Janowicz, K., Schlobach, S., Lambrix, P., Hyvönen, E. (eds.) EKAW 2014. LNCS (LNAI), vol. 8876, pp. 209–224. Springer, Cham (2014). https://doi.org/10.1007/978-3-319-13704-9_17
13. Keet, C.M.: The African wildlife ontology tutorial ontologies. J. Biomed. Semant. **11**, 1–4 (2020)
14. Khodeir, N.A., Elazhary, H., Wanas, N.: Generating story problems via controlled parameters in a web-based intelligent tutoring system. Int. J. Inf. Learn. Technol. **35**(3), 199–216 (2018)

15. Masolo, C., Borgo, S., Gangemi, A., Guarino, N., Oltramari, A.: Ontology library. WonderWeb Deliverable D18 (ver. 1.0, 31-12-2003) (2003). http://wonderweb. semanticweb.org

16. Miller, G.A.: WordNet: a lexical database for English. Commun. ACM **38**(11), 39–41 (1995)

17. Ngomo, A.C.N., Moussallem, D., Bühmann, L.: A holistic natural language generation framework for the semantic web. arXiv preprint arXiv:1911.01248 (2019)

18. Olney, A.M., Graesser, A.C., Person, N.K.: Question generation from concept maps. Dialogue Discourse **3**(2), 75–99 (2012)

19. Papasalouros, A., Kanaris, K., Kotis, K.: Automatic generation of multiple choice questions from domain ontologies. In: Proceedings of the IADIS International Conference on e-learning, pp. 427–434 (2008)

20. Rodríguez Rocha, O., Faron Zucker, C.: Automatic generation of educational quizzes from domain ontologies. In: Proceedings of the EDULEARN, pp. 4024–4030 (2017)

21. Rodríguez Rocha, O., Faron Zucker, C.: Automatic generation of quizzes from DBpedia according to educational standards. In: The 3rd Educational Knowledge Management Workshop, Lyon, France, 23–27 April 2018, pp. 1035–1041 (2018)

22. Sirithumgul, P., Prasertsilp, P., Suksa-ngiam, W., Olfman, L.: An ontology-based framework as a foundation of an information system for generating multiple-choice questions. In: Proceedings of the 25th AMCIS (2019)

23. Vinu, E.V., Sreenivasa Kumar, P.: A novel approach to generate MCQs from domain ontology: considering Dl semantics and open-world assumption. J. Web Semant. **34**, 40–54 (2015)

24. Zhang, L., VanLehn, K.: How do machine-generated questions compare to human-generated questions? Res. Pract. Technol. Enhanc. Learn. **11**(1), 1–28 (2016). https://doi.org/10.1186/s41039-016-0031-7

CoVoMe: New Methodology for Building Controlled Vocabulary

Dominik Tomaszuk[(✉)]

Institute of Computer Science, University of Bialystok, Bialystok, Poland
d.tomaszuk@uwb.edu.pl

Abstract. The use of methodologies in knowledge management and engineering is deeply comprehensive due to their important advantages. In this paper, we propose CoVoMe that is a methodology for building controlled vocabularies. This methodology covers almost all variants of that vocabularies, and it is designed to be close to the currently available languages for creating thesauri, subject headings, taxonomies, authority files, synonym rings, and glossaries.

Keywords: Knowledge organization system · Controlled vocabulary · Methodology

1 Introduction

The term knowledge organization system (KOS) is intended to cover all types of controlled vocabularies (CVs) for organizing information and promoting knowledge management. Compared to free-text searching, the use of a CV can greatly increase the performance and precision of a system. Controlled vocabularies are used in different domains, e.g., libraries [8,27], medicine [26], food [7], art [37], economy [30], etc.

A lot of CVs have been developed by different groups of people, under different approaches, and using different methods and techniques. Unfortunately, there are not too many well-documented activities, life cycles, standardized methodologies, and well-defined design criteria. On the other hand, there are many methodologies for ontologies [14,33,39,40]. At the same time, there are only a few similar, but not so complex, proposals to thesauri, taxonomies, or other controlled vocabularies that support the above features (see the related work in Sect. 4). Moreover, there are no proposals that cover all variants of CVs. The field of CV construction still lacks standardized methodologies that can be adapted to different conditions. The major cause is that most of the methodologies were applied to develop CVs for specific projects and/or types of CV. So, the generalization of the methodology was not proposed for other contexts. In this paper, we propose CoVoMe which is a methodology for building CVs either from scratch or reusing by a process of re-engineering them. This methodology covers almost all variants of the controlled vocabularies. Moreover, it is designed to be close to the currently available languages for creating CVs.

© Springer Nature Switzerland AG 2022
E. Garoufallou et al. (Eds.): MTSR 2021, CCIS 1537, pp. 41–56, 2022.
https://doi.org/10.1007/978-3-030-98876-0_4

The paper is organized as follows. Section 2 contains basic definitions used throughout this paper. In Sect. 3, we describe our methodology. In Sect. 4, we discuss related work. Finally, in Sect. 5, we summarize our findings and outline further research directions.

2   Preliminaries

Controlled vocabularies are used in different forms, such as thesauri [7,26,30], classification schemes [27,28], subject headings [8], taxonomies [10], authority files [16], etc.

A controlled vocabulary is a standardized and organized arrangement of words and phrases used to retrieve content through searching and provide a consistent way to describe data. Metadata and data providers assign terms from vocabularies to improve information retrieval. It should typically have a defined scope or describe a specific domain. In this paper, we define full controlled vocabulary as a broad term. The full controlled vocabulary abstraction is defined to be compatible with all kinds of CVs.

Definition 1 (Full controlled vocabularies). *A full controlled vocabulary is defined as a tuple of the form* $V = \langle RS, C, CS, SR, MP, LD, CO \rangle$, *where*

1. *RS is the set of resources,*
2. $C \subseteq RS$ *is the set of concepts, which are all concepts that are identified by IRIs in the vocabulary namespace,*
3. *CS is the set of concept schemes that aggregate concepts,*
4. *SR is the set of semantic relations that include relations for hierarchies (RH) and relation for association (RA),*
5. *MP is the set of mapping properties that includes properties for hierarchy mapping (HM), association mapping (AM) and similarity (PS) and associate resources with one another,*
6. *LD is the set of labels (L), notation (N), and documentation properties (D),*
7. *CO is the set of unordered and ordered collections.*

Full controlled vocabularies are the basis for other definitions. We start with a simple glossary and end with an advanced thesaurus.

We define a glossary as an alphabetical list of terms, usually in a specific domain with the definitions for those terms.

Definition 2 (Glossaries). *A glossary is defined as a tuple of the form* $G = \langle RS, C, LD \rangle$.

A slightly more expanded form is a synonym ring (also called synset). We define it as a group of terms that are considered semantically equivalent for the purpose of retrieval.

Definition 3 (Synonym rings). *A synonym ring is defined as a tuple of the form* $R = \langle RS, C, RA, LD \rangle$.

Then, we define authority files. An authority file is lists of terms that are used to control the variant names for an object for a particular area. They are also applied to other methods of organizing data such as linkages and cross-references.

Definition 4 (Authority files). *An authority file is defined as a tuple of the form* $A = \langle RS, C, CS, PS, LD \rangle$.

We define a taxonomy as the division of items into categories or classifications, especially a hierarchical classification, based on particular characteristics.

Definition 5 (Taxonomies). *A taxonomy is defined as a tuple of the form* $T = \langle RS, C, CS, RH, LD \rangle$.

Subject heading is slightly more complicated. It provides a group of terms to represent the subjects of items in a collection and sets of rules for connecting terms into headings.

Definition 6 (Subject headings). *A subject heading is defined as a tuple of the form* $H = \langle RS, C, CS, SR, LD \rangle$.

The quite complex form of controlled vocabularies is a thesaurus. We define a thesaurus as collections of terms representing concepts and the hierarchical, equivalence, and associative relationships among them.

Definition 7 (Thesauri). *A thesaurus is defined as a tuple of the form* $S = \langle RS, C, CS, SR, LD, CO \rangle$.

Table 1 presents a summary of the characteristics of the above-defined controlled vocabularies.

Table 1. Features of controlled vocabularies

		Glossaries	Synonym rings	Authority files	Taxonomies	Subject headings	Thesauri	Full controlled vocabulary
Concepts and schemas		y	y	y	y	y	y	y
Lab. and notation		y	y	y	y	y	y	y
Documentation		y	y	y	y	y	y	y
Sem. relations	hrchy.	n	n	n	n	y	y	y
	assoc.	n	y	n	n	y	y	y
Map. properties	hrchy.	n	n	n	y	n	n	y
	assoc.	n	n	n	n	n	n	y
	sim.	n	n	y	n	n	n	y
Collections		n	n	n	n	n	y	y

3   Methodology and Steps

A CoVoMe methodology has eight steps and some of the steps are divided into activities. CoVoMe consists of the following steps:

Step 1: Determine the domain and scope (Subsect. 3.1),
Step 2: Determine the type of controlled vocabulary (Subsect. 3.2),
Step 3: Define the concepts and concept schemas (Subsect. 3.3),
Step 4: Define the terms, labels and notation (Subsect. 3.4),
Step 5: Define the semantic relations (Subsect. 3.5),
Step 6: Define groups of concepts (Subsect. 3.6),
Step 7: Integrate with other controlled vocabularies (Subsect. 3.7),
Step 8: Create the documentation (Subsect. 3.8).

In Subsect. 3.9, we discuss how to evaluate our proposal, and how the chackpoints are connected to CoVoMe steps. Figure 1 shows the steps and activities order.

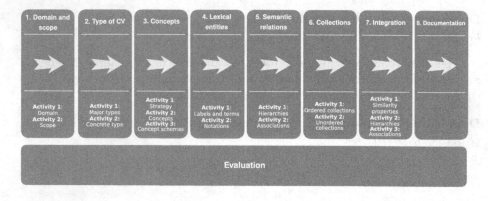

Fig. 1. Sequence of steps in CoVoMe

3.1   Determine the Domain and Scope

In order to define scope, the user should go through two activities. The first one specify some sources that could be used to acquire knowledge for the CV development. In the second activity, a user should use competency questions (CQs) [17] to determine the scope.

In the first activity, a user should acquire a domain knowledge from several sources, such as domain experts, domain literature, other controlled vocabularies, etc. One can also use different techniques, e.g. interviews, brainstorming, mind maps, etc.

In the second activity, based on the first one, the recommended way to determine the scope of the CoVoMe is to sketch a list of CQs that one should be able to answer. CQs are natural language questions outlining and constraining the scope of knowledge represented in a vocabulary. Note that the answers to these questions may change during the process, but at any given time they help limit the scope of the model.

3.2   Determine the Type of Controlled Vocabulary

In this step, one needs to determine what type of controlled vocabulary will be constructed. At this point, users specifies what type of KOS they are building. The first activity at this step is to choose major types of a CV. These major types are based on features such as structure, complexity, relationships among terms, and historical function. According to [19], one can choose three following options:

1. term lists: a CV that emphasizes lists of terms often with definitions,
2. classifications and categories: a CV that emphasizes the creation of subject sets,
3. relationship lists: a CV that emphasizes the connections between terms and concepts.

In the second activity, users should choose the concrete type of CV. According to the definitions in Sect. 2, one can choose:

1. in term lists: glossary, synonym ring or authority file,
2. in classifications and categories: taxonomy or subject headings,
3. in relationship lists: thesaurus or full controlled vocabulary.

Classifications established previously [38] may also be helpful for users in this activity. Note that the selection of a specific type will affect the next steps, e.g. if the user has selected taxonomy, he must complete step 3, 4 and 8, partially step 5, but steps 6 and 7 do not apply to her/him.

In the third activity of this stage in CoVoMe, one should choose vocabulary for building the CV. In this paper, in the steps 3–8, we use SKOS [5], ISO 25964 [21], and MADS [29] that are the most popular. However users are not limited to these vocabularies. Additionally, we suggest which vocabulary elements for building CV may be used in a given step.

3.3   Define the Concepts and Concept Schemas

Partial support: Glossaries, Synonym rings,
Full support: Authority files, Taxonomies, Subject headings, Thesauri, Full controlled vocabularies.

SKOS vocabulary: `dcterms:hasPart`[1], `skos:Concept`, `skos:ConceptScheme`, `skos:hasTopConcept`, `skos:inScheme`, `skos:topConceptOf`,
ISO 25964 vocabulary: `iso25964:CustomConceptAttribute`, `iso25964:CustomTermAttribute`, `iso25964:Thesaurus`, `iso25964:ThesaurusConcept`, `iso25964:TopLevelRelationship`, `iso25964:contains`, `iso25964:isPartOf`,

---

[1] `dcterms:hasPart` is not a part of SKOS but sometimes is used to define coordinations.

MADS vocabulary: mads:Authority, mads:ComplexType, mads:Deprecat-
edAuthority, mads:MADSScheme, mads:MADSType, mads:RWO, mads:Simple-
Type, mads:hasMADSSchemeMember, mads:hasTopMemberOfMADSScheme, m-
ads:identifiesRWO, mads:isTopMemberOfMADSScheme.

In this step, one should denominate ideas, meanings, or objects and events.
In the first activity, users should choose strategy for identifying the concepts.
According to [15], users can decide which option to choose:

- bottom-up: start from the most specific concepts and build a structure by
  generalization,
- top-down: start from the most generic concept and build a structure by specialization,
- middle-out: core concepts are identified and then generalised and specialised
  to a complete list.

In the second activity, one should define the concepts according to the previously selected strategy. In the last step, users should organize and aggregate
concepts into concept schemes.

3.4 Define the Terms, Labels and Notation

Full support: Glossaries, Synonym rings, Authority files, Taxonomies, Subject
headings, Thesauri, Full controlled vocabularies.

SKOS vocabulary: skos-xl:Label[2], skos-xl:altLabel (see footnote 2),
skos-xl:hidden- Label (see footnote 2), skos-xl:prefLabel (see footnote 2), skos:altLabel, skos:hiddenLabel, skos:- notation, skos:
prefLabel,
ISO 25964 vocabulary: iso25964:NodeLabel, iso25964:SimpleNonPrefe-
rredTerm, iso25964:SplitNonPreferredTerm, iso25964:ThesaurusTerm,
iso25964:hasNodeLabel, iso25964:hasNonPreferredLabel, iso25964:h-
asPreferredLabel, iso25964:lexicalValue, iso25964:notation,
MADS vocabulary: mads:CorporateName, mads:Element, mads:Variant, m-
ads:authoritativeLabel, mads:elementList, mads:elementValue, mads-
:hasHiddenVariant, mads:hasVariant.

This step allows, one to describe concepts, terms, and concept schemas in
a way that people and machines can readily understand. The step allows for
the description and link of lexical entities. This step can be divided into two
activities. In the first activity, users should define human-readable labels/terms.
Here it is possible to use different languages. In this activity the preferred string,
maximum one per language tag, should be defined. Optionally users can define
alternative strings.

In the next optional activity, one can define notations. Notations are helpful
for classification codes and can be used to identify a concept within the scope of

---

[2] SKOS-XL is an extension for SKOS.

a given concept scheme, e.g., DD91.0Z can represent Irritable Bowel Syndrome in International Classification of Diseases revision 11. This activity is mainly dedicated machine-readable lexical codes.

3.5 Define the Semantic Relations

Partial support: Synonym rings, Taxonomies,
Full support: Subject headings, Thesauri, Full controlled vocabularies.

SKOS vocabulary: dcterms:references[3], skos:broader, skos:broaderTransitive, skos:narrower, skos:narrowerTransitive, skos:related, skos:semanticRelation,
ISO 25964 vocabulary: gvp:broaderGeneric[4], gvp:broaderInstantial (see footnote 4), gvp:broaderPartitive (see footnote 4), iso25964:AssociativeRelationship, iso2596-4:CompoundEquivalence, iso25964:Equivalence, iso25964:Hierarchic-alRelationship, iso25964:broaderGeneric, iso25964:broaderInstant-ial, iso25964:broaderPartitive, iso25964:narrowerGeneric, iso2596-4:narrowerInstantial, iso25964:narrowerPartitive, iso25964:plusUF, iso25964:plusUSE,
MADS vocabulary: mads:hasBroaderAuthority, mads:hasEarlierEstablishedForm, mads:hasLaterEstablishedForm, mads:hasNarrowerAuthority, mads:hasReciprocalAuthority, mads:hasRelatedAuthority, mads:see, mads:useFor, mads:useInstead.

This step defines ways to declare relationships between concepts within concept schemes. The step is divided into two activities. In the first activity, one should define relations for hierarchies, e.g. *narrower*, *broader* and its variants. Note that depending on the vocabulary used to build the CVs, there may be different deductive rules. Let C_1, C_2, C_3 be concepts, NT be a narrower relation, and BT be a broader relation, some of the following deductive rules that may be taken into account for this activity.

$$\frac{(C_1 \; NT \; C_2)}{(C_2 \; BT \; C_1)} \tag{1}$$

$$\frac{(C_1 \; BT \; C_2)}{(C_2 \; NT \; C_1)} \tag{2}$$

In some vocabularies, NT and BT can be transitive. Then the following rules are also possible.

$$\frac{(C_1 \; NT \; C_2) \; (C_2 \; NT \; C_3)}{(C_1 \; NT \; C_3)} \tag{3}$$

$$\frac{(C_1 \; BT \; C_2) \; (C_2 \; BT \; C_3)}{(C_1 \; BT \; C_3)} \tag{4}$$

---

[3] dcterms:references is not a part of SKOS but sometimes is used to define non-symmetric associative relations.

[4] GVP is an extension of ISO 25964 [1].

In the second activity, users should focus on relations for association, e.g. *related* and its variants. In the activity, the following deductive rule may be taken into account (*RT* is a related relation).

$$\frac{(C_1 \; RT \; C_2)}{(C_2 \; RT \; C_1)} \tag{5}$$

3.6   Define Groups of Concepts

Full support: Thesauri, Full controlled vocabularies.

SKOS vocabulary: skos:Collection, skos:OrderedCollection, skos:member, skos:memberList,
ISO 25964 vocabulary: iso25964:ConceptGroup, iso25964:ConceptGroup-Label, iso25964:ThesaurusArray, iso25964:hasAsMember, iso25964:hasMemberArray, iso25964:hasMemberConcept, iso25964:hasSubgroup, iso25964:hasSubordinateArray, iso25964:hasSuperOrdinateConcept, iso25964:hasSupergroup,
MADS vocabulary: mads:Collection, mads:hasCollectionMember, mads:-isMemberOfCollection.

In this step, user defines groups of concepts that are useful where a collection of concepts have something in common, and it is convenient to group them. The collections can be nested. Depending on the vocabulary chosen for creating CVs, concept schemes can be usually part of a group, but semantic relations cannot apply to these groups.

This step is divided into two activities. In the first activity, a user may collect concepts and concept schemas that are ordered. In the next activity, one should check if the remaining entities can be grouped into unordered collections.

3.7   Integrate with Other Controlled Vocabularies

Partial support: Authority files,
Full support: Full controlled vocabularies.

SKOS vocabulary: skos:broadMatch, skos:closeMatch, skos:exactMatch, skos:mappingRelation, skos:narrowMatch, skos:relatedMatch,
MADS vocabulary: mads:hasBroaderExternalAuthority, mads:hasClose-ExternalAuthority, mads:hasCorporateParentAuthority, mads:hasCorporateSubsidiaryAuthority, mads:hasExactExternalAuthority, mads:-hasNarrowerExternalAuthority, mads:hasReciprocalExternalAuthority.

Some of the practices are acceptable according to the CVs, but having so many acceptable practices makes it more difficult for the consumer of an entity to find their way around. With the goal of standardization and indication of the similar objects in the construction, one might consider the reuse of resources already built into other CVs.

In this step, there are three activities. In the first one, a user defines similarity properties (exact or fuzzy mapping). Let C_1, C_2, C_3 be concepts, EM be an exact relation, some of the following deductive rules that may be taken into account for this activity.

$$\frac{(C_1 \; EM \; C_2)}{(C_2 \; EM \; C_1)} \tag{6}$$

$$\frac{(C_1 \; EM \; C_2) \; (C_2 \; EM \; C_3)}{(C_1 \; EM \; C_3)} \tag{7}$$

In the second activity, one can define hierarchy mapping properties, and in the last activity, mapping properties for association can be defined. Here, deductive rules that may be taken into account are analogous to a rule 1, a rule 2 (second activity), and a rule 5 (third activity). Note that this properties connect concepts from different schemes (in different CVs).

3.8   Create the Documentation

Full support: Glossaries, Synonym rings, Authority files, Taxonomies, Subject headings, Thesauri, Full controlled vocabularies.

SKOS vocabulary: `skos:definition`, `skos:editorialNote`, `skos:example`, `skos:historyNote`, `skos:note`, `skos:scopeNote`,
ISO 25964 vocabulary: `iso25964:CustomNote`, `iso25964:Definition`, `iso-25964:EditorialNote`, `iso25964:HistoryNote`, `iso25964:Note`, `iso2596-4:ScopeNote`, `iso25964:VersionHistory`, `iso25964:hasCustomNote`, `iso-25964:hasDefinition`, `iso25964:hasEditorialNote`, `iso25964:hasHist-oryNote`, `iso25964:hasScopeNote`, `iso25964:refersTo`,
MADS vocabulary: `mads:changeNote`, `mads:definitionNote`, `mads:delet-ionNote`, `mads:editorialNote`, `mads:exampleNote`, `mads:historyNote`, `m-ads:note`, `mads:scopeNote`.

The goal of the documentation step is to catalog the development process and the CV itself. This step, including the maintenance, as well as definitions and examples should be embedded in the code of implemented CV. The languages for creating CVs often support different kinds of human-readable notes, e.g. explanation and information about the intended meaning of a concept, examples, information about historical changes, comments, etc.

3.9 Evaluation

At CoVoMe, we define an evaluation as a technical judgment of the CV and their environment during each step and activity. We distinguish between six different types of errors that can be found in each step:

- coverage level of the topic domain,
- check the completeness of the concepts,
- semantic inconsistency errors,
- lexical errors,
- circularity errors,
- redundancy detection.

Coverage Level of the Topic Domain. The extent to which a CV covers a considered domain is a crucial factor to be considered during the development process. The evaluation that can be employed to achieve this goal can be realized with similarity metrics [2]. This checkpoint is mostly dedicated to step 1 and step 2.

Check the Completeness of the Concept. The aim is to ascertain whether the concepts and/or concept schemas contain as much information as required. For example, errors appear when there are relations missing in the concept. This checkpoint is mostly dedicated to step 3 and step 5.

Semantic Inconsistency Errors. They usually occur because the user makes an incorrect semantic classification, that is, one classifies a concept as a semantic relation of a concept to which it does not really belong. For example, one classifies the *ornithology* concept as related to the *mammal* concept. This checkpoint is mostly dedicated to step 3 and step 6.

Lexical Errors. They occur when a label, a notation, a documentation property is not consistent with the data model because of the wrong value. For example, if we say that *animal* is a preferred label and at the same time *animal* is an alternative label, then the CV has a clash between the preferred and alternative lexical labels. An example rule to check if the preferred label (PL) is the same as the alternative label (AL) is presented below. This checkpoint is mostly dedicated to step 4 and step 8.

$$\frac{(x\ PL\ y)(x\ AL\ y)}{false} \tag{8}$$

Circularity Errors. They occur when a concept and/or concept scheme is defined as a specialization or generalization of itself. For example, if we say that *animal* is a narrower concept of *mammal*, and that *mammal* is a narrower concept of *animal*, then the CV has a circularity error. An example rule to check this error is presented below. This checkpoint is mostly dedicated to step 5 and step 7.

$$\frac{(x\ NT\ y)(y\ NT\ x)}{false} \tag{9}$$

Redundancy Detection. It occurs in CVs when there is more than one explicit definition of any of the hierarchical relations, or when we have two concepts with the same formal definition. For example, when a *dog* concept is defined as a broader concept of *mammal* and *animal*, and *mammal* is defined as a broader concept of *animal*, then, there is an indirect repetition. This checkpoint is mostly dedicated to step 5 and step 7.

4 Related Work

4.1 Construction of Controlled Vocabularies

Guidelines for the construction of controlled vocabularies have evolved over a long period. One of the first recommendations for building thesauri appeared in 1967 [18]. In this publication, the authors first defined terms such as *narrower*, *broader* and *related*. In the 1980s and 1990s, national [4,6,12] and international standards [20] for thesauri and controlled vocabularies were established. Other older guidelines for thesaurus construction have been reviewed by Krooks and Lancaster [25].

In [31], Nielsen analyzes the word association test and discusses whether that method should be included in the process of construction of searching thesauri. This paper presents also three steps for the construction of thesauri: acquisition, analysis, and presentation of concepts and terms. In [35], authors discuss how bibliometric methods can be applied to thesaurus construction. The paper presents semiautomatic and automatic thesaurus construction. Unlike our solution, it focuses on one subject area. The other methods for automatic build of thesauri and/or controlled vocabularies are presented in [9] and [11]. These solutions, unlike CoVoMe, do not have formally described steps.

There are a few approaches that are more formal [21,36]. In [36], nine steps to construct a thesaurus systematically is proposed. Unlike our solution, this proposal only focuses on one vocabulary for building CVs. The next formal approach is ISO 25964-1 [21] that explains how to construct thesaurus, how to display it, and how to manage its development. Unfortunately, this proposal only focuses on one vocabulary for building CVs. That proposal, unlike CoVoMe, describes process of building only one type of CV.

On the other hand, over the years, a considerable amount of research has been performed on user-centered approaches for the construction of thesauri and/or controlled vocabularies. In [32], the author focuses on the situational context that surrounds the user.

In [3], a thesaurus-based methodology is proposed for systematic ontological conceptualization in the manufacturing domain. The methodology has three main phases, namely, thesaurus development, thesaurus evaluation, and thesaurus conversion and it uses SKOS as the thesaurus representation formalism. That proposal, unlike CoVoMe, only focuses on one vocabulary for building CVs. Similar disadvantage can describe a methodology for a Thesauri Quality Assessment [34]. This proposal supports decision makers in selecting thesauri by exploiting an overall quality measure, but support only SKOS.

4.2   Methodologies for Ontology Development

In contrast to the construction of controlled vocabularies approaches, methodologies for ontology development are described more formally. They define steps to meet in the process of ontology development and determine how to document the process. Unfortunately, all the solutions below describe the process of creating an ontology and cannot be easily adapted as methodologies for building CVs.

METHONTOLOGY [14] is a construction methodology for building ontologies. In general, it provides a set of guidelines about how to carry out the activities identified in the ontology development process. It supports the techniques used in each activity, and the output produced by them. METHONTOLOGY consists of the identification of the ontology development process where the main activities are identified, a lifecycle based on evolving prototypes, and the methodology itself, which specifies the steps. Some steps in this methodology are similar to our proposal, e.g., specification can be comparable to step 1, and integration is similar to step 7 in CoVoMe.

On-To-Knowledge [40] is another methodology for building ontologies. It should be used by the knowledge management application because the methodology supports ontologies taking into account how the ontology will be used in further applications. Consequently, ontologies developed with On-To-Knowledge are dependent on the application.

Another methodology for ontology development is NeOn [39]. It supports, among others the reuse of ontologies as well as of non-ontological resources as part of the engineering process. This methodology also proposes detailed guidelines for executing its various activities. In contrast to our proposal, as well as to METHONTOLOGY and On-To-Knowledge that provide methodological guidance for ontology engineering, this methodology rather just recommends a variety of pathways for developing ontologies.

OD101 [33] is an iterative methodology that focuses on guidelines to formalize the subject domain by providing guidance on how to go from an informal representation to a logic-based one. It encompasses not only axiom choice, but also other aspects that affect that. A characteristic feature of this methodology is that, like our proposal, it is close to a vocabulary that can be used to construct an ontology. That proposal, unlike CoVoMe, is strongly connected to OWL. On the other hand, some steps of OD101 can be considered similar to CoVoMe steps, e.g., *define the classes, and the class hierarchy* step can be seen as similar to step 5 in our proposal.

Both NeOn and OD101, like CoVoMe, use Competency Questions [17] in the specification stage. This approach specifies what knowledge has to be entailed in the ontology and thus can be seen as a set of requirements on the content, as well as a way of scoping. We also use CQs in our methodology.

There are many different proposals that relate to the Rational Unified Process (RUP) [22–24]. The first approach [22], in addition to the RUP, is also related to traditional waterfall. The stages proposed by the methodology are based on the METHONTOLOGY. Incremental and Iterative Agile Methodology (IIAM) [23], which is the second proposal, unlike CoVoMe, is the domain-specific solution for the education field. Software Centric Innovative Methodology (SCIM) [24] has five ontology development workflows: requirements analysis, domain analysis, conceptual design, implementation and evaluation. Our proposal, like the above solutions, can integrate into RUP phases and disciplines.

Besides IIAM, there are other domain-specific methodologies, e.g. Yet Another Methodology for Ontology (YAMO) [13]. That methodology provides a set of ontology design guiding principles for building a large-scale faceted ontology for food.

5 Conclusions

In this paper, we have described a controlled vocabulary methodology for knowledge organization systems. We have listed the steps and activities in the CV development process. Our methodology has addressed the complex issues of defining concepts, concept schemas, semantic relations, mapping relations, labels, notation, and documentation. The advantages of CoVoMe are a direct consequence of its generality, including the support for different types of CVs and the possibility to use various vocabularies to create them. The proposed methodology can be used with different vocabularies for building CVs, as well as it flexibly supports different types of CVs.

As part of our future work, we will consider possibilities for enhancement by adding Notation3 rules that can help with evaluation. Furthermore, we intend to work on systematic monitoring of the adoption and use of CoVoMe in different areas, focusing on the problems that will emerge during the CVs creation process.

A   Used Namespaces

Prefix	Namespace	Representation
dcterms	http://purl.org/dc/terms/	RDF
gvp	http://vocab.getty.edu/ontology#	RDF
iso-thes	http://iso25964.org/	XML
	http://purl.org/iso25964/skos-thes#	RDF
mads	http://www.loc.gov/mads/v2	XML
	http://www.loc.gov/mads/rdf/v1#	RDF
skos	http://www.w3.org/2004/02/skos/core#	RDF
skos-xl	http://www.w3.org/2008/05/skos-xl#	RDF

References

1. Alexiev, V., Isaac, A., Lindenthal, J.: On the composition of ISO 25964 hierarchical relations (BTG, BTP, BTI). Int. J. Digit. Libr. **17**(1), 39–48 (2015). https://doi.org/10.1007/s00799-015-0162-2
2. Altınel, B., Ganiz, M.C.: Semantic text classification: a survey of past and recent advances. Inf. Process. Manage. **54**(6), 1129–1153 (2018). https://doi.org/10.1016/j.ipm.2018.08.001
3. Ameri, F., Kulvatunyou, B., Ivezic, N., Kaikhah, K.: Ontological conceptualization based on the simple knowledge organization system (SKOS). J. Comput. Inf. Sci. Eng. (2014)
4. ANSI: American national standard guidelines for thesaurus structure, construction, and use (1980)
5. Bechhofer, S., Miles, A.: SKOS simple knowledge organization system reference. W3C recommendation, W3C, August 2009. https://www.w3.org/TR/2009/REC-skos-reference-20090818/
6. British Standards Institution: British standard guide to establishment and development of monolingual thesauri (1987)
7. Caracciolo, C., et al.: The AGROVOC linked dataset. Semant. Web **4**(3), 341–348 (2013). https://doi.org/10.3233/SW-130106
8. Chan, L.M.: Library of Congress subject headings: principles and application. ERIC (1995)
9. Chen, H., Lynch, K.J.: Automatic construction of networks of concepts characterizing document databases. IEEE Trans. Syst. Man Cybern. **22**(5), 885–902 (1992). https://doi.org/10.1109/21.179830
10. Coulter, N.: ACM's computing classification system reflects changing times. Commun. ACM **40**(12), 111–112 (1997). https://doi.org/10.1145/265563.265579
11. Crouch, C.J.: An approach to the automatic construction of global thesauri. Inf. Process. Manage. **26**(5), 629–640 (1990). https://doi.org/10.1016/0306-4573(90)90106-C
12. Deutsches Institut für Normung: Erstellung und weiterentwicklung von thesauri (1993)
13. Dutta, B., Chatterjee, U., Madalli, D.P.: YAMO: yet another methodology for large-scale faceted ontology construction. J. Knowl. Manage. (2015). https://doi.org/10.1108/JKM-10-2014-0439
14. Fernández-López, M., Gómez-Pérez, A., Juristo, N.: METHONTOLOGY: from ontological art towards ontological engineering. In: Engineering Workshop on Ontological Engineering (AAAI97) (1997)
15. Gandon, F.: Distributed Artificial Intelligence and Knowledge Management: ontologies and multi-agent systems for a corporate semantic web. Ph.D. thesis, Université Nice Sophia Antipolis (2002)
16. Gartner, R.: MODS: metadata object description schema. JISC Techwatch Rep. TSW 03–06 (2003)
17. Grüninger, M., Fox, M.S.: The role of competency questions in enterprise engineering. In: Rolstadås, A. (ed.) Benchmarking — Theory and Practice. IAICT, pp. 22–31. Springer, Boston (1995). https://doi.org/10.1007/978-0-387-34847-6_3
18. Heald, J.H.: The making of TEST thesaurus of engineering and scientific terms. Clearinghouse for Federal Scientific and Technical Information (1967)
19. Hodge, G.: Systems of Knowledge Organization for Digital Libraries: Beyond Traditional Authority Files. ERIC (2000)

20. International Organization for Standardization: Documentation-guidelines for the establishment and development of monolingual thesauri (1985)
21. International Organization for Standardization: Thesauri for information retrieval (2011)
22. John, M.S., Santhosh, R., Shah, N.: Proposal of an hybrid methodology for ontology development by extending the process models of software engineering. Int. J. Inf. Technol. Convergence Serv. 6(1), 37–44 (2016). https://doi.org/10.5121/ijitcs.2016.6104
23. John, S., Shah, N., Smalov, L.: Incremental and iterative agile methodology (IIAM): hybrid approach for ontology design towards semantic web based educational systems development. Int. J. Knowl. Eng. 2(1), 13–19 (2016). https://doi.org/10.18178/ijke.2016.2.1.044
24. John, S., Shah, N., Stewart, C.D., Samlov, L.: Software centric innovative methodology for ontology development. In: 9th International Conference on Knowledge Engineering and Ontology Development (KEOD-2017), pp. 139–146 (2017). https://doi.org/10.5220/0006482901390146
25. Krooks, D.A., Lancaster, F.W.: The evolution of guidelines for thesaurus construction. Libri (1993). https://doi.org/10.1515/libr.1993.43.4.326
26. Lipscomb, C.E.: Medical subject headings (MeSH). Bull. Med. Libr. Assoc. 88(3), 265 (2000)
27. McIlwaine, I.C.: The universal decimal classification: some factors concerning its origins, development, and influence. J. Am. Soc. Inf. Sci. 48(4), 331–339 (1997). https://doi.org/10.1002/(SICI)1097-4571(199704)48:4⟨331::AID-ASI6⟩3.0.CO;2-X
28. Mitchell, J.S., Beall, J., Matthews, W., New, G.: Dewey decimal classification. Encycl. Libr. Inf. Sci. (1996)
29. Needleman, M.: Standards update: some interesting XML standards. Serials Rev. 31(1), 70–71 (2005). https://doi.org/10.1016/j.serrev.2004.11.012
30. Neubert, J.: Bringing the "thesaurus for economics" on to the web of linked data. LDOW 25964, 102 (2009)
31. Nielsen, M.L.: The word association test in the methodology of thesaurus construction. Adv. Classif. Res. Online 8(1), 41–57 (1997). https://doi.org/10.7152/acro.v8i1.12727
32. Nielsen, M.L.: A framework for work task based thesaurus design. J. Documentation (2001). https://doi.org/10.1108/EUM0000000007100
33. Noy, N.F., McGuinness, D.L., et al.: Ontology development 101: A guide to creating your first ontology (2001)
34. Quarati, A., Albertoni, R., De Martino, M.: Overall quality assessment of SKOS thesauri: an AHP-based approach. J. Inf. Sci. 43(6), 816–834 (2017). https://doi.org/10.1177/0165551516671079
35. Schneider, J.W., Borlund, P.: Preliminary study of the potentiality of bibliometric methods for the construction of thesauri. In: Emerging Frameworks and Methods: Proceedings of the Fourth International Conference on Conceptions of Library and Information Science (CoLIS 4), Seattle, pp. 151–165 (2002)
36. Shearer, J.R.: A practical exercise in building a thesaurus. Cataloging Classif. Q. 37(3–4), 35–56 (2004). https://doi.org/10.1300/J104v37n03_0
37. Soergel, D.: The art and architecture thesaurus (AAT): a critical appraisal. Vis. Resour. 10(4), 369–400 (1995). https://doi.org/10.1080/01973762.1995.9658306
38. Souza, R.R., Tudhope, D., Almeida, M.B.: Towards a taxonomy of KOS: dimensions for classifying knowledge organization systems. KO Knowl. Organization 39(3), 179–192 (2012). https://doi.org/10.5771/0943-7444-2012-3-179

39. Suárez-Figueroa, M.C., Gómez-Pérez, A., Fernández-López, M.: The NeOn methodology for ontology engineering. In: Suárez-Figueroa, M.C., Gómez-Pérez, A., Motta, E., Gangemi, A. (eds.) Ontology Engineering in a Networked World, pp. 9–34. Springer, Heidelberg (2012). https://doi.org/10.1007/978-3-642-24794-1_2
40. Sure, Y., Staab, S., Studer, R.: On-to-knowledge methodology (OTKM). In: Staab, S., Studer, R. (eds.) Handbook on Ontologies. INFOSYS. Springer, Heidelberg (2004). https://doi.org/10.1007/978-3-540-24750-0_6

An Ontology to Structure Biological Data: The Contribution of Mathematical Models

Olivier Inizan[1]($\boxtimes$)(iD), Vincent Fromion[1](iD), Anne Goelzer[1](iD), Fatiha Saïs[2](iD),
and Danai Symeonidou[3](iD)

[1] Université Paris Saclay, INRAE, MaIAGE, Jouy-en-Josas, France
olivier.inizan@inrae.fr
[2] LISN, Université Paris Saclay, CNRS UMR9015, Orsay, France
[3] INRAE, SupAgro, UMR MISTEA, Université de Montpellier, Montpellier, France

Abstract. The biology is a research field well known for its huge quantity and diversity of data. Today, these data are still recognized as heterogeneous and fragmented. Despite the fact that several initiatives of biological knowledge representation have been realized, biologists and bioinformaticians do not have a formal representation that, at the level of the entire organism, can help them to organize such a diversity and quantity of data. Recently, in the context of the whole cell modeling approach, the systemic mathematical models have proven to be a powerful tool for understanding the bacterial cell behavior. We advocate that an ontology built on the principles that govern the design of such models, can help to organize the biological data. In this article, we describe the first step in the conception of an ontology dedicated to biological data organization at the level of the entire organism and for molecular scales i.e., the choice of concepts and relations compliant with principles at work in the systemic mathematical models.

Keywords: Ontology · Mathematical models · Biological data

1 Introduction

The recent advances of sequencing technologies lead to a faster and cheaper production of data in the field of biology [14]. Biologists and bioinformaticians have to deal nowadays with a huge quantity and diversity of *omics* data (such as genomics, transcriptomics, proteomics, metabolomics and metagenomics) [8]. These data are mostly obtained in a given context of an experimentation to answer a particular question. From a wider perspective they appear to be heterogeneous and fragmented [2]. Moreover, despite the fact that there are many data available for a given organism, the ability to organize and integrate these data remains a challenge [10]. Such integration can be of great importance, and we can cite, among others, the elucidation of mechanisms to understand and treat diseases [13]. It should also be noticed that, despite an active research

© Springer Nature Switzerland AG 2022
E. Garoufallou et al. (Eds.): MTSR 2021, CCIS 1537, pp. 57–64, 2022.
https://doi.org/10.1007/978-3-030-98876-0_5

activity in biological knowledge representation [12], there is no formal representation dedicated to data organisation for molecular scales, at the level of the organism. The lack of such a representation prevents scientists from exploiting the full potential of these data. Since a decade, the whole cell modelling approach has showed that systemic mathematical models are a powerful tool for describing and understanding the bacterial cell behavior. More precisely, through these models, when fed with biological data, it is possible to identify organizational principles on which (unobserved) cell behavior can be predicted [3,9]. Therefore, there is a real need to develop a new formal representation that can semantically represent the links between biological data while ensuring compliance with biological principles followed in mathematical modelling of biological processes.

In this article we present the first steps in the development of a formal representation dedicated to biological data organisation and designed according concepts that hold in mathematical models. We want to underline that this work is an ongoing research, the tasks realized so far are mainly conceptual and concrete realisations have been done on examples as proof of concepts. The rest of the document is organized as follows. In Sect. 2 we present the state of the art of this work and its main motivation. The concepts and relations of the ontology are described in Sect. 3 and illustrated with an example in Sect. 4. The conclusion and perspectives are provided in Sect. 5.

2 State of the Art and Motivation

To understand the motivation of the present work we have to detail two starting points: the BiPOm and BiPON [5,6] ontologies and the constraints relative to mathematical models.

2.1 BiPON and BiPOm: New Potential Rules and Usage for Bio-ontologies

Biology is a rich field of knowledge where several communities can work on the same object for different purposes. Being able to avoid ambiguities when referring to the same object is then crucial. Consequently, well known bio-ontology projects (for example GO [1]) provide a hierarchy of concepts used as controlled vocabulary. Another usage can be found in the BioPax community [2] where the ontology is designed to collect and exchange data related to biological pathways. In 2017 and 2020, two OWL[1] ontologies, BiPON and BiPOm, have provided new potential rules and usage for bio-ontologies: first, they introduce the systemic approach as a design principle to represent the biological knowledge. This approach originates from the field of engineering science and aims to break down a given system into linked (sub) modules [4]. In this context (Fig. 1a), the notion of systemic module is strictly defined by its inputs, outputs and the function it fulfills. Inputs, outputs and function are then tied together in a mathematical model which gives a formal description of the behavior of the module. The

---

[1] https://www.w3.org/OWL/.

authors of BiPON and BiPOm have showed that the bacteria cell can be considered as a system and be organized in linked and interlocked systemic modules. These systemic modules are OWL concepts typed as *biological processes*. Second, BiPON and BiPOm provide a high level of expressiveness in comparison with other bio-ontologies. From their initial set of concepts, relations, rules and individuals, they exploit the reasoning capacity provided by the OWL language and the Description Logic to infer new relations between individuals. As a result, the authors of BiPON have showed that a wide diversity of biological processes can be described by few concepts of mathematical models.

2.2 The Constraints of Mathematical Models

As presented in Fig. 1b, a mathematical model is associated to a *biological process*. In this section we focus on the constraints that drive the construction of such mathematical models. To understand the importance of these constraints, we first have to detail a little more the notion of biological processes defined in the ontologies BiPON/BiPOm. A biological process has one or several molecules as inputs and also one or several molecules as outputs. We consider that a process *consumes* the inputs and *produces* the outputs. Moreover, a biological process has a function which is the objective to fulfill. Finally, the process has means to transform inputs into outputs and these means are expressed through a mathematical model. In Fig. 1a the general form of a biological process is presented. In Fig. 1b, we represent a simple biochemical reaction (a molecule 'A' is converted into the molecule 'B') and the corresponding biological process.

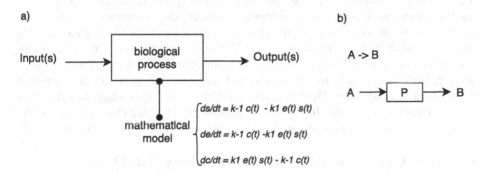

Fig. 1. a) The general form of a biological process and its associated mathematical model. b) A simple biochemical reaction and its process P.

A striking fact in the modeling community is that, whatever the mathematical model being build, three general constraints are always satisfied. Consequently, we consider that (i) these constraints are major and (ii) they drive the construction of mathematical models. These constraints, presented below, will be referred in the sequel as *model constraints*:

1. *The physical causality.* The physical causality states that if the inputs produce the outputs, then the inputs precede the outputs. Since we do not especially consider the time in the formal representation, the causality can be reformulated as follows: if the inputs are present in a sufficient quantity, then the process can consume the inputs and produce the outputs.
2. *The mass conservation.* It is an important constraint of the modelling approach that ensures the consistency of the models.
3. *The concurrency of access.* The biological processes are in concurrence to access the same type of entity. More precisely, the same type of molecule can be consumed or produced by different processes. A classic example is the ATP molecule which provides energy for the cell and that is consequently consumed by different chemical reactions.

It is important to notice that, despite the fact that the concept of the *biological process* is present in BiPON/BiPOm and that mathematical models are represented in BiPON, none of these ontologies considers these model constraints.

2.3   Motivation

Our motivation lies in the fact that the model constraints represent a powerful tool to validate the consistency of the biological knowledge and data relative to an organism. If we want to consider these constraints in a formal representation, we should first provide concepts and relations that allow us to *count* the molecules that are consumed or produced by the biological processes. Consider the simple example of the Fig. 1b: the physical causality states that at *least one* molecule A must be available for the process P. The mass conservation states that *one* molecule A must be converted into *one* molecule B. Considering the concurrence between the processes implies also counting the molecules: consider a second process P' that consumes also a molecule A. If there is *only one* molecule A in the entire cell, P and P' are in concurrence. But if there are *two* molecules A, then P and P' are not in competition. As already mentioned in Sect. 2, BiPON and BiPOm have validated the systemic approach to represent the biological knowledge. However, none of these ontologies allow to count the entities consumed and produced by the processes. This drawback prevents the representation of model constraints and leads us to build a new ontology.

3   First Components of a Bio-ontology for Data and Knowledge Organization

As mentioned in the previous section, we want to provide a representation that takes into account the model constraints that drive the construction of mathematical models. We have shown that, to achieve this goal, we have to count the entities (the molecules) that are consumed or produced by the processes. In this section, we propose a first set of concepts and relations of our bio-ontology that allow counting the entities (see Sect. 3.1). These concepts and relations can help us to give a more formal definition of the biological process. This definition is presented in Sect. 3.2.

3.1   A First Set of Concepts and Relations to Count Entities

In this work, we adopt the formal approach and the concept of *biological process* presented in BiPON/BiPOm. In order to take into account the model constraints (i.e., physical causality, mass conservation and concurrency of access), we use the concepts that are frequently manipulated by the modelers [15]. We first, create the concept *pool* that groups all the molecules of the same biochemical entity into *pools*. For example, all the molecules of water will be grouped in the H2O *pool*. Second, since the *pool* is of a finite volume, the number of molecules is given by the *concentration* of molecules in the *pool*. Third, we state that the *processes* can communicate with each other only via the *pools*. This leads us to create three relations (i.e., *reads, retrieves* and *puts*) and another concept: (i) a *process reads* the *concentration* of the molecules in the *pool* and (ii) the *process retrieves* molecules from the *pool* and/or *puts* molecules into the *pool*. By this way, the *process triggers* a *flow* of molecules. The Fig. 2a illustrates how we represent the concepts of *pool, process, concentration* and *flow*. The relation *triggers* and *reads* are also represented. In the Fig. 2b we represent the simple example showed in Fig. 1b where the *process* P converts the molecule A into the molecule B.

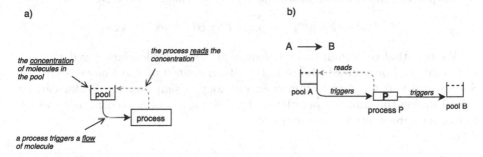

Fig. 2. a) The concepts and relations of the new ontology. b) A simple biochemical reaction represented with these concepts and relations.

The Fig. 2b can be detailed as follows: the *process* P *reads* the *concentration* of molecules in the *pool* A (dashed grey arrow). If there are enough molecules (here only one molecule is required), P *retrieves* this molecule (aka P trigger a *flow* of molecule A (first black arrow)) and *puts* a molecule B in the *pool* B (aka P *triggers* a *flow* of *molecule* B (second black arrow)).

3.2   A Formal Definition of a Biological Process

The set of concepts and relations designed above is a convenient way to go further in the definition of a *biological process* provided by BiPON/BiPOm. These ontologies describe a *biological process* through the relations *has_input* and *has_output* with the molecules that participate in the biochemical reaction. We propose to re-formulate the behavior of the *biological process*. We explain this re-formulation through the example of Figs. 1 and 2. While BiPON/BiPOm state that the *process* P *has_input* the molecule A and *has_output* the molecule B, we state that the *process reads* the *concentration* of molecules A and (if there are enough molecules) *triggers* a *flow* of molecules A and a *flow* of molecules B. Expressing the behavior by this way is more compliant with the constraint stated by the physical causality: the fact that there is enough *concentration* of molecules is the cause of the behavior of the *process* while the *flow* of molecules is considered as its effect. With these considerations we can provide a formal definition of a *biological process*.

A *biological process* is defined as a concept characterized by its inputs and its outputs:

$$BiologicalProcess \equiv \exists has\_input.Input \sqcap \forall has\_input.Input$$
$$\sqcap \exists has\_output.Output \sqcap \forall has\_output.Output \tag{1}$$

An input is the *concentration read* by the *process*:

$$Input \equiv Concentration \sqcap \exists is\_read\_by.BiologicalProcess \tag{2}$$

An output is a *flow* of molecules *triggered* by a biological process:

$$Output \equiv Flow \sqcap \exists triggered\_by.BiologicalProcess \tag{3}$$

We note that the definition of *biological process* is cyclic, since it is defined by the inputs and outputs which are in their turn defined by the *biological process*. Such definitions are very common in ontology design and the cycles can be solved during the ontology population by defining the order according to which individuals are created in the ontology.

4 Illustration on an Example

We illustrate the use of the ontology with the example of a biochemical reaction catalyzed by an enzyme. This biochemical reaction is representative of the metabolic processes within the whole-cell, i.e. one of the most important set of biological processes involving almost one third of the bacterial genes. Therefore, if it can be represented by the concepts and relations introduced in Sect. 3.1, a large part of the biological processes of the cell could be described accordingly, which constitutes a first step in the ontology evaluation. The chemical model of this biochemical reaction proposed by Michaelis and Menten [11] occurs in two reactions:

$$E + S \leftrightarrows [ES] \rightarrow E + P \tag{4}$$

First, the enzyme E binds to the substrate S to form a complex $[ES]$. This reaction is reversible i.e., the complex $[ES]$ can dissociate to release the enzyme E

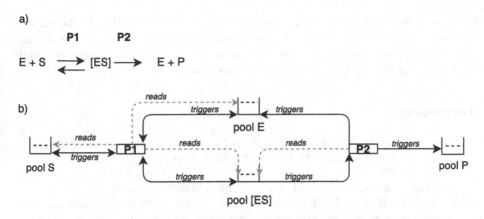

Fig. 3. a) The model provided by Michaelis and Menten b) The representation of the model with the processes, pools and relations.

and the substrate S. In contrast, the second reaction is irreversible: the complex $[ES]$ dissociates to release the enzyme E and the product of the reaction P.

To represent this chemical model with the concepts and relations proposed above, we first design two *processes*, P1 and P2, each one corresponding to the first and second reaction, respectively. We then design four *pools* named S, P, E and ES, one for each type of molecule, i.e., substrate, product, enzyme, and enzyme bound to the substrate, respectively. The *processes*, *pools* and relations are represented in Fig. 3. In Fig. 3b, P2 *reads* the *concentration* of the *pool* ES and (if there is enough molecules of ES) *triggers* a *flow* of molecules E, P and ES. P2 consumes E and P, and produces ES. The *process* P1 represents a reversible reaction. For the forward reaction (E+S $\longrightarrow$ $[ES]$) P1 *reads* the *concentration* of the *pool* E and S and *triggers* a *flow* of E, S and ES. For the reverse reaction ($[ES]$ $\longrightarrow$ E+S), P1 *reads* the *concentration* of the *pool* ES and *triggers* a *flow* ES, E and S. In the ontology, the forward and reverse sub-reactions of P1 are not distinguished: P1 *reads* the *concentrations* of all *pools* (ES, S and E) and for each *pool*, P1 *triggers* a single *flow* (corresponding to the sum of the *flow* of each sub-reactions). By doing so, the constraint of causality is well respected.

5   Conclusion and Perspectives

In this article, we have described the first steps of the development of an ontology dedicated to the organization of biological data. This ontology has been designed according to the constraints that hold in mathematical models. The concepts and relations (i) make possible the representation of quantities, (ii) have been validated on a representative example and (iii) led us to give a new formal definition of a biological process. We plan to populate the ontology with an entire network of reactions [5], using the SBML format [7]. During this population, quantities could be associated with the concepts representing the concentrations and the flows, and the model constraints could be expressed with SHACL[2] language. This work fits in the challenge of making ontologies more expressive including more quantitative knowledge. This will allow us to check the consistency and the validity of knowledge and their associated data.

References

1. Gene Ontology Consortium: The gene ontology resource: 20 years and still GOing strong. Nucleic Acids Res. **47**(D1), D330–D338 (2019)
2. Demir, E., Cary, M.P., Paley, S., et al.: The BioPAX community standard for pathway data sharing. Nat. Bbiotechnol. **28**(9), 935–942 (2010)
3. Goelzer, A., Muntel, J., Chubukov, V., et al.: Quantitative prediction of genome-wide resource allocation in bacteria. Metab. Eng. **32**, 232–243 (2015)
4. Hartwell, L.H., Hopfield, J.J., Leibler, S., et al.: From molecular to modular cell biology. Nature **402**(6761), C47–C52 (1999)
5. Henry, V., Saïs, F., Inizan, O., et al.: BiPOm: a rule-based ontology to represent and infer molecule knowledge from a biological process-centered viewpoint. BMC Bioinform. **21**(1), 1–18 (2020)
6. Henry, V.J., Goelzer, A., Ferré, A., et al.: The bacterial interlocked process ONtology (BiPON): a systemic multi-scale unified representation of biological processes in prokaryotes. J. Biomed. Semant. **8**(1), 1–16 (2017)
7. Hucka, M., Finney, A., Sauro, H.M., et al.: The systems biology markup language (SBML): a medium for representation and exchange of biochemical network models. Bioinformatics **19**(4), 524–531 (2003)
8. Joyce, A.R., Palsson, B.Ø.: The model organism as a system: integrating 'omics' data sets. Nat. Rev. Mol. Cell Biol. **7**(3), 198–210 (2006)
9. Karr, J.R., Sanghvi, J.C., Macklin, D.N., et al.: A whole-cell computational model predicts phenotype from genotype. Cell **150**(2), 389–401 (2012)
10. López de Maturana, E., Alonso, L., Alarcón, P., et al.: Challenges in the integration of omics and non-omics data. Genes **10**(3), 238 (2019)
11. Michaelis, L., Menten, M.L., et al.: Die kinetik der invertinwirkung. Biochem. z **49**(333–369), 352 (1913)
12. Nicolas, J.: Artificial intelligence and bioinformatics. In: Marquis, P., Papini, O., Prade, H. (eds.) A Guided Tour of Artificial Intelligence Research, pp. 209–264. Springer, Cham (2020). https://doi.org/10.1007/978-3-030-06170-8_7
13. Ramon, C., Gollub, M.G., Stelling, J.: Integrating-omics data into genome-scale metabolic network models: principles and challenges. Essays Biochem. **62**(4), 563–574 (2018)
14. Reuter, J.A., Spacek, D.V., Snyder, M.P.: High-throughput sequencing technologies. Mol. Cell **58**(4), 586–597 (2015)
15. Voit, E.O.: Computational Analysis of Biochemical Systems: A Practical Guide for Biochemists and Molecular Biologists. Cambridge University Press, Cambridge (2000)

---

[2] https://www.w3.org/TR/shacl/.

Track on Open Repositories, Research Information Systems and Data Infrastructures

FAIR or FAIRer? An Integrated Quantitative FAIRness Assessment Grid for Semantic Resources and Ontologies

Emna Amdouni[1]([email icon]) [iD] and Clement Jonquet[1,2]([email icon]) [iD]

[1] LIRMM, University of Montpellier and CNRS, Montpellier, France
{emna.amdouni,jonquet}@lirmm.fr
[2] MISTEA, University of Montpellier, INRAE and Institut Agro, Montpellier, France

Abstract. In open science, the expression "FAIRness assessment" refers to evaluating to which degree a digital object is Findable, Accessible, Interoperable, and Reusable. Standard vocabularies or ontologies are a key element to achieving a high level of FAIRness (FAIR Principle I2) but as with any other data, ontologies have themselves to be FAIR. Despite the recent interest in the open science and semantic Web communities for this question, we have not seen yet a quantitative evaluation method to assess and score the level of FAIRness of ontologies or semantic resources in general (e.g., vocabularies, terminologies, thesaurus). The main objective of this work is to provide such a method to guide semantic stakeholders in making their semantic resources FAIR. We present an integrated quantitative assessment grid for semantic resources and propose candidate metadata properties–taken from the MOD ontology metadata model–to be used to make a semantic resource FAIR. Aligned and nourished with relevant FAIRness assessment state-of-the-art initiatives, our grid distributes 478 credits to the 15 FAIR principles in a manner which integrates existing generic approaches for digital objects (i.e., FDMM, SHARC) and approaches dedicated to semantic resources (i.e., 5-stars V, MIRO, FAIRsFAIR, Poveda et al.). The credits of the grid can then be used for implementing FAIRness assessment methods and tools.

Keywords: FAIR data principles · FAIRness assessment · Evaluation grid · Semantic Web · Ontologies · Semantic resources/artefacts · Metadata properties

1 Introduction

In 2014, a group of researchers, research institutions, and publishers (called FORCE 11) defined fundamental guiding principles called FAIR (for Findable, Accessible, Interoperable, and Reusable) to make scientific data and their metadata interoperable, persistent, and understandable for both humans and machines [1]. The FAIR principles emphasize the importance of semantic technologies in making data interoperable and reusable. However, ontologies[1]–the backbone of semantic technologies–have themselves to be

---

[1] In this paper, we will consider the terms ontologies, terminologies, thesaurus and vocabularies as a type of knowledge organization systems [2] or knowledge artefacts [3] or semantic resources [4]. For simplicity, we will sometimes use "ontology" as an overarching word.

© Springer Nature Switzerland AG 2022
E. Garoufallou et al. (Eds.): MTSR 2021, CCIS 1537, pp. 67–80, 2022.
https://doi.org/10.1007/978-3-030-98876-0_6

FAIR. Until recently, not much attention has been made to quantitatively evaluating ontologies using FAIR principles; all related work or state-of-the-art methods regarding ontologies are qualitative i.e., proposing recommendations and best practices without providing a scoring mechanism. It is clear that the development of FAIRness assessment methods–i.e., ways to measure to which level a digital object implements FAIR principles–remains challenging [5], including for ontologies and semantic resources. In fact, the complexity of FAIRness assessment is due to the fact that the FAIR principles are expressed at a very generic level and need to be expanded and projected to specific digital objects to be more explicit. Furthermore, some criteria are very hard to evaluate by a program and sometimes require subjective–human expertise.

For all these reasons, we believe it is essential to define a quantitative method i.e., a metric, for assessing and scoring to which degree a semantic resource is FAIR compliant–for example, to determine if a resource is "not FAIR", "FAIR" or even "FAIRer" than a certain threshold or another resource. The objective of this work is to provide a *grid* dispatching different values of *credits* to each FAIR principle, depending on its importance when assessing the FAIRness of ontologies. We talked about an *integrated grid*, to capture that our grid is aligned and nourished by existing generic approaches for digital objects in general (i.e., FDMM, SHARC) and approaches dedicated to semantic resources or artifacts (i.e., 5-stars V, MIRO, FAIRsFAIR, Poveda et al.). As a result, the proposed grid involves *478 credits* that can be used for implementing FAIRness assessment tools. Such tools will then guide semantic stakeholders in (i) making their semantic resources FAIR and (ii) selecting relevant FAIR semantic resources for use.

The rest of this paper is organized as follows: Sect. 2 presents related work in FAIRness assessment or alike. Section 3 describes the methodology followed to integrate the most prominent existing works into one schema and details the proposed FAIRness assessment grid. Section 4 presents candidate metadata properties–taken from the MOD 1.4 ontology metadata model–to be used to enable FAIRness assessment. Finally, Sect. 5 concludes and gives our perspective of developing a methodology to automatize FAIRness assessment.

2   Overview of Related Work for Assessing FAIRness

We distinguish between two FAIRness assessment approaches: the first category concerns general schemes or generic tools applicable for any kind of digital object; the second category is specific for the description and assessment of ontologies or semantic resources. We review both of them chronologically.

2.1   Generic FAIRness Assessment Approaches

The Research Data Alliance (RDA) *SHARing Rewards and Credit* (SHARC) Interest Group, created in 2017, proposed a FAIRness assessment grid to enable researchers and other data stakeholders to evaluate FAIR implementations and provide the appropriate means for crediting and rewarding to facilitate data sharing [6]. The SHARC grid defines a set of 45 generic criteria with importance levels (essential, recommended, or desirable) evaluated by answering one of four values (Never/NA, If mandatory, Sometimes, Always) to a question; questions are sometimes dependent on one another as in a decision tree.

In 2018, the RDA *FAIR Data Maturity Model* (FDMM) Working Group recommended normalizing FAIRness assessment approaches and enabling comparison of their results [7]. It describes a set of 47 generic criteria derived from each FAIR principle with priorities (essential, important, or useful). Both the SHARC grid and the FDMM recommendation assumed that some FAIR principles were more important than others. We have kept this philosophy in our methodology and kept the SHARC and FDMM outputs as influences on our FAIRness assessment score.

Some FAIRness assessment tools recently appeared, such as FAIRdat tool [8], FAIR self-assessment tool [9], OzNome 5-star tool [10], FAIR Metrics [11], FAIR-Aware [12], F-UJI[2]. We cannot unfortunately detail them here. These tools are relevant but need to be improved in order to provide a clear methodology and a tool to assess any digital object quantitatively.

2.2 Specific FAIRness Assessment Approaches

Before the emergence of the FAIR principles in 2011, Berners-Lee presented the foundational principles for Linked Open Data (LOD) [13] for making data available, shareable, and interconnected on the Web. The FAIR principles have been proposed for similar reasons with a stronger emphasis on data reusability (consideration of license agreement and provenance information). The 5-stars LOD principles were specialized in 2014 for Linked data vocabularies [14] as five rules to follow for creating and publishing "good" vocabularies. Under this scheme, stars denote the quality, leading to better structure (i.e., use of W3C standards) and interoperability for reuse (i.e., metadata description, reuse of vocabularies, and alignment). The proposed 5-star rating system (later called *5-stars V*) for vocabularies is simple. However, no implementation tool was developed for making the assessment automatic, and the principles are not largely referenced today. A study of the degree to which the FAIR principles align, and extend the 5-star LOD principles was proposed first in [15] and later in [16]; we have incorporated this alignment in our methodology.

In 2017, the *Minimum Information for Reporting an Ontology* initiative published the MIRO guidelines for ontology developers when reporting an ontology in scientific reports [17]. The MIRO guidelines aim to improve the information content descriptions' quality and consistency, including development methodology, provenance, and context of reuse information. They define 34 information items (such as "ontology name", "ontology license", "ontology URL") and specify the level of importance "must", "should", "optional" for each. This work was significant, but there have been no studies on how the MIRO properties align with or extend the FAIR principles. However, the MOD 1.4 metadata model (see hereafter) aligned each MIRO guideline and the corresponding metadata properties in MOD. We, therefore, used this alignment in our methodology to influence the FAIRness assessment score with the MIRO guidelines.

---

[2] https://seprojects.marum.de/fuji/api/v1/ui/.

Dutta et al. [18] reviewed and harmonized existing metadata vocabularies and proposed a unified ontology metadata model called MOD (for *Metadata for Ontology Description*) to facilitate manual and automatic ontology descriptions, identification, and selection. MOD is not another standard nor another metadata vocabulary, but more a set of cataloged and regrouped properties one can use to describe a semantic resource. For instance, MOD does not require the use of a specific authorship property but rather encodes that `dc:creator`; `schema:author`, `foaf:maker`, or `pav:createdBy` can be used to say so. The MOD 1.2 model later extended in MOD1.4[3] was used in AgroPortal–a vocabulary and ontology repository for agronomy–to implement a richer, unified metadata model [19]. With this implementation, AgroPortal affirms to recognize 346 properties from 15 relevant metadata vocabularies (such as Dublin Core, Ontology Metadata Vocabulary, VoID, FOAF, Schema.org, PROV-O, DCAT, etc.) and map them to its unified model. Somehow, this previous work on a unified metadata model could be considered as the first step for enabling FAIRness assessment. For example, an ontology developer can focus on his/her responsibility of determining the license to use an ontology, while MOD offers means and recommendations to encode such information in a way machines can assess the level of FAIRness. Based on the MOD model, we produce in this article guidelines on how FAIR principles might be met and evaluated. Section 4 provides a clear alignment between the MOD properties and the FAIR principles. For instance, to assess F1, we rely on the existing MOD properties to encode the identifiers of an ontology (`omv:uri`) and (`dct:identifier`).

In March 2020, the FAIRsFAIR H2020 project delivered the first version of a list of 17 recommendations and 10 best practices recommendations for making semantic artefacts FAIR [3] (later revised in Dec. 2020 in a new deliverable [19]). For each recommendation, the authors provided a detailed description, listed its related semantic Web technologies, and outlined potential technical solutions in some cases. Similarly, best practices are introduced as recommendations that are not directly related to a FAIR principle but contribute to the overall evaluation of a semantic resource. This proposal is currently being discussed in the context of the RDA Vocabulary and Semantic Services Interest Group (VSSIG). The recommendations are also publicly available for comments on GitHub.[4]

Later, in September 2020, Poveda et al. considered some previous works and produced "guidelines and best practices for creating accessible, understandable and reusable ontologies on the Web" [16]. In another position paper [20], they complete a qualitative analysis of how four ontology publication initiatives cover the foundational FAIR principles. They propose some recommendations on making ontologies FAIR and list some open issues that might be addressed by the semantic Web community in the future. These two publications are very relevant for our methodology; our work is a step further. It completes this work and proposes a concrete metric necessary for further work on automatic FAIRness assessment.

Other recent related works on FAIR principles for semantic resources include a list of functional metrics and recommendations for Linked Open Data Knowledge Organization Systems (LOD KOS) products proposed in 2020 [21], a list of ten simple rules for making

---

[3] https://github.com/sifrproject/MOD-Ontology.

[4] https://github.com/FAIRsFAIR-Project/FAIRSemantics/issues/.

a vocabulary FAIR [22]. Finally, the DBPedia Archivo tool [23], an ontology archive also released at the end of 2020 that aims to help developers and consumers in "implementing FAIR ontologies on the Web."

To design our FAIRness assessment methodology, we analyzed and merged relevant related approaches namely FDMM version v0.04, SHARC version v1.1, LOD 5-stars V, MIRO, FAIRsFAIR recommendations, and Poveda et al.'s guidelines. We consider both generic and specific approaches to provide a specialized solution for ontologies but are still influenced by more general concerns, as ontologies are a kind of digital object. The integration was not straightforward because none of the approaches used is simply and strictly aligned with the 15 sub-principles (e.g., FDMM provides 47 criteria). Two of them (i.e., MIRO and 5-stars V) were totally disconnected from the FAIR prism. Table 1 gives a summary of our selection. We classify approaches into three groups: (A) for generic approaches which set priorities for each FAIR principle or sub-principle; for specific approaches for semantic resources which: (B) includes FAIRsFAIR and Poveda et al. as these guidelines do not set priorities; (C) includes LOD 5-stars and MIRO as they are not aligned to the FAIR principles. In the next section, we explain how we proceeded to integrate all these methodologies into the proposed grid.

Table 1. Summary of related works on FAIRness assessment integrated into our approach.

Category	Generic (A)		Specific (B, C)			
Format	Grid		Principles	Scheme	Recommendations	
Approach	SHARC	FDMM	5-stars V	MIRO	FAIRsFAIR	Poveda et al.
Reference	[6]	[7]	[14]	[17]	[3]	[20]
Year	2017	2018	2011	2017	2020	2020
FAIR principles	after	after	before	before	after	After
Priorities	yes	yes	n/a	n/a	no	No

3 Integrated Quantitative FAIRness Assessment Grid for Ontologies

3.1 Methodology

In what follows, we explain how we quantify each approach against the FAIR principles, then for each category (A) and (B-C), and finally determine a set of final FAIR credits that could be used in evaluating any semantic resource.

We chose to provide numerical credits {0;1;2;3} to respectively represent the degree of priorities/qualification of each *indicator* (other names for sub-principle e.g., F1, F2, F3 et F4 for F) within an approach {e.g., "none", "may", "should", "must"}. A "must" represents an essential principle, a "should" means that a principle is important except under some particular circumstance, "may" is an optional requirement, and "none" a

Table 2. Alignment between priorities in related work approaches and credits.

Group	Approach	None (0 credit)	May (1 credit)	Should (2 credits)	Must (3 credits)
A	FDMM	n/a	useful	important	essential
	SHARC	n/a	desirable	recommended	essential
B	FAIRsFAIR	n/a	1 Rec	2 Rec	3 Rec or >
	Poveda et al	n/a	1 Rec	2 Rec	3 Rec or >
C	MIRO	n/a	optional	should	Must
	5-stars V	n/a	1 star	2 stars	3 stars or >

non-revealed/specified qualification of a principle. Table 2 lists the correspondences between the five approaches, their priorities, and their attributed credits.

To determine the FAIR principle credits for each group, we follow certain rules:

- Group A: we calculate the approximate average value of credits per indicator (FDMM) or principle (SHARC). For SHARC, we divide the obtained average value by the number of indicators associated with a principle.
- Group B: we count the number of recommendations to determine the credits.
- Group C: we count the number "must", "should" and "optional" properties for MIRO and the number of the principles for 5-stars V.

The final credits for each sub-principle are the sum of all obtained credits per methodology. An example is provided hereafter:

Example 1: We illustrate how we determine for each group (i.e., A, B and C) the credits of F1 (noted $Credits_{F1}$):

Group A:
- FDMM defines 4 "essential" indicators (F1-01M, F1-01D, F1-02M, and F1-02D). Thus, $Credits_{F1,FDMM} = 3 * 4 = 12$.
- SHARC defines 12 sub-indicators (8 essential, 4 recommended) for F. Thus the approximative $Credits_{F1,SHARC} = (8 * 3 + 4 * 2) \div 4 = 8$.

Group B:
- FAIRsFAIR defines 2 recommendations (P-Rec 1 and P-Rec 2) related to F1 thus, $Credits_{F1,FsF}=2$.
- Poveda et al. define 4 recommendations related to F1 (Rec 1, Rec 2, Rec 3 and Rec 5) thus $Credits_{F1,Poveda\ et\ al.} = 3$.

Group C:
- MIRO refers to 2 "must" properties ("A" category- basics) for F1 sub-principle: ontology version (A.4) and IRI version (A.4). Thus, $Credits_{F1,MIRO}=6$.
- LOD 5-stars V does not especially cover Findability; thus, $Credits_{F1,5-starsV}=0$.

3.2 Results

From a semantic Web perspective, the results obtained emphasize the need for the establishment of agreement about a set of core metadata ontology descriptions, a federation model for ontologies regarding repositories and search engines, clear ontology and metadata ontology perseveration strategies within endpoints, mechanisms for references qualification, and best practices to document and communicate ontologies. Figure 1(c) provides final integrated FAIR credits per indicator; it shows how both generic approaches and semantic resources specific approaches address FAIRness and scores each FAIR indicator.

For example, $Credits_F = 113$. Which is the sum of 41 (F1) + 27 (F2) + 21(F3) + 24(F4).

Figure 1(c) illustrates the importance of each indicator in our integrated method. When doing the final sums, we have chosen a baseline value fixed to 10, to represent the fact that originally, as suggested by the FORCE 11 group, the FAIR principles were not ordered by importance; they were supposed to all contribute equally. The final credits are presented in our integrated FAIRness assessment grid (Table 3); the 478 credits of the grid, dispatched by each sub-principle, can be used for the assessment of any semantic resource or ontologies.

Table 3. Integrated FAIRness assessment grid for semantic resources and ontologies.

Principle		Baseline	SHARC	FDMM	5-stars V	MIRO	FAIRsFAIR	Poveda et al.	Credits	
F	F1	10	8	12	0	6	2	3	41	113
	F2	10	8	2	0	5	1	1	27	
	F3	10	8	2	0	0	1	0	21	
	F4	10	8	3	0	0	2	1	24	
A	A1	10	6	18	3	3	1	2	43	113
	A1.1	10	6	11	0	0	1	0	28	
	A1.2	10	6	5	0	0	1	0	22	
	A2	10	6	3	0	0	1	0	20	
I	I1	10	4	12	1	12	3	2	44	109
	I2	10	4	7	0	9	2	0	32	
	I3	10	4	12	1	3	2	1	33	
R	R1	10	9	3	1	6	0	3	32	143
	R1.1	10	9	12	0	3	2	1	37	
	R1.2	10	9	3	0	12	3	1	38	
	R1.3	10	9	12	0	0	3	2	36	
Total credits										478

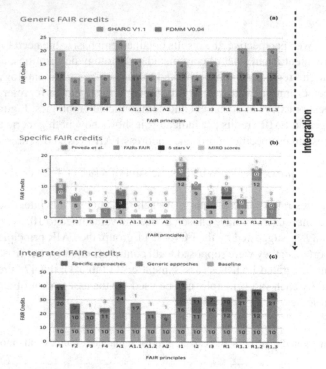

Fig. 1. Credits are assigned to each FAIR principle by generic approaches (a), specific approaches (b), and sums with a common baseline in our integrated grid (c).

A quick analysis of Table 3 and Fig. 1 reveals interesting points:

- The most important principles for generic and specific approaches are not the same. Generic approaches tend to emphasize principles F1 (identifier), A1 (access protocol), R1.1 (license), and R1.3 (community standards), while specific approaches emphasize principles I1 (knowledge representation), R1.2 (provenance), and I2 (use of vocabularies). This confirms our hypothesis that being FAIR is strongly dependent on the type of digital object considered and therefore FAIRness assessment methods must be customized for each type.
- In the integrated grid, F1, A1, and I1 are the three sub-principles with the higher number of credits. These aspects being "generally" well addressed by ontologies, it will contribute to an overall good level of FAIRness.
- Four sub-principles, important for FAIR, were completely ignored/avoided by specific approaches, except the FAIRsFAIR recommendations: F3 (link data-metadata), A1.1 (protocol openness), A1.2 (protocol security), and A2 (long term metadata). Consequently, three of these four keep the minimum number of credits in the integrated grid.
- None of the specific approaches covered all of the FAIR sub-principles. This is not surprising for MIRO and 5-stars V, which preexist the FAIR movement, but it is more surprising for FAIRsFAIR and Poveda et al. whose recommendations were

done specifically for ontologies or semantic resources to be FAIR. Only A1, I1, and I3 were found in the four approaches studied. This point backups our methodology, which mixes both generic and specific approaches.

- Despite differences in credits assigned to the sub-principles, the sums by principles are relatively close, with a mean of 119,5. Only the R group is significantly above the mean. The group I is slightly under, mainly because it is made of only three sub-principles instead of four.
- R being the most important principle may reveal the concern that ontologies and semantic resources, often developed by means of semantic Web technologies (RDFS, OWL, SKOS) are naturally equipped with good findability, accessibility, and inter-operability features (e.g., URIs for identifiers, HTTP for accessibility, W3C standards for knowledge representation, claim to use vocabularies, etc.) whereas they lack reusability.

4 Candidate Metadata Properties for FAIR Ontologies

In the second phase of our work, we elicited candidate metadata properties that can be used to encode information relevant for each FAIR sub-principle. Indeed, we found out most sub-principles (about 93%) might be partially or totally implemented and assessed with a series of metadata properties. In this section, we review candidate metadata properties that could be used by anyone developing (i) an ontology or semantic resource or (ii) a FAIRness assessment tool to obtain associated credits as listed in the previous section.

4.1 Candidate Metadata Properties to Support FAIRness

Here, we reuse the MOD ontology metadata model (v1.4) [24] as a reference to pick up metadata properties. MOD1.4 reviewed 346 metadata properties from 23 standard metadata vocabularies (such as Dublin Core, DCAT, VoID, ADMS, VOAF, Schema.org, etc.) to provide a list of 127 "aligned or crosswalked" properties that can be used to describe an ontology or a semantic resource. MOD allows us to unambiguously identify which property may be used; however, our grid could be implemented with any other metadata standard or combination of standards that cover all the sub-principles.

The outcome of this process is a list of **58 candidate metadata properties** that may be used to support FAIRness assessment and assign some credits from our grid. These metadata properties might help to assign **276 credits** over a total of 478 (57%). We have separated the metadata properties for any principles from the ones for F2, which has to be treated apart. Indeed, F2 ("Data are described with rich metadata") was assigned all the properties that MOD1.4 has reviewed as relevant for ontologies that have not been assigned to another sub-principle. We refer to the first group as *core metadata properties* (Table 4) and to the second group as *extra metadata properties* (Table 5). The idea is that any ontologies using some of the **69 extra metadata properties** in addition to the core 58 ones, will be "FAIRer".

We identified that 46% of the FAIR principles (i.e., F2, I1, I2, R1, R1.1, R1.2, and R1.3) are totally evaluable with metadata properties, 33% are partially evaluable (i.e., F1,

Table 4. List of core metadata properties from MOD1.4 to help make an ontology FAIR.

Principle		Credits	Metadata properties
F	F1	29	owl:ontologyIRI, owl:versionIRI, dct:identifier
	F4	24	schema:includedInDataCatalog
A	A1	36	owl:ontologyIRI, dct:identifier, sd:endpoint
	A2	4	omv:status, owl:deprecated
I	I1	44	omv:hasOntologyLanguage, omv:hasFormalityLevel, omv:hasOntologySyntax, dct:hasFormat, dct:isFormatOf
	I2	22	owl:imports, voaf:hasEquivalenceWith, owl:priorVersion, voaf:similar, voaf:metadataVoc, dct:relation, dct:isPartOf, voaf:specializes, schema:translationOfWork, voaf:generalizes
R	R1	8	mod:prefLabelProperty, mod:synonymProperty, mod:definitionProperty, mod:authorProperty, bpm:obsoleteProperty, mod:hierarchyProperty, mod:obsoleteParent, mod:maxDepth
	R1.1	37	dct:license, dct:rightsHolder, dct:accessRights, cc:morePermissions, cc:useGuidelines
	R1.2	36	dct:creator, dct:ontributor, pav:curatedBy, schema:translator, dct:source, prov:wasGeneratedBy, prov:wasInvalidatedBy, dct:accrualMethod, dct:accrualPeriodicity, dct:accrualPolicy, omv:versionInfo, vann:changes, dct:hasVersion, omv:usedOntologyEngineeringTool, omv:usedOntologyEngineeringMethodology, omv:conformsToKnowledgeRepresentationParadigm, omv:designedForOntologyTask, mod:competencyQuestion, foaf:fundedBy
	R1.3	36	mod:ontologyInUse, omv:endorsedBy, mod:group, dct:accessRights
Total		**276**	**58 metadata properties**

F4, A1, A1.2, and A2). Two principles for which we have not found any metadata property are A1.1 ("*The protocol is open, free, and universally implementable.*") and A1.2 ("The protocol allows for an authentication and authorization where necessary.") because they are completely related to the evaluation of the communication protocol, not the ontology persay. A sub-principle is not totally evaluable with metadata properties when it is about an aspect independent of the ontology itself but related to the library/repository hosting the ontology. For instance: F4 ("*(Meta)data are registered or indexed in a searchable resource.*") concerns also ontology repositories.

F3 ("*Metadata clearly and explicitly include the identifier of the data they describe.*") is excluded from Table 4 as MOD1.4 do not yet offer a property to establish the link between an ontology and its metadata (necessary when metadata are not explicitly included in the same file than the ontology itself). Such a property is currently being discussed in the FAIR Digital Object working group of GO FAIR that shall soon release a new metadata vocabulary including `fdo:hasMetadata` and `fdo:metadataOf` properties. Even if I3 is totally evaluable with metadata, the currently proposed candidate metadata are not covering its evaluation. Here again, we need some extension to MOD to enable encoding all information required by this principle (especially alignment qualification). MOD is currently being extended as a new model compliant with DCAT2 within the RDA VSSIG and H2020 FAIRsFAIR.

Table 5. List of extra metadata properties from MOD1.4 to make an ontology FAIRer.

Principle		Credits	Metadata properties
F	F2	27	omv:acronym, dct:title, dct:alternative, skos:hiddenLabel, dct:description, foaf:page, omv:resourceLocator, omv:keywords, dct:coverage, foaf:homepage, vann:example, vann:preferredNamespaceUri, void:uriRegexPattern, idot:exampleIdentifier, dct:publisher, dct:subject, owl:backwardCompatibleWith, door:comesFromTheSameDomain, mod:sampleQueries, omv:knownUsage, dct:audience, doap:repository, doap:bugDatabase, doap:mailing-list, mod:hasEvaluation, mod:metrics, omv:numberOfClasses, omv:numberOfIndividuals, omv:numberOfProperties, mod:numberOfDataProperties, mod:numberOfObjectProperties, omv:numberOfAxioms, mod:numberOfLabels, mod:byteSize, vann:preferredNamespacePrefix, dct:language, dct:abstract, mod:analytics, dct:bibliographicCitation, rdfs:comment, foaf:depiction, foaf:logo,voaf:toDoList, schema:award, schema:associatedMedia, owl:isIncompatibleWith, dct:hasPart, schema:workTranslation, door:hasDisparateModelling, voaf:usedBy, voaf:hasDisjunctionsWith, omv:keyClasses, void:rootResource, mod:browsingUI, mod:sampleQueries, void:propertyPartition, void;classPartition, void:dataDump, void:openSearchDescription, void:uriLookupEndpoint, schema:comments, dct:created, dct:modified, dct:valid, dct:dateSubmitted, pav:curatedOn, omv:IsOfType
Total		**27**	**69 metadata properties**

4.2 FAIR or FAIRer: How FAIR is a Semantic Resource?

Qualifying the degree of FAIRness of a semantic resource or even comparing it with other semantic resources necessarily implies the use of a metric delimiting the range of values for each qualification (e.g., not FAIR, FAIR, or FAIRer). In that context, our proposed integrated quantitative grid allows for defining *thresholds*. For instance, the median value of the resulting total credits can be considered a minimum threshold to be FAIR. A semantic resource with a degree/score under this threshold will not be considered FAIR. Similarly, a semantic resource might be considered as "FAIRer" if it is described with extra metadata properties. In other words, answering the question: *"how much is a semantic resource FAIR?"* becomes possible with such a metric. In our grid, the total credits are 478, so the *first threshold could be at 240* (478/2 + 1) and the *second threshold at 451* (478–27), as illustrated in Fig. 2.

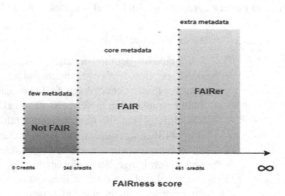

Fig. 2. Not FAIR, FAIR, or FAIRer: using the metric of the integrated quantitative grid.

Clearly, using a metric and threshold is the first required step in making the FAIRness assessment task machine-actionable and enabling the development of automatic FAIR-ness assessment tools. We believe it will also be beneficial for researchers to quantify the FAIRness degree of their semantic resources and compare them with other ones.

5   Conclusions and Perspective

In this paper, we proposed an integrated quantitative grid for assessing the level of FAIRness of semantic resources and ontologies. Moreover, we provided a list of can-didate metadata properties–from the MOD model v1.4–to enable FAIRness assessment and possibly implement systems based on our grid. Our grid was realized by analyzing existing related work (among others, the semantic Web community work before and since the FAIR movement) and summarizing them into one coherent scheme. A distinct feature of our grid is to propose a metric–and thus possible thresholds–for the qualifica-tion of any semantic resource. The grid is conceived in a way that can be customized, extended, or improved by other semantic experts in further studies. This work is a start-ing point for developing machine-actionable FAIRness assessment tools in the semantic Web context.

The motivation of this work was to go beyond the current recommendations to guide semantic stakeholders for making their semantic resources FAIR: We consider these recommendations, harmonize and integrate them to build a grid of 478 credits to assess the 15 FAIR principles.

Currently, we are using the grid to implement a FAIRness assessment tool in Agro-Portal (http://agroportal.lirmm.fr/), a vocabulary and ontology repository dedicated to agri-food and based on the generic and open source OntoPortal technology[5]. However, in the future, this work will need to be further tested in other FAIRness assessment approaches and discussed within some international FAIR initiatives, for instance, RDA, GO FAIR, or projects such as FAIRsFAIR.

Acknowledgments. This work has been supported by the *Data to Knowledge in Agronomy and Biodiversity* project (D2KAB – www.d2kab.org – ANR-18-CE23–0017) and the project ANR *French participation in GO FAIR Food Systems Implementation Network* (FooSIN – https://foo sin.fr – ANR19-DATA-0019). We also thank the VSSIG (Vocabulary and Semantic Services Interest Group) of the Research Data Alliance and the H2020 FAIRsFAIR project T2.2 on "FAIR Semantics" for fruitful discussions and exchanges.

References

1. Wilkinson, M.D., et al.: The FAIR guiding principles for scientific data management and stewardship. Sci. Data **3**(1), Article no. 1 (2016)
2. Zeng, M.L., Mayr, P.: Knowledge organization systems (KOS) in the semantic web: a multi-dimensional review. Int. J. Digit. Libr. **20**(3), 209–230 (2018). https://doi.org/10.1007/s00 799-018-0241-2
3. Le Franc, Y., Parland-von Essen, J., Bonino, L., Lehväslaiho, H., Coen, G., Staiger, C.: D2.2 FAIR Semantics: First recommendations, March 2020
4. Caracciolo, C., et al.: 39 hints to facilitate the use of semantics for data on agriculture and nutrition. Data Sci. J. **19**(1), Article no. 1 (2020)
5. Wilkinson, M.D., Sansone, S.-A., Schultes, E., Doorn, P., Bonino da Silva Santos, L.O., Dumontier, M.: A design framework and exemplar metrics for FAIRness. Sci. Data **5** (2018)
6. David, R., et al.: FAIRness literacy: the achilles' heel of applying FAIR principles. Data Sci. J. **19**(1), Article no. 1 (2020)
7. Bahim, C., et al.: The FAIR data maturity model: an approach to harmonise FAIR assessments. Data Sci. J. **19**(1), Article no. 1 (2020)
8. SurveyMonkey Powered Online Survey. https://www.surveymonkey.com/r/fairdat. Accessed 19 Apr 2021
9. FAIR self-assessment tool, 23 July 2021. https://satifyd.dans.knaw.nl/
10. Cox, S., Yu, J.: OzNome 5-star Tool: A Rating System for making data FAIR and Trustable, October 2017. https://publications.csiro.au/rpr/pub?pid=csiro:EP175062. Accessed 12 Apr 2021
11. Wilkinson, M.D., et al.: Evaluating FAIR maturity through a scalable, automated, community-governed framework. Sci. Data **6**(1) (2019)
12. Mokrane, M., Cepinskas, L., Åkerman, V., de Vries, J., von Stein, I.: FAIR-Aware (2020). https://pure.knaw.nl/portal/en/publications/fair-aware. Accessed 14 Mar 2021
13. Bizer, C., Heath, T., Berners-Lee, T.: Linked Data: The Story so Far. Semantic Services, Interoperability and Web Applications: Emerging Concepts (2011). www.igi-global.com/cha pter/linked-data-story-far/55046
14. Janowicz, K., Hitzler, P., Adams, B., Kolas, D., Vardeman II, C.: Five stars of linked data vocabulary use. Semant. Web **5**(3), 173–176 (2014)

---

[5] https://github.com/ontoportal-lirmm.

15. Hasnain, A., Rebholz-Schuhmann, D.: Assessing FAIR data principles against the 5-star open data principles. In: Gangemi, A., et al. (eds.) ESWC 2018. LNCS, vol. 11155, pp. 469–477. Springer, Cham (2018). https://doi.org/10.1007/978-3-319-98192-5_60

16. Garijo, D., Poveda-Villalón, M.: Best Practices for Implementing FAIR Vocabularies and Ontologies on the Web. ArXiv (2020)

17. Matentzoglu, N., Malone, J., Mungall, C., Stevens, R.: MIRO: guidelines for minimum information for the reporting of an ontology. J. Biomed. Semant. **9**(1), 6 (2018)

18. Dutta, B., Toulet, A., Emonet, V., Jonquet, C.: New generation metadata vocabulary for ontology description and publication. In: Garoufallou, E., Virkus, S., Siatri, R., Koutsomiha, D. (eds.) MTSR 2017. CCIS, vol. 755, pp. 173–185. Springer, Cham (2017). https://doi.org/10.1007/978-3-319-70863-8_17

19. Hugo, W., Le Franc, Y., Coen, G., Parland-von Essen, J., Bonino, L.: D2.5 FAIR Semantics Recommendations Second Iteration, December 2020

20. Poveda-Villalón, M., Espinoza-Arias, P., Garijo, D., Corcho, O.: Coming to Terms with FAIR Ontologies. In: Keet, C.M., Dumontier, M. (eds.) EKAW 2020. LNCS (LNAI), vol. 12387, pp. 255–270. Springer, Cham (2020). https://doi.org/10.1007/978-3-030-61244-3_18

21. Lei Zeng, M., Clunis, J.: FAIR + FIT: Guiding Principles and Functional Metrics for Linked Open Data (LOD) KOS Products, 16 March 2020. https://sciendo.com/article/10.2478/jdis-2020-0008

22. Cox, S.J.D., Gonzalez-Beltran, A.N., Magagna, B., Marinescu, M.C.: Ten simple rules for making a vocabulary FAIR. PLOS Comput. Biol. **17**(6), e1009041 (2021)

23. Frey, J., Streitmatter, D., Götz, F., Hellmann, S., Arndt, N.: DBpedia archivo: a web-scale interface for ontology archiving under consumer-oriented aspects. In: Blomqvist, E., et al. (eds.) SEMANTICS 2020. LNCS, vol. 12378, pp. 19–35. Springer, Cham (2020). https://doi.org/10.1007/978-3-030-59833-4_2

24. Jonquet, C., Toulet, A., Dutta, B., Emonet, V.: Harnessing the power of unified metadata in an ontology repository: the case of AgroPortal. J. Data Semant. **7**(4), 191–221 (2018). https://doi.org/10.1007/s13740-018-0091-5

Towards the FAIRification of Meteorological Data: A Meteorological Semantic Model

Amina Annane[1] , Mouna Kamel[1] , Cassia Trojahn[1(✉)] ,
Nathalie Aussenac-Gilles[1] , Catherine Comparot[1] , and Christophe Baehr[2]

[1] Toulouse University, Toulouse, France
{amina.annane,mouna.kamel,cassia.trojahn,nathalie,aussenac-gilles,
catherine.comparot}@irit.fr
[2] Météo-France, Paris, France
christophe.baehr@meteo.fr

Abstract. Meteorological institutions produce a valuable amount of data as a direct or side product of their activities, which can be potentially explored in diverse applications. However, making this data fully reusable requires considerable efforts in order to guarantee compliance to the FAIR principles. While most efforts in data FAIRification are limited to describing data with semantic metadata, such a description is not enough to fully address interoperability and reusability. We tackle this weakness by proposing a rich ontological model to represent both metadata and data schema of meteorological data. We apply the proposed model on a largely used meteorological dataset, the "SYNOP" dataset of Météo-France and show how the proposed model improves FAIRness.

Keywords: Meteorological data · FAIR principles · Semantic metadata

1 Introduction

Meteorology data is essential in many applications, including forecasts, climate change, environmental studies, agriculture, health and risk management. Their production is based on mathematical models that assimilate different data from several sources including weather stations, satellites and weather radars. While this data has been made available as open data through different portals, such as governmental portals (e.g., MeteoFrance[1], worldweather[2]), or associative or private portals (e.g., infoclimat[3], meteociel[4]), under open licenses, its exploitation is rather limited: it is described and presented with properties that are relevant for meteorology domain experts (data producers) but that are not properly

---

[1] https://donneespubliques.meteofrance.fr/.
[2] http://worldweather.wmo.int/fr/home.html.
[3] https://www.infoclimat.fr.
[4] http://www.meteociel.fr.

© Springer Nature Switzerland AG 2022
E. Garoufallou et al. (Eds.): MTSR 2021, CCIS 1537, pp. 81–93, 2022.
https://doi.org/10.1007/978-3-030-98876-0_7

understood and reusable by other scientific communities. For the latter, one of the challenges is to find relevant data among the increasingly large amount of continuously generated data, by moving from the point of view of data producers to the point of view of users and usages. One way to reach this goal is to guarantee compliance of data to the FAIR principles (Findability, Accessibility, Interoperability, and Reusability) [21]. These principles correspond to a set of 15 recommendations to be followed in order to make data FAIR (Fig. 1). A key step toward improving FAIRness of data is the use of semantic models (i.e., ontologies) for data and metadata representation [9].

While most efforts in data FAIRification are limited to describing data with semantic metadata, such a description is not enough to fully address all FAIR principles [12], in particular for promoting reuse of this data by other scientific communities. We propose to overcome this weakness through a richer representation of the meaning of meteorological data in a formal model which allows for sharing the semantic meaning with third-parties [13]. Contrary to existing works involving ontology population [1,2,14,16,19], and due to the characteristics of meteorological data, we do not transform all data into RDF but rather represent in a fine-grained way the data schema and its distribution structure. The contributions of this paper are as in the following:

- Proposing a semantic model representing both metadata and data schema of meteorological observation data.
- Combining existing vocabularies that follow themselves the FAIR principles.
- Instantiating the proposed model with a real meteorological dataset provided by Météo-France – the official weather service in France.
- Evaluating the FAIRness degree of this dataset without and with the proposed model showing how the proposed model improves the FAIRness degree.

The paper is organized as follows. Section 2 introduces the meteorological data specificities and presents the proposed model. Section 3 shows the instantiation and Sect. 4 presents the evaluation. Section 5 discusses the related work and Sect. 6 ends the paper.

2   Meteorological Semantic Model

In order to develop our model, we have followed the NeOn methodology scenario 3 *"Reusing ontological resources"* [20]: those cases in which ontology developers have at their disposal ontological resources useful for their problem and that can be reused in the ontology development. The methodology includes activities related to the reuse of ontologies (ontology search, ontology assessment, ontology comparison, ontology selection and ontology integration) in addition to the main activities (specification, conceptualization, formalization, implementation). For the sake of space, we focus here on the presentation of the model, without describing in detail the different activities of the methodology. In the following, we summarize the result of specification and knowledge acquisition in Sect. 2.1, and the result of ontology selection and integration in Sect. 2.2.

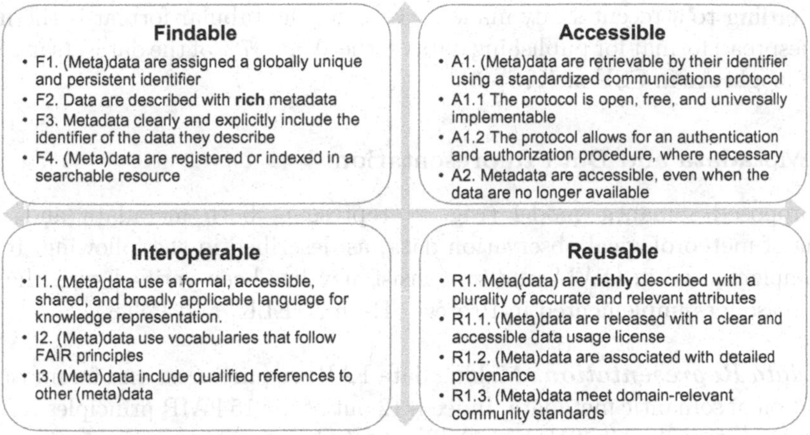

Fig. 1. FAIR principles [21].

2.1 Meteorological Data Characteristics

There exist different types of meteorological data: satellite data, model data that are computed using statistical models such as weather forecast data, radar data, etc. We focus on observation data referred to as "in situ" data. They are direct measurements of various parameters (temperature, wind, humidity, etc.) taken by instruments on the ground or at altitude from predefined locations:

- *Geospatial data:* the measure values must be localised, otherwise it is not fully exploitable. The localisation is usually defined using geospatial coordinates (latitude, longitude and altitude). The interpretation of these coordinates depends on the used coordinate reference system, hence the Coordinate Reference System (CRS) has also to be indicated.
- *Temporal data.* Each measurement is made at a specific time that must be noted with the measurement result (i.e., value). As for the geospatial, the temporal localisation is essential to the right interpretation of measurements.
- *Large volume data:* meteorological data are produced continuously. Within each station, several sensors are installed (thermometer, barometer, etc.). Each sensor generates multiple measure values with a frequency that differs from one measure to another (hourly, trihoral, daily, etc.).
- *Conform to WMO guidelines:* the measurement procedures, the types of sensors to use, the quality standards, and many other specifications are defined by the World Meteorological Organization (WMO). The latter provides detailed guides, such as *the guide to meteorological instruments and observation methods*[5] where there is a chapter for each measure describing all details about it. Nevertheless, to our knowledge, no semantic version of these guides exists.
- *Tabular data:* observation data are usually published in tabular format where measure values are organized according to spatio-temporal dimension.

---

[5] https://library.wmo.int/doc_num.php?explnum_id=10179.

According to a recent study made by Google, the tabular format is the most widespread format for publishing data on the Web (37% of the datasets indexed by Google are in CSV or XLS) [3].

2.2 Metadata and Data Representation

The proposed semantic model (Fig. 2) represents both metadata and data schema of meteorological observation data, as described in the following. It has been implemented in OWL[6] and its consistency has been verified with the different reasoners implemented in Protégé (Hermit, ELK, and Pellet).

Metadata Representation. Making data FAIR requires first and foremost the generation of semantic metadata. Indeed, 12 out of the 15 FAIR principles refer to metadata as described in [21] (Fig. 1). This metadata must remain accessible even if the data itself is no longer accessible. These 12 principles provide guidance on the categories of metadata: (i) descriptive metadata for data indexing and discovery (title, keywords, etc.); (ii) metadata about data provenance; (iii) metadata about access rights and usage licenses. Particularly for publishing data on the web, W3C recommends three other categories of metadata: (i) version history; (ii) quality; (iii) structure. Our goal is therefore to propose metadata model that covers these different categories, thus ensuring adherence to the principle on rich metadata. For metadata representation, our proposition relies on GeoDcat-AP, except structural metadata that are covered by CSVW.

GeoDcat-AP. It is a specification of the DCAT-AP vocabulary which is a specification of the W3C DCAT (Data CATalog vocabulary) recommendation. The choice of GeoDCAT-AP is motivated by the richness of the vocabulary metadata. In addition to allowing to describe data catalogs, it offers specific properties required to correctly interpret spatial data such as the geographical area covered by the data (`dct:spatial`), the reference coordinate system used (`dct:conformsTo`) to be chosen from a list defined by the OGC[7], as well as the spatial resolution (`dcat:spatialResolutionInMeters`) of the data. GeoDCAT-AP is also recommended by W3C/OGC to describe geospatial data on the Web [4].

CSVW. As pointed out in [12], it is essential for data reuse to represent the internal structure of the data. Since observation data are mostly tabular data, CSVW[8] is a suitable vocabulary. It resulted from the work of the W3C group on publishing tabular data on the web. It allows to define the different columns `csvw:Column` of a given `csvw:Table` (i.e., csv file) via the `csvw:Schema` concept. Moreover, it represents the interdependence between two tables. Indeed, it allows to represent if a column (or a set of columns) in a given csv file is a foreign key `csvw:ForeignKey` that references a column (or columns) of another CSV file.

---

[6] https://w3id.org/dmo.
[7] http://www.opengis.net/def/crs/EPSG/.
[8] https://www.w3.org/ns/csvw.

Web Annotation Ontology (oa). It is a W3C recommendation for representing data annotations. As discussed in Sect. 2.1, all WMO members (i.e., states) use the same guides developed by WMO. It is used here to annotate parts of these guides that describe relevant metadata about measures. We use mainly three classes: (i) `oa:Annotation`, (ii) `oa:SpecificResource` to represent the annotated document, and (iii) the document-part annotated via the class `oa:RangeSelector`.

Data Representation. We have made the choice to not transform all data into RDF because it is: (i) expensive: transforming the data archived for decades requires human and physical resources, and (ii) not effective: it would result in a huge RDF graph that would not be effective for querying and accessing the data [11]. We rather represent the data schema and the RDF data cube (qb) vocabulary has been considered for that. In addition to qb, we have reused several domain and cross-domains ontologies for making explicit the semantics of measures and dimensions using concepts from the meteorological domain. It is worth to mention that we use CSVW to represent the syntactical structure of a tabular dataset distribution, while we use RDF data cube and domain ontologies to represent the semantics of the dataset independently of any data format.

RDF Data Cube (qb). It is a W3C vocabulary [4][9] dedicated to the representation of multi-dimensional data. qb is suitable in our case since observation data is multi-dimensional data organized according to spatio-temporal dimensions. It describes the multidimensional data schema using three subclasses of `qb:ComponentProperty`: (i) measures `qb:MeasureProperty`, (ii) dimensions `qb:DimensionProperty` according to which the measures are organized, and (iii) attributes to represent metadata `qb:AttributeProperty`. The `qb:concept` property allows to link a `qb:ComponentProperty` (i.e., measure, dimension or attribute) to the corresponding concept to explicit its semantics. We use this property to associate component properties to domain ontologies.

Domain Ontologies. Meteorological data refers to concepts from the meteorological domain such as atmospheric parameters (e.g., temperature, wind speed), sensors (e.g. thermometer, barometer), etc. For expliciting their semantics, the following domain and cross-domain ontologies are used: SOSA [10] (Sensor, Observation, Sample, and Actuator), the reference ontology to represent observations; ENVO (Environment ontology) [5] and SWEET (Semantic Web Earth and Environment Technology ontology) [17], to designate the atmospheric parameters represented with qb as measurements; aws (ontology representing weather sensors)[10], to designate the type of weather sensor used to measure each atmospheric parameter; and QUDT, to specify the unit of measurement of each measurement.

2.3   New Entities

In order to be able to fully address the ontology requirements, we have introduced the following entities:

---

[9] https://www.w3.org/TR/eo-qb/.

[10] https://www.w3.org/2005/Incubator/ssn/ssnx/meteo/aws.

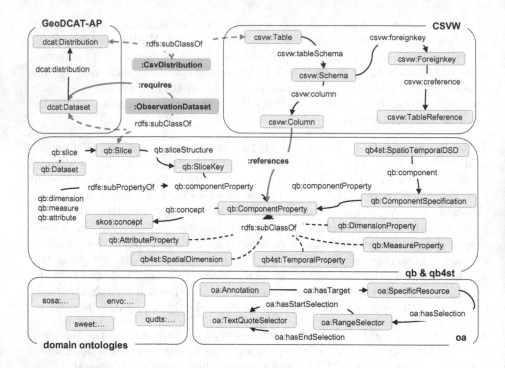

Fig. 2. Proposed modular ontology.

- *":ObservationDataset" concept*: given the continuous production of observation data, it is usually archived as fragments, where each fragment contains data of a given period (day, month, etc.). qb allows to represent the notion of a dataset (`qb:Dataset`) with multiples fragments (`qb:Slice`). However, GeoDCAT-AP offers only the possibility to represent a given dataset as a whole (`dcat:Dataset`). Since it is the same dataset fragment that we describe with GeoDCAT-AP and RDF data cube, we have defined a new concept `:ObservationDataset` that is a subclass of both `qb:Slice` and `dcat:Dataset`.
- *":CsvDistribution" concept*: it represents distributions in csv format. It is a subclass of both `csvw:Table` and `dcat:Distribution`.
- *":requires" property*: when a dataset X requires another dataset Y to be exploited, it is essential to enable the reuse of X to represent this dependency relation. As GeoDCAT-AP does not offer the possibility of representing such a relation between two datasets, we have added this new property.
- *":references" property*: it allows to associate each `csvw:Column` to an qb component property (i.e., `qb:MeasureProperty` or a `qb:DimensionProperty`): Thus, we explicit the link between the structural components (i.e., columns) and the data schema components (i.e., measures and dimensions). Moreover, data schema components are associated to domain ontology concepts, thereby explicit the semantic of each column too.

Table 1. Extract from SYNOP data.

numer_sta	date	pmer	ff	t	...
7005	20200201000000	100710	3.200000	285.450000	...
7015	20200201000000	100710	7.700000	284.950000	...
7020	20200201000000	100630	8.400000	284.150000	...
...	...	...	...	...	...

3   Use Case: SYNOP Dataset from Météo-France

3.1   Overview of SYNOP Dataset

The SYNOP dataset is an open meteorological datasets provided by Météo-France on its data portal. It includes observation data from international surface observation messages circulating on the Global Telecommunication System (GTS) of the World Meteorological Organization (WMO). The choice of this dataset is motivated by the fact that this data is open and free, and it concerns several atmospheric parameters measured (temperature, humidity, wind direction and force, atmospheric pressure, precipitation height, etc.). These parameters are important for many scientific studies. The dataset[11] is described by seven items: (i) *description*: natural language summary that describes the content of the dataset, (ii) *conditions of access*: Etalab license[12] for the data, (iii) *means of access*: specifies that the data can be accessed via direct download, (iv) *download*: possibility offered to the user to download the data in csv format for a given date, (v) *download archived data*: similar to the previous item, but for a given month, (vi) *station information*: list of stations (station id, name) accompanied by a map displaying the location of these stations, and (vii) *documentation*, links to a data dictionary, to CSV and JSON files listing the meteorological stations of Météo-France (id_station, name, latitude, longitude, altitude). Table 1 shows an extract of the SYNOP data. The file contains 59 columns, the first two correspond to the station number and the date of the measurements made, the other 57 columns to the meteorological measurements.

3.2   Model Instanciation

The SYNOP data archive consists of a set of monthly files since January 1996, where each file covers only the observations made in one month. The data of each monthly file corresponds to an instance of the :ObservationDataset. :synop_dataset_feb20 is the instance corresponding to the SYNOP dataset of February 2020 (Table 1). For sake of space, we present a fragment of the instantiated model that show both metadata and data representation. It corresponds to

---

[11] https://donneespubliques.meteofrance.fr/?fond=produit&id_produit=90&id_rubrique=32.

[12] https://www.etalab.gouv.fr/wp-content/uploads/2014/05/Licence_Ouverte.pdf.

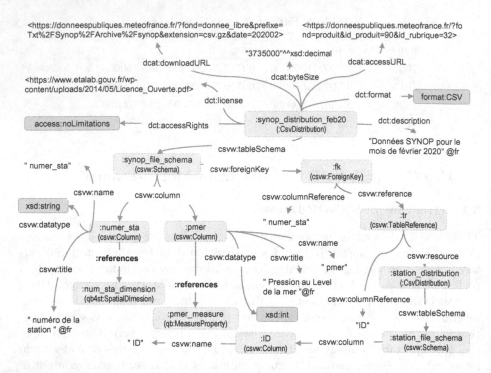

Fig. 3. Representing Synop_20 distribution using GeoDCAT-AP and CSVW.

the representation of a distribution of the dataset: `:synop_distribution_feb20` (`:CsvDistribution`), as shown in Fig. 3. This distribution is accessible and downloadable via URLs specified with properties `dcat:accessURL` and `dcat:downloadURL`; it is subject to an open license, the value of the `dct:license` property. Finally, the columns (e.g., `numer_sta` and `pmer`) of this file are characterized by their name (`csvw:name`), their label (`csvw:title`), their type (`csvw:datatype`) from the schema `:synop_file_schema` (`csvw:tableSchema`), etc. Note the representation of the foreign key `:fk` which connects the column "numer_sta" of the SYNOP data, to the column "ID" of the station data (`:station_distribution`) by passing through the instance `:tr` of `csvw:TableReference`.

In order to express the fact that all the monthly data are part of the same SYNOP dataset, we represent it as an instance of `qb:Dataset` (Fig. 4). We have defined one spatial dimension `:station_dimension` and three temporal dimensions: `:year_dimension`, `:month_dimension`, and `:date_dimension`. The spatial or temporal nature of a dimension is specified using the concepts of the qb4st vocabulary `qb4st:SpatialDimension` and `qb4st:TemporalProperty`, respectively. Note that the year and month dimensions do not refer to existing columns, but are included in the date column. We have added them to instantiate `qb:Slice`. Indeed, the instantiation of a `qb:Slice` requires the definition

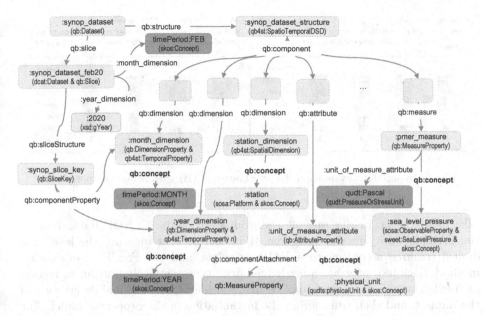

Fig. 4. Representing Synop_feb20 data using RDF data cube and domain ontologies.

of dimensions with fixed values, which are specified using the `qb:SliceKey` concept. In our case, the fixed dimensions for a monthly dataset are the year and the month, which have the values `month:FEB` and `year:2020` for the instance `:synop_dataset_feb20`. In addition, although the station dimension is not directly a geographic coordinate, it is defined as an instance of `qb4st:spatialDimension` because it provides access to geospatial coordinates contained in the station file. Each dimension or measure is associated with a concept from domain ontologies via the `qb:concept` property. Thus, the measure `:pmer_measure` (the only one represented here while all 57 measures have been instantiated) is associated to the concepts `sosa:observableProperty` and `sweet:SeaLevelPressure` to explicit its meaning. Similarly, the measure t (see Table 1) is associated to the concept `ENVO:ENVO_09200001` which represents the `air temperature`. We have defined two attributes attached to `qb:Measure`: (i) `:unit_of_measure_attribute` associated to `qudts:physicalUnit` to represent the unit of measurement of each `qb:Measure`. This makes it possible to specify that the unit of measurement of `pmer_measure` is `qudt:Pascal`; (ii) `:method_of_measure_attribute` associated to `sosa procedure` to represent the procedure of measurement of each measure according to WMO guides that are digital books.

4 Evaluation

To evaluate the degree of FAIRness, we have chosen the framework *FAIR data maturity model* (FAIR data maturity model) proposed by the RDA [18]. For

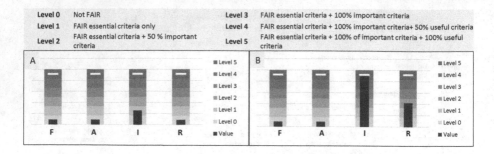

Fig. 5. Synop data evaluation: (A) without and (B) with semantic metadata.

sake of space, we briefly present the evaluation of the SYNOP dataset using
the FAIR maturity model using the 41 indicators that measure the level of a
digital resource according to a FAIR principle, and the Fail/Pass evaluation
method. Each indicator has a predefined priority: essential, important or recommended. The indicators were applied first considering the original description of
the dataset, and then considering the instantiation of the proposed model. The
reader car refer to Zenodo[13] for a detailed evaluation report.

The first evaluation of the SYNOP dataset consisted in evaluating its original
description (without the semantic model). This evaluation resulted in: i) level
0 for principles "F", "A" and "R", because at least one essential indicator was
not satisfied for each of them; ii) level 1 for principle "I", because no indicator is
essential for this principle (Fig. 5(A)). As it stands, the SYNOP dataset is not
FAIR. The data has been **re-evaluated** after generating the semantic metadata
that describes it. This metadata significantly improves the FAIRness level, especially for the "I" and "R" principles (Fig. 5(B)). Although the re-evaluation of
the "F" principle did not show any improvement, the model allows representing
"rich" indexing metadata that satisfy "F2" principle. However, improving the
"F" and "A" degree requires satisfying essential indicators that are beyond the
abilities of any semantic model e.g., the generation of persistent and unique identifiers ("F1"), persistent metadata ("A2"), publishing metadata on searchable
resources ("F4"), etc.

5 Related Work

Hereafter, we present a summary on works related to the main subjects addressed
in this work, focusing on works related to geospatial data.

Metadata Representation. The importance of sharing geospatial data and
describing them with rich metadata has been recognized for decades. Indeed,
in 1999, Kim has published a comparative analysis of eight already existing
metadata schemes for geospatial data. The INSPIRE (2007) directive defined

---

[13] doi.org/10.5281/zenodo.4679704.

a metadata schema, mainly based on the previous standards for describing the European geospatial data on web portals. Later, with the emergence of semantic web, semantic vocabularies have been developed to describe dataset metadata such as Dublin core, VoID, schema.org and DCAT. DCAT-AP was designed to ensure interoperability between European data portals. GeoDCAT-AP was initially developed to enable interoperability between geospatial data portals implementing the INSPIRE directive, and those implementing DCAT-AP, by developing a set of mappings between the metadata schemes. In December 2020, a new version of GeoDCAT-AP was released, making this vocabulary a full-fledged specification for describing geospatial data catalogs on the Web[14].

Data Representation. Several works have focused on the semantic representation of geospatial data [1,2,14,16,19]. The proposed models are generally a combination of a set of reference ontologies. In [14] the authors combined qb and SOSA to represent 100 years of temperature data in RDF. Similarly, in [19], the ontologies SOSA, GeoSPARQL, LOCN and QUDTS have been reused to represent a meteorological dataset with several measures (temperature, wind speed, etc.). In our case, given the characteristics of the meteorological data (Sect. 2.1), we did not transform Météo-France data into RDF. Representing all the data in RDF generates a huge graph which is not effective for querying the data [11]. Moreover, such a choice would require Météo-France to convert all its archives (some of them date back to 1872), which can turn out to be very expensive. Close to ours, [13] propose the Semantic Government Vocabulary, based on the different ontological types of terms occurring in the Open Government Data. They show how the vocabularies can be used to annotate Open Government Data on different levels of detail to improve "data discoverability".

FAIR Principles and FAIRness Evaluation. As discussed in [8,15], semantic web technologies are the most in compliance to the implementation of FAIR principles. Since the appearance of FAIR principles in 2016, several frameworks have been proposed to evaluate the FAIRness degree of a given digital object. In most cases, the evaluation is performed by answering a set of questions – also called metrics or indicators in some works – or fill in a checklist[15] such as the "FAIR Data Maturity Model" [18] or "FAIRshake" [6]. Other works have proposed automated approaches for FAIRness evaluation [7,22] based on small web applications that test digital resources against some predefined metrics.

6   Conclusion

This paper has presented an ontological model to represent both metadata and data schema of observational meteorological datasets. We have shown how the proposed model improves the adherence to FAIR principles. This work is part of an approach that aims to make meteorological data FAIR in general, and that of

---

[14] https://semiceu.github.io/GeoDCAT-AP/releases/2.0.0/.
[15] https://fairassist.org/#!/.

Métééo-France in particular. The next step is to study the specifics of the data from the statistical models to enrich the current model if necessary. We plan as well to use the final model to generate the metadata and index it in data portals.

References

1. Arenas, H., Trojahn, C., Comparot, C., Aussenac-Gilles, N.: Un modèle pour l'intégration spatiale et temporelle de données géolocalisées. Revue Int. de Géomatique **28**(2), 243 (2018)
2. Atmezing, G., et al.: Transforming meteorological data into linked data. Semant. Web **4**(3), 285–290 (2013)
3. Benjelloun, O., Chen, S., Noy, N.: Google dataset search by the numbers. In: Pan, J.Z., et al. (eds.) ISWC 2020. LNCS, vol. 12507, pp. 667–682. Springer, Cham (2020). https://doi.org/10.1007/978-3-030-62466-8_41
4. van den Brink, L., et al.: Best practices for publishing, retrieving, and using spatial data on the web. Semant. Web **10**(1), 95–114 (2019)
5. Buttigieg, P.L., Morrison, N., Smith, B., et al.: The environment ontology: contextualising biological and biomedical entities. J. Biomed. Semant. **4**, 43 (2013)
6. Clarke, D., et al.: FAIRshake: toolkit to evaluate the FAIRness of research digital resources. Cell Syst. **9**(5), 417–421 (2019)
7. Devaraju, A., Huber, R., Mokrane, M., et al.: FAIRsFAIR data object assessment metrics, October 2020. https://doi.org/10.5281/zenodo.4081213
8. Jacobsen, A., et al.: FAIR principles: interpretations and implementation considerations. Data Intell. **2**(1–2), 10–29 (2020)
9. Guizzardi, G.: Ontology, ontologies and the "I" of FAIR. Data Int. **2**(1–2), 181–191 (2020)
10. Janowicz, K., Haller, A., Cox, S.J., Le Phuoc, D., Lefrançois, M.: SOSA: a lightweight ontology for sensors, observations, samples, and actuators. J. Web Semant. **56**, 1–10 (2019)
11. Karim, F., Vidal, M.-E., Auer, S.: Compact representations for efficient storage of semantic sensor data. J. Intell. Inf. Syst. **57**(2), 203–228 (2021). https://doi.org/10.1007/s10844-020-00628-3
12. Koesten, L., Simperl, E., Blount, T., Kacprzak, E., Tennison, J.: Everything you always wanted to know about a dataset: studies in data summarisation. Int. J. Hum. Comput. Stud. **135**, 102367 (2020)
13. Kremen, P., Necaský, M.: Improving discoverability of open government data with rich metadata descriptions using semantic government vocabulary. J. Web Semant. **55**, 1–20 (2019). https://doi.org/10.1016/j.websem.2018.12.009
14. Lefort, L., Bobruk, J., Haller, A., Taylor, K., Woolf, A.: A linked sensor data cube for a 100 year homogenised daily temperature dataset. In: Proceedings of the 5th International Workshop on Semantic Sensor Networks, vol. 904, pp. 1–16 (2012)
15. Mons, B., Neylon, C., Velterop, J., et al.: Cloudy, increasingly fair; revisiting the FAIR data guiding principles for the European open science cloud. Inf. Serv. Use **37**(1), 49–56 (2017)
16. Patroumpas, K., Skoutas, D., Mandilaras, G.M., Giannopoulos, G., Athanasiou, S.: Exposing points of interest as linked geospatial data. In: Proceedings of the 16th International Symposium on Spatial and Temporal Databases, pp. 21–30 (2019)
17. Raskin, R.: Development of ontologies for earth system science. In: Geoinformatics: Data to Knowledge. Geological Society of America (2006)

18. RDA Fair Data Maturity Model Working Group: FAIR Data Maturity Model. Specification and Guidelines, June 2020. https://doi.org/10.15497/rda00050
19. Roussey, C., Bernard, S., André, G., Boffety, D.: Weather data publication on the LOD using SOSA/SSN ontology. Semant. Web **11**(4), 581–591 (2020)
20. Suárez-Figueroa, M.C., Gómez-Pérez, A., Fernández-López, M.: The neon methodology framework: a scenario-based methodology for ontology development. Appl. Ontol. **10**(2), 107–145 (2015). https://doi.org/10.3233/AO-150145
21. Wilkinson, M., Dumontier, M., Aalbersberg, I.J., et al.: The FAIR guiding principles for scientific data management and stewardship. Sci. Data **3**(1), 1–9 (2016)
22. Wilkinson, M., Dumontier, M., Sansone, S.A., et al.: Evaluating FAIR maturity through a scalable, automated, community-governed framework. Sci. Data **6**(1), 1–12 (2019)

A Practical Approach of Actions for FAIRification Workflows

Natalia Queiroz de Oliveira$^{(\boxtimes)}$, Vânia Borges , Henrique F. Rodrigues ,
Maria Luiza Machado Campos , and Giseli Rabello Lopes

Federal University of Rio de Janeiro, Rio de Janeiro, Brazil
{natalia.oliveira,mluiza}@ppgi.ufrj.br, {vjborges30,
hfr}@ufrj.br, giseli@ic.ufrj.br

Abstract. Since their proposal in 2016, the FAIR principles have been largely discussed by different communities and initiatives involved in the development of infrastructures to enhance support for data findability, accessibility, interoperability, and reuse. One of the challenges in implementing these principles lies in defining a well-delimited process with organized and detailed actions. This paper presents a workflow of actions that is being adopted in the VODAN BR pilot for generating FAIR (meta)data for COVID-19 research. It provides the understanding of each step of the process, establishing their contribution. In this work, we also evaluate potential tools to (semi)automatize (meta)data treatment whenever possible. Although defined for a particular use case, it is expected that this workflow can be applied for other epidemical research and in other domains, benefiting the entire scientific community.

Keywords: FAIRification workflow · FAIR (meta)data · ETL4FAIR

1 Introduction

Since its publication in 2016 [1], the FAIR principles have been guiding best practices on publishing scientific research data and their associated metadata to make them Findable, Accessible, Interoperable, and Reusable by humans and especially by machines. The international GO FAIR[1] initiative aims at implementing the FAIR principles through Implementation Networks (INs)[2], which operate as FAIR drivers, collaboratively involving communities, institutions, and countries. As a sense of urgency due to the rapidly COVID-19 pandemic spread, the Data Together initiative involving the Committee on Data for Science and Technology (CODATA)[3], Research Data Alliance (RDA)[4], World Data System (WDS)[5], and GO FAIR was established, including a joint effort, the Virus

---

[1] https://www.go-fair.org/.
[2] https://www.go-fair.org/implementation-networks/.
[3] https://codata.org/.
[4] https://rd-alliance.org/.
[5] https://world-datasystem.org/.

© Springer Nature Switzerland AG 2022
E. Garoufallou et al. (Eds.): MTSR 2021, CCIS 1537, pp. 94–105, 2022.
https://doi.org/10.1007/978-3-030-98876-0_8

Outbreak Data Network IN (VODAN-IN[6]). The initial goal is to develop a federated data infrastructure to support the capture and use of data related to epidemic outbreaks, both for the current situation and future epidemics.

Initiatives such as VODAN-IN attempt to deliver FAIR data, in the original sense of the acronym, but also in the sense of "Federated, AI-Ready"[7] data, therefore readable and machine actionable. The first IN of GO FAIR Brazil [2], GO FAIR Brazil Health[8], is a thematic network responsible for developing strategies for the implementation of the FAIR principles in the health domain. VODAN BR[9] is the first pilot of GO FAIR Brazil Health, aiming to collect and implement a data management infrastructure for COVID-19 hospitalized patients' cases, according to the FAIR principles. The published scientific research data and their associated metadata should be as open as possible and as closed as necessary, to protect participant privacy and reduce the risk of data misuse.

The attempt of adopting the FAIR principles has led many scientific disciplines, which value the importance of research data stewardship [3], to consider: "Which knowledge is needed to make my data FAIR?" or "What solutions could be used?". The process of making data FAIR is called FAIRification and the VODAN BR pilot has been using the FAIRification workflow [4] for the transformation and publication of FAIR (meta)data. This general workflow describes a process that applies to any type of data and can be extended, adapted, and reused in different domains. However, in the VODAN BR pilot, we verified the need for specific actions to be defined in a more detailed FAIRification process, as a basis for implementation choices that needed to be carried out to support it.

Based on the recommendations of the original FAIRification process, this paper presents a practical approach for actions associated with the transformation of data and metadata, which are being tested in the VODAN BR pilot to ensure the publication of FAIR (meta)data on COVID-19. To systematize some of the established actions, we experimented and analyzed potential solutions to support FAIRification.

The remainder of this paper is organized as follows: Sect. 2 presents an overview of the FAIRification workflow; Sect. 3 describes the actions established for each step of the workflow for the VODAN BR pilot; Sect. 4 presents support solutions analyzed during the study of the steps, aiming at the systematization of the process; Sect. 5 presents a discussion about the relevant aspects treated in this work and concludes with final comments for future work.

2   FAIRification Workflow

The generic workflow proposed in [4] aims to facilitate the FAIRification process comprising three defined phases: pre-FAIRification, FAIRification and post-FAIRification. The phases are further divided into seven steps: 1) identify the FAIRification objective;

---

[6] https://go-fair.org/wp-content/uploads/2020/03/Data-Together-COVID-19-Statement-FINAL.pdf.

[7] https://www.go-fair.org/implementation-networks/overview/vodan/.

[8] https://www.go-fair-brasil.org/saude.

[9] https://portal.fiocruz.br/en/vodan-brazil.

2) analyze data; 3) analyze metadata; 4) define semantic model for data (4a) and metadata (4b); 5) make data (5a) and metadata (5b) linkable; 6) host FAIR data; and 7) assess FAIR data.

From these multiple steps, the authors describe how data and metadata can be processed, which knowledge is required, and which procedures and tools can be used to obtain FAIR (meta)data. The FAIRification workflow was defined based on discussions and experimentations from a series of workshops (Bring your own device - BYOD) [5] and is applicable to any kind of data and metadata.

FAIRification is in fact a complex process, requiring several areas of expertise and data stewardship knowledge. Our adaptation follows the steps of the generic FAIRification workflow and, according to our understanding, steps 6 and 7 have been renamed to 6) host FAIR data and metadata and 7) assess FAIR data and metadata. The reason is to emphasize the importance of storing, publishing, and evaluating both FAIR data and metadata.

In the literature review we found related studies and experiments discussing the FAIRification process. In [6], a retrospective form of FAIRification approach is presented, using two related metabolic datasets associated with journal articles to curate and re-annotate data and metadata using interoperability standards. However, the work does not follow the generic FAIRification workflow approach.

The work of [7] details the FAIRification process[10] proposed by GO FAIR, which aims to facilitate the conversion of spreadsheets into FAIR databases, with the help of the NMDataParser tool [8]. This tool supports data aggregation block levels, developed to speed up the mapping of the original file into the eNanoMapper[11] semantic model.

In [9], the authors present an architecture, following the GO FAIR FAIRification process, and addressing identified gaps in the process when dealing with datasets from the health domain. Another paper [10] proposes the De-novo FAIRification method, based on an Electronic Data Capture (EDC) system, where the steps of the generic FAIRification workflow are incorporated into the data collection process for a registration or research project.

We verified that these related works present approaches with guidelines for FAIRification proposed by the generic workflow and for the FAIRification process of GO FAIR. However, none of the works present the detail of associated actions for the FAIRification in a delimited and specific way, justifying implementation choices to support the transformation and publishing of FAIR (meta)data.

3   Set of Actions for FAIRification

3.1   VODAN BR Pilot

The VODAN BR pilot has been using the adapted FAIRification workflow, in a platform acting as a FAIR solution for COVID-19 clinical data. This platform is not only concerned with the process of data transformation and metadata generation, but also with support solutions to host and publish FAIR (meta)data. Figure 1 shows a diagram of the platform,

---

[10] https://www.go-fair.org/fair-principles/fairification-process/.
[11] https://search.data.enanomapper.net/.

with the (meta)data flow from the original source to the target FAIR Data Point, associated with the steps of the adapted FAIRification workflow.

For the pilot, the platform captures COVID-19 patients' datasets, in CSV format (1), applying the pre-FAIRification phase (a) steps. This dataset and the results of the performed analyses are used in steps 4a and 4b of the FAIRification phase (b), establishing the semantic models. Following the actions specified by steps 5a and 5b, the Extract, Transform and Load (ETL) process, designated in this work as ETL4FAIR (2), is responsible for transforming data and metadata to the RDF representation.

Hosting of (meta)data follows step 6, with the linkable (meta)data published in a triplestore (3). A triplestore Application Programming Interface (API) can be made available for access to (meta)data. The metadata schemas for the dataset and its distributions are provided in a FAIR Data Point (5). The distribution metadata schemas can provide an URL to download the RDF file published in the repository (4) and/or an SPARQL endpoint to the triplestore.

Finally, step 7, intended for the assessment of FAIR (meta)data, in the post-FAIRification phase (c), allows the (meta)data FAIRness evaluation and verifying the suitability of the established platform.

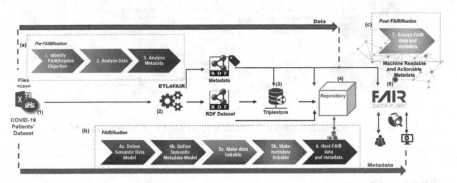

Fig. 1. VODAN BR pilot platform, with associated steps of the adapted FAIRification workflow.

3.2 Phases, Steps and Actions

In the platform, we transformed the recommendations from each step of the adapted FAIRification workflow into a practical set of actions enabling the implementation of the FAIR principles, improving the FAIRness evaluation and, consequently, the reuse of (meta)data. Representing a continuous evolution for the FAIRification workflow, this approach can be used as a reference framework. The set of delimited actions is presented below according to each phase of the FAIRification workflow.

Pre-FAIRification Phase
The actions established for step 1 (Identify FAIRification Objective) seek to propose a view of the expected results to be achieved through FAIRification. It requires access to data, followed by a preliminary analysis of data and associated metadata. Based on these,

it is possible to set goals for the treatment to be performed, identifying the objectives to obtain FAIR (meta)data and defining a set of competency questions that allows it to validate the FAIRification process.

For step 2 (Analyze Data), the actions aim to analyze the data representation according to their format and semantics, the FAIRness evaluation, to check the FAIR maturity level, for example, according to RDA [11], and, finally, to define a relevant subset of the analyzed data for FAIRification.

The actions for step 3 (Analyze Metadata) analyze the metadata associated with the relevant subset of data defined in the previous step and their FAIRness evaluation. It is important to identify the provenance metadata that should be collected for each step of the adapted FAIRification workflow. Figure 2 presents the set of associated actions, for each step of the Pre-FAIRification phase.

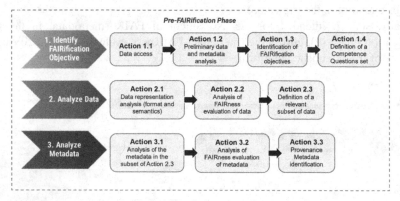

Fig. 2. Set of associated actions for each step of the Pre-FAIRification phase.

FAIRification Phase

Steps 4a (Define Semantic Data Model) and 4b (Define Semantic Metadata Model) are responsible for the specification of semantic models for data and metadata by identifying and evaluating whether any semantic models already exist and could be reused for them. For cases where no semantic model is available, a new one should be created for the representation of data or metadata.

In steps 5a (Make Data Linkable) and 5b (Make Metadata Linkable), the actions highlight the importance of choosing an RDF framework, as a major step to make (meta)data interoperable and machine-accessible with the association of the semantic models defined in step 4. In step 5b, it is worth mentioning the importance of representing and transforming provenance metadata into a machine-readable and actionable language.

For step 6 (Host FAIR Data and Metadata), the actions make data and metadata available for human and machine use, through various interfaces, such as the adoption of a triplestore for RDF triples and also a FAIR Data Point for metadata storage. The FAIR Data Point adoption facilitates transparent and gradually controlled access over the metadata through four different hierarchical layers: starting with metadata from the FAIR Data Point itself, followed by metadata from the catalog, from the datasets, and from the distributions [12]. Figure 3 presents the set of associated actions for each step of the FAIRification phase.

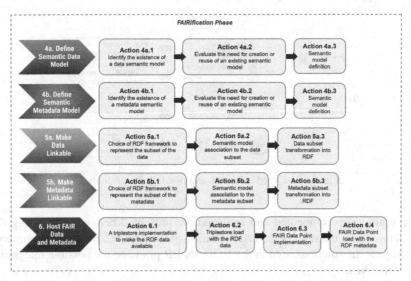

Fig. 3. Set of associated actions for each step for the FAIRification phase.

Post-FAIRification Phase

Finally, the actions of step 7 (Assess FAIR Data and Metadata) contemplate the assets of the Post-FAIRification process, verifying the objectives and answering the competence questions defined in step 1. Another relevant aspect refers to the assessment of the FAIRness evaluation of data and metadata after the completion of all actions in the adapted FAIRification workflow. Figure 4 shows the set of associated actions for each step in the Post-FAIRification phase.

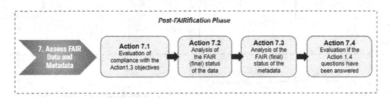

Fig. 4. Set of associated actions for each step for the Post-FAIRification phase.

4 Solutions to Support the FAIRification Phase

During this study, we investigated solutions capable of supporting and systematizing the FAIRification process, aiming to reduce human errors. The analysis of them helped to understand the recommendations associated with the steps (4a, 4b, 5a, 5b, and 6) of the FAIRification phase. The solutions contributed to validate the actions, promoting the automated support of some steps in the workflow.

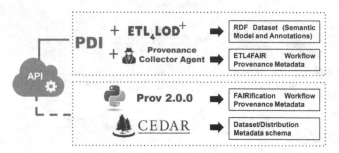

Fig. 5. Analyzed solutions and possible integrations.

The solutions experimented and analyzed are presented below, emphasizing their potential to support the steps of the FAIRification phase. Figure 5 presents a summary of the heterogeneous solutions used in the VODAN BR pilot and the possible integrations through their API.

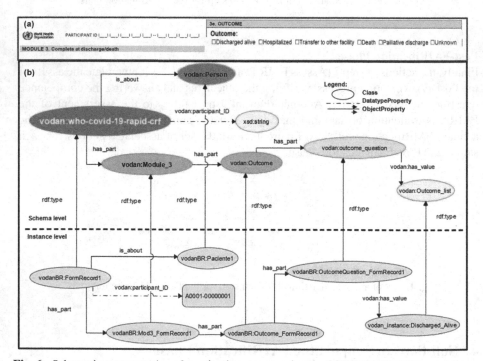

Fig. 6. Schematic representation of a patient's outcome using the COVIDCRFRAPID semantics.

For the experiments and analyses of the solutions, we considered the transformation of (meta)data referring to the questions presented in the WHO Case Record Form (CRF-WHO) [13], using the COVIDCRFRAPID semantic model. CRF-WHO was developed by experts to collect relevant anonymous information related to patients with COVID-19. It has three modules: the first one collects the patient's data on the admission day to the health center; the second one, the follow-up, collects daily information such as ICU admission and laboratory results; and the last one summarizes the medical care and collects the outcome information. Figure 6 highlights: (a) the CRF-WHO outcome questions present in "Module3: Complete at discharge/death"; and (b) the semantic model excerpt that handles these questions, associated with instances (example).

4.1 ETL4LOD+ Framework

The ETL4LOD+[12] framework provides data cleansing and triplification solutions in the context of Linked Open Data. The framework is an extension of the Pentaho Data Integration (PDI) tool, also known as Kettle, widely used in data ETL processes. This framework provides searching and selecting terms of ontologies and interlinks to other data.

According to our experiments and analyses ETL4LOD+ assists the FAIRification process contributing to the systematization of steps 5a and 5b. Figure 7 shows an example using ETL4LOD+ to transform a patient's outcome data as shown in Fig. 6(b). The framework components organize data obtained from the sources into triple (RDF format), according to the respective semantic model, connecting to vocabularies or ontologies (which can be imported).

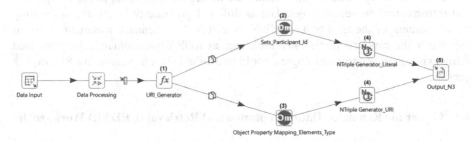

Fig. 7. Triplification extract for outcome questions using ETL4LOD+.

To create triplified data, ETL4LOD+ provides several components. In the process depicted in Fig. 8, to generate the required URI, we use the "Formula - fx" (1) component. Then, data are annotated with the CRF-OMS ontology. The "Data Property Mapping - Dm" (2) component deals with literal values related to the answers. We also use the "Object Property Mapping - Om" (3) component for other ontology-related items. After mapping, the "NTriple Generator - N3" (4) component serializes the data in N-triples format. Finally, the serialized data is unified in a file through the "File Output" (5) component.

---

[12] https://github.com/Grupo-GRECO/ETL4LODPlus.

In step 5b, the tool can collect metadata related to the data processing, using solutions such as the Provenance Collector Agent (PCA) (detailed in Sect. 4.2). The associated metadata are obtained in triple format. Furthermore, the tool gathers and organizes other metadata such as the FAIR Data Point dataset and distribution metadata schemas, both generated by the CEDAR tool (detailed in Sect. 4.3), employing the "REST Client" PDI step. In step 6, the tool contributes to the last part of the ETL process, enabling automatic loading of triplified data into a triplestore (currently Virtuoso[13]) or generating an output in files with RDF data serialized in N-Triples. These files can be published in different triplestores.

4.2 ETL4LinkedProv Approach

The purpose of the ETL4LinkedProv[14] approach is to manage the collection and publication of provenance metadata with distinct provenance granularity as Linked Data. The approach uses ETL workflows and employs the Provenance Collector Agent (PCA) component, capturing prospective and retrospective provenance metadata. To support the semantic publication of provenance, ETL4LinkedProv approach uses a set of existing ontologies as PROV-O[15], OPMW[16] and COGS[17] [14].

Through initial analyses and simulation working with the ETL4LOD+ framework, the PCA showed potential to collect provenance metadata associated with an ETL workflow. Our simulation was not as detailed as it was planned due to the version mismatch between ETL4LinkedProv and ETL4LOD+ framework used in the VODAN BR pilot. Therefore, an update of ETL4LinkedProv is currently under development to experiment with the FAIRification process.

As shown in Fig. 8, PCA could contribute to steps 5b and 6, capturing prospective and retrospective provenance metadata at different granularity levels and supporting the assessment of the quality and reliability of FAIR provenance metadata. Thus, at the step 6, the captured provenance metadata, as RDF triples semantically annotated using existing provenance ontologies, could be available in a triplestore for SPARQL[18] queries.

4.3 Center for Expanded Data Annotation and Retrieval (CEDAR) Workbench

CEDAR Workbench[19] provides a suite of Web-based tools that allows users to build and populate metadata templates, generate high-quality metadata, and share and manage these resources through an API based environment [15]. This solution can assist steps 5b and 6 with respect to metadata schemas established for the FAIR Data Point [12]. Through CEDAR, it is possible to create metadata schemas as templates. These templates

[13] https://virtuoso.openlinksw.com/.
[14] https://github.com/rogersmendonca/provenance_collector.
[15] http://www.w3.org/TR/2013/REC-prov-o-20130430/.
[16] https://www.opmw.org/model/OPMW/.
[17] http://vocab.deri.ie/cogs.
[18] https://www.w3.org/TR/rdf-sparql-query/.
[19] https://metadatacenter.org/.

Fig. 8. ETL4LinkedProv approach representing the provenance metadata in steps 5a, 5b and 6.

must be instantiated with the metadata for the dataset and distribution to be generated. The generated metadata schemas, in RDF N-Quad or JSON-LD, can be accessed directly or through the API and published in the FAIR Data Point. Our experiment used the "REST Client" PDI with CEDAR to collect the metadata schemas of the COVID-19 dataset and its RDF distribution that will be published on the FAIR Data Point.

4.4 Prov Python (Prov 2.0.0)

According to our metadata provenance analyses, it was observed the importance of also capturing the provenance of the macro process. For the study of this high-level provenance, the Prov.2.0.0[20] was selected. Prov Python is a library for the implementation of the W3C PROV Data Model[21], with support for serialization in PROV-O (RDF), PROV-XML and PROV-JSON [16].

The experiment and analysis identified a potential solution for steps 5b and 6. In step 5b, the solution provided provenance information, capturing provenance of each step, and it could even collect details of the actions themselves. Figure 9 illustrates a representation of provenance metadata of the step 5b obtained with Prov Python. In step 6, the provenance workflow can be published in a repository or accessed by the ETL4LOD+ tool and joined with the triples of the data file.

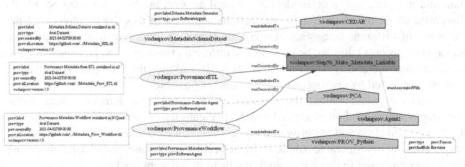

Fig. 9. An extract from the provenance metadata for step 5b with Prov Python. (Color figure online)

---

[20] https://openprovenance.org.
[21] https://www.w3.org/TR/prov-dm/.

Figure 9, due to space limitations, only shows an extract of the workflow provenance metadata based on PROV-O Model, generated by Prov Python. This extract highlights the solutions, represented as software agents (orange pentagons), used in step 5b, the activity (blue rectangle), for metadata generation, and the entities (yellow ovals).

5 Discussion and Conclusion

In the VODAN BR pilot, we verified the need for specific actions to be defined in a more detailed FAIRification process, justifying implementation choices of the domain. The rapid spread of the COVID-19 pandemic accelerated the discussion on technology support to publish FAIR (meta)data, although there are still many questions and open issues, especially in the context of metadata management and support. Complementary, it is important to consider a set of best practices from a great number of projects experimenting with the FAIRification process of (meta)data related not only to virus outbreaks, but to life sciences data in general.

This work analyzed the recommendations proposed by the generic workflow for FAIRification and it established an approach inspired by a group of well-delimited actions to support researchers and data stewardship in the generation of FAIR (meta)data. This proposal is being tested in the VODAN BR pilot to guarantee the publication of FAIR data and metadata about COVID-19 hospitalized patients' cases with the support provided by the ETL4FAIR framework. The framework promotes integration between heterogeneous tools to support the process, providing a (semi-)automated workflow for users and reducing error-prone situations.

The first lesson learned along this work is that FAIRification is a complex process in which a multidisciplinary team involvement is extremely important. FAIRification requires several areas of expertise as well as domain knowledge to support each step of the process. Establishing roles and responsibilities for the mapped actions is also important. The second lesson learned is that transforming data and metadata aligned with the FAIR principles is not an easy task. Identifying, choosing, and adapting appropriate data and metadata semantic models are critical actions, as there are many standards disseminated on the Web. Finally, the actions analyzed in this work emphasized the existence of different categories of metadata (for data, data transformation process, and applied process) that can be presented at different granularity levels, contributing to reuse and interoperability. These metadata should be captured throughout a FAIRification process, supported by appropriate tools, whenever possible.

From the exposed context, the importance of establishing actions to define and discuss implementation choices aligned with FAIRification is observed. This contributes to a better organization and maturity of a process that could be assisted by a group of heterogeneous but interoperable solutions. In the near future, we are considering improving the actions proposed in this paper, applying them in different domains.

Acknowledgements. This work has been partially supported with students grants from CAPES (Process numbers 223038.014313/2020–19 and 88887.613048/2021–00), CNPq (Process number 158474/2020–1) and INOVA UNIRIO PROPGPI/DIT Program.

References

1. Wilkinson, M., Dumontier, M., Aalbersberg, I., Appleton, G., Axton, M., Baak, A., et al.: The FAIR guiding principles for scientific data management and stewardship. Sci Data. **3**, 160018 (2016). https://doi.org/10.1038/sdata.2016.18.2
2. Sales, L., Henning, P., Veiga, V., Costa, M.M., Sayão, L.F., da Silva Santos, L.O.B., et al.: GO FAIR Brazil: a challenge for brazilian data science. Data Intell. **2**(1–2), 238–245 (2020). https://doi.org/10.1162/dint_a_00046
3. Jansen, P., van den Berg, L., van Overveld, P., Boiten, J.-W.: Research data stewardship for healthcare professionals. In: Kubben, P., Dumontier, M., Dekker, A. (eds.) Fundamentals of Clinical Data Science, pp. 37–53. Springer, Cham (2019). https://doi.org/10.1007/978-3-319-99713-1_4
4. Jacobsen, A., Kaliyaperumal, R., da Silva Santos, L.O.B., Mons, B., Schultes, E., Roos, M., et al.: A generic workflow for the data FAIRification process. Data Intell. **2**(1–2), 56–65 (2020). https://doi.org/10.1162/dint_a_00028
5. Hooft, R., Goble, C., Evelo, C., Roos, M., Sansone, S., Ehrhart, F., et al.: ELIXIR-EXCELERATE D5.3: bring your own data (BYOD). https://zenodo.org/record/3207809, Accessed 16 June 2021
6. Rocca-Serra, P., Sansone, S.A.: Experiment design driven FAIRification of omics data matrices, an exemplar. Sci. Data. **6**(1), 271 (2019). https://doi.org/10.1038/s41597-019-0286-0
7. Kochev, N., Jeliazkova, N., Paskaleva, V., Tancheva, G., Iliev, L., et al.: Your spreadsheets can Be FAIR: a tool and FAIRification workflow for the eNanoMapper database. Nanomaterials **10**(10), 1908 (2020). https://doi.org/10.3390/nano10101908
8. Jeliazkova, N., Doganis, P., Fadeel, B., Grafström, R., Hastings, J., Jeliazkov, V., et al.: The first eNanoMapper prototype: a substance database to support safe-by-design. In: 2014 IEEE International Conference on Bioinformatics and Biomedicine (BIBM), pp. 1–9 (2014)
9. Sinaci, A., Núñez-Benjumea, F., Gencturk, M., Jauer, M., Deserno, T., et al.: From raw data to FAIR data: the FAIRification workflow for health research. Methods Inf Med. **59**(S 01), e21–e32 (2020). https://doi.org/10.1055/s-0040-1713684
10. Groenen, K., Jacobsen, A., Kersloot, M., Vieira, B., van Enckevort, E., Kaliyaperumal, R., et al.: The de novo FAIRification process of a registry for vascular anomalies. Orphanet J. Rare Dis. **16**(1), 1–10 (2020). https://doi.org/10.1101/2020.12.12.20245951
11. FAIR Data Maturity Model Working Group (2020) FAIR Data Maturity Model. Specification and Guidelines. https://doi.org/10.15497/rda00050
12. FAIRDataTeam. FAIR Data Point Metadata Specification. https://github.com/FAIRDataTeam/FAIRDataPoint-Spec/blob/master/spec.md, Accessed 16 June 2021
13. World Health Organization. (2020). Global COVID-19 clinical platform: rapid core case report form (CRF). https://apps.who.int/iris/handle/10665/333229
14. Mendonça, R., Cruz, S., Machado, M.L.C.: ETL4LinkedProv: managing multigranular linked data provenance. J. Inf. Data Manag. **7**, 70–85 (2016)
15. Gonçalves, R.S., et al.: The CEDAR workbench: an ontology-assisted environment for authoring metadata that describe scientific experiments. In: d'Amato, C., et al. (eds.) ISWC 2017. LNCS, vol. 10588, pp. 103–110. Springer, Cham (2017). https://doi.org/10.1007/978-3-319-68204-4_10
16. Moreau, L., Freire, J., Futrelle, J., McGrath, R.E., Myers, J., Paulson, P.: The open provenance model: an overview. In: Freire, J., Koop, D., Moreau, L. (eds.) IPAW 2008. LNCS, vol. 5272, pp. 323–326. Springer, Heidelberg (2008). https://doi.org/10.1007/978-3-540-89965-5_31

On Metadata Quality in Sceiba, a Platform for Quality Control and Monitoring of Cuban Scientific Publications

Eduardo Arencibia[1]([✉]) [iD], Rafael Martinez[1] [iD], Yohannis Marti-Lahera[2] [iD], and Marc Goovaerts[3] [iD]

[1] CRAI at University of Pinar del Río "Hermanos Saíz Montes de Oca", 300 Martí, Pinar del Río 20100, Pinar del Rio, Cuba
{eduardo.arencibia,rafael.martinez}@upr.edu.cu

[2] Central Library of Havana University, San Lazaro and L, 10400 Havana, Cuba
yohannis@dict.uh.cu

[3] Hasselt University, Martelarenlaan 42, 3500 Hasselt, Belgium
marc.goovaerts@uhasselt.be

Abstract. It is introduced a platform for quality control and monitoring of Cuban scientific publications named Sceiba. To this end, it needs to collect scientific publications comprehensively at the national level. Metadata quality is crucial for Sceiba interoperability and development. This paper exposes how metadata quality is assured and enhanced in Sceiba. The metadata aggregation pipeline is worked out to collect, transform, store and expose metadata on Persons, Organizations, Sources, and Scientific Publications. Raw data transformation into Sceiba's internal metadata models includes cleaning, disambiguation, deduplication, entity linking, validation, standardization, and enrichment using a semi-automated approach aligned with the findability, accessibility, interoperability, and reusability principles. To meet the requirements of metadata quality in Sceiba, a three-layer structure for metadata is used, including 1) discovery metadata, which allows the discovery of relevant scientific publications by browsing or query, 2) contextual metadata, which allows a) rich information on persons, organizations and other aspects associated with publications, b) interoperation among common metadata formats used in Current Research Information Systems, journals systems or Institutional Repositories; 3) detailed metadata, which is specific to the domain of scientific publication evaluation. The example provided shows how the metadata quality is improved in the Identification System for Cuban Research Organizations, one of Sceiba´s component applications.

Keywords: Current research information system · Metadata quality · Scientific publication quality

1 Introduction

Metadata topics, usually understood as data about data, are receiving a lot of attention in the realm of Information Systems research. Metadata can be defined as "structured,

© Springer Nature Switzerland AG 2022
E. Garoufallou et al. (Eds.): MTSR 2021, CCIS 1537, pp. 106–113, 2022.
https://doi.org/10.1007/978-3-030-98876-0_9

encoded data that describe characteristics of information bearing entities to aid in the identification, discovery, assessment, and management of the described entities" [8].

The use of metadata models and standards are key to Current Research Information Systems (CRIS), especially in achieving higher levels of interoperability with internal and external systems. At the same time, it is needed to assure metadata quality in this endeavour. Wiley [11] and Allen [1] define metadata quality criteria: completeness, accuracy, consistency, standardization, machine-processable, and timely. Also, FAIR (Findability, Accessibility, Interoperability, and Reusability) principles [12] must be considered since they are crucial for metadata quality in CRIS.

Empirical studies [2–4] state that metadata quality should be enhanced by cleaning, disambiguation, deduplication, enrichment and validation of metadata. These processes are related to metadata curation that should be carried out after metadata collection. The peril of ignoring metadata standards and its quality in a CRIS have several implications in the performance of research organizations [9]. Even research assessment can be affected by metadata quality due to the need for all institutional research outputs to be collected and described in a standardized way in a single system [3] at regional, national and institutional levels.

A VLIR-UOS[1] Joint project entitled "Improving quality control and monitoring of scientific publications on national and institutional levels" was launched to address this and other issues related to scientific publications. The project is developed through the cooperation of six universities from Cuba, Belgium and Peru: University of Havana, University of Pinar del Rio, National Agrarian University of La Molina, University of San Ignacio Loyola, Hasselt University and Antwerp University. With the general objective of "Enhancing the quality of scientific publications as part of the research output", in Cuba the project faces the problem of setting up a system capable of gathering comprehensively the research output metadata at national level. The Sceiba[2] platform aims to be the answer to this problem. Metadata quality is a key element to consider by the platform.

This paper introduces the Sceiba platform, focusing on the processes by which metadata quality is assured. Section 2 gives a general description of the structure, the metadata model and the metadata aggregation pipeline of Sceiba. Section 3 exposes how metadata quality is ensured and enhanced in Sceiba, using as an example the application Identification System for Cuban Research Organizations. Final considerations, main challenges and further developments are presented in Sect. 4.

2   Sceiba Structure, Pipeline and Metadata Model

The Sceiba platform is powered by Invenio[3], an open-source framework to build repositories. It follows the next-generation repositories principles from COAR[4]. Sceiba emerges

---

[1] Vlaamse Interuniversitaire Raad - Universitaire Ontwikkelingssamenwerking' (VLIR-UOS), more information about the project can be found in https://www.vliruos.be/en/projects/project/22?pid=4202.

[2] Sceiba is a word that arises from the combination of the Latin "sci" and Ceiba, a leafy tree considered sacred by several Cuban traditions.

[3] https://invenio.readthedocs.io/en/latest/.

[4] https://www.coar-repositories.org/news-updates/what-we-do/next-generation-repositories/.

as an open system, acting as a framework to build applications for evaluating and monitoring scientific publications. The platform collects and manages scientific publication metadata and metadata linked to identification systems for organizations and persons. Metadata standardization relies on using controlled vocabularies and persistent identifiers where possible.

Sceiba is divided into the following components:

- Sceiba Core: manages scientific publications and main sources.
- Organizations Identification System: manages research organizations profiles.
- Persons Identification System: manages research related persons' profiles.
- System for Controlled vocabularies: manages vocabularies related to research data and metadata.
- Tools for monitoring and evaluation

Sceiba applies a three-layer Metadata Architecture, as proposed by Jeffery [6], to ensure the quality of metadata. Sceiba's feeding sources use heterogeneous metadata standards and schemas like DCMI (DC terms), Qualified DC, CERIF or ontologies. Others, like domestic developed systems, do not assume international and recognized standards. The metadata standards used in the discovery metadata (first layer) have the advantage of enabling the easy linkage of large numbers of scientific publications. However, they insufficiently describe the relationships between those publications, persons and organizations involved in publications as research outputs. "The syntax of flat metadata standards is often insufficiently formal, the semantics presented are rudimentary, they do not handle multilingualism well, they do not respect referential integrity, and they do not handle temporal relationships well" [13].

Because of the disadvantages of flat metadata standards, it was chosen to add contextual metadata (second layer) that offers structured relationships inspired by the CERIF [7] and GRID models[5], mainly based on persistent identifiers usage (see Fig. 1). The contextual metadata allows rich information on many publications' aspects, including the required metadata fields about the context, provenance, organizations, and persons. Also, detailed metadata from the domain (third layer) is needed, with the use of rich semantics in the contextual metadata layer and the ability to crosswalk from one semantic term to another. The domain metadata layer is oriented, but not limited to, the quality of scientific publications or criteria related to their visibility and impact.

The three-layer metadata architecture and metadata quality have a significant impact on the metadata aggregation process implementation. Therefore, an aggregation metadata pipeline (see Fig. 2) is in development with four general stages:

- Collection of data from primary and secondary sources with heterogeneous metadata models and standards.
- Transformation of raw data into Sceiba's internal metadata models. This stage includes processes like cleaning, disambiguation, deduplication, entity linking, validation, standardization, and enrichment using a semi-automated approach aligned to FAIR principles.

---

[5] https://grid.ac/format.

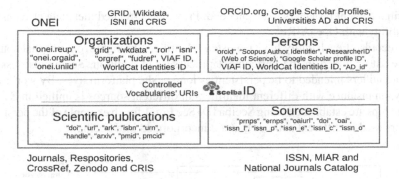

Fig. 1. Identifiers in Sceiba

- Storing the metadata considering the most probable scenarios for recovering by persistent identifiers, text fields, and relationships between publications and other entities included metadata model (see Fig. 3).
- Exposure of metadata using standards to guarantee interoperability and reusability.

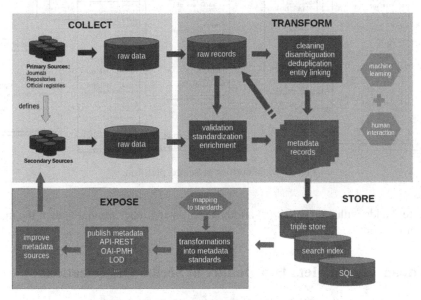

Fig. 2. Sceiba metadata aggregation pipeline

The Sceiba metadata model involves entities like Persons, Organizations, Sources, and Scientific Publications (see Fig. 3). Sceiba Core works as an aggregator at the national level and therefore requires, in each metadata record, additional source information from the original content providers to be encoded. Provenance-related metadata also ensures compatibility with OpenAIRE[6].

All records of each entity have persistent identifiers, brought from original sources if they exist or added in the enrichment processes. In addition, Sceiba also assigns unique identifiers intended to be persistent as long as the platform lives. By working in this way, an instance with different identifiers in different sources is unified in Sceiba. Relationships are established using Sceiba ID (See Fig. 1 for an example of the persistent identifiers used in different sources that are incorporated into Sceiba).

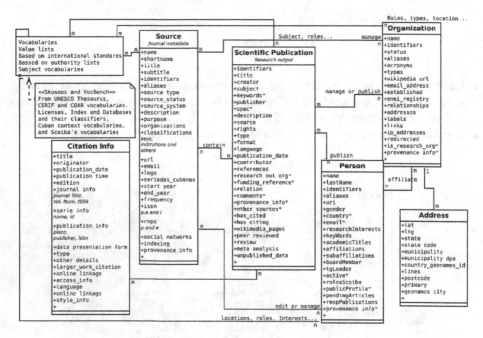

Fig. 3. Main entities in Sceiba platform.

Note: Fields with an asterisk (*) are those following other standards than the main used for each entity.

3   Enhancing the Metadata Quality in Sceiba Organizations

Sceiba includes the development of an Identification System for Cuban Organizations called Sceiba Organizations (see Sceiba components in Sect. 2). It aims to enable connections between organization records in various systems. This application component only includes officially registered research organizations as listed by the National Office of Statistics and Information of Cuba (ONEI, Spanish acronym). The data is collected

---

[6] https://guiasopenaire4.readthedocs.io/es/latest/use_of_oai_pmh.html#formato-de-los-met adatos.

automatically from public Microsoft Excel documents, and cross-walked into the Sceiba data model. There are several types of organizations in the official ONEI registry (primary and authority source), so those that are of interest in the context of scientific publications are selected by a cleaning process.

Constraints emerge from the use of the ONEI source: although the data is accessed openly, international metadata standards or internationally recognized persistent identifiers are not used. Besides, its structure is not intuitive and is dispersed over several files. Because of these and other issues, it was needed to add a contextual metadata layer. This second layer was developed using the GRID[7] data model, the Cuban organizations context and the wikidata registries. The project is considering the integration of ROR's data[8], as GRID is passing the torch to ROR. Both are a great inspiration for this Sceiba's component application.

Disambiguation has been more labour intensive for organizations' metadata of coming from ONEI and GRID, because of the initial absence of persistent identifiers in the ONEI metadata. The enrichment will come from other sources such as Wikidata, ROR and ISNI. Wikidata is gaining popularity in libraries as an open and collaborative global platform for sharing and exchanging metadata [10]. The Sceiba organizations identification system is able to collect data from every Cuban research organization, and with more options possible when a Wikidata ID is available. For instance, the Sceiba integration with Wikidata allows to expose statistical graphs with data from Wikipedia about the organizations and link them to more details in Scholia[9] website.

Enrich metadata through curation is a process that can't be fully automated, therefore, to put a human in the loop, user interface was designed to allow actions such as duplicate detection, disambiguation and enrichment of records. The user interface allows selecting a master organization, searches for possible duplicates and disambiguates and merges fields when applicable.

The algorithms for duplicate detection are based on external identifiers. In case of any match they are considered as the same organization. Sceiba keeps ONEI codes, already transformed into URIs and links unequivocally with common persistent identifiers used internationally for organizations identification (see Fig. 1), when possible. Offering this way a service to identify them more easily henceforth. Therefore, if reviewers find inconsistency they can correct them through the curation user interface.

The project is working on an approach which combines rule-based, machine learning and manual approach to connect heterogeneous author affiliations in scientific publications to known research organizations. Thus, possible duplicates of organizations will be detected applying the parametrized finite-state graphs method proposed by Gálvez & Moya-Anegón [5] and through human processing. Using this mixed disambiguation method would reduce the amount of manual reviewing to the most difficult cases, increase the precision of disambiguation in organization-scientific publication relationships and facilitate more accuracy in control and monitoring of scientific publication at institutional and national levels.

---

[7] https://grid.ac/.

[8] https://ror.org/.

[9] https://scholia.toolforge.org/.

Updating organization information and managing organizational hierarchies is a challenging issue during enrichment processes. Subordination relationships are represented between organizations already included in the ONEI registry. How to get a deeper and comprehensive representation of organizational hierarchy is a pending task in the project. Much more work needs to be done to clarify workflows and methods.

Also, the self-update procedure by organizations to improve the content curation of metadata is still in development. Sceiba proposes a follow-up report on the completeness of organizations' metadata. Organizations will be required to complete the mandatory and recommended metadata according to the Sceiba metadata model on a periodic basis.

The quality control process in the transformation of the data, seeks to ensure not only that it is complete but also that its syntactic and semantic value, and its overall compliance with the aforementioned quality metadata criteria and FAIR principles (e.g. the use of the OpenAire validator to confirm that it complies with OpenAire guidelines) is realized. Thanks to the use of international standards and this FAIRification workflow, quality metadata related to Cuban organizations will be reusable, looking for improving records in domestic systems and feeding other organization identification systems (e.g. ROR) to improve Cuban organizations visibility on those international databases.

4 Challenges and Further Work

The paper focuses on the challenges about metadata quality. Improving the quality of metadata will always be essential to achieve Sceiba's objectives. It means the further development of the Sceiba metadata model to include other entities such as projects and other research outputs besides scientific publications, going deeper on details in the domain of research systems, the improvement of curation and transformation operations of metadata and the exposure of metadata for reuse in the context of open data and open science. Crucial in this process will be cooperation with data creators on improving records and metadata.

The project is also developing policies and workflows for quality control and monitoring of scientific publications, taking in account the specificity of Spanish-speaking countries like Cuba and Peru, with a large scientific production that is not taken in account in the international citation databases. A vision has been worked out about policy and guidelines to ensure the sustainability and adoption of Sceiba principles for quality control and monitoring of Cuban scientific publications at the national and institutional levels. The policy and guidelines will be the subject of another paper.

The challenges for the project will be to address the development of the platform, with a strong focus on metadata standards and quality, while implementing the specific policies and workflows developed by Sceiba.

Acknowledgements. The work of the Sceiba project was supported by the 'Vlaamse Interuniversitaire Raad - Universitaire Ontwikkelingssamenwerking' (VLIR-UOS), Belgium. The authors are team members of the Sceiba project. They like to thank Sadia Van Cauwenbergh (Hasselt University) and Raf Guns (Antwerp University) for their suggestions on the article and to the Sceiba team of the University of Pinar del Rio for their contribution to the development of the Sceiba platform.

References

1. Allen, R.: Metadata for social science datasets. In: Rich Search and Discovery for Research Datasets: Building the Next Generation of Scholarly Infrastructure, pp. 40–52. Sage (2020)
2. Alma'aitah, W.Z.A., Talib, A.Z., Osman, M.A.: Opportunities and challenges in enhancing access to metadata of cultural heritage collections: a survey. Artif. Intell. Rev. **53**(5), 3621–3646 (2020)
3. Bryant, R., Clements, A., Castro, P., de Cantrell, J., Dortmund, A., Fransen, J., et. al.: Practices and patterns in research information management: findings from a global survey (2020). https://doi.org/10.25333/BGFG-D241
4. Fernandes, S., Pinto, M.J.: From the institutional repository to a CRIS system. Qual. Quant. Methods Libr. **7**(3), 481–487 (2019)
5. Galvez, C., Moya-Anegón, F.: The unification of institutional addresses applying parametrized finite-state graphs (P-FSG). Scientometrics **69**, 323–345 (2006). https://doi.org/10.1007/s11192-006-0156-3
6. Jeffery, K., Houssos, N., Jörg, B., Asserson, A.: Research Information management: the CERIF approach. Int. J. Metadata Semant. Ontol. **9**, 5–14 (2014). https://doi.org/10.1504/IJMSO.2014.059142
7. Jörg, B., Jeffery, K., Dvorak, J., Houssos, N., Asserson, A., Grootel, G., et.al.: CERIF 1.3 Full Data Model (FDM): introduction and specification (2012)
8. Ma, J.: Managing metadata for digital projects. Libr. Collect. Acquis. Tech. Serv. **30**, 17–23 (2006)
9. Schriml, L.M., Chuvochina, M., Davies, N., Eloe-Fadrosh, E.A., Finn, R.D., Hugenholtz, P., et al.: COVID-19 pandemic reveals the peril of ignoring metadata standards. Sci. Data **7**(1), 188 (2020). https://doi.org/10.1038/s41597-020-0524-5
10. Tharani, K.: Much more than a mere technology: a systematic review of Wikidata in libraries. J. Acad. Librarianship **47**(2), 102326 (2021). https://doi.org/10.1016/j.acalib.2021.102326
11. Wiley, C.: Metadata use in research data management. Bull. Assoc. Inf. Sci. Technol. **40**(6), 38–40 (2014). https://doi.org/10.1002/bult.2014.1720400612
12. Wilkinson, M.D., Dumontier, M., Aalbersberg, I.J., Appleton, G., Axton, M., Baak, A., et al.: The FAIR guiding principles for scientific data management and stewardship. Sci. Data **3**(1), 1–9 (2016). https://doi.org/10.1038/sdata.2016.18
13. Zuiderwijk, A., Jeffery, K., Janssen, M.: The potential of metadata for linked open data and its value for users and publishers. J. e-Democracy Open Gov. **4**(2), 222–244 (2012). https://doi.org/10.29379/jedem.v4i2.138

Managing and Compiling Data Dependencies for Semantic Applications Using Databus Client

Johannes Frey[✉][iD], Fabian Götz, Marvin Hofer[iD], and Sebastian Hellmann

Knowledge Integration and Linked Data Technologies (KILT/AKSW), DBpedia Association/InfAI, Leipzig University, Leipzig, Germany
{frey,gotz,hofer,hellmann}@informatik.uni-leipzig.de

Abstract. Realizing a data-driven application or workflow, that consumes bulk data files from the Web, poses a multitude of challenges ranging from sustainable dependency management supporting automatic updates, to dealing with compression, serialization format, and data model variety. In this work, we present an approach using the novel Databus Client, which is backed by the DBpedia Databus - a data asset release management platform inspired by paradigms and techniques successfully applied in software release management. The approach shifts effort from the publisher to the client while making data consumption and dependency management easier and more unified as a whole. The client leverages 4 layers (download, compression, format, and mapping) that tackle individual challenges and offers a fully automated way for extracting and compiling data assets from the DBpedia Databus, given one command and a flexible dependency configuration using SPARQL or Databus Collections. The current vertical-sliced implementation supports format conversion within as well as mapping between RDF triples, RDF quads, and CSV/TSV files. We developed an evaluation strategy for the format conversion and mapping functionality using so-called round trip tests.

Keywords: Data dependency management · Data compilation · Data release management platform · Metadata repository · ETL

1 Introduction

With the growing importance of transparent, reproducible, and FAIR publishing of research results as well as the rise of knowledge graphs for digital twins in corporate and research environments in general, there is on the one hand an urging demand for (research) data infrastructure and management platforms to publish and organize produced data assets. On the other hand, there is a huge potential for plenty of research that depends on workflows using a variety of internal and external data dependencies or that creates applications which consume large amounts of data and try to make use of it (e.g. AI-based algorithms).

One major reason for the introduction of the Semantic Web was to make data on the Web more useful for machines such that they could automatically

E. Garoufallou et al. (Eds.): MTSR 2021, CCIS 1537, pp. 114–125, 2022.
https://doi.org/10.1007/978-3-030-98876-0_10

discover, access, read, understand and process it. While the Linked Data design principles provide a guideline to browse Linked (Open) Data in an automated and decentralized fashion, when it comes to workflows and applications that are driven by a variety of high volume data (bulk file dumps) and that aim to be automatically deployed and updated, several challenges arise with respect to managing and consuming these data dependencies.

Although data repositories or management platforms with rich homogeneous metadata catalogs like the DBpedia Databus [2] allow to manage, find, and access files in a unified way, difficulties arise if consumers want to use data from different publishers and domains. These files can be released in various serialization formats (e.g. RDF can be represented in more than 8 formats) and compression variants, that typically can not be read all by an application or workflow without any prior conversion. Moreover, in many research disciplines, data is stored in relational databases and exported into tabular-structured data formats (e.g. CSV) or specialized community-specific formats. Loading this data alongside knowledge graphs requires a mapping process to be performed on the consumer side. However, this mapping effort is usually lost on the local infrastructure or in a GitHub repository, where it is hard to find and reuse. Even if data dependencies are not fed manually into the system, plenty of custom scripted solutions per application becoming quickly chaotic tend to grow, making applications harder to maintain and reproduce, finally leaving users and consumers with the resulting decreased reusability and unclear provenance.

While some of the conversion to popular formats is already performed by publishers, we argue that this should not be the burden of the data provider in general. Instead, we envision a software client, that - given a dependency configuration - can dump any data asset registered on a data management platform and converts it to a format supported by the target infrastructure. A client that can execute different applications and ingest *compiled* data automatically, such that data is only one command away, like in traditional software dependency, built, and package management systems. Analogous to compiling of software, we define *compiling* of data as the process that converts, transforms or translates data geared to the needs of a specific target application.

This work introduces a conceptual approach implemented within the DBpedia Databus Client, that facilitates a more natural consumption and compiling of data from the DBpedia Databus and brings us one step closer towards our vision. Our main contributions are: a modular and extendable client that leads in combination with the Databus platform to less format conversion publishing effort (w.r.t. storage and time), enables easier and systematic data consumption with less conversion issues, allows for realizing data-driven apps using automatically updating data dependencies with clear provenance, and improves findability and reuse of mapping definitions.

The remainder of the paper is structured as follows: in the next section we sketch the process of data release and dependency management leveraging the DBpedia Databus. In Sect. 3 we present the conceptual design of the client, followed by the description of its implementation in Sect. 4. We evaluate the approach in Sect. 5 and compare it to other related work in Sect. 6. We conclude with a discussion and future work.

2   DBpedia Databus Release Management Platform

Inspired by paradigms and techniques successfully applied in (Java) software release management and deployment, we started to think how we could transfer these to data engineering and management. Additionally driven by the need for a flexible, heavily automatable dataset management and publishing platform for a new and more agile DBpedia release cycle [5], we initiated the development of the DBpedia Databus Platform[1] over 3 years ago.

The Databus [2] uses the Apache Maven concept hierarchy *group, artifact, version* and ports it to a Linked Data based platform, in order to manage data pipelines and enable automated publishing and consumption of data. *Artifacts* form an abstract identity of a dataset with a stable dataset ID and can be used as entry point to discover all *versions*. A *version* usually contains the same set of *files* for each release. These concepts are embedded in the personal IRI (Internationalized Resource Identifier) space that is issued by the Databus for every user. The full IRI `https://databus.dbpedia.org/<publisher>/` `<group>/<artifact>/<version>/<file>` can be used as a stable ID for a particular dataset *file* in a particular *version*. *Groups* provide a coarse modularization or bundling of datasets forming (useful) units to improve overview and consumption. The overall structure is very flexible as software libraries, but once defined should be as fixed as software to prevent applications from breaking, if they update on a new version.

Additionally, every *file* can be described by key-value records (so-called *content-variants*) which allow another level of granularity as well as addressing and querying for particular files (e.g. split labels of entities based on their language into different files).

Databus metadata is represented with an extension of the DataID core vocabulary for *group, artifact, version,* and *file* entities that allows for flexible, fine-grained, as well as unified metadata access using SPARQL. Based on `dcat:downloadURL` links in this metadata, Databus file IDs form a stable (but redirectable) abstraction layer independent of file hosting (similar to w3id.org). Provenance can be added by specifying Databus IDs of the input data on *version* or *file* level.

Moreover, users can create automatically updating or stable catalogs of data assets via so-called Databus collections[2], which encode the information need or asset selection via SPARQL queries. Collections can be created and refined via a faceted browsing UI on the Databus Website similar to a shopping cart and used as easy way to specify data input dependencies while recording provenance.

An example collection which consists of 2 *artifacts* from 2 different publishers (a crawl of the German Energy Market Core Register (MaStR) filtered to files

---

[1] https://databus.dbpedia.org.

[2] https://www.dbpedia.org/blog/databus-collections-feature/.

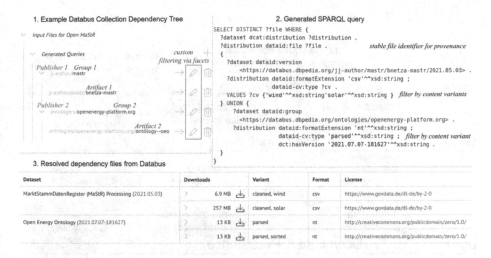

Fig. 1. Data dependency definition using Databus Collections

with wind and solar units, as well as parsed files of the Open Energy Ontology from DBpedia Archivo [4]) is shown as dependency tree in Fig. 1. Using the dedicated collection identifier, it is possible to retrieve the generated SPARQL query which encodes the dependency tree and optional filters based on the facet selection. When issuing this query against the Databus SPARQL endpoint, a list of Databus files will be returned, which is also displayed in the Collection view on the Databus website.

3 Databus Client Concept

The Databus Client is designed in a modular way to achieve high reusability, which means that the components and functionalities such as the downloading component, and compression converter can be used separately and interchangeably. It leverages 4 functionality layers depicted in Fig. 2.

The fundamental **Download-Layer** is supposed to download exact copies of data assets via the DBpedia Databus in a flexible way. It can be understood as a simple extraction phase of the ETL (Extract-Transform-Load) process. Moreover, it is supposed to persist the input data provenance by recording stable file identifiers and additional metadata. The data assets to be downloaded can be selected in a fine-grained way via an interoperable data dependency specification. and optional compiling configurations tailored to the needs of a consuming app or workflow.

If any conversion process is required, the **Compression-Layer** takes action. It sniffs for the input compression format and decompresses the file. If the input file format differs from the output file format, the decompressed file is passed to the Format-Layer. The Compression-Layer takes the decompressed file, which

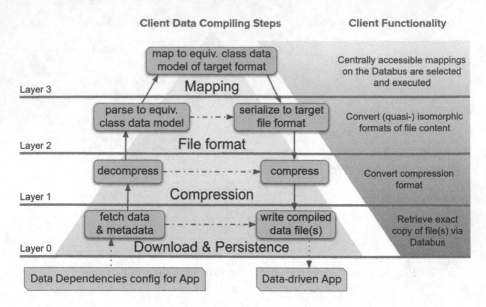

Fig. 2. Layers of the databus client data compiling process.

may be format converted by the Format-Layer or Mapping-Layer, and compresses it to the requested output compression format. This compressed file is passed back to the Download-Layer, after the conversion process has finished.

Within the data format conversion process, the Databus Client utilizes the Format-layer and the Mapping-Layer where required. The **Format-Layer** receives the uncompressed file and parses it to a unified internal data structure of the corresponding (format) equivalence class. Such an equivalence class contains all serialization formats that can be used interchangeably while representing the same amount of information, given a defined common data model for the class (e.g. a set of triples for RDF triple formats, a table of Strings for tabular-structured data formats). Subsequently, the Format-Layer serializes the internal data structure to the desired output file format. It passes the serialized data back to the Compression-Layer.

Whenever the input file format and the requested output file format are in different equivalence classes (e.g. Turtle/RDF triples and TSV/tabular-structured data), the **Mapping-Layer** is additionally used. However, it could also be used to manipulate the data of the same equivalence class (e.g. ontology mapping). With the aid of mapping configurations, the Mapping-Layer transforms the data represented using the internal data structure of the input equivalence class, to data of the internal data structure of the equivalence class of the target file format. After that process has finished, the data is passed back to the Format layer.

The Compression-Layer, File-Format-Layer, and Mapping-Layer represent the transformation-phase of the ETL process.

4   Implementation

We implemented a vertical slice of the four conceptional layers in the command-line tool *Databus Client*[3]. It is written in Scala and using Apache Maven. Subsequently, it is executable within a Java Virtual Machine (JVM) or a Docker[4] container, allowing it to be run on almost any machine and to be interoperable to a broad amount of applications. In addition, we provide a Maven package with interfaces to invoke the functions of the Databus Client from other JVM-based applications.

Depending on the data compilation command parameters, the client applies different methods at each layer, either passing already processed data (as file, stream, or object) to the next higher layer or returning it to the one beneath.

Layer 0 (Download & Persistence) manages the data handling between the Databus, the Compression Layer, and the local file system. Its implementation consists of two modules: 1) the Download-Module that queries file metadata using the Databus, retrieves the files by accessing their download URLs, and finally verifies the download process; 2) the Persistence-Module which generates local provenance metadata and stores the target files in the correct file structure.

The Databus Client can download any file registered on the Databus as exact copy and verifies it according to its corresponding Databus metadata (using the SHA256 checksum). The files to be downloaded are specified via a SPARQL query or a Databus collection.

The Persistence-Module receives the target data as stream or file from either the Compression-Layer or directly from the Download-Module and stores the data on the local file system reproducing a directory structure similar to the Databus hierarchy /<account>/<group>/<artifact>/<version> /<fileName>. In addition, it creates a summary file tracking provenance of the Databus file identifiers and processing information, like applied mappings.

The **Compression-Layer** is implemented using Apache Commons Compress[5]. This library provides functions to detect and decompress several file compression formats, like *gzip, bzip2, snappy-framed, xz, deflate, lzma*, and *zstd*. The Compression-Module can either read/write from the local file system or a byte stream, getting data from the Download-Module and passing data to the Persistence-Module.

The **Format-Layer** that handles the format conversion within an equivalence class, currently supports three equivalence classes: 1) quad-based RDF formats, 2) triple-based RDF formats, and 3) Tabular structure formats.

For RDF formats, the implementation uses Apache Jena[6] either leveraging Jena's StreamRDF in combination with Apache SPARK[7] or the RDF Model/Dataset API, supporting various formats (see Table 1). Apache Spark

---

[3] https://github.com/dbpedia/databus-client.
[4] https://www.docker.com/.
[5] https://commons.apache.org/proper/commons-compress/.
[6] https://jena.apache.org/.
[7] https://spark.apache.org/.

utilizes Resilient Distributed Datasets (RDD) [10], which provide several relational algebra operations to transform and combine this kind of data structure in a salable way. A significant benefit of an RDD is that it can be partitioned and distributed over several computing nodes, including swapping (spill) partitions to disk to avoid out-of-memory exceptions that larger datasets could introduce. The inner type of an RDD can be any serializable JVM Object. In our case, the internal data structure of triple-based RDF formats is an instance of RDD[Triple], and the internal data structure of quad-based RDF formats is an instance of RDD[Quad].

For tabular-structured data, the conversion methods of Apache Spark's IO library are utilized, allowing to handle configurable CSV formats (specified by delimiter and escape characters). The internal representation of Tabular structured data is an instance of RDD[Row]. The Format-Layer is either passing the internal representation of an equivalence class to the Mapping-Layer, or a stream of the target format back to the Compression-Layer.

Mapping-Layer. To convert formats between different equivalence classes, the Format-Layer passes the internal data structure of an equivalence class to the Mapping-layer. With the aid of additional mapping information, the client can transform data between different equivalence classes. At the time of writing, the client supports conversion from tabular-structured data to RDF triples, or from RDF to tabular-structured data, or between RDF quads and triples.

Tabular to RDF. For mapping tabular-structured data to RDF triples, the client utilizes the Tarql[8] mappings language. Currently, the Tarql library only supports the mapping of tabular data to RDF triple formats. RDF quad formats can be supported in the future by using the RDF Mapping Language (RML)[9]. There are three strategies to apply a mapping from a table to RDF using the Databus Client: 1) a generic transformation from CSV to RDF, that generates a resource URI for each row and creates a triple for each column and its corresponding value (the column header is appended to a generic base URI to specify the property). The value is represented either as an IRI if it can be parsed as valid IRI or a literal value otherwise. 2) Databus managed - The Databus can be requested to find matching mapping files for the given Databus file identifiers. Users can associate mapping files (e.g., a published Tarql file) using metadata in a flexible way with Databus groups, versions, or file identifiers, allowing anyone to reuse and apply these with the client automatically. 3) manual mapping - The user can specify a mappings file for the Databus file selection (query, collection) with a command-line parameter.

RDF to Tabular. The client implements a generic approach for mapping RDF into a wide table. Each RDF triple <subject, predicate, object> is mapped

---

[8] https://tarql.github.io/.
[9] https://rml.io/.

to one or more table cells, whereas each row contains information about one subject/entity. The first column of the table contains the subject's IRI. Then, for each occurring property of the source dataset, either one or two columns are created depending on the stored value. In case of an IRI, one column is created. Otherwise, two columns are created, one with the lexical form and a separate one to encode the original value's datatype or language tag information.

In addition to the resulting tabular file, the process generates a Tarql file that contains information for mapping the resulting table back to the original RDF structure.

RDF to RDF. The Databus Client can also convert between RDF triples and RDF quads formats. The mapping of RDF triples to RDF quads assigns a configurable graph name to the triples. The graph name setting can be given via a command-line option.

RDF quads to RDF triples are converted by splitting the input (quads) file into multiple triple files, one for each named graph.

Table 1. Equivalence class implementation overview: Reported are the equivalence classes with their supported serialization formats and mapping strategies between each other (inter equivalence class mapping)

Equivalence class		Supported mapping strategy		
Name	Serial. formats	to Quads	to Triples	to Tabular
RDF Quad	trig, trix, nquads, json-ld	–	File split	Wide table
RDF Triple	turtle, ntriples, rdf-xml	Conf. graph	–	Wide table
Tabular	tsv, csv	N/A	Tarql	–

5 Evaluation

We created a test suite and performed so-called round trip tests to verify the correctness of the file compiling for the reading and writing functionalities for every supported input/output format combination. We distinguish between round trip format conversion tests (Layer 2) and round trip mapping tests (Layer 3). Layer 0 and 1 are tested with regular unit tests.

A **round trip format conversion test** runs as follows. We take a file i and read it into the internal data structure of its equivalence class. Subsequently, that internal data structure is serialized to a file o, which is of the same format as file i. If the information in both files is equal, the round trip test succeeds. Within a **round trip mapping test**, we take a file i and convert it to file c of the format of another equivalence class before we convert c back to file o of the same format as i. Therefore, i first has to be read into the internal data structure of the equivalence class of i (see (1) in Fig. 3). Then this data is mapped to the internal data structure of the equivalence class of c (2) before it is written out to c (3). Next, c is read into the internal data structure of its equivalence class (4). That resulting data is mapped back to the internal data structure of the equivalence class i (5). In the last step (6), this internal data structure data is written out to o. If the information of the input file i is equal to the information of output file o, the round trip test succeeds.

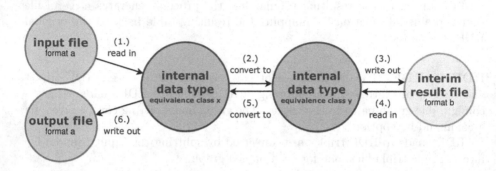

Fig. 3. Walk-through of a round trip mapping test

A round trip test is considered successful if we detect equality in the amount of information between the input and output file. There may be differences in syntax especially if no canonical version of the format is available. As a consequence, the files are parsed (ideally using a different software library) into some kind of internal/abstract data model again to be compared. In case of a non-bijective mapping between two equivalence classes (mapping is not reversible without information loss), these predictable losses have to be taken into account when evaluating the amount of information. We call this "quasi"-equal.

The layer design and round trip test approach reduce the quadratic amount of transformation/compiling combinations to be probed, and therefore help to realize a reliable and sustainable way to extend the client with other formats while maintaining/ensuring quality and correctness with a manageable effort. The number of tests performed on format layer is $T_f = n_{e_1} + n_{e_2} + ... + n_{e_{x-1}} + n_{e_x}$, whereas n_{e_i} is the number of formats in equivalence class e_i and x the total number of classes. Currently, the Databus Client has three implemented equivalence classes (see Table 1), which add up to $4 + 3 + 2 = 9$ format round trip tests that need to be performed.

To test the correctness of the mapping layer, we pick one format for each class and do a round trip mapping test for every (ordered) pair of equivalence classes. If we have two classes e_1 and e_2 we perform one mapping round trip test starting with a format from e_1 and a second test starting with a format from e_2. Picking one format is sufficient since we already tested the format conversion process within the equivalence classes for Layer 2. In summary, for x equivalence classes, the number of round trip mapping tests can be calculated by $T_m = \frac{x!}{(x-2)!}$. However, this formula assumes that there is exactly one mapping implementation in every direction from/to every class. There could be cases where two equivalence classes can not be mapped or only in one direction (because the underlying data models differ too much), or multiple implementations for one mapping transition exist (that would need to be tested additionally).

When having 3 equivalence classes using exactly one mapping implementation between every class $\frac{3!}{(3-2)!} = 3! = 6$ round trip mapping tests need to performed. Since there is currently no mapping from tabular to RDF quads, 5 tests were performed.

Round trip tests allow to automate the conversion test, but they also have a limitation in spotting two interfering, systematic implementation errors, (e.g. one in the parser and one in the serializer), that counteract themselves. However, we consider them as sufficient in the scope of this work, especially when using frameworks that are broadly used and already tested in itself.

6 Related Work

The following section reports related work that also aims to improve the consumption of Linked Data into applications.

With the aid of **HTTP content negotiation**, HTTP clients can request files in formats that suite best for their demands, sending a list of weighted MIME types in the Accept header. Content negotiation is considered best practice for consuming Linked Data [8]. By using an Accept-Encoding header, the compression can be additionally specified. However, all conversion and implementation overhead as well as the complexity is on the server/publisher side, while leaving the consumer with the resulting technical heterogeneity, failures, and varying availability for common formats and compressions.

HDT [1] addresses a similar problem as the Databus Client, making RDF accessible better for consumers while being more efficient for the party hosting the data. It decomposes the original data into three components: Header, Dictionary, and Triples. With the help of the dictionary it realizes a compression, and makes additional compression of RDF files obsolete. An optional index can speed up simple lookup queries on the file. Unfortunately, there is no widespread native reading support for semantic applications and tools (SPARQL stores, reasoners, etc.). However, HDT parsing support could be integrated into the Databus Client, to allow transparent consumption of HDT files for applications.

OntoMaven [7] uses Maven repositories to release ontologies and optionally its dependencies (i.e. imported ontologies). As a consequence, transitive imports can be resolved and downloaded locally (using the Maven client) and then rewritten to use the locally mirrored (transitive) imports via a Maven plugin.

Although we were not able to find any announced public repository, the ontology organization structure is very similar to the one that is realized on the Databus using DBpedia Archivo [4] and which can be leveraged in combination with the Databus Client to manage and consume over 1300 ontologies as dependencies alongside instance data.

While plenty of ETL frameworks exist, we mention **UnifiedViews** [6] as an open-source ETL framework that supports RDF and ontologies. A data processing pipeline in UnifiedViews, consists of one or more data processing units (DPUs) and data flows between them. The DPUs offer basic functions that obtain data from external sources (e.g. CSV, XLS, RDF), convert data between various formats (e.g., CSV files to RDF, relational tables to RDF), perform data transformations (such as executing SPARQL Construct queries, XSLT, linking/fusing RDF data), and load the data to various (RDF) databases and file sinks.

While UnifiedViews has more powerful options in the individual steps, it has a weakness when it comes to provenance and repeatability (e.g. when the sources have changed). In contrast, the Databus Client harnesses the clear versioning and provenance model of the DBpedia Databus.

DataHub.io[10] is a data management platform, based on CKAN . A command line tool is provided that can download a single dataset alongside its datapackage JSON metadata file. A rudimentary versioning strategy allows to download the latest or an older version of a dataset. Furthermore, DataHub converts tabular data into normalized CSV and JSON files. However, the rich DataID metadata Model of the Databus in combination with collections or SPARQL queries provide a much more flexible and fine-grained download configuration method for the Databus Client.

7   Discussion and Future Work

In this work, we presented a concept and vertical-focused implementation of an interoperable and modular Databus Client, that shifts effort from the servers to the client while making data consumption and dependency management easier and more unified as a whole. The Databus Client offers a fully automated way for extracting and compiling data assets from the DBpedia Databus. Data that is only available in one RDF or tabular format can be used for many different semantic applications that support only a subset of these formats. Publishers can save storage and processing power of servers as well as human effort for publishing data in multiple formats, and instead invest resources in organizing the release and registering it with appropriate metadata.

The client's modular layer structure allows to implement, test, and use different functionalities individually and extend the client easily in the future. We can imagine to add one or multiple integration layers which normalize and merge schema and entity identifiers [3]. Moreover, we can support more formats (e.g. HDT, Manchester Syntax) and more mapping frameworks (like RML) by expanding existing layers.

While the Databus Client allows a flexible and via DataID metadata fine-grained access to files, this granularity is still dependent on the file partitioning strategy of the dump publisher. Although a monthly DBpedia release is separated into over 3,000 files, if information for only a small set of entities is

---

[10] https://datahub.io.

consumed by an application, a SPARQL or Linked Data fragments [9] endpoint is more convenient. We plan to extend the current file-based focus of the client to an even more flexible extraction phase that can use e.g. SPARQL to filter the compiled data.

At the current stage, the Databus Client is considered passive in the loading phase of the ETL process. The interface to consume data is on file/folder level, which is simple and powerful, but for better flexibility and complex workflows we see potential in advancing the client to orchestrate the loading phase as well.

Acknowledgments. This work was partially supported by grants from the Federal Ministry for Economic Affairs and Energy of Germany (BMWi) to the projects LOD-GEOSS (03EI1005E) and PLASS (01MD19003D).

References

1. Fernández, J.D., Martínez-Prieto, M.A., Gutiérrez, C., Polleres, A., Arias, M.: Binary RDF representation for publication and exchange (HDT). J. Web Semant. **19**, 22–41 (2013). https://doi.org/10.1016/j.websem.2013.01.002
2. Frey, J., Hellmann, S.: Fair linked data - towards a linked data backbone for users and machines. In: WWW Companion (2021). https://doi.org/10.1145/3442442.3451364
3. Frey, J., Hofer, M., Obraczka, D., Lehmann, J., Hellmann, S.: DBpedia FlexiFusion the best of wikipedia > wikidata > your data. In: Ghidini, C., et al. (eds.) ISWC 2019. LNCS, vol. 11779, pp. 96–112. Springer, Cham (2019). https://doi.org/10.1007/978-3-030-30796-7_7
4. Frey, J., Streitmatter, D., Götz, F., Hellmann, S., Arndt, N.: DBpedia archivo: a web-scale interface for ontology archiving under consumer-oriented aspects. In: Blomqvist, E., et al. (eds.) SEMANTICS 2020. LNCS, vol. 12378, pp. 19–35. Springer, Cham (2020). https://doi.org/10.1007/978-3-030-59833-4_2
5. Hofer, M., Hellmann, S., Dojchinovski, M., Frey, J.: The new dbpedia release cycle: increasing agility and efficiency in knowledge extraction workflows. In: Semantic Systems (2020). https://doi.org/10.1007/978-3-030-59833-4_1
6. Knap, T., et al.: Unifiedviews: an ETL tool for RDF data management. Semant. Web **9**(5), 661–676 (2018). https://doi.org/10.3233/SW-180291
7. Paschke, A., Schäfermeier, R.: OntoMaven - maven-based ontology development and management of distributed ontology repositories. In: Nalepa, G.J., Baumeister, J. (eds.) Synergies Between Knowledge Engineering and Software Engineering. AISC, vol. 626, pp. 251–273. Springer, Cham (2018). https://doi.org/10.1007/978-3-319-64161-4_12
8. Sauermann, L., Cyganiak, R.: Cool uris for the semantic web. W3c interest group note, W3C (2008). https://www.w3.org/TR/cooluris/
9. Verborgh, R., Sande, M.V., Colpaert, P., Coppens, S., Mannens, E., de Walle, R.V.: Web-scale querying through linked data fragments. In: Proceedings of the 7th Workshop on Linked Data on the Web, vol. 1184. CEUR (2014). http://ceur-ws.org/Vol-1184/ldow2014_paper_04.pdf
10. Zaharia, M., et al.: Resilient distributed datasets: a fault-tolerant abstraction for in-memory cluster computing. In: USENIX Symposium on Networked Systems Design and Implementation (NSDI 2012), pp. 15–28. USENIX Association (2012). https://www.usenix.org/conference/nsdi12/technical-sessions/presentation/zaharia

KG-Visual: A Tool for Visualizing RDF Knowledge Graphs

Devanshika Ghosh$^{(\boxtimes)}$ and Enayat Rajabi

Cape Breton University, Sydney, NS, Canada
{cbu19cgx,enayat_rajabi}@cbu.ca

Abstract. RDF Knowledge graphs are semantic networks to infer information from data based on RDF triples using SPARQL queries. Querying RDF Knowledge graphs using visualization allows different views of the graph and provides more insights. A new visualization tool, KG-Visual is developed in this paper using Python dashboard, JavaScript and RDF libraries. This tool tackles the limitations of existing tools by providing a customizable and reliable visualization for RDF knowledge graphs. In addition to the essential functionalities such as search, drag and drop nodes, zoom-in and zoom-out over a knowledge graph, the tool holds the capability to run SPARQL queries and visualize the results on the knowledge graph, which makes this open-source tool a potential candidate amongst most RDF visualization tools.

Keywords: Visualizaion · Knowledge graph · RDF · SPARQL

1 Introduction

Diverse web content has been growing at leaps and bounds in the past decade. Today, the Web has access to loads of information that can be collected, processed and analyzed to discover key insights, and obtain knowledge. With the inception of the semantic Web, W3C initiated a common platform that acted as a framework for data to be used and shared by multiple applications. Some common standards have been created to ensure that data is managed and represented interoperably and uniformly. To understand and make use of the data available on the Web, knowledge graphs are used. Knowledge graphs have recently become a popular, efficient, and compelling way to organize structured information on the Web [1]. They are being implemented in various domains such as bioscience for research-orientated organizations, finance to improve retail banking and customer protection, retail and e-commerce to make better profitable decisions [2]. They have become pivotal in extracting knowledge and inferring what can be learnt from the data. Several machine learning models are also using knowledge graphs as input to explore patterns, and relationships [3].

However, as the volume of data has been increasing, knowledge graphs are becoming complex. Each entity can be linked to multiple other entities through various relationships. This focuses the attention of this study on a very key

E. Garoufallou et al. (Eds.): MTSR 2021, CCIS 1537, pp. 126–136, 2022.
https://doi.org/10.1007/978-3-030-98876-0_11

concept which is visualizing the knowledge graph. It is imperative that we have access to the tools that help knowledge graph consumers visualize the knowledge graphs from different viewpoints. Visualizing data in the form of graphs makes data more tangible, intuitive and valuable. There are several tools and options available for exploring knowledge graphs visually. However, most of these tools are either paid or have limitations that prevent extensive exploration of RDF knowledge graphs.

The objective of this report is to develop a visualization tool that accepts knowledge graphs in RDF format. RDF serves as a uniform structure to express any information using simple statements. This uniform structure represents information by connecting data piece by piece and allows for any resource to be identified and linked [4]. The presented tool in this report can filter and query results from an RDF knowledge graph using SPARQL. It also has a search box where the user can highlight objects and their relationships in the knowledge graph and visually understand how they are linked. The presented tool in this paper is open source, can be customized and hence be reused to discover different semantic relationships in a knowledge graph that may be difficult or impossible to identify. The source code of the tool is publicly available on GitHub[1].

The report comprises of the following sections. Section 2 discusses the existing tools available for visualizing knowledge graphs and their limitations. Section 3 outlines the methodology of the visualization and explains the technology used for the presented tool. Section 4 presents a case study where we can see the potential application of the tool for visualizing any knowledge graph, followed by a conclusion in Sect. 5.

2   Background

Visual data exploration is beneficial when little is known about the source data, and the analysis goals are vague [5]. There are various tools available to visualize using graph visualization techniques. Some of these tools are development tools, which give developers a chance to code and program a graph according to customization. Other tools can be used to reveal patterns in the data and explore hidden relationships. The following technologies have been investigated in this report.

2.1   Visualization Tools

One popular development tool for network visualizations is Neo4J Browser [6]. It gives the user options to choose different file formats for the knowledge graph like GraphML and RDF. To support RDF format, it makes use of a plugin called neosemantics. It also has its own graph database to store and manage data. Neo4J Browser has a query language called Cypher, which is different from SPARQL. However, the Cypher queries limit the exploration in a knowledge graph as they work for simple queries and do not support complex relationships in an RDF

---

[1] https://github.com/Devanshika/RDF-SPARQL-Visualization.

knowledge graph. Neo4J Bloom[2] offers a more friendly user interface and more options for visualization but it does not support SPARQL. There are a few proprietary products that provide visualization for knowledge graphs. Cambridge Intelligence [7] is a commercial tool that has three enterprise products namely, KeyLines, ReGraph and KronoGraph. All these visualization tools were developed in JavaScript and React. They have been designed to build compelling visualizations for knowledge graphs using link analysis, customizing apps and integrating them with APIs. The products also implement the social network analysis for graph visualizations. Another promising visualization tool is Gephi [8]. It is an open-source tool that offers a variety of options to customize a knowledge graph and understand the information. It also uses social network analysis like degree centrality, betweenness centrality, page rank and range, to change the layout of a graph so that more connections in the network are interpreted. Gephi currently does not support RDF format or SPARQL. Although an attempt was made to build an RDF plugin that can accept RDF data, Gephi's developers stopped updating their repository for this plugin. OptiqueVQS [9] is another visual query formulation tool for expressing information needs in terms of queries over ontologies. OptiqueVQS is composed of an interface and a navigation graph extracted from the underlying ontologies. The tool isn't specifically designed for knowledge graphs. The user interface is complex, and it doesn't allow many viewpoints of data, making it difficult to find indirect relationships.

2.2   Libraries

Many python libraries are used for making dashboards and visualizations. In particular, Dash [10] is a python library that can be used along with JavaScript libraries to create interactive applications. It is open source and can efficiently run on any browser. This Python library aims at the development of dashboards flexibly. Dash has been described as pure Python abstraction around HTML, CSS, and Javascript in the official documentation.

Several open-source JavaScript libraries are designed especially for graph and network visualizations. Javascript can run client-side, which makes it fast. The latency of callbacks between the backend and frontend is minimal. It is compatible with all browsers and easy to debug. JavaScript loads and executes web pages quickly. It does all the processing work, reduces dependency and the load factor on the server [11]. *D3* and *vis.js* are two popular JavaScript libraries that offer a range of customizable options for knowledge graphs. However, D3 is heavier than vis.js. Simple functionalities like clicking, zooming in and zooming out, dragging nodes are tedious to implement in D3 compared to vis.js. The above research became the motivation for KG-Visual. Heim et al. [12] worked on a similar visualization tool that discovers relationships between different knowledge bases. However, their tool is built on adobe flash, and the only way to fetch the data in their tool is through SPARQL endpoints. The tool presented in this paper, on the contrary, has the feature where users can upload an RDF

---

[2] https://neo4j.com/product/bloom/.

knowledge graph. In addition to the essential tool functionalities like search, drag and drop nodes, zoom in and zoom out, KG-Visual holds the capability to run SPARQL queries. These queries help users filter results to obtain several views of a knowledge graph, thereby facilitating its visualization.

3   Methodology

After an extensive study on available knowledge graph visualization tools, we developed a tool by using Dash for its highly flexible nature and vis.js for its lightweight simplicity. To keep the codebase of this tool more understandable for developers without programming knowledge, two main files have been created. This also satisfies the need to keep visualization on the client-side for speed and the dashboard functionality on a local server for data security.

3.1   Features of the Tool

The tool requires being able to read and understand an RDF knowledge graph. Given that an RDF file is available in multiple formats, the tool allows users to choose the RDF file format. As RDF knowledge graphs tend to have a large number of triples, it is essential to enable users to filter the graph using SPARQL queries. The tool should also be customizable enough to allow for different viewpoints. It should allow users to fix nodes, identify their relationships with other nodes, search for specific nodes, highlight some nodes, and search for particular relationships to highlight the interconnected nodes. Both abstraction and display of important information to users have been considered in the tool design.

3.2   Application Structure

Dashboards need to be intuitive, customizable and clear so that information is communicated quickly. They should use available space effectively, and important information should be presented properly [13]. The dashboard uses a bootstrap column structure to define a two-column menu and an eight-column visualization section. There are two one-column empty *divs* to provide space from the edges of the screen. This has been done to allow for a margin between relevant information in the dashboard.

3.3   Dashboard Menu

The menu is arranged vertically in order of functional requirement. The first interactive element is a drop-down to select the format of the RDF file, followed by an upload file option. RDFlib library [14] is used to read the RDF file in the chosen format and create a Graph object from it. The triples function in the RDFlib makes it easier to read the triple structure from the RDF files. The Graph object allows access to all RDF triples and exposes query functionality to allow filtering using SPARQL. The menu also features a textbox that takes

CONSTRUCT SPARQL queries to create filtered RDF triples that can be visualized in the visualization section. Given that the knowledge graphs tend to be huge in size, the tool gives the user an explicit option as a button *Generate Graph* to generate the graph instead of auto-generating it. The filtered graph is then set as an active "Graph object". Since "Graph objects" need to have triples, only CONSTRUCT queries can be used to filter the graphs. If the original graph is required, a *Clear Graph* button can be clicked, and that would remove the visualization and reset the "Graph object" to the original graph.

Once the visualization is active, the rest of the menu options can be used to customize the visualization. The tool has a search bar to allow highlighting of nodes and their relationships. There is a drop-down provided to customize the search functionality. It has two options, namely, *Search by Subject/Object* and *Search by Predicate*. *Search by Subject/Object* searches for the search string in the node and highlights nodes that contain search string and their connected nodes. *Search by Predicate* searches for the search string in the edges and highlights the nodes connected by the edge.

3.4 Visualization

The visualization uses vis.js Network library, which creates and displays a graph written in JavaScript and allows faster response on the client-side. Once the Python code generates a dictionary-like structure of nodes and edges from RDF triples, the dictionary is passed as JSON to the frontend, i.e. JavaScript. The JavaScript code initializes the network graph using the following options:

```
{options = {clickToUse : true, height : '650px', width :
            '100%', nodes : {font : {size : 0}, shape : 'dot'},
            edges : {font : {size: 0}, width : 2, smooth : {enabled
            : true, type : 'continuous', roundness : 0.6}}, physics
            : {solver : 'forceAtlas2Based', forceAtlas2Based :
            {avoidOverlap : 0.6, springConstant : 0.01, springLength
            : 300, gravitationalConstant : -150}, minVelocity : 0,
            maxVelocity : 50, stabilization : true}, interaction : {
            navigationButtons : true}}}
```

The above options use forceAtlas2[3] as the physics solver and add navigation buttons like zooming, centring and moving the graph. The nodes of the vis.js Network graph can be dragged and fixed to allow different viewpoints, and double clicking a fixed node returns it to the physics simulation. There is also a convenience button to return all fixed nodes to the physics simulation.

4 Case Study

To demonstrate the functionality and usability of the tool, a case study is presented in this section to make use of a knowledge graph consisting of statistical

---

[3] https://visjs.github.io/vis-network/docs/network/physics.html.

information of diseases in Canadian provinces (i.e. Nova Scotia and Alberta) in different years. The data is a RDF turtle file which comprises of a total of 4,254 triples.[4] All the data is acquired from open data portals of Nova Scotia and Alberta. Relationships like *isa* and *hasdisease* are part of the triples to infer details about disease hierarchy. The subject and objects in the triples contain year, region and disease name which create the entities for the knowledge graph. Number of cases and rate per 100k population for diseases were also part of the objects in the triples. We get individual information about the datasets when we glance them from the open data portals[5]. The tool makes it possible to view the information from several datasets in such a way that we can discover how one dataset information can be closely related to the other datasets in the knowledge graph. The tool can successfully find similarities between certain diseases and classify them. Other visualization tools were not adept at discovering these relationships. Tools like Gephi had multiple limitations when it came to uploading RDF data and running SPARQL. Others like OptiqueVQS had a less user friendly interface. KG-Visual is able to overcome these issues and is a simple to use application that performs effective visual filtering. It also has features like search and SPARQL execution. We were able to explore the following queries in this case study with the help of KG-Visual:

- Find relationships between diseases.
- Comprehend disease hierarchy and classifying diseases.
- Exploring hidden relationships in the data through visualization.

To fetch all nodes from the knowledge graph, we used the following SPARQL query:

```
CONSTRUCT  {?s ?p ?o} WHERE {?s ?p ?o}
```

We can also make use of the Limit keyword to restrict the number of nodes making the graph on the screen. Since the data is about diseases, we searched for "disease" keyword and nodes containing related information got highlighted. Using the zoom in and zoom out keys at the bottom right of the graph panel, the nodes and the edges can be viewed in more detail.

Query 1: Find diseases prominent in Nova Scotia

```
CONSTRUCT { ?s sdmx_dimension:refPeriod ?o; sdmx_dimension:refArea
          ?area;rdfs:label ?la.?area rdfs:label ?a. ?o rdfs:label ?l.}
WHERE { ?s sdmx_dimension:refPeriod ?o; sdmx_dimension:refArea ?area,
     geo:6091530;rdfs:label ?la. ?area rdfs:label ?a. ?o rdfs:label ?l.}
```

Figure 1 shows all diseases in the province of Nova Scotia. In addition to the list of diseases, the graph also shows the year in which the diseases occurred. The

---

[4] https://github.com/Devanshika/RDF-SPARQL-Visualization/blob/master/data. ttl.

[5] http://data.novascotia.ca.

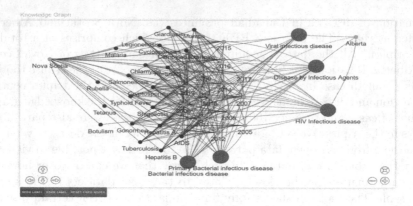

Fig. 1. Diseases occurring in Nova Scotia

tool is able to visualize the diseases in broader disease categories which makes it better for us to understand the disease hierarchy. Another hidden relationship which can be seen here is the connection of the nodes to Alberta. It can be inferred that both Nova Scotia and Alberta had HIV Infectious Disease as a common disease.

Query 2: Identifying relationships between diseases

```
CONSTRUCT { ?s sdmx\_dimension:refPeriod ?o; rdfs:label ?l;
            :isa ?v. ?o rdfs:label ?d. ?v rdfs:label ?u.}
WHERE { ?s sdmx_dimension:refPeriod ?o; rdfs:label ?l; :isa
        ?v, doid:0050117. ?o rdfs:label ?d. ?v rdfs:label ?u.}
```

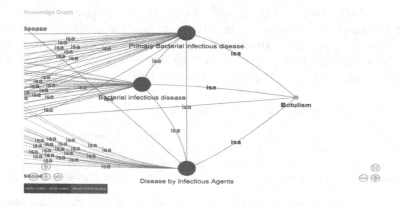

Fig. 2. Identifying type of disease

Relationships in knowledge graphs help us understand the data better. In this case study, triples have a *is-a* relation, which determines the type of disease. Using the tool's predicate search feature, we can directly look at specific relationships in the graph. In Fig. 2, it can be seen that *Botulism* is a type of *Primary Bacterial Infectious Disease* which is also a *Bacterial Infectious Disease* which is a *Disease by Infectious Agents.*

This makes *Botulism* a part of all the above disease types. This information can be fetched for other diseases as well. The same query can also be used to get all diseases of a disease type. Figure 4 shows all primary bacterial infectious diseases like Shigellosis, Tuberculosis, Tetanus, etc. (Fig. 3).

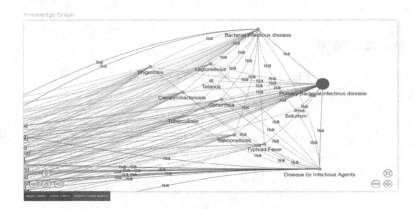

Fig. 3. Identifying type of disease

Query 3: Exploring a particular disease

```
CONSTRUCT { ?s :hasdisease ?o; rdfs:label ?l; :numberofcases
            ?cases. ?o rdfs:label ?d. }
WHERE { ?s :hasdisease ?o, doid:1116; rdfs:label ?l;
            :numberofcases ?cases. ?o rdfs:label ?d.}
```

Using this query, the tool retrieves all data nodes to *DOID:1116* which is *Pertussis*. A simple keyword search for *Pertussis* highlights all the information connected to Pertussis. Figure 4 shows Pertussis node highlighted in pink. All connected nodes give us information like the year and number of cases. We can also infer inverse relationship from this graph like the year 2008 *hasdisease* Pertussis with 14 *numberofcases* (Fig. 5).

Query 4: Filtering the graph using Number of Cases measure

```
CONSTRUCT{ ?s sdmx_dimension:refPeriod ?o; sdmx_dimension:refArea ?area;
            rdfs:label ?la;:numberofcases ?cases. ?area rdfs:label ?a.
            ?o rdfs:label ?l. }
WHERE{ ?s sdmx_dimension:refPeriod ?o; sdmx_dimension:refArea ?area,
            geo:6091530; rdfs:label ?la; :numberofcases ?cases. ?area
            rdfs:label ?a. ?o rdfs:label ?l. FILTER (?cases > 100) }
```

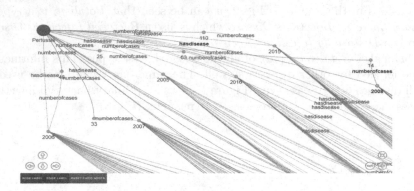

Fig. 4. Exploring data of Pertussis

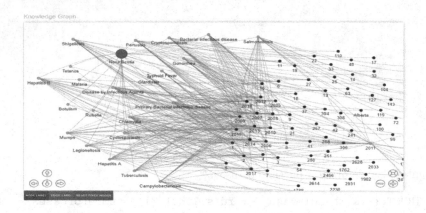

Fig. 5. Diseases without using filter

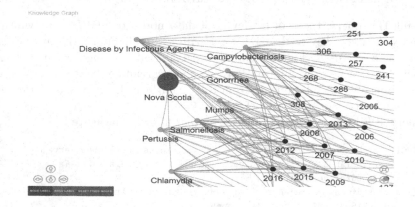

Fig. 6. Diseases with using filter

Knowledge graphs can be expansive and it can become tedious to retrieve information. With the help of this query, we filtered all diseases in Nova Scotia that had more than 100 cases per year. Figure 6 shows all diseases in Nova Scotia without the use of FILTER and Fig. 6 shows the change in graph after applying the FILTER of number of cases greater than 100. All nodes connected to Nova Scotia are highlighted using the tool's keyword search feature.

Just like the above case study, different RDF files can be uploaded to this tool. With the help of the SPARQL queries, parts of the graph can be filtered to get enhanced visualizations. Many other questions can be formulated and answered with the ability of the tool to search for predicates as well as object values. The tool is scalable to an extent and can handle sufficiently large knowledge graphs with minimal lag.

We conducted a user test according to ISO 9241-11:2018 [15] standard to evaluate the usability of the designed tool. This standard defines usability as "the effectiveness, efficiency and satisfaction of the user's interaction with the object of interest", and introduces the following metrics for evaluating a tool:

- Effectiveness as "the accuracy and completeness with which users achieve specified goals", where accuracy is how well the outcome matches the intended outcome, and completeness is how well users are able to achieve all intended outcomes.
- Efficiency as "the resources used in relation to the results achieved", where resources could be time, money, effort or similar.
- Satisfaction as "the extent to which the user's physical, cognitive and emotional responses that result from use of a system, product or service, meet user's needs and expectations".

As the KG-visual successfully finds the hidden relationships between the data points, easily classifies them based on their relationship and explore already existing relationships, it is fair to conclude that the tool effectively achieves all intended outcomes. In terms of efficiency, KG-visual works very well for small to medium sized knowledge graphs. However, the efficiency of tool should be further investigated when it comes to knowledge graphs with more than 4,000 nodes.

5   Conclusion

The paper discusses various tools and techniques that are used to visualize knowledge graphs. It also explains the limitations of existing visualization tools when it comes to visualizing RDF based knowledge graphs. There are many technologies and tools available for visualization, however keeping dashboards simple while providing as much relevant information as possible is important. KG-Visual was developed in this study to visualize an RDF based knowledge graph and filter it using SPARQL queries. A case study using an open government dataset was presented as the proof of concept.

Acknowledgement. The work conducted in the study has been funded by NSERC (Natural Sciences and Engineering Research Council) Discovery Grant (RGPIN-2020-05869).

References

1. Ehrlinger, L., Wöß, W.: Towards a definition of knowledge graphs. SEMANTiCS (Posters, Demos, SuCCESS) **48**(1–4), 2 (2016)
2. Visualizing knowledge graphs. https://cambridge-intelligence.com/use-cases/knowledge-graphs, Accessed 14 Aug 2021
3. Lecue, F.: On the role of knowledge graphs in explainable AI. Semant. Web **11**(1), 41–51 (2020)
4. Ontotext. https://www.ontotext.com/knowledgehub/fundamentals/what-is-rdf, Accessed 14 Aug 2021
5. Gómez-Romero, J., Molina-Solana, M., Oehmichen, A., Guo, Y.: Visualizing large knowledge graphs: a performance analysis. Future Gener. Comput. Syst. **89**, 224–238 (2018)
6. Neo4j documentation. https://neo4j.com/docs, Accessed 14 Aug 2021
7. How to understand social networks. https://info.cambridge-intelligence.com/social-network-visualization-white-paper, Accessed 14 Aug 2021
8. Learn how to use gephi. https://gephi.org/users, Accessed 14 Aug 2021
9. Soylu, A., et al.: Qptiquevqs: a visual query system over ontologies for industry (2018)
10. Creating python dashboards: Dash vs bokeh. https://www.activestate.com/blog/dash-vs-bokeh/, Accessed 14 Aug 2021
11. Benefits of using javascript in front end and back end. https://www.turtlejet.net/benefits-using-javascript-front-end-back-end, Accessed 14 Aug 2021
12. Heim, P., Hellmann, S., Lehmann, J., Lohmann, S., Stegemann, T.: RelFinder: revealing relationships in RDF knowledge bases. In: Chua, T.-S., Kompatsiaris, Y., Mérialdo, B., Haas, W., Thallinger, G., Bailer, W. (eds.) SAMT 2009. LNCS, vol. 5887, pp. 182–187. Springer, Heidelberg (2009). https://doi.org/10.1007/978-3-642-10543-2_21
13. Dashboard design - considerations and best practices. https://www.toptal.com/designers/data-visualization/dashboard-design-best-practices. Accessed 14 Aug 2021
14. Rdflib documentation. https://rdflib.readthedocs.io/_/downloads/en/4.2.2/pdf, Accessed 14 Aug 2021
15. ISO 924111:2018(e) ergonomics of human-system interaction -part 11: Usability: Definitions and concepts. Standard. Geneva, CH. International Organization for Standardization (2018)
16. Simplea. A brief introduction to the technical standards of the semantic web. https://simplea.com/Articles/what-is-the-semantic-web (2018)
17. Visjs documentation. https://github.com/visjs/vis-network, Accessed 14 Aug 2021

Track on Knowledge IT Artifacts (KITA) and Decentralized Applications, Blockchains and P2P Systems, and General Session

KERMIT*viz*: Visualizing Neural Network Activations on Syntactic Trees

Leonardo Ranaldi[1]([✉])(iD), Francesca Fallucchi[1](iD), Andrea Santilli[2](iD),
and Fabio Massimo Zanzotto[3](iD)

[1] Department of Innovation and Information Engineering, Guglielmo Marconi University,
Rome, Italy
{l.ranaldi, f.fallucchi}@unimarconi.it
[2] Department of Computer Science, Sapienza University Rome, Rome, Italy
santilli@di.uniroma1.it
[3] Department of Enterprise Engineering, University of Rome Tor Vergata, Rome, Italy
fabio.massimo.zanzotto@uniroma2.it

Abstract. The study of symbolic syntactic interpretations has been the corner-stone of natural language understanding for many years.

Today, modern artificial neural networks are widely searched to assess their syntactic ability, through several probing tasks.

In this paper, we propose a neural network system that explicitly includes syntactic interpretations: Kernel-inspired Encoder with Recursive Mechanism for Interpretable Trees *Visualizer* (KERMIT*viz*). The most important result is that KERMIT*viz* allows to visualize how syntax is used in inference. This system can be used in combination with transformer architectures like BERT, XLNet and clarifies the use of symbolic syntactic interpretations in specific neural networks making the black-box neural network neural networks explainable, interpretable and clear.

Keywords: Natural Language Processing · Explainable AI · Neural Networks

1 Introduction

While systems based on natural language processing (NLP) and neural network (NN) are achieving extraordinary success, the lack of *interpretation* and NN transparency from the representations learned to the underlying decision-making process, is an important problem to be addressed.

Understanding why a model does not correctly classify test data instances or performs incorrectly is a challenging task. Many works propose techniques such as data augmentation [15] or analysis of available features [10] to improve results. Despite the good results that can be obtained on these challenging tasks, usually methodologies do not consider the investigation of the reasons why the model made predictions.

In fact, when human uses an application, that is based on learning to make critical decisions, not having the perception of what is going on, it calls into question the model's *reliability*. To address this problem, researchers have introduced many different techniques to help interpret what is happening in the NNs. Techniques range from

© Springer Nature Switzerland AG 2022
E. Garoufallou et al. (Eds.): MTSR 2021, CCIS 1537, pp. 139–147, 2022.
https://doi.org/10.1007/978-3-030-98876-0_12

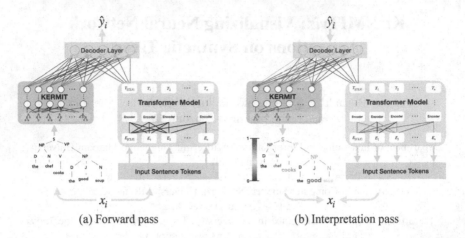

(a) Forward pass   (b) Interpretation pass

Fig. 1. The KERMIT+Transformer architecture. During the interpretation pass KERMIT*viz* is used to produce *heat parse trees*, while a transformer's activation visualizer is used for the remainder of the network.

features important explanations [2,14,16] to prototypes and criticisms [1,3]. Feature Importance Explanations methods, given input with features, explain model's decision by assigning a score to each feature that indicates its contribution in the decision making. Prototype methods seek a minimal subset of samples that can use as condensed view of a data set. In the NLP world, we have word importance explanations. Feature Importance techniques can be categorized into three categories: perturbation-based techniques [14], gradient-based techniques [16], and decomposition-based techniques [2]. However, such techniques are meaningless, specially in the case of NLP, if they are not surrounded by a good method of visualisation that is simple and comprehensible to humans. Many works use these techniques to generate static images, such as *attention maps* [11,19,21] and *heat maps* [9] for image classification, indicating which parts of an image are most important for classification. Interaction has also been incorporated into the process of understanding the model through *visual analytics* tools. For example, *ActiVis* [9] offers a view of neuron activations and can be used to view interactive model interpretations of large heterogeneous data formats such as images and text. However *ActiVis* doesn't support recurrent architectures, a common type of architecture in natural language tasks. For this extent, Ming et al. [11] and Strobelt et al. [19] proposed respectively dedicated visualizers for *recurrent neural networks (RNNviz)* and *long short-term memory networks (LSTMviz)* that are able to inspect the dynamic of the hidden state. These systems are very high performance, provide a very good explanation of what happened and are aimed at both a programmer and an ordinary user, so they are user-friendly. Both *RNNviz* and *LSTMviz* unfortunately do not support specialised RNN-based models, such as memory networks or attention models.

Recently, with the advent of transformer models [20], a lot of work has been done in order to interpret activations of attention heads [7,21,22]. All these transformer visualizers allow to view the magnitude of softmax attention heads correlated with input tokens to interpret model's decisions. By the way of example we selected *BERTviz*

[21] as the representative for this category of Transformer visualizers, it is very difficult to use and its outputs are quite difficult to interpret if you are not familiar with the underlying model. A solution to the problem arising from the difficulty of the task has been proposed by [17,23] that have exploited the basic structure of Transformer to add symbolic syntactic information. Although the symbolic syntactic information is clearer and has allowed good results to be obtained in the downstream tasks, it has not proved useful in terms of explainability. Finally, *Embedding Projector* [18] is an interactive tool for visualizing and interpreting *embeddings*. This tool uses different dimensionality reduction techniques to map high-dimensional embedding vectors into low-dimensional output vectors that are easier to visualize. It can be used to analyze the geometry of words and explore the *embedding space*, although it can't be used directly to explain a neural network model.

In this paper, we present KERMITviz (Kernel-inspired Encoder with Recursive Mechanism for Interpretable Trees *Visualizer*), which is integrated into the KERMIT system [25]. KERMITviz allows researchers to embed symbolic syntactic parse trees into artificial neural networks and to visualize how syntax is used in inference. We use the Layer-wise Relevance Propagation (LRP) [2] (Sect. 2), which is a technique of Feature Importance Explanations. Along the interpretation pass (Fig. 1), using LRP combined with special visualization algorithms, we provide an easy and user-friendly tool to see how syntax is used in inference.

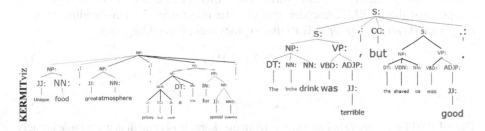

Fig. 2. KERMITviz interpretations over KERMITviz using BERT on two sample sentences where the word *but* is correlated or not with the final polarity.

2 System Description

This section introduces our visualizer KERMITviz stemming from KERMIT [25], a lightweight encoder for universal syntactic interpretations that can be used in combination with transformer-based networks such as BERT [5] (Fig. 1). It follows some preliminary notations (Sect. 2.1), a presentation of KERMIT model (Sect. 2.2), an introduction to KERMITviz (Sect. 2.3) and an overview of heat parse trees (Sect. 2.4).

2.1 Preliminary Notation

Parse trees, $\mathcal{T}$, are core representations in our model. Parse subtrees τ are recursively represented as trees $t = (r, [t_1, ..., t_k])$ where r is the label representing the root of the tree and $[t_1, ..., t_k]$ is the list of child trees t_i. Leaves t are represented as trees $t = (r, [])$.

On parse trees $\mathcal{T}$, our model KERMIT requires the definition of three sets of subtrees: $N(\mathcal{T})$, $\overline{S}(\mathcal{T})$ and $S(\mathcal{T})$. For defining the last two sets we used subtrees defined in [4]: $N(\mathcal{T})$ contains all the complete subtrees of $\mathcal{T}$ and $\overline{S}(\mathcal{T})$ contains all the valid subtrees of $\mathcal{T} = (r, [t_1, ..., t_k])$. The set $S(\mathcal{T})$ is the union of $\overline{S}(t)$ for all the trees $t \in N(\mathcal{T})$ and it contains the subtrees used during training and inference.

Finally, to build the untrained KERMIT encoder, we use the properties of random vectors drawn from a multivariate Gaussian distribution $v \sim \mathcal{N}(0, \frac{1}{\sqrt{d}}\mathbb{I})$. We compose these vectors using the shuffled circular convolution $u \otimes v$.

These vectors are drawn from a multivariate Gaussian distribution which guarantees that $(u \otimes v)^T u \approx 0$, $(u \otimes v)^T v \approx 0$ and $(u \otimes v) \neq (v \otimes u)$. This operation is a circular convolution $\star$ (as for Holographic Reduced Representations [13]) with a permutation matrix Φ: $u \otimes v = u \star \Phi v$.

2.2 The Encoder for Exploiting Parse Trees and Sub-network

KERMIT is a neural network that allows to encode and directly use syntactic interpretations in neural networks architectures. The KERMIT neural network has two main components: the KERMIT encoder, that encodes parse trees $\mathcal{T}$ in embedding vectors, and a multi-layer perceptron (MLP) that exploits these embedding vectors:

$$y = \mathcal{D}(\mathcal{T}) = W_{dt}x \tag{1}$$

$$z = mlp(y) \tag{2}$$

The KERMIT encoder $\mathcal{D}$ in Eq. 1 stems from tree kernels [4] and distributed tree kernels [24]. It gives the possibility to represent parse trees in vector spaces $\mathbb{R}^d$ that embed huge spaces of subtrees $\mathbb{R}^n$.

These encoders may be seen as linear transformations $W_{dt} \in \mathbb{R}^{d \times n}$ (similarly to Transformation in [8]). These linear transformations embed vectors $x^{\mathcal{T}} \in \mathbb{R}^n$ in the space of tree kernels in smaller vectors $y^{\mathcal{T}} \in \mathbb{R}^d$:

$$y^{\mathcal{T}} = W_{dt}x^{\mathcal{T}} \tag{3}$$

Columns w_i of W_{dt} encode subtree $\tau^{(i)}$ and are computed with an encoding function $w_i = \Upsilon(\tau^{(i)})$ as follows:

$$\Upsilon(t) = \begin{cases} r & \text{if } \tau^{(i)} = (r, []) \\ r \otimes \Upsilon(\tau^{(i)}) \otimes ... \otimes \Upsilon(\tau^{(k)}) & \text{if } t = (r, [\tau_1^{(i)}, ..., \tau_k^{(i)}]) \end{cases}$$

As for tree kernels also for distributed tree encoders, linear transformations W_{dt}, vectors $x^{\mathcal{T}} \in \mathbb{R}^n$ are never explicitly produced and encoders are implemented as recursive functions [24].

2.3 Heat Parse Trees and Activation

Heat parse trees (HPTs), similarly to "heat trees" in biology [6], are heatmaps over parse trees (see the colored tree in Fig. 1). The underlying representation is an *active tree* $\bar{t}$, that is a tree where each node $\bar{t} = (r, v_r, [\bar{t}_1, ..., \bar{t}_k])$ has an activation value $v_r \in \mathbb{R}$ associated. HPTs are graphical visualizations of active trees $\bar{t}$ where colors and sizes of nodes r depend on their activation values v_r.

As we will see in Sect. 3, this module is used with the Transformers-models architecture but we specify that this part is frozen during this pass, because this analysis is purely syntactic. We compute activation value v_r in *active tree* $\bar{t}$ by using Layer-wise Relevance Propagation (LRP) [2].

LRP is a framework to explain the decisions of a generic neural network using local redistribution rules and is able to explain which input features contributed most to the final classification.

In our case, is used as a sort of inverted function of the MLP in Eq. 2,

$$\boldsymbol{y}_{LRP} = mlp_{LRP}^{-1}(\boldsymbol{z}). \tag{4}$$

The property in Eq. 1, that enables the activation of each subtree $t \in \mathcal{T}$ to be computed back by transposing the matrix $\boldsymbol{W}_{dt}$, that is:

$$\boldsymbol{x}_{LRP} = \boldsymbol{W_r}^T \boldsymbol{y}_{LRP} \tag{5}$$

To make the computation feasible, $\boldsymbol{W}_{dt}^T$ is produced on-the-fly for each tree $\mathcal{T}$. Finally, activation values v_r of nodes $r \in \mathcal{T}$ are computed by summing up values $x_{LRP}^{(i)}$ if $r \in t^{(i)}$.

2.4 Visualizing Activation in Heat Parse Trees

KERMIT*viz* give the possibility to visualize the activation of parse trees. To make the active trees understandable we use *heat maps*. We use this tool to visualize how much a subtree affects the final decision of an NN classifier Fig. 2. We define the *Heat parse trees* as a graphical visualization of heatmaps over active trees $\bar{t}$ where colors and sizes of nodes r depend on their relevance values v_r. The module allows us to explain which nodes have contributed most to the final classification of a model through the visualization of the Heat parse trees.

3   KERMIT*viz* - System Overview

KERMIT*viz* is a visualizer to inspect how syntax is used in taking final decisions in specific tasks. We showed that KERMIT can effectively embed different syntactic information and KERMIT*viz* can explain KERMIT's decisions. KERMIT*viz* offers two main features: the visualization tool and a tutorial on how to quickly build and visualize a sample KERMIT encoder network[1].

---

[1] The code is available at https://github.com/ART-Group-it/KERMIT.

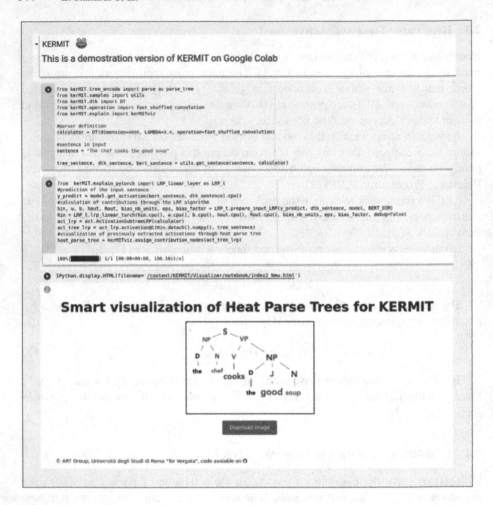

Fig. 3. KERMIT's notebook with integrated KERMIT*viz* is available on google colab.

In this paper, we focus specifically on these two use cases: an example of the advantages provided by the *heat parse tree* produced by KERMIT*viz* (Fig. 2), and an example on how to generate an *heat parse tree* given a sentence (see Fig. 3).

Hereafter, are described these use cases and demonstrate them in Sect. 3.1 and Sect. 3.2.

3.1 KERMIT*viz* - Example

KERMIT*viz* allows to visualizes activation as *heat parse trees* to help justify the choices of the model based on the relevance of the fragments of a sentence, as shown in Fig. 2. In this figure (Fig. 2), colors and sizes identify the relevance value v_r of node r. The range of values: $v_r \in [0, 1]$ and colour range goes from *black* for v_r tending to 0 and *red* for v_r tending to 1.

3.2 KERMIT*viz* - Demo

Interacting and testing KERMIT*viz* is very easy. We produced a jupyter notebook to explain how to get an *heat parse tree* given sentence. We also give users the opportunity to try out this system without the need to download and install everything, using of Google Colaboratory (GC)[2]. In Fig. 3 are represented some important steps of KERMIT*viz* on the GC platform. More precisely, we can observe the encoding of the sentence in the constituent tree, the encoding in vectors introduced in Sect. 2.2, the application of the LRP algorithm in Sect. 2.3 and finally the visualisation using the *heat parse trees* Sect. 2.4.

4   Conclusion

KERMIT*viz* is a simple visualizer that allows us to explain how syntactic information is used in classification decisions within networks combining KERMIT and BERT.

KERMIT*viz* has a clear description of the used syntactic subtrees and gives the possibility of visualizing how syntactic information is exploited during inference, this opens consequently the possibility of devising models to include explicit syntactic inference rules in the training process.

Our future goal is to combine KERMIT*viz* with a *rule control mechanism* of a [12] neural network in order to have full control over the decisions of a fully explainable neural network.

References

1. Ancona, M., Ceolini, E., Öztireli, C., Gross, M.: Towards better understanding of gradient-based attribution methods for deep neural networks (2018)
2. Bach, S., Binder, A., Montavon, G., Klauschen, F., Müller, K.R., Samek, W.: On pixel-wise explanations for non-linear classifier decisions by layer-wise relevance propagation. PLoS ONE **10**(7), 1–46 (2015). https://doi.org/10.1371/journal.pone.0130140
3. Bien, J., Tibshirani, R.: Prototype selection for interpretable classification. Ann. Appl. Stat. **5**(4) (2011). https://doi.org/10.1214/11-aoas495. http://dx.doi.org/10.1214/11-AOAS495
4. Collins, M., Duffy, N.: New ranking algorithms for parsing and tagging: kernels over discrete structures, and the voted perceptron. In: Proceedings of ACL 2002 (2002)
5. Devlin, J., Chang, M.W., Lee, K., Toutanova, K.: BERT: pre-training of deep bidirectional transformers for language understanding. CoRR abs/1810.0 (2018). http://arxiv.org/abs/1810.04805
6. Foster, Z.S.L., Sharpton, T.J., Grünwald, N.J.: Metacoder: an R package for visualization and manipulation of community taxonomic diversity data. PLoS Comput. Biol. **13**(2) (2017). https://doi.org/10.1371/journal.pcbi.1005404
7. Hoover, B., Strobelt, H., Gehrmann, S.: exBERT: a visual analysis tool to explore learned representations in transformers models. arXiv e-prints arXiv:1910.05276, October 2019
8. Johnson, W., Lindenstrauss, J.: Extensions of Lipschitz mappings into a Hilbert space. Contemp. Math. **26**, 189–206 (1984)

---

[2] https://colab.research.google.com.

9. Kahng, M., Andrews, P.Y., Kalro, A., Chau, D.H.: ActiVis: visual exploration of industry-scale deep neural network models. CoRR abs/1704.01942 (2017). http://arxiv.org/abs/1704.01942
10. Liang, B., Yin, R., Gui, L., Du, J., He, Y., Xu, R.: Aspect-invariant sentiment features learning: Adversarial multi-task learning for aspect-based sentiment analysis. In: Proceedings of the 29th ACM International Conference on Information amp; Knowledge Management, CIKM 2020, New York, NY, USA, pp. 825–834. Association for Computing Machinery (2020). https://doi.org/10.1145/3340531.3411868
11. Ming, Y., et al.: Understanding hidden memories of recurrent neural networks. CoRR abs/1710.10777 (2017). http://arxiv.org/abs/1710.10777
12. Onorati, D., Tommasino, P., Ranaldi, L., Fallucchi, F., Zanzotto, F.M.: Pat-in-the-loop: declarative knowledge for controlling neural networks. Future Internet **12**(12) (2020). https://doi.org/10.3390/fi12120218. https://www.mdpi.com/1999-5903/12/12/218
13. Plate, T.A.: Holographic reduced representations. IEEE Trans. Neural Networks **6**(3), 623–641 (1995). https://doi.org/10.1109/72.377968
14. Ribeiro, M.T., Singh, S., Guestrin, C.: "Why should i trust you?": explaining the predictions of any classifier (2016)
15. Rizos, G., Hemker, K., Schuller, B.: Augment to prevent: short-text data augmentation in deep learning for hate-speech classification. In: Proceedings of the 28th ACM International Conference on Information and Knowledge Management, CIKM 2019, New York, NY, USA, pp. 991–1000. Association for Computing Machinery (2019). https://doi.org/10.1145/3357384.3358040
16. Selvaraju, R.R., Cogswell, M., Das, A., Vedantam, R., Parikh, D., Batra, D.: Grad-CAM: visual explanations from deep networks via gradient-based localization. Int. J. Comput. Vision **128**(2), 336–359 (2019). https://doi.org/10.1007/s11263-019-01228-7. http://dx.doi.org/10.1007/s11263-019-01228-7
17. Shen, Y., Lin, Z., Huang, C.W., Courville, A.: Neural language modeling by jointly learning syntax and lexicon (2018)
18. Smilkov, D., Thorat, N., Nicholson, C., Reif, E., Viégas, F.B., Wattenberg, M.: Embedding projector: interactive visualization and interpretation of embeddings. arXiv preprint arXiv:1611.05469 (2016)
19. Strobelt, H., Gehrmann, S., Huber, B., Pfister, H., Rush, A.M.: Visual analysis of hidden state dynamics in recurrent neural networks. CoRR abs/1606.07461 (2016). http://arxiv.org/abs/1606.07461
20. Vaswani, A., et al.: Attention is all you need. In: NIPS (2017)
21. Vig, J.: A multiscale visualization of attention in the transformer model. In: ACL 2019–57th Annual Meeting of the Association for Computational Linguistics, Proceedings of System Demonstrations, pp. 37–42 (2019)
22. Wallace, E., Tuyls, J., Wang, J., Subramanian, S., Gardner, M., Singh, S.: AllenNLP Interpret: a framework for explaining predictions of NLP models. In: Empirical Methods in Natural Language Processing (2019)
23. Wang, Y., Lee, H.Y., Chen, Y.N.: Tree transformer: integrating tree structures into self-attention. In: Proceedings of the 2019 Conference on Empirical Methods in Natural Language Processing and the 9th International Joint Conference on Natural Language Processing (EMNLP-IJCNLP), Hong Kong, China, pp. 1061–1070. Association for Computational Linguistics, November 2019. https://doi.org/10.18653/v1/D19-1098. https://www.aclweb.org/anthology/D19-1098
24. Zanzotto, F.M., Dell'Arciprete, L.: Distributed tree kernels. In: Proceedings of the 29th International Conference on Machine Learning, ICML 2012, vol. 1, pp. 193–200 (2012). http://www.scopus.com/inward/record.url?eid=2-s2.0-84867126965&partnerID=MN8TOARS

25. Zanzotto, F.M., Santilli, A., Ranaldi, L., Onorati, D., Tommasino, P., Fallucchi, F.: KER-MIT: complementing transformer architectures with encoders of explicit syntactic interpretations. In: Proceedings of the 2020 Conference on Empirical Methods in Natural Language Processing (EMNLP), pp. 256–267. Association for Computational Linguistics, November 2020. https://doi.org/10.18653/v1/2020.emnlp-main.18. https://www.aclweb.org/anthology/2020.emnlp-main.18

BERT Model-Based Approach
for Detecting Racism and Xenophobia
on Twitter Data

José Alberto Benitez-Andrades[1(✉)] [iD], Álvaro González-Jiménez[2] [iD],
Álvaro López-Brea[2] [iD], Carmen Benavides[1] [iD], Jose Aveleira-Mata[3] [iD],
José-Manuel Alija-Pérez[3] [iD], and María Teresa García-Ordás[3] [iD]

[1] SALBIS Research Group, Department of Electric, Systems and Automatics
Engineering, Universidad de León, Campus of Vegazana s/n, 24071 León, Spain
jbena@unileon.es
[2] Universidad de León, Campus of Vegazana s/n, 24071 León, Spain
[3] SECOMUCI Research Group, Escuela de Ingenierías Industrial e Informática,
Universidad de León, Campus de Vegazana s/n, 24071 León, Spain

Abstract. The large amount of data generated on social networks makes the task of moderating textual content written by users complex and impossible to do manually. One of the most prominent problems on social networks is racism and xenophobia. Although there are studies of predictive models that make use of natural language processing techniques to detect racist or xenophobic texts, a lack of these has been observed in the Spanish language. In this paper we present a solution based on deep learning models and, more specifically, models based on transfer learning to detect racist and xenophobic messages in Spanish. For this purpose, a dataset obtained from the social network Twitter has been created using data mining techniques and, after a preprocessing, it has been labelled into racist messages and non-racist messages. The trained models are based on BERT and were called BETO and mBERT. Promising results were obtained showing 85.14% accuracy in the best performing model.

Keywords: Natural language processing · BERT · Deep learning · Hate speech · Racism · Social networks

1 Introduction

Some social media such as forums and also social networks such as Twitter or Facebook are showing day after day conversations and texts related to hate among users [14,38,39]. One of the reasons for this is the fact that users can send messages anonymously. This leads to a spread of hate speech [6].

Among the studies on hate speech, there are studies mainly focused on xenophobic and racist crimes [29,32]. It has been observed that in the UK there is hate speech focused on different Muslim communities and other immigrants

E. Garoufallou et al. (Eds.): MTSR 2021, CCIS 1537, pp. 148–158, 2022.
https://doi.org/10.1007/978-3-030-98876-0_13

[4,36]. This has increased as Brexit has progressed and also with the Manchester bombings. On the other hand, in Spain, the national government has approved a non-legislative proposal to prevent the dissemination of hate on the Internet [16]. It can be seen that the analysis of racism and xenophobia is an important issue at the international level.

Currently, some studies have worked on the classification of texts for the detection of racism or xenophobia [2,3,11,13,27]. To do this, they have used different techniques in the field of artificial intelligence and, more specifically, within natural language processing. One of the most widely used techniques for this purpose is sentiment analysis on different datasets obtained from some social networks, Twitter being one of the most widely used [17,28,31,33].

Thanks to artificial intelligence, and, more specifically, thanks to natural language processing, there are studies that are working on detecting racism and xenophobia in speeches [2,3,11,13,27]. Among the most widely used techniques within the field of text mining is sentiment analysis on different datasets. Generally these discourses are obtained from social networks, especially from Twitter [17,31].

Machine learning and deep learning techniques are often used to create predictive models capable of classifying texts according to their content. Among the deep learning techniques most commonly used today are Bidirectional Long Short-Term Memory Networks (BiLSTM). The BiLSTMs that show the best results are those known as BERT.

However, one of the problems currently existing in the detection of this type of racist or xenophobic messages is the language in which they are written. There are machine learning and deep learning models that detect this discourse in English. However, no pre-trained models capable of solving the problem in Spanish have been found.

This research proposes the creation of a dataset obtained from Twitter related to racism and xenophobia in Spanish. After this data collection and labelling work, different deep learning models capable of classifying these texts with adequate accuracy are proposed.

The paper is organized as follows. Related work is presented in Sect. 2. The methodology of the different proposed techniques is detailed in Sect. 3. In Sect. 4 is explained the setup of different deep learning techniques and the results, showing a comparative between the different techniques. Finally, results have been discussed in Sect. 5 and we conclude in the same section.

2   Related Work

2.1   Datasets About Racism and Xenophobia

First of all, there are a couple of datasets in Spanish that are related to hate speech: HaterNet [26] and HatEval [7]. However, they do not focus exclusively on the problem of racism or xenophobia.

HaterNet [26] consists of a total of 6,000 tweets including texts related to hate speech. Among these tweets there are some tweets that do relate to racism and xenophobia, but they represent a very low percentage and could not help us to solve the problem proposed in this research. This dataset would not allow us to obtain valid predictive models.

On the other hand, there is HatEval [7], composed of two datasets, one of them in English and one of them in Spanish. The Spanish dataset consists of a total of 5,000 tweets, of which 1,971 are related to racism. Within this dataset, it was observed that a high percentage of tweets labelled as racist did not actually contain racist tweets, but were tweets that mentioned racism.

For all of the above reasons, it was decided to generate a new dataset for the present research.

2.2   Predictive Models to Detect Hate Speech on Spanish

The most commonly used techniques for sentiment analysis are divided into three groups: conventional machine learning, deep learning and transfer learning.

Among the different conventional machine learning techniques, Support Vector Machines (SVMs) [12] have proven to be accurate and effective in text classification [1,19]. There are also studies applying logistic regressions with good results in their predictions [9,22].

In the field of deep learning techniques, the articles that make use of Convolutional Neural Networks (CNN) [24,30], Recurrent Neural Networks (RNNs) [25] and Long Short-Term Memory Network (LSTM) [8,18,23,35] stand out.

Finally, the most recent studies that show the highest accuracy and precision are those that make use of transfer learning techniques such as BERT [15].

Of all the techniques mentioned, the most important study was found in [27]. This article compares the performance of different models classifying tweets from the HatEval dataset. Among the models they compare are SVM, linear regression (LR), Naive Bayes (NB), decision trees (DT), LSTM and lexicon-based classifier.

A second study [5] compares the performance of different NLP models between tweets from HaterNet and HatEval. This time they include more advanced deep learning techniques such as LSTM, BiLSTM, CNN, and transfer learning techniques such as mBert, XLM and BETO.

After analysing the existing models, it was verified that there are no models specifically developed to connect racism and xenophobia in sets of texts written in Spanish, which justifies the development carried out in this research.

3   Material and Methods

3.1   Dataset

A proprietary dataset was constructed by obtaining the messages from the Twitter platform. The Python Tweepy library was used for this purpose.

The keywords shown below were selected: *moro, mora, gitano, gitana, gypsy, puto simio, negro de mierda, negra de mierda, puto negro, puta negra, inmigración, inmigrante, patera, mena, panchito, panchita, sudaca.*

The dataset obtained consisted of a total of 26,143 tweets dated between 2nd November 2020 and 21st December 2020. The following metadata was obtained from each tweet collected in the dataset: tweet message, location, number of people the user follows, number of followers, user creation date, total number of tweets written by the user, tweet creation date, number of retweets and hashtags.

After collection, the data was preprocessed and labelled. For this purpose, (i) various tweets containing little information, i.e. they were too short; (ii) tweets containing ironic messages were deleted; (iii) texts with excessive spelling and grammar mistakes were removed; (iv) texts were converted to lowercase; (v) various unnecessary characters and stopwords were removed.

After this preprocessing, 2,000 tweets were manually tagged by two computer engineers. Subsequently, a committee composed by 8 experts trained in psychology subsequently reviewed these labels. Each pair of experts individually analysed a subset of 500 tagged tweets. They then pooled their judgements and reached agreement on the most controversial tags.

Of the 2,000 selected tweets obtained, tweets that were considered racist and tweets that were not racist were labelled, resulting in a balanced set consisting of 48% of tweets labelled as racist versus 52% of non-racist tweets.

In selecting the subset of 2,000 tweets, consideration was given to a variety of terms in the subset. Several terms were more popular, but tweets containing a multitude of terms were selected. In addition, consideration was also given to the possible double meaning of some words that, in other contexts, would not be racist slurs.

3.2 BERT Models

BERT models [15] were deep learning models created by researchers at Google and the University of Toronto in 2017 to solve particular problems within natural language processing. These models make use of what are known as Transformers [37].

Transformers are designed to work with sequential data, as is the case with recurrent neural networks (RNN). These Transformers are able to process natural language in much the same way as humans do. While RNNs process sequential data in order, in the case of Transformers this is not necessary.

When receiving a text as input, it is not necessary to process the beginning of the text before the end, thus allowing training times to be reduced. Transformers make use of a mechanism known as the attention mechanism. Its main function is to memorise long sentences in machine translation tasks.

Transformers are based on an encoder-decoder architecture. Encoders iteratively process the input of one layer after another, while decoders perform decoding in the same way. A high-level representation of Transformers can be seen in Fig. 1.

Transformers have become the best solution to NLP problems since their emergence. The first differentiating factor of BERT is the difference with older embedding generation techniques, such as Word2Vec, Glove or FastText.

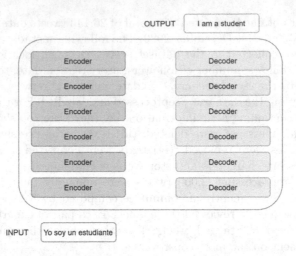

Fig. 1. High-level representation of Transformers.

3.3 Metrics to Evaluate Results

To evaluate the results obtained in each of the models developed, 3 different metrics have been used: Precision (P), Recall (R) and F1-score (F1).

Precision. Precision is a metric used to calculate what percentage of the positive samples (which in this particular case equals the samples labelled as racist) have been properly classified. The formula used to calculate this metric is as follows, where c is equal to the class (0 = Non-racist, 1 = Racist), TP = True positive, FP = False positive and FN = False negative:

$$P(c) = \frac{TP}{TP + FP} \tag{1}$$

Recall. Recall, in turn, is a metric used to calculate what percentage of the samples classified as positive have been properly classified. The formula used to calculate this metric is as follows, where c is equal to the class (0 = Non-racist, 1 = Racist), TP = True positive and FN = False negative:

$$R(c) = \frac{TP}{TP + FN} \tag{2}$$

F1-Score. F1-score is a metric used to calculate the effectiveness of a classifier by taking into account its accuracy and recall values. F1 assumes that the two metrics used are of equal importance in calculating effectiveness. If one of them is more important than the other, a different formula F_β would have to be used. The formula used to calculate this metric is as follows, where P equals the precision value and R equals the recall value:

$$F_1 = \frac{2 * P * R}{P + R} \tag{3}$$

4 Experiments and Results

4.1 Experimental Setup

As part of the development of this project, a total of 2 different predictive models
have been developed. All of them are transfer learning models: a model based
on BETO, a model very similar to BERT trained in Spanish, and a model based
on mBERT, a BERT checkpoint that can be used on texts in a large number of
different languages.

For these experiments, the data were divided into a training set (70%) and
a test set for model validation (30%).

BETO Model. BETO [10] is a model that, like BERT, belongs to the transfer
learning class. The particularity of this model is that the language of the texts
with which it has been trained is Spanish. This model has 12 layers of encoders in
its architecture, so it should be noted that they are very similar. BETO has two
models, one trained with words written in upper or lower case (original form)
and the other trained only with lower case. In this case, tests were carried out
with both, obtaining a difference of 1.0% in favour of the model trained with
only lowercase letters.

mBERT Model. On the other hand, mBERT (Multilingual BERT) [15] is also
a transfer learning model trained with Wikipedia texts that have been written in
104 different languages, among them, Spanish. It also has a very similar architecture to the BERT base consisting of 12 layers of encoders. It also has a version
trained with lowercase words and another version trained with original texts
that combine uppercase and lowercase letters. On this occasion, better results
were obtained with the model trained with upper and lower case.

One of the problems with multilingual models is that they do not easily
detect which language the text is in, as they do not usually have a system that
detects the language in which the input texts are written. With this in mind,
various tests were carried out by adjusting the hyperparameters of the models.
The most important hyperparameters were modified according to the [34] study,
as shown below:

- Type of model: Cased or uncased.
- Number of epochs: 2, 4 and 8. The number of epochs dictates the number of
  times the model will process the entire training set.
- Batch size: 8, 16, 32 and 64. This parameter indicates the number of samples
  to be processed by the model until an internal update of the model weights
  is performed.

- Optimiser: Adam and Adafactor. Mechanisms used to manage the update of the model weights.
- Learning rate: 0.00002, 0.00003 and 0.00004. Parameter that determines the step size when performing an update in the model with a view to approaching a minimum in a loss function.

The different possible combinations tested (a total of 144) and the best parameters found for each of the two models can be found in the Table 1.

Table 1. The best transfer learning hyperparameters

Hyperparameter	Options	BETO	mBERT
Model type	[Cased, uncased]	Uncased	Cased
Epochs	[2, 4, 8]	8	4
Batch size	[8, 16, 32, 64]	8	8
Optimizer	[Adam, Adafactor]	Adam	Adam
Learning rate	[2e−5, 3e−5, 4e−5]	4e−5	4e−5

The most optimal configurations coincide in three hyperparameters and differ in the type of model (cased, uncased) and in the number of epochs.

4.2 Results

The following Table 2 shows the results obtained after numerous runs of the various predictive models.

Table 2. Results obtained for all models

Model	Non-racist			Racist			Macro-averaged		
	P (%)	R (%)	F1 (%)	P (%)	R (%)	F1 (%)	P (%)	R (%)	F1 (%)
BETO	**84.28**	**87.30**	**85.76**	**86.17**	**82.94**	**84.52**	**85.22**	**85.12**	**85.14**
mBERT	83.28	81.11	82.18	80.73	**82.94**	81.82	82.00	82.02	82.00

BETO offers the best results in each and every one of the metrics calculated, obtaining a wide advantage over the rest of the models.

The model with the best results in all the calculated metrics is BETO, with an average accuracy (macro average F1-score) of 85.14%.

The confusion matrices of the mBERT and BETO models are shown below in Fig. 2.

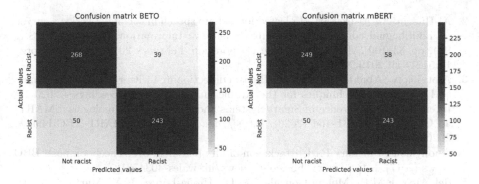

Fig. 2. Confusion matrices of the mBERT and BETO models.

5   Discussion and Conclusions

The BETO and mBERT models have provided fairly high accuracy results within the context of this research, both exceeding 81.99%, while the most accurate predictive model in [27] was 74.20%. Even so, the results obtained show that the native model (BETO) performs better than the multilingual model (mBERT). This fact has an explanation related to the following two aspects: (i) the difference in vocabulary between the two models and (ii) the difference in tokenisers.

Regarding the first fact, the difference in vocabulary, it should be noted that the BETO model has a higher percentage of different words in Spanish than the mBERT model. Moreover, as they are transfer models, the results obtained with less generic models are usually better [20,21], and this is also the case in our research.

With regard to the difference in tokenisers, BETO tokenises only texts written in Spanish, whereas mBERT has a generic tokeniser which, moreover, does not have a system for detecting the language in which the texts are written. This means that mBERT recognises some words from other languages as if they were Spanish.

Taking this into account, BETO obtains better results, being the model that best solves the problem posed in this research. In addition, it is important to highlight the importance of developing learning models that make use of the native language of the problem to be solved, as they tend to obtain better results.

Future research will increase the dataset, adding new languages and integrating these models into web applications that can be useful to society.

Funding. This research was funded by the Junta de Castilla y León grant number LE014G18.

References

1. Ahmad, M., Aftab, S., Bashir, M.S., Hameed, N.: Sentiment analysis using SVM: a systematic literature review. Int. J. Adv. Comput. Sci. Appl. **9**(2), 182–188 (2018). https://doi.org/10.14569/IJACSA.2018.090226

2. Al-Hassan, A., Al-Dossari, H.: Detection of hate speech in social networks: a survey on multilingual corpus. In: Computer Science & Information Technology (CS & IT), pp. 83–100. AIRCC Publishing Corporation, February 2019. https://doi.org/10.5121/csit.2019.90208

3. Alotaibi, A., Abul Hasanat, M.H.: Racism detection in Twitter using deep learning and text mining techniques for the Arabic language. In: Proceedings - 2020 1st International Conference of Smart Systems and Emerging Technologies, SMART-TECH 2020, pp. 161–164 (2020). https://doi.org/10.1109/SMART-TECH49988.2020.00047

4. Anonymous: Finsbury Park attack: son of hire boss held over Facebook post. BBC News (2017). https://www.bbc.co.uk/news/uk-wales-40347813/

5. del Arco, F.M.P., Molina-González, M.D., Ureña-López, L.A., Martín-Valdivia, M.T.: Comparing pre-trained language models for Spanish hate speech detection. Expert Syst. Appl. **166**, 114120 (2021). https://doi.org/10.1016/j.eswa.2020.114120, https://www.sciencedirect.com/science/article/pii/S095741742030868X

6. Barlett, C.P.: Anonymously hurting others online: the effect of anonymity on cyberbullying frequency. Psychol. Pop. Media Cult. **4**(2), 70–79 (2015). https://doi.org/10.1037/a0034335

7. Basile, V., et al.: SemEval-2019 task 5: multilingual detection of hate speech against immigrants and women in Twitter. In: Proceedings of the 13th International Workshop on Semantic Evaluation, Minneapolis, Minnesota, USA, pp. 54–63. Association for Computational Linguistics, June 2019. https://doi.org/10.18653/v1/S19-2007

8. Bisht, A., Singh, A., Bhadauria, H.S., Virmani, J., Kriti: Detection of hate speech and offensive language in Twitter data using LSTM model, pp. 243–264. Springer, Singapore (2020). https://doi.org/10.1007/978-981-15-2740-1_17

9. Br Ginting, P.S., Irawan, B., Setianingsih, C.: Hate speech detection on Twitter using multinomial logistic regression classification method. In: 2019 IEEE International Conference on Internet of Things and Intelligence System (IoTaIS), pp. 105–111 (2019). https://doi.org/10.1109/IoTaIS47347.2019.8980379

10. Cañete, J., Chaperon, G., Fuentes, R., Ho, J.H., Kang, H., Pérez, J.: Spanish pre-trained BERT model and evaluation data. In: PML4DC at ICLR 2020 (2020)

11. Chaudhry, I.: Hashtagging hate: using Twitter to track racism online. First Monday, vol. 20, no. 2 (2015). https://doi.org/10.5210/fm.v20i2.5450https://journals.uic.edu/ojs/index.php/fm/article/view/5450

12. Cortes, C., Vapnik, V.: Support-vector networks. Mach. Learn. **20**(3), 273–297 (1995). https://doi.org/10.1023/A:1022627411411

13. Criss, S., Michaels, E.K., Solomon, K., Allen, A.M., Nguyen, T.T.: Twitter fingers and echo chambers: exploring expressions and experiences of online racism using Twitter. J. Racial Ethn. Health Disparities **8**(5), 1322–1331 (2020). https://doi.org/10.1007/s40615-020-00894-5

14. Del Vigna, F., Cimino, A., Dell'Orletta, F., Petrocchi, M., Tesconi, M.: Hate me, hate me not: hate speech detection on Facebook. CEUR Workshop Proc. **1816**, 86–95 (2017)

15. Devlin, J., Chang, M.W., Lee, K., Toutanova, K.: BERT: pre-training of deep bidirectional transformers for language understanding. In: Proceedings of the 2019 Conference of the North American Chapter of the Association for Computational Linguistics: Human Language Technologies, Volume 1 (Long and Short Papers), Minneapolis, Minnesota, pp. 4171–4186. Association for Computational Linguistics, June 2019. https://doi.org/10.18653/v1/N19-1423

16. de los diputados, C., Government, S., October 2020. https://www.parlamento2030.es/initiatives/3381886de6b06a9ab93ac0bed74cbc61d9259c1c
17. Garcia, K., Berton, L.: Topic detection and sentiment analysis in Twitter content related to COVID-19 from Brazil and the USA. Appl. Soft Comput. **101**, 107057 (2021). https://doi.org/10.1016/j.asoc.2020.107057, https://www.sciencedirect.com/science/article/pii/S1568494620309959
18. García Nieto, P.J., García-Gonzalo, E., Paredes-Sánchez, J.P., Bernardo Sánchez, A., Menéndez Fernández, M.: Predictive modelling of the higher heating value in biomass torrefaction for the energy treatment process using machine-learning techniques. Neural Comput. Appl. **31**(12), 8823–8836 (2019). https://doi.org/10.1007/s00521-018-3870-x
19. Hasan, M.R., Maliha, M., Arifuzzaman, M.: Sentiment analysis with NLP on Twitter data. In: 2019 International Conference on Computer, Communication, Chemical, Materials and Electronic Engineering (IC4ME2), pp. 1–4 (2019). https://doi.org/10.1109/IC4ME247184.2019.9036670
20. Kalaivani, A., Thenmozhi, D.: SSN_NLP_MLRG at SemEval-2020 task 12: offensive language identification in English, Danish, Greek using BERT and machine learning approach. In: Proceedings of the Fourteenth Workshop on Semantic Evaluation, Barcelona, pp. 2161–2170. International Committee for Computational Linguistics (online), December 2020. https://aclanthology.org/2020.semeval-1.287
21. Kumar, P., Singh, A., Kumar, P., Kumar, C.: An explainable machine learning approach for definition extraction. In: Bhattacharjee, A., Borgohain, S.K., Soni, B., Verma, G., Gao, X.-Z. (eds.) MIND 2020. CCIS, vol. 1241, pp. 145–155. Springer, Singapore (2020). https://doi.org/10.1007/978-981-15-6318-8_13
22. Lakshmi, R., Divya, S.R.B., Valarmathi, R.: Analysis of sentiment in Twitter using logistic regression. Int. J. Eng. Technol. **7**(233), 619–621 (2018). https://doi.org/10.14419/ijet.v7i2.33.14849
23. Menéndez García, L.A., Sánchez Lasheras, F., García Nieto, P.J., Álvarez de Prado, L., Bernardo Sánchez, A.: Predicting benzene concentration using machine learning and time series algorithms. Mathematics **8**(12), 2205 (2020). https://doi.org/10.3390/math8122205
24. Nedjah, N., Santos, I., de Macedo Mourelle, L.: Sentiment analysis using convolutional neural network via word embeddings. Evol. Intell. (2019). https://doi.org/10.1007/s12065-019-00227-4
25. Paetzold, G.H., Zampieri, M., Malmasi, S.: UTFPR at SemEval-2019 task 5: hate speech identification with recurrent neural networks. In: Proceedings of the 13th International Workshop on Semantic Evaluation, Minneapolis, Minnesota, USA, pp. 519–523. Association for Computational Linguistics, June 2019. https://doi.org/10.18653/v1/S19-2093
26. Pereira-Kohatsu, J.C., Quijano-Sánchez, L., Liberatore, F., Camacho-Collados, M.: Detecting and monitoring hate speech in Twitter. Sensors **19**(21) (2019). https://doi.org/10.3390/s19214654
27. Plaza-Del-Arco, F.M., Molina-González, M.D., Ureña López, L.A., Martín-Valdivia, M.T.: Detecting misogyny and xenophobia in Spanish tweets using language technologies. ACM Trans. Internet Technol. **20**(2) (2020). https://doi.org/10.1145/3369869
28. Rastogi, S., Bansal, D.: Visualization of Twitter sentiments on Kashmir territorial conflict. Cybern. Syst. **52**, 642–669 (2021). https://doi.org/10.1080/01969722.2021.1949520

29. Rodríguez Maeso, S.: "Europe" and the narrative of the "true racist": (un-)thinking anti-discrimination law through race. Oñati Socio-Legal Ser. **8**(6), 845–873 (2018). https://doi.org/10.35295/osls.iisl/0000-0000-0000-0974

30. Roy, P.K., Tripathy, A.K., Das, T.K., Gao, X.: A framework for hate speech detection using deep convolutional neural network. IEEE Access **8**, 204951–204962 (2020)

31. Saha, B.N., Senapati, A., Mahajan, A.: LSTM based deep RNN architecture for election sentiment analysis from Bengali newspaper. In: 2020 International Conference on Computational Performance Evaluation (ComPE), pp. 564–569 (2020). https://doi.org/10.1109/ComPE49325.2020.9200062

32. Sayan, P.: Enforcement of the anti-racism legislation of the European Union against antigypsyism. Ethnic Racial Stud. **42**(5), 763–781 (2019). https://doi.org/10.1080/01419870.2018.1468568

33. Singh, M., Bansal, D., Sofat, S.: Who is who on Twitter-spammer, fake or compromised account? A tool to reveal true identity in real-time. Cybern. Syst. **49**(1), 1–25 (2018). https://doi.org/10.1080/01969722.2017.1412866

34. Sun, C., Qiu, X., Xu, Y., Huang, X.: How to fine-tune BERT for text classification? In: Sun, M., Huang, X., Ji, H., Liu, Z., Liu, Y. (eds.) CCL 2019. LNCS (LNAI), vol. 11856, pp. 194–206. Springer, Cham (2019). https://doi.org/10.1007/978-3-030-32381-3_16

35. Talita, A., Wiguna, A.: Implementasi algoritma long short-term memory (LSTM) untuk mendeteksi ujaran kebencian (hate speech) pada kasus pilpres 2019. MATRIK: Jurnal Manajemen, Teknik Informatika dan Rekayasa Komputer **19**(1), 37–44 (2019). https://doi.org/10.30812/matrik.v19i1.495

36. Travis, A.: Anti-Muslim hate crime surges after Manchester and London bridge. The Guardian (2017). https://www.theguardian.com/society/2017/jun/20/anti-muslim-hate-surges-after-manchester-and-london-bridge-attacks

37. Vaswani, A., et al.: Attention is all you need. In: Guyon, I., et al (eds.) Advances in Neural Information Processing Systems, vol. 30. Curran Associates, Inc. (2017). https://proceedings.neurips.cc/paper/2017/file/3f5ee243547dee91fbd053c1c4a845aa-Paper.pdf

38. Watanabe, H., Bouazizi, M., Ohtsuki, T.: Hate speech on Twitter: a pragmatic approach to collect hateful and offensive expressions and perform hate speech detection. IEEE Access **6**, 13825–13835 (2018). https://doi.org/10.1109/ACCESS.2018.2806394

39. Zhang, Z., Luo, L.: Hate speech detection: a solved problem? The challenging case of long tail on Twitter. Semantic Web **10**(5), 925–945 (2019). https://doi.org/10.3233/SW-180338

Topic Identification of Instagram Hashtag Sets for Image Tagging: An Empirical Assessment

Stamatios Giannoulakis[✉][ID] and Nicolas Tsapatsoulis[ID]

Department of Communication and Internet Studies, Cyprus University of
Technology, 30, Arch. Kyprianos Street, 3036 Limassol, Cyprus
{s.giannoulakis,nicolas.tsapatsoulis}@cut.ac.cy

Abstract. Images are an important part of collection items in any digital library. Mining information from social media networks, and especially the Instagram, for Image description has recently gained increased research interest. In the current study we extend previous work on the use of topic modelling for mining tags from Instagram hashtags for image content description. We examine whether the hashtags accompanying Instagram photos, collected via a common query hashtag (called 'subject' hereafter), vary in a statistically significant manner depending on the similarity of their visual content. In the experiment we use the topics mined from Instagram hashtags from a set of Instagram images corresponding to 26 different query hashtags and classified into two categories per subject, named as 'relevant' and 'irrelevant' depending on the similarity of their visual content. Two different set of users, namely trained students and generic crowd, assess the topics presented to them as word clouds. To invest whether there is significant difference between the word clouds of the images considered as visually relevant to the query subject compared to those considered visually irrelevant. At the same time we investigate whether the word cloud interpretations of trained students and generic crowd differ. The data collected through this empirical study are analyzed with use of independent samples t-test and Pearson rho. We conclude that the word clouds of the relevant Instagram images are much more easily interpretable by both the trained students and the crowd. The results also show some interesting variations across subjects which are analysed and discussed in detail throughout the paper. At the same time the interpretations of trained students and the generic crowd are highly correlated, denoting that no specific training is required to mine relevant tags from Instagram hashtags to describe the accompanied Instagram photos.

Keywords: Digital libraries · Topic modelling · Instagram hashtags · Image tagging · Visualisation

© Springer Nature Switzerland AG 2022
E. Garoufallou et al. (Eds.): MTSR 2021, CCIS 1537, pp. 159–170, 2022.
https://doi.org/10.1007/978-3-030-98876-0_14

1   Introduction

Metadata and tagging are key factors in digital libraries. They are used to describe and organize resources [21] allowing the library users to effectively locate and retrieve digital items. On the other hand, adding manual description to digital items, such as images, is time-consuming and subject to human interpretation. The text that describes images, in many digital library collections, is poor and limits retrieval effectiveness due to dissimilarities between the terms users use to locate images and the (limited) or maybe irrelevant text used to describe those images [16]. Thus, alternative techniques that can reduce human subjectivity and enrich image descriptions in digital libraries are highly desirable and led to dedicated research field known as Automatic Image Annotation.

Social media, and especially the Instagram, contain huge amounts of images which are commented through hashtags by their creators/owners [6]. In a previous work [9] we have found that a portion of 55% of Instagram hashtags are directly related with the visual content of the photos they accompany. Since then, in a series of studies we have proposed several Instagram hashtag filtering techniques to effectively identify those Instagram hashtag subsets [8,10]. An innovative topic modelling scheme is one of our newest developments towards that aim [2,20].

Probabilistic topic models (PTM) algorithms can discover the main themes for a vast and unstructured collection of documents. Thus, we can use PTM to organize several documents based on the identified themes. PTM is suitable for any kind of data, and researchers used these algorithms to locate patterns in genetic data, images, and social networks. Topic modelling is an effective way to organize and summarize electronic archives something impossible to achieve with human annotation [4].

Let us now assume that we want to create a set of Instagram photos in order to collect the hashtags and locate the relevant photos. Instagram has a search box and you can locate based on account name and Instagram hashtags. So, we queried with specific hashtag (i.e. #dog), which in the current work we name *subject*. Hashtags accompany images were collected automatically using the Beautiful Soup[1] library of Python We can see the hashtags of an Instagram image as a textual representation of it and in this way Instagram hashtag collections of images can be seen as textual documents. So we can analyse via topic modelling techniques once textual preprocessing, such as word splitting is applied first. Since with topic modelling we can measure the most relevant terms of a topic we can assume that by applying topic modelling on the hashtags sets [20] we can derive a set of terms best describing the collection of images based on a specific subject.

Word clouds are used to depict word frequencies derived from a text or a set of text documents. The size of each depicted word in the cloud depends on its frequency: words that occur often are shown larger than words with rare appearance while stopwords are removed. Thus, a Word cloud can be seen as a

---

[1] https://www.crummy.com/software/BeautifulSoup/bs4/doc/.

synopsis of the main themes contained in textual information [3,13]. Word clouds became popular in practical situations and are commonly used for summarizing a set of reviews presented as free texts (i.e., "open questions").

In order to construct a classic word cloud it is necessary to calculate the word frequencies in a text or set of texts. However, word frequencies can be replaced by any other measure that reflects the importance of a word in a text document. In that respect word clouds can be used for the visualisation of topics derived from a collection of texts. Topic models infer probability distributions from frequency statistics, which can reflect co-occurrence relationships of words [7]. Through topic modeling we can reveal the subject of a document or a set of documents and present in a summarized fashion what the document(a) is/are about. This is why topic modeling is, nowadays, a state-of-the-art technique to organize, understand and summarize large collections of textual information [1].

In this paper we investigate how the crowd and students understands the topics derived from the hashtag sets of Instagram photos that were grouped together by a common query hashtag which we call subject. The topics are illustrated as word clouds with the queried hashtags (subjects) hidden and the crowd is asked to guess the hidden hashtag providing their best four guesses. The aim of the current work is to examine the performance accuracy interpretation, in topic modeling we created from Instagram hashtags, between crowd and the students and second, to investigate if there is significant correlation on the way the crowd and the students interpret the word clouds of Instagram hashtags. If crowd and students choice coincide with the subject of the word cloud, we have a good indication that the word cloud words, indeed, related with the subject. We believe that through this meta-analysis we gain useful insights on whether we can use words mined form Instagram hashtags [9] as description metadata for digital libraries. To the best of our knowledge this is the first study that examine how to locate the relevant Instagram hashtags for image metadata description in digital libraries.

2 Related Work

Ibba and Pani in their research to formalize knowledge through the creation of a metadata taxonomy they developed a method to integrate and combine Instagram metadata and hashtags [12]. Ibba and Pani also mention our previous work [9] that 55% Instagram hashtags are related to the visual content of the image but the researchers do not analyse how we can locate only the relevant hashtags. Sfakakis et al. [18] propose document subject indexing with the help of Topic Modeling and automated labeling processes. The authors implemented LDA toping modelling to a corpus of papers in order to produce the topic models. To evaluate the topic models they created the researchers asked an expert to label the same corpus of papers and they concluded that human labeling is similar to topic modelling.

Suadaa and Purwarianti [19] in their study they aim to solve the problem of document classification they examined a combination of LDA and Term

Frequency-Inverse Cluster Frequency. To conduct their experiment the used Indonesian digital library documents, 113 documents from digital library of STIS and 60 documents from digital library of ITB. The researchers propose LDA in combination with Term Frequency-Inverse Cluster Frequency is the best option for labeling. Hall *et al.* [11] they focus on automatic clustering techniques and if we can use them to support the exploration of digital libraries. The researchers investigated LDA, K-Means and OPTICS clustering using collection of 28,133 historical images with meta-data provided by the University of St Andrews Library. They created models for the three aforementioned algorithms based on photos title and description and those models were evaluated by the crowd. The authors concluded that we can apply LDA-based models in large digital libraries.

Rohani *et al.* [17] used topic modeling to extract topic facets from a dataset consisting of 90527 records related with the domain of aviation and airport management. They developed an LDA topic modeling method while the data were pre-processed by removing punctuation and stop words. They identified five main topics and then they examined which one of the topics was the dominant each date. The performance of topic modelling was qualitatively evaluated by domain experts who were asked to investigate the detected topics along with the discovered keywords and compare the results with their own interpretation about the top topics of studied datasets. The topics assigned by domain experts are similar to the LDA topic modeling.

The previous discussion shows that topic modelling is suitable techniques to locate/derive appropriate summary description and/or tags for documents and images. Word clouds have been mainly used for visualisation purposes but the appropriateness of this visualisation format was never assessed. Thus, in addition to the application perspective of our work, which emphasizes on mining terms from Instagram hashtags for image tagging, the crowd-based and student-based meta analysis of word clouds provides also useful insights about their appropriateness for topic visualisation. Some of the reported works applied topic modelling to summarize textual information using the classic LDA approach. Our topic modeling algorithm [20] is quite different and tailored to the specific case of Instagram posts. Photos and associated hashtags are modelled as a bipartite network and the importance of each hashtags is computed via its authority score obtained by applying the HITS algorithm [10].

3   Word Clouds Creation

As already mentioned the main purpose of the current work is to investigate and discuss the crowd-based and student-based interpretation of word clouds created from Instagram hashtags. A dataset of 520 Instagram posts (photos along with their associated hashtags) was created by querying with 26 different hashtags (see Table 1) which in the context of the current work are called *subjects*. For each subject we collected 10 visually relevant to the subject and 10 visually irrelevant image posts to the subject (images and associated hashtags) leading to a total of 520 (260 relevant and 260 non-relevant) images and 8199 hashtags (2883 for relevant images and 5316 non-relevant images).

All collected hashtags were undergone preprocessing so as to derive meaningful tokens (words in English). Instragram hashtags, are unstructured and ungrammatical, and it is important to use linguistic processing to (a) remove stophashtags [8], that is hashtags that are used to fool the search results of the Instagram platform, (b) split a composite hashtag to its consisting words (e.g. the hashtag '#spoilyourselfthisseason' should be split into four words: 'spoil', 'yourself', 'this', 'season'), (c) remove stopwords that are produced in the previous stage (e.g. the word 'this' in the previous example), (d) perform spelling checks to account for (usually intentionally) misspelled hashtags (e.g. '#headaband', '#headabandss' should be changed to '#headband'), and (e) perform lemmatization to merge words that share the same or similar meaning. Preprocessing was conducted with the help of Natural Language ToolKit (NLTK - https://www.nltk.org/), Wordnet[2] and personally developed code in Python.

By finishing all pre-processing steps we ended up with a token set for each one of the 520 Instagram photos. Instagram photos and the associated hashtag sets belonging to a common subject were grouped together and modeled as a bipartite network. Then, topic models were created for each one of the subjects following the approach described in [20]. A total of 52 (26 relevant and 26 irrelevant) different topic models were developed. The importance of each token within a topic model was assessed by applying the HITS algorithm as described in [10]. For each one of the topics a word cloud was created. The token corresponding to the associated subject (query hashtag) was excluded in order to examine whether the crowd and students would guess it correctly (see Sect. 4 for the details). Word clouds visualization was done with the help of WordCloud[3] Python library.

4   Interpretation of Word Clouds

Crowd-based interpretation of word clouds was conducted with the aid of the *Appen*[4] crowdsourcing platform (see Fig. 1a) and student-based interpretation was performed with the aid of the learning platform *Moodle*[5] (see Fig. 1b). We choose the interpretation from cloud because we want to take advantage of the collective intelligence. The viability of crowdsourced image annotation was examined and verified by several researchers ([5, 14, 15]). Moreover, the student interpretation was conducted by undergraduate students of the department of Communication & Internet Studies of the Cyprus University of Technology. Students received a treatment of training to perform annotation of word clouds. During a course the students were informed about word cloud creation and topic model.

The word clouds were presented to crowd participants which were asked to select one to four of the subjects that best match the shown word cloud

---

[2] https://wordnet.princeton.edu/.
[3] https://amueller.github.io/word_cloud/.
[4] https://appen.com/.
[5] https://elearning.cut.ac.cy/.

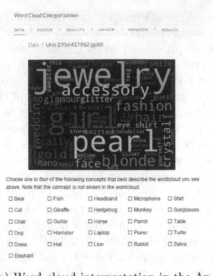

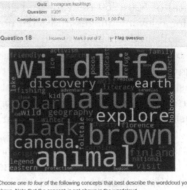

(a) Word cloud interpretation in the Appen crowdsourcing platform

(b) Word cloud interpretation in Moodle

Fig. 1. Question examples for *Appen* and *Moodle*

according to their interpretation. The participants were clearly informed that the token corresponding to the correct subject was not shown in the cloud. The same questions were presented to the students and had to choose between one to four subjects that best match the word cloud they see. Also, we informed the students that the correct subject was not included in the word cloud.

Every word cloud for the crowd was judged by at least 30 annotators (contributors in Appen's terminology) while eight word clouds were also used as 'gold questions' for quality assurance, i.e., identification of dishonest annotators and task difficulty assessment. The correct answer(s) for the gold clouds were provided to the crowdsourcing platform and all participants had to judge those clouds. However, gold clouds were presented to the contributors in random order and they could not know which of the clouds were the gold ones. A total of 165 contributors from more than 25 different countries participated in the experiment. The cost per judgement was set to $0.01 and the task was completed in less than six hours. A total of 25 students annotations were collected.

Not all word clouds present the same difficulty in interpretation. Thus, in order to quantitatively estimate that difficulty per subject we used the typical accuracy metric, that is the percentage of correct subject identifications by the crowd and the students. By correct identification we mean that a contributor or a student had selected the right subject within her/his one to four choices. We see for instance in Table 1 that the accuracy for crowd of the guitar word cloud is 93%. This means that 93% of the contributors included the word 'guitar' in their interpretation for that word cloud, regardless the number (1 to 4) of contributor choices. The accuracy above was also employed for irrelevant word clouds. For instance, 44% of students chose in their interpretation 'lion' for irrelevant word cloud that derived based on the hashtag #lion, and the posts were visually irrelevant with that subject.

Table 1. Topic identification accuracy for word clouds created using visually relevant (Relev.) and irrelevant (Irre.) Instagram photos

Subject	Relevant		Irrelevant	
	Crowd (%)	Student (%)	Crowd (%)	Student (%)
Guitar	93	88	87	84
Piano	70	80	47	72
Microphone	57	92	67	80
Bear	43	76	0	0
Elephant	37	48	0	0
Giraffe	63	72	3	16
Lion	60	76	67	44
Monkey	33	36	0	0
Zebra	57	68	3	0
Dress	80	84	60	76
Hat	7	40	3	52
Headband	30	24	17	80
Shirt	33	48	53	56
Sunglasses	67	68	13	36
Chair	43	60	47	80
Laptop	100	96	80	92
Table	73	84	77	84
Cat	90	92	17	60
Dog	87	92	0	0
Fish	100	92	93	84
Hamster	3	40	7	36
Parrot	87	88	90	84
Rabbit	77	72	7	0
Turtle	20	60	20	52
Hedgehog	0	12	0	0
Horse	87	88	7	4

5   Results and Discussion

The accuracy of interpretation for all word clouds is presented in Table 1 while summary statistics are presented in Table 2. In order to better facilitate the

Table 2. Summary statistics for the accuracy of identification

Subject	Mean (%)	St. Dev. (%)	Min (%)	Max (%)
Student relevant	68	23	12	96
Crowd relevant	58	30	0	100
Student irrelevant	45	35	0	92
Crowd irrelevant	33	34	0	93

Table 3. Independent samples t-test, $N = 26$ subjects in all cases

Group	Mean (%)	St. Dev. (%)	Stan. Err. (%)	t	p
Relevant (Students)	68	23	5	25	.003
Irrelevant (Students)	45	35	7	25	
Relevant (Crowd)	58	30	6	25	.001
Irrelevant (Crowd)	33	34	6	25	

discussion that follows the subjects (query hashtags) were divided into six categories: (a) **Music**: Guitar, Piano, Microphone (b) **Wild animals**: Bear, Elephant, Giraffe, Lion, Monkey, Zebra (c) **Fashion**: Dress, Hat, Headband, Shirt, Sunglasses (d) **Office**: Chair, Laptop, Table, (e) **Pets**: Cat, Dog, Fish, Hamster, Parrot, Rabbit, Turtle (f) **Miscellaneous**: Hedgehog, Horse.

In order to answer the main research questions of our study formulate three null hypotheses as follows:

H_{01}: *There is no significant difference of word cloud interpretation of hashtags sets mined from relevant and irrelevant images by the trained students.*

H_{02}: *There is no significant difference of word cloud interpretation of hashtags sets, mined from relevant and irrelevant images, by the generic crowd.*

H_{03}: *There is no significant correlation on the way the generic crowd and trained students interpret the word clouds mined from Instagram hashtags.*

In Table 3 we see the paired-sampled t-test with the aid of SPSS was conducted to compare the interpretation in relevant and irrelevant word clouds conditions in both the crowd and students. There was a significant difference in the scores for relevant (Mean Crowd = 68%, Mean Student = 58%) and irrelevant (Mean Crowd = 33%, Mean Student = 45%). Thus the null hypotheses H_{01} and H_{02} are rejected at a significance level $a = .003$ for students and $a = .001$ for the crowd.

Regarding the third null hypothesis, for a significant level $a = 0.01$ the critical value for the correlation coefficient (two tail test, $df = 50$) is $r_c = 0.354$. By computing the correlation coefficient (Pearson rho) of the mean accuracy values per subject of the crowd and the students we find $r = 0.861$. Thus, $r > r_c$ and the null hypothesis (H_{03}) is rejected at a significance level $a = 0.01$, denoting that the way word clouds are interpreted by the trained students and the crowd is highly correlated.

We see in Table 1 that the interpretation accuracy varies within and across categories. As we explain later through specific examples, there are three main parameters which affect the difficulty of interpretation. The first one is the conceptual context for a specific term. It is very easy, for instance, to define a clear conceptual context for the term fish but very difficult to define clear conceptual contexts for terms such as hat and hedgehog. This difficulty is, obviously, reflected in the use of hashtags that accompany photos presenting those terms. As a result the corresponding word clouds do not provide the textual context and hints that allow the correct interpretation of word clouds. Thus, textual context and key tokens in the word clouds is the second parameter affecting the difficulty of interpretation. Concepts such as dog, cat and horse are far more familiar to everyday people and students than concepts such as hedgehog and hamster.

In the following we present and discuss some representative/interesting examples for each one of the six categories mentioned above.

The word clouds in the Music category have very high scores of interpretation accuracy. Music related terms share a strong conceptual context which results in clear textual contexts in the Instagram hashtags. In Fig. 2a we see the word cloud for the subject 'microphone'. Tokens like band, singer, music, singer and stage create a strong and clear textual content. Thus, the annotators, 57% for crowd and 92% for students, correctly chose microphone to interpret the word cloud. Moreover, the 'microphone' word cloud tokens had as a results the crowd and the students to choose also guitar and piano.

(a) Word cloud for the 'microphone' subject   (b) Word cloud for the 'monkey' subject

Fig. 2. Word clouds for the 'microphone' and 'monkey' subject

The monkey word cloud (see Fig. 2b) was in fact a confusing one. The most prominent tokens were art, animal and nature while some other terms such as artist, artwork, and work could also confuse the crowd and the students. As a result the accuracy for that category is 33% for crowd and 36% for the students.

In the case of subject 'hat' (see word cloud in Fig. 3) we have a situation where there are many different conceptual contexts. As a result, the hashtags appeared in different Instagram photos differ significantly and the resulting word cloud is confusing. We see that the most prominent tokens in the cloud are blogger, style, sun, and beach (obviously these are concepts shown in some of the Instagram photos grouped under the subject 'hat'). There is no doubt that the subject 'hat' fits well with those terms. However, the same terms fit well or even better to other subjects such as 'sunglasses' and dress that had as result the accuracy was not high for students and crowd (7% for crowd and 40% for students).

(a) Word cloud for the 'hat' subject   (b) Word cloud for the 'chair' subject

Fig. 3. Word clouds the subjects 'hat' and 'chair'

The case of hedgehog is a classic example showing that the familiarity with a concept affects the difficulty in interpretation of the word cloud derived from Instagram hashtags. While in the word cloud (see Fig. 4a) the words pygmy, pet and animal are by far the most important ones none of the participants selected the right subject. It appears that the contributors and students were non-familiar with the word pygmy. The African pygmy hedgehog is the species often used as pet.

(a) Word cloud for the 'hedgehog' subject (b) Word cloud for the 'hamster' subject

Fig. 4. Word clouds for the subjects 'hedgehog' and 'hamster'

6   Conclusion

In the current work we have presented a crowd-based and student-based interpretation of word clouds created from Instagram hashtags. The main purpose was to examine if we can locate appropriate tags from Instagram photos that share (and grouped together) a common hashtag (called subject in the current work) for image metadata description. A statistical significant difference between the interpretation accuracy of relevant and irrelevant word clouds was found. This mean that Instagram images of similar visual content share hashtags that are related to the subject. In addition to these we concluded that there is correlation in interpretation of trained students and the generic crowd, denoting that no specific training is mandatory to mine relevant tags from Instagram to describe photos. Moreover, since there is no difference in the interpretation accuracy performance of generic crowd and trained students we have an indication that indeed these hashtags can describe an image. In the results analysis we concluded that there is significant variation in the difficulty of interpretation of word clouds corresponding to different terms and we named three parameters affecting this interpretation: conceptual context, textual context and familiarity with concept. Terms that have a clear conceptual context ('fish', 'guitar', 'laptop'), can be easily identified. On the contrary, term without clear conceptual context like 'hat' confused students and the crowd. In addition, terms like 'hedgehog' that students and crowd were no familiar had a difficult to interpret. The main conclusion is that we can use topic model to mine information from Instagram tags for image description metadata.

References

1. Alami, N., Meknassi, M., En-nahnahi, N., El Adlouni, Y., Ammor, O.: Unsupervised neural networks for automatic Arabic text summarization using document clustering and topic modeling. Expert Syst. Appl. **172**, 114652 (2021)
2. Argyrou, A., Giannoulakis, S., Tsapatsoulis, N.: Topic modelling on Instagram hashtags: an alternative way to Automatic Image Annotation? In: 13th International Workshop on Semantic and Social Media Adaptation & Personalization (SMAP 2018), pp. 61–67, IEEE, Piscataway (2018)
3. Atenstaedt, R.: Word cloud analysis of the BJGP: 5 years on. Br. J. Gen. Pract. **67**(658), 231–232 (2017)
4. Blei, D.: Probabilistic topic models. Commun. ACM **55**, 77–84 (2012)
5. Cabrall, C., et al.: Validity and reliability of naturalistic driving scene categorization Judgments from crowdsourcing. Accid. Anal. Prev. **114**, 25–33 (2018)
6. Daer, A., Hoffman, R., Goodman, S.: Rhetorical functions of hashtag forms across social media applications. Commun. Des. Q. **3**, 12–16 (2015)
7. Fu, X., Wang, T., Li, J., Yu C., Liu, W.: Improving distributed word representation and topic model by word-topic mixture model. In: Durrant, R.J., Kim, K.-E.b (eds.) Proceedings of the Asian Conference on Machine Learning, vol. 63, pp. 190–205 (2016)

8. Giannoulakis, S., Tsapatsoulis, N.: Defining and identifying stophashtags in insta-gram. In: Angelov, P., Manolopoulos, Y., Iliadis, L., Roy, A., Vellasco, M. (eds.) INNS 2016. AISC, vol. 529, pp. 304–313. Springer, Cham (2017). https://doi.org/10.1007/978-3-319-47898-2_31

9. Giannoulakis, S., Tsapatsoulis, N.: Instagram hashtags as image annotation meta-data. In: Chbeir, R., Manolopoulos, Y., Maglogiannis, I., Alhajj, R. (eds.) AIAI 2015. IAICT, vol. 458, pp. 206–220. Springer, Cham (2015). https://doi.org/10.1007/978-3-319-23868-5_15

10. Giannoulakis, S., Tspatsoulis, N.: Filtering Instagram hashtags through crowd-tagging and the HITS algorithm. IEEE Trans. Comput. Soc. Syst. 6(3), 592–603 (2019)

11. Hall, M., Clough, P., Stevenson, M.: Evaluating the use of clustering for auto-matically organising digital library collections. In: Zaphiris, P., Buchanan, G., Rasmussen, E., Loizides, F. (eds.) TPDL 2012. LNCS, vol. 7489, pp. 323–334. Springer, Heidelberg (2012). https://doi.org/10.1007/978-3-642-33290-6_35

12. Ibba, S., Pani, F.E.: Digital libraries: the challenge of integrating instagram with a taxonomy for content management. Future Internet 8(2), 16 (2016)

13. Lohmann, S., Heimerl, F., Bopp, F., Burch, M., Ertl, T.: ConcentriCloud: word cloud visualization for multiple text documents. In: Banissi, E., et al. (eds.) Pro-ceedings of the 19th International Conference on Information Visualisation, pp. 114–120. IEEE, Piscataway (2015)

14. Maier-Hein, L., et al.: Can masses of non-experts train highly accurate image classifiers? In: Golland, P., Hata, N., Barillot, C., Hornegger, J., Howe, R. (eds.) MICCAI 2014. LNCS, vol. 8674, pp. 438–445. Springer, Cham (2014). https://doi.org/10.1007/978-3-319-10470-6_55

15. Mitry, D., et al.: The accuracy and reliability of crowdsource annotations of digital retinal images. Transl. Vis. Sci. Technol. 5, 6 (2016)

16. Petrelli, D., Clough, P.: Analysing user's queries for cross-language image retrieval from digital library collections. Electron. Libr. 30, 197–219 (2012)

17. Rohani, V., Shayaa, S., Babanejaddehaki, G.: Topic modeling for social media content: a practical approach. In: 3rd International Conference on Computer and Information Sciences (ICCOINS) a Conference of World Engineering, Science & Technology Congress (ESTCON), pp. 397–402. IEEE, Piscataway (2016)

18. Sfakakis, M., Papachristopoulos, L., Zoutsou, K., Tsakonas, G., Papatheodorou, C.: Automated subject indexing of domain specific collections using word embed-dings and general purpose Thesauri. In: Garoufallou, E., Fallucchi, F., William De Luca, E. (eds.) MTSR 2019. CCIS, vol. 1057, pp. 103–114. Springer, Cham (2019). https://doi.org/10.1007/978-3-030-36599-8_9

19. Suadaa, L., Purwarianti, A.: Combination of Latent Dirichlet Allocation (LDA) and Term Frequency-Inverse Cluster Frequency (TFxICF) in Indonesian text clus-tering with labeling. In: 4th International Conference on Information and Commu-nication Technology. IEEE, Piscataway (2016)

20. Tsapatsoulis, N.: Image retrieval via topic modelling of Instagram hashtags. In: 15th International Workshop on Semantic and Social Media Adaptation & Person-alization, pp. 1–6. IEEE, Piscataway (2020)

21. Xie, I., Matusiak, K.: Metadata. Discover Digital Libraries: Theory and Practice, pp. 129–170. Elsevier, Amsterdam (2016)

Integration of Ontologies with Decentralized Autonomous Organizations Development: A Systematic Literature Review

María-Cruz Valiente(✉) and David Rozas

Institute of Knowledge Technology, Universidad Complutense de Madrid, Madrid, Spain
{mcvaliente,drozas}@ucm.es

Abstract. This paper presents a systematic literature review of the integration of ontologies into the Decentralized Autonomous Organization (DAO) development process. The review extracted data from 34 primary studies dealing with ontologies in the blockchain domain. DAO has become a key concept for the development of blockchain-based decentralized software systems. DAOs are seen as a positive alternative for organizations interested in the adoption of decentralized, reliable and transparent governance, as well as attracting the interest of academic research. However, there is no common understanding or generally accepted formal definition of a DAO, and the guidelines that provide support for the adoption and development of DAOs are limited to a few key references that lack the computational semantics needed to enable their automated validation, simulation or execution. Thus, the objective of this paper is to provide an unbiased and up-to-date review related to the integration of ontologies within DAOs which helps to identify new research opportunities and take advantage of this integration from a blockchain-based decentralized perspective.

Keywords: Ontology · DAO · Decentralized autonomous organization · Blockchain · Smart contract · Systematic literature review

1 Introduction

In the last decade, Decentralized Autonomous Organizations (DAOs) have gained increasing attention in industry and, in general, in the academic and public debate (e.g. American CryptoFed DAO[1] has been officially registered as the first DAO in Wyoming [1]). DAOs are being explored as a means of supporting organizations that ensure sharing, security, transparency, and auditability, making their governance or business models truly global without any central controlling authority or middleman.

DAOs appeared in the context of decentralized solutions with the creation of Ethereum [2], a general-purpose blockchain-based computing platform, as a way to explore new governance rules which could be automated, immutable and transparently embedded in a blockchain.

---

[1] https://www.americancryptofed.org/.

© Springer Nature Switzerland AG 2022
E. Garoufallou et al. (Eds.): MTSR 2021, CCIS 1537, pp. 171–184, 2022.
https://doi.org/10.1007/978-3-030-98876-0_15

In Ethereum, through the use of smart contracts (i.e. small pieces of code deployed on the blockchain and executed in a decentralized way by all the nodes in the network), DAOs can implement governance models and provide services (or resources) to third parties without the need for any intermediary [3].

However, DAO is still a term under development and it can be understood differently depending on the domain and the platform used [4, 5]. In this context, Liu et al. [6] identify and classify different proposals and perspectives closely related to the combination of DAO and blockchain technologies. Although this work could be a valuable source of information for the creation of ontologies related to DAO development, the review is not focused on the formalization process of this domain.

Currently, Moloch DAO [7], a DAO created to fund Ethereum 2.0 grants, and Aragon [8], a DAO that has implemented the most popular Ethereum-based framework for building DAOs, could be considered as de facto references, but they lack the computational semantics needed to enable their automated validation, simulation or execution.

In order to address this problem, ontologies have the potential to provide an agreed and common understanding of the term. Ontologies are widely used in the area of Software Engineering dealing with the process of software modeling aimed at the improvement of the software development process. An ontology is a formal term with a specific meaning from the real world and a related set of assumptions about that meaning [9]. More formally, an ontology defines the vocabulary of a problem domain and a set of constraints (axioms or rules) on how terms can be combined to model specific domains. Furthermore, ontologies are machine-processable models that have been used for decades to represent knowledge from our surroundings, producing domain-specific abstractions and an agreed understanding of the domain of interest.

Therefore, it seems that the integration of ontologies within the DAO domain may help software engineers and researchers understand, manage and build these types of complex blockchain-based decentralized organizations. That is, ontologies may provide a shared domain of conceptualizations representing knowledge that enable software engineers to model the problem as well as the solution for the subject of their investigations. As a result, ontologies have the potential to foster interoperability and support the extension of practices. In the existing literature, we find discussions about the contributions of ontologies to the implementation of decentralized approaches, for example, the research carried out by [10–13], among others.

Since we are interested in providing new solutions which deliver real benefits to developers of DAOs using ontologies, it is important to determine what type of research is being carried out and how it is conducted. Therefore, this paper presents a systematic literature review of the existing research related to the integration of ontologies into DAO development. The systematic literature review has been carried out following and adapting the protocols proposed in [14].

In this paper, Sect. 2 describes the plan of this systematic literature review, the research question, the sources used for the selection of primary studies, the search strings, the selection criteria and process, and the data that were considered for each primary study. Subsequently, Sect. 3 lists the selected primary studies. Based on the research questions, the discussion of the results is presented in Sect. 4. Finally, Sect. 5 contains the conclusion.

2 Systematic Literature Review Planning

2.1 Research Question

Since the objective of this systematic literature review is the identification of solutions related to the integration of ontologies into DAO development, the research question that was addressed by this work was the following: How can we use ontologies with blockchain-based decentralized technologies in order to support the adoption and building of DAOs?

2.2 Search Strategy

The selection of primary studies was based on a search of exclusively electronic sources. The primary studies selected were acquired from the following sources (in alphabetic order): (1) ACM Digital Library, (2) Elsevier Science Direct, (3) Google Scholar (this source was only used for searching specific papers that were cited in other primary studies), (4) IEEE Xplore, and (5) SpringerLink. These electronic sources were selected because they represent an important reference for software engineers and the industry in general.

From the research question, several search strings were defined: (1) "DAO" AND "Ontology"; (2) "Decentralized application" AND "Ontology"; (3) "Smart contract" AND "Ontology"; (4) "DAO" AND "Knowledge Graph"; (5) "Decentralized application" AND "Knowledge Graph"; and (6) "Smart contract" AND "Knowledge Graph".

It is worth highlighting two aspects regarding the search strategy. Firstly, the term "knowledge graph" was included since it was employed as a synonym of the term "ontology" in several articles. Secondly, the sources do not distinguish between singular and plural forms of the terms (e.g. ACM Digital Library). As a result, only singular terms were employed.

2.3 Primary Studies Selection

As recommended by [14], the primary studies selection was based on specific inclusion and exclusion criteria. The inclusion criteria considered studies where ontologies are used in blockchain-based decentralized approaches concerning the development of DAOs. These studies must provide contributions of ontologies to the DAO development process.

On the other hand, the exclusion criteria considered studies about DAO development and ontologies, in which there was no relation between them, or papers about blockchain-based decentralized approaches and ontologies, in which there was no relation to DAO development. Papers in which ontologies are used to improve the building of blockchain-based decentralized applications, but whose improvement is not related to the integration of ontologies within the DAO do-main, were also excluded.

The inclusion and exclusion criteria were applied to the title and abstract in order to determine if the research was considered relevant for the goals of this systematic literature review. However, when the title and abstract alone proved insufficient to determine the relevance of a text, the full text was reviewed.

The selection process for studies entailed several steps: (1) one researcher (the first author of this paper) applied the search strategy to identify potential primary studies, (2) several researchers checked titles and abstracts of all potential primary studies against the inclusion and exclusion criteria. If the title and abstract were not enough to determine how relevant a primary study was, then researchers reviewed the full text, and (3) any uncertainty in primary studies was discussed among the authors of this paper or with other researchers who have expertise in this domain. Each primary study remaining after the selection process of the systematic literature review was reviewed in detail and a review summary was written for each paper. The information of a review summary is defined in Table 1.

Table 1. Paper review summary.

Property	Value
Reference	Primary study ID
Source	The electronic source(s) where the primary study was found
Relevance	The relevance of the primary study to the research question (i.e., how well the primary study answers the research questions): {low, medium, high}
Title	The title of the primary study
Authors	The author(s) of the primary study
Publication	The details of the publication
Abstract	A summary of the primary study
Comments	Remarks and additional notes about the primary study

3 Data Synthesis

In recent years, there has been a growing effort to formalize the knowledge that under-lies blockchain-based decentralized applications. However, it has been difficult to find relevant contributions and real implementations in this field of study. Most of them were blockchain-based conceptual or theoretical contributions pending validation or imple-mentation of the proposed solutions. However, we included papers that, although focused on other topics not directly associated with DAOs, were considered as references for the integration of ontologies into the DAO development process.

The electronic sources provided 682 results. After applying the inclusion and exclu-sion criteria, 34 papers were considered to be primary studies for the research question. The total number of papers and the number of primary studies obtained from each electronic source can be seen in Table 2.

Table 2. Relevant information obtained from the electronic sources.

Electronic source	Papers (*)	Primary studies (**)
ACM Digital Library	61 ("DAO" AND "Ontology") 3 ("Decentralized application" AND "Ontology") 19 ("Smart contract" AND "Ontology") 5 ("DAO" AND "Knowledge Graph") 1 ("Decentralized application" AND "Knowledge Graph") 3 ("Smart contract" AND "Knowledge Graph")	9
Elsevier ScienceDirect	258 ("DAO" AND "Ontology") 15 ("Decentralized application" AND "Ontology") 56 ("Smart contract" AND "Ontology") 2 ("DAO" AND "Knowledge Graph") 2 ("Decentralized application" AND "Knowledge Graph") 9 ("Smart contract" AND "Knowledge Graph")	6
Google Scholar		2
IEEE Xplore	11 ("DAO" AND "Ontology") 3 ("Decentralized application" AND "Ontology") 10 ("Smart contract" AND "Ontology") 0 ("DAO" AND "Knowledge Graph") 0 ("Decentralized application" AND "Knowledge Graph") 0 ("Smart contract" AND "Knowledge Graph")	8
SpringerLink	41 ("DAO" AND "Ontology") 4 ("Decentralized application" AND "Ontology") 134 ("Smart contract" AND "Ontology") 17 ("DAO" AND "Knowledge Graph") 5 ("Decentralized application" AND "Knowledge Graph") 23 ("Smart contract" AND "Knowledge Graph")	9

(*) Date of search: June 2021.
(**) For a specific source, primary studies that were found in another source are not counted as primary studies.

The complete paper review summaries are excluded from this paper due to space limitation restrictions. Therefore, Table 3 shows the list of primary studies (Authors, Title, Relevance and Source) that were selected after the selection process.

Table 3. Selected studies grouped by source and publication date.

Authors	Title	Relev.	Source
Alex Norta, Anis Ben Othman, Kuldar Taveter	Conflict-Resolution Lifecycles for Governed Decentralized Autonomous Organization Collaboration	High	ACM [10]
Allan Third, John Domingue	Linked Data Indexing of Distributed Ledgers	High	ACM [15]
Michal R. Hoffman	Can Blockchains and Linked Data Advance Taxation?	Medium	ACM [16]
Marco Crepaldi	Why blockchains need the law	Low	ACM [17]
Leepakshi Bindra, Changyuan Lin, Eleni Stroulia, Omid Ardakanian	Decentralized Access Control for Smart Buildings Using Metadata and Smart Contracts	High	ACM [18]
Roberto García, Rosa Gil	Social Media Copyright Management using Semantic Web and Blockchain	High	ACM [19]
Manoharan Ramachandran, Niaz Chowdhury, Allan Third, John Domingue, Kevin Quick, Michelle Bachler	Towards Complete Decentralised Verification of Data with Confidentiality: Different ways to connect Solid Pods and Blockchain	Low	ACM [20]
Haan Johng, Doohwan Kim, Grace Park, Jang-Eui Hong, Tom Hill, Lawrence Chung	Enhancing Business Processes with Trustworthiness using Blockchain: A Goal-Oriented Approach	High	ACM [21]
Hongman Wang, Yongbin Yuan, Fangchun Yang	A Personal Data Determination Method Based On Blockchain Technology and Smart Contract	Low	ACM [22]
Athina-Styliani Kleinaki, Petros Mytis-Gkometh, George Drosatos, Pavlos S. Efraimidis, Eleni Kaldoudi	A Blockchain-Based Notarization Service for Biomedical Knowledge Retrieval	Low	Elsevier [23]
Zhengxin Chen	Understanding Granular Aspects of Ontology for Blockchain Databases	Low	Elsevier [24]

(continued)

Table 3. (*continued*)

Authors	Title	Relev.	Source
Wout J. Hofman	A Methodological Approach for Development and Deployment of Data Sharing in Complex Organizational Supply and Logistics Networks with Blockchain Technology	High	Elsevier [25]
Alex Roehrs, Cristiano André da Costa, Rodrigo da Rosa Righi, Valter Ferreira da Silva, José Roberto Goldim, Douglas C. Schmidt	Analyzing the performance of a blockchain-based personal health record implementation	High	Elsevier [26]
Hans Weigand, Ivars Blums, Joost de Kruijff	Shared Ledger Accounting - Implementing the Economic Exchange pattern	High	Elsevier [27]
Xiaochi Zhou, Mei Qi Lim, Markus Kraft	A Smart Contract-based agent marketplace for the J-Park Simulator - a knowledge graph for the process industry	Low	Elsevier [28]
Henry M. Kim, Marek Laskowski	Toward an Ontology-Driven Blockchain Design for Supply Chain Provenance	High	Google [11]
Henry M. Kim, Marek Laskowski, Ning Nan	A First Step in the Co-Evolution of Blockchain and Ontologies: Towards Engineering an Ontology of Governance at the Blockchain Protocol Level	High	Google [12]
Darra L. Hofman	Legally Speaking: Smart Contracts, Archival Bonds, and Linked Data	High	IEEE [29]
Olivia Choudhury, Nolan Rudolph, Issa Sylla, Noor Fairoza, Amar Das	Auto-Generation of Smart Contracts from Domain-Specific Ontologies and Semantic Rules	High	IEEE [30]
Alex Norta	Self-Aware Smart Contracts with Legal Relevance	High	IEEE [31]
Hamza Baqa, Nguyen B. Truong, Noel Crespi, Gyu Myoung Lee, Franck Le Gall	Semantic Smart Contracts for Blockchain-based Services in the Internet of Things	High	IEEE [32]

(*continued*)

Table 3. (*continued*)

Authors	Title	Relev.	Source
Mengyi Li, Lirong Xiay, Oshani Seneviratne	Leveraging Standards Based Ontological Concepts in Distributed Ledgers: A Healthcare Smart Contract Example	High	IEEE [33]
Wim Laurier	Blockchain Value Networks	High	IEEE [34]
Seung-Min Lee, Soojin Park, Young B. Park	Formal Specification Technique in Smart Contract Verification	High	IEEE [35]
Panos Kudumakis, Thomas Wilmering, Mark Sandler, Víctor Rodríguez-Doncel, Laurent Boch, Jaime Delgado	The Challenge: From MPEG Intellectual Property Rights Ontologies to Smart Contracts and Blockchains	High	IEEE [36]
Alex Norta	Creation of Smart-Contracting Collaborations for Decentralized Autonomous Organizations	Low	SpringerLink [37]
Alex Norta, Lixin Ma, Yucong Duan, Addi Rull, Merit Kõlvart and Kuldar Taveter	eContractual choreography-language properties towards cross-organizational business collaboration	High	SpringerLink [38]
Nanjangud C. Narendra, Alex Norta, Msury Mahunnah, Lixin Ma, Fabrizio Maria Maggi	Sound conflict management and resolution for virtual-enterprise collaborations	High	SpringerLink [39]
Elena García-Barriocanal, Salvador Sánchez-Alonso, Miguel-Angel Sicilia	Deploying Metadata on Blockchain Technologies	Low	SpringerLink [40]
Joost de Kruijff, Hans Weigand	Understanding the Blockchain Using Enterprise Ontology	High	SpringerLink [41]
Joost de Kruijff, Hans Weigand	Ontologies for Commitment-Based Smart Contracts	High	SpringerLink [42]
Jan Ladleif, Mathias Weske	A Unifying Model of Legal Smart Contracts	Low	SpringerLink [43]
Elena García-Barriocanal, Miguel-Ángel Sicilia, Salvador Sánchez-Alonso	The Case for Ontologies in Expressing Decisions in Decentralized Energy Systems	Medium	SpringerLink [44]

(*continued*)

Table 3. (*continued*)

Authors	Title	Relev.	Source
Diogo Silva, Sérgio Guerreiro, Pedro Sousa	Decentralized Enforcement of Business Process Control Using Blockchain	High	SpringerLink [13]

4 Discussion

In this section, we present the relevant information gathered that answers the research question of this systematic literature review: How can ontologies be used with blockchain-based decentralized technologies in order to support the adoption and building of DAOs?

After the analysis and evaluation of the primary studies, we found several approaches that could apply ontologies to DAO development. Most of the studies use ontologies in the context of governance. For example, Garcia and Gil [19] propose the use of an ontology in order to formalize key copyright concepts that, although not applied to DAOs, is suitable for rights management modeling in a specific DAO. Another example can be found in Kim et al. [12], who propose a conceptual design of a governance ontology represented as meta-data tags to be embedded and instantiated in a blockchain-based smart contract solution. We can also find several studies related to the formalization of legal aspects involved in smart contracts such as the implementation of a socio-technical system of rules as established by legal theorists [17], aspects related to the tax gap [16], decentralized peer-to-peer (P2P) economy in terms of obligations and rights [31] and a semantic legal layer [29, 32].

Another line of research is focused on cross-organizational businesses whose governance involves the use of DAOs. In this line, DAOs are employed in the management of eCommunities [10], to access cloud computing services [37], to allow contractual flexibility [38], and to support conflict resolution management [39], to name but a few. In the same context, Silva et al. [13] present a proposal that tackles the problem of traceability and management in collaborative business processes.

Another common approach is the of use ontologies for domain modeling through the implementation of smart contracts which are part of a DAO (e.g. business transactions [25], distributed and interoperable personal records [26] and accounting and financial reporting [27]).

Finally, another general approach, although less explored, proposes ontologies for the modeling of blockchain (and smart contract) concepts such as the work presented in [15], which could provide support for technical issues concerning DAO development.

Figure 1 shows the number of studies focused on each research topic according to the publication year. Since legal aspects and governance rules may be successfully described by ontologies, the 'governance' category represents the most important research topic related to DAO development [45]. It is worth noting that research related to governance started to gain importance particularly since the appearance of the Ethereum platform and the concept of DAO. On the other hand, due to the proliferation of blockchain-based decentralized applications, such as DAOs, research related to domain modeling has seen increasing interest in the last two years.

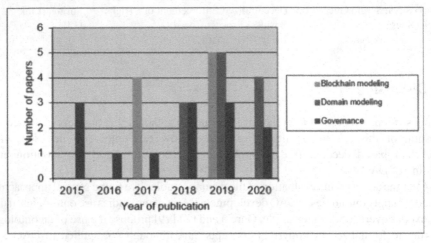

Fig. 1. Number of studies covering each topic based on the publication year.

In summary, from a DAO development perspective, although we could not find proposals that explicitly apply ontologies in the formalization of the term, ontologies could be integrated within DAOs in three ways: (1) using ontologies as a tool for the management of governance in decentralized organizations; (2) using ontologies for business domains or governance rules modeling; and, at a general level, (3) using ontologies as a formalization of technical aspects concerning blockchain technology.

5 Conclusions

Our research responds to an increasing interest in and adoption of DAOs as a new approach for the implementation of blockchain-based online organizations, where establishing a consensus and a common understanding without ambiguities and contradictions (i.e. formalization) is of major importance.

In this paper, we have answered the research question presented in Sect. 2 by offering an insight into recent research on the integration of ontologies into DAO development in order to identify new research challenges to be explored.

This systematic literature review provides up-to-date information on how ontologies could be integrated within DAOs from a blockchain-based decentralized perspective. The findings reveal:

- The contribution that ontologies make to DAO development. That is, how ontologies may help to describe knowledge related to blockchain-based decentralized applications that could be reused to build similar or more complex ones.

- Ontology-based approaches that can be applied across several interrelated blockchain-based decentralized application knowledge areas (e.g. legal aspects, governance rules modeling, technical issues), and that could be extrapolated to DAOs in a seamless manner.
- The existing ontologies created to define specific domains aimed at solving different problems and gaps related interoperability and data sharing in several business scenarios in a blockchain-based decentralized way (e.g. personal and health data, supply and logistics information, and energy systems).

These results indicate a growing interest in the integration of ontologies with different aspects of blockchain-based decentralized applications. We have observed that ontologies could play an important role in the DAO development process. Moreover, the formalization of this term could help to improve the development of tools and frameworks that provide support to adopt this new governance approach.

Acknowledgments. This work was partially supported by the project P2P Models (https://p2p models.eu) funded by the European Research Council ERC-2017-STG [grant no.: 759207]; and by the project Chain Community funded by the Spanish Ministry of Science, Innovation and Universities [grant no.: RTI2018-096820-A-100].

References

1. America's First Legal DAO Approved in Wyoming, 5 July 2021. https://decrypt.co/75222/americas-first-dao-approved-in-wyoming. Accessed 16 Aug 2021
2. Buterin, V.: A next-generation smart contract and decentralized application platform. https://blockchainlab.com/pdf/Ethereum_white_paper-a_next_generation_smart_cont ract_and_decentralized_application_platform-vitalik-buterin.pdf. Accessed 16 Aug 2021
3. Hassan, S.: P2P Models white paper. Decentralized Blockchain-based Organizations for Bootstrapping the Collaborative Economy (2017). https://p2pmodels.eu/wp-content/uploads/whi tepaper_p2pmodels.pdf. Accessed 16 Aug 2021
4. Hassan, S., De Filippi, P.: Decentralized autonomous organization. Internet Policy Rev. **10**(2) (2021). https://doi.org/10.14763/2021.2.1556
5. El Faqir, Y., Arroyo, J., Hassan, S.: An overview of decentralized autonomous organizations on the blockchain. In: Proceedings of the 16th International Symposium on Open Collaboration (OpenSym 2020), New York, NY, USA, Article 11, pp. 1–8. Association for Computing Machinery (2020). https://doi.org/10.1145/3412569.3412579
6. Liu, L., Zhou, S., Huang, H., Zheng, Z.: From technology to society: an overview of blockchain-based DAO. IEEE Open J. Comput. Soc. **2**(1), 204–215. (2021). https://doi.iee ecomputersociety.org/10.1109/OJCS.2021.3072661
7. MolochDAO. https://molochdao.com/. Accessed 16 Aug 2021
8. Aragon. https://aragon.org/. Accessed 16 Aug 2021
9. Guarino, N.: Formal Ontology and Information Systems (1998). http://www.loa.istc.cnr.it/old/Papers/FOIS98.pdf. Accessed 16 Aug 2021
10. Norta, A., Othman, A.B., Taveter, K.: Conflict-resolution lifecycles for governed decentralized autonomous organization collaboration. In: Proceedings of the 2015 2nd International Conference on Electronic Governance and Open Society: Challenges in Eurasia - EGOSE 2015, St. Petersburg, Russian Federation, pp. 244–257. ACM Press. (2015). https://doi.org/10.1145/2846012.2846052

11. Kim, H.M., Laskowski, M.: Towards an ontology-driven blockchain design for supply chain provenance. Int. Syst. Account. Finance Manag. (2018). https://doi.org/10.1002/isaf.1424
12. Kim, H.M., Laskowski, M., Nan, N.: A first step in the co-evolution of blockchain and ontologies: towards engineering an ontology of governance at the blockchain protocol level. arXiv:180102027 (2018)
13. Silva, D., Guerreiro, S., Sousa, P.: Decentralized enforcement of business process control using blockchain. In: Aveiro, D., Guizzardi, G., Guerreiro, S., Guédria, W. (eds.) EEWC 2018. LNBIP, vol. 334, pp. 69–87. Springer, Cham (2019). https://doi.org/10.1007/978-3-030-06097-8_5
14. Kitchenham, B.: Guidelines for performing systematic literature reviews in software engineering (Version 2.3). EBSE Technical report: EBSE-2007-01. Software Engineering Group, School of Computer Science and Mathematics, Keele University, Staffordshire (2007)
15. Third, A., Domingue, J.: Linked data indexing of distributed ledgers. In: Proceedings of the 26th International Conference on World Wide Web Companion - WWW 2017 Companion, Perth, Australia, pp. 1431–1436. ACM Press (2017). https://doi.org/10.1145/3041021.305 3895
16. Hoffman, M.R.: Can blockchains and linked data advance taxation. In: Companion of the Web Conference 2018 - WWW 2018, Lyon, France, pp. 1179–1182. ACM Press (2018). https://doi.org/10.1145/3184558.3191555
17. Crepaldi, M.: Why blockchains need the law: Secondary rules as the missing piece of blockchain governance. In: Proceedings of the Seventeenth International Conference on Artificial Intelligence and Law, Montreal, QC, Canada, pp. 189–193. ACM Press (2019). https://doi.org/10.1145/3322640.3328780
18. Bindra, L., Lin, C., Stroulia, E., Ardakanian, O.: Decentralized access control for smart buildings using metadata and smart contracts. In: 2019 IEEE/ACM 5th International Workshop on Software Engineering for Smart Cyber-Physical Systems (SEsCPS), Montreal, QC, Canada, pp. 32–38. IEEE (2019). https://doi.org/10.1109/SEsCPS.2019.00013
19. García, R., Gil, R.: Social media copyright management using semantic web and blockchain. In: Proceedings of the 21st International Conference on Information Integration and Web-Based Applications & Services, Munich Germany, pp. 339–343. ACM (2019). https://doi.org/10.1145/3366030.3366128
20. Ramachandran, M., Chowdhury, N., Third, A., Domingue, J., Quick, K., Bachler, M.: Towards complete decentralised verification of data with confidentiality: different ways to connect solid pods and blockchain. In: Companion Proceedings of the Web Conference 2020, Taipei Taiwan, pp. 645–649. ACM (2020). https://doi.org/10.1145/3366424.3385759
21. Johng, H., Kim, D., Park, G., Hong, J.-E., Hill, T., Chung, L.: Enhancing business processes with trustworthiness using blockchain: a goal-oriented approach. In: Proceedings of the 35th Annual ACM Symposium on Applied Computing, pp. 61–68 (2020). https://doi.org/10.1145/3341105.3374022
22. Wang, H., Yuan, Y., Yang, F.: A personal data determination method based on blockchain technology and smart contract. In: Proceedings of the 2020 4th International Conference on Cryptography, Security and Privacy, Nanjing China, pp. 89–94. ACM (2020). https://doi.org/10.1145/3377644.3377656
23. Kleinaki, A.-S., Mytis-Gkometh, P., Drosatos, G., Efraimidis, P.S., Kaldoudi, E.: A blockchain-based notarization service for biomedical knowledge retrieval. Comput. Struct. Biotechnol. J. 16, 288–297 (2018). https://doi.org/10.1016/j.csbj.2018.08.002
24. Chen, Z.: Understanding granular aspects of ontology for blockchain databases. Procedia Comput. Sci. 162, 361–367 (2019). https://doi.org/10.1016/j.procs.2019.11.296
25. Hofman, W.J.: A methodological approach for development and deployment of data sharing in complex organizational supply and logistics networks with blockchain technology. IFAC-Pap. 52, 55–60 (2019). https://doi.org/10.1016/j.ifacol.2019.06.010

26. Roehrs, A., da Costa, C.A., da Rosa Righi, R., da Silva, V.F., Goldim, J.R., Schmidt, D.C.: Analyzing the performance of a blockchain-based personal health record implementation. J. Biomed. Inform. **92**, 103140 (2019). https://doi.org/10.1016/j.jbi.2019.103140

27. Weigand, H., Blums, I., de Kruijff, J.: Shared ledger accounting - implementing the economic exchange pattern. Inf. Syst. **90**, 101437 (2020). https://doi.org/10.1016/j.is.2019.101437

28. Zhou, X., Lim, M.Q., Kraft, M.: A Smart Contract-based agent marketplace for the J-Park Simulator - a knowledge graph for the process industry. Comput. Chem. Eng. **139**, 106896 (2020). https://doi.org/10.1016/j.compchemeng.2019.106577

29. Hofman, D.L.: Legally speaking: smart contracts, archival bonds, and linked data in the blockchain. In: 26th International Conference on Computer Communication and Networks, Vancouver, BC, Canada, pp. 1–4 (ICCCN). IEEE (2017). https://doi.org/10.1109/ICCCN. 2017.8038515

30. Choudhury, O., Rudolph, N., Sylla, I., Fairoza, N., Das, A.: Auto-generation of smart contracts from domain-specific ontologies and semantic rules. In: 2018 IEEE International Conference on Internet of Things (IThings) and IEEE Green Computing and Communications (Green-Com) and IEEE Cyber, Physical and Social Computing (CPSCom) and IEEE Smart Data (SmartData) , Halifax, NS, Canada, pp. 963–970. IEEE (2018). https://doi.org/10.1109/Cyb ermatics_2018.2018.00183

31. Norta, A.: Self-aware smart contracts with legal relevance. In: 2018 International Joint Conference on Neural Networks (IJCNN), Rio de Janeiro, pp. 1–8. IEEE (2018). https://doi.org/ 10.1109/IJCNN.2018.8489235

32. Baqa, H., Truong, N.B., Crespi, N., Lee, G.M., le Gall, F.: Semantic smart contracts for blockchain-based services in the internet of things. In: IEEE 18th International Symposium on Network Computing and Applications (NCA), pp. 1–5 (2019). https://doi.org/10.1109/ NCA.2019.8935016

33. Li, M., Xia, L., Seneviratne, O.: Leveraging standards based ontological concepts in distributed ledgers: a healthcare smart contract example. In: IEEE International Conference on Decentralized Applications and Infrastructures, Newark, CA, USA, pp. 152–157. IEEE (2019). https://doi.org/10.1109/DAPPCON.2019.00029

34. Laurier, W., Kiehn, J., Polovina, S.: REA2: a unified formalisation of the Resource-Event-Agent ontology. Appl. Ontol. **13**, 201–224 (2018). https://doi.org/10.3233/AO-180198

35. Lee, S.-M., Park, S., Park, Y.B.: Formal specification technique in smart contract verification. In: International Conference on Platform Technology and Service (PlatCon) , Jeju, Korea (South), pp. 1–4. IEEE (2019). https://doi.org/10.1109/PlatCon.2019.8669419

36. Kudumakis, P., Wilmering, T., Sandler, M., Rodriguez-Doncel, V., Boch, L., Delgado, J.: The challenge: from MPEG intellectual property rights ontologies to smart contracts and blockchains [standards in a nutshell]. IEEE Signal Process. Mag. **37**, 89–95 (2020). https:// doi.org/10.1109/MSP.2019.2955207

37. Norta, A.: Creation of smart-contracting collaborations for decentralized autonomous organizations. In: Matulevičius, R., Dumas, M. (eds.) BIR 2015. LNBIP, vol. 229, pp. 3–17. Springer, Cham (2015). https://doi.org/10.1007/978-3-319-21915-8_1

38. Norta, A., Ma, L., Duan, Y., Rull, A., Kõlvart, M., Taveter, K.: eContractual choreography-language properties towards cross-organizational business collaboration. J. Internet Serv. Appl. **6**(1), 1–23 (2015). https://doi.org/10.1186/s13174-015-0023-7

39. Narendra, N.C., Norta, A., Mahunnah, M., Ma, L., Maggi, F.M.: Sound conflict management and resolution for virtual-enterprise collaborations. SOCA **10**(3), 233–251 (2015). https:// doi.org/10.1007/s11761-015-0183-0

40. García-Barriocanal, E., Sánchez-Alonso, S., Sicilia, M.-A.: Deploying metadata on blockchain technologies. In: Garoufallou, E., Virkus, S., Siatri, R., Koutsomiha, D. (eds.) Metadata and Semantic Research. CCIS, vol. 755, pp. 38–49. Springer, Cham (2017). https:// doi.org/10.1007/978-3-319-70863-8_4

41. de Kruijff, J., Weigand, H.: Understanding the blockchain using enterprise ontology. In: Dubois, E., Pohl, K. (eds.) Advanced Information Systems Engineering. LNCS, vol. 10253, pp. 29–43. Springer, Cham (2017). https://doi.org/10.1007/978-3-319-59536-8_3
42. de Kruijff, J., Weigand, H.: Ontologies for commitment-based smart contracts. In: Panetto, H., et al. (eds.) On the Move to Meaningful Internet Systems. OTM 2017 Conferences. LNCS, vol. 10574, pp. 383–398. Springer, Cham (2017). https://doi.org/10.1007/978-3-319-69459-7_26
43. Ladleif, J., Weske, M.: A unifying model of legal smart contracts. In: Laender, A.H.F., Pernici, B., Lim, E.-P., de Oliveira, J.P.M. (eds.) ER 2019. LNCS, vol. 11788, pp. 323–337. Springer, Cham (2019). https://doi.org/10.1007/978-3-030-33223-5_27
44. García-Barriocanal, E., Sicilia, M., Sánchez-Alonso, S.: The case for ontologies in expressing decisions in decentralized energy systems. In: Garoufallou, E., Sartori, F., Siatri, R., Zervas, M. (eds.) Metadata and Semantic Research. CCIS, vol. 846, pp. 365–376. Springer, Cham (2019). https://doi.org/10.1007/978-3-030-14401-2_35
45. Risius, M., Spohrer, K.: A blockchain research framework. Bus. Inf. Syst. Eng. 59(6), 385–409 (2017). https://doi.org/10.1007/s12599-017-0506-0

Track on Digital Humanities and Digital Curation, and General Session

FAIR Metadata: A Community-Driven Vocabulary Application

Christopher B. Rauch[1]([✉])[iD], Mat Kelly[1][iD], John A. Kunze[2][iD],
and Jane Greenberg[1][iD]

[1] Drexel University, Philadelphia, PA 19104, USA
{cr625,mkelly,jg4233}@drexel.edu
https://cci.drexel.edu/mrc
[2] California Digital Library, University of California, Oakland, CA 94612, USA
jak@ucop.edu
https://cdlib.org

Abstract. FAIR metadata is critical to supporting FAIR data overall. Transparency, community engagement, and flexibility are key aspects of FAIR that apply to metadata. This paper presents YAMZ (Yet Another Metadata Zoo), a community-driven vocabulary application that supports FAIR. The history of YAMZ and its original features are reviewed, followed by a presentation of recent innovations and a discussion of how YAMZ supports FAIR principles. The conclusion identifies next steps and key outputs.

Keywords: Metadata · Standardization · FAIR · Metadata quality · Community driven

1 Introduction

FAIR data sharing principles have taken hold and continue to be adopted across a wide diversity of communities. While grounded in open data and data sharing, the FAIR principles further apply to sensitive data. The principles bring even more communities together to build sustainable, trusted data sharing infrastructure. Metadata is essential to FAIR, and researchers have underscored its role in key documentation [12], exemplifying what Riley calls value-added data [11]. Selected example metadata applications supporting FAIR principles include [5,7,13]. One area requiring further attention is the need to facilitate metadata standards development, specifically agreement on and durable reference to semantics.

In further supporting FAIR, there is a need for an open service that supports community-driven evolution, consensus-building, and permalinked references to metadata semantics currently siloed by discipline or institution type. Such an application could help communities to define, reference, and test semantics before issuing a standard based upon them. Communities could also share their semantics with other communities, learning from and borrowing prior art,

© Springer Nature Switzerland AG 2022
E. Garoufallou et al. (Eds.): MTSR 2021, CCIS 1537, pp. 187–198, 2022.
https://doi.org/10.1007/978-3-030-98876-0_16

avoiding duplication of effort between communities, and reducing the proliferation of metadata standards with overlapping semantics. Foundational work for
this type of application was initiated with the YAMZ (Yet Another Metadata
Zoo) project [4].

YAMZ was initiated as part of the NSF DataONE Datanet initiative [8]
through a collaborative effort of the Metadata Preservation and Metadata Working Groups. It is important to acknowledge that YAMZ preceded the development of FAIR, although the underlying vision [4] echoes a number of foundational principles guiding today's FAIR efforts. YAMZ development is focusing
on enhancing application features that integrate community member expertise
to: 1) determine a canonical set of metadata terms, and 2) analyze and improve
the quality of related metadata. This notion builds on the ranking/feedback loop
that underlies community driven systems such as Stack Overflow[1] and Reddit[2].

This paper presents some of these YAMZ enhancements. We first review
the history of YAMZ, its original features, and the initial ranking methodology.
Next, we report on recent innovations and plans, followed by a discussion of how
YAMZ supports FAIR principles. The paper closes with a summary of the work
presented and identifies next steps.

2   Background: The History of YAMZ

YAMZ was developed through the efforts of the NSF DataONE Preservation, Metadata and Interoperability Working Group (PMWG). This working
group was charged with developing solutions to prevalent, growing, and anticipated cyberinfrastructure preservation and metadata-related challenges. Part of
DataONE's mission is to facilitate data sharing and interoperability among a
diversity of earth science communities and to further bring together a growing
number of community member repositories (currently 44). From the start, the
DataONE PMWG took on the challenge of advancing the expensive conventional
"panel of experts" process of developing shared metadata standards by turning
to social computing, particularly inspired by community driven forums.

3   Original YAMZ

The YAMZ metadata dictionary permits any authenticated user to propose
terms for inclusion with a corresponding definition and example. The user can
comment on the terms submitted by other contributors, attach tags to definitions, or provide examples. During the prototype evaluation period, a sample
group contributed terms to the dictionary and voted on contributed terms.

The terms are scored according to a heuristic that models consensus-based
quality evaluation. Community votes influence ranking on a numerical scale

---

[1] https://stackoverflow.com/.
[2] https://www.reddit.com/.

intended to reflect the appropriateness or deficiency of the proposed term's definition and usage examples. Contributor reputation influences the score in that votes for terms proposed by users who have made prior contributions or comments, or that have participated in voting activity receive additional weight.

The YAMZ consensus ranking system, described in detail at [9], begins with the percentage of users who cast an up-vote for a term, where u is the number of up-votes and d the number of down-votes. If every user casts a vote, then a term's score (S) is

$$S = \frac{u}{u+d}$$

Since not every user will cast a vote, the weight of a user's vote is adjusted by that user's reputation. Let R_i be the reputation acquired by user i, let R be the total reputation of the users who have voted on a particular term, and let $r_i = R_i/R$ for each user i who voted on the term. The weight w_i of a user's vote is then based on their reputation by the formula

$$w_i = 1 + r_i\,(t - v)$$

where t is the total number of users in the community and v the number of votes cast.

The scores are updated by a regularly scheduled process to account for changes in user reputation. Terms are assigned a stability rating depending on how long they remain unaltered by their contributor and are classified into one of three types: *vernacular, canonical,* and *deprecated*. A term is designated *vernacular* by default. After the term has exceeded a certain stability threshold (remains unaltered for an assigned duration), it becomes canonical if the consensus of the community, as indicated by the score (voting consensus), exceeds a designated threshold (75%). A term is deemed *deprecated* if its score (S) falls below 25%. These formulations are initial values and their adjustment is the subject of the ongoing enhancements as discussed in subsequent sections. Before the enhancements reported in the next section, the dictionary contained approximately 2,778 terms contributed by 158 users.

4   Ongoing Enhancements

This section presents YAMZ enhancements supporting metadata quality evaluation and refinement. Primarily, the proposed changes involve additional variables added to consensus ranking algorithms and the expansion of social features to facilitate community interaction. We also outline some changes in approach to the data model, such as representing subject and object terms as equivalent and relationships as predicates.

4.1   Equivalency of Terms

The RDA Metadata Principles assert that the only difference between metadata and data is mode of use [6]. The data model of the revised metadictionary will reflect this distinction. In the proposed enhancements, a term is represented as a first-class object and corresponding examples are other terms related to that object.

Although the application of the term metadata is contextual [6], a practical distinction is possible between collections of data that exist for categorical object description and the descriptions themselves. This distinction is represented by the schematization of metadata terms by various committees or industry groups and their promulgation as standard vocabularies versus terms from those vocabularies as assigned to objects in a collection. As linked data, the resulting relationships of vocabulary terms to objects yields a set of predicates. When a set of terms is encoded according to these relationships, it can represent categorical metadata within the associated domain. By default, the categorized terms inherit the ontological status of the primary subject relative to the represented domain [10]. In the new data model, the relationships between the terms are stored separately using the RDF subject, predicate, object syntax. This supports the addition of terms organized with different schemas.

4.2 Scoring Terms

Scoring is intended to facilitate metadata quality analysis, and the enhancements retain the ability to score terms in various contexts. The stability and appropriateness (applicability) scores encompass the metrics used to determine the category of vernacular, canonical, or deprecated assigned to a term. If a term was imported from a formal schema, the term is stable by default. When imported in this way, the source URL is recorded. When the record of a term is accessed for display, the source document is hashed and compared with a stored hash value. If the two values are the same, then stability is not affected. If they differ, the score is reduced by a set percentage, and the term is flagged. If the original document is no longer accessible, the stability score is further reduced. There are default values for the magnitude of the reduction or increase, although these may be changed in the management interface. Initial values are arbitrary but as part of a pilot project, a test group will help to adjust those weights and compare the rankings achieved by vocabularies that have been assessed for quality by a manual or semi-automated process.

When a schema is imported manually or terms are entered individually, they may languish over time as new ones become popular. Terms that are neither edited by their author nor scored by the user community lose applicability over time. Scoring can both increase or reduce the numerical quality of a term (a heuristic for appropriateness). It is increased by some amount by interaction but may decrease or increase depending on an up or down vote from a registered user and their corresponding reputation.

Retrieving lists of terms within a given stability threshold is a resource-intensive task but implementing a message queue rather than relying on database polling makes these queries feasible. Future plans include the incorporation of additional available XSEDE[3] provided resources to facilitate text analysis based on sets of terms from the dictionary and integrations with externally hosted classification tools that expose an API (Fig. 1).

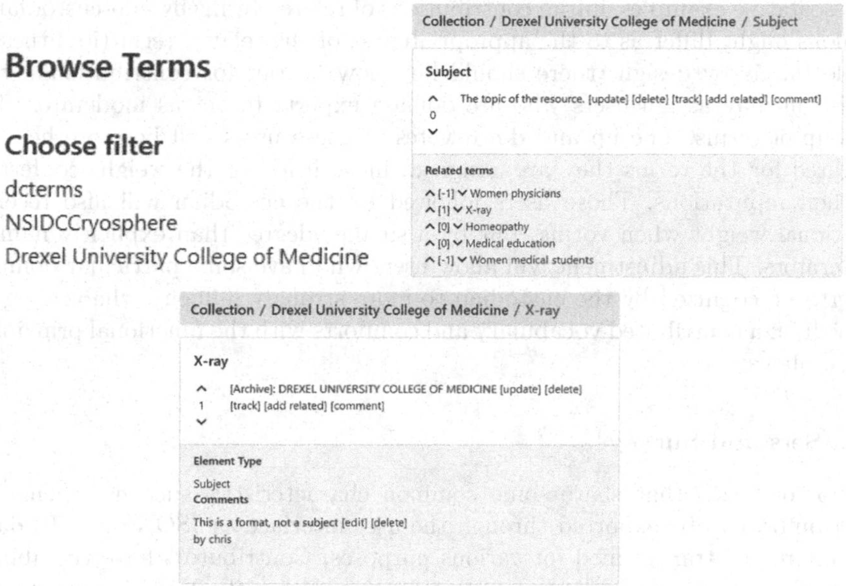

Fig. 1. Terms filtered by collection and refined by subject in three steps. 1. The user chooses from a list of filters. 2. The filtered vocabulary terms are presented. 3. Users vote and comment on the appropriateness of the term relative to the filters.

4.3   Adding and Importing Terms

New subject terms can be added manually or by parsing an imported schema. Vocabulary (object terms) can be imported by parsing RDF or XML representations of records encoded according to an imported schema. Bulk import from a collection can facilitate an analysis of metadata quality if the collection is designated with a unique identifier.

The RDA Metadata Standards Catalog is an open directory of metadata standards maintained by the Research Data Alliance and hosted by the University of Bath.[4]

---

[3] The Extreme Science and Engineering Discovery Environment (XSEDE) is an NSF-funded organization that coordinates the sharing of digital services.
[4] https://github.com/rd-alliance/metadata-catalog-v2/blob/live/openapi.yaml.

4.4   Moderation of Terms and Concepts

The originator of a vocabulary term or a set of terms imported by schema or by inference from XML or RDF records becomes the default custodian of those terms. Since anyone in the community can comment on these terms and add representative examples, initial contributions of related terms by non-custodians, opinions might differ as to the appropriateness of the related term (its fitness). While this is by design (there should be a low barrier for contributions), the custodian may assign users who are domain experts to act as moderators for a group of terms. The up and down votes of these users will be more heavily weighted for the terms they are assigned, in addition to the weight conferred by their reputations. Those users followed by the custodian will also receive additional weight when voting, but by a smaller degree than explicitly named moderators. This adjustment will allow users who have some particular domain expertise recognized by the custodian to more strongly influence the vetting of terms from a contributed vocabulary and comports with the functional principles stated above.

4.5   Sets and Surveys

Groups of terms that share some common characteristics such as schema or contributor, can be exported through the user interface as JSON or XML data and filtered or transformed for various purposes. Contributors have the ability to send surveys to their followers by notification within the YAMZ environment or by sharing a link with potential participants. These surveys can be prepared and distributed ad hoc or as part of proceeding with a specific goal, such as a metadata review session or conference.

4.6   User Profiles and Comments

Although users are not expected to create detailed profiles, the profile section permits linking to external services such as ORCID or LinkedIn to provide some context to the value of their contribution. Completing a profile increases the numerical value representing user reputation which will, in turn, increase the weight of a user's vote when ranking quality and, to a lesser extent, stability. The votes of more active users (those who have logged on frequently and more recently, voted or commented) will receive additional weight. Users may also follow other users, and the number of followed and followers affects reputation score.

4.7   Term Tracking and Notification

As in the prototype, users can elect to track terms of interest and choose to receive notifications of varying levels of activity associated with those and, optionally, related terms. An activity might include an author or administrator's update of a term (or related term), the addition of a related term, change

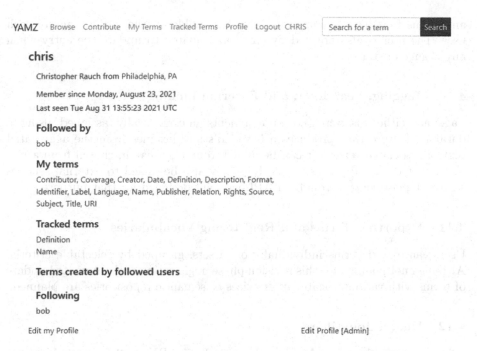

Fig. 2. User profiles display activity information, followers, contributed terms, tracked terms and users followed.

in stability/quality within a given threshold, or a notification of a survey involving a followed term. Notifications appear in the user's profile page and can be sent by email in either a scheduled digest or as they are generated (Fig. 2).

4.8 Rights

Contributions to the YAMZ metadictionary are dedicated to the public domain under the terms of CC0 (No Rights Reserved) [1]. Imported terms are governed by the rights statements assigned by their proponent organization. Whenever possible, this is extracted from the rights statements encoding in a metadata schema, but at a minimum, a link to the source is maintained with every term entry, so that usage rights are discoverable.

4.9 Versioning

Updates (edits) to terms are tracked as versions, and version history can be displayed by selecting the appropriate option in the display screen of the relevant term. Currently, each discrete update is stored separately (a separate entry is created each time the term definition is edited), but versioning will eventually incorporate a more efficient approach. Terms can be submitted for review to their contributors with the posting of a comment. A list of down-voted terms and terms that have become deprecated is visible on the profile page of each user. The user is also notified by email and invited to update the entry when any change of status occurs.

4.10   Tagging, Searching, and External Linking

Tags are either user-created in comments, automatically assigned using a database feature that produces a list of distinct lexemes from the aggregated text of associated terms, or can be added from a by search, chosen from a list, or suggested with type-ahead [2]. Tags may also be linked to external services such as OpenRefine[5] through an API endpoint designed for that purpose.

4.11   Exporting Terms and Registering Vocabularies

Users can export terms individually or in sets, grouped by selectable criteria. Although not planned for this revision phase, registration and automated update of terms with various vocabulary services or semantic repositories are planned.

4.12   Unique Identifiers

All terms are assigned an Archival Resource Key (ARK) that uniquely identifies them and allows for their resolution (if they are resolvable) through the N2T service of the California Digital Library[6]. Imported schemas, collections, and manually added terms also receive an identifier. The ARKs carry with them persistence data that can be retrieved by adding a suffix to their URL. This data is determined from metadata relating to the terms versioning and categorization and presented as a persistence statement.

5   Discussion

Metadata scheme development and supporting metadata interoperability remain among two of the most time demanding challenges for researcher communities that seek to share, reuse, and integrate data from multiple sources. The metadata ecosystem is extensive and research points to the development of overlapping schemes that have been developed in silos. Further, there are reports of researchers spending over 80% of their time managing their data and less than 20% of their time pursuing their science. As presented above, an application like YAMZ can help address these challenges and help advance metadata activities in connection to FAIR.

---

[5] https://openrefine.org.
[6] https://n2t.net/.

5.1 How YAMZ Helps FAIRNness

YAMZ leverages social computing technology, the spirit of open science, and ultimately the notion of the wisdom of the crowds for metadata scheme development. The original vision that helped to shape YAMZ called for a low barrier for contributions, transparency in the review process, collective review and ownership, expert guidance, voting capacity, and overall stakeholder engagement. These aspects are reflected in FAIR principles with the support of data being findable, accessible, interoperable, and reusable. The FAIR community also recognizes the significance of vocabularies and how these principles are exhibited in metadata schemes. Cox et al. [3] identify and discuss ten rules that support FAIR vocabularies, covering governance, licensing, quality issues, persistence, and other key aspects.

The rules present a rubric for showing how YAMZ aligns with FAIR principles.

Rules 1 and 2. (Governance)
In YAMZ, the identification of the content custodian is multifaceted. Contributions are made under CC0 terms but rights holders of imported schemas retain ownership rights.

The unique style of governance offered by the metadictionary model that incorporates crowd-sourced ranking with the ability to import both canonical (schema elements) and vernacular (as vocabulary terms). The status of these can be adjusted by vote, comment, moderation and usage examples. YAMZ governance represents an attempt to expose as much content as possible to the public domain while recognizing that not all contributors can grant that right. Origin and commensurate publishing rights are assumed to be with a term contributor and thereby in the public domain as established by the contribution. Imported schemas will always retain a link to the original source or a stored version of the document. An effort is underway to incorporate data sharing agreements into the submissions process for proprietary vocabularies, but this is in the early planning stage.

Rule 3 (Consistency)
One of the goals of the project is to facilitate metadata quality analysis. Accuracy and consistency are attributes that can be voted on and commented on. Contributors can filter a particular corpus of records representing objects imported from collections as a way to focus quality evaluation and facilitate group work. This approach works best when analyzing terms that have repositories in common, but can also be initiated as a survey with invited participants. This process facilitates consistency checking.

Rule 4 (Maintenance Environment)
Facilitating vocabulary maintenance is a primary goal of the project. The ranking algorithms together with the group work features and versioning capabilities ensure that changes to definitions or categorization are recorded with their

associated events (either responding to a comment, author edit of recharacterization of a term by stability, category, and fitness metrics.

Rule 5 (Unique Identifiers)
Archival Resource Keys are appropriate identifiers for contributed terms. They are flexible enough to assign to any type of term and produce a resolvable identifier. ARKs can be minted as terms are added. When terms change, the metadata associated with object persistence that can be retrieved via an ARK inflection is updated to reflect the date and time of the change (last updated).

Rule 6 (Machine Readable Versions)
The dictionary will feature both REST APIs for returning data over HTTP in various formats and the ability to respond to ARK-related metadata requests. The bulk of terms will be imported and machine-readability is therefore assumed from successful import, but individual terms can also be manipulated and extracted through the API.

Rule 7 (Vocabulary Metadata)
The assignment of metadata is inherent in the contribution process. Provenance information includes, at the least, a record of the contributor of a term. Versioning-related metadata is recorded each time a database transaction occurs or there is user activity. Permanence statements that are retrievable by their ARK ids represent term metadata as does the association of related terms in the subject-object-predicate pattern.

Rule 8 (Register the Vocabulary)
The dictionary will be registered manually with various vocabulary services and semantic repositories as suggested.

Rule 9 (Accessibility)
The dictionary makes terms viewable by humans with an HTML representation that includes the definition with related terms. Machine access is facilitated by the API and the ability to export selected sets of terms in various formats or conventions such as JSON, XML, RDF, and SKOS.

Rule 10 (Publishing)
Versioning information is available at API endpoints corresponding to the following terms (at a minimum) suggested by Cox.

- **dcterms:created-date** or date-time that the vocabulary or term was initially created
- **dcterms:modified-date** or date-time that the vocabulary or term was last updated
- **dcterms:isReplacedBy** - to point to a superseding vocabulary or term
- **dcterms:replaces** - to point to a prior version of a vocabulary or term
- **owl:deprecated** = 'true' if the vocabulary or term is no longer valid
- **owl:priorVersion** - to point to a previous version of a vocabulary

– **owl:versionInfo** - general annotations relating to versioning
– **skos:changeNote** - modifications to a term relative to prior versions
– **skos:historyNote** - past state/use/meaning of a term

6 Conclusion

The conventional approach to developing metadata standards is slow, expensive, and compromised by egos and the limited number of people available to review, travel to, and endure endless consensus discussions. Social computing technology offers new opportunities for enabling a more inclusive, transparent approach to metadata standards development. Moreover, social computing offers community features that can be leveraged to support FAIR and reduce duplication of effort in metadata silos. The YAMZ prototype serves as a demonstration for such an approach, and increased interest in and adoption of FAIR principles present a rubric for enhancing YAMZ as described in this paper.

YAMZ was created before the articulation and adoption FAIR, but the current prototyping enhancements map well to FAIR principles and metadata rules. Next steps include demonstrating and testing these new features, following by a set of formal evaluations. The results of these activities will be folded into future releases of YAMZ.

References

1. CC0 - Creative Commons. https://creativecommons.org/share-your-work/public-domain/cc0/. Accessed 31 Aug 2021
2. typeahead.js. https://twitter.github.io/typeahead.js/. Accessed 31 Aug 2021
3. Cox, S.J., Gonzalez-Beltran, A.N., Magagna, B., Marinescu, M.C.: Ten simple rules for making a vocabulary fair. PLoS Comput. Biol. **17**(6), e1009041 (2021)
4. Greenberg, J., et al.: Metadictionary: advocating for a community-driven metadata vocabulary application (2013)
5. Jacobsen, A., et al.: A generic workflow for the data fairification process. Data Intell. **2**(1–2), 56–65 (2020)
6. Jeffery, K.G., Koskela, R.: RDA metadata principles and their use, November 2014
7. Kunis, S., Hänsch, S., Schmidt, C., Wong, F., Weidtkamp-Peters, S.: OMERO.mde in a use case for microscopy metadata harmonization: facilitating fair principles in practical application with metadata annotation tools. arXiv preprint arXiv:2103.02942 (2021)
8. Michener, W., Vieglais, D., Vision, T., Kunze, J., Cruse, P., Janée, G.: DataONE: data observation network for earth-preserving data and enabling innovation in the biological and environmental sciences. D-Lib Mag. **17**(1/2), 12 (2011)
9. Patton, C.: YAMZ metadata dictionary, September 2014. https://github.com/nassibnassar/yamz
10. Plaisance, C.A.: Textual realities: an Aristotelian realist ontology of textual entities (14), 23–40. https://doi.org/10.4000/variants.932. https://journals.openedition.org/variants/932. Number: 14 Publisher: European Society for Textual Scholarship

11. Riley, J.: Understanding metadata. National Information Standards Organization, Washington DC, United States 23 (2017). http://www.niso.org/publications/press/UnderstandingMetadata.pdf
12. Wilkinson, M.D., et al.: The fair guiding principles for scientific data management and stewardship. Sci. Data **3**(1), 1–9 (2016)
13. Wilkinson, M.D., et al.: Evaluating fair maturity through a scalable, automated, community-governed framework. Sci. Data **6**(1), 1–12 (2019)

Best of Both Worlds? Mapping Process Metadata in Digital Humanities and Computational Engineering

Kerstin Jung[1]([✉])[iD], Björn Schembera[2,3][iD], and Markus Gärtner[1][iD]

[1] Institute for Natural Language Processing, University of Stuttgart,
Stuttgart, Germany
{kerstin.jung,markus.gaertner}@ims.uni-stuttgart.de
[2] High-Performance Computing Center (HLRS), University of Stuttgart,
Stuttgart, Germany
schembera@hlrs.de
[3] Institute of Applied Analysis and Numerical Simulation, University of Stuttgart,
Stuttgart, Germany
bjoern.schembera@mathematik.uni-stuttgart.de

Abstract. Process metadata constitute a relevant part of the documentation of research processes and the creation and use of research data. As an addition to publications on the research question, they capture details needed for reusability and comparability and are thus important for a sustainable handling of research data. In the DH project SDC4Lit we want to capture process metadata when researchers work with literary material, conducting manual and automatic processing steps, which need to be treated with equal emphasis. We present a content-related mapping between two process metadata schemas from the area of Digital Humanities (GRAIN, RePlay-DH) and one from Computational Engineering (EngMeta) and find that there are no basic obstacles preventing the use of any of them for our purposes. Actually a basic difference rather exists between GRAIN on the one hand and RePlay-DH and EngMeta on the other, regarding the treatment of tools and actors in a workflow step.

Keywords: Process metadata · Metadata mapping · Literary studies

1 Introduction

For compliance with the FAIR data principles [12], it is not only important to store research data and results generated in the research process, but also to document the process itself. Such process metadata enable potential researchers to decide whether a resource is suitable for their research question and can enable greater comparability of research results. Decisions that seem subordinate or irrelevant in the original research process usually do not find their way into publications or a documentation, even if they might be relevant for reuse.

E. Garoufallou et al. (Eds.): MTSR 2021, CCIS 1537, pp. 199–205, 2022.
https://doi.org/10.1007/978-3-030-98876-0_17

Process metadata as part of larger metadata models often describe processes by sequentially executed individual steps and are usually designed to enable automated execution, especially in natural sciences, life sciences, and engineering. In contrast, for the Digital Humanities (DH) it is crucial to capture and treat automatic and manual steps with equal importance. The manual steps include annotation, interpretation, extraction, or selection, while the automatic steps include the execution of computational tools for annotation, analysis, or visualization. Dedicated provenance metadata like PROV [8] are more general and descriptive, however focus on a specific object, while process metadata focus on the process leading to several or also no results. The work presented in this paper is conducted within the DH project SDC4Lit [2], which aims to build a sustainable data life cycle for data in digital literary studies, including handling of process metadata. The primary data in this project is stemming from (a) born digitals, i.e. digital inheritances (Nachlasse) of authors, which usually include digital carriers such as hard drives and CDs, but even aged media, such as floppy disks, which could contain valuable research data. Primary data may also originate from (b) net literature, such as digital literature or literary blogs. In case (a), when a new inheritance is received, curation steps are to be performed. For example, the content of the received hard disk has to undergo an laborious manual review and a transfer to state of the art storage technology. In case (b) web resources containing literature, such as blogs or interactive web sources are repeatedly crawled and archived. After these curation steps and the ingestion of the data into a repository, it can be reused for scientific purpose, generating research data. For example, automatic methods like entity recognition or topic modeling are used on the primary data. Furthermore manual steps are included in the research process, such as selection/extraction of works or free text annotation. In these analysis steps, process metadata is generated, which will eventually be ingested to a repository along with the research data.

The research presented in this paper aims for a recommendation for process metadata for SDC4Lit and for its use within the repositories, which will be deployed with Dataverse [7], and is organized as follows. In Sect. 2. we are considering three process metadata schemas from diverse fields that base each step on a structural triplet of input, operation, and output: EngMeta [11] from Computational Engineering, GRAIN [6] from Computational Linguistics, and RePlay-DH [5] with a focus on Digital Humanities. While EngMeta is originally not developed for the Digital Humanities, it is investigated since there is experience with its integration into Dataverse. Finding cross-sections between the three models, or, the two worlds of Engineering and DH, and mapping them we deem beneficial for finding optimal process metadata, which is presented in Sect. 3. Moreover, the mapping between the schemas considered here is intended to show how similar or different assumptions about required process metadata are and thus which applications they enable. In addition to equal coverage of manual and automatic steps, attention is also paid to the flexibility of the structure contents, so that, for example, input and output can also be empty. An evaluation of the mapping results is presented in Sect. 4. Section 5 summarizes and concludes the results of this paper.

2   Related Work

GRAIN. GRAIN is a collaboratively created corpus with many annotation layers, automatically and manually created ones. To keep track of the workflow steps in the creation of the corpus the applied JSON process metadata schema equally captures manual and automatic steps by means of input, output and the description of workflow steps including operators. The operators can be human individuals as well as tools and operator components capture specific versions of trained models or annotation guidelines.

EngMeta. The metadata schema EngMeta (Engineering Metadata) originates from computational engineering [10,11], especially aerodynamics and thermodynamics. Since there are very few manual work steps involved in the workflows of this discipline, which primarily uses computer simulation, the focus is primarily on recording the automatically generated process metadata. In EngMeta, these include an annotation of the research data with information about the computer environment and software, the experimental device, the simulation method and its parameters and variables. However also people involved and the input and output data that have accrued within the process step are taken into account. Much of this information is automatically provided in the step of conducting (i.e. preparing, running and analyzing) the computer simulation. In the field of computational engineering, in addition to subject-specific and technical metadata, process metadata in particular can be easily extracted automatically [9].

RePlay-DH. The metadata schema of RePlay-DH [4] is part a desktop application [5] meant to aid researchers in documenting their workflows. The RePlay-DH Client builds on top of Git as version control to track changes in a user's workspace and uses the Git commits to directly store process metadata for individual workflow steps as text in JSON format. RePlay-DH is focused primarily on users in the DH and as such needs to account for very heterogeneous workflows, comprising manual steps like annotation, curation or commenting as well as fully automated processing or any mixture in between. Similar to GRAIN, it also models workflows as graphs of individual steps that are composed of optional input and output resources and which may involve tools or persons. This explicit distinction between tools and human individuals involved in the workflow is one of the differences between RePlay-DH and GRAIN and attributed to the target audience of DH. Elicitation of metadata is performed semi-automatic, with the RePlay-DH Client assisting the user with information obtained from workflow tracking via the underlying version control. For interoperability process metadata stored with RePlay-DH can be exported in several formats, e.g. $\tilde{P}$ROV.

3   Mapping

First the two JSON formats of RePlay-DH and GRAIN and the XML schema of EngMeta are translated to tree representations. The XML tree resembles the DOM tree of a respective instance where each optional and multipliable element appears exactly once. The value layer is only included if the element node would not be the leaf anyway. EngMeta includes recursion (for the description of affiliations) which is stopped on the first level. JSON schemas allow by default additional properties, i.e. as long as they are not explicitly excluded. Since we only take elements specified in the schemas into account, we only add those where RePlay-DH makes use of explicitly restricted additional properties. For all schemas we assume that element order does not add to the semantics.

The mapping is then conducted unidirectionally from one tree to another, by including edges between the trees which document the possible mapping quality: **MAP_FULLY**, **MAP_NEARLY**, **MAP_PARTIALLY**. Nodes from one tree with information that cannot be mapped to the other tree at all (**NO_MAP**) are realized by the absence of a mapping edge. Thereby the goal is not to answer the question if the content from one tree can be automatically mapped to the other, but to find out, if the information which is covered by one schema could also be covered by the other schema, even if information has to be split, combined or mapped to different elements based on the actual content. Due to different mapping options, some leafs are part of several mapping categories.

Due to the diverging discipline of EngMeta, we only consider the mapping from GRAIN and RePlay-DH to EngMeta, not the other way around. For the project it is not relevant, if all instruments or simulation details of EngMeta can be captured. However it is relevant, if EngMeta could represent the same information as GRAIN or RePlay-DH, even if leaving EngMeta elements unused.

3.1 GRAIN to RePlay-DH

GRAIN and RePlay-DH base on the same ideas and are thus rather similar. Of GRAIN's 10 leafs, 3 provide for a full map, 6 for a near map and 4 for a partial map into RePlay-DH. The two major differences are that (i) GRAIN allows for several workflow steps to be captured by one instance of the schema, while a RePlay-DH instance describes exactly one step and (ii) RePlay-DH handles human actors separately from tools, while GRAIN combines them under the idea of operators, allowing for a parallel handling of automatic and manual steps. Regarding (i) processing steps might not have an output object, e.g. because the output is a change of state or was immediately redirected to the input of the next operator. GRAIN reflects this by describing several steps within one instance. However RePlay-DH allows for empty input and output, thus a follow-up of workflow steps without intermediate result objects can be handled by filling several instances. With respect to (ii), the operator parameters of GRAIN can only be mapped in case of automatic operators, since RePlay-DH's *persons* does not provide for additional descriptions beside a role, and the additional properties on workflow step level, not allowing to link the properties to specific actors, especially for different actors with different properties.

3.2 RePlay-DH to GRAIN

RePlay-DH comes with more than twice the number of leafs of GRAIN (22 to 10). Due to GRAIN's flexibility and the possibility to combine values into single strings, 11 leafs come with a full map in this direction. One near map and one partial map leave 9 leafs unmapped. Of these, two unmapped leafs contain metadata about the schema and the time of step recording, which relates to the RePlay-DH Client tool and is thus not relevant for the content mapping. Three unmapped leafs contain checksums for input, output and tool, which have not been taken into account as a concept for GRAIN, asking for explicit version information instead. For input, output and tool RePlay-DH describes a resource type based on DataCite [3], which is also not included in GRAIN. The remaining unmapped leaf stands for the free additional properties, where single instances might be mappable to GRAIN categories depending on the content, however only on a by-case basis. For the partial mapping, the environment in RePlay-DH takes local architecture, operation system etc. for local executables into account. Depending on the content, this information might fit GRAIN's operator component description consisting of version, type and name.

3.3 GRAIN to EngMeta

EngMeta is the largest schema with 91 leafs. Thus, the flexibility of more general elements like *operator* or *component* in GRAIN is expressed in EngMeta with a set of concrete options (e.g. describing a tool by a link, a repository or the source code). From GRAIN to EngMeta there are 3 full and 6 near matches. 5 partial maps are mostly due to the several possibilities of mapping parameters, of mapping components, including the default option to treat them as additional input, and of mapping operator name, which can refer to a human actor or a tool, each of which comes with several description options in EngMeta. However, though with the many specific options many of the cases in GRAIN can be handled, there might be parameters which do not find their mapping in EngMeta, especially in the case of manual workflow steps.

3.4 RePlay-DH to EngMeta

RePlay-DH and EngMeta are similar in their distinction of tool and actor. For the RePlay-DH leafs there are 6 full and 10 near mappings. For the RePlay-DH tool parameters, there are again several options in EngMeta, thus it is part of full and partial maps. However there are 6 RePlay-DH leafs which with no mapping, two of which are again the metadata related to the RePlay-DH Client. One is the placeholder for all kinds of additional properties, which might or might not find a mapping on a by-case basis. The three others refer to the resource type of input, output and tool, however the checksum property of these three concepts is reflected in RePlay-DH and EngMeta.

4   Evaluation

For the project, it is of major importance that manual and automatic steps can be captured by the process metadata. For example selecting and exploring data from the repository, such as a specific version of a work or a net literature object, is a crucial step which should be documented. This is the case by design for GRAIN and RePlay-DH, however it is also expressible in EngMeta, due to the same actor/tool split as in RePlay-DH. Neither RePlay-DH nor EngMeta capture GRAIN's flexible actor parameters, so their importance has to be taken into account for a decision in the project. On the other hand, RePlay-DH and EngMeta come with more specific options which support better search than the general categories from GRAIN. All three schemas allow for a flexible handling of sequential steps, either within one or by means of several instances, and all schemas allow for empty input and output. Table 1 shows the sizes of the different mapping categories. Taking the content from GRAIN there is not much of a difference between the two targets RePlay-DH and EngMeta. Thus a decision between RePlay-DH and EngMeta can also take parameters like experience and implementation into account. The results of the unidirectional mappings allow to answer the question how much of the *information* encoded in one schema can be represented in the other, without restricting the setting to automatically mappable information.

Table 1. Quantitative summary of unidirectional mappings. The percentage of the mappings refer to the number of leafs in the source schema, i.e. the nodes to be mapped. Values in brackets are the absolute numbers. Some nodes have several options for mappings and appear in more than one mapping category.

From	(leafs)	To	(leafs)	FULLY	NEARLY	PARTIALLY	NO_MAP
GRAIN	(10)	RePlay-DH	(22)	30% (3)	60% (6)	40% (4)	0
RePlay-DH	(22)	GRAIN	(10)	50% (11)	4,5% (1)	4,5% (1)	41% (9)
GRAIN	(10)	EngMeta	(91)	30% (3)	60% (6)	50% (5)	0
RePlay-DH	(22)	EngMeta	(91)	27% (6)	45% (10)	4,5% (1)	27% (6)

5   Summary and Conclusion

We presented a set of mappings between two process metadata schemas in the DH and from Computational Engineering. Making use of three different qualities of mapping instances we get an overview about the overlap in content semantics between GRAIN and RePlay-DH and from these two into EngMeta. This study has been conducted to provide decision criteria to substantiate a selection and implementation for the DH project SDC4Lit dealing with manual and automatic text analysis based on different kinds of literature works. We discussed which aspects are relevant or get lost in the individual mappings. The decision which schema to choose can then be based on this findings and the results of user studies conducted within the project. It can also take decisions of fellow projects into account, since SDC4Lit is part of a group of infrastructure projects from different disciplines [1], some of which also take (parts from) EngMeta into account. Overall the successful mappings of the DH content into EngMeta argue for an underlying consensus on an abstract workflow structure even over discipline borders.

References

1. Axtmann, A.: Data center 4 science: Disziplinspezifische und disziplinübergreifende Forschungsdateninfrastrukturen und abgestimmte Bearbeitung von Querschnitts-themen in Baden-Württemberg. In: Poster at E-Science-Tage 2021: Share Your Research Data, Heidelberg (2021). https://doi.org/10.11588/heidok.00029607
2. Blessing, A., et al.: SDC4Lit - a science data center for literature. In: Poster at DH 2020, Ottawa (2020). http://dx.doi.org/10.17613/cyg5-3948
3. DataCite Metadata Working Group. DataCite Metadata Schema Documentation for the Publication and Citation of Research Data. Version 4.0. (2016). DataCite e.V. http://doi.org/10.5438/0012
4. Gärtner, M.: RePlay-DH Process Metadata Schema (2019). https://doi.org/10.18419/darus-474
5. Gärtner, M., Hahn, U., Hermann, S.: Preserving workflow reproducibility: the RePlay-DH client as a tool for process documentation. In: Calzolari, N., et al. (eds.) Proceedings of the Eleventh International Conference on Language Resources and Evaluation (LREC 2018). European Language Resources Association (ELRA), Paris (2018)
6. Jung, K., Gärtner, M., Kuhn, J.: Fine-GRAINed process metadata. In: Garoufal-lou, E., Fallucchi, F., William De Luca, E. (eds.) MTSR 2019. CCIS, vol. 1057, pp. 373–378. Springer, Cham (2019). https://doi.org/10.1007/978-3-030-36599-8_33
7. King, G.: An introduction to the Dataverse network as an infrastructure for data sharing. Sociol. Methods Res. **36**(2), 173–199 (2007). https://doi.org/10.1177/0049124107306660
8. Lebo, T., et al.: PROV-O: the PROV ontology. In: W3C Recommendation, World Wide Web Consortium, United States (2013)
9. Schembera, B.: Like a rainbow in the dark: metadata annotation for HPC applications in the age of dark data. J. Supercomput. **77**(8), 8946–8966 (2021). https://doi.org/10.1007/s11227-020-03602-6
10. Schembera, B., Iglezakis, D.: The genesis of EngMeta - a metadata model for research data in computational engineering. In: Garoufallou, E., Sartori, F., Siatri, R., Zervas, M. (eds.) MTSR 2018. CCIS, vol. 846, pp. 127–132. Springer, Cham (2019). https://doi.org/10.1007/978-3-030-14401-2_12
11. Schembera, B., Iglezakis, D.: EngMeta: metadata for computational engineering. Int. J. Metadata Semant. Ontol. **14**(1), 26–38 (2020)
12. Wilkinson, M.D., et al.: The FAIR guiding principles for scientific data management and stewardship. Sci. Data **3**(1), 1–9 (2016). https://doi.org/10.1038/sdata.2016.18

MEtaData Format for Open Reef Data (MEDFORD)

Polina Shpilker[1], John Freeman[1], Hailey McKelvie[1], Jill Ashey[2],
Jay-Miguel Fonticella[1], Hollie Putnam[2], Jane Greenberg[3],
Lenore Cowen[1], Alva Couch[1], and Noah M. Daniels[4(✉)]

[1] Department of Computer Science, Tufts University, Medford, MA, USA
[2] Department of Biological Sciences, University of Rhode Island, Kingston, RI, USA
[3] Department of Information Science, Drexel University, Philadelphia, PA, USA
[4] Department of Computer Science and Statistics, University of Rhode Island,
Kingston, RI, USA
noah_daniels@uri.edu

Abstract. Reproducibility of research is critical for science. Computational biology research presents a significant challenge, given the need to track critical details, such as software version or genome draft iteration. Metadata research infrastructures, while greatly improved, often assume a level of programming skills in their user community, or rely on expert curators to ensure that key information is not lost. This paper introduces MEDFORD, a new human-readable, easily-editable and templatable metadata language for scientists to collocate all the details relevant to their experiments. We provide an overview of the underlying design principles, language, and current and planned support infrastructure for parsing and translating MEDFORD into other metadata formats. MEDFORD 0.9 has been specifically designed for the coral research community, with initial metadata generated from RNA-Seq analyses of coral transcriptomes and coral photo collections. Notably, the format is generally applicable and useful for many types of scientific metadata generated by non-computer science experts.

Keywords: Metadata · Research accessibility · Coral reef data

1 Introduction

Corals comprise thousands of different organisms, including the animal host and single celled dinoflagellate algae, bacteria, viruses, and fungi that coexist as a holobiont, or metaorganism [2]. Thus, corals are more like cities than individual animals, as they provide factories, housing, restaurants, nurseries, and more for an entire ecosystem. Research on coral reefs is ever more pressing, given their local and global contributions to marine biodiversity, coastal protection, and economics, plus their sensitivity to climate change [6,16]. Research in this area requires integration of interdisciplinary data across multiple environments and

E. Garoufallou et al. (Eds.): MTSR 2021, CCIS 1537, pp. 206–211, 2022.
https://doi.org/10.1007/978-3-030-98876-0_18

a range of data types: 'omic data such as gene expression data generated using RNA-Seq (RNA transcript sequencing), image and time-lapse video, and physical and environmental measurements including light and water temperature, to name but a few. The coral research community has long been committed to sharing and open data formats, and both individual researchers and large funding agencies have invested heavily in making data available [4,9,11,17].

Effective data sharing for coral research, as in all data-intensive domains, requires metadata, which is essential for data organization, discovery, access, use, reuse, interoperability, and overall management [8]. The growing amount of digital data over the last several decades has resulted in a proliferation of metadata standards supporting these functions [1,12]. However, the mechanisms to create metadata have been focused primarily on ease of machine parsing and have tolerated schema that are cumbersome and difficult for humans to understand. If creating metadata in the appropriate format is difficult, or requires expert curators, then fewer scientists can comply with metadata standards, leading to loss of scientific data if neither discoverable nor reusable. Meanwhile, much scientific data in multiple countries now falls under mandated data sharing policies that include metadata requirements. Thus, there is a need for a format that streamlines the process of providing what is mandated by law and policy.

We propose to address this need by developing and implementing MEta-Data Format for Open Reef Data (MEDFORD). The MEDFORD markup language is simultaneously human and machine writable and readable. MEDFORD is designed to work in conjunction with the BagIt [10] filesystem convention, enabling easily accessible and interoperable bundles of data and metadata.

MEDFORD is initially targeted at coral holobiont transcriptomics data and coral image collections, with the subsequent goal of supporting metadata for additional research fields. The urgent need for international collaboration around saving coral reefs, plus the sheer complexity of the types and modalities of data the coral scientific community generates (from omics data, to image data with geospatial and temporal components, to temperature and color measurements), make corals a good domain choice. This short paper provides the rationale for current work and introduces the MEDFORD (version 0.9) metadata scheme.

MEDFORD will enable interdisciplinary coral reef data to be discoverable, accessible, and interoperable. Further, we are currently building the back-end infrastructure to translate between MEDFORD and make it compatible with other databases and systems such as Resource Description Framework (RDF) [7], ultimately supporting the interopability and reusability in FAIR [15] as well.

2   MEDFORD Design Principles

MEDFORD's design principles are informed by the those underlying highly successful metadata standards, such as the Dublin Core [14], Ecological Metadata Language (EML) [5], and the Data Document Initiative (DDI) [13], while addressing additional requirements enabling ease of metadata creation and other aspects. The design requirements for creating MEDFORD are, generally, to have a mechanism scientists can use at the point of data collection which is a simple, human-readable format with a simple syntax that does not require programming expertise. In addition, we wish for scientists to be able to create and reuse templates to minimize manual effort, use editing tools of their choice, and be able to produce output in a number of machine-readable formats including Resource Description Format (RDF), Extensible Markup Language (XML), and JavaScript Object notation (JSON), as well as database formats.

These requirements reflect the work of metadata experts [12]. Web-based metadata interfaces can become cumbersome when one is entering metadata for many similar data files or publications. The machine-readable formats XML, RDF, and JSON are difficult to understand and edit for scientists who are not programmers, and error messages for these formats are cryptic. Plain-text specification of metadata, such as the NSF's BCO-DMO resource [3] must then be manually translated into machine-readable form. Thus, the evidence is clear that there is a need for an intermediate format that is both machine-readable and human-readable and understandable by the scientists most qualified to specify the metadata correctly.

MEDFORD is aimed specifically at solving the problems of specifying interdisciplinary research metadata and is first applied to coral reef omics data. In general, however, the principles above apply to any scientific metadata specification problem, and the specific extensions identified here may be supplemented for other scientific disciplines. Thus MEDFORD can be used as a tool for metadata creation in any scientific discipline. These requirements are realized by MEDFORD by adding design elements that satisfy the above principles: first, a contextual grammar, devoid of parentheses or lexical scopes; second, a simple concept of a metadata definition statement: starting with an '@', a keyword, and a value; third, a simple concept of hierarchy, in which subparts of a clause start with the same keyword prefix; and fourth, a simple concept of user-extensible formatting, in which metadata details not covered by the main keywords can be added via notes.

All MEDFORD files are defined in reference to a BagIt [10] bag (where there is a special use case where the MEDFORD file refers only to external data by reference). The BagIt bag binds a set of files to the MEDFORD file, where these files can be any type: including source code, scientific papers, or raw data, each represented by a major tag. The provenance of that file is marked using a secondary major tag, where the tag can represent that the bag is the primary and authoritative source for the data or resource. Other secondary major tags describe the file as either a copy of an existing source, or simply a pointer to a URI where the resource can be obtained.

3   The MEDFORD File Format

MEDFORD's file format is plain text, with tags starting with the @ character. Anything after an @ character, until the next space in the file, is read as a tag. There are two other protected symbols that have special meanings: # which is treated as a comment character: characters after a # on the same line are ignored and do not carry through to any destination format. Finally, the $$ string (two dollar signs) is used to delimit a string to be parsed by LaTeXmath mode.

The following design principles are important in MEDFORD file syntax: MEDFORD files use the ASCII character set whenever possible. The characters @, #, and $$ are reserved and protected (@ only when it starts a string; # only when followed by a space). MEDFORD tags are referred to as @tags and always start with the @ character. Particular @tags are given meanings and specific recommended or required rules. The MEDFORD parser passes any unfamiliar @tags and their associated text through verbatim. Here, we present an excerpt from a MEDFORD description for a coral paper.

```
# This is just some example fragments of the MEDFORD file we built to
# record the metadata associated with this publication.

@Paper_Primary Coral bleaching response is unaltered following
acclimatization to reefs with distinct environmental conditions
@Paper_Primary-DOI https://doi.org/10.1073/pnas.2025435118
@Paper_Primary-Journal PNAS

@Contributor Katie L. Barott
@Contributor-ORCID 0000-0001-7371-4870
@Contributor-Role First Author, Corresponding author
@Contributor-Contribution Wrote paper, designed & performed research, analyzed data
@Contributor-email kbarott@sas.upenn.edu

@Contributor Hollie M. Putnam
@Contributor-ORCID 0000-0003-2322-3269
@Contributor-Contribution designed research, analyzed data

@Data_Primary Reef Seawater Sample No. 1
@Data_Primary-Location Kane'ohe Bay lagoon
@Data_Primary-Coord 21.4343°N, 157.7991°W
@Data_Primary-ResidenceTime 30+ days
@Data_Primary-ShoreDistance 0.75km
@Data_Primary-SampleDepth 2m

@Data_Reference Paper supplement
@Data_Reference-DOI 10.5281/zenodo.4315627
@Data_Reference-Notes Raw data and R scripts used for statistical analysis and PCA
```

4 Reusability

MEDFORD supports several features aimed at reusability of metadata among projects or datasets. The first of these is tag extensibility; MEDFORD has a set of pre-defined tags, but also accepts user-defined tags with no declaration needed. The MEDFORD parser will infer structure from the tag and any sub-tags. MEDFORD also supports templates; a MEDFORD file can be partially filled out, saved, and re-used. For instance, a lab may create a template containing common contributors and funding sources, which can be used for future contributions. MEDFORD recognizes an "invalid data" token, [..] that can ensure users complete all fields of a template, such as @Image-Date [..]. MEDFORD also supports macros, similar to a variable defined in Bash or a #define in C, a macro is a string name that is directly substituted with another, longer string. Finally, MEDFORD can act as a common source format for many possible destination formats; users may wish to submit their data to a database such as BCO-DMO [3]. Other formats can be added to the MEDFORD parser easily; tutorials will be available in the github repository. The ability of MEDFORD to act as an intermediary allows for a lab to write a single MEDFORD file to describe their research and export it to a multitude of different formats.

5   Availability

The MEDFORD parser is open-source and available under the MIT license at https://github.com/TuftsBCB/medford. The authors welcome suggestions for other output formats that may be beneficial for data storage submissions through the Issues tab on GitHub. Some example MEDFORD files are available at https://github.com/TuftsBCB/medford-examples.

6   Discussion and Future Work

This manuscript presents MEDFORD, a lightweight metadata format initially targeted at coral reef research data, intended to be easy for researchers without programming expertise to create and maintain. Initially supporting interoperability and reuse, MEDFORD aims to support all FAIR [15] principles. MEDFORD is currently at version 0.9; we intend to begin testing with users in the coral research community by the time this paper appears, and have already received input from potential users. We are working on finishing initial versions of the basic documentation and the parser.

Currently, MEDFORD relies on editing ASCII or UTF-8 text, but it is capable of extracting text content from Microsoft Word files. One possible critique of MEDFORD is the variety of possible tags. A rich template library can mitigate this, by providing examples that a user can simply fill in. A searchable template library portal (similar to LaTeX's CTAN) would enable users to find applicable templates as the template ecosystem grows.

A visual user interface for writing, editing, and viewing MEDFORD files is also in early stages of development. Another goal will be the development of a front-end tool that does identifier lookup from authoritative sources, such as ORCID, Grant ID, DOI, populating all redundant data fields.

A major future goal will be output of RDF and support for linked open data; EML [5] is another reasonable target specification. We hope to add the ability to translate a MEDFORD file (and created bag, if applicable) to RDF, as well as the data-1 compliance this involves.

Acknowledgment. The authors thank the anonymous reviewers for their valuable suggestions. This work is supported in part by funds from the National Science Foundation under grants NSF-OAC #1939263, #1939795 and #1940233.

References

1. Ball, A., Greenberg, J., Jeffery, K., Koskela, R.: RDA metadata standards directory working group (2016)
2. Bosch, T.C.G., McFall-Ngai, M.J.: Metaorganisms as the new frontier. Zoology **114**(4), 185–190 (2011)
3. Chandler, C.L., et al.: BCO-DMO: stewardship of marine research data from proposal to preservation. American Geophysical Union 2016:OD24B-2457 (2016)
4. Donner, S.D., Rickbeil, G.J.M., Heron, S.F.: A new, high-resolution global mass coral bleaching database. PLoS One **12**(4), e0175490 (2017)
5. Fegraus, E.H., Andelman, S., Jones, M.B., Schildhauer, M.: Maximizing the value of ecological data with structured metadata: an introduction to ecological metadata language (EML) and principles for metadata creation. Bull. Ecol. Soc. Am. **86**(3), 158–168, e0175490 (2005)
6. Hughes, T.P., et al.: Coral reefs in the anthropocene. Nature **546**, 82–90, e0175490 (2017)
7. Lassila, O., Swick, R.R., et al.: Resource description framework (RDF) model and syntax specification (1998)
8. Leipzig, J., Nüst, D., et al.: The role of metadata in reproducible computational research. CoRR, abs/2006.08589 (2020)
9. Liew, Y.J., Aranda, M., Voolstra, C.R.: Reefgenomics. Org - a repository for marine genomics data. Database **12**, baw152 (2016)
10. Littman, J., Madden, L., Vargas, B.: The BagIt file packaging format (v0. 97) draft-kunze-bagit-07. txt (2012)
11. Madin, J.S., et al.: A trait-based approach to advance coral reef science. Trends Ecol. Evol. **31**(6), 419–428, e0175490 (2016)
12. Qin, J., Ball, A., Greenberg, J.: Functional and architectural requirements for metadata: supporting discovery and management of scientific data. In: International Conference on Dublin Core and Metadata Applications, pp. 62–71 (2012)
13. Vardigan, M.: The DDI matures: 1997 to the present. IASSIST Quart. **37**(1–4), 45–45, e0175490 (2014)
14. Weibel, S.L., Koch, T.: The Dublin core metadata initiative. D-lib Magaz. **6**(12), 1082–9873, e0175490 (2000)
15. Wilkinson, M.D., Dumontier, M., et al.: The FAIR guiding principles for scientific data management and stewardship. Sci. Data **3**(1), 1–9, e0175490 (2016)
16. Woodhead, A., et al.: Coral reef ecosystem services in the anthropocene. Funct. Ecol. **33**(6), 1023–1034, e0175490 (2019)
17. Yu, L., Li, T., Li, L., et al.: SAGER: a database of symbiodiniaceae and algal genomic resource. Database **07**, baaa051 (2020)

Edumeres Toolbox: Functional, Technical, Architectural Analysis

Ernesto William De Luca[1,2,3], Francesca Fallucchi[1,2(✉)],
and Cristian Nobili[2]

[1] Leibniz Institute for Educational Media, Georg Eckert Institute,
Freisestraße 1, 38118 Braunschweig, Germany
{deluca,fallucchi}@gei.de
[2] Guglielmo Marconi University, via Plinio 44, Rome 00193, Italy
[3] Otto von Guericke University, Universitätsplatz 2, Magdeburg, Germany

Abstract. Edumeres Toolbox is a tool that helps researchers in the quantitative and qualitative analysis of large textbook collections. It belongs to the family of CAQDAS products: tools that allow text research to be simplified through automated text analysis. This paper analyses how the product is structured, its functionality and its architecture. It then reviews the architectural and technical aspects of this software, starting with a definition of a grid of architectural and software engineering design principles. The purpose is to identify its strengths and the improvements that should be made. This paper may be useful for an exploration of the application of software engineering principles and modern architectures (typical of commercial enterprise contexts) in software that supports research.

Keywords: Quantitative analysis · Qualitative analysis · Digital humanities · Software architecture · Software design · Software engineering

1 Introduction

Qualitative analysis is a scientific method that consists of the collection and evaluation of data in order to describe its contents and to enable researchers to provoke deeper thought and question attitudes and motivations. Quantitative analysis consists of a set of statistical-mathematical methods applied to a dataset with the aim of building a general model. Both of these types of research can be supported by software that helps simplify the researcher's work. CAQDAS (Computer Aided Qualitative Data Analysis Software) or QDA (Qualitative Data Analysis), for example, provide a set of data analysis tools which enable information to be cataloged and organised in a single database that can be explored using search engines which integrate information from heterogeneous sources [1].

© Springer Nature Switzerland AG 2022
E. Garoufallou et al. (Eds.): MTSR 2021, CCIS 1537, pp. 212–223, 2022.
https://doi.org/10.1007/978-3-030-98876-0_19

Edumeres Toolbox [2] belongs to this family, as its goal is to offer support tools for both qualitative and quantitative analysis of texts, even large selections. Software that aims to manage a large amount of data from heterogeneous sources, and that should also be extensible over time by incorporating new features to analyse that data, poses problems of design and development that fall within the scope of software engineering. Several quality attributes are considered important in this area, such as efficiency, consistency, maintainability, expandability, and last but not least, reliability. Identifying an effective solution to meet these quality objectives requires action at the design level to determine the shape of the product and enable its development in terms of functionality and extensions [10].

This paper will therefore describe how the Edumeres Toolbox solution is structured in terms of design, how the above issues have been addressed, and what the strengths and improvement points are of the solution adopted. An in-depth study of some more general software engineering aspects, in particular related to architecture and design, will also provide a methodological reference for the analysis and further elements for the design of comparable software. The goal is to describe: what are good design principles and why they are so important and how Edumeres Toolbox fulfills good design principles.

2   Related Work

Qualitative and quantitative analysis software began to be developed in the 1980s and the first commercial products date back to the 1990s [1]. Within a short time they have become real software suites that are rich in features, both in terms of data processed and types of data analysis. Today there are many products available on the market that offer solutions for research institutes: both on-site and, in the last decade, as cloud solutions through PaaS services. MAXQDA[1] and Provalis[2] are commercial tools that support qualitative and quantitative analysis; Atlas.ti[3] is a commercial workbench for the qualitative analysis of large bodies of textual, graphic, audio and video data [21] (as are as NVivo [18] or Quirkos[4]). Diacollo ia a software tool developed in the context of CLARIN for the efficient extraction, comparison and interactive visualisation of material from a diachronic text corpus [22]. Another popular tool is Voyant tools [23]. It is an open source, web-based, text mining solution. Other open source tools for quantitative and qualitative analysis of texts are Aquad[5], RQDA[6], Taguette[7], NLTK[8], OpenNLP[9], etc.

---

[1] https://www.maxqda.com.
[2] https://provalisresearch.com.
[3] https://atlasti.com.
[4] https://www.quirkos.com.
[5] http://www.aquad.de.
[6] https://rqda.r-forge.r-project.org.
[7] https://www.taguette.org.
[8] https://www.nltk.org.
[9] https://opennlp.apache.org.

Edumeres Toolbox currently offers a set of tools with which to organise large collections of documents (with their metadata) from research corpora, and which includes an OCR and text analysis service. It also offers utilities for quantitative text analysis, such as word frequency, co-occurrences, and distribution of words in the text. This solution therefore differs somewhat from commercial products (such as MAXQDA [19] and Atlas.ti [20]) which are designed for heterogeneous data collections. It also differs from other research products (such as Voyant Tools [23] and Diacollo [22]) because it aims not only to manage analytical activities but also the organisation of textual sources themselves, including their metadata.

From a software engineering perspective, Edumeres Toolbox is related to established commercial products (such as Atlas.ti [21]) that have large budgets and multidisciplinary teams dedicated to the design, development and collection of requirements, but it is a solution proposed by a research institute and therefore closer to the research context, where resources and expertise are more limited. Its goal is to provide an all-in-one tool focused on organising even large collections of text books, in a on-premise solution, thus giving a large collection of digital books to the researcher.

This software needs be analysed in strict terms of engineering and software architecture, defined in this document, but also placed in the context in which it is developed, so as to better understand not only its strengths and improvements, but also the applicability of future improvements and functionality [11–13].

3   Functional and High Level Design

Edumeres Toolbox [2] is an application developed by the George Eckert Institute, which conducts research in the area of educational and school texts at GEI [14–17] It is a web-based application that supports research activities based on the analysis of documents. The application uses collections of documents that are divided into research projects and corpora, i.e. groupings of texts that are the subject of specific research. More specifically, Edumeres Toolbox offers the following functions:

- importing digital documents from different sources
- pre-processing documents by extracting information, including OCR, meta-data collection and text analysis
- organising documents into collections and corpora
- performing automated, corpus-level, asynchronous analysis tasks that generate reports
- a tool for searching within collections, documents, and individual corpora
- tools for the visualisation and analysis of the extracted information, such as word frequency and co-occurrencies research.

Figure 1 shows a summary of the main functionalities.

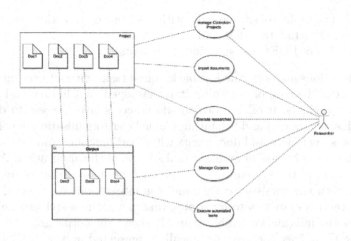

Fig. 1. Edumeres Toolbox main functionalities

3.1   Software and Model Design

The Edumeres Toolbox consists of a set of interconnected applications, which together offer user interaction and document import workflow functionality. Firstly, a web application offers the user a dashboard with the functionalities seen above. There is then a set of applications that carry out the pre-processing activities according to a predefined pipeline. The documents are uploaded to Edumeres Toolbox in different ways before being available for analysis: via web, FTP, external supports, etc. There are also different methods for associating metadata, such as the use of CSV-Excel or databases in Dublin Core, MARC and Pica+ formats. A pre-processing phase takes place prior to the uploading of the document (scheduled to run constantly, not interactive). This consists of text analysis and information extraction, in order to make the text and information available to the researcher. The pre-processing is structured as a "staged machine" , i.e. a series of cascading processes, as in an assembly line, that carry out the extraction process and manipulation for a single document. The application framework is completed by a set of external services, such as a database, search engine and file system where texts are stored. The application accesses the collections of several libraries for text analysis and processing, especially for Natural Language Processing. In detail, Edumeres Toolbox (dashboard web) is a java web application implemented upon toolbox API that runs on a Java servlet container (Apache Tomcat). It ias based upon Java PrimeFaces (a popular JavaServer Faces (JSF) UI framework that uses a MVC architecture (where M stands for modelisations, i.e. documents, corpora, users etc., V stands for "views", like html pages, and C stands for Controllers, the glue that keeps holds it all together).

Import Tools are java command line tools that manage the processing phase where documents are submitted and inserted into the database. They offers various functions:

216   E. W. De Luca et al.

- Extraction of topic, token, named entities, sentence extraction, etc.;.
- extraction of metadata, OCR and post-correction;
- manipulation of PDFs (i.e. splitting documents)

These functions are performed as background tasks without user interaction. API Toolbox is the core of the suite: it is developed as a library and included in the other products. It offers both the data access layer (access to database, search engine, filesystem) and the busines logic layer (organisation of collections, corpora, users, metadata and documents with NLP functions and text analysis). Figure 2 shows the high level architectural scheme of the application. API Toolbox is the heart of the system and is therefore the main object of analysis, as it contains both the persistence logic and the integrations to external libraries (for the extraction of metadata for topics, tokens and the search engine). Figure 3 illustrates the information architecture. It shows the entity graph used internally in the Edumeres Toolbox (technically represented in a SQL RDBMS and mapped into entities in API Toolbox). It is possible to divide this entity model into three areas:

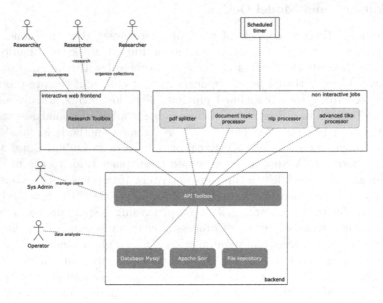

Fig. 2. Software high level architecture

- a documents area, which collects information (content, metadata, NLP-related information, tokens);
- a projects area related to corpora and to the management of automatic tasks;
- an area related to users and research projects (digital libraries).

3.2   Software Design Principles

It is necessary to identify and explain what the engineering and architectural criteria for software design and development are [3]. In software engineering literature there is a particular emphasis on the fact that a good architecture must divide the software into appropriately chosen modules in order to obtain a low outward coupling between modules and a high internal cohesion in the single module [4]. The goal is for the sub-parts of the product to be as independent as possible and for the release to be as atomic as possible, so as to simplify the product and make it modular, extensible, easily modifiable and evolvable over time. Cost is also an essential aspect of good architecture and adherence to software design principles as maintenance alone can amount to 75% of the cost of software development. To achieve this, the space domain must be taken into account. Two strategies are possible here, one based on decoupling by levels (for example, separating the UI operating rules and data access) or based on use cases (a module for each functionality) [8]. The time domain must also be taken into account. In software development, it is necessary to distinguish between three phases: compile time, build time and runtime, which correspond to a different level of abstraction and composition for distinct modules. A subdivision of the modules at compile time produces a monolithic model, a subdivision at build time produces a library model and a subdivision at runtime produces a service model. It is then necessary to hold account to put to disposition, in base to the identified strategy and the model of development, an adequate infrastructure that allows to always manage at least an environment of production and one or more environments of development, test, testing, also using the virtualization and the sharing of some parts of infrastructure between more environments. In order to industrialise the process, it is necessary to provide adequate deployment automation through Continuous Integration and Continuous Delivery [7].

An effective architectural model (used in models like MVC-MVP-MVVM-Hexagonal-VIPER-BCE-DCI, etc.) requires the software to be subdivided by abstraction levels [5].

The entities represent the information architecture, operational rules with the logics, adapters, and controllers that contain the logics that allow operational rules to be translated for external use, as well as the drivers and views that allow actual interfacing with external users. This model guarantees a software product that is independent of other technology, languages, and external libraries but which can also be tested and released for any strategy or model in both the time and space domains. It is important to underline how such a model generates a set of dependencies that are directed towards the "inside", i.e. towards the core components of the application, while the flows are bidirectional. We will explain below how this apparent contradiction is overcome. It is, however, not enough to divide the application from the outside in, into layers based on a generic abstraction. Further internal structuring constraints must be fixed in each layer and its components: in modern programming languages they can be composed of concrete classes, abstract classes and interfaces (or the functional equivalent). When designing these components, 3 architectural principles must be observed:

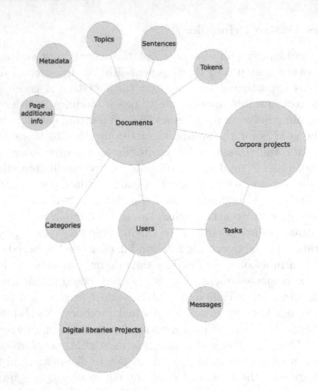

Fig. 3. Information architecture

1. The dependency graph must be oriented and acyclic, to avoid mutual dependencies;
2. Each component is defined by its instability $I = \frac{F_o ut}{F_i n + F_o ut}$, where $F_i n$ (Fan in) are the incoming dependencies and $F_o ut$ (Fan out) the outgoing dependencies, which can be expressed as the ratio of outgoing dependencies that quantitatively expresses a measure of a component's attitude to change. The principle requires that dependencies should always have decreasing instability in order to avoid or minimize a cascading effect following a change.
3. The concept of abstraction must be defined $A = \frac{N_a}{N_c}$, where N_a are the abstract classes/functions and N_c are the total classes/functions of the component. The principle defines a local rule for which the distance $D = |A+I-1|$ must be close to 0. The goal is to provide an adequate level of abstraction for the most stable components, since having many dependencies makes them difficult to modify if they are fixed.

The next phase, that of software development, is to work within the context of the constraints defined at the design level. Since it is not always easy to see the general design at the code level, the SOLID principles that define clear rules for writing classes and interfaces (or their functional counterparts) are a useful tool for the programmer:

1. SRP: each class must implement only one responsibility.
2. OCP: each class must be open to extension but not change
3. LSP: each class must be replaceable by one of its subclasses
4. ISP: each class must be associated with a public interface
5. DIP: each class must depend on abstractions or interfaces.

The inversion of control principle is also associated with these principles and is intended to overcome the apparent contradiction mentioned above. Since dependencies must be inward, but flows are bidirectional, the inner modules must include public interfaces to the outside, which will then be implemented by concrete components contained in the outer modules.

Another important local rule is Demeter's law, which limits the objects visible in a class to only those objects directly instantiated or referenced by the class itself (and therefore not their dependencies) [9]. The next phase after development is testing, where it is necessary to formally define a level of testing for each component created (static testing at compile time, and unit testing at build time) taking into account the development model (integration testing at runtime), the final stage is functional testing, or end-to-end testing when modules are released separately [6]. It is possible to speed up the process by skipping all or some of these guidelines. However, this creates a form of "debt" , which consists of the costs of solving problems at a later date. These costs also incur interest", i.e., additional costs that arise as the complexity of the software grows, known as "code smell" (code that shows design weaknesses) and "code erosion" (code that is unable to handle complexities for which it was not originally designed). To counter this phenomenon, continous refactoring techniques must be adopted: a development strategy that consists of a standardised process of code quality control, use of static analysis tools, coverage of unit testing, and modification of existing code when adding functionality.

4 Edumeres Toolbox: Project Design Analysis

Having explained the guidelines, it is now possible to go deeper into the analysis of the Edumeres Toolbox in order to highlight its strengths and weaknesses.

4.1 Development Strategies

Edumeres Toolbox is a suite of applications that consists of a library (Toolbox API) where the application logic resides, a web application with user interface (Dashboard), and several tools used in document processing (Tika processor, PDF splitter, Topic processor, NLP processor). A strategy of decoupling emerges from this subdivision, as can be seen in Fig. 4. Both by levels (Edumeres Toolbox and API Toolbox are to all intents and purposes two distinct levels) and by use cases (the preprocessing tools). If we compare the use cases with the modules used, we can see that this strategy is largely consistent with the decoupling principle stated above, i.e., components that change for homogeneous and independent reasons are generally grouped together.

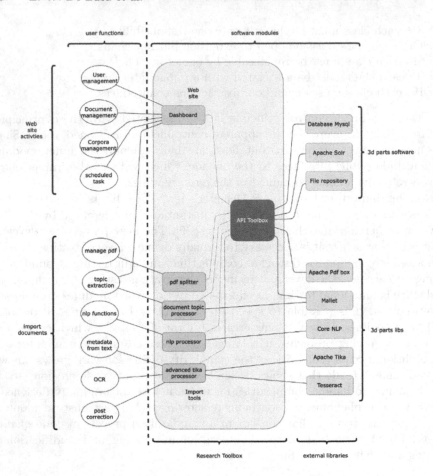

Fig. 4. Coupling between functions and modules

API Toolbox is a module that is released as a library. In contrast, the other applications are released as stand-alone command line applications or as web applications. API Toolbox is developed with its own codebase and release cycle; the API Toolbox build is exported as a library and used by other applications at build time. This allows separation in terms of the development cycle, without the complexity of managing an additional release. This mechanism is effective on the one hand because in the current state of development it would be an unjustified cost to create a service, since there is neither a separate team nor a public API to access Edumeres Toolbox, and on the other hand it may not be efficient to further split the API toolbox into multiple, separately releasable, modules since the information architecture (based on users, documents and collections) would be impacted by each different functionality.

The toolbox currently provides two environments: the programmer's development environment, and the production environment. They share the database (and search engine) with a single production instance. At the code level there is a separate repository for the API Toolbox and for the web dashboard. The import software tools are not under source control, which is a weakness that can cause problems in managing multiple development and release tasks at the same time (e.g. bugfix and new features). The can be solved by the creation of a development environment, independent from production, where all code is placed under source control in a multi-branch workflow (such as gitflow). Solutions to these issues are currently being studied, such as a smaller database and a parametric configuration.

4.2   Architectural Model

The API Toolbox and web dashboard can be logically divided into more modules using the structure illustrated in Fig. 5. The high-level architectural model respects the principles of clean architecture. Internally the web dashboard uses a MVC Framework, while the API Toolbox has a custom architecture model.

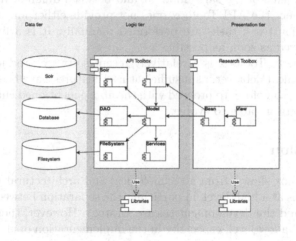

Fig. 5. Edumeres toolbox modules

This scheme therefore means that the current division into modules, with dependencies, is effective and constitutes a good compromise between complexity and separation of layers by abstraction. Thanks to this structure it is finally possible to plan new developments, such as a web API layer that would expose Toolbox API functionality.

At the level of detail architecture, the API Toolbox shows a component structure that exhibits a set of limitations and points of improvement with respect to the above architectural principles:

– cyclic paths are present in the dependency graph between classes;

- the dependencies present numerous cases of dependencies from more stable to less stable components;
- in general, little use is made of abstract classes and interfaces, meaning that code modifications are always rather expensive.

In this sense there is a situation of little maturity of the code, and the need for a refactoring activity of the classes.

If we analyse the individual classes, we see that the SOLID principles are poorly respected, as there is a lack of interfaces and abstract classes. The result at source level is that there are extremely complex classes (especially in document and corpora management) that include many functionalities in a single concrete object that have a strong coupling not borrowed from abstractions. Although the layers are separated at a macro-architectural level, this separation is not respected at code level with regards to an inversion of control, with the result that classes of business logic depend from classes that interact with the database, with dependences therefore that go towards the outside. The solution is to introduce abstract classes and interfaces to guarantee a better separation between components of the same module, and between different modules.

At the moment the API Toolbox does not provide either unit tests or automated integration tests; tasks are performed manually. It is a limitation that should be resolved as soon as possible.

Since Edumeres Toolbox is a relatively recent software product, we cannot talk about technical debt yet, as insufficient new features have been introduced. The intention is, therefore, to proceed with the above mentioned changes in order to make this software able to evolve.

5   Conclusion

Edumeres Toolbox shows, from a technological and architectural point of view, several strengths at a high level, in particular the separation between application and UI logics and the development-release strategy. However, there is room for improvement at a low level, especially in the implementation of classes, which at the moment may appear unimportant but are the basis of a significant technical debt. Edumeres Toolbox is constrained by being a project with limited budget resources in an already well-developed sector, where there are highly expert competitors. However, improvements to the product are still possible, especially in the long term.

Future development of Edumeres Toolbox should consist in making the improvements mentioned above. It may also be useful to develop a detailed work plan and to create a document based on that plan in which to verify the results. This paper, and its guidelines in particular, may be a useful reference for future studies on other products similar to Edumeres Toolbox, in particular those dedicated to the management of large amounts of data, that provide APIs to external users, and manage import flows and the use of third-party libraries to analyse documents. Software design (which is not limited to software engineering but embraces fields such as service design, user experience and digital transformation in general) is still an essential field of study regardless of the software product to be developed.

References

1. Wolski, U.: The History of the Development and Propagation of QDA Software. University of Northampton (2018)
2. De Luca, E.W., Fallucchi, F., Ligi, A., Tarquini, M.: A Research Toolbox: A Complete Suite for Analysis in Digital Humanities, vol. 1057. CCIS (2019)
3. Garlan, D.: Software Architecture: A Roadmap. Carnegie Mellon University (2000)
4. Sommerville, I.: Software Engineering. Pearson (2015)
5. Martin, R.: Clean Architecture. Prentice Hall (2017)
6. Schach, S.: Object Oriented and Classical Software Engineering. McGraw-Hill (2010)
7. Nygard, M.: L arte del rilascio. Apogeo (2018)
8. Martin, R.C.: Agile Software Development. Prentice Hall (2002)
9. Hunt, A., Thomas, D.: The Pragmatic Programmer. Addison-Wesley (2000)
10. Beck, K.: Test-Driven Development: By Example. Addison-Wesley (2002)
11. Fowler, M., Beck, K.: Refactoring: Improving the Design of Existing Code. Addison-Wesley (2018)
12. Gamma, E., Vlissides, J., Helm, R., Johnson, R.: Design Patterns: Elements of Reusable Object-Oriented Software. Addison-Wesley (1994)
13. Fowler, M.: Patterns of Enterprise Application Architecture (2002)
14. De Luca, E.W., Spielhaus, R.: Digital transformation of research processes in the humanities. In: Garoufallou, E., Fallucchi, F., William De Luca, E. (eds.) MTSR 2019. CCIS, vol. 1057, pp. 343–353. Springer, Cham (2019). https://doi.org/10.1007/978-3-030-36599-8_30
15. Fallucchi, F., Steffen, H., De Luca, E.W.: Creating CMDI-Profiles for Textbook Resources, vol. 846 (2019)
16. Fallucchi, F., De Luca, E.W.: Connecting and Mapping LOD and CMDI Through Knowledge Organization, vol. 846 (2019)
17. Fallucchi, F., De Luca, E.W.: CMDIfication process for textbook resources. Int. J. Metadata Semant. Ontol. 14(2), 135–148 (2020). https://doi.org/10.1504/IJMSO.2020.108331
18. Kausar Alam, M.: A systematic qualitative case study: questions, data collection. NVivo analysis and saturation. Qual. Res. Organ. Manag. (2020). ISSN:1746–5648
19. Marjaei, S., Yazdi, F.A., Chandrashekara, M.: MAXQDA and its application to LIS research. In: Library Philosophy and Practice, pp. 1–9 (2019). https://www.proquest.com/scholarly-journals/maxqda-application-lis-research/docview/2236131089/se-2?accountid=11064
20. Muhr, T.: ATLAS.ti – a prototype for the support of text interpretation. In: Tesch, R. (ed) Qualitative Sociology, vol. 14, pp. 349–371. Human Science Press, New York (1991)
21. Smit, B.: Atlas.ti for qualitative data analysis: research paper. Perspective in Education (2002)
22. Jurish, B.: DiaCollo: on the trail of diachronic collocations. Brandenburgische Akademia del Wissenschaften, Berlin (2018)
23. Miller, A.: Text mining digital humanities projects: assessing content analysis capabilities of Voyant Tools. J. Web Librarianship 12(8), 169–197 (2018)

Expressing Significant Others by Gravitation in the Ontology of Greek Mythology

Juan-Antonio Pastor-Sánchez[1] (iD), Sándor Darányi[2] (iD),
and Efstratios Kontopoulos[3]([✉]) (iD)

[1] University of Murcia, Murcia, Spain
pastor@um.es
[2] Swedish School of Library and Information Science, University of Borås, Borås, Sweden
sandor.daranyi@hb.se
[3] Catalink Limited, Nicosia, Cyprus
e.kontopoulos@catalink.eu

Abstract. To help close the gap between folksonomic knowledge vs. digital classical philology, based on a perceived analogy between Newtonian mechanics and evolving semantic spaces, we tested a new conceptual framework in a specific domain, the Ontology of Greek Mythology (OGM). The underlying Wikidata-based public dataset has 5377 entities with 289 types of relations, out of which 34 were used for its construction. To visualize the influence structure of a subset of 771 divine actors by other means than the force-directed placement of graph nodes, we expressed the combination of semantic relatedness plus objective vs. relative importance of these entities by their gravitational behaviour. To that end, the metaphoric equivalents of distance, mass, force, gravitational potential, and gravitational potential energy were applied, with the latter interpreted as the structuration capacity of nodes. The results were meaningful to the trained eye, but, given the very high number of contour maps and heatmaps available by our public tool, their systematic evaluation lies ahead.

Keywords: Ontology · Knowledge graph · Greek mythology · Gravitation · Wikidata

1 Introduction

Classic graphical visualization of semantic data models (i.e., ontologies and knowledge graphs – KGs) is very useful, and possibly the most efficient way to understand their elements. However, one of the main problems is the layout of individuals and relationships, when their number exceeds a certain threshold. In these cases, the mere display of nodes and edges leads to problems in understanding the structure of the ontology.

We rephrase this point of departure as the intersection of two shortcomings. First, ontology content visualization is problematic because of the often extreme size of KGs vs. the importance of small details, where different kinds of nodes vs. types of relations make such recognition even more difficult. The matter of consideration here is how to

E. Garoufallou et al. (Eds.): MTSR 2021, CCIS 1537, pp. 224–235, 2022.
https://doi.org/10.1007/978-3-030-98876-0_20

stress similarity or semantic relatedness *and* importance of content at the same time in one interactive visualization. Secondly, when it comes to elaborate fields of knowledge, like, e.g., Greek mythology, the classically trained eye is even more helpless to spell out the above, falling back on subjective relativities.

To remedy this combination of research problems, we call in classical mechanics as a metaphor, using gravity to express similar and socially significant ontology content for visualization in a novel way. This paper shows that using physical metaphors is not foreign to graph processing, including KGs, and applying the concept of gravitation as a modelling tool to visualize evolving structures of semantic content results in new insights and methodological opportunities. We see our contribution as an effort to close the gap between Wikidata-based folksonomic knowledge vs. digital classical philology, one that can assist scholars in asking new questions in their fields of specialisation.

2   Related Work

2.1   Visualization of Ontologies and KGs

As indicated by recent surveys of ontology visualization tools and techniques, human users face substantial challenges when attempting to visualize and navigate KGs containing more than a few hundred nodes [1–3]. Interestingly, relevant works addressing the visualization of large KGs (e.g., [4, 5]) do not focus on this user-related perspective but discuss the performance and technical issues of visualizing large graphs instead. In the same vein, other recent proposals involve the creation of spatial partitions of vertex sets [6] or the generation of summarized models [7], thus avoiding dealing with the whole structure. Finally, in an attempt to improve the user's cognition when traversing a large KG, some approaches propose the use of different colours for indicating the semantic relatedness between a chosen entity and other entities in the graph [8, 9]. Thus, after studying the existing approaches, one can easily conceive of the gap in current ontology visualization tooling with regards to: (a) visualizing large collections of items, (b) indicating the objective (vs. the relative) importance of nodes/entities in the graph.

2.2   Forces, Language, KGs, and Classical Mechanics

The idea of force-directed placement (FDP) goes back to [10]. Their purpose was to position the nodes of a graph in two- or three-dimensional space, so that all the edges are of more or less equal length with as few crossing edges as possible. They assigned forces among the sets of edges and nodes based on their relative positions, using these forces either to simulate the motion of the edges and nodes, or to minimize their energy [11]. Force-directed graph drawing algorithms do the same to a set of edges and a respective set of nodes. Typically, spring-like attractive forces based on Hooke's law are used to attract pairs of endpoints of the edges towards each other, while simultaneously attractive and repulsive forces like those of electrically charged particles based on Coulomb's law are used to separate all pairs of nodes until equilibrium. Applying FDP to model the inner dynamics of KGs is a popular application domain too [12–14].

The idea to compare content-based grouping behaviour to the impact of a gravitation-like force is not new either [15]. Ma et al. [16] reported good results with a gravity-based centrality index to identify influential spreaders in complex networks by means of considering each node's k-shell [17–20] value as its mass, and the shortest path distance between two nodes viewed as their distance. A similar idea was proposed in [21], with the hypothesis that the dynamics of semantic drifts can be modelled on a relaxed version of Newtonian mechanics. By using term distances as a measure of semantic relatedness [22] vs. their centrality, prominently PageRank values indicating social importance and applied as term mass, gravitation as a metaphor to express changes in the semantic content of a vector field lends new perspectives for experimentation.

3   Background: Wikidata and the OGM

We applied our above considerations to a specific dataset in Wikidata about Greek mythology. Wikidata is a KG that uses its own RDF-compliant data model. Its main elements are items with a unique identifier (starting with "Q") and described by uniquely identified properties (starting with "P"). Properties define relations between items, or refer to literal values (strings, numbers, dates).

One of the most complex aspects of Wikidata is the use of qualifiers, references, and rankings. Qualifiers are used to make claims about a statement. Rankings specify which one of the statements about the same property is preferred. Statements can have references to information sources associated to verify the source of the data. Qualifiers, rankings, and references are defined using a mechanism similar to RDF reification, which reinforces Wikidata's compatibility with this data model, and therefore its representation in the Linked Data context. Wikidata includes in its data model the number of Wikimedia sites (sitelinks) in which items have equivalences.

Wikidata has no explicitly defined classes differentiated from the rest of the items. Instead, some items play the role of class according to their membership in a taxonomy of classes and subclasses defined by connecting items via property P279 (subclass of). Membership of items to other item-classes is done using property P31 (instance of).

The OGM [23] is an ontology about Greek mythology created from Wikidata. The data model was developed through the analysis of the properties from 5377 items defined as instances of "mythological Greek character (Q22988604)" and "group of Greek myth-ical characters (Q28061975)". After analysing the 289 properties used to describe these items, a set of 34 properties relevant to the domain was defined on the basis of [24]. The OGM is available at http://purl.org/umu/ogm. A tool called Wikidata Ontologizer was also developed and is provided at https://skos.um.es/gmwdo.

4   Material and Method

The point of departure for our working hypothesis was the observation that the very moment change or behavior is to be observed in them, vector space-based methods of content grouping should be reinterpreted in terms of vector fields. In such an environment, semantic relatedness between entities is expressed by distance [25], but due to content dislocation over time, concept velocity vs. concept acceleration can be detected as well, random drift patterns reminding one of the Brownian motion of particles. Given the general resemblance between Newton's second law, $F = ma$, i.e., force being equal to the product of mass and acceleration, and the above situation, one can envisage the dynamics of semantic space due to some force-like impact whose nature can be modelled as soon as one can compute m, i.e., term mass. From this it also follows that Newton's general law of gravitation should apply. As similarity between any two items in Wikidata is measured by the proportion of their shared vs. specific intensions, this invites social significance for the role of mass, another important variable successfully used in machine learning and document retrieval, expressed by measures of centrality [26–28]. Experiment design by these parameters means that items which are *both* similar and popular should be grouped together. As soon as all these parameters can be operationalized for an experiment, our working hypothesis can be tested.

For this work, all the relevant relations in Wikidata between the items in OGM were retrieved via SPARQL queries to the Wikidata Query Service (WDQS). The obtained results were processed to create an undirected graph by Neo4j. In this way, it was possible to calculate the proximity between items even if no direct interrelationships were there (i.e., both were connected via an intermediate node). The resulting graph was processed to calculate the PageRank of each node and the distance matrix between all nodes. Apart from their PageRank values, we also wanted to express the importance of the retrieved items in relation to Wikimedia Foundation projects. This information is provided by Wikidata sitelinks that indicate the number of equivalent articles an item has in different editions of Wikipedia (or other Wikimedia projects). Therefore, our metaphoric mass for each item was calculated as follows:

$$m_i = PageRank_i \times log_e(sitelinks_i)$$

The logarithmic weighting of the sitelinks expresses the importance of an item by its persistence in the Wikimedia corpus without causing high variations in its PageRank value. Another additional advantage of this method is that thereby more heterogeneous values are obtained, i.e., it cannot occur that two items end up with the same mass.

The next step calculated the gravitational force between all pairs of nodes in the graph. To that end, the equation of Newton's law of universal gravitation was used, without the gravitational constant (G), meaningless in this context. The masses (m) of all the items calculated in the previous step were used. We considered the distance between any two nodes (r) as the number of edges between them. When there is a direct relation between two nodes, the value of r is 1. The type of semantic relation between nodes was not taken into account to calculate the distance. This implies that the distance between two nodes is calculated from the number of edges between them, although the edges correspond to different types of relations. This way, the gravitational force between two pairs of nodes in the graph was computed as:

$$F(a, b) = \frac{m_a \times m_b}{r^2(a, b)}$$

Gravitational potential energy (U) is the energy that a mass possesses according to its position in space. U is caused by the gravitational attraction between two masses. Consequently, a greater force of attraction between masses implies greater gravitational potential energy. As the distance between two masses decreases, the gravitational potential energy also decreases since gravitational attraction is greater and therefore the energy necessary to bring these masses closer also decreases. The gravitational potential energy between all pairs of nodes (U) was calculated as:

$$U(a, b) = -\frac{m_a \times m_b}{r(a, b)}$$

All the calculations this far refer to aspects of every node (such as m) or the relationships between pairs of nodes (e.g., F, U, r). Next, the gravitational potential (V) was calculated for every node. The main difference between gravitational potential (V) and gravitational potential energy (U) is that every point in a gravitational field has a value of V, while U is the energy that a mass acquires when placed at that point. The average distance of each node in relation to the rest of the nodes of the graph (r_{avg}) was also calculated. Both measures provided an overview of the relationship of a node with all other nodes in the graph. The gravitational potential, at a point when there are several masses around it, follows the principle of superposition, and for a particular node it is calculated as the sum of the V values of each of the surrounding masses. Considering n as the total number of nodes in the graph, the following equations were applied:

$$V(a) = \sum_{k=1}^{n} \frac{m_k}{r(a, k)}$$

$$r_{avg}(a) = \frac{\sum_{k=1}^{n} r(a, k)}{n}$$

The calculation of the metric z (used in the plots of Sect. 5) to express findings was based on the distance that separates the node for which we are representing the contour plot from other nodes displayed in the plot. We fell back on using the $1/r$ metric because applying r directly one gets the opposite effect, highlighting the most distant items. In this way, as r increases, the value of z is getting smaller and vice versa.

5   Results

The first SPARQL query in WDQS retrieved 839 items and 3109 relations. Because this first graph was relatively compact and small, we obtained very similar PageRank values for many items that had practically no presence in the Wikimedia corpora compared to other items with a higher presence. For this reason, we considered weighting the PageRank values based on the number of sitelinks for every item. This weighting is only possible if there is some level of correlation between both variables. The Pearson and Spearman correlation coefficients showed the following results:

$$r_{Pearson}(PageRank, sitelinks) = 0.2812587$$

$$r_{Spearman}(PageRank, sitelinks) = 0.4366637$$

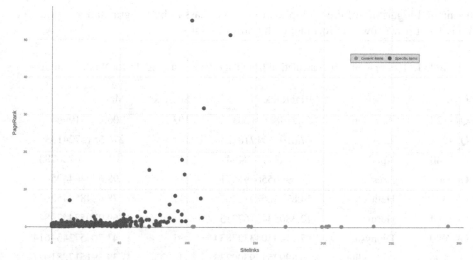

Fig. 1. PageRank vs. sitelinks distribution before revision with identification of specific vs. generic items. Source: own dataset.

These values hinted at a possible non-linear correlation between both variables. Visualizing their distribution via a scatter plot (see Fig. 1) revealed a few generic topic items (in red) with a low PageRank value and a high number of sitelinks.

We decided not to use these items because OGM includes relations such as "*Appears in the form of*", "*Domain of the deity*", "*Uses*", "*Wears*", etc., linking specific items of Greek mythology with other generic ones that distorted the results. A new SPARQL query was submitted, ignoring these relations and, after repeating the process, the Spearman correlation index was calculated again, obtaining a value of 0.5337093. Compared to the initial version of the graph, this 20% increase confirmed a certain relationship between the PageRank value and the number of sitelinks. After recalculating the PageRank, the equation from Sect. 4 was applied. An example of the obtained values ordered by mass is shown in Table 1.

We developed two web applications to represent results based on the Plotly JavaScript Open Source Graphing Library. The first one is a contour plot generator and viewer to study the relations of a specific item A with the rest of the items in the KG. The user can limit the number of items, with the location of the retrieved items in the plot expressed as coordinates in F, V and $1/r$. The application allows various combinations of mass and gravitational potential with or without logarithmic scales. Gravitational potential on the y-axis compensates for the existence of a very small set of items with a large mass and improves the visualization. Table 2 shows results from the analysis of the percentile distribution for mass m and different ways to express gravitational potential V.

The table shows how the mass distribution tends to show items with predominantly large mass on the y-axis (even if a logarithmic scale is used). This is evident in the distribution of the 95th percentile, where most of the items with the greatest mass are located. It is possible to compensate for this by using the gravitational potential V whose distribution is more homogeneous. Finally, the default configuration for the y-axis uses the natural logarithm of the multiplication of the mass m by the gravitational potential V. The last row shows the formula with optimal results.

Table 1. Example of mass calculation from PageRank and sitelinks for Wikidata items.

Item	Label	PageRank	Sitelinks	Mass
Q41127	Poseidon	54.2198663120373	103	306.03811996433
Q34201	Zeus	47.0101791718628	131	276.55157241336
Q37340	Apollo	31.583977419494	113	181.17196226783
Q40901	Ares	17.6996556191571	96	98.670464495844
Q134270	Helios	14.8238268011202	72	78.424854453935
Q41484	Hermes	12.3805345167315	98	69.270574429841
Q41680	Dionysus	7.91493043327834	91	43.704572454614
Q35500	Aphrodite	6.89925729300233	110	39.391517881021
Q44384	Hephaestus	5.25671113648196	87	28.79277743093
Q2631851	Manes	7.0123068035716	13	25.518186471048
Q40730	Demeter	3.92363381107958	93	21.749858832496
Q159168	Themis	4.00281620958408	69	21.0087618308
Q38012	Hera	3.24091017419886	97	18.100377924193
Q93172	Gaia	3.25400362284996	80	17.553557092584
Q102884	Mnemosyne	2.86364329268765	63	14.773200939423
Q44204	Cronus	2.460767530201	87	13.478452585043

Table 2. Distribution of the 25th, 50th, 75th, 95th and 100th percentiles of values obtained from equations that include the mass and/or gravitational potential for all the items in the dataset.

	25	50	75	95	100
m	1177.534	2189.244	4170.850	11919.537	587974.487
$\log_e(m)$	−0.03929022	0.57524850	1.12357927	2.09257192	5.72370967
V	1143.741	1332.626	1434.121	1522.358	2727.449
$\log_e(V)$	7.042059	7.194907	7.268308	7.328016	7.911122
$\log_e(m) \times \log(V)$	−0.2723836	4.0805415	8.1124609	15.1975413	43.0790417
$\log_e(m \times V)$[a]	**7.071167**	**7.691312**	**8.335875**	**9.385929**	**13.284439**

The z-axis of the contour plot is interpreted as the closeness between items in the knowledge graph. The application offers a variation of formulae to compute the z value, taking into account the average distance of items retrieved from the rest of the items in the graph, so as to highlight those that are on the periphery of the graph and close to item A. The application is available at: https://skos.um.es/gmwdo/contour.php.

The second web application shows the relationships of a set of selected items with the rest of the items in the dataset based on a heatmap plot. The x-axis of the heatmap lists the labels of the selected items vs. the y-axis labels of all items in the dataset. It is possible to limit the number of items to be displayed on the y-axis by indicating the number of items we want according to their mass. The z-axis in heatmaps represents the force or distance between the items. In this case, the same equations used for the x-axis and the z-axis of the contour plot are offered. This is possible because each element on the z-axis of the heatmap refers to a variable between two items, be it the force of attraction (F) or the distance between items ($1/r$). The application is available at: https:// skos.um.es/gmwdo/heatmap.php.

Table 3 shows a summary of the equations used in each of the axes in both plots. The tools allow selecting any possible combination. The table also shows the optimal equations to configure each axis.

Table 3. Equations used in each of the axes in contour and heatmap plots.

Axis	Contour plot	Heatmap plot
x	$x = \log_e(F(m_a \times m_b))^a$	Label of selected items
	$x = F(m_a \times m_b)$	
y	$y = \log_e(m_b \times V(m_b))^a$	Label of retrieved items
	$y = \log_e(m_b) \times \log_e(V(m_b))$	
	$y = \log_e(m_b)$	
	$y = m_b$	
	$y = m_b \times V(m_b)$	
z	$z = 1/r(m_a,m_b)^a$	$z = \log_e(F(m_a \times m_b))^a$
		$z = 1/r(m_a,m_b)$
	$z = r_{avg}(m_b)/r(m_a,m_b)$	$z = (F(m_a \times m_b)$
		$z = r_{avg}(m_b)/r(m_a,m_b)$

[a]Default configurations

Figure 2 displays the status of Medusa (from her perspective, i.e., not in the plot), against prominent actors in her story, indicated by high values. The map correctly states that key figures are Poseidon in the upper right corner vs. Perseus, Chrysaor and Pegasus in the lower left one, namely Medusa was turned into a monster by Pallas Athene after having had sex in her temple with Poseidon; on the other hand, it was Perseus who decapitated her, with Chrysaor, a giant wielding a golden sword, and Pegasus, a winged horse, born from her blood. The space where the relations among actors are expressed is that of semantic relatedness combined with perceived importance as force F; gravitational potential V, i.e., the structuration capacity of a node with respect to all other nodes; and distance metrics to highlight the relative impact of central vs. peripheral nodes. Figure 3 confirms the same key actors in the plot as above, but redraws contour

lines according to the increased importance of peripheral nodes in the graph after picking
the non-default option for z.

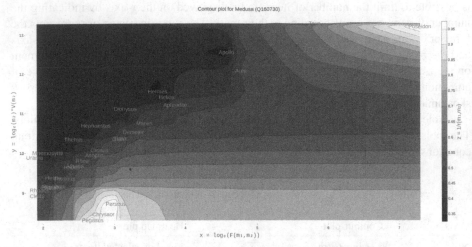

Fig. 2. Contour plot for Medusa. Original: Query Q160730 with default x,y,z parameters at https://
skos.um.es/ogm/contour.php. Legend: x = force value between the "observer" vs. other actors; y
= gravitational potential energy of the actors in the plot; z = central vs. peripheral node impact
regulation.

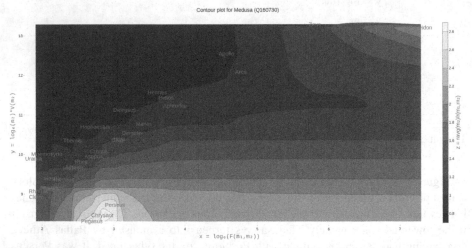

Fig. 3. Contour plot for Medusa. Original: Query Q160730 with default x,y and non-default z
parameters, at https://skos.um.es/ogm/contour.php. Legend: x = force value between the "observer" vs. other actors; y = gravitational potential energy of the actors in the plot; z = central vs.
peripheral node impact regulation.

Out of several generative options, Fig. 4 shows the heatmap of 771 divine figures vs.
the 12 Olympians (in fact 13 of them, because accounts differ if Hestia or Dionysus was

accepted as the 12th one). Cells in the table express the strength of attractive force between any two entries, with columns ranked according to their average values. This particular parametrization suggests that in terms of celebrity status measured by influence and connectedness, except for Aphrodite, goddesses in Greek mythology were considered secondary to gods, because Demeter, Hera, Athena, Artemis and Hestia were placed to the right side of the heatmap. On the other hand, the goddess of love was inserted among dominant males on the left, preceding Dionysos, the youngest god and latest arrival on Mt. Olympus [29], and limping Hephaistus as the least influential males. Of course, other parameter choices allow for less radical interpretations as well.

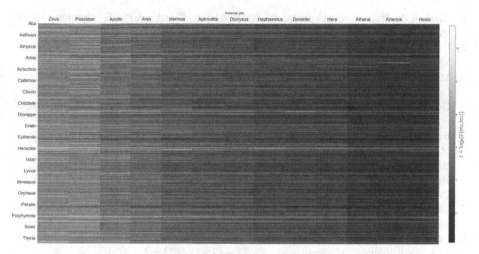

Fig. 4. Heatmap of the attractive force F between 771 divine actors and the 12 Olympians.

6 Conclusion and Future Work

Based on a perceived analogy between Newtonian mechanics and evolving semantic spaces, we tested gravity as a new conceptual framework in a specific domain, the Ontology of Greek Mythology. The results were meaningful for the trained eye and providing new insights for KG visualization by means of two public tools and a public dataset, but their systematic evaluation lies ahead.

We see our contribution as an effort to close the gap between Wikidata-based folksonomic knowledge vs. digital classical philology [30], one that can assist scholars in asking new questions in their fields of specialisation [31–37]. At the same time, the current parametrization options over 771 divine actors in the OGM allow for 12336 contour maps, making their manual evaluation practically impossible. Nevertheless, their factual accuracy in terms of Wikidata vs. classical sources will have to be systematically scrutinized, eventually considering how to translate the often conflicting content of myth variants into visual landscapes by drilling down in the material. Another priority will be to continue the fine-tuning of our algorithms during the process.

In a broader context, and with an eye for other application domains, the concept of gravitational potential energy as a property of KG nodes in this framework corresponds to *change (structuration) capacity*. This follows from the fact that semantic content evolution, with its temporal implications, requires a field – rather than a spatial-only – representation, implemented by a combination of semantic relatedness expressed by distance vs. relative social or semantic importance expressed by centrality. Changes in these components then can model engagement, activation, update, fashion, and more.

References

1. Katifori, A., Halatsis, C., Lepouras, G., Vassilakis, C., Giannopoulou, E.: Ontology visualization methods—a survey. ACM Comput. Surv. **39**(4), 10 (2007)
2. Dudáš, M., Lohmann, S., Svátek, V., Pavlov, D.: Ontology visualization methods and tools: a survey of the state of the art. Knowl. Eng. Rev. **33** (2018)
3. Mikhailov, S., Petrov, M., Lantow, B.: Ontology visualization: a systematic literature analysis. In: BIR Workshops (2016)
4. Gómez-Romero, J., Molina-Solana, M., Oehmichen, A., Guo, Y.: Visualizing large knowledge graphs: a performance analysis. Futur. Gener. Comput. Syst. **89**, 224–238 (2018)
5. Bikakis, N., Sellis, T.: Exploration and visualization in the web of big linked data: a survey of the state of the art. arXiv preprint arXiv:1601.08059 (2016)
6. Bikakis, N., Liagouris, J., Krommyda, M., Papastefanatos, G., Sellis, T.: GraphVizdb: a scalable platform for interactive large graph visualization. In: 2016 IEEE 32nd International Conference on Data Engineering (ICDE), pp. 1342–1345. IEEE (2016)
7. Ghorbel, F., Hamdi, F., Ellouze, N., Métais, E., Gargouri, F.: Visualizing large-scale linked data with memo graph. Procedia Comput. Sci. **112**, 854–863 (2017)
8. Le, D.H.: UFO: a tool for unifying biomedical ontology-based semantic similarity calculation, enrichment analysis and visualization. PloS One **15**(7), e0235670 (2020)
9. Nguyen, Q.H., Le, D.H.: Similarity calculation, enrichment analysis, and ontology visualization of biomedical ontologies using UFO. Curr. Protoc. **1**(4), e115 (2021)
10. Fruchterman, T.M., Reingold, E.M.: Graph drawing by force-directed placement. Softw. Pract. Exp. **21**(11), 1129–1164 (1991)
11. Kobourov, S.G.: Spring embedders and force directed graph drawing algorithms. arXiv preprint arXiv:1201.3011 (2012)
12. Huang, Z., Wu, J., Zhu, W., Wang, Z., Mehrotra, S., Zhao, Y.: Visualizing complex networks by leveraging community structures. Phys. A Statist. Mechan. Appl. **565**, 125506 (2021)
13. Basole, R.C., Accenture, A.I.: Mining logomaps for ecosystem intelligence. In: HICSS, pp. 1–10 (2021)
14. Nararatwong, R., Kertkeidkachorn, N., Ichise, R.: Knowledge graph visualization: challenges, framework, and implementation. In: 2020 IEEE 3rd International Conference on Artificial Intelligence and Knowledge Engineering (AIKE), pp. 174–178. IEEE (2020)
15. Paijmans, H.: Gravity wells of meaning: detecting information-rich passages in scientific texts. J. Document. **53**(5), 520–536 (1997)
16. Ma, L.L., Ma, C., Zhang, H.F., Wang, B.H.: Identifying influential spreaders in complex networks based on gravity formula. Physica A **451**, 205–212 (2016)
17. Carmi, S., Havlin, S., Kirkpatrick, S., Shavitt, Y., Shir, E.: A model of Internet topology using k-shell decomposition. Proc. Natl. Acad. Sci. **104**(27), 11150–11154 (2007)
18. Kitsak, M., et al.: Identification of influential spreaders in complex networks. Nat. Phys. **6**(11), 888–893 (2010)

19. Garas, A., Schweitzer, F., Havlin, S.: A k-shell decomposition method for weighted networks. New J. Phys. **14**(8), 083030 (2012)
20. Zeng, A., Zhang, C.J.: Ranking spreaders by decomposing complex networks. Phys. Lett. A **377**(14), 1031–1035 (2013)
21. Darányi, S., Wittek, P., Konstantinidis, K., Papadopoulos, S., Kontopoulos, E.: A Physical Metaphor to Study Semantic Drift. arXiv preprint. arXiv:1608.01298 (2016)
22. Pedersen, T., Pakhomov, S.V., Patwardhan, S., Chute, C.G.: Measures of semantic similarity and relatedness in the biomedical domain. J. Biomed. Inform. **40**(3), 288–299 (2007)
23. Pastor-Sánchez, J.-A., Kontopoulos, E., Saorín, T., Bebis, T., Darányi, S.: Greek mythology as a knowledge graph: from chaos to zeus and beyond. Seman. Web J. Rev. (2021)
24. Syamili, C., Rekha, R.V.: Developing an ontology for Greek mythology. Electron. Lib. **36**(1) (2018)
25. Wittek, P., Darányi, S., Kontopoulos, E., Moysiadis, T., Kompatsiaris, I.: Monitoring term drift based on semantic consistency in an evolving vector field. In: 2015 International Joint Conference on Neural Networks (IJCNN), pp. 1–8. IEEE (2015)
26. Mai, G., Janowicz, K., Yan, B.: Support and centrality: learning weights for knowledge graph embedding models. In: Faron Zucker, C., Ghidini, C., Napoli, A., Toussaint, Y. (eds.) EKAW 2018. LNCS (LNAI), vol. 11313, pp. 212–227. Springer, Cham (2018). https://doi.org/10. 1007/978-3-030-03667-6_14
27. Brank, J., Leban, G., Grobelnik, M.: Semantic annotation of documents based on Wikipedia concepts. Informatica **42**(1), 23–31 (2018)
28. Hamdam, H., Ganascia, J.G.: Graph Centrality Measures for Boosting Popularity-Based Entity Linking. arXiv. arXiv:1712.00044 (2017)
29. Kerényi, K.: Die Mythologie der Griechen: Götter, Menschen und Heroen. Klett-Cotta, Stuttgart (1997)
30. Berti, M. (ed): Digital classical philology. In: Ancient Greek and Latin in the Digital Revolution. De Gruyter, Berlin (2019)
31. Zgoll, C.: Tractatus Mythologicus. De Gruyter, Berlin (2019)
32. Zgoll, A., Zgoll, Ch. (eds): Mythische Sphärenwechsel: Methodisch neue Zugänge zu Antiken Mythen in Orient und Okzident. De Gruyter, Berlin (2020)
33. McConnell, J., Hall, E.: Ancient Greek Myth in World Fiction Since 1989. Bloomsbury, London (2016)
34. Versnel, H.S.: Coping With the Gods: Wayward Readings in Greek Theology. Brill, Leiden (2011)
35. Frenzel, E.: Motive der Weltliteratur: Ein Lexikon dichtungsgeschichtlicher Längsschnitte. Alfred Kröner Verlag, Stuttgart (1976)
36. Frenzel, E.: Stoffe der Weltliteratur: Ein Lexikon dichtungsgeschichtlicher Längsschnitte. Alfred Kröner Verlag, Stuttgart (1970)
37. Seigneuret, J.C. (ed.): Dictionary of Literary Themes and Motifs, vols. 1–2. Greenwood Press, New York (1988)

Semantic Information Extraction in Archaeology: Challenges in the Construction of a Portuguese *Corpus* of Megalithism

Ivo Santos[(✉)] [iD] and Renata Vieira [iD]

CIDEHUS, University of Évora, Palácio do Vimioso - Largo do Marquês de Marialva, no. 8, Apartado 94, 7000-809 Évora, Portugal
{ifs,renatav}@uevora.pt
http://www.cidehus.uevora.pt

Abstract. Archaeological records are a central part of this discipline research. It is essential that the records include the relationship between its parts to allow better understanding among man and machine. Here we present the challenges of applying NLP and Information Extraction to Archaeological data with a case study: Megalithism.

Keywords: Information Extraction · Natural Language Processing · Archaeology · Megalithism

1 Introduction

In archaeological works, it's necessary to obtain certain information to characterize the object of study, for example: a list of archaeological sites from a chronological period and/or in a certain region; in which sites an artifact of a specific typology was exhumed; or which archaeological sites whose architecture has certain characteristics (for example, the shape of the plant or even the dimensions). The compilation of this information can be obtained through public management databases, or by contacting pairs, or by checking possible references in the bibliography. Studies, in general, are naturally conditioned to the exhaustion of this collection and the effort to carry out supralocal studies is progressively greater. Ultimately, when there is no data sharing, the community multiplies into isolated efforts with the same purpose and we can assume the existence of difficulties in the reproducibility of conclusions. Besides, part of archaeology research is destructive, by nature, which makes the archaeological records even more important. Ideally, everything that can be registered should be registered. We agree with Cripps that "without the data model capable of adequately describing not only the archaeological data contained within records but the archaeological processes used to

This work is funded by national funds through the Foundation for Science and Technology, under the project UIDB/00057/2020.

generate records, any database is limited in terms of its capabilities and suitability for reporting, assessment and analysis ultimately its suitability as an archive" [5]. Thus, from the point of view of information, we consider essential for the record to include relationships between all parts to understand the semantic relationship between existing data. Ideally, a database for archaeological management would benefit from the possibility of carrying out searches with Booleans (for example, the presence/absence of a certain artifact), but also by characterizing the relationships between the data and, undoubtedly, by the possibility of applying inference mechanisms. To achieve such level it is necessary to apply Natural Language Processing methods for archaeological Information Extraction (IE). Here we present the constitution of a Portuguese corpus of Megalithism, one of the most important categories of European prehistoric monuments, and the most common in the south of Portugal, to serve as a basis for our research about information extraction from such Portuguese records.

2 Related Works

Pushed forward by several international Conventions and initiatives (e.g. INSPIRE), the distribution of information and the sharing of digital data within the global scientific community has become key elements of heritage conservation policy, as well as a tool that points out to the sustainable use of historical resources or even a prerequisite for their preservation [6,11,19].

Noor et al. [13] argue that approaches using ontologies are not always adopted due to specific requirements and limitations of the archaeological projects themselves. However, at European level, structuring projects that use this technology have emerged (for example, ARIADNE) [20]. At the same time, the application of sophisticated documentation (e.g. 3D) and mapping technologies is being increasingly used, generating data sets with interest beyond their immediate purpose. Without standards, this increasing data sets can be generally conceived as "data silos" with limited mechanisms for discovery, visualization, download and reuse [10]. To avoid it, some authors assume the need of standard formats [8] and tried to understand the user requirements [6,7], to normalize data and attempt to integrate 3D models in Spatial Data Infrastructures (SDI) [1,7,12].

From our knowledge, there's no published attempt to apply NLP to extract information from archaeology Grey literature written in Portuguese. Most of the international bibliography refer rule-based approaches or Machine Learning (ML). From those, we should mention projects such as Archeotools [9,16] and STAR [20] , works like [4] and the application to other languages, such as Dutch [14,15]. In Italian reports, [3] describes the domain of archaeology as "strong Semantic Expansion (SE), being strictly interlinked with other domains" and applies an Ontology-based Information Extraction. Recently, the work presented in [2] leads to the use of BERT models for the first time in archaeology achieving the best results in NER in this domain.

238   I. Santos and R. Vieira

Previously, we proposed a data model aligned with the CIDOC-CRM[1] in conjunction with the open access software ARCHES to build a digital atlas for Megalithism [17]. In that work, we synthesized the various concepts related to the Megalithism of the Iberian Peninsula and identified the use of imported concepts and the use of synonyms. With regard to academic works related to Megalithism, it was found that the original data are often not available for reuse and confirmation of interpretations, drastically limiting the scientific process.

There are different perspectives and approaches in the literature, due to the specificities inherent to the subdomain dealt with, we do not know yet which one will better adapt to our use-case, or even if a greater reliability will be achieved in the combination of the different approaches reported. On the other hand, from the point of view of NLP, the use of specific concepts from Portuguese archaeology (PT-PT) makes it difficult to use models created from general texts in PT-BR, such as the BERT model for Portuguese [18]. The case of "Anta" is one of the best examples: in PT-BR models "anta" is a mammal, but it also appears in social contexts as a negative reference to a person's intelligence; and it is a megalithic monument to Portuguese archaeology. Therefore, an adaptation with fine tune techniques may be required.

3   The Data Collection

In order to constitute a Portuguese *corpus* of Megalithism, for the extraction of archaeological information through NLP methods, we considered the main sources of information (reports of archaeological works, academic theses and specialized bibliography) available. Among these sources, the Portal do Arqueólogo (Archaeological Data Management Tool) stands out for housing structured information, as well as brief descriptions and reports of archaeological work. The decision of starting from these portal and its reports is due to the fact that the formal characteristics of the reports are regulated and, thus, they will possibly form a dataset more appropriate to our objectives. These reports constitute, nevertheless, a *data pit* of unknown characteristics.

The Archaeologist's Portal does not have a thesaurus directly linked to the page itself but, there is a reference on the introductory page of the Directorate General for Cultural Heritage (DGPC) for a PDF with the title "Lists of terms to fill in the fields from the database - Endovélico" which proposes 158 typologies of sites[2]. With regard to Megalithism, we verified the use of terms that could be considered synonymous (for example, "Dolmen" and "Anta"), but also the use of ambiguous nomenclature (as is the case of "Megalithic Monument"). However, in the database itself, 9 typologies are used that are not present in the *Thesaurus*, with emphasis on the introduction of "Anta/Dolmen". In formal terms, the information on the Portal do Arqueólogo is distributed in three main groups: sites, works and projects. A project can be made up of several jobs and

---

[1] http://www.cidoc-crm.org.
[2] http://www.patrimoniocultural.gov.pt/static/data/patrimonio_arqueologico/listade campos.pdf.

Table 1. General features (June, 2021)

Type	General			Megalithism		
	n	Reports	With error	n	Reports	With error
Sites	36275	5855	1151	4640	826	107
Works	39947			5494		

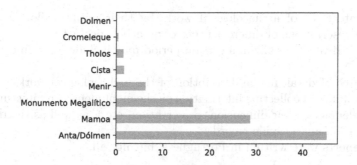

Fig. 1. Number of occurrences of each typology corresponding to Megalithism

a job can refer to one or more sites. It is possible to visualize the exact location of the sites on a map, without coordinates, but registered users "must keep the information on the location of archaeological sites confidential" [21] and it is possible to access some digitized reports.

As of June 2021, there are 36275 records of archaeological sites and 39947 works, of which 5855 have a link to a report in digital format. It was found that 1151 of the links to the reports do not work by error. As for Megalithism, 4640 site records were identified (about 12.8%), 5494 works and 826 reports. However, 107 reports are inaccessible, as summarized in Table 1. To identify such reports on this first steps, we used the presence of keywords on the record. Figure 1 presents the number of occurrences of each of the categories that correspond to a megalithic concept. It was found that the "Anta/Dolmen" typology is the most common in the records, but, on the other hand, the only occurrence of "Dolmen" possibly corresponds to an error. From the metadata of these records we collected information about geographical distribution, chronological periods and year of deposit. We can consider that, in general, the geographic distribution of the works present on the Portal, possibly reflects the occurrence of safeguard works accompanying the large public works, especially in the districts of Évora and Beja (Alqueva and associated Irrigation System). Likewise, the geographic distribution of the records of sites attributed to Megalithism corroborates what is defended in the specialized bibliography, in general. The geographic distribution shows some predominance in certain districts, mainly in Évora, Portalegre and Viseu. As for the chronological periods attributed to megalithic sites, there is, as expected, a predominance of Neo-Chalcolithic, Neolithic and Chalcolithic. Chronologies to which the construction of these monuments in currently Portuguese territory is normally attributed. Noteworthy is the representativeness of the "Undetermined" in the attribution of the classification of Mamoa and Megalithic Monuments.

4   Challenges and Next Steps

Some characteristics of the data are profiled as challenging:

- some categories of archaeological work, by their nature, allow reports to include descriptions of different types of archaeological sites;
- archaeological sites built in a certain period may include reuse in other periods.
- the degree of detail in the description of the archaeological works will limit the possibility of collecting information on the monument's architecture (number of elements, their dimension, preservation, etc.), as well as the degree of preservation and graphic records;
- most reports were written in Portuguese, but not all.

The main objective of the work presented here is to constitute a corpus from grey literature to test the information mapping for a data model aligned with the CIDOC-CRM, as previously proposed by [17]. We will also explore the inclusion of scientific articles and academic works to the corpus. This model seeks to respond to the community's requirements for an archaeology management tool, thus, it is essential to successfully adapt the archaeological data collected to the FAIR principles (Findable, Accessible, Interoperable and Reusable).

Among the information to be collected from the corpus, the following stand out:

- elements that allow characterizing the monument's architecture and its constituent parts;
- listings of collected artifacts;
- associated bibliography;
- references to the existence of other analyzes (archaeosciences) for later inclusion.

To achieve our goals, we will continue to process information trying to identify those texts that include references to Megalithism but are not identified as such. For this, on the one hand it may suffice to identify keywords, on the other hand it may be useful to use data summarization and similarity approaches to reports in general.

References

1. Billen, N., Auer, M., Zipf, A., Richards-Rissetto, H., Reindel, M., von Schwerin, J.: Development of a 4D-webgis for archeological research. In: Proceedings of the AGILE (2013)

2. Brandsen, A., Verberne, S., Lambers, K., Wansleeben, M.: Can BERT Dig It? – named entity recognition for information retrieval in the archaeology domain. J. Comput. Cult. Herit. (2021). https://doi.org/10.1145/3497842
3. di Buono, M.P.: Information extraction for ontology population tasks. An application to the Italian archaeological domain. Int. J. Comput. Sci. Theor. Appl. **3**(2), 40–50 (2015)
4. Byrne, K., Klein, E.: Automatic extraction of archaeological events from text. In: Proceedings of Computer Applications and Quantitative Methods in Archaeology. Archaeopress, Oxford (2010)
5. Cripps, P.J.: Places, people, events and stuff; building blocks for archaeological information systems. In: CAA 2012 (2011)
6. De Kleijn, M., et al.: Towards a user-centric SDI framework for historical and heritage European landscape research. Int. J. Spatial Data Infrastruct. Res. **9**, 1–35 (2014)
7. de Kleijn, M., de Hond, R., Martinez-Rubi, O.: A 3D spatial data infrastructure for mapping the Via Appia. Digit. Appl. Archaeol. Cult. Herit. **3**(2), 23–32 (2016)
8. Fiedukowicz, A., et al.: Map portal as a tool to share information on cultural heritage illustrated by the National Heritage Board Geoportal. In: Ioannides, M., Martins, J., Žarnić, R., Lim, V. (eds.) Advances in Digital Cultural Heritage. LNCS, vol. 10754, pp. 48–64. Springer, Cham (2018). https://doi.org/10.1007/978-3-319-75789-6_4
9. Jeffrey, S., et al.: The archaeotools project: faceted classification and natural language processing in an archaeological context. Philos. Trans. Roy. Soc. A Math. Phys. Eng. Sci. **367**(1897), 2507–2519 (2009)
10. McKeague, P., Corns, A., Shaw, R.: Developing a spatial data infrastructure for archaeological and built heritage. Int. J. Spatial Data Infrastruct. Res. **7**, 38–65 (2012)
11. Migliorini, S., et al.: An interoperable spatio-temporal model for archaeological data based on ISO standard 19100. J. Comput. Cult. Heritage **11**(1), 1–28 (2017)
12. Naranjo, J.M., Parrilla, Á., de Sanjosé, J.J.: Geometric characterization and interactive 3D visualization of historical and cultural heritage in the province of Cáceres (Spain). Virt. Archaeol. Rev. **9**(18), 1–11 (2018)
13. Noor, S., et al.: Knowledge retrieval of historic concepts using semantic web. Clust. Comput. **22**(3), 7321–7332 (2019)
14. Paijmans, H., Brandsen, A.: What is in a name: recognizing monument names from free-text monument descriptions. In: Proceedings of the 18th Annual Belgian-Dutch Conference on Machine Learning (Benelearn), pp. 2–6. Citeseer (2009)
15. Paijmans, J., Brandsen, A.: Searching in archaeological texts: problems and solutions using an artificial intelligence approach. PalArch's J. Archaeol. Egypt/Egyptol. **7**, 1–6 (2010)
16. Richards, J., et al.: The archaeology data service and the archaeotools project: faceted classification and natural language processing. Archaeology **2**, 31–56 (2011)
17. Santos, I. de J.F. dos: Um atlas digital para o megalitismo: uma infraestrutura de dados espaciais (sudoeste da Península Ibérica). Universidade de Évora (2018)
18. Souza, F., et al.: BERTimbau: pretrained BERT models for Brazilian Portuguese. In: 9th Brazilian Conference on Intelligent Systems, BRACIS, Rio Grande do Sul, Brazil, 20–23 October (to appear). (2020)
19. Tchienehom, P.: ModRef project: from creation to exploitation of CIDOC-CRM triplestores. In: The Fifth International Conference on Building and Exploring Web Based Environments (WEB 2017) (2017)

20. Vlachidis, A., Tudhope, D.: A knowledge-based approach to information extraction for semantic interoperability in the archaeology domain. J. Assoc. Inf. Sci. Technol. **67**, 1138–1152 (2016)
21. Portal do Arqueólogo. https://arqueologia.patrimoniocultural.pt

Track on Digital Libraries, Information Retrieval, Big, Linked, Social and Open Data

Scholarly Artifacts Knowledge Graph: Use Cases for Digital Libraries

Fidan Limani[✉][iD], Atif Latif[iD], and Klaus Tochtermann[iD]

Leibniz Information Centre for Economics, Düsternbrooker Weg 120, 24105 Kiel,
Germany
{f.limani,a.latif,k.tochtermann}@zbw.eu
https://www.zbw.eu/en/research/science-2-0/fidan-limani

Abstract. Scholarly communication process is constantly evolving to
include new artifacts that present a part of the research. The traditional
practice of conference and journal publications being the key artifacts
to publish have changed to include new or complementary artifacts that
help the audience grasp the research outcomes as much as possible as a
single unit or whole. We also witnessed this trend with the library community, where different stakeholders – users, library patrons, or management – require that new research artifacts, such as scientific blogs,
datasets, or citation links, be included in the library catalogs alongside
existing artifacts. Knowledge Graphs (KG) have been applied as means
to bring together data from heterogeneous sources, within or across multiple domains, and this has shown to be an effective approach. In this
work, we adopt them to bring research artifacts of different types in a
more compact research unit. This includes the approach to specify it and
its components considering the library environment, and the accompanying methodology used to implement it. Finally, we explore the value
and potential use cases from this integration for the library community
in the domain of economics.

Keywords: Knowledge graph · Scholarly artifacts · Digital libraries ·
Semantic Web

1 Introduction

Opening up the research process represents an important development for scholarly communication. Regardless of the extent (include data, source code, scientific workflow implementation, and more), there is evidence of benefits from
its adoption by researchers [17]. Moreover, initiatives like the FAIR principles
[19] also go in this direction as they provide guidelines for research artifacts
(research data, in this case) to increase their re-usability for both humans and
machines. Thus, as the Open Science movement and relevant practices build
momentum, more research artifacts will be managed (created, described, stored,

Leibniz Information Centre for Economics.

etc.), become part of the scholarly communication process, and become valuable assets for research communities.

Research communities employ different, often dedicated, dissemination platforms for their research deliverables. This creates a distributed infrastructure of artifacts which often requires the same effort to publish and access artifacts like dataset, citation link, open notebook, etc., in the corresponding platforms. Libraries are important scholarly infrastructure hubs and in a good position to start to address this opportunity. Thus, as new research artifacts become available, they have an opportunity to offer a more comprehensive research picture, i.e., the ability to provide complementary aspects of a research work as well.

We faced a similar requirement at our library institution – requirements from both authors and library users – for more research artifacts as part of the library collections or catalogs. In this paper we conceptualize and conduct a preliminary exploration of the role of Knowledge Graphs (KG) as means to bring different research artifacts – publications, datasets, blogs, and citations – in a more centralized, one-stop fashion for a library environment.

The paper is structured as follows: In Sect. 2 we provide the research motivation for this work, and the related work in Sect. 3. We then present the datasets selected for the work (Sect. 4), and our technical approach to the KG components in Sect. 5. In Sect. 6 we present few use case scenarios from our data, and make our conclusions in Sect. 7.

2   Research Motivation

In the library context, artifact collections are the single most important asset. While the Open Science is gaining ground, library users are not only generating more artifacts themselves, but they also expect richer research artifact collection from libraries. Libraries, then, should be capable to bring a range of research artifacts together that may consist of different type, metadata standards, research practices, etc., and be able to cope with new artifacts in the future.

Two use case categories we treat in this work revolve around accessing resources that (1) originate from the same research work, or (2) are relevant to a topic of interest:

1. Search for related artifacts: The user is interested to find all the available artifacts that stem from a single research work. For example, given a research publication from a library catalog, she might want to explore the dataset(s), implementation scripts/code, cited publications, etc., used. Moreover, comments on social channels from the scientific community about the paper, such as blogs, could also be of use.
2. Cross-artifacts search: Here the user is interested in a single type of artifact and wants to find relevant artifacts of any type, based on certain criteria (author, topic, publication venue, etc.), thus a cross-artifacts scenario. For example, she might want to know the most cited dataset (on a topic, or any criterion) in a given year; the dataset(s) cited in a research publication;

the number of citations for a publication; the datasets or blog posts on a certain topic or authored by certain authors; most commented publications (by analyzing blog posts from the domain); and so on.

Understandably, a lot of the use case scenarios depend on the available artifact metadata (for e.g., if bibliographic citations are missing, one could not conduct citation analysis). However, we see this only as a current shortcoming for at least 2 reasons: (1) as the Open Science picks up momentum, there will be more artifacts across domains, thus potential use cases will increase; and (2) libraries have a selection process in place to include research artifacts of interest as part of their catalogs, which matches well with the previous trend.

3 Related Work

Going beyond the publications, many initiatives already strive to capture and express as more complete (with as many artifacts) a research picture as possible. The term "enhanced publication" is often referred to as an umbrella term for this idea. It focuses on "compound digital objects" [18] that capture the different facets of research via its constituting artifacts.

The library domain has seen examples of KG adoption for the similar requirements and goals that other domains have adopted KGs. Haslhofer & Simon [12] point out the continuation and "readiness" of libraries for the adoption of KGs. In terms of the potential benefits, they state that "knowledge graphs can be vehicles for connecting and exchanging findings as well as factual knowledge", which is in line with the benefits generally observed with the KG adoption across domains. In addition, Zhang [20] notes KGs will enable libraries to move from "knowledge warehouses" to "acquisition tools". In the same work he presents the typical structure of such a KG, as well as the (automatic) means to create it. Hienert et al. [13] provide an integrated approach of scholarly resources from social sciences, typically found on multiple platforms, for a digital library. They focus on publications, data, and provide a finer granularity of the data, considering the domain requirements, such as survey details. Angioni et al. [4] apply the KG to unify research deliverables such as articles, research topics, organizations, and types of industry, all from different sources, in order to measure the impact that academic research has on the industry. A final library example, the Open Research KG proposes a model and an architecture to represent research outputs, with an initial focus on survey articles [11,14]. The way the scholarly output is modeled is through the (classes of) *research problem*, *research method*, and *research result*, all part of the *research contribution* under consideration. This allows a more structured and granular comparison between survey articles, such as based on the hypothesis tested, research methods, and so on.

In the context of infrastructure-like providers, Atzori et al. [6] report on a research infrastructure, materialized via its Information Space Graph – a graph representation of scholarly collection that constitutes of different artifacts, such as articles, datasets, people (authors), funders, and grants. In both KG examples, the Semantic Web technologies play an important part of the technical infrastructure and implementation. Another publishing entity – Springer Nature – offers an enhanced access to its aggregation of scholarly resources, including publications, conferences, funders, research projects, etc., via its SciGraph [1]. Moreover, one of the largest infrastructure institutions in the domain of social sciences is embarking on an infrastructure project, the core of which will be a social sciences KG, bringing together all the collections of this institution, as well as establish links to external collections [2].

In the more academic umbrella of projects, the Microsoft Academic Graph models entities from the scholarly communication (authors, publications, datasets, citations, and other aspects), and represents them as a single graph, whereas the PID Graph connects persistent identifiers (PID) of different research artifacts, across PID schemes, in a single graph for new insights of the research ecosystem [8]. Finally, Aryani et al. [5] report on the graph of datasets linked with other relevant scholarly deliverables, such as publications, authors, and grants, and a corresponding model to represent these artifacts.

Despite the upwards trend of research on KG applications, often even for overlapping scholarly artifacts, the domain of interest, the scope of artifacts, or specific requirements often drive the need for new KG adoptions. We explore such a case to bring (the metadata of) scholarly artifacts in a machine-readable representation for the domain of economics.

4   Dataset Selection

We include several research artifact types in our KG, such as (scientific) blog posts, open access research publications, research data, and citation links. The artifacts were selected based partially on the complementarity they bring, as well as the user interest in a library environment. Next, we present some key descriptions of these 4 collections.

a) **(Open Access) Publications** remain one of the primary means of scholarly communication. They often represent the starting point from where researchers (including library users) search for relevant information. For this artifact type we rely on an Open Access collection of publications from EconStor[1], a publishing platform for scholarly publications from the domain of economics and business administration at the Leibniz Information Centre for Economics[2] (ZBW). The types of publications in this collection include journal articles, conference proceedings, draft papers, and so on. The collection contains more than 108 K publications, and is provided as an RDF data dump, which suits our technology of choice for materializing the Artifacts Graph, as the Semantic Web technology provides a key element in it (see Sect. 5 for more).

---

[1] https://www.econstor.eu/.
[2] https://www.zbw.eu/.

b) **Research data** are seeing a surge in importance in the scholarly communication. As a result, the ZBW is also engaging in supporting it in its data holdings, such as its engagement with the Journal Data Archive[3] or Project GeRDI. Project GeRDI [3], a research data infrastructure, focused on providing research data management support for long tail research data. It targeted many disciplines, such as social sciences and economics, life sciences and humanities, marine sciences, and environmental sciences. During its 3-year run, it harvested more than 1.1 M dataset metadata, and had 9 pilot research communities to help specify the project requirements for its infrastructure services. Having a multidisciplinary research scope, albeit at different extents (life sciences contributions dominate the collection), provides means to potentially conduct cross-disciplinary use cases, and this is one of the reasons we included it as part of the dataset. We use the RDF version of the dataset, which is publicly available from Zenodo [16].

c) **Links between scholarly artifacts** can be quite complementary in a KG that contains publications and datasets because this enables one to check if a publication or dataset has been cited or not. For the purpose of this work we use the link collection from OpenAIRE's Data Literature Interlinking service, Scholexplorer[4], originally containing more than 126 M citation links – both literature-to-dataset and dataset-to-dataset, and 17 providers that contribute to the collection. For our use cases section, we rely only on a subset of this large collection, also available as an RDF data dump [15].

d) **Blog post collection** Social scientific collections, such as blogs and wikis, are another type of artifact that we have explored in the past as they have become an interesting development of scholarly communication. Blog authors often contact the ZBW to offer their collection to any of its publishing platforms. Moreover, as with many of the emerging research artifacts, different blogs on the topic of economics have been considered for integration. For this artifact type we chose the blog post collection from VoxEU[5], as a portal that provides analysis and articles on more than 30 economic topics. We harvested 8.5 K blog posts, including the ones published as late as April 11 of this year.

5   Artifacts Knowledge Graph: A Technical Perspective

Although the number of projects and research on the topic is increasing, there is still not a commonly accepted definition what a KG is [9]. We adopt the definition from Färber et al., who "use the term knowledge graph for any RDF graph" [10]. In this section we provide our KG adoption approach, starting with its architecture, semantic modeling of the datasets, and the KG instantiation.

---

[3] https://journaldata.zbw.eu/.
[4] http://scholexplorer.openaire.eu/.
[5] https://voxeu.org/.

5.1 KG Architecture

The debate about KGs does not end with their definition, and different approaches exist for their architecture design as well. We adopt the so called "Enterprise KG" architecture from Blumauer and Nagy [7, pp.146], which specifies 3 key "layers" of an KG:

1. Data sources: This layer contains the dataset, and the datasets can be of different representation, metadata description, and so on. In our case, we deal with structured (RDF) and unstructured (information retrieved from Web pages) representations.
2. Enterprise KG Infrastructure: Represents the core of the a KG and typically includes the graph database used to store (and query) datasets; AI/ML activities to populate, maintain, enrich, etc., the data layer; any KG management tasks that might be required, and so on. In our case, we rely on an RDF triple store for the database operations, and apply enrichment with one artifact collection.
3. Data consumers. This is the layer used by end users – developers, data scientists, etc., which offers different services for this purpose. In our case, we rely on the SPARQL service to retrieve artifacts of interest (as defined in the use cases).

Based on these suggestions, we adopted the architecture in Fig. 1. Starting from the data sources, since we are dealing with a variety of data provisions, including RDF and JSON data dumps, and HTML pages, we implement dedicated adapters to access the sources. Data ingestion, then, provides the resulting (meta)data. The Extract Transform Load-like process allows us to conduct different task on this metadata, such as pre-processing or enriching it (when applicable), before finally converting it to RDF – our model of choice – and a single graph representation. We organize, store, and maintain the resulting RDF in a triplestore, which approximately matches layer 2 above. In this layer we also plan for other graph-based technologies, such as the Property Graph, especially when it comes to graph analysis, hence its depiction (although not in use yet). Finally, in layer 3, different set of services can be developed (so far, we only rely on retrieval via SPARQL for our use cases).

5.2 Semantic Modeling of Artifacts

We were directly involved with the conversion of the last three collections, but we are familiar with that of the first one. Next we present the selection of vocabularies/ontologies for the datasets:

1. **Publications** This collection is already provided in RDF. Being that its metadata are mainly of descriptive nature, the Dublin Core Metadata Initiative (DCMI) is used to model the larger part of the collection, with more than 30 properties – both using the DC Elements and the DC Terms specifications. In few of the cases, there are more vocabularies that cover the same artifact

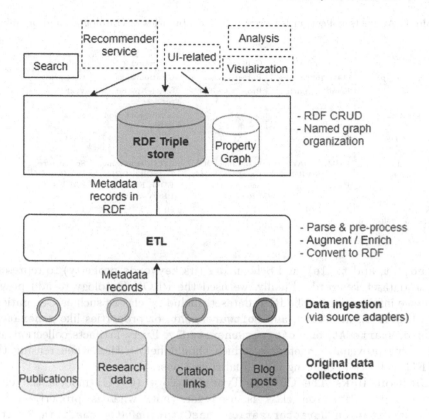

Fig. 1. The knowledge graph components

attribute. For example, to denote the author of a publication, in addition to DCMI, the maker from Friend of a Friend (FOAF) and author from the Semantic Web Conference Ontology (SWRC) have been used, as have the classes for Document (FOAF), Paper (SWRC), and Item from Semantically-Interlinked Online Communities (SIOC), for every literature item. Finally, the Bibliographic Ontology (BIBO) is used to capture additional bibliographic aspects, such as DOI and handle identifiers, ISSN, and so on.

2. **Research data** The type of an artifact is important during retrieval. We use the BibFrame Initiative (its Dataset class) for this purpose; targeting bibliographic descriptions, it supports a wide range of types (13 such types in its latest version), able to accommodate new scholarly artifacts in the future. To represent dataset identifiers, we relied on the DataCite Ontology: PrimaryResourceIdentifier class for identifiers of type DOI, and AlternateResourceIdentifier class for the rest. Due to the fact that the datasets come from different institutions or providers, we used the Europeana Data Model (EDM) to specify the dataset provider, specifically the class Agent to denote the provider. For the descriptive aspects of the datasets, we used the DCMI specification (creator, date, description, format,

Table 1. Artifacts collection features: Size, Vocabularies & Ontologies, and organization

	Collection 1	Collection 2	Collection 3	Collection 4
Artifact type	OA Publications	Research data	Citation links	Blog posts
Source	EconStor portal	Project GeRDI	ScholeXplorer service	VoxEU
Total items	>108 K	>1.1 M	>126 M citation links	8,752
Total RDF triples	3.6 M	24.2 M	3.9 B	396 K
Vocabularies/ collection	DCMI, FOAF, SIOC, SWRC, and BIBO	BiBFrame, DCMI, DataCite, EDM, Schema.org, PROV-O	CiTO, BibFrame, DataCite, DCMI, EDM, FRBR, PROV-O	Schema.org, DCMI, SIOC, PROV-O
Named graphs/collection	1	11	30	1

subject, and title), and Schema.org (its keywords property) to represent the dataset keywords. Finally, we used the PROV Ontology to add provenance information to the RDF dataset, including classes such as Generation, Collection, Activity, and SoftwareAgent, or properties like generated, used, startedAt, endedAt, wasGeneratedBy. Every artifacts collection has its own provenance metadata, which should help wither when reusing the (KG) collection, or using individual collections.

3. **Citation links** The Citation Type Ontology (CiTO) models the citation links. Citation class is used for that, whereas properties such as hasCitationCharacterization, hasCitationDate, hasCitingEntity, hasCitedEntity, capture the type of the link (references, relates to, supplements, etc.) between source and target. BibFrame and DataCite Ontology are used as before: to define the type of the resources being linked (publications and datasets) and the representation of identifiers; the same goes with the DCMI and PROV Ontology, too. EDM is also used as before, with the addition of the isRelatedTo property, used to model a citation type in the collection. The last vocabulary, Functional Requirements for Bibliographic Records (FRBR), is used to provide few link types that the previous ontologies did not support – supplement and supplementOf.

4. **Blog posts**: There are no new elements to model for this collection – classes or properties – as its items resemble the artifacts we already modeled previously, especially research publications and datasets. SIOC's BlogPost class denotes a blog post, whereas its content property denote the blog post content. The major metadata of every item are covered by DCMI, with Schema.org covering the blog post keywords, and the PROV Ontology providing support for the collection's provenance information.

Table 1 contains some information about the source collections, such as their size, number of RDF triples after the conversion, vocabularies/ontologies used, as well as the number of named graphs used to organize them in the triplestore. Deciding on the number of named graphs typically depended on the source data.

Namely, the research data are organized based on the data providers, whereas the citation link collections is organized based on its source files (30 in total).

5.3   KG Instantiation

The Semantic Web and Linked Data (LD) provide a great conceptual and technological fit for this research undertaking. Among other things, they are well suited for bringing heterogeneous collections in a common representation model (RDF, in this case), which fits well with the KG definition we referred to earlier.

We rely on the data ingestion and Extract, Transform, Load (ETL) components of the KG to harvest, enrich or linked up artifacts with external collections. In our case, we applied this for the blog post collection, as it provided enough text to engage in tasks such as automatic term assignment; link citations and research data, due to the short (textual) values for their metadata, did not lend themselves to such activities. Given that the ZBW has adopted the Thesaurus for Economics[6] to describe its data collections (EconStor dataset, for example), we decided to apply automatic term assignment (using Maui indexer[7]) to blog posts based on it, and add up to 3 terms to every blog post.

In this way, regardless of the term vocabulary used to describe the blog posts, we assign terms from a vocabulary that the library already uses. This bridges (to some extent) the terminology gap between heterogeneous collections (in this case EconStor publications and blog posts). In addition, this task enables us to explore the different components of instantiating KGs based on the domain practices – STW thesaurus and the domain of economics, in our case. Finally, we provide access to the resulting RDF data of the KG via SPARQL or as data dumps.

For the RDF conversion, its storage to a triplestore, and querying, we relied on Apache Jena Framework[8], and its TDB storage component[9]. We provide all our datasets based on the Creative Commons BY-NC 4.0 license[10]; due to the large collection (especially that of citation links), we only provide a subset and few exemplary SPARQL queries online[11].

6   Use Cases: Explored Scenarios

Generally, the use cases revolve around (fine-grained) search and involve different metadata elements across artifacts, such as: publication date, resource provider, persistent identifier, resource type of the resource and dataset size, etc.

---

[6] https://zbw.eu/stw/.
[7] https://github.com/zelandiya/maui.
[8] https://jena.apache.org/.
[9] https://bitbucket.org/fidanLimani/workspace/projects/KG.
[10] https://creativecommons.org/licenses/by-nc/4.0/.
[11] https://zbw.eu/beta/sparql-lab/about.

Publications and Data. GeRDI dataset collection contains a provider from social sciences that we can use to demonstrate cross-artifact search. After retrieving the subject terms for the datasets from this provider, we select the *"household composition"* to search the publications collections with. We find 2 publications that are also described with this subject term (*Inputs, Gender Roles or Sharing Norms? Assessing the Gender Performance Gap Among Informal Entrepreneurs in Madagascar*, and *The analytical returns to measuring a detailed household roster*). This is relatively specific subject for this provider, but if we want to check for *earnings*, another subject from the dataset collection, this gives us more than 200 matches. On the other hand, *health and satisfaction indicators* does not have an exact match from publications, although *health indicators* provides 3 matching publications.

In a user study, for example, while a user is checking a dataset on the topic of "household composition", we can show her two publications from EconStor on this topic. For the cases where there are more results, we can apply additional metadata to further filter the results (publication date, text similarity, or resource identifiers, for example).

On another scenario, the user retrieves the RD that directly support (as a primary source of data) the research paper at hand. If she wants to further specify the result, she can refine the query to include the most re-used RD in the collection (based on the number of times it has been cite). On the other hand, if the results are scarce or the user wants to broaden the search, she could also retrieve all the RD by the same author of the paper. In another scenario, a user can retrieve the "trending" RD (RD being cited the most in a more recent time frame) – and their corresponding publications – for a quick impression of what her community is currently working on. In a final scenario for this part, the user can rely on the "subject term" to search for a field of interest across link providers for a more interdisciplinarity search scenario (search for a fish type to see its fishing quotas, market fluctuations in a certain period, as well as the impact from climate conditions on its habitat).

Importantly, the DL collection we are working with primarily supports publications, thus in presented scenarios we assume the user first selects a publication and then proceeds to find RD. This aspect can easily be reversed (start with RD of interest, and find publications and/or RD).

Publications and Blogs. Another search across artifacts could be between publications and blog posts. On the topic of *health*, for example, there are 134 matches from the relatively small blog post collection, one matching dataset from one of the dataset providers (from social sciences), and many more (>700) from the literature collection.

Similar examples, with many more elements, can be devised to search across all the different collections, but due to space limit, we will provide such examples alongside the SPARQL service for the KG (see the link above).

Generic Use Case Scenarios: This set of scenarios provides more general information, which, although not the first use case of choice, could turn useful to the researchers. Few list examples are:

– List resources that are linked by the same publisher, publication date, domain, and other relevant metadata.
– Based on links that cite my research artifacts (publications or RD), who is using my RD? In what scenarios and context (information you get after reading a citing paper or RD, for example)? This question would apply both to individual researchers and institutions.
– Show the potential of relevant resources based on a certain criteria such as: classification terms for the subject of coverage, resources type, number of files that constitute a resources, etc.

While the trends of combining different types of research artifacts are already emerging, finding the right artifact collections to demonstrate the possible reuse scenarios is always challenging. This is so even within the same/similar research domains. More of these use cases will only be possible if sufficient information is present within the KG, specifically the new sources it will harvest.

7   Conclusion and Future Work

In this work we explored the role of a KG in providing more holistic view of research deliverables. Moreover, we specified the components and an approach to instantiate the KG with data from the social sciences domain. The KG developed in this work represents a nice basis for future work, including the following:

– Showing an approach to bring emerging research artifacts (links, datasets, blog posts, etc.) to a library environment based on KGs;
– The possibility to explore new use cases for this environment, important before adopting any new (KG) strategy for an interested institution;
– Domain-specific operations that aid with the resource (re)usage, such as the automatic term assignment based on a common thesaurus;
– Contribute with a KG with resources from social sciences, and provide new/emerging research artifacts to the research community;

Summing it up, providing a more holistic access to research deliverables is a good research direction. By adopting KGs as means to do it, in addition to the listed outcomes above, one supports extensibility for new artifacts, as well as means to exchange with other (open) KGs. In the future, we would like to tackle the aspects of scalability (especially when introducing new artifacts), as well as UI to enable an exploration from a broader set of users.

References

1. SN SciGraph: A Linked Open Data platform for the scholarly domain. https://www.springernature.com/gp/researchers/scigraph. Accessed 20 Aug 2021

2. Knowledge Graph Infrastructure. https://www.gesis.org/en/research/applied-computer-science/knowledge-graph-infrastructure. Accessed 24 Aug 2021
3. GeRDI: Generic Research Data Infrastructure. https://www.gerdi-project.eu/. Accessed 30 Feb 2020
4. Angioni, S., Osborne, F., Salatino, A., Reforgiato Recupero, D., Motta, E.: Integrating knowledge graphs for comparing the scientific output of academia and industry (2019)
5. Aryani, A., et al.: A research graph dataset for connecting research data repositories using rd-switchboard. Sci. Data 5(1), 1–9 (2018)
6. Atzori, C., Bardi, A., Manghi, P., Mannocci, A.: The OpenAIRE workflows for data management. In: Italian Research Conference on Digital Libraries (IRCDL), Modena, Italy (2017, September 25). https://doi.org/10.5281/zenodo.996006
7. Andreas, B., Helmut, N.: The Knowledge Graph Cookbook Recipes That Work. Edition mono/monochrom, Vienna (2020)
8. Cousijn, H., et al.: Connected research: the potential of the PID graph. Patterns 2(1), 100180 (2021)
9. Ehrlinger, L., Wöß, W.: Towards a definition of knowledge graphs. SEMANTiCS (Posters, Demos, SuCCESS) 48, 1–4 (2016)
10. Färber, M., Bartscherer, F., Menne, C., Rettinger, A.: Linked data quality of dbpedia, freebase, opencyc, wikidata, and yago. Semant. Web 9(1), 77–129 (2018)
11. Fathalla, S., Vahdati, S., Auer, S., Lange, C.: Towards a knowledge graph representing research findings by semantifying survey articles. In: Kamps, J., Tsakonas, G., Manolopoulos, Y., Iliadis, L., Karydis, I. (eds.) TPDL 2017. LNCS, vol. 10450, pp. 315–327. Springer, Cham (2017). https://doi.org/10.1007/978-3-319-67008-9_25
12. Haslhofer, B., Isaac, A., Simon, R.: Knowledge graphs in the libraries and digital humanities domain. arXiv preprint arXiv:1803.03198 (2018)
13. Hienert, D., Kern, D., Boland, K., Zapilko, B., Mutschke, P.: A digital library for research data and related information in the social sciences. In: 2019 ACM/IEEE Joint Conference on Digital Libraries (JCDL), pp. 148–157. IEEE (2019)
14. Jaradeh, M.Y., et al.: Open research knowledge graph: next generation infrastructure for semantic scholarly knowledge. In: Proceedings of the 10th International Conference on Knowledge Capture, pp. 243–246 (2019)
15. Limani, F.: OpenAIRE ScholeXplorer data dump in RDF (0.1.0) [Data set]. Zenodo. https://doi.org/10.5281/zenodo.3820026
16. Limani, F.: Project GeRDI collection in RDF (0.3.0) [Data set]. Zenodo. https://doi.org/10.5281/zenodo.4104280
17. McKiernan, E.C., et al.: Point of view: how open science helps researchers succeed. elife 5, e16800 (2016)
18. Vernooy-Gerritsen, M.: Enhanced Publications: Linking Publications and Research Data in Digital Repositories. Amsterdam University Press, Amsterdam (2009)
19. Wilkinson, M.D., et al.: The FAIR guiding principles for scientific data management and stewardship. Sci. Data 3(1), 1–9 (2016)
20. Zhang, L.: Describe library resources with knowledge graph (2017)

A Web-Based Recommendation Mechanism for Learning Objects Combining Ontologies and Zero-Shot Learning

Dimitrios K. Charalampopoulos and Dimitrios A. Koutsomitropoulos$^{(\boxtimes)}$

Computer Engineering and Informatics Department, University of Patras, 26500 Patras, Greece
{charalamp,koutsomi}@ceid.upatras.gr

Abstract. Content management, selection and reuse is a difficult task especially for educational purposes. Flat metadata aggregations lack semantic interoperability and content is often poorly indexed thus making its discovery and integration troublesome. In this paper we propose a web interface for managing learning objects that leverages ontologies, automated subject classification and scoring to aid users and curators overcome these obstacles. We examine and document requirements and design decisions spanning data handling, storage, display, and user interaction. Through research and comparative evaluation, we choose an appropriate database layer and corresponding web framework for the application's development. The app is capable of consuming metadata from other repositories but also maintains a local pool of learning object metadata where users can collaboratively contribute on content indexing and recommendation.

Keywords: Ontologies · Learning objects · Metadata · JavaScript frameworks

1 Introduction

Vast data availability can make it challenging for someone to store, search and find the exact thing one is looking for [16]. For this reason, digital libraries containing nearly every type of data have been created. More importantly, educational information is stored in chunks of data, so it can be easily accessed by everyone. These chunks of data are called Learning Objects (LOs) and they contain metadata for the educational subject they are addressing [7]. As rich as the object's metadata may be, there is however a considerable semantic gap between annotations originating from different sources. Consequently, content searching, selection and further indexing is hampered and often requires manual resolution.

Building on previous work [12, 11] in this paper we propose a web-based front-end for a learning object repository based on dynamic web frameworks using JavaScript (JS) and Node.js. We primarily focus on creating a web interface that would ideally be implemented for use in all educational levels [3]. First, by leveraging the notion of a Learning Object Ontology Repository (LOOR), we have shown that it is possible to search through various educational repositories' metadata and amalgamate their

© Springer Nature Switzerland AG 2022
E. Garoufallou et al. (Eds.): MTSR 2021, CCIS 1537, pp. 257–267, 2022.
https://doi.org/10.1007/978-3-030-98876-0_23

semantics into a common LO ontology [12]. Then we commenced with automatic subject classification of LOs using keyword expansion and referencing standard taxonomic vocabularies for thematic classification [11]. The proposed front-end takes advantage of the LOOR and gives users the ability to display, manage and enrich LOs. In addition, it adds a persistency layer that allows for content already sought for and indexed by curators to be available for others to reuse. Finally, it integrates with a novel validation service that checks semantic similarity between subject tags proposed by the LOOR and the LO itself and produces recommendations that can help users in selecting content and deciding on the most appropriate keywords. Source code and a demo of our implementation are available at: https://github.com/Dcharalamp/React-LOR.

The main contributions of the work presented in this paper are summarized as follows:

- Comparative assessment of the available JS frameworks and selection based on our needs.
- Design and implementation of a LOOR web interface based on the chosen framework that provides for improved and collaborative management, selection and indexing of LOs.
- Development of a management system ideal for LO integration. This will help with discovery, reusability, and enhancement of each LO.
- A novel recommendation and scoring mechanism for subject tags that is based on zero-shot machine learning [21] and is therefore light on resources.

To give a more thorough understanding of what follows, we first analyze the base concepts and review related work in the field (Sect. 2). Next, in Sect. 3 we present the design and architecture of our application. We compare JavaScript web frameworks to identify what is the best suited one for our purposes. After that, we discuss a series of requirements our front-end to the LOOR may fulfill, as well as the reasoning for their implementation. In Sect. 4, we examine some indicative use cases that exemplify the functionality of our approach. Finally, in the last section we discuss our conclusions and future work.

2 Background and Related Work

An LO is a collection of combined information and data that aim to be used for educational purposes [7]. Most of the time, LOs do not stand on their own, but they are well organized in big collections inside repositories. A popular standard for describing LOs is the IEEE Learning Object Metadata (LOM) model. The purpose of LOM is to support the reusability of learning objects, to aid discoverability as well as to facilitate their interoperability, search, evaluation and acquisition [9].

Based on LOM we identify a least common set of elements available on various educational repositories, including MERLOT II, a large archive of LOs [14], Europe PubMed Central, a major repository of biomedical literature [5], ARIADNE finder, a European infrastructure for accessing and sharing learning resources [18] and openarchives.gr, the entry point for Greek scholarly content. This set includes LOM properties such as lom:title, lom:description, lom:keyword and lom:identifier and forms the basis for a *Learning Object Ontology Schema* to be used for immediate ingestion of learning objects into the LOOR [12]. This schema serves the metadata "semantification" process, i.e., the transformation of the textual information captured by a metadata instance into a semantically enriched and thus machine-understandable format [8]. For the LOM-specific entities, the official LOM namespace has been used (http://ltsc.ieee. org/xsd/LOM/, prefix lom:).

Similar to our approach, many researchers have long proposed the use of an ontology for describing both the content and structure of LOs, as well as of an ontology for modelling LO categories [6]. In addition, earlier research focuses on comparative studies involving different metadata standards [15]. The authors are addressing the need of metadata annotations for efficient retrieval of learning materials within learning object repositories. They also identify the advantages of annotating the documents with some standard metadata schemas for making the former reusable and interoperable between different learning systems.

Next, we review some LO repositories that are oriented towards educational purposes, so as to identify common ground as well as differences to our approach. The first example we will discuss is the MIT repository for open courses, called MIT OpenCourseWare [4]. If someone visits this repository one can clearly see that there is a search option based on the title of the LO. As far as we know, there are no other metadata involved in the search operation, nor any advanced search option. A typical pagination of the results can be seen but with no filtering or sorting option. Last but not least, there is no option to alter the LOs in any way or add/delete LOs and also there is no ability to search for LOs from an external source.

We also consider a more advanced repository, the Multimedia Educational Resource for Learning and Online Teaching also known as MERLOT. It provides access to curated learning tools and subjects and it is addressed mostly to professors and students of the highest educational level [14]. In this case, the search function takes into consideration way more metadata fields than before. An interesting feature is the scoring of the LOs by the users themselves. This provides additional information for the quality of the given object. Regarding the ability to alter LOs and their metadata, the repository states that signed users are permitted to upload new LOs but there is no option to delete or edit existing ones. Finally, fetched results are both from the repository itself and external sources, like other libraries or the Web.

From the discussion above, we get a clear view of what features need to be present and what new features will be desirable additions. Our approach is more comparable with the 2nd example we discussed. The web interface is going to be used mostly by students; therefore, a variety of options and pagination features is more suitable than a restricted approach. We also like the idea of fetching objects from an external source, but with some differences. We would like to give our users the ability to add external resources to our own repository. This way, the intellectual wealth of the LOOR will increase and users will be able to reuse the LOs more easily. If we follow this approach however, a way to handle the duplicate ontology entries that may occur is advised.

In earlier work we have investigated and documented the positive effects of query expansion when harvesting Open Educational Resources (OERs) and for subject classification for example, boosting recall of retrieval by a factor of 4–8 [11]. Initial search keywords are reused to discover matching and related terms within domain knowledge thesauri, such as the Medical Subject Headings (MeSH) [19]. These matches are injected as semantic subject annotations into selected LOs, using the lom:keyword property of the LO Ontology Schema. To assess the quality of discovered subject tags, we tap into deep language models based on word embeddings, including BART [20] and XLM-RoBERTa (XLM-R) [1] and acquire validation scores for each tag that can be displayed and stored through the proposed application. To keep low on training resources we employ the idea of zero-shot classification, that is, to assign an appropriate label to a piece of text, irrespective of the text domain and the aspect described by the label. Effectively, zero-shot classification attempts to classify text even in the absence of labeled data.

3 Design and Architecture

In this section we describe the design process we followed for creating the web interface. First, we present a brief workflow of the interface's architecture.

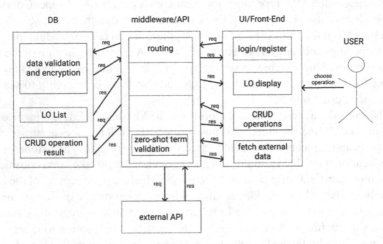

Fig. 1. Brief UML case diagram of the application.

As can be seen from Fig. 1, our architecture consists of 3 main axes: The database, where all information about user login and registration is stored, as well as every LO's metadata and its corresponding CRUD (Create, Remove, Update, Delete) operations; the middleware, which consists of API routes that direct the requests and the responses of each operation; and finally, the front-end from where the user can interact with the features of the interface. We selected MongoDB as our database because, thanks to its document-oriented nature, it can handle this type of data efficiently and can also cooperate with any JS framework we choose. What every route has in common, is that they are directly associated with an API call. We will focus on each step and each route of the workflow later in this section.

3.1 JavaScript Web Frameworks

Before proceeding with the implementation, an important matter that should be taken into consideration is the selection of an appropriate web framework for developing such a web application and the criteria which this choice should be based upon. Undeniably, Because of the proliferation of current web frameworks, we decided to focus on the most popular ones, by taking into consideration criteria such as the number of stars in GitHub, google trends, stability etc. [2]. The 3 most popular JS frameworks appear to be Angular, React and Vue [2, 17, 13].

Angular

It is a Typescript focused framework that follows the Model-View-Controller (MVC) architecture. Angular is a complete framework. It does not require additional libraries or tools to create a feature. This at first glance sounds like an important advantage, but in reality, can lead to problems. The huge space of its library can cause performance problems and slow apps, especially on simple interfaces with 2–3 ordinary features. Scheduled updates for the framework are taking place every 6 months. Most of the time, these updates introduce important changes that alter the behavior of current working apps [2]. Therefore, we cannot rely on this framework for stability in our apps, especially in the long run.

React

It is an open-source framework designed by Facebook. It does not follow the MVC architecture; rather, it is based on single-direction data flow which can provide greater control during a project. It is especially suited for creating single-page web applications. The downside of this framework is that it is not complete. Because it is a mostly UI-focused framework, certain features are not available and use of third-party libraries is mandatory. React's library size is small but tends to grow in size based on the needs of the application. The creators have stated that the stability of this framework is highly important for them, because large companies use this framework on a big scale [17].

Vue

It is an open-source framework for creating single-page interfaces and it is the newest amongst them. The big advantage this framework has is its size. With a library size of 20 KB, it can offer high speeds in software development. Evidently, a lot of plug-ins are missing from the main core of its library but, like React, additions can be made. Vue is not supported or used by large companies and its community is entirely open-source driven [13]. Therefore, although its creators have stated that updates will not be a problem in the future, we cannot be entirely sure about the stability of our apps, especially in the long run.

Since we aim to create an application that is going to be used for educational purposes, stability is very important. Another thing we must consider is the target-group this application aims for. The majority are going to be students, so having a very strong UI-focused framework that handles single-page interfaces better than others will certainly help. In terms of library size, our application is not going to be too feature-heavy, therefore a framework that easily allows to plug/unplug desired tools and libraries will be the better choice. Based on all the above, we decided that the best JS framework to use for these purposes is React.js.

3.2 Design Requirements

Most features should be oriented towards the application's target-group, that is, students and instructors. Not all features will be available to everyone: users will be separated in 2 different levels of accessibility. Simply put, faculty and curators will have full control of CRUD operations upon LOs, where students will mostly have read-only rights. Finally, we need to implement a feature where external repositories can contribute in some way to the local repository. We also need to find a solution about possible duplicates that might occur. A different coloring scheme seems to be a method of handling such problems.

LO Search and Recommendation. Apart from CRUD operations, users should have the ability to search for specific LOs based on keywords. These keywords are searched against specific metadata fields as they are expressed within the LO Ontology Schema. Given the least common subset of elements (Sect. 2), our approach is to use the ontology properties `lom:title`, `lom:keyword` and `lom:description` for faceted search. The same approach will be followed when fetching LOs from an external online repository. In this case, however, we have to take into consideration possible duplicate (or semi-duplicate) results that might occur during this fetch. Duplicates may occur when metadata fetched from external repositories are already stored locally but may contain different subject assignments. For this reason, we plan to create a recommendation system that informs the user about the metadata that each repository suggests. For example, let's say that a LO in our repository has the subject keywords "viruses" and "defective". The same LO gets fetched from an external repository but this time it has "viruses" and "vaccine" as its subject keywords. The metadata record will not be replicated twice; instead, our interface will inform the user which repository recommends which keywords with different coloring for a better and more user-friendly experience.

Persistent Storage and Reusability. Reusability of the LOs is highly important for the design procedure. We would like to provide direct ways in which the LOs are being displayed so reusability will be straightforward task. New LOs should be added manually but results from external repositories should be also accommodated. For this reason, a user can search an external repository, select some of the results and store them to the database. The metadata fields completed manually or fetched from another repository populate the LO Ontology Schema and are stored within the local database. That way, the LO and its annotations are being replicated locally and reused easier, faster and following a more direct approach. On top of that, we want to combine this feature with a strategy to export either the LOs themselves or the entire way the data is being saved and managed. To this end, we can take advantage of REST APIs and facilitate metadata export for interoperability purposes. We have created multiple routings, each covering a different option: if a user wants to export the entire DB, with the right API call, all data is displayed to the user in the same shape and form that are stored inside the DB (JSON format). On the other hand, when the user wants to export specific LOs based on their unique id, this can also be achieved by calling the appropriate API URL.

Semantic Indexing and Zero-shot Learning. Another important feature is the ability to select and/or edit the subject annotations of available learning resources. Typically, a curator would be responsible for entering appropriate subject tags, possibly originating from a controlled vocabulary, a process that would streamline further discovery and reuse by other users. To this end, the LOOR provides a set of automatic subject keywords through the semantic matching process described in Sect. 2. Further, each keyword is coupled with a validity score produced by zero-shot classification (zero-shot term validation in Fig. 1). To fetch scores, we leverage the Huggingface model hub Inference API [10]. Out of the models available on the hub that implement zero-shot inference we have chosen *bart-large-mnli* and *xlm-roberta-large-xnli*, which exhibits, among others, multilingual capabilities. Taking advantage of these suggestions and accompanying scores, a user, without having any previous knowledge upon the subject of an item, can classify the object itself through the recommended tags and decide on which they should keep and which to discard.

4   Functionality and Use Cases

In this section, we present a series of use cases and corresponding examples for the LOOR and the LO ontology. For the purposes of this, we use a specific LOOR implementation[1] that fetches data from the various data sources mentioned in Sect. 3.2 and uses, among others, the MeSH taxonomy for the automated subject annotations (keywords). Some trivial but nevertheless important use cases are not going to be described in detail, such as login/register, pagination, sorting, and all sorts of quality-of-life features as well as the initialization of the application. We will focus on the users that have access to CRUD operations, as this supersedes use cases for which users have read-only rights.

4.1   CRUD Operations

Adding a Learning Object. There are multiple ways a user can add a new LO to the repository. The first, most common method is by filling a form. As shown in Fig. 2, another way one can add objects to the database is via file upload. This way the user can concurrently add many LOs. After the file is uploaded, some validation checks occur (file needs to have the correct extension and objects inside it need to have proper form) and duplicates are filtered out. The progress bar on top of the form will inform the user when the upload is completed. The final option is to add an object that was fetched from an external online repository. This is another use case (*fetching data from external online repository*) and is explained in Sect. 4.2.

---

[1] https://github.com/swigroup/federated-semantic-search.

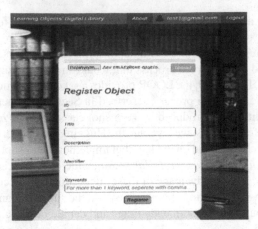

Fig. 2. Adding an LO's metadata to the local repository.

Delete a Learning Object. Since users have the option to add LOs to the database, they should also be able to remove them. When the user clicks the "delete object" button, a pop-up warning message will appear, notifying him about this irreversible action. When the user confirms the action, the LO and its metadata are removed from the database.

Update a Learning Object. Similar to adding, we also provide a variety of features for updating an object. We separated the update feature into 2 sub-features. The first one is responsible for the updating of the least-significant metadata fields of the LO. These include the title, the description as well as the identifier. The second is responsible for updating the most-significant metadata field of the LO, the subject keywords.

4.2 Fetching Data from External Online Repository

One of the most important features of the application is fetching LOs from an external source. The user types in the search bar (upper left in Fig. 3) the term that wants to see results for. Then, LOs from the external repository are fetched based on their subject keywords. The interface currently accepts external data in XML/OWL or JSON format, provided that they follow the LO Ontology Schema. As documented in [11] however, this is highly configurable and additional mappings can be specified to accommodate any other repository or metadata format. Results are rendered as shown in Fig. 3. Selecting the *DB* button under *options* opens a popup window, asking the user to confirm addition to the database. Notice that duplicate objects are highlighted with a different background color.

A fetched object is marked as duplicate when there is an object in the database with identical title, description, and identifier. When a duplicate LO is selected for addition to the database, an *update current saved object* pop-up window will appear instead (Fig. 4). There, the user will be able to choose which keywords to keep and which to reject.

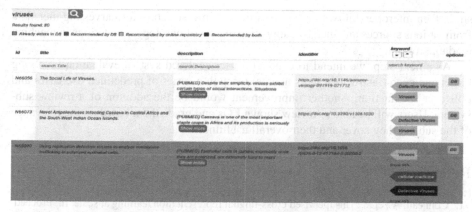

Fig. 3. Duplicate LOs and keywords appear with different colors.

The keywords on the duplicate objects have different colors to stand out. The blue labeled keywords are the ones already stored in the local DB, the yellow labeled keywords are recommended by the LOOR through semantic matching (Sect. 3.2) and finally, the black labeled keywords occur in both (Fig. 4). For the keywords originating from the LOOR, there is also a validation score available below their lexical representation based on the zero-shot classification procedure described previously.

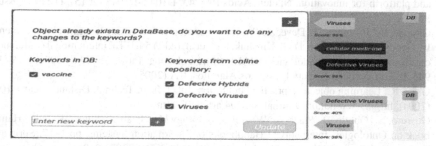

Fig. 4. Left: Update duplicate LO with keywords from external repository. Right: Labels and scores of LOs

5 Conclusions and Future Work

We have presented the design and development of a web interface, through which users are able to interact in a variety of ways with different learning objects and their metadata respectively. Through this process, users can access learning objects in both the interface's database (local repository) and ones in an online, external repository. The ability to produce and validate automated classification suggestions is also integrated into the application. This is combined with collaborative features where authorized users can edit subject annotations and decide on their inclusion to the local pool for others to discover and reuse thus enabling a form of collective intelligence. Finally, our approach can strengthen interoperability, first by providing an infrastructure for harvesting metadata from various sources and then by supporting export of ontology annotations in machine readable format.

As a next step, we intend to conduct a user-centered system evaluation involving target audience (instructors and students) through a series of predefined use-cases and poll user satisfaction. Another improvement would be the addition of a review sub-system. Users will be able to review shown LOs and grade them based on the relevance of the subject they cover and their overall usefulness.

References

1. Conneau, A., et al.: Unsupervised cross-lingual representation learning at scale. In: Proceedings of the 58th Annual Meeting of the Association for Computational Linguistics (ACL), pp. 8440–8451 (2019)
2. Daityari, S.: Angular vs React vs Vue: Which Framework to Choose in 2021. Codeinwp (2021). https://www.codeinwp.com/blog/angular-vs-vue-vs-react/
3. Downes, S.: New models of open and distributed learning. In: Jemni, M., Kinshuk, Khribi M. (eds.) Open Education: from OERs to MOOCs. LNET, pp. 1–22. Springer, Berlin, Heidelberg (2017). https://doi.org/10.1007/978-3-662-52925-6_1
4. d'Oliveira, C., Carson, S., et al.: MIT opencourseware: unlocking knowledge, empowering minds. Science **329**(5991), 525–526 (2010).https://doi.org/10.1126/science.11826962
5. Europe PMC Consortium: Europe PMC: a Full-Text literature database for the life sciences and platform for innovation. Nucleic Acids Res. **43**, D1042–D1048 (2015). Database issue PMC
6. Gasevic, D., Jovanovic, J., Devedzic, V., et al.: Ontologies for reusing learning object content. In: Goodyear, P., Sampson, D.G., Kinshuk, D.J., et al. (eds.) 5th IEEE international conference on advanced learning technologies (ICALT '05), Kaohsiung, Taiwan, 5–8 July 2005, pp. 944–945. IEEE Computer Society Press, Los Alamitos, CA (2005)
7. Greal, R.: Learning objects: a practical definition. Int. J. Instr. Technol. Distance Learn. **1**(9) (2004). http://www.itdl.org/Journal/Sep_04/article02.htm
8. Guarino, N., Oberle, D., Staab, S.: What is an ontology? In: Staab, S., Studer, R. (eds.) Handbook on Ontologies. International Handbooks on Information Systems, pp 1–17. Springer, Berlin, Heidelberg (2009). https://doi.org/10.1007/978-3-540-92673-3_0
9. Hodgins, W., Duval, E.: Draft standard for learning object metadata. Institute of Electrical and Electronics Engineers (2002)
10. Huggingface (2021): Accelerated Inference API (online). https://api-inference.huggingface.co/docs/python/html/index.html
11. Koutsomitropoulos, D.: Semantic annotation and harvesting of federated scholarly data using ontologies. Digit. Libr. Perspect. **35**(3/4), 157–171 (2019). https://doi.org/10.1108/DLP-12-2018-0038
12. Koutsomitropoulos, D., Solomou, G.: A learning object ontology repository to support annotation and discovery of educational resources using semantic thesauri. IFLA J. **44**(1) (2017). https://doi.org/10.1177/0340035217737559
13. Mariano, C.: Benchmarking JavaScript Frameworks. Masters dissertation (2017).https://doi.org/10.21427/D72890
14. McMartin, F.: MERLOT: a model for user involvement in digital library design and implementation. J. Digit. Inf. **5**(3) (2006, online)

15. Roy, D., Sarkar, S., Ghose, S.: A comparative study of learning object metadata, learning material repositories, metadata annotation & an automatic metadata annotation tool. Adv. Semant. Comput. **2**, 103–126 (2010)
16. Sabarmathi, G., Chinnaiyan, R., Ilango, V.: Big data analytics research opportunities and challenges-a review. Int. J. Adv. Res. Comput. Sci. Softw. Eng. **6**(10), 227–231(2016)
17. Satrom, B.: Choosing the right JavaScript framework for your next web application. Vitbok RITM0012054. Progress Software Corporation (2018). https://softarchitect.files.wordpress. com/2018/03/choose-the-right-javascript-framework-for-your-next-web-application_whitep aper1.pdf
18. Ternier, S., et al.: The ariadne infrastructure for managing and storing metadata. IEEE Internet Comput. **13**(4), 18–25 (2009)
19. U.S. National Library of Medicine. Medical Subject Headings (2021). https://www.nlm.nih. gov/mesh/meshhome.htmlLewis
20. Lewis, M., et al.: BART: Denoising sequence-to-sequence pre-training for natural language generation, translation, and comprehension (2019). arXiv preprint arXiv:1910.13461
21. Yin, W., Hay, J., Roth, D.: Benchmarking zero-shot text classification: Datasets, evaluation and entailment approach. In: Proceedings of the 2019 Conference on Empirical Methods in Natural Language Processing (EMNLP 2019), pp. 3914–3923 (2019)

Ontology of Experimental Variables as an Extension of Infrastructure for Behavioral Research Data FAIRification

Alena Begler[1]([✉]) [iD], Grigoriy Anufriev[2] [iD], and Irina Leshcheva[1] [iD]

[1] St. Petersburg State University, St. Petersburg 199034, Russia
`alena.begler@gmail.com`
[2] Higher School of Economics, Moscow 101000, Russia

Abstract. Data sharing is becoming a common practice in behavioral research. Thousands of experimental datasets can be found in open repositories; however, most of them cannot be properly reused due to lack of documentation. We present a structured review of ontologies for experimental research data with a description of 16 ontologies that we divided into three groups according to their approach to variable descriptions: general data description with no attention to variables, scientific research description with either abstract representation of variables or focus on their measurement, and domain-specific ontologies with classes for biological and cognitive fields. The structured resources review can be found at https://doi.org/10.17632/xw288mx2ws.1. We propose an Empirion ontology that provides a variables description that makes it possible to integrate variables from different datasets. To do this, the ontology inherits three-level variable description and enriches it with (1) connections with information about the variable's measurements, and (2) typology of variables based on their role in the experiment. The ontology source code together with supportive materials can be found at our GitHub repository: https://github.com/jimijimiyo/empirion.

Keywords: Ontology · Conceptual modeling · FAIR data · Research data · Experimental data integration

1 Introduction

Thousands of social science datasets obtained by different research groups can be found in open repositories; however, the quality of data sharing is considerably low. For example, dataset files are not always accompanied by the metadata and license files necessary for data understanding and reuse. Poor data documentation increases the perceived effort of data reuse (Yoon and Kim 2017), reduces data consumer satisfaction (Faniel et al. 2019) and might even prevent the reuse of a dataset that has already been explored (Yoon 2016). Moreover, it increases the time and effort entailed in already time-consuming data preparation work.

The improvement of data reuse is one of the goals of the FAIR principles (Wilkinson 2016). A set of data FAIRification initiatives has been successfully implemented;

© Springer Nature Switzerland AG 2022
E. Garoufallou et al. (Eds.): MTSR 2021, CCIS 1537, pp. 268–279, 2022.
https://doi.org/10.1007/978-3-030-98876-0_24

however, an important part of data management is still absent. While most developed models focus on a dataset as a whole, there is a need for variable-level metadata schemas (Dumontier 2019). Detailed variable description makes it possible not only to interpret a dataset but also to integrate several datasets obtained in similar research and test preliminary hypotheses. And the use of semantic technologies is recommended for the implementation of FAIRification initiatives (Jacobsen et al. 2020).

Our contribution is twofold. Firstly, we present a structured review of ontologies for experimental research data (Sect. 2). Secondly, we propose Empirion ontology that describes the variables common to behavioral research datasets in a way that allows for their integration (Sect. 3).

2 Structured Review of Ontologies for Experimental Data

To find related ontologies, we performed a structured resources review in accordance with Campos et al. (2020) methodology. We used the terms "ontology" and "vocabulary" and their synonyms to find literature on structured resources and the terms "experimental variable(s)" and "experimental data (set)" with synonyms to indicate domain field. The query string together with the raw materials can be found at https://doi.org/10.17632/xw288mx2ws.1.

Overall, 69 publications were retrieved by Google Scholar to the query string. Of these, 9 publications mentioned structured resources. These publications were checked for the papers that cited them (using Google Scholar), resulting in 88 more papers that were analyzed using the same procedure, which added another 9 relevant papers. The reference lists of the 9 papers from the initial search (a total of 78 publications) were also analyzed and yielded in 14 more relevant papers.

The resulting 32 papers were analyzed for structured resources selection. We walked through the papers and checked all the references and footnotes regarding structured resources (ontologies, thesauri, metadata schemas, and so on). We did not include unstructured resources (like university websites or guidelines). If we encountered an unstructured resource that could contain structured resources (like a data repository that might use some ontology), we searched for such structured resources. Nor did we include meta-models of metadata such as OWL or METS that provide language for metadata schemas. If the webpage in the source paper was inaccessible, we tried to find a new website.

Of the resulting 97 structured resources, 10 addressed experimental datasets or variables description and were available in OWL or RDF. Additionally, 6 more resources were found beyond the structured data analysis and were also included in the resulting list of structured resources. Thus, we found 16 ontological resources that describe experimental variables or datasets. We divided them into three groups according to their scopes.

2.1 Ontologies for General Data Description

The majority of generic ontologies for data description are not concerned with the description of dataset parts such as variables: IAO defines a dataset as an information entity that describes some part of reality, DCAT denotes that a single dataset can have several forms, cube focuses on dataset structure as a set of observations that have some attributes and dimensions, and the VoID approach appears inapplicable to experimental data representation, as such data are rarely published as RDF datasets.

- **Information Artifact Ontology (IAO)** (Smith and Ceusters 2015) is a mid-level ontology that extends Basic Formal Ontology (BFO) (Arp et al. 2015) for the description of information entities like *information content entity* and *data set*.
- **Data Catalog Vocabulary (DCAT)** (Albertoni et al. 2020) is a W3C Recommendation for the description of data catalogs. It provides classes for the representation of any digital asset, including *Dataset* and its physical representations (*Distribution*).
- **RDF Data Cube Vocabulary (cube)** (Cyganiak and Reynolds 2014) is a W3C recommendation for the publication of multi-dimensional data in RDF format. It contains entities for the description of datasets (*DataSet*), which consist of observations (*Observation*), their different parts (e.g. *Slice*) and structures (*DataStructureDefinition*).
- **Vocabulary of Interlinked Datasets (VoID)** (Alexander et al. 2011) describes a dataset (*dataset*) as linked data with a particular RDF serialization (*technical feature*).

2.2 Ontologies for Scientific Research Description

The ontologies in this group follow two different approaches to variable description: by their role in the experiment (EXPO and SIO) and by the notion of measurements (OoEVV and disco). The other ontologies in this group (EXACT2, HAScO, ro) do not provide concepts for variables description.

- **An ontology of scientific experiments (EXPO)** (Soldatova and King 2006) describes scientific experiments. The ontology provides classes for *ScientificExperiment* characteristics (*ExperimentalResults, ExperimentalGoal, ExperimentalDesign*, etc.) and contains a typology of variables with respect to their role in the experiment: it distinguishes *TargetVariable, ObservableVariable, InferableVariable, ExperimentalFactor* and *CalculableVariable*. The ontology uses SUMO as upper-level ontology and is designed to be further extended with domain-specific ontologies.
- **DDI-RDF Discovery Vocabulary (disco)** (Bosch et al. 2013) for the description of survey datasets. It represents datasets at two levels: data content (*LogicalDataSet*, subclass of *dcat:Dataset*), which is organized using *Variables* and physical data (*qb:DataFile*, subclass of *dcat:Distribution*). It provides three-level representation: any variable has its instance in a tabular dataset (*Variable*), its representation with particular values such as a list of codes (*Representation*) and a dataset-independent description of what it is (*RepresentedVariable*). Each variable is also a *skos:Concept*, and *Representation* is either a *skos:ConceptScheme* (for variables represented with codelists) or *rdfs:Datatype* (for variables with numeric values). The variable should be connected to a dataset (*LogicalDataSet*) or *Study*.
- **Experiment Action Ontology (EXACT2)** (Soldatova et al. 2014) is dedicated to biomedical protocols description. Its core classes are *Experimental action, Descriptor of experimental action, Experimental procedure, Experimental protocol*. Thus, it

makes it possible to describe an experiment as a process and its properties. It is compliant with upper-level BFO ontology and uses several domain-specific OBO Foundry ontologies as extensions of the corresponding classes.

- **Human-Aware Science Ontology (HAScO)** (Pinheiro et al. 2018) for scientific data annotation, created for HADatAc platform[1] support. It describes the *Data Acquisition* process, such as empirical experiment, which is described with a *Data Acquisition Schema* and conducted using some instruments (*Deployment*). The ontology addresses datasets only through SIO that HAScO uses as upper-level ontology.

- **Ontology of Experimental Variables and Values (OoEVV)** (Burns and Turner 2013) was created for the description of experimental variables in neuroimaging experimental studies. It includes classes for the *ExperimentalVariable* contained in the *OoevvElementSet* and for the information on how they were measured: *MeasurementScale* with subclasses presenting types of scales and *MeasurementValue* with subclasses presenting the types of values that the variable can take. The ontology is aligned with BFO and IAO and uses CogPO for domain-related concepts.

- **Research Objects (ro)** (Belhajjame et al. 2015) is an ontology for the description of research objects in the research workflow. It is part of a family of ontologies that supports tools for research objects management such as myExperiment portal[2]. The ro ontology extends Annotation Ontology and ORE and represents any *ResearchObject* without further differentiation.

- **Semanticscience Integrated Ontology (SIO)** (Dumontier et al. 2014) is an upper-level ontology that was created for research data integration in the biomedical field. Similarly to the BFO and IAO, it contains a *dataset* as a type of *information content entity* and as a collection of *data items*. It distinguishes *dataset* from *scientific data* and captures information about a dataset's origins as a result of some *purposeful process*, for example – an *experiment*. In the SIO, dataset is understood as a *computational entity* while *variable* is understood as a *mathematical entity* that is divided into *control*, *independent* and *dependent variable*.

2.3 Domain-Specific Ontologies for Experimental Data Description

These ontologies extend BFO and IAO with a description of experimental procedures and, partially – experimental data. They contain classes that can be used for variables description in the biomedical (EFO, OBI, SP) and cognitive (CogPO, cogat) domains, CogPO additionally contains a relatively general typology of experimental variables.

- **Experimental Factor Ontology (EFO)** (Malone et al. 2010) is a huge ontology describing biological samples. It uses BFO as upper ontology; it is compliant with OBI and uses several other domain ontologies as extensions. It was designed as an application ontology for the description of genomics data and provides tools for this.

- **Ontology of Biomedical Investigation (OBI)** (Bandrowski et al. 2016) is a community standard that provides entities for biomedical research description, including the research processes and the entities participating in them. It is part of OBO Foundry

---

[1] http://www.hadatac.org/.
[2] https://www.myexperiment.org/.

(Smith et al. 2007), uses BFO and IAO as upper and mid-level ontologies together with other more domain-specific OBO ontologies.

- **SMART Protocols (SP) Ontology** (Giraldo et al. 2014) describes a research process. It uses BFO1 as upper ontology and extends IAO classes with domain-specific subclasses.
- **Cognitive Paradigm Ontology (CogPO)** (Turner and Laird 2012) was created to describe human behavior experiments. It collaborates with several cognitive science projects[3] and uses BFO as upper ontology and extends *obi:planned process* with *Behavioral Experimental Paradigm* and *Behavioral Experimental Paradigm Condition*. It also contains relatively universal classes for behavioral experiment design such as *Instruction, Response, Stimulus Modality*.
- **Cognitive Atlas Ontology (cogat)** (Poldrack et al. 2011) is a domain-specific ontology for cognitive science experiments that was created for Cognitive Atlas portal[4] support. It extends some CogPO classes with domain-specific concepts.

2.4 Part of the Infrastructure for Variables Description

The majority of the reviewed ontologies are interconnected and form infrastructure clusters. For example, cogat extends some CogPO classes that in turn extend *obi:planned process*, which is a subclass of *bfo:process*.

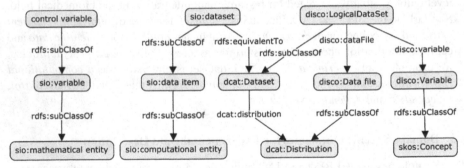

Fig. 1. Part of the infrastructure for experimental variables description.

Some of the ontologies form part of the infrastructure providing a sizable set of variables characteristics (Fig. 1); however, not all of the ontologies that mention variables are connected: while disco and SIO provide connection with DCAT for the description of a variable as part of a dataset, CogPO and EXPO do not describe variables this way, using other upper-level ontologies instead (BFO and SUMO, respectively). The OoEVV sees variables as part of a dataset but isn't connected to other models. Thus, despite the fact that existing ontologies provide a set of useful variables characteristics (different abstraction levels in disco, role in SIO and EXPO, type in CogPO, and measurements in OoEVV), to connect variables from different datasets, these characteristics should be

[3] http://www.cogpo.org/.
[4] https://www.cognitiveatlas.org/.

provided simultaneously, and this is not always possible when a bunch of models must be used. The Empirion ontology is aimed at filling this gap.

3 Empirion Ontology

During the structured resources review, we looked at the ontological landscape for open research data and identified an issue preventing research data integration: lack of a variables description allowing for the integration of variables from different datasets into a single one. In the Empirion ontology, we combined existing models for variable description and added several connections to provide such an opportunity.

3.1 Development Methodology

Ontology development followed Scenario 3 of the NeOn methodology (Suárez-Figueroa et al. 2012): Reusing ontological resources.

The main ontology **requirement** is the ability to provide terminology for the integration of datasets obtained in behavioral experiments. Researchers in this field might be interested in answering questions such as the following: "How do the parameters of a certain type of stimulus influence reaction time?" or "In what context was a particular concept studied?" In other words, there are some hypotheses related to experimental parameters that can be investigated with the re-analysis of existing datasets.

For the **conceptualization** of ontology vocabulary, we applied a combination of top-down and bottom-up modeling styles (Uschold and Grüninger 1996). We started with an analysis of the datasets we found in open research repositories and derived a list of preliminary concepts. This allowed us to derive groups of variables that included most of the identified terms. Then, we matched these groups with candidate ontologies for **reuse:** the already-existing ontologies that were identified at the structured resource review stage and contained variable descriptions (see Sect. 2). Finally, to formulate upper-level classes, we rethought metadata classification into embedded, associated and physical (Duval et al. 2002).

We **formalized** the Empirion ontology with Ontology Web Language using Protégé ontology editor (Musen 2015) and **populated** it with the help of a set of Python modules (Leshcheva and Begler 2020); this stage is ongoing.

3.2 Ontology Structure

To describe variables in a way allowing for the integration of variables from different datasets, two aspects of variables representation should be presented in an ontology simultaneously: their connection to the information necessary for their interpretation (i.e. how the variables are represented in a dataset), and their role in the experiment (i.e., what they are from the experiment design point of view). In this section, we briefly describe the main design decisions for Empirion ontology; its full structure can be found at our GitHub repository: https://github.com/jimijimiyo/empirion.

By the structure of their representation, variables can be divided into three types based on their values: (1) values described by the list, for example, correctness of answer as correct and incorrect; (2) values measured in certain units, for example, reaction time in seconds or milliseconds; (3) string values (for open questions) or dimensionless values (for marks). This typology is not directly reflected in the ontology's structure, but it shapes the population process: for the first type of variables, a list of values should be created and linked to reference values; for the second type, a connection to measurement unit should be added; the third type is a simple string.

To provide such information, the Empirion ontology inherits disco's three-level variable description and enriches it by connecting variables to the information necessary for their interpretation and physical representation (Fig. 2):

- *disco:Variable* is dedicated for the variables as they are in the dataset. Individuals of this class are variables as they are in a dataset.
- *disco:Representation* connects variable representation with *MeasurementUnit* or value list (corresponding individuals in the *RepresentationValue* class should be created). It makes it possible to make a comparison of two variables reflecting the same experimental aspect with different instruments. For example, if in the one experiment reaction time was measured in milliseconds, and in the other in seconds, this information will be explicitly presented in the ontology.
- *disco:RepresentedVariable* is a most abstract variable representation that is not depended on variables exact representation in the dataset and is connected with abstract representations of all known variable values: particular cases of the variable values in the particular dataset contained in the *RepresentationValue* class are connected to the corresponding values of *RepresentedVariableValue* class with *owl:sameAs*, thereby providing an opportunity for the interpretation of values in different datasets.

By their role in the experiment, variables can be dependent (reaction time), independent (stimulus characteristics) or characteristics of something in the experiment (like subject age). This difference is reflected in the Empirion ontology by the *disco:Variable* subclasses structure (part of it can be seen in Fig. 4), including:

- *cogpo:Stimulus* and *cogpo:Response* for presented stimulus (independent variable) and participant's reactions (dependent variable).
- *cogpo:StimulusRole* and *cogpo:ResponseRole* for the role of the variable in the experiment. For example, a stimulus may be a prime – to which any reaction is anticipated, or a target – to which a reaction is supposed.
- *StimulusCharacteristic* and *ResponseCharacteristic* for different modifications of responses and stimuli, respectively.
- *SubjectCharacteristic* for information about the participant.
- *ExperimentPartCharacteristic* for information about different experiment parts: the simplest part of any experiment is the trial (the simplest part of the experiment reflecting a single record comprised of a participant's stimulus and reaction), while some experiments have a more complex design with blocks representing different sets of trials inside the experiment.

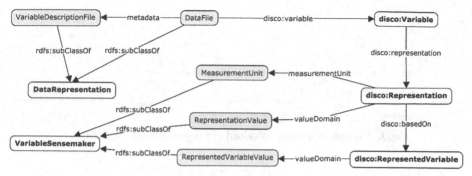

Fig. 2. Empirion ontology main classes and properties. Upper-level classes in white figures.

3.3 Usage Scenario

Imagine that we're interested in re-analyzing several datasets obtained in the flanker task experiment (Eriksen and Eriksen 1974). This task is common for modern experimental studies of perception, as it models the simplest form of cognitive conflict. During the experiment, the participant sits in front of a computer screen and presses a button corresponding to a central sign in a stimulus. The stimuli in the task are rows of objects (for example, letters), while the flanker objects might either be the same as the central objects or different. If all of the objects in a row are the same, the stimulus is called congruent; if they're different – it's called incongruent. For example, the stimulus "$<<<<<$" is congruent (as the target symbol "$<$" is the same as the flanker symbols), and the stimulus "$<<>><$" is incongruent (as the target symbol "$>$" is different from the distractor stimulus). The result of the participant's performance in an experiment is a record of stimuli, responses and their parameters. Such datasets are often presented in tabular (.csv or.xlsx) format and can be found in open repositories. An example of such a dataset is depicted in Fig. 3.

Variables in the exemplar datasets have different types and their values can be either codified or accompanied by measurement units. The variables also differ by type, and they should instantiate different subclasses of *disco:Variable* class. An example of such instantiation of two real datasets is shown in Fig. 4. Both datasets were found with a "flanker task" keyword search at figshare (Dataset 1[5]) and OSF (Dataset 2[6]) research repositories. For the sake of readability, the column order was changed.

In addition to the depicted mapping, the variables should be connected to the information necessary for their interpretation. For example, the variable *Condition* in Dataset 1 and variable *flanker_type* in Dataset 2 provides the same information about stimulus congruence but with different codifications. To say in the ontology that "incongruent and noncongruent means the same stimulus condition; namely – its noncongruence," we applied a three-level variables description (Fig. 5): we preserved both codification vocabularies and for every item created an *owl:sameAs* connection with reference vocabulary.

---

[5] https://figshare.com/articles/dataset/The_Role_of_Sustained_Attention_in_the_Produc
tion_of_Conjoined_Noun_Phrases/1517601.

[6] https://osf.io/pzxq6/.

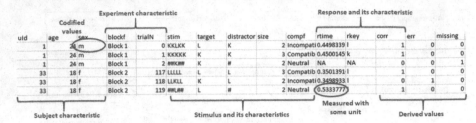

Fig. 3. Example of a dataset obtained in a cognitive study experiment.

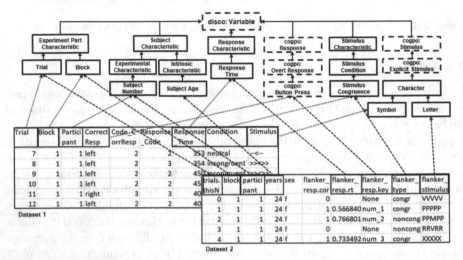

Fig. 4. Mapping of two datasets to the Empirion ontology. Imported classes are in the dashed rectangles. Black arrows represent class-subclass relations. Dashed and dotted arrows represent instantiation.

The proposed approach makes it possible to fully describe a variable from the experimental study dataset because it allows for the preservation of both its meaning in the experiment (with subclasses of *disco:Variable*) and the information necessary for its values interpretation (with three-level representation).

4   Discussion and Conclusion

Empirion ontology builds on efforts towards experimental variables description for the better reusability of datasets. While existing ontologies are focused either on variable measurements or on the high-level variable-type definition, Empirion connects these approaches and adds some details (see Table 1 for comparison).

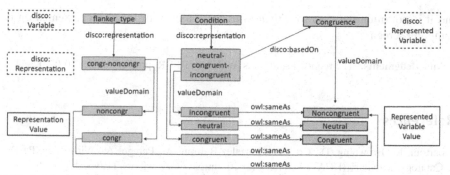

Fig. 5. Representation of variable values in Empirion ontology. Imported classes are in the dashed rectangles. Instances are filled with grey.

Table 1. Comparison of Empirion with existing ontologies

Existing ontology	Variable's description	Empirion difference
EXPO	By role (e.g., target variable)	For now, Empirion does not classify variables by role. It is partially superseded by type classification. Additions on raw and inferred variables differentiation are to be added
SIO	By role (e.g., control variable)	
disco	By abstraction level (e.g., variable, represented variable)	Empirion borrows this approach with three additions: (1) direct connection with measurements and list values; (2) types of variables added; (3) variables are not *skos:Concept* but individuals of classes for the corresponding types
OoEVV	By measurement (e.g., measurement scale and value)	In the Empirion ontology, measurements of variables are presented not by scales but by units of measurement and lists of values
CogPO	By type (e.g., response, stimulus modality)	These types were reused in Empirion and formed an extension of *disco:Variable* class

For now, Empirion ontology has not been integrated with any upper-level ontology. Despite the fact that many research ontologies use BFO as an upper-level ontology, we decided not to stick to it at this time. Our main concern was that our reuse of some ontologies that are already BFO-IAO mapped might prevent integration. For example, CogPO classifies *Stimulus* as an *object aggregate*. This is, in our opinion, a questionable decision, as *object aggregate* is a subclass of BFO *material entity* (i.e. physical object) and it is not often the case for *Stimulus* as the majority of them are presented on the computer screen.

Acknowledgments. The reported study was funded by RFBR, project number 20-07-00854.

References

Albertoni, R., Browning, D., Cox, S., Gonzalez-Beltran, A., Perego, A., Winstanley, P.: Data Catalog Vocabulary (DCAT)-Version 2 (2020). https://www.w3.org/TR/vocab-dcat-2/

Alexander, K., Cyganiak, R., Hausenblas, M., Zhao, J.: Describing Linked Datasets with the VoID Vocabulary (2011). https://www.w3.org/TR/void/

Arp, R., Smith, B., Spear, A.D.: Building Ontologies with Basic Formal Ontology. MIT press, Cambridge (2015)

Bandrowski, A., et al.: The ontology for biomedical investigations. PloS One **11**(4), e0154556 (2016)

Belhajjame, K., et al.: Using a suite of ontologies for preserving workflow-centric research objects. J. Web Semant. **32**, 16–42 (2015)

Bosch, T., Gregory, A., Cyganiak, R., Wackerow, J.: DDI-RDF discovery vocabulary: a metadata vocabulary for documenting research and survey data. In: Proceedings of the WWW2013 Workshop on Linked Data on the Web (LDOW2013), p. 996 (2013). http://ceur-ws.org/Vol-996/papers/ldow2013-paper-12.pdf

Burns, G.A.P.C., Turner, J.A.: Modeling functional magnetic resonance imaging (fMRI) experimental variables in the ontology of experimental variables and values (OoEVV). Neuroimage **82**, 662–670 (2013)

Campos, P.M.C., et al.: Finding reusable structured resources for the integration of environmental research data. Environ. Model. Softw. **104813**(August), 104813 (2020)

Cyganiak, R., Reynolds, D.: The RDF Data Cube Vocabulary (2014). https://www.w3.org/TR/vocab-data-cube/

Dumontier, M.: Accelerating biomedical discovery with an Internet of FAIR data and services (2019)

Dumontier, M., et al.: The semanticscience integrated ontology (SIO) for biomedical research and knowledge discovery. J. Biomed. Semant. **5**(1), 1–11 (2014)

Duval, E., Hodgins, W., Autodesk, S.F., Sutton, S., Weibel, S.L.: Metadata principles and practicalities. D-Lib Mag. **8**(4), 15 (2002)

Eriksen, B.A., Eriksen, C.W.: Effects of noise letters upon the identification of a target letter in a nonsearch task. Percept. Psychophys. **16**(1), 143–149 (1974)

Faniel, I.M., Frank, R.D., Yakel, E.: Context from the data reuser's point of view. J. Doc. **75**(6), 1274–1297 (2019)

Giraldo, O., García, A., Corcho, O.: SMART protocols: SeMAntic representation for experimental protocols. In: Proceedings of the 4th Workshop on Linked Science 2014–Making Sense Out of Data (LISC2014) Co-Located with the 13th International Semantic Web Conference (ISWC 2014), vol. 1282, pp. 36–47. CEUR Workshop Proceedings (2014)

Jacobsen, A., et al.: FAIR principles: interpretations and implementation considerations. Data Intell. **2**(1–2), 10–29 (2020)

Leshcheva, I., Begler, A.: A method of semi-automated ontology population from multiple semi-structured data sources. J. Inf. Sci. 0165551520950243 (2020)

Malone, J., et al.: Modeling sample variables with an experimental factor ontology. Bioinformatics **26**(8), 1112–1118 (2010)

Musen, M.A.: The protégé project: a look back and a look forward. AI Matters 1(4), 4–12 (2015)

Pinheiro, P., et al.: HADatAc: a framework for scientific data integration using ontologies. In: Proceedings of the ISWC 2018 Posters & Demonstrations, Industry and Blue Sky Ideas Tracks Co-Located with the 17th International Semantic Web Conference (ISWC 2018), Monterey, USA, October 8th to 12th 2018, p. 2180 (2018). http://ceur-ws.org/Vol-2180/paper-49.pdf

Poldrack, R.A., et al.: The cognitive atlas: toward a knowledge foundation for cognitive neuroscience. Front. Neuroinform. 5(September), 1–11 (2011)

Smith, B., et al.: The OBO foundry: coordinated evolution of ontologies to support biomedical data integration. Nat. Biotechnol. 25(11), 1251–1255 (2007)

Smith, B., Ceusters, W.: Aboutness: towards foundations for the information artifact ontology. In: Proceedings of the International Conference on Biomedical Ontology, vol. 1515, pp. 1–5 (2015)

Soldatova, L.N., King, R.D.: An ontology of scientific experiments. J. R. Soc. Interface R. Soc. 3(11), 795–803 (2006)

Soldatova, L.N., et al.: EXACT2: the semantics of biomedical protocols. BMC Bioinform. 15(14), S5 (2014)

Suárez-Figueroa, M.C., Gómez-Pérez, A., Fernández-López, M.: The NeOn methodology for ontology engineering. In: Suárez-Figueroa, M., Gómez-Pérez, A., Motta, E., Gangemi, A. (eds.) Ontology Engineering in a Networked World, pp. 9–34. Springer, Berlin, Heidelberg (2012). https://doi.org/10.1007/978-3-642-24794-1_2

Turner, J.A., Laird, A.R.: The cognitive paradigm ontology: design and application. Neuroinformatics 10(1), 57–66 (2012)

Uschold, M., Grüninger, M.: Ontologies: principles, methods and applications. Knowl. Eng. Rev. 11(2), 93–136 (1996)

Wilkinson, M.D.: Comment: the FAIR guiding principles for scientific data management and stewardship. Sci. Data 3, 160018 (2016)

Yoon, A.: Red flags in data: learning from failed data reuse experiences. Proc. Assoc. Inf. Sci. Technol. 53, 1–6 (2016)

Yoon, A., Kim, Y.: Social scientists' data reuse behaviors: exploring the roles of attitudinal beliefs, attitudes, norms and data repositories. Libr. Inf. Sci. Res. 39(3), 224–233 (2017)

Publishing LOD Vocabularies in Any Schema with Semantics.gr

Haris Georgiadis(✉) , Georgia Angelaki , Elena Lagoudi ,
Nikos Vasilogamvrakis , Kostas Stamatis , Agathi Papanoti ,
Alexia Panagopoulou , Katerina Bartzi , Dimitris Charlaftis , Eleni Aggelidi ,
Poly Karagianni, Despina Hardouveli , and Evi Sachini

National Documentation Center (EKT), Vasileos Konstantinou 48 Avenue 116 35,
Athens, Greece
{hgeorgiadis,angelaki,elena.lagoudi,nikvasil,kstamatis,apapano,
apanagopoulou,bartzi,dharlaftis,eage,pkarag,dxardo,
esachin}@ekt.gr

Abstract. Semantics.gr is an innovative, cutting-edge platform developed by the National Documentation Centre (EKT) for the creation, curation, interlinking and publishing of vocabularies, thesauri, classifications and authority files (collectively referred to as *Vocabularies* in this paper) as Linked Open DataQuery.

Besides SKOS, Semantics.gr can accommodate vocabularies of any data model that can be expressed as an OWL ontology. Through a user-friendly GUI, a user can represent a particular data model (i.e. SKOS or MADS/RDF) by configuring the relevant OWL classes and properties and setting appropriate constraints as a *Vocabulary Schema*. The Vocabulary Schema, in turn, provides the blueprint for the term forms through which a user adds or updates individual terms.

To date, we have represented various established data models in Semantics.gr, such as SKOS, EDM's contextual classes, MADS/RDF (for person names and organizations) and Schema.org, creating, in parallel, several custom Vocabulary Schemas capturing specialized vocabulary needs. We have also developed several Vocabularies that we use, on one hand, as controlled vocabulary lists in our digital repositories as well as to enrich 3rd party data in the national cultural aggregator, SearchCulture.gr, and the scientific data aggregator, OpenArchives.gr. Vocabularies are published as RDF and also via a Web API under an open license and are, therefore, free for any entity to reuse for their purposes in their own systems. Semantics.gr is launching as a free service to organizations that wish to create and publish their vocabularies as LOD, with the intention to become a central public platform for publishing and re-using authoritative LOD Vocabularies and to develop an active community around the service.

Keywords: LOD Vocabularies · Thesauri · Authority files · Linked data · Semantic enrichment · RDF · Vocabulary publishing service

1 Introduction

Semantics.gr is an innovative platform for the development, curation and interlinking of vocabularies, thesauri, classification schemes and authority files- collectively hereby

© Springer Nature Switzerland AG 2022
E. Garoufallou et al. (Eds.): MTSR 2021, CCIS 1537, pp. 280–291, 2022.
https://doi.org/10.1007/978-3-030-98876-0_25

called *Vocabularies-* and their publication as Linked Open Data (LOD). The infrastructure is developed in-house by the National Documentation Centre in Greece (EKT), alongside other services and tools, as per the organization's mission statement and its long-term strategy.

The platform has been in development since 2015 and was initially built with the scope to cater for in-house needs, i.e. to serve as a central infrastructure where EKT staff would develop the vocabularies that were being used to support the cataloguing and enrichment requirements of the organization's content repositories (such as the National PhD theses Archive, the EKT's Institutional Repository, the cultural and scientific data aggregators SearchCulture.gr and OpenArchives.gr, etc.) using semantic knowledge representation technologies.

The platform provides a smart, user-friendly interface that can be used even by non-experts in RDF, thus significantly lowering the barrier for institutions to publish vocabularies using semantic web technologies in a standardized way. The long-term goal for Semantics.gr is to become a central public platform for publishing LOD vocabularies, especially scientific terminology and authority files that can be further used by any third party in order to enhance the quality and the interoperability of their digital resources.

The platform is in production release available at https://www.semantics.gr. It currently includes all the functionality described in this paper as well as more than 40 published vocabularies freely available under open licenses for re-use. Some functionalities, such as the configuration of data models and schemata are currently available only to EKT personnel but the development and publishing of vocabularies will soon be also available, for free, to selected 3rd party legal entities (public, not-for-profit or commercial) that wish to develop and publish their own vocabularies as Linked Data. In the present article we examine the platform, its functionality and workflows for custom design of data models and vocabulary schemata and the development and publication of vocabularies. We also highlight some of the vocabularies developed by EKT scientific staff and how these are being used to homogenize and enrich our content repositories.

2   A Mechanism for Representing Data Models in a Customizable Way

Semantics.gr can support the publication of vocabularies that conform to any data model which can be expressed as an OWL ontology. This is achieved thanks to a user-friendly customization mechanism for the registration of data models and their specializations as concrete documentation schemata that adhere to the basic standards and specifications of the Semantic Web and LOD (RDF, OWL ontology, classes and properties). The mechanism is aimed to support the development of vocabularies that are conformant either to the mainstream data models and ontologies or to customized data models that correspond to specialized documentation needs. A number of commonly used data models have already been integrated in the platform, such as SKOS[1], MADS/RDF[2],

---

[1] https://www.w3.org/2004/02/skos/.
[2] https://www.loc.gov/standards/mads/rdf/.

the contextual classes of EDM[3] and part of Schema.org[4]. At the same time, new data models have been developed such as oadm[5] which was created by EKT as a model for the description of scientific resources and catriseu that was developed by the EU CatRIS project[6] consortium as a model to describe research infrastructure services.

The data model chosen in each case generates the template on which a *Vocabulary Schema* is based to be created. The vocabulary schema in turn stipulates in detail the structure of the vocabulary that will be created in the infrastructure. In practice, the vocabulary schema defines the entry-update form through which the user adds or updates terms. These user-friendly forms are then used by authorized users assigned with the role of a *Vocabulary Curator* who creates and curates vocabularies. The forms possess control mechanisms that safeguard the constraints that are set for the individual properties by the chosen vocabulary schema. The forms can also be used for the curation of terms even by non-experts in RDF and OWL technologies.

Vocabulary curators can publish the vocabularies they have created as LOD following the adoption of a suitable open license. A published vocabulary is publicly searchable through the platform and is made available to third parties via the Web API and as a Linked Data.

2.1 Registering Data Models

Users with admin rights (currently EKT personnel) can represent any data model by specifying and customizing the OWL properties and then grouping them into OWL classes. A registered data model can then be used to produce the documentation schema that contains the exact structure and constraints underpinning the creation of one or more vocabularies.

In the user-friendly Administrator Environment the admin can register data models by configuring their namespaces, properties and classes. After the necessary namespaces (such as dc, dcterms and skos) are defined the admin can proceed to register properties by setting their namespaces, labels and constraints. For example, one can configure a particular property as referential, which means that it can be populated only with referential values (via their URIs) or with other nested resources (embedded resources, often without URIs which are depended on a parent resource) or even with language labels (via the xml:lang property in RDF/XML).

Figure 1 for example, depicts the skos:broader property registration form as defined by the SKOS data model. This property is referential, which means that it takes as value a URI that refers to another resource. An additional constraint is set in this particular case, which is that the resource referenced should pertain to the same vocabulary. Finally, as the skos:broader property is an expression of the bilateral relationship "generalization-specialization", the inverted property of the relationship is also defined, that is skos:narrower.

---

[3] https://pro.europeana.eu/page/edm-documentation.

[4] https://schema.org/.

[5] OpenArchives Data Model (OADM), described here (in greek): http://ariadne.ekt.gr/ariadne/handle/20.500.12776/16660.

[6] Catalogue for Research Infrastructure Services (Catris): https://www.portal.catris.eu/home.

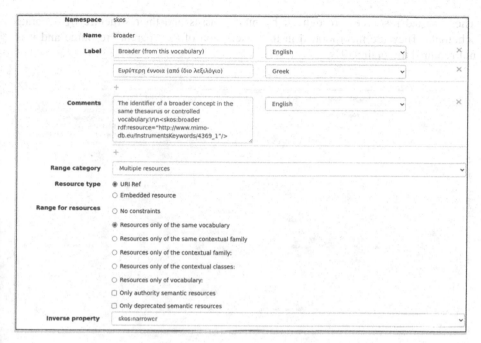

Fig. 1. The property editing form

Next, the admin can register OWL classes by setting their namespace and labels as well as the properties they contain.

Established classes and properties (under third-party namespaces), such as SKOS, are registered in Semantics.gr only with the purpose to support the creation and dissemination of vocabularies whose concrete schemata are based on these classes and properties. EKT personnel, who are granted with the permission to register data models and create schemata based on them, are responsible to respect the original semantics and specifications of the established data models and any possible configuration shall conform to that.

2.2 Building Vocabulary Schemata

After the classes and properties are registered, the user can configure a vocabulary schema which conveys the exact structure and additional constraints that will support the development of one or more separate vocabularies.

Initially, the user selects the basic class and any additional classes that the vocabulary terms will correspond to and decides which of their properties will be included in the schema. For every property, the user can select additional constraints. For example, they can narrow a referential property's value range to terms from a specific vocabulary published in Semantics.gr.

Figure 2 shows the vocabulary schema entry/editing form that is based on the MADS/RDF model and particularly on the PersonalName class that is used to describe persons. In the schema quite a few properties take "nested" resources as their values.

These nested resources are defined by other classes and their structure by separate schemata. They are incorporated in the description of the "parent" resource and it is not required to obtain URIs.

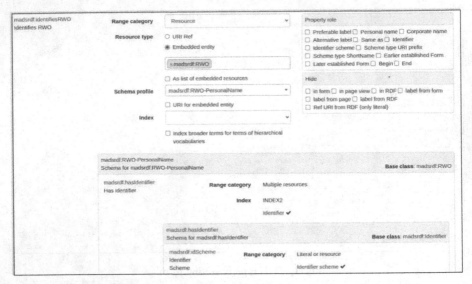

Fig. 2. Configuration of a property that incorporates a "nested" resource

Given the high level of complexity the functions described so far are accessible only to administrators from the EKT personnel who can represent and configure established or custom data models and vocabulary schemata and their adaptations in Semantics.gr. Upon request EKT admins can create new or adapt existing schemata to better serve any specific documentation needs of a third party that uses Semantics.gr to develop their own vocabularies.

The functions described in the following sections are accessible by vocabulary curators after they are granted the relevant permissions. Vocabulary curators can create and publish their own vocabularies using one of the pre-configured vocabulary schemata.

3   Creating and Publishing Vocabularies

In order to start creating a new vocabulary, a vocabulary curator first selects the vocabulary schema that it pertains to and enters some descriptive properties such as creator(s), contributor(s), domain of application and license.

Then he/she can start creating and curating terms. As described before, the term editing forms are particularly easy to use and include all the property constraints that have been defined in the schema.

Figure 3 shows the term editing form for a MADS/RDF PersonalName vocabulary whereby the property madsrdf:identifiesRWO takes as value a nested resource (of Class madsrdf:Identifier) that in turn includes several properties (fields) and Fig. 4 shows the

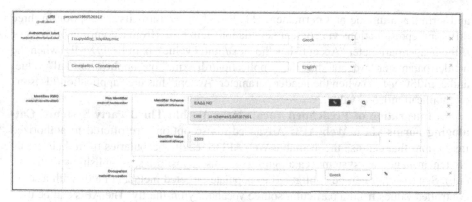

Fig. 3. Editing form for a madsrdf:PersonalName resource

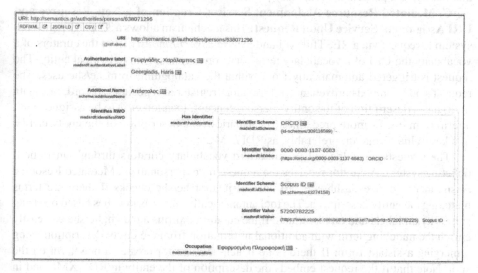

Fig. 4. A MADS/RDF PersonalName resource page

term page that includes the term URI, as well as all the terms' properties and values. URI references appear as hyperlinks that link to other resources. The user can also see the RDF representation of the term, either as RDF/XML or as JSON-LD serialization.

4   Access, Re-use and Integration Mechanisms

Below we present the different channels through which vocabularies or individual terms hosted in Semantics.gr can be searched online and served for use or integration in third party systems.

   A. Linked Data Endpoints: A published vocabulary is publicly accessible as Linked Data. The RDF/XML and J-SON LD representations are available for every vocabulary or term, in the vocabulary's page or resource's page, respectively. Every vocabulary and term has a unique and permanent HTTP URI that returns its description in three different representations via content negotiation: a. in html (from a common browser or if the header parameter "Accept" has the "text/html" value), b. in RDF/XML (when the header parameter "Accept" has the "application/rdf+xml" or "application/xml" value) and c. in JSON-LD (when the header parameter "Accept" has the "application/ld+json" or "application/json" value).

B. Integration of Predefined Vocabularies Within Third Party Systems' Cataloging Forms via a Web API: Advanced re-use options are offered to authorized institutions that can use the available Web API to recall vocabularies from their digital content management systems (cataloguing systems, repositories, e-publishing platforms, etc.). Semantics.gr can be configured to populate targeted metadata fields with a set of controlled values from a particular source vocabulary on-the-fly. The APIs can be used in a cataloguing/archiving form to enable the user to insert values from controlled terms that pertain to a particular vocabulary published in Semantics.gr.

C. Mediated Resource Assignment Service: Creation of a New Resource and URI Assignment Service Upon Request: This mechanism allows a 3rd party registered system to request via a RESTful API and receive *asynchronously* from the curators of a vocabulary the URI of a vocabulary term[7] that corresponds to an individual entity. The request is triggered automatically from within the cataloguing form he/she uses. The request's body embeds provenance information (registered repository, record, metadata field) and a description of the entity (person, concept, location etc.) to be assigned with a term from one or more predefined vocabularies. The description of the entity can be in a key-value format or, preferably, as RDF/XML.

The requests are allocated to authorized vocabulary curators through an in-built ticketing system. A curator receives the request in the personalized Mediated Resource Assignment Service dashboard. To process it, first he/she checks if there are terms matching the entity description. The tool automatically suggests matches based on string similarity on labels and on identifiers. If the curator confirms a match, he/she can easily enrich the matching term with additional information from the entity description using a merging assistant form. If there is no match, the curator creates a new term on the spot. Note that if the request embeds the description of the entity in RDF/XML and in the exact same data model as the vocabulary's, then the form for creating a new (or merging/enriching an existing) term is automatically filled with values obtained by the RDF/XML representation. The description of a person entity, for example, may include the preferred and alternative names, ORCID id and other identifiers, affiliation etc. This significantly eliminates the need for new data entry making the entire process faster. In either case, upon resolving a request the 3rd party registered system is notified via a webhook in order to handle the assignment appropriately (for example to enrich the metadata record with the term URI).

This service provides a simple and fast mechanism for 3rd parties that wish to integrate LD in their systems but need an additional curation step from an expert who checks for them if a term already exists in the designated vocabulary or creates a new

---

[7] We use the word *term* for any entity/resource part of a vocabulary or catalogue, even for persons/legal bodies.

term when needed. This is also beneficial for the institution that owns the vocabulary since it facilitates the expansion of a vocabulary in a controlled and curated way.

D. A Mapping Tool for Enriching Content *En Masse:* This tool can be used to define mappings in order to perform bulk data enrichment in aggregator databases and repositories. The GUI environment includes advanced automated functionalities that help the curator easily define mappings from source datasets (resources/terms from vocabularies, metadata records or aggregated metadata values) to terms from a target vocabulary. The tool incorporates a self-improving automatic suggestion mechanism and additionally supports the curator when intervening in the mapping process. After mappings for a dataset are finalized they can be served on request via a RESTful API in JSON format which can be used by the aggregator or repository to enrich the actual dataset easily and en masse. The tool is thoroughly described in [1].

5 How EKT Leverages Semantics.gr to Enrich and Integrate Its Content

Until today there are 48 Vocabularies published on Semantics.gr covering different various thematic areas and scientific topics. Most of these vocabularies have been developed by EKT's staff and by EU-funded projects' consortia. The majority are original Vocabularies while some are adaptations and extensions of existing popular vocabularies with labels translated in Greek.

Vocabularies currently hosted in Semantics.gr are grouped around four categories based on their area of application: i) Persons/Corporate bodies (supported models: MADS/RDF PersonalName/CorporateName and edm:Agent) ii) Historical periods (supported models: edm:Timespan from EDM), iii) concepts (supported models: SKOS) and iv) Geographical locations (supported models: edm:Place from EDM).

We use the vocabularies that we have developed in-house to enrich our scientific and cultural content repositories and aggregators with Linked Data resources. These activities have already significantly improved the quality and the efficiency of our content cataloguing, have boosted semantic interoperability and data integration across our distributed infrastructures and have improved the overall user search and browsing experience in our content discovering websites.

So far, we are using Semantics.gr in the following content infrastructures that are maintained by EKT:

- **SearchCulture.gr** | https://www.searchculture.gr: the national cultural data aggregator (more than 720K + items/ records from 72 Greek institutions)
- **OpenArchives.gr** | https://www.openarchives.gr: the biggest Greek aggregator of scientific literature (770K + items records, such as scholarly publications and gray literature, from 78 institutions)
- **National Archive of PhD Theses** | https://www.didaktorika.gr: collects in digital form doctoral dissertations awarded by Higher Education Institutions (HEIs) or to Greek scholars by foreign HEIs (46K + thesis).
- **ePublishing** | https://epublishing.ekt.gr: EKT's open access scholarly communication service for the Greek academic community (20K + articles).

- **Ariadne** | http://ariadne.ekt.gr: EKT Institutional Repository (3K + items)

Next, we highlight our most representative vocabularies that are used in the above infrastructures:

Cultural Heritage Item Types Vocabulary [8]: A SKOS-based original vocabulary using the skos:Concept class to describe different types of cultural artifacts. It is hierarchical, bilingual and the majority of the terms are linked to the Getty Art and Architecture Thesaurus. The vocabulary is being used to enrich SearchCulture.gr collections as per item types using the *Mapping Tool* [1] (see Sect. 5, D).

UNESCO Thesaurus (EKT Version) [9]: Vocabulary adapted from the UNESCO thesaurus. We followed the original hierarchical thesaurus structure whose concepts are grouped in 7 broad thematic areas. For the EKT version, 1387 terms were selected that are particularly suitable for the SearchCulture.gr collections. The vocabulary was used to enrich SearchCulture.gr items as per their subjects using the *Mapping Tool* [1].

Greek Historical Periods [10]: A vocabulary constructed according to the semantic class edm:Timespan of Europeana's EDM model. It contains 94 terms that cover Greek history from 8.000 BC to today. It is hierarchical, bilingual, it covers the Greek territory and some values in the 3rd and 4th level correspond to individual civilizations. The vocabulary is used to enrich the content in SearchCulture.gr as per historical periods using the *Mapping Tool* [1].

Significant Figures in Greek History and Culture [11]: A vocabulary of approximately 7,500 names of historical figures and influential persons from across Greek history and culture conforming to the edm:Agent class of Europena's EDM. Each entity is assigned a unique URI, enriched with basic biographical information and links to other reputable databases such as VIAF. It is also enriched with links to a hierarchical bilingual vocabulary of professions/occupations (e.g. politicians, clergy, artists, scientists, etc.) that we developed for this purpose. The vocabulary, which is not published yet, is being currently used to enrich SearchCulture.gr items with creators or persons they are related to. The *Mapping Tool* is also used for this type of enrichment.

EKT Scientific Disciplines [12]: we have also developed a vocabulary of scientific disciplines based on the OECD 2015[13]. It aligns with the FORD classification with regards to the six 1st-level broad thematic areas and forty-two 2nd-level thematic areas. EKT information scientists expanded the 2nd-level thematic areas creating a 3rd fine-grained level based on a series of valid scientific resources. The resulting SKOS vocabulary

---

[8] https://www.semantics.gr/authorities/vocabularies/ekt-item-types.

[9] https://www.semantics.gr/authorities/vocabularies/ekt-unesco.

[10] http://semantics.gr/authorities/vocabularies/historical-periods.

[11] http://semantics.gr/authorities/vocabularies/searchculture-persons.

[12] https://www.semantics.gr/authorities/vocabularies/EKT-voc.

[13] OECD FORD Research and Development classification fields.https://unstats.un.org/unsd/classifications/Family/Detail/1039.

comprises of 474 unique bilingual subject terms covering the principal areas of Science, Technology & Development. The vocabulary is being used in the National PhD Archive repository where PhD holders select the subject areas that their dissertation relates to. The vocabulary will be further used for classifying the content of OpenArchives.gr and ePublishing.

Catalogue of Authors of Scientific Publications: A list of authors from across EKT's scientific repositories such as the National PhD Archive repository, ePublishing and Ariadne. The vocabulary conforms to the MADS/RDF ontology (madsrdf:PersonalName class) and currently consists of more than 53k authors, initially imported from the National PhD Archive.

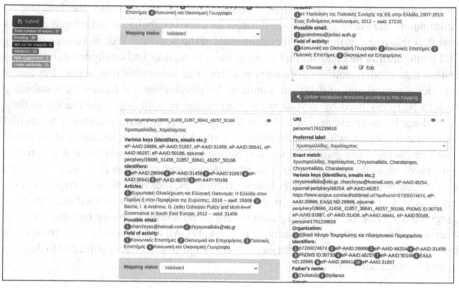

Fig. 5. Mapping authors from an ePublishing journal to the Catalogue of Authors of Scientific Publications

Our aim is to enrich the publications' records with the authors and contributors' URIs and to integrate a person's scientific and research output from across a range of different platforms. For new records we will integrate our scientific repositories with the *Resource Assignment Service* (described in Sect. 4, E). The National PhD Archive is the first platform fully integrated with this service allowing PhD theses records to get enriched with Person URIs from the catalogue prior to publication. For existing content, we are using the Mapping Tool to map author names to persons from the Catalogue and to enrich the Catalogue with new persons when there is no match. We have started this process with the authors of articles of selected journals from the ePublising platform. Figure 5 illustrates the mapping form of the tool, where authors from a specific journal (left part) are mapped to authors from the Catalogue (right part).

6 Related Work and Discussion

There are many vocabulary publishing tools, both open source and commercial. Most of them support only SKOS [2, 5] or a limited pre-defined set of data models [3]. There are also platforms and research tools that support ontology and Linked Data resource management, such as VocBench [4] and Protégé [6] that focus more on ontology engineering leveraging OWL expressiveness for building ontology-based systems and are rather geared towards advanced users. These systems are also enabled with reasoning and SPARQL endpoint services confirming the consistency and information retrieval functionality of data models.

Semantics.gr on the other hand is not meant as an ontology engineering tool nor has it been purposed as a Triplestore service. It puts at the centre the development of a vocabulary network to be used by interested parties and therefore the building of a community network. This is done through an easy vocabulary creation and curation workflow that respects the reusability principles of the Semantic Web and a user-friendly GUI configuration mechanism that enables users to register and configure standard and custom data models and/or application profiles. The innovative trait about it is that it provides a central and uniform environment for developing and housing a vocabulary bank to be freely used by anyone who is interested in applying vocabularies to their collections. It can create dedicated forms for updating or creating vocabulary terms that conform to a schema, which in turn reflects or specializes the specifications of an established or custom data model. Moreover, Semantics.gr embeds advanced mechanisms that enable external platforms such as repositories and aggregators to link and align their content with respect to vocabularies, taxonomies, thesauri and authority files. This can be achieved either for newly created content via a Web API or a mediated resource assignment service or for existing content via an advanced mapping tool that embeds semi-automatic workflows (see Sects. 4, B, C and D). All these not only set Semantics.gr as a core vocabulary publication service but also align with its wider objective to develop an active community around it.

7 Conclusions

With the development of Semantics.gr, it is the first time at national level in Greece, that state-of-the-art semantic knowledge representation technologies and methodologies have been applied to such a scale in scientific and cultural data infrastructures of national importance, for the homogenization, standardization, enrichment and integration of information resources.

The key innovation of Semantics.gr lies in that it enables even non-experts in semantic web technologies to harness the benefits of the Semantic Web to publish authoritative Vocabularies as Linked Data. The publication and re-use of Linked Data Vocabularies in digital infrastructures enhance the quality and interlinking of resources as well as the interoperability of the systems, while improving search and browsing functionalities, adding multilinguality and helping lower the costs of documentation. EKT aspires that Semantics.gr develops into a central public platform, where authoritative semantic vocabularies can be curated and published for everyone to re-use in Greece and beyond, building an active community around vocabularies. In the new, open linked environments these semantic tools can provide a powerful conduit for research and discovery of digital resources.

Acknowledgments. The work presented in this article has been partly supported by the project "National Research Information and Technology System: Digital Content Aggregation, Documentation and Dissemination Infrastructure ensuring interoperability, long-term preservation and open access" of the Operational Programme "Reform of the Public Sector" (NSFR), co-funded by Greece and the European Union.

References

1. Georgiadis, H., Papanoti, A., Paschou, M., Roubani, A., Chardouveli, D., Sachini, E.: Using type and temporal semantic enrichment to boost content discoverability and multilingualism in the Greek cultural aggregator SearchCulture.gr. Int. J. Metadata Semant. Ontol. **13**(1), 75–92 (2018)
2. Suominen, O., et al.: Publishing SKOS vocabularies with Skosmos. Manuscript submitted for review (2015)
3. TemaTres. https://www.vocabularyserver.com/index.html
4. Stellato, A., Fiorelli, M., Turbati, A., et al.: VocBench 3: a collaborative semantic web editor for ontologies, thesauri and lexicons. Semant. Web **11**(5), 855–881 (2020). https://doi.org/10.3233/SW-200370
5. Tuominen, J., Frosterus, M., Viljanen, K., Hyvönen, E.: ONKI SKOS server for publishing and utilizing SKOS vocabularies and ontologies as services. In: Aroyo, L., et al. (eds.) ESWC 2009. LNCS, vol. 5554, pp. 768–780. Springer, Heidelberg (2009). https://doi.org/10.1007/978-3-642-02121-3_56
6. Musen, M.A.: The protégé project: a look back and a look forward. AI Matters **1**(4), 4–12 (2015). https://doi.org/10.1145/2557001.25757003

Enabling Publishing and Reuse of Government Data Through the Republic of Cyprus Open Data Portal

Christos Rodosthenous[1]([✉])[iD] and Dimitris Michail[2]([✉])[iD]

[1] Open University of Cyprus, Nicosia, Cyprus
christos.rodosthenous@ouc.ac.cy
[2] Public Administration and Personnel Department, Nicosia, Cyprus
dmichail@papd.mof.gov.cy

Abstract. In this work, we present the Republic of Cyprus Open Data Portal for promoting the publishing and reuse of government data. In particular, we present the design and implementation options for the portal and how this is used to enable access and reuse of government data. A brief overview of the state-of-affairs of open data in Cyprus is presented and how the deployment of the revamped national portal facilitated the reuse of government data, followed by a presentation of the design requirements of the portal and the steps followed to deploy it. We also present the current state of the portal in terms of datasets and usage statistics, as well as some of the innovative features now available to the users, such as visualizations and conversion of tabular data to application programming interfaces. The paper concludes with a brief presentation of the key findings of a user satisfaction survey that recorded the perceptions of expert users (programmers) after using the new version of the open data portal.

Keywords: Public sector data · Reuse of public data · Government portal

1 Introduction

The concept of open data in Cyprus dates back to 2006 with the introduction of the first national Public Sector Information Re-Use legislation. Since then, the island's public administration has formulated and implemented two five-year open data strategic plans for the promotion of open data in Cyprus, the latest of which covers the period 2017-2021 [10]. The plan consists of four main pillars that cover legal framework and governance, national portal and infrastructure, training and capacity building and promotion of open data reuse to the private, public, and academic sectors.

The development of the latest edition of the national open data portal[1] is an integral part of the second pillar of the aforementioned strategic plan, the

---

[1] The portal is available at https://www.data.gov.cy/.

© Springer Nature Switzerland AG 2022
E. Garoufallou et al. (Eds.): MTSR 2021, CCIS 1537, pp. 292–303, 2022.
https://doi.org/10.1007/978-3-030-98876-0_26

implementation of which contributed to Cyprus being viewed as one of the top performing countries in the EU according to recent European Data Portal (EDP) Open Data Maturity Reports. The portal itself was ranked 1st in the report of 2018 [6] and 4th in 2019 [7].

The national portal is seen as the central point for delivering data created by government agencies for further use. Its main goal is to provide the means for easy and quick search and access to both processed and raw data of the public sector in order to enable the reuse of these data in contexts other than the ones they were originally intended. The availability and accessibility of these data through the national portal promotes the creation of added value, innovative services and products that boost economic growth and/or enhance transparency. In this work we present the national portal and its features for enabling access and reuse of government data.

The portal hosts datasets, from almost all government agencies, as well as from other government related organizations and local administration authorities. These datasets can be searched through the portal's catalog using several methods, such as title, thematic category, organization, format, licence etc.

The portal, in its current form, was developed in 2018 using DKAN, a community-driven, free and open-source platform which handles both data and metadata and provides intuitive visualizations and search methods. For developing the portal, a memorandum of understanding between the Public Administration and Personnel Department, which has the overall responsibility for the formulation and application of open data policies in Cyprus and the Open University of Cyprus was signed in late 2016, promoting collaboration between the two parties. The portal is also directly connected to the European Data Portal [8], which harvests datasets from all EU member states' national portals and makes them available for searching in a single point of access.

In the next sections we present related work on open data portals, and the development process of the new portal followed by a brief overview of its features, which allow easy access and reuse of open government data. We also present results from a user satisfaction questionnaire which was presented to the participants of the 2018 Cyprus Open Data Hackathon[2].

2   Related Work

Currently, there are a number of systems available which are used to create data portals. During the design phase of the project, the project team investigated possible solutions for deploying the new open data portal. Through this investigation, a number of good practises were revealed by other European countries who mostly used the CKAN and DKAN systems. There were also examples of North American portals who were based on Socrata [9]. In the following paragraphs we present a number of systems that are available and were considered for developing the Republic of Cyprus Open Data Portal.

---

[2] The Hackathon website is available at https://opendatacy.com/.

CKAN[3] is a web-based open-source data management system (DMS) which is used for the storing, cataloguing and sharing of open data. CKAN is supported by the Open Knowledge Foundation[4], a non-profit organization, with best practice policies on governing openly and for use of the CKAN trademark. The platform can be self-hosted using a web and database server or it can be cloud hosted through one of the available providers. There is a plethora of available plugins that can be added, allowing additional functionality and of course new features can be added by anyone as its source code is available under a GNU Affero General Public License (AGPL) v3.0[5] license. There are several open data portals developed using CKAN, such as the European data portal [8] (the new version of the portal moved away from CKAN), the Irish open data portal, the Australian and Canada's Government portal. CKAN is also used for research data distribution [13]. In terms of technology, CKAN is based on Python with dependencies on Solr for search and PostgreSQL for data storage. It includes ready-made APIs for accessing the datasets and resources. In terms of metadata, it supports the DCAP-AP v1.1 schema through some additional extensions (e.g., the ckanext-dcat extension).There is also a large community of developers and users who collaborate for the development of the system and for supporting users.

DKAN[6] is also a popular open-source data management system. It delivers an open data catalog with similar features as CKAN and is bundled in one of the popular Content Management System (CMS), Drupal. It provides native support for RDF metadata, such as Dublin Core and DCAT and in particular the DCAT-AP metadata schema and offers a number of out-of-the-box visualizations of data. Both the datasets and the resources are exposed using the system's API through the internal datastore. The use of Drupal as the front-end provides the flexibility to deliver content along with data using data stories, articles, etc. In terms of technology, the requirements are the same with that of a typical Drupal installation using PHP, a database server (e.g., MySQL, MariaDB, PostgreSQL), a web server (e.g., Apache, Nginx). There is also a package for direct deployment of the system using a fully-made DKAN codebase which is hosted at the DKAN DROPS-7[7] repository. DKAN also has a large community supporting it and it is used by a number of open data portals, such as the Italian open data portal[8], and the Russian[9] open data portal.

Socrata[10] is a proprietary cloud-based open data catalog platform. It delivers an API for accessing data, a catalog, a datastore and a number of tools for handling data. There is also an open-source version of the system, the "Socrata

[3] CKAN is available at: https://ckan.org/.
[4] https://okfn.org/.
[5] http://www.fsf.org/licensing/licenses/agpl-3.0.html.
[6] https://getdkan.org/.
[7] https://github.com/GetDKAN/dkan-drops-7.
[8] https://www.dati.gov.it.
[9] https://data.gov.ru/.
[10] http://www.socrata.com/.

Open Data Server - Community Edition"[11]. The system supports RDF metadata such as Dublin Core and DCAT. The system is mainly used in North America where most of its installations exist.

Another system that gain attention through the years is udata[12] which is maintained by the French public agency in charge of open data (Etalab). The system is mostly found in production in France and in Luxembourg. The system is developed in Python and depends on MongoDB, ElasticSearch and Redis.

The above systems are not the only available, but are the ones that are widely used by other Government portals, offer a wide range of features, and provide support for the DCAT metadata schema. Furthermore, these systems also find application in research oriented portals which follow an open access to data model [11].

3   The Republic of Cyprus Open Data Portal

In this section we provide an overview on the steps used to design and implement the national open data portal which aims to promote the use of open data in the Republic of Cyrus. The importance of software to provide technical solutions to the open data community is high and this is also stressed in the work of [5].

3.1   Requirements for the Portal

For designing the new open data portal, a requirements document was prepared, and an analysis of possible solutions was performed, taking into consideration other European and North American portals that were available at that time and their corresponding features. The document drafted included a number of requirements, such as 1) the support for the DCAT Application Profile (DCAT-AP) [4] for data portals in Europe which allows metadata integration to the European data portal [8] and exchangeability of metadata with other data portals, 2) the existence of a quality assurance mechanism, where the content uploaded by government agencies and the metadata added would be moderated before made available to the public, ensuring reusability in terms of the format of data available and metadata quality, 3) the ability to hold a datastore to convert tabular data to application programming interfaces (APIs) for promoting the reuse of data in third-party applications and possible combinations with other data from other sources, and 4) the ability to automatically create visualizations, facilitating the view of data in formats which can be easily understood by the public.

In terms of more technical requirements, the new open data portal was expected to use open-source software to promote the openness of both the data and the technologies, and to provide a user management system for granular access and a user authentication mechanism for government agencies' liaison

---

[11] https://open-source.socrata.com/.
[12] https://github.com/opendatateam/udata.

officers. Moreover, it was expected to also be accessible from any device and by any user, following accessibility guidelines [3] and a responsive template.

As far as the availability of languages is concerned, the portal was envisaged to primarily provide content and the interface in Greek language and additionally to provide an option for English language for the interface and core documentation.

In terms of deployment, the new portal was required to be developed in-house and hosted in a datacenter in the Republic of Cyprus to promote internal expertise, which could be used to assist other initiatives of open data in the country.

3.2   Selecting an Appropriate Platform for the Portal

Following the review of the mainstream platforms available (cf. Sect. 2) we focused on two of the most popular data portals that matched all the requirements set, i.e., CKAN and DKAN. When it came to the final decision of which of the two platforms would be used, the team decided to choose the one that they had more expertise in, i.e., the opendata team was more familiar with DKAN's technology stack and this was a benefit, as it would allow the customization of the portal and also overcome possible obstacles. Furthermore, DKAN was available as an all-in-one solution, which could handle both the requirements for open data distributions, such as the DCAT-AP v1.1 support for metadata, the data catalogue and datastore and the presentation and impact creation requirements, such as the data stories, the portal like features, the social media sharing of datasets and the support section. The rest of the solutions would require the setup of a CMS to meet these requirements.

3.3   Data Migration From the Previous Version of the Portal

For migrating data from the old portal, the team decided to apply a manual migration process, allowing filtering of the existing data, as a substantial percentage of the existing datasets were either limited in metadata or available only in proprietary formats, making the reuse and usefulness of these very limited. In particular, a number of datasets, which included only links to agencies websites and information documents were removed.

The remaining datasets were manually added to the updated open data portal by both the team and the agencies' liaison officer, following the updated process depicted in Fig. 1.

3.4   Portal Deployment and Features

For implementing the new national open data portal, the DKAN open-source system was selected and setup using a scalable virtual infrastructure of web servers, database servers and storage. Next the ability to allow multilingual interface, i.e., both Greek and English was introduced. In terms of content, twelve topics/themes were introduced to categorize datasets, including health, energy, transport, environment, etc. The next step was the creation of the government agencies as entities in the portal (approximately 90 organizations) and assigning a liaison officer to each one of these entities. The liaison officer is the person responsible for coordinating the creation and maintenance of datasets for data produced by their agency.

For ensuring the quality of data and metadata hosted in the national portal, an approval/rejection workflow process is put in place. Liaison officers create a dataset and add the relevant resources to the portal following the open government data-lifecycle [1]. For each agency there is a moderator who has the role of checking the conformance of the data uploaded regarding the file formats and the metadata. Where such a role does not exist within the agency, officers from the Public Administration and Personnel Department take this responsibility. There are three states in this workflow, the "draft" state of the dataset, available only to the creator, the "waiting approval" state, where the moderator needs to take action to accept or reject the publishing of the dataset and the "published" state where the dataset is made available to the public. This workflow is depicted in Fig. 1.

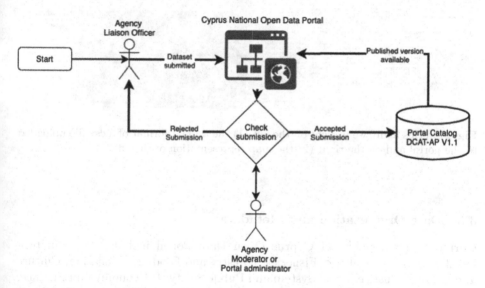

Fig. 1. Dataset publishing workflow, including the various actors and the different states of the dataset, based on the decision made by the agency moderator.

The portal allows publishing of datasets using three types of creative commons licenses: 1) the Creative Commons Attribution 4.0 International (CC BY 4.0) license, 2) the Creative Commons Attribution-ShareAlike 4.0 International (CC BY-SA 4.0) license and for special cases of datasets, where some limitations exist 3) the Creative Commons Attribution-NonCommercial 4.0

International (CC BY-NC 4.0) license. The majority (>99.9%) of datasets are published under the first two license types.

One of the innovative features of the platform is the automatic conversion of tabular file formats, e.g., spreadsheets and csv files into API, which is provided directly from the portal. This is one of the most prominent features, delivered through the portal, as it promotes reuse of data by third-parties even when the government agency does not have the technical capability to offer these data in an API directly.

In a similar fashion, the portal can create visualizations of tabular data either in graph format or a map representation, for cases where the data include geographical information (coordinates). This feature provides liaison officers with the ability to promote their data by delivering meaningful visualizations to their users. In Fig. 2 we present an example of a dataset, which includes a resource in csv format with geographical coordinates. This is represented on a map so that users of the portal do not have to download the dataset and then use an external application to visualize the data.

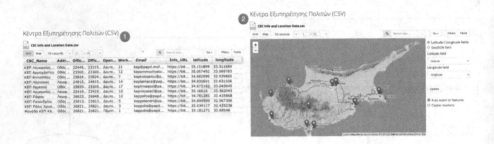

Fig. 2. In this figure we present on the left (1) the tabular format of a csv file uploaded to the portal and on the right (2) the map representation of that file.

3.5 Data Organization and Metadata

Currently the Republic of Cyprus Open Data Portal includes 12 main topics/themes: 1) Agriculture, Fisheries, Forestry and Food, 2) Education, Culture and Sport, 3) Justice, Legal System and Public Safety, 4) Economy and Finance, 5) Energy, 6) Environment, 7) Government and Public Sector, 8) Health, 9) Population, Society and Employment, 10) Science and Technology, 11) Regions, Cities and Zoning, and 12) Transport. All available datasets are categorized under these topics, allowing multiple assignments of topics for a dataset.

For each dataset, a number of metadata, following the DCAT-AP schema are available and exposed. In Table 1 a list of all the metadata fields available in the dataset and distribution classes are presented.

The portal follows the DCAT-AP v1.1 metadata schema which was modified to make mandatory the following dataset properties: contact point (name

Table 1. The list of metadata available in the portal for the dataset and distribution class. On the left is the URI of the metadata field, followed by the range of the field and a description. URIs with an asterisk (*) are mandatory in the Cyprus National Metadata Schema which follows the DCAT-AP v1.1 schema [4].

Dataset		
URI	Range	Description
dct:title (*)	rdfs:Literal	A name given to the item.
dct:description (*)	rdfs:Literal	A free-text description of the dataset.
dcat:keyword	rdfs:Literal	A keyword or tag describing the dataset.
dct:modified	rdfs:Literal typed as xsd:date or xsd:dateTime	Most recent date on which the dataset was changed, updated or modified. Automatically set by the portal.
dct:issued (*)	rdfs:Literal typed as xsd:date or xsd:dateTime	Date of formal publication of the dataset. Automatically set by the portal.
dct:publisher (*)	foaf:Agent	The entity responsible for making the item available. The value is filled by a predefined list of available agencies in the portal.
dcat:theme (*)	skos:Concept	The main category of the dataset. A dataset can have multiple themes. This is filled by a predefined list of 12 topics.
dct:spatial (*)	dct:Location	The geographical area covered by the dataset.
dct:accrualPeriodicity (*)	dct:Frequency	The frequency in which the dataset is published: Continuously, Daily, Weekly, Semimonthly, Monthly, Quarterly, Semiannual, Annually, Irregularly, Decennial.
dct:temporal (*)	dct:PeriodOfTime	The period of time the dataset covers.
adms:contactPoint (*)	vcard:Kind	The name of the liason officer and its email.
dct:language (*)	dct:LinguisticSystem	The language of the Dataset.
dcat:distribution (*)	dcat:Distribution	This field links the Dataset with a distribution. A Dataset can have multiple distributions.
Distribution		
URI	Range	Description
dcat:accessURL (*)	rdfs:Resource	A URL that gives access to a Distribution of the Dataset.
dct:title (*)	rdfs:Literal	A name given to the distribution.
dct:description	rdfs:Literal	A free-text description of the dataset.
dct:format (*)	dct:MediaTypeOrExtent	The file format of the Distribution
dct:licence (*)	dct:LicenceDocument	A legal document under which the dataset is made available. The list of available licenses is presented in Sect. 3.4.

and email), dataset distribution, publisher, theme/category, frequency, language, temporal coverage, spatial/geographical coverage, and the following distribution properties: title, format and licence.

4 Support, Training, Impact, and User Satisfaction

Beyond the technical aspect of the portal, great effort is put into providing support and training to the liaison officers of each organisation and programmers who want to use the portal's APIs to consume data. A special part of the open data portal is dedicated to showcase applications developed by both governmental and private organizations by using data from the portal.

An important aspect of the deployment of the new portal is the training of liaison officers and the documentation of the portal's features. Several training workshops were organized with participants from all government agencies who took hands-on sessions of the functionality of the new portal and the quality assurance processes that are in place. Moreover, detailed documentation both for the liaison officers and for programmers who want to use the portal's API were published[13].

The portal also serves as an information and dissemination point for showcasing applications developed using government open data and publishing news about the state-of-affairs of the open data community in Cyprus. In particular, there are more than 40 known applications developed, re-using data from the portal which is one of the goals of the policy for open data. These application include among others: A web app which provides information related to electric cars in Cyprus (charging stations, yearly savings when choosing an electric vehicle), the official application for Cyprus bus schedules, an application for visualizing election results and an application for monitoring fuel prices in Cyprus.

It also offers a contact form for the public to submit requests for new datasets and request information on existing datasets. In Fig. 3 we present the number of requests made per semester and the number of known UseCases for datasets available in the portal. One can identify the increase when the new portal was published.

4.1 Current State of the Portal

In its current state, the Republic of Cyprus Open Data Portal hosts 1108 datasets and 3010 resources (results retrieved at 13/08/2021). In Fig. 4 we present the increase of the number of datasets per year/semester, indicating the points where the preparation of the new portal started and when the new portal was released. In terms of availability of data, the largest contributions of data are from the Statistics service of Cyprus, the Department of Lands and Surveys, and the Department of Environment. The three most popular datasets are the "Current capacity of the dams", "Maps of Land and Division", and "Companies Registry in Cyprus".

---

[13] https://www.data.gov.cy/node/3902?language=en.

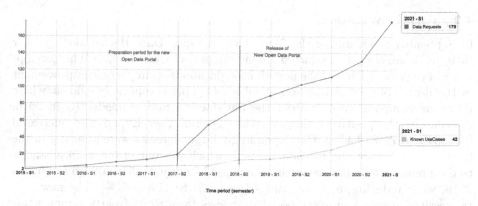

Fig. 3. In this figure we present the number of requests made per semester and the number of known UseCases for datasets available in the portal.

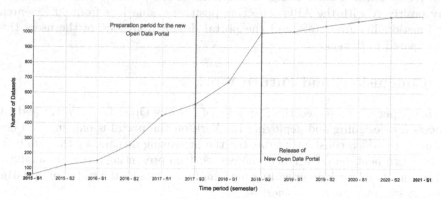

Fig. 4. In this figure we present the increase of the number of datasets per year/semester, indicating the points where the preparation of the new portal started and when the new portal was released.

The majority of these resources are in tabular format, and hence delivered through an API or are natively available as a webservice. In fact, 49% of resources are available in tabular format (csv format) and 17.3% as a webservice (SOAP, wms, esri REST, wfs). In terms of agencies uploading data to the portal, there are currently 91 governmental and municipal agencies registered.

From June 2018 until the end of May 2021 there were more than 1,000,000 pageviews from 251,000 users. Most of these views are from Cyprus, Greece, Spain, and Russia. Based on the period, specific datasets are in more demand than others. For example, during the covid-19 pandemic the daily disease cases dataset had a particularly high demand.

4.2 Portal Evaluation

In September 2018, during the 2-day Cyprus Open Data Hackathon[14], a user satisfaction survey was conducted among the participants (n = 27). The development of the new version of the portal, brought about an important improvement in the degree of user satisfaction at all levels. This is especially evident where there are comparative data from the Satisfaction Survey conducted in 2016. Specifically, the positive ratings for the "Overall User Experience" increased from 34% to 74% (+40%). Correspondingly large increases were observed in the field of data distribution formats, an issue which was one of the main obstacles to data reuse, where positive ratings increased from just 25% in 2016 to 56% in 2018, while reducing negative ratings from 72% to 15% (–57%). The new portal received positive and very positive reviews from 89% of participants, while the percentage of positive and very positive reviews for the government open data policy reached 96%. The new functions of the portal were also evaluated very positively with the APIs collecting positive evaluations from 60%, searching functionality from 74% and the portal design from 93% of the users that participated in the survey.

5 Conclusions and Future Work

In this paper we presented the Republic of Cyprus Open Data Portal and the process for designing and deploying it. Work on the portal is ongoing and new features are added constantly to match the increasing demand by the public for open government data. Currently there is work on presenting metadata analytics in the portal and work on providing meaningful reports on the status of updating datasets by government agencies.

Based on the statistics, the number of requests for new datasets and the results of the user satisfaction survey, indicate that the portal provides the means for further reuse and promotion of government open data. Furthermore, the current state in terms of published datasets and requests for data shows that the updated portal has increased the impact of open data in the Republic of Cyprus and this is also verified by the fact that the EDP reports rank the new Republic of Cyprus Open Data Portal in the top positions.

The need for public open data is more prominent today than ever before, since Artificial Intelligence researchers and innovators use these data to develop applications and train machine learning models [12]. Journalists and social scientists use visualizations to present these data for promoting transparency. Furthermore, public open data are a step forward to the European Open Science Cloud [2].

Acknowledgement. The Republic of Cyprus Open Data Portal was developed by the Cyprus Open data team which was formed by the Public Administration and Personnel Department (Dimitris Michail and Mantalena Tsoukka) and the Open University of Cyprus (Christos Rodosthenous, Michalis Epiphaniou, Stathis Mavrotheris).

---

[14] http://opendatacy.com/.

References

1. Attard, J., Orlandi, F., Scerri, S., Auer, S.: A systematic review of open government data initiatives. Gov. Inf. Q. **32**(4), 399–418 (2015). https://doi.org/10.1016/j.giq.2015.07.006
2. Budroni, P., Claude-Burgelman, J., Schouppe, M.: Architectures of knowledge: the European open science cloud. ABI Technik **39**(2), 130–141 (2019). https://doi.org/10.1515/abitech-2019-2006
3. Caldwell, B., Cooper, M., Reid, L.G., Vanderheiden, G.: Web Content Accessibility Guidelines (WCAG) 2.0 (2018)
4. Dragan, A.: DCAT Application Profile for data portals in Europe Version 1.2. Technical report (2018)
5. Enríquez-Reyes, R., Cadena-Vela, S., Fuster-Guilló, A., Mazón, J.N., Ibáñez, L.D., Simperl, E.: Systematic mapping of open data studies: classification and trends from a technological perspective. IEEE Access **9**, 12968–12988 (2021). https://doi.org/10.1109/ACCESS.2021.3052025
6. European Commission: Open Data Maturity in Europe. Report 2018. Technical report (2018)
7. European Commission: Open Data Maturity in Europe. Report 2019. Technical report (2019)
8. Kirstein, F., Dittwald, B., Dutkowski, S., Glikman, Y., Schimmler, S., Hauswirth, M.: Linked data in the European data portal: a comprehensive platform for applying DCAT-AP. In: Lindgren, I., et al. (eds.) EGOV 2019. LNCS, vol. 11685, pp. 192–204. Springer, Cham (2019). https://doi.org/10.1007/978-3-030-27325-5_15
9. Kubler, S., Robert, J., Neumaier, S., Umbrich, J., Le Traon, Y.: Comparison of metadata quality in open data portals using the Analytic Hierarchy Process. Gov. Inf. Q. **35**(1), 13–29 (2018). https://doi.org/10.1016/j.giq.2017.11.003
10. Public Administration and Personnel Department: Open Data Strategic Plan 2017–2021 (2019). https://doi.org/10.5281/zenodo.5594120
11. Tzitzikas, Y., Pitikakis, M., Giakoumis, G., Varouha, K., Karkanaki, E.: How can a university take its first steps in open data? Metadata Semant. Res. **1355**, 155–167 (2020). https://doi.org/10.1007/978-3-030-71903-6_16
12. Wang, K.: Opportunities in open science with AI. Front. Big Data **2**, 26 (2019). https://doi.org/10.3389/fdata.2019.00026
13. Winn, J.: Open data and the academy: an evaluation of CKAN for research data management (2013)

Track on European and National Projects, and General Session

E-Government and COVID-19: An Empirical Study in Greece

Chrysanthi Chatzopoulou[1]([⊠]) [iD], Dimitrios Tsolkanakis[1], Symelia M. Vasileiadou[1], Konstantinos Kyriakidis[1], Konstantina Skoutzouri[1], Despina Kirtikidou[1], Syed Iftikhar Hussain Shah[1] [iD], and Vassilios Peristeras[1,2]

[1] School of Science and Technology, International Hellenic University, Thessaloniki, Greece
chatzopoulou.c@gmail.com
[2] Council of the European Union, General Secretariat, Brussels, Belgium

Abstract. E-government and the implementation of ICT technologies in the public sector has been in the center of interest for a few decades now, but it is a fact that the Covid-19 pandemic and the worldwide lockdowns have given a boost on their prosecution in our everyday lives. The aims of this study were to i) examine the implementation of digital transformation best practices utilized by the governments globally and ii) take a thorough look in the case of Greece, to determine whether and to what extent the Greek government adopted similar practices and initiatives, allowing the use of online digital services to citizens in a wide array of public sector areas during the Covid-19 pandemic. Initially, we sent a questionnaire to 202 people in Greece, via email and social media platforms. In response, 150 useable questionnaires were received with response rate of 74%. We gathered responses were gathered between May and June 2021, and data gathered were analyzed with PSPP statistical program. The results showed that the majority of the practices used by the government were well communicated, as most of the digital services were acknowledged by the participants even if they had not used them. In particular, the taxation portal and the central digital portal for governmental services were used in percentages of 76% and 66% respectively. In terms of use and satisfaction, responses were also quite encouraging, with 72% of the participants mentioning being very satisfied with the speed and quality of the new digital services, though leaving room for further research to conclude on improvement methods. After in-depth examination of the global and Greek progress of digital transformation during the COVID-19 pandemic, it is essential to state that all governments have shown tremendous improvement in order to cover citizens' needs, while using the majority of the available digital channels.

Keywords: E-government · Digital government · Digital services · Public sector · Greece

Supplementary Information The online version contains supplementary material available at https://doi.org/10.1007/978-3-030-98876-0_27.

E. Garoufallou et al. (Eds.): MTSR 2021, CCIS 1537, pp. 307–321, 2022.
https://doi.org/10.1007/978-3-030-98876-0_27

1 Introduction

The evolvement of world wide web in the last decades has caused tremendous effects in all business environments, with more and more companies adopting web-based technologies for the automation of their everyday tasks. In the contrary, although there have been several models for incorporating such a change in public organizations, governmental agencies have been more conservative and idle to adopting new technologies [1]. To be more accurate, the idea of citizens being treated as customers has been introduced in 1992, by Osbourne and Gaebler [2], to convince public organizations to adopt a more customer centric point of view while delivering their services. Although in 2005 Torres et al. refer to e-government being a global trend with new web-based technologies [3], we can now say there has been little change in the public sector, until e-government has become an absolute necessity with the Covid-19 outburst.

Luckily, the Digital Agenda for Europe had set among its targets the development of more efficient public services since 2010, with the last decade being essential for the positive exploitation of Information and Communication Technologies (ICT) in all private and public sectors for foreseeing problems and opportunities of the digital outburst [4], which was crucial for the confrontation of all physical, economical, and managerial boundaries caused by the worldwide Covid-19 lockdowns. It is undoubtable that despite the difficulties, the majority of businesses, organizations and people had the appropriate background in ICT, both knowledge wise and in physical infrastructure, so that most of their everyday tasks will not be ceased but continue to occur with the most normal possible flow in a digital form. The aim of this paper is to study and present the boost of the ICT usage in public sectors and e-government progress, and how their operations transformed through the Covid-19 outburst, setting Greece under the microscope to acknowledge the work done so far and identify best practices for future adoption.

2 Background

Analyzing some studies on the e-government implementation, it is observed that in the first steps of incorporating ICT in public organizations some findings come to an opposition to the overall e-government vision and scope, which has always been the elimination of discrimination between citizens, the provision of equal, fast services and treatment for all, and the performance excellence of public administration providing services with convenience, efficiency, and transparency [5].

In a general view of e-government implementation, Mishra analyzes the "Digital India" program, a program which aims to make India a truly and fully digital country after the Covid-19 outbreak and the new demand rules it has brought, introducing the implementation of ICT with a series of policies, initiatives, and excellence centers, that would offer services to citizens on demand [6]. During this program India has managed to digitize all departments to achieve the offering of digital services to all citizens, though several other problems are presented for the full success of the program, such as infrastructure, connectivity in rural areas, the amendment of restrictive regulations and most important, the digital literacy both of the citizens and the governmental employees [6]. Furthermore, Burlacu et al. [7] and Scupola [8] analyze the Covid-19 e-government management in Romania and Denmark respectively, and identify similar issues. In the first study, it is suggested that effective e-government practices can be implemented in a 5-step process, which includes the creation of webpages for all organizations and institutions, the extent of information coverage, the online availability of forms or facilities requested by citizens, followed by the possibility of obtaining/issuing important documents via the internet, and the overall expansion of services offered digitally [7]. Though the problems identified in both studies also concern the socio-economic status of a big portion of both countries' population, meaning that there are cases of inefficient knowledge or infrastructure to access those services [7, 8] – to be more accurate, apart from concerns on data protection in Romania, public workers have proven not to be ready to completely embrace such a change [7] and more than a quarter of Denmark's population still lacks basic digital skills [8].

During the beginning of the pandemic, China has demonstrated a few successful practices on the improvement of everyday life though e-government too [9–13]. Studies have shown that most online interaction happens though mobile phones, online health information seeking behavior has also increased – especially during Covid-19, where isolation was essential, and hence many governments attempted to achieve social media presence by even using celebrities and word of mouth as a tool, in order to provide health guidance to people [9]. The role of e-government and word of mouth on spreading messages has proven to be very effective during quarantine, as the Chinese government has taken full advantage of the ability to be online present, and not only spreading messages for personal hygiene and social distancing, but also for promoting even more digital transactions [10, 11]. Though it should be mentioned that Chinese government had already incorporated basic e-government operations in one of Chinas most popular social media platforms/applications, WeChat, before the pandemic. Such mechanisms included messaging for payments and similar electronic transactions, thus the online presence of government increased the usage of this service [11]. Additional practices that were used since 2018 in 80% of China's republics also included distance education and health, and were already suggested as best practices to be adopted by other countries too, though they require an extended combination of e-governance innovative use on advanced technologies and citizen participation to maximize the advantages of this effort, and the effective confrontation of the fact that 85% of the global population are still using the 3G network, which in many cases may not be quite efficient [11, 12]. Agostino et al. have also identified social media as a more powerful tool for the digitization of public service deliveries over other ground-breaking tools, focusing on the digitization of cultural services. In their study they have identified that the usage of social media has changed from simple communication with users in a more creative and effective way, such as performing virtual tours or educational initiatives in order not to fend off their core operation [13].

Some further best practices that were identified in the public sector focus on the development of communication strategies and initiatives performed online, also based in the fact that most of the world population uses the internet and social media for fast and up to date information retrieval. In order to avoid miscommunication and the spread of misleading information regarding Covid-19, many governments proceeded with collaboration with digital companies and mass media [14]. Furthermore, some governments have even developed multi-purpose applications, such as the case of Italy, where collaboration with private companies was accomplished in order to provide free online services and internet access to the public during the lockdown [14]. Most of the countries have even developed mobility tracing applications to contact tracing of people entering the country and ensure that all quarantine measures were kept, as well as ensuring that the appropriate Covid-19 tests were performed so that people could act accordingly [15]. Regarding public sector capacity though, studies have shown that governments need to be more adaptive and attentive to people's needs, aligning public services to emergency situations. For instance, investment and coordination in public and private health sectors working remotely has proven to be effective, but public sector workers' needs should be taken more seriously under consideration, since there has been tremendous change in the way they work, and assistance was substantial [16, 17]. Schuster et al. support that surveys of public servants are an important tool for such an implementation, as they can identify problems and provide solutions on online and remote interactions that are now needed for the completion of their everyday tasks. Furthermore, technical equipment and safe remote workplace environments can be more easily ensured, as well as best practices can be identifying by keeping constant communication and satisfaction measure of public workers [17]. In addition to this opinion, Cohen et al. suggest that user-friendly e-learning programs need to be organized by universities, for accounting systems in the public sector to acquire technical support, efficiently qualified staff and to achieve bridging the gap of academic and practitioner knowledge on the digital environment that navigates the current operation of the system [18].

From the aspect of public services in healthcare, education and news media, China was once again an example to follow, as great technological evolution occurred in a very short period of time to effectively confront the emergency situation. Numerous artificial intelligence (AI) and 5G applications were developed as a window to a whole new world of possibilities. 5G smart hospitals were established, with their operation being mainly based on cloud-working robots to eliminate human interaction. Their role was to perform important everyday actions such as temperature measurement, disinfection and cleaning of medical spaces and drug delivery, mainly with drones and especially to vulnerable populations [19–21]. Moreover, with 5G offering wider and faster connectivity, many private companies have cooperated with governments introducing innovative health applications accompanying existing services. For example, there were cases of ambulances converted to smart ambulances, that would offer pre-hospital emergency treatment using video consultation during the transmission to the hospital, and what is even more worth mentioning is that during the pitch of the pandemic they performed even double daily trips than the traditional ambulances [20, 22]. Similarly, many applications were also developed to provide eHealth literacy in older adults and their families or caregivers, ensuring that as vulnerable populations they would not be left sidelined [23]. In terms of e-learning capabilities, the necessity of remote education was also highlighted by the use of 5G, as there have also been cases of private companies cooperating with governments for providing full access to 5G networks and custommade platforms, for live distance classrooms or clouds, aiming to better connectivity and synchronized classes without technical issues [19, 24, 25]. It is worth mentioning though that the pandemic has effected not only the traditional classroom operation, but also the adjacent functions supporting education. Research conducted in Bridgewater State University Library clearly presents the adjustments made in the academic library sector to continue operating as an auxiliary pillar to student's distance education, with a series of tasks including digitization of automated tasks, launching new digital services in the library's web page and even through social media, and online research consultations [26].

3 Research Method

Research methodology in this study was designed aiming to acknowledge digitization best practices adopted by governments around the world, and dive in the case of Greece, to identify similar practices and explore whether and how efficiently enough, Greek government established initiatives enabling the usage of online digital services to citizens in various public sector areas, during the Covid-19 pandemic. Empirical studies are an important methodology for evaluating real-life phenomena on specific issues, thus was identified as the best choice for performing research to evaluate public opinion on the extend of performance excellence this digitization attempt had throughout the last year. For this aim, quantitative research was conducted, and primary, descriptive data were gathered and analyzed with PSPP statistical program (2018 version).

For the development of the questionnaire a thorough search was conducted in governmental sites, aiming to identify the practices used for the digitization of existing services and the development of new digital functions for remote citizens' service. A questionnaire of 17 questions was developed based on the eGovernment practices identified, including only closed-ended questions of mainly 'yes' or 'no' answers, multiple-choice questions (with single and multi-selection answers), and Likert scale questions for the measurement of satisfaction of the services (full questionnaire available in the Supplementary file).

Survey questionnaire was created in Greek, data were collected via Google Forms, and distribution of the questionnaire occurred via e-mail and social media platforms. The questionnaire was initially tested with 10 people, and once finalized distributed to the public, in 202 people in total. Usable responses from 150 people were gathered between May and June 2021. Several covariates were used in the analysis included sociodemographic characteristics (sex, age, number of kids, working in private or public sector etc.) to identify the use of public services of each participant in accordance with their needs. The questionnaire was divided into six sections (including demographics), referring to measures related to eGovernment practices on information spread for Covid-19 pandemic, public agencies & remote services, public health services, cultural services, and remote work and education. Participation in the research was voluntarily and completion of the questionnaire was anonymous. All questionnaires were fully responded, and hence all data gathered were included in the analysis.

4 Results

In order to identify whether the eGovernment practices followed during the Covid-19 pandemic in Greece were well communicated to citizens and successful in substituting the physical services, a total of 150 questionnaires were included in the analysis. To begin with, 72% of the participants were female, and almost half of the total sample (44%) were people aged between 19–25 years old. Regarding the occupation area of the participants, sample was split in three parts, were almost one third were private sector employees (34.67%), second part was students (34%), and the third part was distributed between public sector workers (16%), self-employed (8%) and unemployed (7.33%) people (Table 1).

Table 1. Demographics (N = 150).

	N	%
Sex		
Male	39	26
Female	108	72
Prefer not to say	3	2
Age		
<18	6	4
19–25	66	44
26–35	45	30
36–45	9	6
>46	24	16
Occupation		
Public sector worker	24	16
Private sector employee	52	34.67
Self-employed	12	8

Table 2. Citizen's familiarization on e-government practices for information spread during the covid-19 pandemic evolution (N = 150).

Digital means of information	Yes		No	
	N	%	N	%
TV/radio advertisements	117	78	33	22
Cooperation with celebrities (Word of Mouth)	84	56	66	44
New governmental websites (e.g., live COVID-19 map)	50	33.33	100	66.67
Email/phone/SMS for increased risk areas	64	42.67	86	57.33
Social media governmental profiles	76	50.67	74	49.33

The second section of the questionnaire was related to eGovernment practices for information spread during the Covid-19 pandemic evolution. Participants had the option to choose multiple means of information and practices that they were familiarized with.

All means and practices mention were identified, though TV and radio advertisements appeared to be more popular with 78% percentage of acknowledgement, while new governmental sites such as the live Covid-19 map streaming increased risk areas and restrictions, was in the last position with 33.33% (Table 2).

In relation with public agencies and remote services, an attempt was made to identify both the most frequently digital public service used, and user satisfaction. It is worth mentioning that 85.33% of the participants were not aware of digital transformation bible of Greece, which is a holistic digital transformation strategy for the Greek society and economy, but they were familiar with most of the digital services launched during Covid-19 pandemic (Table 3).

Table 3. Public agencies & remote services awareness (N = 150).

Awareness of the bible of digital transformation for Greece	N		%	N	%
Yes	22		14.67	22	14.67
No	128		85.33	128	85.33

Remote use of public services	Total use	Degree of satisfaction				
	N (%)	Not satisfyied (%)	Slightly satisfied (%)	Neutral (%)	Satisfied enough (%)	Very satisfied (%)
Digital services of citizen's service center (myKEPlive)	13 (8.67)	15.38	0.00	23.08	46.15	15.38
Digital services of manpower employment organization (myOAEDlive)	8 (5.33)	0.00	12.50	0.00	75.00	12.50
Taxation services (TaxisNet)	114 (76.00)	0.88	7.89	24.56	50.00	16.67
Central digital portal (Gov.gr)	99 (66.00)	2.02	7.07	25.25	47.47	18.18
Municipality digital services (myDimoslive)	5 (3.33)	20.00	0.00	20.00	60.00	0.00

(continued)

Table 3. (*continued*)

Awareness of the bible of digital transformation for Greece		N		%	N	%
Digital services for occupational safety (e-EFKA)	53 (35.33)	0.00		5.66	22.64	52.83	18.87
Public payments (e-fees, state pensions etc.)	50 (33.33)	4.00		8.00	20.00	52.00	16.00
ERGANI (portal for work insurances, movement certificates of employees etc.)	58 (38.67)	1.72		5.17	32.76	43.10	17.24
Comparison to physical presence use of Public services		N		%		
My request was successfully completed easier and faster with the online services		109		72.67		
My request was completed but the online services were complicated/not easy to use/took longer than usual		35		23.33		
My request was not completed, and I had to book a physical appointment with the service		6		4		

As mentioned in the table above, taxation services (TaxisNet) and the central digital portal (Gov.gr) were the most used digital services during the pandemic, with 76% and 66% use, respectively. From people using TaxisNet, 50% were satisfied enough with the portal, while 77, 19% mentioned that their request was completed easier and faster compared to the physical presence services in tax offices. Similarly, 47.47% and 18.18% of those who used Gov.gr were satisfied enough and very satisfied, while only 2.02% mentioned that their request was not complete through the portal. The least popular digital service was MyDimosLive, which is related to municipal issues and was used by only 3.33% of the participants. In the total point of view of satisfaction, users were satisfied enough with most of the digital services, and 72.67% mentioned that their request was completed easier and faster with the remote services. Regarding user experience, ERGANI was rated as the one with the most successful services with a percentage of 81.03% completed requests.

The fifth section of the questionnaire was related to public health services, as they were transformed by the government to serve people with as less interaction as possible. The most used digital service related to health appears to be the self-test declaration platform (39.33%), followed by the individual electronic health record for intangible prescription via emails and electronic appointments with health scientists (26.67%). On the contrary, medicine delivery to remote areas was a service that the majority of the participants were not even aware of (62.67%), followed by the automated procedures initiated in specific hospitals (such as measurements and chatbots for the diagnostic initiation), with 54.67%.

On the cultural services, 92 of 150 participants were aware of digital events performance, and 53.33% of them mentioned that they did not attend any digital cultural event during the quarantines. Among the rest 46.67%, most people attended online concerts and live theater plays (33.33%), fewer attended virtual tours in museums (18%) and art exhibitions (6%), and only 6.67% attended an online reading event. Participants mentioned that they were satisfied with their digital experience in general, with the highest rates of satisfaction being in virtual tours in museums (48.15% were satisfied enough, and 40.74% very satisfied) (Tables 4 and 5).

Table 4. Public health digitization services during covid-19 pandemic (N = 150).

Remote use of public health services	I am aware of this service and I have used it		I am aware of this service, but I have not used it		I am not aware of this service	
	N	%	N	%	N	%
Individual Electronic Health Record (for intangible prescription via sms/emails, electronic appointments, etc.)	40	26.67	58	38.67	52	34.67
Self-test declaration platform	59	39.33	71	47.33	20	13.33
Online appointments at Primary Health Care Units (idika.gr)	29	19.33	72	48	49	32.67
E-consultation/distance support of Covid-19 patients (EODY)	13	8.67	90	60	47	31.33
Medicine delivery to remote areas or vulnerable populations (with drones or other means)	6	4	50	33.33	94	62.67
Automated temperature measurements/chatbots as a diagnostic initiation	16	10.67	52	34.67	82	54.67

Table 5. Digitization of cultural services (N = 150).

N (%)		Not satisfied (%)	Slightly satisfied (%)	Neutral (%)	Enough satisfied (%)	Very satisfied (%)
Virtual tours in museums	27 (18.00)	0.00	0.00	11.11	48.15	40.74
Virtual tours in art exhibitions	9 (6.00)	11.11	33.33	0.00	33.33	22.22
Online concerts/Live theater plays	50 (33.33)	4.00	8.00	28.00	34.00	26.00
Online reading events	7 (4.67)	14.29	42.86	14.29	14.29	14.29
I did not attend any event	80 (53.33)	–	–	–	–	–

Regarding remote work and education, it is observed that 66% of public sector employees did work remotely during the Covid-19 lockdowns, though only 31.25% of them mentioned that they received the appropriate technological and infrastructure assistance from the government so that they can be as productive as in their offices. For students and freelancers, it is observed that a percentage of 100% stated that they had to work or follow their courses remotely, while 40.38% of private sector employees (21 from 52 participants) proceeded with teleworking (Table 6).

Table 6. Remote work and education (N = 150).

	N	%
Performance of remote Working/education		
Private sector employee	21	40.38
Public sector worker	16	66.67
Freelancer	12	100.00
Student	51	100.00
Assistance of government for remote working in public sector workers		
Yes	3	18.75
No	13	81.25

Most used applications for teleworking and online education during the pandemic were zoom (63%) and webex (29%), while in Fig. 1 it is presented that eGovernment means assisting distance work and online education were not very popular among citizens. A total of 42.70% were not aware of any of these assisting tools introduced by the

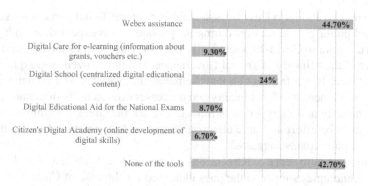

Fig. 1. Awareness of tools supporting remote working/education.

government, while from the rest 57.30% webex assistance gained cognition of 44.70% between participants, and the digital school 24%. On the contrary, the cognition percentages of citizens' digital academy (a tool for adult education on digital skills to be promoted for the pandemic needs) were very low (6.70%).

5 Discussion

The whole pandemic situation has caught everyone by surprise. It has exposed many deficiencies and brough up many functionality issues of everyday operations, while causing irreparable damages to the economy and society [27]. In the contrary, such situations that lead to radical changes usually cause versatile effects, both negative and positive ones. In the case of the pandemic, technological innovations and procedures have been rapidly sped up and it has been showcased how the next normal might look like, at least for the majority of our world.

Having proceeded with a closer look on the global and Greek landscape of digital transformation during Covid-19, it can be stated that all governments have done a remarkable effort, using multiple channels to cover citizens' needs. As multiply stated, during the pandemic the information flow was accelerated, making it difficult for many people to distinguish which information should be seriously taken under consideration and which not [28–30]. Undoubtedly, social media platforms have gained more ground with the passage of time and their purpose becomes more and more serious than just entertainment. According to our results, Greek government has taken good advantage of the opportunities they offer, although their high popularity of 50.67% among participants to ensure valid information on Covid-19 evolution may also be justified by the fact that almost half of the sample size (44%) in the research was aged among 19–25 years old, which is the most active group on such platforms [31]. Additionally, similarly to what is indicated by Yasir A. et al. [10], governmental appearance using the technique of Word of Mouth was also quite effective in the case of Greece, as it was acknowledged by 56% of the participants in the research. In Greece though, TV and radio advertisements still remain people's top choice when it comes to information, as they are by far the most approachable means of information.

The fact that taxation services (TaxisNet) and the central digital portal (Gov.gr) were the most used public digital services during the pandemic was expected, as both portals had been in use prior to Covid-19, specifically since the European Union financed 2014–2020 project of the Ministry of Digital Governance, and thus citizens were quite aware of their existence. It is a fact though that the pandemic operated as a cornerstone that sped up the enrichment, the functionality and processes offered for both portals, leading to higher popularity in a short period of time. In overall, the Greek government's online services seem to be effort and time effective compared to the physical use of them as 72.67% of the participants suggested.

In relation to health services, Greece did not proceed with any massive changes or disruptive technologies similar to the ones identified for the case of China [19–22]. In a few hospitals though innovative technologies such as automated measurements were established, but as they were isolated cases they were not widely spread and advertised, thus most of the citizens were not even aware of such services. Though an ambitious effort has been made with the introduction of the individual e-consultation services and self-declaration tests platform (73% and 86.66% of awareness respectively), as well as the individual electronic health record (65.34%) and the platform for online appointments at primary health care units (67.33%).

On cultural services point of view, even though the majority were aware with actions taken from organizations not to eliminate their presence in everyday life, participation rates were rather low. Regarding satisfaction of the alternatives offered, virtual museum tours achieved really high scores though satisfaction was neutral in relation to live concerts (28%) and low for reading events (42.86%), which means that virtual experience is far from replacing the real-life experience related to entertainment, although this might not be the case for all countries. For example, Bin E. et al. have performed a research of 750 people (mainly located in Italy, Sweden, and India) and identified that there is high likelihood of keeping their new habits related to free time after the pandemic period, too [32].

5.1 Limitations

This study has some limitations. First of all, further research could be done with a bigger sample size, also considering the confidence interval estimation, to ensure greater liability for our conclusions. Achieving a bigger sample size would also help to identify broader eGovernment practices, as according to what has already been mentioned, 44% of the current sample were students aged 19–25 years old, thus they might not have the same needs and demands on public services as working adults (for example on taxation on insurance services). Finally, due to limited possibilities of the PSPP statistical analysis package, dependent and independent variables were not taken under consideration during the analysis.

6 Conclusion

The Covid-19 pandemic has brought up enormous changes in everyday life operations, both in public and private sectors. It has to be acknowledged that all governments have made huge efforts to correspond in the demanding situation and isolation requirements, without though seizing their activities. More or less measures taken around the world followed similar patterns, though differentiation in each country's background led to diverse results in each case. Factors such as infrastructure, economy, citizens' status and education should seriously be considered before the implementation and further development of digital services, in order for e-government not to result in being a means of discrimination. For the case of Greece, it could be mentioned that e-government practices were quite acknowledged by the public in relation to the hustle under which they were implemented, though for sure there is room for further improvement, as there has been observed a difference in citizens knowledge and satisfaction while using the e-government services.

6.1 Future Research

With this study a spherical point of view is presented on what digital means were implemented through the pandemic in Greece and whether they were well communicated with citizens, though since each service has multiple functions, it would require an indepth qualitative research to measure accurate satisfaction, and identification of flaws or strong points on their operation.

References

1. Davison, R.M., Wagner, C., Ma, L.C.K.: From government to e-government: a transition model. Inf. Technol. People **18**(3), 280–299 (2005). https://doi.org/10.1108/095938405106 15888
2. Osbourne, D., Gaebler, T.: reinventing government: how the entrepreneurial spirit is transforming the public sector. Plume (1992)
3. Torres, L., Pina, V., Royo, S.: E-government and the transformation of public administrations in EU countries: beyond NPM or just a second wave of reforms? Online Inf. Rev. **29**(5), 531–553 (2005). https://doi.org/10.1108/14684520510628918
4. European Commission. Communication From The Commission To The European Parliament, The Council, The European Economic And Social Committee And The Committee Of The Regions: A Digital Agenda for Europe (2010). Accessed 1 May 2021, https://eur-lex.europa. eu/legal-content/en/ALL/?uri=CELEX%3A52010DC0245
5. Six, D.P.: The scope of E-governance. In: E-governance. Palgrave Macmillan (2004). https:// doi.org/10.1057/9780230000896_2
6. Mishra, M.K.: Digital transformation of public service and administration. Leibniz Information Centre for Economics (2020). Accessed 1 May 2020, https://www.econstor.eu/bit-str eam/10419/222522/1/Digital%20Transformation%20of%20Public%20Ser-vice%20and% 20Administration.pdf
7. Burlacu, S., Patarlageanu, S.R., Diaconu, A., Ciobanu, G.: E-government in the era of globalization and the health crisis caused by the Covid-19 pandemic, between standards and innovation. SHS Web Conf. **82**, 08004 (2021). https://doi.org/10.1051/shsconf/20219208004
8. Scupola, A.: Digital transformation of public administration services in Denmark: a process tracing case study. J. NBICT **1**, 261–284 (2019). https://doi.org/10.13052/nbjict1902-097X. 2018.014

9. Imhof, M.A., Schmalzle, R., Renner, B., Schupp, H.T.: Strong health messages increase audience brain coupling. Neuroimage **216**, 116527 (2021). https://doi.org/10.1016/j.neuroi mage.2020.116527

10. Yasir, A., Hu, X., Ahmad, M., Rauf, A., Shi, J., Nasir, S.A.: Modeling impact of word of mouth and E-government on online social presence during COVID-19 outbreak: a multi-mediation approach. Int. J. Environ. Res. Public Health. **17**, 2954 (2020). https://doi.org/10.3390/ijerph 17082954

11. Ullah, A., Pinglu, C., Ullah, S., Abbas, H.S.M., Khan, S.: The role of e-governance in combating COVID-19 and promoting sustainable development: a comparative study of China and Pakistan. Chin. Polit. Sci. Rev. **6**, 86–118 (2021). https://doi.org/10.1007/s41111-020-001 67-w

12. Shaw, R., Kim, Y.K., Hua, J.: Governance, technology and citizen behavior in pandemic: Lessons from COVID-19 in East Asia. Progr. Disast. Sci. **6**, 100090 (2020). https://doi.org/10. 1016/j.pdisas.2020.100090

13. Agostino, D., Arnaboldi, M., Diaz, L.M.: New development: COVID-19 as an accelerator of digital transformation in public service delivery. Public Money Manag. **41**(1), 69–72 (2021). https://doi.org/10.1080/09540962.2020.1764206

14. Lovari, A., D'ambrosi, L., Bowen, S.A.: Re-connecting voices: the (new) strategic role of public sector communication after the Covid-19 crisis. PACO **2**(13), 970–989 (2020). https:// doi.org/10.1285/i20356609v13i2p970

15. European Commission. Travel during the coronavirus pandemic: Mobile contact tracing applications. Accessed 4 June 2021, https://ec.europa.eu/info/live-work-travel-eu/corona-virus-res ponse/travel-during-coronavirus-pandemic_en

16. Mazzucato, M., Kattel, R.: COVID-19 and public-sector capacity. Oxf Rev. Econ. Policy **36**(S1), S256–S269 (2020). https://doi.org/10.1093/oxrep/graa031

17. Schuster, C., Weitzman, L., Mikkelsen, K.S., et al.: Responding to COVID-19 through surveys of public servants. Public Adm. Rev. **80**(5), 792–796 (2020). https://doi.org/10.1111/puar. 13246

18. Cohen, S., Rossi, F.M., Caperchione, E., Brusca, I.: Debate: If not now, then when? covid-19 as an accelerator for public sector accrual accounting in Europe. Public Money Manag. **41**(1), 10–12 (2021). https://doi.org/10.1080/09540962.2021.1834714

19. Chunming, Z., He, G.: 5G applications help China fight against COVID-19. Accessed 5 May 2021, http://www.caict.ac.cn/english/re-search/covid19/study/202004/P02020042637 1477971478.pdf

20. Mbunge, E., Akinnuwesi, B., Fashoto, S.G., Metfula, A.S., Mashwama, P.: A critical review of emerging technologies for tackling COVID-19 pandemic. Hum. Behav. Emerg. Technol. **3**, 25–39 (2020). https://doi.org/10.1002/hbe2.237

21. Ting, D.S.W., Carin, L., Dzau, V., Wong, T.W.: Digital technology and COVID-19. Nat Med. **26**, 459–461 (2020). https://doi.org/10.1038/s41591-020-0824-5

22. Ren, H., Shen, J., Tang, X., Feng, T.: 5G healthcare applications in COVID-19 prevention and control. ITU Kaleidoscope Ind.-Driven Digital Transf. (ITU K) **2020**, 1–4 (2020). https:// doi.org/10.23919/ITUK50268.2020.9303191

23. Xie, B., Charness, N., Fingerman, K., Kaye, J., Kim, M.T., Khurshid, A.: When going digital becomes a necessity: ensuring older adults' needs for information, services, and social inclusion during COVID-19. J. Aging Soc. Policy **32**(4–5), 460–470 (2020). https://doi.org/ 10.1080/08959420.2020.1771237

24. Ruize, O.: 5G's indispensable role in China's fight against COVID-19. CGTN (2020). Accessed 7 May 2021, https://news.cgtn.com/news/2020-07-09/5G-s-indispensable-role-in-China-s-fight-against-COVID-19-RXRu9TlZ9S/index.html

25. Xue, Y.: China's online education drive to boost demand for PCs, tablets, 5G and cloud services, says IDC. South China Morning Post (2020). Accessed 7 May 2021, https://www.scmp.com/tech/policy/article/3079782/chinas-online-education-drive-boost-demand-pcs-tablets-5g-and-cloud

26. Mehta, D., Wang, X.: COVID-19 and digital library services – a case study of a university library. Digit. Libr. Perspect. **36**(4), 351–363 (2020). https://doi.org/10.1108/DLP-05-2020-0030

27. Venkatachary, S.K., Prasad, J., Samikannu, R., Baptist, L.J., Alagappan, A., Ravi, R.: COVID-19 - an insight into various impacts on health, society and economy. Int. J. Econ. Finan. Issues **10**(4), 39–46 (2020). https://doi.org/10.32479/ijefi.9925

28. Mensah, K.I., Adams, S., Adjei, K.J., Mwakapesa, D.S:. Drivers of egovernment adoption amidst COVID-19 pandemic: the information adoption model (IAM) approach. Inf. Dev. (2021). https://doi.org/10.1177/02666669211010872

29. Dhar, S.A., Wani, Z.A., Shiekh, S.: Will Trust Survive the COVID Pandemic? Sage, New York (2020)

30. World Health Organization. Information dissemination during a global pandemic: Experiences from WHO (2020). Accessed 9 May 2021, https://extra-net.who.int/kobe_centre/en/news/UNU

31. Percentage of adults in the United States who use social networks as of February 2019, by age group. Statista (2021). Accessed 9 May 2021, https://www.statista.com/statis-tics/471370/us-adults-who-use-social-networks-age/

32. Bin, E., Andruetto, C., Susilo, Y., Pernestål, A.: The trade-off behaviours between virtual and physical activities during the first wave of the COVID-19 pandemic period. Eur. Transp. Res. Rev. **13**(1), 1–19 (2021). https://doi.org/10.1186/s12544-021-00473-7

Ontology-Based Interestingness
in COVID-19 Data

C. B. Abhilash$^{(\boxtimes)}$ and Kavi Mahesh

Indian Institute of Information Technology Dharwad, Dharwad, India
{abhilashcb,director}@iiitdwd.ac.in

Abstract. This paper describes an approach to mining interestingness in data by designing domain ontology, COKPME and populating it with anonymized COVID-19 data from private hospital in Karnataka State, India. In general, association rules applied to healthcare data generate a large number of rules. These generated rules may not guarantee interestingness of the generated knowledge. To address this, we propose an ontology-based interestingness measure using the association rule mining algorithm. With the association rule, the implicit relationship between different categories of data attributes is captured. Our approach is to design the domain ontology, populate with data instances and operate association rules for semantic and non-semantic data to discover interesting facts.

Keywords: Interestingness · Ontology mining · Knowledge base · Association rule mining · Interestingness metrics

1 Introduction

Widespread use of ontologies to describe data has resulted in access to large ontology-based datasets. Ontologies are the building blocks for encoding the appropriate knowledge from a domain. Many repositories in BioPortal [5] and OBO Foundry [24] have various ontologies that can be used for data integration, query, and building a decision support system. Ontology-based decision systems are used to produce accurate and reliable results [14].

In this paper, we identify the relationships involved in COVID-19 data of Karnataka State private hospital patients. We represent the data by manually listing the meta data information and build the relationships between the concepts and use it for designing the ontology. COKPME is an ontology designed and developed for analysing COVID-19 Karnataka State private hospital data. The data instances are converted to semantic triple form. The association rule mining algorithm is applied on the semantic triple data to generated set of rules that satisfies the minSup (minimum support) and minConf (minimum confidence), we name it the rule repository (Rule REPO).

Interestingness is an important aspect of data [1], here we explore interestingness in COVID-19 data using the COKPME ontology is illustrated with a

© Springer Nature Switzerland AG 2022
E. Garoufallou et al. (Eds.): MTSR 2021, CCIS 1537, pp. 322–335, 2022.
https://doi.org/10.1007/978-3-030-98876-0_28

case study. The ontology is designed by integrating concepts from schema.org[1], a friend of a friend vocabulary FOAF[2] for modeling concepts like person, organization, gender, age, and related properties. Also, OBO is used for clinical symptoms and other findings. CODO ontology is used as the reference ontology for designing COKPME ontology [10].

The association rule generates interesting patterns based on metrics like support, confidence, lift, and rule length [21]. Thus, Association rules represent implicit relationship from frequent patterns. The widely used association rule mining algorithm, is the Apriori algorithm [15]. The ontology is a semantic data model, and ontology encodes the knowledge in a machine-understandable manner. The concepts of the domain, their meaning (semantics), and their properties and relationships, along with the annotation of data helps, represent the knowledge in a highly usable way. Ontology-based association rule mining improves the quality of generated rules by incorporating semantics. Also, invalid and inconsistent rules can be pruned and filtered [23].

The paper is organized as follows: Sect. 2 provides the related work considering rule mining, ontology-based mining techniques, and existing COVID-19 ontologies. Section 3 describes the data, and the methodology followed. Section 4 deals with the results and discussion on the proposed methodology under different criteria. Section 5 concludes the paper with scope for future enhancements[3].

2   Related Work

COVID-19 ontology for cases and patient information (CODO)[4] is a model designed to collect and analyze COVID-19 data. The ontology is standards-based and can incorporate data from multiple sources. Data are represented using OWL and W3C standards so that other ontologies and software systems can be used accordingly. CODO [10] follows the FAIR (findable, accessible, interoperable, and reusable) principles. In addition, it provides a semantic-based data retrieval that can be further used for deeper insights. Several other ontologies related to COVID-19 are also discussed. Using CODO, COVID-19 data is represented in OWL so that other ontologies can inherit these features [10]. Table 1 illustrates the existing COVID-19 related ontologyies.

2.1   Ontology Based Mining

The metadata, which is machine-readable descriptions of the data, is available for all data sets in public repositories. However, the metadata creation process is time-consuming, and also it lacks validation process. Considering these, a method has been developed to streamline the metadata creation process that enables to enter the metadata quickly and accurately by using association rule mining

---

[1] https://schema.org/.
[2] http://xmlns.com/foaf/spec/.
[3] https://bioportal.bioontology.org/ontologies/COKPME.
[4] https://bioportal.bioontology.org/ontologies/CODO.

Table 1. Summary of existing COVID-19 ontology

Ontology	Description	Reference
CIDO	It mainly concerned with medical diagnosis	[14]
CODO	Collecting and analyzing COVID data.	[10]
COVI-19 Surveillance Ontology	Traces medical case and respiratory symptoms from the electronic health record (EHR)	[17]
DRUGS4COVID-19	Medication and its relation to COVID-19	[4]
COVIDCRFRAPID	Semantic data model. It analyzes the rapid case records and answers certain questions	[5]
Kg-COVID-19 and Linked COVID-19	Semantically designed and have a software interface	[22]

coupled with ontology-based semantic mappings to discover hidden association among the metadata [21].

RDF data is extracted in various ways using "mining configuration [2]. Association rules mining at RDF statement level is an interesting field for further research, as there are remaining configurations to be elaborated and combined for other interesting use cases.

The ontology is also used for the association rule mining technique for extracting knowledge from text. Ontology-based keyword extraction and revised Association Rules based on weighting scheme was used [3].

An existing ontology can be populated with the instances of information present in natural language texts. Once the relevant ontology domain is selected, the related information is processed and updated to their existing ontology [3]. The data is appended to the existing ontology by converting the semantic class instances of extracted data to their existing ontology (OBIE) [27].

2.2   Association Rule Based Mining

Association rule (AR) mining is a very significant method in the extraction of information from databases. Huge amounts of data in any domain can make the entire process of data management and interpretation very cumbersome. Having a knowledge base provides a space to store unstructured and complicated data elements for information processing [15].

Ontology knowledge mining approach to rank semantically interesting association rules is used for incorporating semantics to the mined rules. The semantic correlation of the data elements influences semantic interestingness measures. The basic approach is to establish the concepts of ontology into a hierarchical structure portraying the conceptual clusters of the target subject. Here each cluster summarizes similar concepts which may suggest a specific category of the corresponding domain. If the corresponding clusters are different, it essentially defines the interestingness of the association rules [2].

Apriori algorithm is the most commonly used algorithm for AR's mining. Suppose the parameters used in the Apriori algorithm like minConf, and minSup, are high. In that case, it leads to more robust rules, but they are few in number, and some useful information might be ignored. If the parameters are set too low, the algorithm will generate huge rules with uninteresting information. To overcome this limitation, we must identify the parameter values and threshold values to select the most interesting rules out of the whole set, depending on the ontology [12].

The AMIE algorithm [11] is another second-generation algorithm aimed at the specific application of Knowledge base refinement. A systematic approach to mine ARs from ontology-based semantic trajectory data.

2.3   FAIR Principles

A good way of thinking and making data available is using FAIR principles published on scientific data in 2016 [26]. The FAIR principles has four aspects - It should be **findable, accessible, interoperable,** and **reusable.**

In the context of ontology, findability is achieved by having rich metadata defined. Furthermore, the accessibility of data via URI makes it easier and conflict-free. Interoperability is indirectly achieved by having findability and accessibility. The data interoperability makes the systems talk to each other for data exchange. Data reusability is achieved by incorporating data standards in different domains. With FAIR principles, knowledge integration with existing data is achieved [25].

3   Data and Methods

Besides general data analytics and knowledge engineering methods, the ontology-based approach stands aside and has unique significance. The ontology-based approach is the key aspect for semantic data integration and interoperability. With the knowledge gained from our literature, we have modeled a unique way to find interestingness in data. By the motivation from our previous study, where we had used a graph-based approach for finding interestingness in COVID-19 contact tracing data [6] and [7], we use an ontology-based framework and FAIR principles of data, to make the system more reliable and efficient.

3.1   Data Interestingness

This section describes the methodology adopted in our study. It illustrates the data collection, ontology design process, and knowledge distillation for interestingness in data. The high-level architecture illustrating the methodology is presented in Fig. 1.

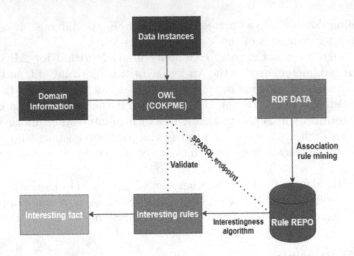

Fig. 1. Architectural view of the methodology.

By using COKPME ontology, the data instances are converted to RDF form. A set of association rule is also generated for the data instances using the association rule mining algorithm and is named as "Rule REPO." Using RDF data and rule repository, we manually extract the set of interesting rules using the defined interestingness algorithm. SPARQL query for the set of the interesting rules is written to validate the rules with the COKPME ontology.

3.2 Ontology Design

Motivation from [18], we model the ontology considering the domain of interest, reusing the existing ontology like schema.org and SNOMED CT and OBO for integrating certain concepts [8]. In COKPME ontology, we have integrated Friend of Friend (FOAF) [13] for person as patient and Schema.org is used to model gender and location. SNOMED CT and OBO are sued for modeling clinical findings and symptoms. To design the ontology, we follow well known procedures. Domain information is identified considering the data and its dependencies. In our study we use anonymized COVID-19 data of private hospital from Karnataka State. The domain information is extracted by understanding the structure of the data. CODO ontology which is a universal data integration ontology for COVID-19 data is used as the reference model for our ontology design. To develop COKPME ontology, the following steps were followed. Firstly, listing the possible classes that match the domain information like patient, symptom, diagnosis, healthcare facility, and location as indicated in Fig. 2. This was done by analyzing the data and domain information. Secondly, the classes were arranged in systematic order to match the sub class hierarchy. A schematic class diagram approach was used to validate the class, sub-class hierarchy. Next, for each class the annotation of type **rdf:label** and **dcterms**[5] were used. The next step is to define data properties and object properties and their cardinalities. The relationships between the concepts in domain are: "has_a", "Is_a", "Suffer_from", "others_comorbid_conditions", "reported_on".

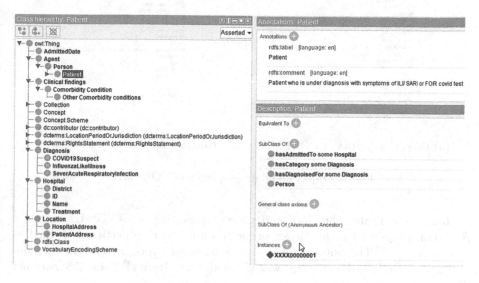

Fig. 2. Class with assertion properties.

Ontology Development Process- The competency questions for developing COKPME are listed in Sect. 4.2.

- Step1: We identify the scope and purpose
- Step2: Competency question determined by the application or data. (i.e., The question the ontology should be able to answer).
- Step3: Consider reusing existing ontology.
- Step4: Using the data attributes, we identify the concepts and their properties
- Step5: Using step4, we define the class of the designated domain.
- Step6: Using step4, we define the set of properties.
- Step7: Property constraints are described.
- Step8: Create instances for the classes.
- Step9: Documentation and validation using WIDOCO.

The purpose of ontology evaluation is to see how well the ontology adheres to the design goals. There is no simple or automatic technique to assess an ontology. Reasoners can validate the ontology's syntactic structure and coherence but not its domain knowledge or structure. One of the most common ways is manual evaluation by domain experts [9,16]. Data instances were imported using the Cellfie plugin in Protégé. We used SPARQL queries to evaluate the competency questions mentioned in Sect. 4.2 to validate the COKPME ontology.

---

[5] https://www.dublincore.org/specifications/dublin-core/dcmi-terms/.

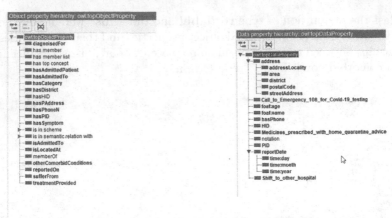

(a) Object properties of COKPME.   (b) Data properties of COKPME.

Fig. 3. Object and data properties of COKPME.

Figure 3 indicates the data and object properties of COKPME ontology. Assertion property for the object properties and data properties is defined as shown in Fig. 4. The ontology design is done using Protégé tool and the consistency of COKPME ontology was checked using HermiT 1.4.3.456 reasoner [20].

3.3   Data Instances

Data collection is the first step. The data used in this study is gathered from the Department of Health and Family Welfare Service, Karnataka Government, for research purposes only. The data is in a structured format with patient demographic and clinical symptom details. The data was provided by anonymizing the patient demographic details. The sample data for experimental use is available at GitHub repository[6].

Figure 4 indicates the data concepts considered for COKPME ontology. The data is in a well-structured format for capturing the COVID-19 patient's information at the healthcare facility. Patients are diagnosed into three categories - ILI (influenza-like illness), SARI (severe acute respiratory infection), and COVID-19 Suspect. Based on the diagnosed category, the prescription is provided, as shown in the Fig. 4. In general, ILI patients are prescribed necessary medicines and advised for self-home quarantine. SARI is a critical condition where a patient's saturation level will not be at a constant rate. So as a precautionary measure, they are sifted to the hospital with the required facility. Certain patients are symptomatic or asymptomatic, probable COVID-19. They are sent for the COVID-19 test and marked as COVID-19 suspects. Interestingly, the majority of patients suffer from other comorbid conditions. This enables researchers to discover more insight and possible causes for infections.

---

[6] https://github.com/abhilashcb8/COKPME.

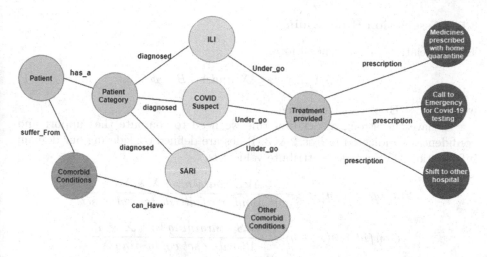

Fig. 4. Data concepts for COKPME ontology.

3.4   Ontology Population, Evaluation and Visualization

The data instances are imported using the cellfie-plugin of the Protégé tool. The transformation rules are defined to add the data instances from the spreadsheet to the class and its instances. In the COKPME ontology, we transformed each row into an individual of the Patient class. We transformed values in each row, such as the PID, date of diagnosis, suffering from and comorbid conditions, etc., into the appropriate property values. Since the data size is rather large for Protégé to handle, we have added only 500 individuals covering all aspects of the domain of interest for testing purposes. The complete data of 700,000 instances was added to the graph database as an alternative. The graph database is faster and more convenient to handle the RDF data store. Figure 5 shows the hierarchical view of COKPME. COMKPME ontology documentation and validation are done using WIDOCO[7]. WebVOWL is used to visualize the COKPME ontology[8].

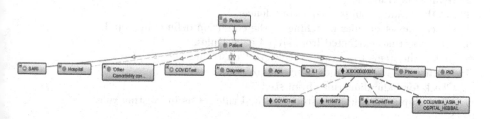

Fig. 5. Hierarchical view of patient class with properties.

---

[7] https://github.com/dgarijo/Widoco.
[8] http://vowl.visualdataweb.org/webvowl.html.

3.5 Association Rule Mining

The association rule in general form:

$$Let\, A \subseteq X, B \subseteq X, and\, A \cap B = \phi \tag{1}$$

we call **A → B** as association rule.

To have the strong association rule we need to compute the support and confidence as indicated in Eqs. 2 & 3. Rules are defined considering our domain information. AVS refers to attribute value set.

$$Support(x \rightarrow y) = \frac{AVS\ containing\ X\ \&\ Y}{Total\ number\ of\ attributes\ value\ set} \tag{2}$$

$$Confidence(x \rightarrow y) = \frac{AVS\ containing\ both\ X\ \&\ Y}{All\ value\ set\ containing\ X} \tag{3}$$

Rules do not take away the preference of an individual, but rather find links between a set of elements.

3.6 Interestingness algorithm

There is no optimal measure that can be used to evaluate the extracted association rules. The interestingness of a rule depends on the context and individual perspectives. With the motivation from [19], here we attempt to generalize the approach by introducing the algorithm for mining interestingness by incorporating the domain ontology. The algorithm takes the rule set generated by association rule mining as input data discussed in Sect. 3.5 and also the owl defined constraints key words which are manually selected from the COKPME data instances considering the object and data properties.

Algorithm 1. Interestingness algorithm

1: Start: Input Rule REPO.
2: Input Constraint set.
3: Set the required support and confidence.
4: Check the set of rules matching to the condition defined in step 3.
5: Store the rules extracted from step 4 as T-Rules.
6: Match the items from the T- Rules to Constraints set.
7: Extract the relevant rules from step 6.
8: Check for redundant rules from step 7.
9: Filter duplicate rules and store the final rule set as Interesting rules.
10: Stop.

---

4   Result and Discussions

The experimental results were executed on Intel(R) Core(TM) i7-8565U CPU @ 1.80 GHz machine with 16 GB RAM. The software platforms and tools used include Protégé for designing the owl ontology and generate RDF data, the GraphDB- graph database tool for processing the SPARQL query on RDF data. The rule generation and interestingness mining algorithms discussed in Sect. 3 are coded in python on Google Colaboratory. Ontology documentation by WIDOCO, visualization by WebVOWL[9].

4.1   Association rule generation

We compare both traditional association rule mining and ontology based methods to bring deeper insights from the data for interestingness.

AR's for Non-semantic and Semantic Triple Data. Applying the AR's with set of minimum support and minimum confidence draws the following results as show in Table 2. The abbreviations used are - minimum support - MS, minimum confidence - MC, minimum lift - ML, minimum length - LN, semantic rule set - S-RS, non-semantci - N-RS.

Table 2. Rule set: RS for different parameters of interest

	I	II	III	IV	V	VI	VII	VIII	IX	X	XI	XII
MS	0.005	0.003	0.006	0.005	0.005	0.003	0.009	0.005	0.1	0.0045	0.005	0.003
MC	0.5	0.7	1	0.9	1	0.9	1	1	0.2	0.5	0.9	0.7
ML	2	2	2	2	2	2	2	2	2	2	3	2
LN	5	3	3	3	3	3	3	3	3	4	3	2
N-RS	534	1184	214	826	676	179	321	112	302	535	926	1184
S-RS	240	590	90	390	356	70	150	210	139	289	521	590

The interestingness measure from Table 2:

$$< MS \ < MC = > RS \tag{4}$$

$$> MS \ > MC = < RS \tag{5}$$

For the data with 12 attributes and 700,000 data instances, we recorded the number of rules generated by considering different values for support and confidence. Table 2 indicates the influence of support and confidence with different threshold values. With the minSup of 0.003 and minConf of 0.7, 590 rules for semantic data and 1184 for non-semantic data are generated. Considering

---

[9] https://github.com/abhilashcb8/COKPME.

Table 3. Rule set: RS for different parameters of interest

Non semantic AR's	Semantic AR's
['Medicines prescribed with home quarantine advice',' ILI']	['COVID-19-positive', 'CallEmergency-Covid-19-test']
['Others (Mention Disease)' , 'ILI']	['INFECTIVE-ETIOLOGY-OF-VIRAL-ORIGIN', 'Referred to other hospital']
[Fever-Cough, 'ILI','None']	[Fever-Cough-Breathlessness',' SARI']
['Contact With COVID positive patient', 'ILI']	['Covid-19-(Suspect)' , 'Call-to-Emergency-108-for-Covid-19-testing',' NIL']

the interestingness metrics, we vary the parameters of interest and generate the aggregated rule set for both semantic and non-semantic data. Further, for creating the aggregated rule set, we can merge the rules from various columns like II, III, VIII, IX, XI by removing the redundant rule called aggregated rule set. The aggregated rule set is used in generating interesting facts.

From Table 3, We can differentiate the semantic and non-semantic rules generated. The semantic rules are generated based on the user-defined constraints along with interestingness metrics. The traditional methods generate rules that are more general. Ontology based method generates more relevant rules that are based on user interest. We can conclude that semantic data discover more interesting patterns compared to non-semantic data.

4.2 RDF Data Processing

The competency questions listed here are queried using SPARQL:

- How many people are with symptom S in place L.
- How many people reported on nth day with comorbid condition C.
- List the patient P with category PC and comorbid condition C.
- Given the symptom S and age A with pin code PK. Find the most identified patient category in that pin code PK.
- Find all the patient P who are all admitted to hospital H and belongs to the same pin code PK.
- Identify the most common hospital patient admitted to considering the Pin code PK.

4.3 Interestingness From Data

We have indicated a few interesting facts along with the interesting pattern from the interestingness Algorithm 1.

- The most common symptom is "Common FLU," and the average age group is 30.
- Diabetic symptom - the average age is 53.
- Hypertension, Hypothyroid, breathing problem and asthma is commonly seen symptom for age group of 45-55.
- 15% of patients suffer from Allergic bronchitis (age 37).
- Acute febrile illness (AFI) for age group 33.
- Lower respiratory tract infection (LTRI) is also a widely seen symptom.
- On 21st May - Only two districts of Karnataka has reported Acute Febrile illness (AFI) as major symptom.
- Diabetic with low oxygen saturation is reported under SARI.
- Common Flu, Breathlessness, Heart disease, Hypertension, and respiratory infections are major symptoms indicated.

4.4   An Interesting Case

Our method discovered several interesting facts, one of which is as follows.
Considering the Confidence
We discover a high confidence rule for ILI → MP-HQA - 80% of all patients who suffer from ILI also suffer from common FLU. (Fever-headache-body pain-cold-cough). Hypothesis: Patients who are ILI category and are likely to have other symptoms as "Common FLU"
Implicitly: more likely than patients not under Common FLU.

5   Conclusion and Future Enhancement

This paper presented a novel ontology-based interestingness method using association rule mining. First, the domain ontology COKPME is designed by manually extracting the terms, concepts from the dataset and building implicit relationships. Then, using the designed COKPME ontology, the data instances are converted to RDF triples. Next, an association rule mining algorithm with defined parameters of interest generates the rules for the non-semantic and semantic data. Further, using the proposed interestingness algorithm based on the Apriori algorithm, interesting rules are extracted considering the concepts from COKPME ontology. Finally, the generated rules are validated with the domain ontology to get interesting facts using the SPARQL query on GraphDB[10]. Our experiment results show that semantic data gives more relevant and useful facts than non-semantic datasets.

In the future, we would like to extend our approach to automatically select the rules and parallelize the task of generating interesting facts for many large semantic datasets.

Acknowledgements. This work was supported in part by the Department of Health and Family Welfare Services (HFWS), Government of Karnataka, India. We also extend our special thanks to the E-Health section of HFWS, Government of Karnataka, India, for providing all the necessary support and encouragement.

---

[10] https://www.ontotext.com/products/graphdb/.

References

1. Abhilash, C., Mahesh, K.: Interesting patterns from covid-19 dataset using graph-based statistical analysis for preventive measures. Comput. Intell. Healthcare Inf., 325–358 (2021)
2. Afolabi, I., Sowunmi, O., Daramola, O.: Semantic association rule mining in text using domain ontology. Int. J. Metadata Semant. Ontol. 12(1), 28–34 (2017)
3. Anantharangachar, R., Ramani, S., Rajagopalan, S.: Ontology guided information extraction from unstructured text. arXiv preprint arXiv:1302.1335 (2013)
4. Badenes-Olmedo, C., et al.: Drugs4covid: drug-driven knowledge exploitation based on scientific publications. arXiv preprint arXiv:2012.01953 (2020)
5. Bonino, L.: Who covid-19 rapid version CRF semantic data model. BioPortal (2020)
6. Abhilash, C., Mahesh, K.: Graph analytics applied to covid19 Karnataka state dataset. In: 2021 The 4th International Conference on Information Science and Systems, pp. 74–80. Association for Computing Machinery, New York (2021). https://doi.org/10.1145/3459955.3460603
7. Abhilash, C.B., Mahesh, K.: Interesting patterns from covid-19 dataset using graph-based statistical analysis for preventive measures. Comput. Intell. Healthcare Inf. 1, 325 (2021)
8. Donnelly, K., et al.: SNOMED-CT: the advanced terminology and coding system for ehealth. Stud. Health Technol. Inf. 121, 279 (2006)
9. Dutta, B.: Examining the interrelatedness between ontologies and linked data. Library Hi Tech (2017)
10. Dutta, B., DeBellis, M.: Codo: an ontology for collection and analysis of covid-19 data. arXiv preprint arXiv:2009.01210 (2020)
11. Galárraga, L.A., Teflioudi, C., Hose, K., Suchanek, F.: Amie: association rule mining under incomplete evidence in ontological knowledge bases. In: Proceedings of the 22nd International Conference on World Wide Web, pp. 413–422 (2013)
12. Geng, L., Hamilton, H.J.: Interestingness measures for data mining: a survey. ACM Comput. Surv. (CSUR) 38(3), 9-es (2006)
13. Graves, M., Constabaris, A., Brickley, D.: FOAF: connecting people on the semantic web. Cataloging Classif. Q. 43(3–4), 191–202 (2007)
14. He, Y., et al.: Cido, a community-based ontology for coronavirus disease knowledge and data integration, sharing, and analysis. Sci. Data 7(1), 1–5 (2020)
15. Idoudi, R., Ettabaa, K.S., Solaiman, B., Hamrouni, K.: Ontology knowledge mining based association rules ranking. Procedia Comput. Sci. 96, 345–354 (2016)
16. Lozano-Tello, A., Gómez-Pérez, A.: Ontometric: a method to choose the appropriate ontology. J. Database Manag. (JDM) 15(2), 1–18 (2004)
17. de Lusignan, S., et al.: Covid-19 surveillance in a primary care sentinel network: in-pandemic development of an application ontology. JMIR Public Health Surveill. 6(4), e21434 (2020)
18. Mahesh, K.: Ontology development: ideology and methodology. Technical Report MCCS-96-292, Computing Research Laboratory, New Mexico . . . (1996)
19. Mahesh, K., Karanth, P.: Smart-aleck: an interestingness algorithm for large semantic datasets. Algorithms 2, 3 (2015)
20. Musen, M.A.: The protégé project: a look back and a look forward. AI Matters 1(4), 4–12 (2015)
21. Petri, A.C.F., Silva, D.F.: Towards logical association rule mining on ontology-based semantic trajectories. In: 2020 19th IEEE International Conference on Machine Learning and Applications (ICMLA), pp. 586–591. IEEE (2020)

22. Reese, J.T., et al.: Kg-covid-19: a framework to produce customized knowledge graphs for covid-19 response. Patterns **2**(1), 100155 (2021)
23. Shen, B., Yao, M., Wu, Z., Zhang, Y., Yi, W.: Ontology-based association rules retrieval using protege tools. In: Sixth IEEE International Conference on Data Mining-Workshops (ICDMW 2006), pp. 765–769. IEEE (2006)
24. Smith, B., et al.: The obo foundry: coordinated evolution of ontologies to support biomedical data integration. Nat. Biotechnol. **25**(11), 1251–1255 (2007)
25. Wikipedia contributors: Fair data – Wikipedia, the free encyclopedia (2021). https://en.wikipedia.org/w/index.php?title=FAIR_data&oldid=1038845392, Accessed 24 Aug 2021
26. Wilkinson, M.D., et al.: The fair guiding principles for scientific data management and stewardship. Sci. Data **3**(1), 1–9 (2016)
27. Wimalasuriya, D.C., Dou, D.: Ontology-based information extraction: an introduction and a survey of current approaches (2010)

GAP: Enhancing Semantic Interoperability of Genomic Datasets and Provenance Through Nanopublications

Matheus Pedra Puime Feijoó[1]([✉]) [ID], Rodrigo Jardim[3] [ID],
Sergio Manuel Serra da Cruz[1,2] [ID], and Maria Luiza Machado Campos[1] [ID]

[1] Universidade Federal do Rio de Janeiro (PPGI/UFRJ), Rio de Janeiro, Brazil
feijoo@ufrj.com, {serra,mluiza}@ppgi.ufrj.br
[2] Federal Rural University of Rio de Janeiro (UFRRJ), Seropédica, Brazil
[3] Oswaldo Cruz Foundation (LBCS/IOC), Rio de Janeiro, Brazil

Abstract. While the publication of datasets in scientific repositories has become broadly recognised, the repositories tend to have increasing semantic-related problems. For instance, they present various data reuse obstacles for machine-actionable processes, especially in biological repositories, hampering the reproducibility of scientific experiments. An example of these shortcomings is the GenBank database. We propose GAP, an innovative data model to enhance the semantic data meaning to address these issues. The model focuses on converging related approaches like data provenance, semantic interoperability, FAIR principles, and nanopublications. Our experiments include a prototype to scrape genomic data and trace them to nanopublications as a proof of concept. For this, (meta)data are stored in a three-level nanopub data model. The first level is related to a target organism, specifying data in terms of biological taxonomy. The second level focuses on the biological strains of the target, the central part of our contribution. The strains express information related to deciphered (meta)data of the genetic variations of the genomic material. The third level stores related scientific papers (meta)data. We expect it will offer higher data storage flexibility and more extensive interoperability with other data sources by incorporating and adopting associated approaches to store genomic data in the proposed model.

Keywords: Nanopublication · FAIR principles · Data provenance · Genomic data · Reusability · Interoperability

1 Introduction

Datasets and reproducibility of research play a crucial role in modern data-driven research. Scientific data management has become increasingly complex and is gaining traction in the research community, mainly when spotlighting data and metadata's share, reuse, and interoperation, particularly for machine-actionable processes [1]. Genomic databases are classic examples of this scenario.

© Springer Nature Switzerland AG 2022
E. Garoufallou et al. (Eds.): MTSR 2021, CCIS 1537, pp. 336–348, 2022.
https://doi.org/10.1007/978-3-030-98876-0_29

Researchers often upgrade their databases with diverse data and metadata to map as sequence new genes, fomenting new biological investigations [2]. These databases store either partial sequences of genes or complete genomes of organisms. However, data reusability-related issues challenge researchers. Sometimes data are unnecessarily duplicated, inconsistent, inaccurate, incomplete, and even obsolete, to name a few of these issues [3, 4]. Consequently, these drawbacks aggravate whenever researchers need to find, access, interoperate, and reuse data using machine-actionable processes, requiring a fully semantic-aware scenario [5].

Our work investigates two core issues related to data reuse. First, machine-driven processes cannot understand the real meaning of stored data in repositories, generating an inflexible interoperable scenario. Second, the lack of data standardisation and provenance [6, 7] makes understanding the data more error-prone and time-consuming. This paper claims that we can address both issues with an innovative approach to managing data provenance while ensuring semantic interoperability based on nanopublication technologies; we present the Genome Assembly nanoPublication (GAP) approach.

Nanopublications [8] (a.k.a nanopub) are a formalized and machine-readable way of communicating the smallest possible units of publishable information. A nanopub is the materialisation model of Linked Data (LD) concepts representing small statements attached with data provenance and metadata. According to [9], it creates a uniform, self-supporting, and machine-readable information ecosystem. Nanopubs is a novel and reliable approach for extending scientific insights, notably in the biomedical fields [10]. However, the current nanopubs suffer from the absence of the data provenance of the assertions and the nanopub itself, like incorrect authorship information [11].

This article discusses the feasibility of a novel data model to enhance the control of genomic data by injecting descriptive and structural semantically enriched metadata. The devised model uses convergent approaches and techniques such as controlled vocabularies, ontologies, W3C PROV standard [12], and FAIR data principles [5] to mitigate the nanopubs related issues. As proof of concept, we have created an operational prototype of GAP to transform genomic data into nanopubs. In order to evaluate the proposal, the nanopubs were confronted with the real-world scenario of reusing genomic (meta)data and other well-known nanopubs repositories to verify the potential of data provenance and interoperability enrichment in this machine-actionable context.

Our computational experiments consider the GenBank Assembly Database (GBAD) as a use case to compose this novel data model. Among all GenBank databases, GBAD is one of the most used [13]. The data it stores are manually published and curated by researchers or scientific organisations. These publishers usually store data related to the assembly of organisms, containing the composition of assembled genomes, additional metadata, statistical reports, and genomic sequence data [14].

The paper is organised as follows. First, we present the background and discuss related works in Sect. 2. Then, in Sect. 3, we detail the proposed approach, the Genome Assembly nanoPublication (GAP) data model. Next, we report our implementation and discussion in Sect. 4 and conclude the paper in Sect. 5.

2 Background and Related Work

2.1 FAIR Data Principles and Nanopublications

The FAIR data principles (FDP) [5] focus on reusing data and metadata of any kind. These principles stress the role of Open Science with a focus on '(meta)data', where authors use this term in cases that apply to metadata and data. FAIR stands for: Findable, Accessible, Interoperable, and Reusable. The principles based on these characteristics, up-to-date data resources, tools, vocabularies, and foundations should manifest to support exploration and reuse by third parties through the Web [5].

Reusability and interoperability are quintessential goals for Web data: data resources should be explicitly designed to be reused by either humans or machines. The interoperability in data infrastructures maximises the value of information artefacts retrieved from different data silos. However, a much broader and deeper analysis must have a reliable and solid data association.

Several proposals report the lack of semantic interoperability, undocumented data models, poor provenance, and data reuse. In the context of scientific repositories, the nanopublication model can address some of these problems.

Nanopubs follow the FDP and exploit the LD to represent any digital object using minimal statements with its context and provenance. A typical nanopub uses the Resource Description Framework (RDF), persistent identifiers, use licenses, the Web Ontology Language (OWL), and the nanopub schema. Initially, a nanopub consists of four RDF graphs: head, assertion, provenance, and publication info [8].

Figure 1 represents a nanopublication with the following assertion of "Malaria is transmitted by mosquito." The assertion is the core section in a nanopub, represented by at least one RDF triple. This assertion constitutes two concepts (Malaria and Mosquito) and a relationship (Transmitted by). Therefore, the RDF statement triple is displayed as Subject (Malaria), Predicate (Transmitted by), and Object (Mosquito).

```
@prefix cw: <http://conceptwiki.org/index.php/Concept> .
@prefix orcid: <http://orcid.org> .
@prefix np: <http://www.nanopub.org/nschema#> .
@prefix pav: <http://purl.org/pav/> .
sub:Head{
    this: np:hasAssertion sub:Assertion ;
        np:hasProvenance sub:Provenance ;
        np:hasPublicationInfo sub:Pubinfo ;
        a np:Nanopublication .
}
sub:assertion{
    cw:malaria cw:Trasmitted_by cw:mosquitoes.
}
sub:provenance{
    sub:assertion pav:authoredBy cw:BobSmith ;
        pav:createdOn "2008-08-05"^^xsd:date .
}
sub:pubinfo{
    this: dct:created "2019-05-03"^^xsd:dateTime ;
        pav:createdBy orcid:0000-0002-1144-6265 .
}
```

Fig. 1. Example of a typical nanopub [8]. (Color figure online)

In Fig. 1, the blue box illustrates the assertion graph, the smallest unit of a statement. The orange box represents the assertion provenance, and it describes how the assertion was generated and the methods used to compose it. The publication info graph comprises the information regarding the nanopub, like assertion subject, authors, rights information, and creation date, represented in the yellow box. Finally, the head graph represents the relation between the cited graphs and a triple to identify the file as a nanopub [8]. Kuhn et al. [15] report that the FDP and the LD approach are utterly necessary for scientific data management. Nevertheless, up to now, we do not yet have a robust, portable set of technologies to manage and steward data resources.

2.2 The Impact of Poor Data Curation in Genomics

Genbank[1], Uniprot[2], ENA[3], and DDBJ[4] are traditional genomic databases used world-wide. Despite that, they have well-known issues reported by researchers [3]. For instance, GenBank is one of the most used. Despite being constituted by many databases, it still lacks several data controls and management issues [16].

Historically, data modelers or data experts did not contribute to designing genomic databases. Consequently, today's researchers who need to reuse genomic data (a.k.a, data reusers) often make intense efforts to discover and obtain datasets. Usually, they extract and test data trustworthiness by doing hand-made scripts. However, they frequently need to interoperate datasets with other databases and even refactor, parse or filter the data. Thus, duplication, inconsistency, inaccuracy, incompleteness, and outdatedness are frequent labour-intensive problems genomic researchers face [4].

Our previous work [17] has investigated data issues in some genomic databases, considering two data reusers personas: humans and machines. We scrutinised the FDP as the theoretical foundation to compose an evaluation framework for these genomic databases. The framework focused on the features of digital genomic objects to facilitate their discovery, access, interoperability, and reuse by data reusers. We created an evaluation framework on seven well-known genomic databases; the experimental results were below their beliefs and expectations. For instance, GenBank was only the sixth database compliant with the evaluation process, showing poor interoperability and reusability results for the machine-readable scenario [17].

2.3 Related Works

Several approaches addressing reusability for digital objects are present in the literature. One exemplary project is the nanopublication dataset of monogenic rare gene-disease associations (DisGeNET) [18]. It contemplates more than one million nanopubs referring to manually curated disease-gene associations following the DisGeNET model. The nanopubs are generated by automatically extracting the existing DisGeNET dataset, making them machine-automatable and ensuring immutable, permanent, and verifiable digital objects.

---

[1] https://www.ncbi.nlm.nih.gov/genbank/.
[2] https://www.uniprot.org/.
[3] https://www.ebi.ac.uk/ena/browser/home.
[4] https://www.ddbj.nig.ac.jp/index-e.html.

WikiPathWay is another nanopub project that stores assertions of biological pathway models, including metabolic, signalling, and genetic pathways [19]. The project's curators highlighted that nanopubs increase findability and reusability due to data provenance and the adoption of Globally Unique and Persistent Identifiers (GUPI).

NeXtProt employs nanopubs focusing on knowledge integration. In this case, human proteins (meta)data are extracted from the UniProtKB/Swiss-Prot database (one of the most used biological databases) and incorporated into the nanopub statements with other relevant information [20]. This approach focuses on provenance to increase discoverability and to establish quality thresholds. Provenance plays a crucial part in the judgment of data reliability, mainly when dealing with machine-actionable processes.

Prospective and retrospective data provenance has an essential role for nanopubs, representing two graphs (provenance and publication info graphs) of the four required in the original schema. Developing a nanopub schema that devotedly reflects the provenance associated with the data demands some effort when attending highly consolidated standards such as PROV-O.

Nevertheless, Asif et al. [11] state that a substantial part of nanopublications does not guarantee provenance and still has obstacles associated with semantic interoperability. The non-use of a suitable methodology, the possible limited data and expertise about the related domain, and the concepts of nanopubs may compromise the captured data and the nanopub itself. Additionally, the authors state that many nanopubs misunderstand the authoring roles, as they do not cite the assertion author(s), only the author(s) of the nanopub. In addition, the authors argue that a more profound analysis during the development and generation of data models for nanopubs is needed.

A well-founded reusability and interoperability approach for machine-readable processes may have a critical role in advancing knowledge discoverability, preventing information loss, reducing time, labour, and cost for data producers [21]. Initiatives like the FAIR principles are not new, although they can create a more robust and concise data reuse scenario for the existing data dilemmas. The convergence of semantic-related concepts and technologies is essential to mature this scenario and make data more understandable. The use of ontologies, controlled vocabularies, LD technologies, and other theories can provide this context [21, 22].

This paper proposes an approach to provide a well-established data model for GenBank genomic data. As previously mentioned, GenBank was one of the lowest in compliance with FAIR principles. Thus, we choose it as a use case. As pointed earlier, there is necessary to build a more reliable data environment for data interoperation and reuse.

Nanopubs can be very useful to circumvent the issues mentioned in this section. Nevertheless, there is still room for improvements in the data provenance and semantics of the nanopub data. Based on this, we propose an enhanced nanopub model to manage genomic data centered on semantic interoperability and provenance-aware concerns.

3   GAP (Genome Assembly NanoPublication)

The GAP approach combines related approaches to store GBAD data, emphasising data provenance, semantic interoperability, and machine-readable formats. We adopt the nanopublication approach to propose the GAP data model due to its naturalness of generating a more interoperable, reusable, and flexible data environment. To compose the GAP model, we needed to understand the meaning of each (meta)data stored and the data reusability scenario. As a first step, a genomic specialist contributed to better acknowledging the data and composing a data draft to generate the GAP model. Next, we recognised that supplementary metadata associated ought to be added to the schema.

These metadata stand for identifying the related genomic organism of GBAD (stored in NCBI taxonomy database) and articles that cite the data stored in GBAD (stored in PubMed articles database). This supplementary metadata is crucial to understand the stored information better and to increase knowledge discoverability.

To support that, we upgraded the GAP model to three different levels of nanopubs schemas (Fig. 2): (i) GBAD nanopub schema, referring to the metadata stored in GBAD (in green); (ii) the Organism nanopub schema referring to the organism taxonomy metadata (in purple); and (iii) the Article nanopub schema, related to scientific publications that cite the stored assembly data (in orange).

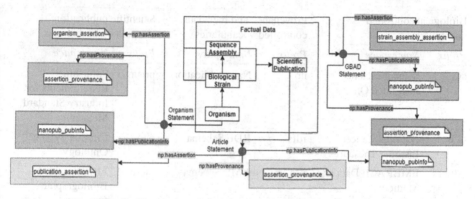

Fig. 2. Nanopubs schema diagrams (Color figure online)

The next step was to specify how to represent the metadata. Besides, how this should be implemented adequately and which ontologies could be used to reproduce the semantical environment of GBAD data. To support enhanced semantics, the model used domain-controlled vocabularies. We adopted GUPI, avoided data literals (only used in particular cases such as publisher names), and provided a schema of nanopubs concentrating on their metadata provenance.

We used a total of 20 controlled vocabularies to deal with the complexity of representing three levels of the GAP model. The main ontologies to represent the biological data were the Semantic science Integrated Ontology (SIO) [23], the EMBRACE Data And Methods (EDAM) ontology [24], and the National Cancer Institute Thesaurus (NCIt) [25]. These ontologies are some of the most used when representing biological data. In addition, we adopted seven other biological ontologies to support the terms associated with GBAD metadata. Another significant point is the composition of the nanopubs schema for scientific articles. In this case, we utilised four additional ontologies related to semantic aggregation for the domain of scientific publications.

During the composition of the three nanopubs schemas, we established vocabularies to describe provenance and metadata in the nanopublication graphs. To compose and control provenance and publication info on nanopub graphs, we follow the W3C standard PROV ontology (PROV-O) [12]. PROV-O provides clear upper classes, relationships, and restrictions to frame any provenance. The nanopub graphs follow the Entity, Activity, and Agent concepts defined by the PROV model.

In addition, we used the Provenance, Authoring, and Versioning (PAV) ontology to describe authorship, curation, and digital creation of online resources [26], and we used DC terms for general metadata. Table 1 shows a summary of the most used semantic controlled vocabularies in the three-level data model. We use RDF to compose the nanopub data models to represent Genbank (meta)data. The three-level data model is serialised in TriG syntax to follow the pattern of the nanopub concept.

Table 1. Prefixes and descriptions of the most common namespaces

Biological controlled vocabularies		Provenance and metadata controlled vocabularies		Scientific publication controlled vocabularies	
Prefix	*Namespace*	*Prefix*	*Namespace*	*Prefix*	*Namespace*
sio	Semanticscience Integrated Ontology	np	Nanopublication	prism	Publishing Requirements for Industry Standard Metadata
ncit	National Cancer Institute Thesaurus	rdfs	RDF Schema	cito	Citation Typing Ontology
edam	EMBRACE Data and Methods	xsd	XML Schema	fabio	FBBR-aligned Bibliographic Ontology
pato	The Phenotype and Trait Ontology	prov	Provenance Ontology	data	DataCite Ontology
so	Sequence Ontology	pav	Provenance, Authoring and Versioning		
fbcv	FlyBase Controlled Vocabulary	dcterms	DCMI Metadata Terms		

Figure 2 illustrates that the different levels of the model are complementary. Associations were established within the nanopubs by referencing GUPI. Furthermore, it was essential to transform most data literals into identifiers to compose a semantically interoperable environment. Kuhn et al. [27] cite that the fewer literals there are in nanopublications, the better the use of machine-actionable processes will be.

Figure 3 illustrates the core section of the data model, the GBAD nanopub schema (following the colour schema present in Fig. 1). The complete versions of the Organism, GBAD, and Article nanopubs data models are available in a Github repository[5].

The GBAD nanopub assertion graph (blue box) stores all the (meta)data related to an organism assembly. All the (meta)data were transformed following the domain ontologies to obtain a fully semantic understandable scenario. In order to associate the related metadata present in the Organism nanopub, the SIO concept "SIO_000628" was used. This concept states a reference between two correlated nanopubs, the GBAD nanopub and the Organism nanopub (in this case, represented as "org_npub:5693").

The provenance graph (red box) comprises four different blocks of triples obeying concepts of PROV-O ontology, two entities generated by an automatic assertion and attributed to the submitter, the National Center for Biotechnology Information (NCBI), the owner of GenBank databases. To generate direct access to original and other related data, PROV concept "prov:hadPrimarySource" is used to connect to the FTP directory of the stored assembly data, which contains raw data, Genomic GenBank Format (.GBFF), and other associated files.

The publication info graph (yellow box) follows the same PROV-O concepts and stores the nanopub provenance in five distinct triples blocks of Entity, Activity, and Agent. Besides data for nanopub provenance, this schema differentiates the authors of the assertion from the curators of the nanopublication (using ORCID unique digital identifier). Additionally, in "dcterms:dateSubmmitted", we prioritise using URIs instead of literals to identify related dates. By doing this, we may apply much faster filters when accessing the nanopubs by machine-readable processes [27].

Besides the assertion graph, the Organism and Article nanopub models follow the same head, provenance, and publication info template graphs present in the GBAD example. Additionally, in their publication info graphs, all nanopub levels within the GAP model use the "dcterms:subject" concept. The adoption of this concept aims to achieve better information discovery at the three levels of nanopubs and distinguish the content present between the levels.

4   Computational Experiments

We designed and executed a computational experiment composed of scripts to scrape and transform the GenBank (meta)data to nanopublications to evaluate the nanopublication models. Subsequently, we analyse the results with the real scenario of extracting (meta)data from GenBank and compare it with well-known nanopub datasets.

4.1   From Scraping Genomic Data to Generating Nanopublications

We developed Python scripts to automatically access, scrape, crawl and transform the collected GBAD data using the created nanopub schemas. We used the scripts to generate nanopubs related to assembly data of *Trypanosoma cruzi* and *Leishmania* diseases to test the schema. Additionally, we used the Scrapy framework to crawl and scrape the

---

[5] https://github.com/MatheusFeijoo/Genome-Assembly-nanoPublication.

```
@prefix this: <https://github.com/GenKnowlets/genknowlets/>.
@prefix sub: <https://github.com/GenKnowlets/genknowlets/>.
@prefix dcterms: <http://purl.org/dc/terms/>.
@prefix prov: <http://www.w3.org/ns/prov#>.
@prefix pav: <http://purl.org/pav/>.
...
@prefix edam: <http://edamontology.org/page>.

sub:GCA_015033655_Head {
  this: np:hasAssertion sub:GCA_015033655_assertion;
  np:hasProvenance sub:GCA_015033655_provenance;
  np:hasPublicationInfo sub:GCA_015033655_PublicationInfo;
  a np:Nanopublication.
}

sub:GCA_015033655_provenance {
  sub:GCA_015033655_assertion a prov:Entity;
  prov:wasGeneratedBy sub:GCA_015033655_automaticAssertion;
  prov:wasAttributedTo sub:GCA_015033655_submitter;
  pav:curatedBy sub:GCA_015033655_submitter;
  prov:hadPrimarySource <https://www.ncbi.nlm.nih.gov/assembly/>;
  dcterms:accessRights <https://www.ncbi.nlm.nih.gov/home/about/policies/>;
  eco:ECO_0000501 <https://www.ncbi.nlm.nih.gov/assembly/GCA_015033655.1/>;
  prov:wasDerivedFrom sub:GCA_015033655_ftp.
  sub:GCA_015033655_submitter a foaf:organization, prov:Agent;
  foaf:name "University of Georgia"@en.
  sub:GCA_015033655_automaticAssertion a prov:Activity;
  rdfs:type eco:ECO_0000203;
  prov:wasAssociatedWith ncit:C45799, sub:GCA_015033655_submitter;
  dcterms:dateSubmitted "DATETIME"^^xsd:datetime;
  npubDate:creationDay npubDate:20201103;
  npubDate:creationMonth npubDate:202011;
  npubDate:creationYear npubDate:2020.
  sub:GCA_015033655_ftp a prov:Entity;
  rdfs:type dcterms:dataset;
  pav:curatedBy sub:GCA_015033655_submitter;
  prov:hadPrimarySource <https://ftp.ncbi.nlm.nih.gov/genomes/all/GCA/015/033/655/GCA_015033655.1_ASM1503365v1>.

sub:GCA_015033655_assertion {
  ncbi_asbID:GCA_015033655 rdfs:type edam:data_2292, edam:data_0925;
  sio:SIO_000628 sub:GCA_015033655_strain;
  prov:wasGeneratedBy sub:GCA_015033655_gbAssembly;
  prov:wasGeneratedBy sub:GCA_015033655_wgs;
  edam:data_3273 <https://www.ncbi.nlm.nih.gov/biosample/SAMN12275290/>;
  ncit:C175890 <https://www.ncbi.nlm.nih.gov/bioproject/PRJNA554625/>.
  sub:GCA_015033655_strain sio:SIO_000628 sio:SIO_010055;
  edam:data_1046 "Y done C6"@en;
  sio:SIO_000497 org_npub:s693.
  org_npub:s693 sio:SIO_000628 sio:SIO_010000.
  sub:GCA_015033655_gbAssembly sio:SIO_000628 so:SO_0001248;
  rdfs:type fbcv:FBcv_0003237;
  ncit:C25554 so:SO_0000340;
  ncit:C71460 "SMRT Link v. 5.0.1"@en;
  obi:OBI_0001939 "130.0x"@en;
  efo:EFO_0003739 "PacBio Sequel; Illumina NextSeq"@en;
  rdfs:type pav:latest_version.
  sub:GCA_015033655_wgs sio:SIO_000628 ncit:C101294;
  dcterms:identifier <https://www.ncbi.nlm.nih.gov/nuccore/WNWY00000000.1/>;
  pav:version "WNWY01"@en.
}

sub:GCA_015033655_PublicationInfo {
  this: a prov:entity;
  prov:wasGeneratedBy sub:GCA_015033655_automaticAssertion;
  prov:wasAttributedTo sub:GCA_015033655_software, sub:GCA_015033655_npubCreators;
  prov:wasDerivedFrom ncit:C45799;
  prov:hadPrimarySource <https://www.ncbi.nlm.nih.gov/assembly/>;
  dcterms:accessRights <http://opendatacommons.org/licenses/odbl/1.0/>;
  dcterms:subject so:SO_0001248, sio:SIO_010055.
  sub:GCA_015033655_automaticAssertion a prov:Activity;
  rdfs:type eco:ECO_0000203;
  prov:wasAssociatedWith ncit:C45799, prov:softwareAgent, ncit:C122473;
  dcterms:dateSubmitted "DATETIME"^^xsd:datetime;
  npubDate:creationDay npubDate:20210515;
  npubDate:creationMonth npubDate:202105;
  npubDate:creationYear npubDate:2021.
  ncit:C45799 a foaf:organization, prov:Agent;
  foaf:name "NCBI - National Center for Biotechnology Information"@en.
  sub:GCA_015033655_software a prov:softwareAgent;
  rdfs:type prov:softwareAgent;
  foaf:name "genscraper"@en;
  pav:version "v1";
  pav:createdBy <ORCID creator>;
  dcterms:source <https://github.com/GenKnowlets>;
  edam:data_1188 <https://doi.org/10.5281/zenodo.4818638>.
  sub:GCA_015033655_npubCreators a prov:Agent;
  rdfs:type ncit:C122473;
  pav:createdBy <ORCID creators>.
}
```

Fig. 3. GBAD nanopub example in RDF/TriG notation using GAP data model. (Color figure online)

data from GBAD and related databases. Figure 4 illustrates the conceptual processes and the steps designed to generate the nanopubs.

The initial step receives as input the URL referring to an assembly of the diseases stored in GBAD and the ORCID of the data curators. The script analyses and searches for existing nanopubs referring to the instance in GBAD and its organisms. If there are no nanopubs, the following step extracts (meta)data referring to this organism in NCBI databases and scrapes (meta)data referring to the GBAD.

Simultaneously, a routine begins scraping GBAD instances (meta)data associated with the given organism. From there, all related GBAD registers are concentrated and stored in a JSON backup file. The subsequent step scrapes the PubMed database, aiming to collect (meta)data from scientific papers referencing the gathered instances.

After completing the previous steps, three JSON files are produced, each related to the levels of the nanopubs model. The following step begins converting the collected (meta)data to nanopubs based on the created model with those files.

The first level, transform the referenced organism (meta)data following the data model. Then, add the provenance related to the extraction and generation of the nanopub. In this transformation, the script creates a GUPI referring to the nanopub following the NCBI Taxonomy id of the organism.

As the second level, the code converts the data collected from the GBAD. The GBAD nanopub model includes all possible fields that can be stored. However, GBAD data are entered manually, and the entire model was not used. In this conversion, the GUPI of GBAD nanopublication follows the id present on GBAD. The GUPI referring to the organism nanopub is inserted into the nanopub, as mentioned in Sect. 3.

Finally, at the last level, data referring to scientific papers that cite the collected GBAD instances are transformed to nanopubs. To relate these nanopubs with the GBAD nanopubs, the GUPI created for the GBAD nanopubs is used. The PubMed *id* is used on the creation of the GUPI of this nanopub.

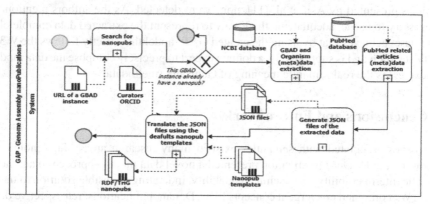

Fig. 4. The conceptual process to scrape, crawl and transform genomic data to nanopubs.

4.2 Nanopub Dataset

The nanopub dataset corresponds to two nanopubs of a given organism, 54 nanopubs of GBAD, and 14 nanopubs of scientific papers represented by 6.139 RDF triples. We can standardise the extracted (meta)data to be semantically understandable by machines by adopting the GAP data model. Only 12,99% of the (meta)data presented in the generated dataset are literals. In this case, they represent data about scientific publication tags, abstract text, names of provenance agents and insert data manually. We highlight that they are hard to format due to their heterogeneity.

It is possible to use SPARQL data query systems after converting the data to a machine-understandable format. Several works embrace extracting (meta)data from GenBank using unique approaches to perform the extractions [28, 29]. Each approach offers different results that are often not reused by other works.

This scenario can generate two problems: (i) increase in the amount of specific (meta)data and (ii) increase the effort to develop (meta)data extraction applications for specific GenBank scenarios. Our dataset is an example that circumvents these two problems, as it provides semantic-understandable (meta)data present in GenBank and eases the effort in producing new approaches for automatic (meta)data extraction. Additionally, the nanopub dataset can exploit the Linked Open Data (LOD) scenario to interoperate with other machine-readable data resources. LOD can be crucial in the genomic field by generating new knowledge, increasing information quality, and reducing gaps.

Another observation is about the provenance control improvement in nanopubs. Our results are comparable with the ones obtained by Asif et al. [11]. The authors evaluate the (meta)data quality of five well-known biologic nanopub repositories. Asif et al. state a lack of detailed data provenance in the provenance and publication info graphs of the analysed repositories, which may be related to the mechanism when capturing the data.

Additionally, Asif et al. found issues in the publication info graphs of the dataset. Data curators misunderstand when they designate the authors of a statement, curators, and creators of nanopublications [11]. When comparing our dataset with the types of problems presented by Asif et al. [11], none were detected. As the authors mention, it is necessary to use an adequate methodology to represent the extracted data completely. Our dataset achieves that by using the created GAP model that strictly follows the W3C PROV standard and is supported by a domain expert to precisely compose the data model that expresses the real semantic meaning of GenBank (meta)data.

5   Conclusions and Future Work

Data issues associated with semantics exist in many research areas; the genomic is just one example. Our investigation presented a novel data model approach to augment semantic interoperability for machine readability, indicating a feasible solution to these issues. We combined convergent concepts like LD, nanopublications, retrospective data provenance, FDP, and Web Ontology Language to mitigate machine data reuse issues. We developed a novel nanopub data model to transform and inject semantic meaning in one of the most used and problematic genomic databases, the GenBank.

Unlike the traditional scenario experienced by genomic data reusers, the GAP model increases the data semantic meaning and interoperability by using controlled vocabularies ontologies and consolidated models for data interchange. It can contribute to solving the data issues and constitutes a more robust way to represent data provenance in nanopubs. As future work, we intend to improve the data model to support: (i) better authoring, provenance representation, and interoperability between data silos; (ii) to scrape, transform and publish GenBank data in a machine-readable scenario; and (iii) to adapt the created model to use in other genomic databases; (iv) evaluate our approach in other knowledge domains.

Acknowledgements. This study was financed in part by the National Council for Scientific and Technological Development (CNPq), Programa de Educação Tutorial (PET), Conselho Nacional de Pesquisa – Grant Number 315399/2018-0 and Coordenação de Aperfeiçoamento de Pessoal de Nível Superior – Brasil (CAPES) – Finance Code 001.

References

1. Hey, T., Trefethen, A.: The data deluge: an e-science perspective. In: Grid Computing: Making the Global Infrastructure a Reality. Wiley-Blackwell (2003). https://doi.org/10.1002/047086 7167.ch36
2. Bayat, A.: Bioinformatics: science, medicine, and the future. Bioinformatics (2002). https://doi.org/10.1136/bmj.324.7344.1018
3. Koh, J., Lee, M., Brusic, V.: A classification of biological data artifacts. In: Workshop on Database Issues in Biological Databases, pp. 53–57 (2005)
4. Fan, W.: Data quality: from theory to practice. In: Proceedings of the ACM SIGMOD International Conference Management Data, vol. 44, pp. 7–18 (2015). https://doi.org/10.1145/285 4006.2854008
5. Wilkinson, M., Dumontier, M., Aalbersberg, I., Appleton, G., et al.: The FAIR Guiding Principles for scientific data management and stewardship. Sci Data (2016). https://doi.org/10.1038/sdata.2016.18
6. Buneman, P., Khanna, S., Tan, W.-C.: Data provenance: some basic issues. In: Kapoor, S., Prasad, S. (eds.) FSTTCS 2000. LNCS, vol. 1974, pp. 87–93. Springer, Heidelberg (2000). https://doi.org/10.1007/3-540-44450-5_6
7. Cruz, S.M.S., Campos, M.L.M., Mattoso, M.: Towards a taxonomy of provenance in scientific workflow management systems (2009). https://doi.org/10.1109/services-i.2009.18
8. Mons, B., Velterop, J.: Nanopublication in the e-science era. In: Proceedings of the Workshop on Semantic Web Applications in Scientific Discourse (2009)
9. Groth, P., Gibson, A., Velterop, J.: The anatomy of a nanopublication. Inf. Serv. Use, 51–56 (2010). https://doi.org/10.3233/ISU-2010-0613
10. Chichester, C., Gaudet, P., Karch, O., Groth, P., et al.: Querying neXtProt nanopublications and their value for insights on sequence variants and tissue expression. JWS **29**, 3–11 (2014)
11. Asif, I., Chen-Burger, J., Alasdair, J.: Data quality issues in current nanopublications. In: IEEE 14th e-Science (2019). https://doi.org/10.1109/eScience.2019.00069
12. PROV-O: The PROV Ontology. https://www.w3.org/TR/prov-o/
13. Qingyu, C., Justin, Z., Karin, V.: Duplicates, redundancies and inconsistencies in the primary nucleotide databases: a descriptive study. Database (2017). https://doi.org/10.1093/database/baw163
14. Attwood, K., Agit, B., Ellis, L.: Longevity of biological databases. Embnet **21**, 803 (2015)
15. Kuhn, T., Peñuela, A., Malic, A., et al.: Nanopublications: a growing resource of provenance-centric scientific linked data. In: IEEE 14th e-Science (2018)
16. Gonçalves, R., Musen, M.: The variable quality of metadata about biological samples used in biomedical experiments. Sci Data (2019). https://doi.org/10.1038/sdata.2019.21
17. Feijoo, M., Jardim, R., Cruz, S.M.S., Campos, M.: Evaluating FAIRness of genomic databases. In: Grossmann, G., Ram, S. (eds.) Advances in Conceptual Modeling. ER 2020. LNCS, vol. 12584, pp. 128–137. Springer, Cham (2020). https://doi.org/10.1007/978-3-030-65847-2_12
18. Queralt-Rosinach, N., Kuhn, T., Chichester, C., Dumontier, M., Sanz, F., Furlong, L.: Publishing DisGeNET as nanopublications. Semantic Web **7**, 519–528 (2016)
19. Martens, M., Ammar, A., Riutta, A., et al.: WikiPathways: connecting communities. Nucleic Acids Res. (2020). https://doi.org/10.1093/nar/gkaa1024
20. Chichester, C., Karch, O., Gaudet, P., et al.: Converting neXtProt into Linked Data and Nanopublications, pp. 147–153. IOS Press (2015). https://doi.org/10.3233/SW-140149
21. Sielemann, K., Hafner, A., Pucker, B.: The reuse of public datasets in the life sciences: potential risks and rewards. PeerJ (2020). https://doi.org/10.7717/peerj.9954
22. de Boer, V., Bonestroo, I., Koolen, M., Hoekstra, R.: A linked data model for data scopes. In: Garoufallou, E., Ovalle-Perandones, M.-A. (eds.) MTSR 2020. CCIS, vol. 1355, pp. 345–351. Springer, Cham (2021). https://doi.org/10.1007/978-3-030-71903-6_32

23. Dumontier, M., Baker, C., et al.: The Semanticscience Integrated Ontology (SIO) for biomedical research and knowledge discovery. J. Biomed. Semantic **5**, 1–11 (2014)
24. Ison, J., Kalaš, M., Jonassen, I., et al.: EDAM: an ontology of bioinformatics operations, types of data and identifiers, topics and formats. Bioinformatics **29**, 1325–1332 (2013)
25. NCIT Thesaurus. https://ncithesaurus.nci.nih.gov/ncitbrowser/
26. PAV Ontology. https://pav-ontology.github.io/pav/
27. Kuhn, T., Taelman, R., Emonet, V., Antonatos, H., et al.: Semantic micro-contributions with decentralised nanopublication services. PeerJ Comput. Sci. **7**, e387 (2021)
28. Magge, A., Weissenbacher, D., O'Connor, K., Tahsin, T., Gonzalez, G., Scotch, M.: Geo-Boost2: a natural language processing pipeline for GenBank metadata enrichment for virus phylogeography. Bioinformatics (2020). https://doi.org/10.1093/bioinformatics/btaa647
29. Yin, Y., Du, L., Yue, B.: GenScalpel: an application for sequence retrieval and extraction from the GenBank flat file. J. Hered. (2012). https://doi.org/10.1093/jhered/ess052

A Semantic Technologies Toolkit for Bridging Early Diagnosis and Treatment in Brain Diseases: Report from the Ongoing EU-Funded Research Project ALAMEDA

Christoniki Maga-Nteve[1] , Efstratios Kontopoulos[2(✉)] , Nikos Tsolakis[1] ,
Ioannis Katakis[3] , Evangelos Mathioudis[3] , Panagiotis Mitzias[3] ,
Konstantinos Avgerinakis[2] , Georgios Meditskos[4] , Anastasios Karakostas[1],
Stefanos Vrochidis[1] , and Ioannis Kompatsiaris[1]

[1] Centre of Research and Technology, Information Technologies Institute, Hellas, Greece
{chmaga,tsolakin,akarakos,vrochidis,ikom}@iti.gr
[2] Catalink Limited, Nicosia, Cyprus
{e.kontopoulos,koafgeri}@catalink.eu
[3] Department of Computer Science, School of Sciences and Engineering, University of Nicosia,
2417 Nicosia, Cyprus
katakis.i@unic.ac.cy, {mathioudis.e,mitzias.p}@live.unic.ac.cy
[4] School of Informatics, Aristotle University of Thessaloniki, Thessaloniki, Greece
gmeditsk@csd.auth.gr

Abstract. Semantic Web technologies are increasingly being deployed in various e-health scenarios, prominently due to their inherent capacity to harmonize heterogeneous information from diverse sources and devices, as well as their capability to provide meaningful interpretations and higher-level insights. This paper reports on ongoing work in the recently started EU-funded project ALAMEDA towards a semantic toolkit for bridging the gap between early diagnosis and treatment in a variety of brain diseases. The toolkit comprises (a) a semantic model serving as the underlying knowledge base for the toolkit; (b) a flexible semantic data integration framework; (c) a semantics-enabled conversational agent for interacting with human users and other components of the ALAMEDA system.

Keywords: Ontologies · Semantic data integration · Conversational agent · Brain disease · e-health

1 Introduction

Semantic Web technologies are rapidly gaining popularity in the domain of e-health applications, where these technologies substantially facilitate the harmonization of data coming from multiple sources and devices, as well as its meaningful interpretation, providing, thus, context awareness and access to rich higher-level interpretations and insights. This paper reports on ongoing work within the context of the ALAMEDA EU-funded project (https://alamedaproject.eu/) aimed at the development of a sophisticated

© Springer Nature Switzerland AG 2022
E. Garoufallou et al. (Eds.): MTSR 2021, CCIS 1537, pp. 349–354, 2022.
https://doi.org/10.1007/978-3-030-98876-0_30

semantic toolkit for bridging the gap between early diagnosis and treatment in a variety of brain diseases: Parkinson's Disease, Multiple Sclerosis, and stroke. The key component of the toolkit is the ALAMEDA semantic model, which consists of a set of interconnected ontologies, for semantically representing all domain-pertinent concepts and entities. Operating on-top of the semantic model, two additional components of the toolkit are also presented: (a) the semantic data integration framework for populating the ontology with instance data from sensors and analysis components, and (b) the conversational agent that utilizes the ontology as a common vocabulary, facilitating interaction with human users and other components of the ALAMEDA system. Our ambition is to deliver a cutting-edge toolkit of semantics-enabled components that will facilitate medical practitioners in better monitoring the development of the end user's condition in a non-intrusive and ubiquitous fashion.

2   Conceptual Semantic Model

The overarching goal of our semantic model is to represent information that is made available via the questionnaires and the monitoring modules in the ALAMEDA system, as well as to establish semantic interoperability between the system components.

2.1   Related Work: Relevant Ontologies in Healthcare

Some of the most commonly used healthcare models for exchanging healthcare information are FHIR-HL7 (http://hl7.org/fhir/) and ICD-10 (https://bioportal.bioontology. org/ontologies/ICD10). Moreover, the Systematized Nomenclature of Medicine-Clinical Terms (SNOMED CT) [1] is a standardized, multilingual vocabulary of clinical terminology for the storage, retrieval, and exchange of electronic health data and for the representation of medical concepts. There also exist disease-specific ontologies, like the PDON Parkinson's Disease ontology [2], MSO, a multiple sclerosis ontology [3], and the Dem@care ontologies (https://demcare.eu/ontologies/) for representing knowledge relevant to dementia.

Compared to the aforementioned ontologies that can cover a subset of the respective domains, the ALAMEDA ontology seeks to address multiple aspects, consisting of modules for representing various needs, and can be easily adjustable and reusable.

2.2   Ontology Design

We relied on the *NeOn methodology* [4] for designing and developing the ALAMEDA ontology. The first phase involves the definition of the ontology requirements and the retrieval of the *Ontology Requirements Specification Document (ORSD)*. At this point, the contribution of the domain experts was crucial, as they define the use cases and propose optimal matching to ontology requirements. These requirements correspond to a set of *Competency Questions (CQs)* [5], which specify what knowledge must be entailed in the ontology. The second phase involves the development of the ontology at a primary level, where the existing ontologies that will be (re)used are defined. The final phase contains the implementation and enrichment of the ALAMEDA ontology.

2.3 Ontology Modules

The ALAMEDA model contains six modules and a main ontology: *Model* is the parent of all the hierarchical relations in ALAMEDA:

- *Home* provides information about the behavioural interpretation and reported difficulties in the home environment.
- *Lab* indicates the types of information relevant to the tests, assessments, patient's clinical and experimental records in the lab environment.
- *Person* refers to human users' sociodemographic data and represents information about persons, diseases, gender, educational levels and languages.
- *Event* provides information relevant to the entities and activities that take place in the context of the ALAMEDA use cases. Its design is based on the Event Model F [6] and the Event Ontology[1].
- *Sensors* describes information concerning the type and properties of the sensors used in the ALAMEDA system, which may be fixed on wearable. Its design was strongly influenced by SSN/SOSA [7] and the Smart Home Ontology [8].
- *Time* represents the temporal dimension, namely, the time, duration, and information of the tasks/events taking place within the ALAMEDA context.

3 Semantic Data Integration

The integration of the inputs from the various heterogeneous sources into the ALAMEDA semantic model are handled by *CASPAR (Structured Data Semantic Exploitation Framework)*[2], our domain-agnostic semantic data integration framework. CASPAR is based on the ontology population methodology and approach presented in previous works of ours [9–11]. The tool deploys the following set of interconnected mechanisms for ingesting data into a semantic model: *automated acquisition* of structured data from APIs, databases, message buses; *mapping* of input data fields to semantic entities (concepts, relationships, etc.); *semantic integration* of knowledge into a semantic repository; *semantic enrichment* of existing knowledge from Linked Open Data sources; *rule-based semantic reasoning* to unveil underlying or generate new knowledge.

CASPAR defines mappings between input data fields and respective ontology concepts for the integration of knowledge through a flexible methodology using a Domain-Specific Language (DSL) based on JSON syntax. The building blocks of a mapping are templates, individuals, and properties. A *template* serves as the mechanism for focusing on specific parts of the input. Since large pieces of input can be handled by CASPAR, defining several templates within a mapping that target specific parts allows easier maintenance of the mapping itself. A template contains a set of *individuals*, which declare the nodes that need to be created or updated in the Knowledge Graph (KG). From the perspective of using an ontology as the KG schema, an individual is an instance of one or more classes. A *property* indicates a desired edge that needs to be created in the KG, connecting a node with another node or with a literal value. Properties in mappings

---

[1] http://motools.sourceforge.net/event/event.html.
[2] https://caspar.catalink.eu/.

are defined by a set of *predicates*, meaning the relationship types of the ontology, and *objects*, which indicate the value that will be given to the property.

4 Conversational Agent

Nowadays, more and more chatbot platforms are emerging with the aim to provide personalized health services. Through a chat with the patient the chatbot gathers information related to the symptoms and the person's condition and then provides a report to the clinician, assisting this way in better managing the patient's health condition.

4.1 Related Work: Chatbots in Healthcare

There exist several chatbot applications in healthcare. Puffbot is a conversational agent that helps people with asthma [12]. EVA is another chatbot that helps people to self-manage their diabetes, by educating them, interacting with them, and giving them recommendations [13]. HOLMeS, on the other hand, serves as a medical recommendation system designed to autonomously handle discussions with patients and chat and act like a human physician helping patients in choosing their disease prevention pathway [14].

4.2 A Chatbot for Brain Diseases in the ALAMEDA Project

The *ALAMEDA chatbot* will gather lifestyle data generated from static and wearable sensors and will identify changes in the users' lifestyle. Unusual measurements will trigger the agent to ask the patient questions, and categorize these measurements based on the ALAMEDA semantic model (see Sect. 2). We have identified the following requirements for the ALAMEDA chatbot:

- *Non-intrusive*: The conversational agent should not interfere with the patients' daily activities. It should be up to the user to define how much information she wants to share and when is the appropriate time to be inquired for information.
- *Adaptive and personalized*: The agent should be unique, tailored for its user (patient or caregiver), and should be able to adapt based on their needs. Based on a sentiment analysis component [15], the agent will be able to sense the user's dissatisfaction.
- *Information disambiguation*: In the cases of missing, erroneous, or conflicting input, the conversational agent should be able to resolve the issue by sending an appropriate enquiry to the user [16].

In order for all the intelligent ALAMEDA components to communicate, a common semantic dictionary is necessary. In the case of the agent, such a resource is necessary whenever communication with human participants is required. The ALAMEDA semantic model (see Sect. 2) serves as the common language between artificial agents and humans (patients and caregivers) (see Fig. 1).

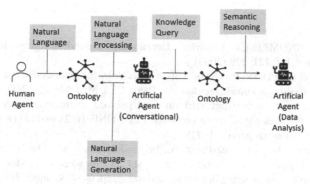

Fig. 1. The ALAMEDA ontology as a common vocabulary between human and artificial agents.

In order to illustrate the orchestration of the above components, let us present the following use-case scenario:

1. **(Intention)** User wishes to report to the chatbot that he feels his heart pacing fast.
2. **(Natural Language)** User types *"I feel my heart pacing fast"* in the chatbot app.
3. **(Natural Language Understanding)** The conversational agent identifies the intent that the user wants to declare an event of type: `increased_heart_rate`.
4. **(Knowledge Query)** As a knowledge management process, an `increased_heart_rate` event declared by the user initiates a knowledge query. The system has to confirm the event with the sensors.
5. **(Semantic Reasoning)** The Semantic Reasoning component retrieves the patient's data (stored in their mobile device) to check if there are *recent* sensor data annotated with the `increased_heart_rate` event entity from the event ontology.
6. **(Natural Language Generation)** If not, the chatbot reassures the user that everything looks normal, and suggests relaxing. The heart rate will be monitored again in five minutes and reported back to the patient.

5 Conclusions and Next Steps

This paper reported on ongoing work within the ALAMEDA EU-funded project involving the deployment of a toolkit based on semantic technologies that will constitute the backbone of the overall e-health system for brain diseases. We presented the current state of the ALAMEDA semantic model, the semantic data integration framework, and the conversational agent. The first iteration of the semantic toolkit is scheduled for release in early 2022; we will then start working closely with our medical partners towards practically deploying the involved modules in the project's use cases.

Acknowledgment. ALAMEDA has received funding from the European Union's Horizon 2020 research and innovation programme under grant agreement No GA101017558.

References

1. Donnelly, K.: SNOMED-CT: the advanced terminology and coding system for eHealth. Stud. Health Technol. Inf. **121**, 279 (2006)
2. Younesi, E., et al.: PDON: Parkinson's disease ontology for representation and modeling of the Parkinson's disease knowledge domain. Theor. Biol. Med. Model. **12**(1), 1–17 (2015)
3. Malhotra, A., et al.: Knowledge retrieval from pubmed abstracts and electronic medical records with the multiple sclerosis ontology. PLoS ONE **10**(2), e0116718 (2015). https://doi.org/10.1371/journal.pone.0116718
4. Suárez-Figueroa, M.C., Gómez-Pérez, A., Fernández-López, M.: The NeOn methodology for ontology engineering. In: Suárez-Figueroa, M.C., Gómez-Pérez, A., Motta, E., Gangemi, A. (eds.) Ontology engineering in a networked world, pp. 9–34. Springer, Heidelberg (2012). https://doi.org/10.1007/978-3-642-24794-1_2
5. Bezerra, C., Freitas, F., Santana, F.: Evaluating ontologies with competency questions. In: 2013 IEEE/WIC/ACM Int. Joint Conf. on Web Intelligence (WI) and Intelligent Agent Technologies (IAT), Vol. 3, pp. 284–285. IEEE (2013)
6. Scherp, A., Franz, T., Saathoff, C., Staab, S.: A core ontology on events for representing occurrences in the real world. Multimed. Tools Appl. **58**(2), 293–331 (2012)
7. Haller, A., et al.: The modular SSN ontology: a joint W3C and OGC standard specifying the semantics of sensors, observations, sampling, and actuation. Semantic Web **10**(1), 9–32 (2019)
8. Sezer, O.B., Can, S.Z., Dogdu, E.: Development of a smart home ontology and the implementation of a semantic sensor network simulator: an Internet of Things approach. In: 2015 Int. Conf. on Collaboration Technologies & Systems, pp. 12–18. IEEE (2015)
9. Kontopoulos, E., Mitzias, P., Riga, M., Kompatsiaris, I.: A domain-agnostic tool for scalable ontology population and enrichment from diverse linked data sources. In: DAMDID/RCDL, pp. 184–190 (2017)
10. Riga, M., Mitzias, P., Kontopoulos, E., Kompatsiaris, I.: PROPheT – ontology population and semantic enrichment from linked data sources. In: Kalinichenko, L., Manolopoulos, Y., Malkov, O., Skvortsov, N., Stupnikov, S., Sukhomlin, V. (eds.) Data Analytics and Management in Data Intensive Domains: XIX International Conference, DAMDID/RCDL 2017, Moscow, Russia, October 10–13, 2017, Revised Selected Papers, pp. 157–168. Springer International Publishing, Cham (2018). https://doi.org/10.1007/978-3-319-96553-6_12
11. Kontopoulos, E.; et al.: An extensible semantic data fusion framework for autonomous vehicles. In: 15th Int. Conf. on Advances in Semantic Processing, pp. 5–11 (2021)
12. Teixeira, M.S., Maran, V., Dragoni, M.: The interplay of a conversational ontology and AI planning for health dialogue management. In: 36th Annual ACM Symposium on Applied Computing, pp. 611–619 (2021)
13. Anastasiadou, M., Alexiadis, A., Polychronidou, E., Votis, K., Tzovaras, D.: A prototype educational virtual assistant for diabetes management. In: 2020 IEEE 20th Int. Conf. on Bioinformatics and Bioengineering (BIBE), pp. 999–1004. IEEE (2020)
14. Amato, F., et al.: Chatbots meet eHealth: automatizing healthcare. In: WAIAH@AI*IA, pp. 40–49 (2017)
15. Agathangelou, P., Katakis, I.: A hybrid deep learning network for modelling opinionated content. In: 34th ACM/SIGAPP Symp. on Applied Computing, pp. 1051–1053 (2019)
16. Panagiotou, N., et al.: Intelligent urban data monitoring for smart cities. In: Berendt, B., et al. (eds.) Machine Learning and Knowledge Discovery in Databases: European Conference, ECML PKDD 2016, Riva del Garda, Italy, September 19-23, 2016, Proceedings, Part III, pp. 177–192. Springer International Publishing, Cham (2016). https://doi.org/10.1007/978-3-319-46131-1_23

Track on Cultural Collections
and Applications, and General Session

Publishing Cultural Heritage Collections of Ghent with Linked Data Event Streams

Brecht Van de Vyvere[1]($\boxtimes$)(iD), Olivier Van D'Huynslager[2], Achraf Atauil[3],
Maarten Segers[3], Leen Van Campe[3], Niels Vandekeybus[3], Sofie Teugels[2],
Alina Saenko[4], Pieter-Jan Pauwels[3], and Pieter Colpaert[1](iD)

[1] IDLab, Department of Electronics and Information Systems,
Ghent University - imec, Ghent, Belgium
{brecht.vandevyvere,pieter.colpaert}@ugent.be
[2] Design Museum Gent, Ghent, Belgium
{olivier.vandhuynslager,sofie.teugels}@stad.gent
[3] District09, Ghent, Belgium
{achraf.atauil,maarten.segers,leen.vancampe,
niels.vandekeybus,pieter-jan.pauwels}@district09.gent
[4] Meemoo, Ghent, Belgium
alina.saenko@meemoo.be
https://idlab.technology/, https://www.designmuseumgent.be/,
https://district09.gent/, https://www.meemoo.be/

Abstract. Cultural heritage institutions maintain digital artefacts of their collections using Collection Management Software (CMS). In order to attract new audiences, these data should be interoperable with and reusable within other Web APIs. In this article, we explain how we applied Flemish Linked Data Standards (OSLO) to make the data within the Axiell Collections CMS interoperable, and how we applied the method of Linked Data Event Streams (LDES) for making the data reusable. The LDES has been successfully adopted by third parties to then host subject pages, a SPARQL endpoint, a substring fragmentation for autocompletion purposes, and a IIIF enriched LDES. To this end, we see LDES as the core Web API of a CMS, allowing third parties to take up other querying and processing tasks on their own machines.

Keywords: Collection Management Software · Linked Data Event Streams · Cultural information publication

1 Introduction

Digital cultural heritage can play an important role in tackling urban societal issues, such as social inclusion. To this end, Collections of Ghent[1] (CoGhent)

---

[1] Collections of Ghent is co-financed by the European Regional Development Fund through the Urban Innovative Actions (UIA) initiative. More info: https://www.collectie.gent/.

© Springer Nature Switzerland AG 2022
E. Garoufallou et al. (Eds.): MTSR 2021, CCIS 1537, pp. 357–369, 2022.
https://doi.org/10.1007/978-3-030-98876-0_31

explores the role and capacity of the collections from four museums and one archive in the City of Ghent[2]. Together with stories coming from the communities themselves, these will be displayed on a multi-voice platform to spark new conversations and relations between cultural heritage organizations (CHOs) and their communities, thus fostering a more inclusive reading of our cultural heritage. The collections of the CHOs and the communities' digitized stories need to be integrated into this platform by replicating and synchronizing the data. Currently, these CHOs use the Collections Management Software (CMS) Axiell Collections (AC)[3], which exposes their collection objects' metadata with an Application Programming Interface (API). This API offers different functionalities, such as an advanced search language statement and autocompletion. However, the platform of Coghent needs to integrate data from heterogeneous sources and therefore requires the usage of persistent identifiers and Linked Data at the source, which are not supported by the CHO's version (Adlib Xplus 4.3), and the Linked Data must be exposed with a replication and synchronization API to efficiently create an up-to-date copy of the data. In this article, we will explain how such a Linked Data API can be created on top of AC, and how, among others, a Digital Asset Management System (DAMS) can use this API to enrich the images of objects with metadata stored in AC.

Since 1999, replicating and synchronizing the data repository of a CHO has been performed with the Open Archives Initiative Protocol for Metadata Harvesting (OAI-PMH) protocol [1]. By executing specific HTTP calls in a linear fashion, the whole repository can be retrieved in XML format. One major drawback of this approach is that Representational State Transfer (REST) API design [2] is not implemented decoupling client and server in a stateless fashion. With OAI-PMH, clients can ask sets of records within any time interval and when the response is too big to send over one response, the first part of the result is returned with a resumption token. With this token, the client can request the next part and so forth. As a consequence, the server must maintain the state of every client separately. Also, this approach is not suited for the replication and synchronization of specific resources, such as updates from paintings. In 2012, ResourceSync solved these gaps by specifying different methods (Resource List, Resource Dump, Change List, Change Dump) to retrieve updates from resources [3]. These methods are described with a sitemap allowing clients to discover changes in a hypermedia-driven approach. However, sitemaps are originally created for search engines and do not use the Resource Description Framework (RDF) [4], which is a requirement for Linked Data publishing[4]. Starting from publishing Linked Data with data dumps, subject pages or SPARQL endpoints, it became clear that Linked Data can be published in several ways and in 2014, the term 'Linked Data Fragments' (LDF) was introduced to define how a dataset is fragmented and which hypermedia controls and metadata are added [5]. With this LDF vision, data publishers need to decide on trade-offs whether to put

---

[2] Design Museum Gent, STAM, Industriemuseum, Huis van Alijn, and Archief Gent.

[3] https://www.axiell.com/nl/oplossingen/product/axiell-collections/.

[4] https://5stardata.info/en/.

all the data processing effort on the server-side (SPARQL endpoint) or apply a more fragmented data strategy (subject pages, Triple Pattern Fragments [5]) shifting part of the querying cost to clients. In 2019, the Linked Data Event Streams (LDES) specification was created for the replication and synchronization of Linked Data [6]. Although a one-dimensional pagination strategy is put forward as best practice, similar to Hydra [7], Activity Streams[5] and International Image Interoperability Framework (IIIF) Change Discovery[6] [8], other fragmentation strategies can be researched using the TREE hypermedia specification[7]. As a result, LDES does not only allow third parties to integrate the data into their own systems, it also gives third parties the opportunity to take part of the publication effort with derived LDESs, reusable indexes and query services.

Given this background, the main issues addressed in this paper are a) how cultural heritage institutions can extend their AC CMS with LDES and b) how integrating LDES by a third party leads to integrated advanced services. This article begins by giving an overview of the TREE and LDES specifications. It will then explain how CoGghent's CHOs created an LDES on top of their AC instance and give an overview of derived query services. Finally, we conclude how LDES tackles the challenges related to the management of cultural information.

2 Background

TREE Specification. The hypermedia specification TREE (see footnote 7) allows to publish objects of a collection, called members. A member is part of a collection that describes the data graph of its member using shapes[8], and can broadly be defined as prov:Entity being a physical, digital, conceptual, or other kind of thing with some fixed aspects; entities may be real or imaginary[9]. This way, TREE can be used cross-domain for slow (cultural heritage objects) and fast (sensor observations) moving data. The collection's members are published over multiple pages on the Web where each page can be seen as a node of a traversable tree and contains qualified relations to other nodes. A TREE relation describes which property and value of members can be expected when a client follows the relation to another node. Specific TREE relations are available, such as *GreaterThanRelation* and *GeospatiallyContainsRelation*, to compare strings, geospatial features and time literals giving clients the ability to prune the search tree. Another aspect of TREE is that the collection can have multiple views where the view refers to the root node from where all members can be retrieved

---

[5] https://www.w3.org/TR/activitystreams-core/.
[6] https://iiif.io/api/discovery/1.0/.
[7] https://w3id.org/tree/specification.
[8] Shapes can be described with Shapes Constraint Language (SHACL) or Shape Expressions (ShEx).
[9] https://www.w3.org/TR/prov-o/#Entity.

thus multiple fragmentation strategies can be applied to one collection, such as geospatial clusters to search efficiently (speed, bandwidth) over certain regions [9], and prefix trees to solve text search queries on the client-side [10].

Linked Data Event Streams. An LDES is a specific type of TREE collection where its members are immutable. If objects need life cycle management, such as cultural heritage objects, immutability is achieved through versioned objects. Each time an object changes, a new immutable version is created. As a consequence, a client only needs to fetch the objects once and can maintain a cache of processed members. It is the responsibility of the data publisher to maintain LDESs for their collections of objects from where other parties can replicate and synchronize. LDES is positioned in a three-layered architecture (LDES, indexes and query services) by the Semantic Interoperability Community (SEMIC)[10] where third parties can offer indexes and query services using an LDES as base data source. For example, LDES is implemented by the Flemish government for the publication of base registry data, such as address related information [6].

3   Extending Axiell Collections API with Linked Data Event Streams

In this section, we will describe how we implemented an LDES on top of an AC API. Our method is composed of two steps. First, an Extract Mapping and Loading (ETL) pipeline is used to generate the versioned Linked Data objects. Then, another LDES building block bundles these objects inside hypermedia-driven LDFs. Figure 1 illustrates the various stages of the process, which we will discuss in depth hereafter. This section also describes four query services that use an LDES with cultural heritage data as input.

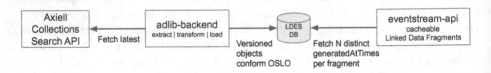

Fig. 1. Creating an LDES from Axiell collections uses two building blocks and an LDES DB.

3.1   Extraction, Transformation and Loading

The LDES generation component "eventstream-api" (Sect. 3.2) requires querying over the list of immutable objects of the LDES collection to bundle these objects in fragments. An ETL pipeline called "adlib-backend" is created that i)

---

[10] https://w3id.org/ldes/specification.

periodically fetches the latest objects from an AC API, ii) maps the objects to a Linked Data model and iii) loads them in a relational database, which we will call the LDES DB.

Extraction. The ETL pipeline needs to periodically run to fetch the latest objects from the AC CMS. The AC Search API is used and allows, among others, to configure an output format (JSON or XML), a database, pagination size and search parameters. To simplify explaining how the latest objects can be fetched, we will use in the rest of the examples for the query parameters as shown in Listing 1.1: JSON as format (format=json), "collection objects" as database (database=objecten), and a page size of 10 objects (start=0&limit=10). For the search parameters, we will set the institution's name, e.g. "Het Huis van Alijn (Gent)", and web publication flag (webpublication=EUROPEANA). The latter is used by the institutions of CoGhent to indicate that the object metadata may be used as Open Data.

Listing 1.1. Base query parameters used.

```
?output=json&database=objecten&startFrom=0&limit=10
&search=webpublication=EUROPEANA
AND institution.name='Het Huis van Alijn (Gent)' AND ...
```

On the first run, no objects from the institution's database have been retrieved thus running the query in Listing 1.2 can be used in a loop by increasing the startFrom parameter. When objects are already harvested in the LDES DB, the generatedAtTime of the latest versioned object is retrieved and must be used in the Modified search parameter:

Listing 1.2. Search parameters to retrieve the latest objects.

```
Modified > 'timestamp-last-retrieved-object'
```

However, in AC, records are sorted by their internal identifier (priref record number) and not by their modified time. As a result, when a run has not been completed, records will be missed in the next run. Therefore, before running the query from Listing 1.3, an extra query needs to retrieve all records that were modified before the last retrieved object and that has a priref identifier that is greater than the last retrieved object's priref (Listing 1.3):

Listing 1.3. Search parameters to complete the previous run.

```
Modified <= 'timestamp-last-retrieved-object'
AND priref > 'last-retrieved-priref'
```

Transformation. The extracted Adlib records are returned in JSON format and need to be transformed to standardized Linked Data information models to achieve semantic interoperability with other related Linked datasets. In the next paragraphs, we will describe how this is done i) by creating URIs and ii) mapping to Linked Data models.

The first step in creating Linked Data is the usage of HTTP URIs as identifiers for entities instead of the local identifier (priref). For LDES, two URIs need to be created: the version object URI and the persistent object URI. A field is reserved in AC where the institution can fill in the persistent URI when this is available. For example, when institutions host their own URIs using a resolver. If a persistent URI is available, the versioned object URI will extend this URI with a timestamp. When this is empty, the following URI template is used based on the Flemish URI standard[11]: https://{domain}/{type}/{concept}(/{reference-basic})+(/{reference-version}). CoGhent makes use of the https:// protocol and uses the domain of the City of Ghent's website (stad.gent). All entities are given 'id' as *type* to clarify that the URIs are identifiers. The *concept* depends on the type of entity. For example, human-made objects have the concept 'mensgemaaktobject' (Dutch for human-made object). Two *reference-basics* are used. First, a namespace is given per collection, which aligns with the database name in AC. Second, an MD5 hash will be generated based on the local identifier (*priref*) and the record's creation time. In the current version, the second reference basic is set to the local identifier only. *Reference-version* is used for versioned objects and contains the record's modification time. For example, an object of Design Museum Gent (dmg) that has been modified at 2021-08-15T01:56:04.152Z has a URI https://stad.gent/id/mensgemaaktobject/dmg/530027447/2021-08-15T01:56:04.152Z.

The second step towards Linked Data is mapping the extracted Adlib records to, among others, the CIDOC-Conceptual Reference Model (CRM) information model [11]. CIDOC-CRM provides the concepts and relations to describe entities in the cultural heritage domain and has been an official ISO standard since 2006. In Flanders (Belgium), its usage is promoted with the use of two Application Profiles (APs) created by the Open Standards for Linked Organizations (OSLO) standardization programme [12]. While both OSLO and Linked Art[12] use CIDOC-CRM as a semantic layer, OSLO is an inter-domain effort using the same approach for non-cultural heritage domains. An AP operates in the context of use cases and specifies which concepts and relations of vocabularies need to be reused. Also, a closed-world assumption is created by adding cardinality constraints. The first AP[13] focuses on static concepts, such as a human-made object, information object, work, expression and collection, while the second AP[14] focuses on cultural heritage related activities, such as the creation and acquisition of an object. JavaScript Object Notation Linked Data (JSON-LD) is used as the format and uses a JSON-LD context file for each AP. Listing 1.4 demonstrates the mapping of a human-made object, which refers to the two context files and indicates when the versioned object has been created (prov:generatedAtTime) and the persistent, non-versioned URI of the object (dcterms:isVersionOf). How OSLO maps JSON-LD terms to URIs is

---

[11] https://data.vlaanderen.be/cms/VlaamseURI-StandaardVoorData_V1.0.pdf.
[12] https://linked.art/.
[13] https://data.vlaanderen.be/doc/applicatieprofiel/cultureel-erfgoed-object.
[14] https://data.vlaanderen.be/doc/applicatieprofiel/cultureel-erfgoed-event.

also exemplified by repeating the class "MensgemaaktObject" in the context to its CIDOC-CRM URI. Furthermore, the institution that maintains the object ("MaterieelDing.beheerder") is demonstrated. To allow semantic reconciliation, contextualisation and alignment across institutions, URIs referring to external vocabularies, such as Wikidata and Getty's AAT, ULAN and TGN, were added to AC. Mapping relations between source and target models are established by creating a JSON object in the Javascript programming language to which JSON-LD mappings can be added. A Javascript function is created for each feature (descriptions, associations, iconography) and appends JSON-LD objects that are aligned with the OSLO context files to the main JSON object. With this mapped JSON-LD object in mind, the last step of the ETL pipeline can be performed.

Listing 1.4. Snippet of a versioned human-made object.

```
{
"@context": [
  "https://apidg.gent.be/opendata/adlib2eventstream/v1/
      context/cultureel-erfgoed-object-ap.jsonld",
  "https://apidg.gent.be/opendata/adlib2eventstream/v1/
      context/cultureel-erfgoed-event-ap.jsonld",
  {
    "dcterms": "http://purl.org/dc/terms/",
    "prov": "http://www.w3.org/ns/prov#",
    "MensgemaaktObject": "http://www.cidoc-crm.org/
        cidoc-crm/E22_Man-Made_Object"
  }
],
"@id": "https://stad.gent/data/mensgemaaktobject/dmg/53
    0027447/2021-09-11T01:56:30.635Z",
"@type": "MensgemaaktObject",
"dcterms:isVersionOf": "https://stad.gent/id/
    mensgemaaktobject/dmg/530026077",
"prov:generatedAtTime": "2021-09-11T01:56:30.635Z",
"MaterieelDing.beheerder": "http://www.wikidata.org/
    entity/Q1809071"
}
```

Load. Mapped JSON-LD objects are stored in the payload column of the "Members" table in a relational database (Table 1). Next to inserting the URI, institution, generation time and AC database name, also the software version number of adlib-backend at the time of running the ETL pipeline is inserted. Institutions may request new features to the mapping algorithm, such as adding links to other external thesauri. When this happens, the ETL pipeline needs to extract every object again and append the mapped objects to the LDES. This way, older version objects are preserved and the life cycle of an object can be retained.

Detecting whether the mapping algorithm has changed requires checking if the software version of "adlib-backend" has changed since the latest software version in the database (version column). In the next section, we will describe how an LDES can be constructed on top of the Members table.

Table 1. Columns of the members table.

Column name	Definition
URI	Web identifier of versioned object
Version	Software version of adlib-backend
Institution	Institution name
adlibDatabase	Database name of Adlib
generatedAtTime	Timestamp when versioned object was created
Payload	JSON-LD mapping of object

3.2 Linked Data Event Stream

The LDES generation component[15] called "eventstream-api" needs to construct an LDES by applying a fragmentation strategy over the version objects in the Members table. We will explain in this section how we implemented this strategy following the three parts of a Linked Data Fragment [5]: i) data: which objects will be selected per fragment, ii) controls: the relationships added between fragments, and iii) metadata: data about the knowledge graph.

Data. The term 'data' is used here for the objects in an LDES. To emphasize the autonomy and decentralized nature of an institution, we decided in the CoGhent project to create an LDES of collection objects per institution. This selection is performed by filtering on the "institution" and "adlibDatabase" columns. Filtering also needs to be performed to limit the number of objects per fragment. A one-dimensional fragmentation based on the generation time of the version object has been implemented, because clients will only need to subscribe to the latest page to retrieve updates. New versions are generated during the working hours of an institution, thus fragmenting with static time periods, e.g. every 10 min, would lead to a large number of empty fragments. To evenly spread objects over fragments, we group N distinct generatedAtTime timestamps T per fragment ($N > 0$) from the sorted list of distinct Ts. As a result, every fragment corresponds with N Ts and contains the version objects that have a T greater or equal than the fragment's lowest T and less than the next fragment's lowest T.

---

[15] Available as Open Source: https://github.com/StadGent/node_service_eventstream-api.

Controls. Hypermedia controls are added between fragments following the TREE specification. Every fragment has two TREE relations: to go forward and backward in time. These relations are qualified links indicating to clients which objects of the LDES collection can be expected when the link is followed. Listing 1.5 demonstrates a LessThanRelation between two fragments, which are instances of *tree:Node*, to retrieve objects that contain T before '2021-08-15T01:52:51.561Z'. Also, the number of remaining items is added to each relation to indicate how many objects can be retrieved through that link.

Listing 1.5. Example of a TREE relation to retrieve version objects with a generatedAtTime value less than 2021-08-15T01:52:51.561Z.

```
{
  @id: "https://apidg.gent.be/opendata/adlib2
    eventstream/v1/dmg/objecten?generatedAtTime=2021-
    08-15T01:52:51.561Z",
  @type: "tree:Node",
  tree:relation: {
    @type: "tree:LessThanRelation",
    tree:node: "https://apidg.gent.be/opendata/adlib2
      eventstream/v1/dmg/objecten?generatedAtTime=202
      1-08-15T01:51:51.569Z",
    tree:path: "prov:generatedAtTime",
    tree:value: "2021-08-15T01:52:51.561Z",
    tree:remainingItems: 1325
}
```

Metadata. Every object in the LDES is linked with the LDES collection through a tree:member relation. By dereferencing the collection URI, a Data Catalog Application Profile (DCAT-AP) description is returned where data about the LDES can be retrieved, such as title, license, and maintainer. Figure 2 shows how the three layers (metadata, controls, and data) are linked with each other: an LDES corresponds with a DCAT dataset and all objects can be retrieved by following the accessURL on a distribution or by choosing a TREE view directly. Version objects of the information model are embedded inside fragments thus do not require an explicit link with its *tree:Node*.

3.3 External Query Services

In the CoGhent project, the two LDES generation components from previous sections are deployed on behalf of the institutions by the ICT partner of Ghent (District09) in a production environment with the use of Docker containers[16]. By replicating and synchronizing with these LDESs, which can be done with the

---

[16] https://github.com/StadGent/docker_adlib2eventstream.

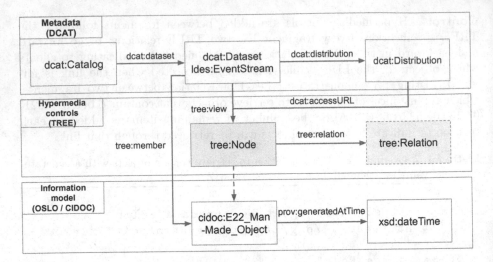

Fig. 2. Overview how metadata, hypermedia controls and information objects are linked.

LDES client[17], other actors in the ecosystem can create derived query services. In this section, we describe how query services are created by three different organizations (the City of Ghent, Inuits[18], and IDLab) in the context of CoGhent.

Subject Pages. The transformation step in Sect. 3.1 creates HTTP URIs using the cities' domain, because the city is responsible for resolving the URIs with relevant information (Linked Data principle 3). To make this possible, the City of Ghent hosts a Virtuoso triple store for Linked Open Data publication and has created a Linked pipes configuration to import an LDES[19]. From this triple store, a service returns subject pages with relevant triples when a URI containing https://stad.gent/ is dereferenced.

SPARQL Endpoint. The city of Ghent also exposes a SPARQL endpoint[20] on top of their triple store to publish cross-domain semantic data related to the city, such as public services, news articles, and parking availability. All version objects of the object from Listing 1.4 can now be retrieved with a SPARQL query having following triple pattern: $?version < http : //purl.org/dc/terms/isVersionOf >< https : //stad.gent/id/mensgemaaktobject/dmg/530027447 >$. This query can be used when the version URI from Listing 1.4 does not work anymore as the city decides which versions to preserve. If a third party wants to set up their own SPARQL

---

[17] Available as library: https://github.com/TREEcg/event-stream-client.
[18] https://inuits.eu/.
[19] https://github.com/district09/ldes-to-linkedpipes/.
[20] https://stad.gent/sparql.

endpoint: an open source Software Development Kit (SDK) is being developed to deploy multiple services that replicate and synchronize with LDESs[21]. One of these services is to set up a GraphDB triple store[22]. From there, a SPARQL endpoint can be deployed.

IIIF Enriched LDES. AC is used for the management of collection metadata. However, high-resolution images of objects still need to be maintained in a dedicated Digital Asset Management System (DAMS). The DAMS used by the CoGhent institutions have the LDESs integrated to link images with their corresponding object metadata using the object identifier[23]. As a result, the DAMS will publish derived LDESes where the versioned objects contain links to the IIIF image API (3.0) and presentation API (3.0). These enriched LDESes will serve for the creation of innovative applications (multi-voice platform, cocreation funding, hackathons) in the context of Coghent.

Substring Index. One of the benefits of LDES is the use of the allround hypermedia specification TREE. Instead of describing TREE relations to traverse in time, also other fragmentations, such as geospatial and text-based fragmentations, can be expressed. A substring index has been created to demonstrate how (thesauri) objects of an LDES can be fragmented by substring[24]. For example, a fragment B contains a limited set of objects having a label starting with "b". With a Substring relation having a value "bo", objects having a label starting with "bo" can be retrieved. These relations are especially useful for autocompletion applications[25].

4   Conclusion and Future Work

In CoGhent, semantic and technical interoperability is achieved using interdomain efforts: the OSLO APs are used to semantically align the cultural information within the broader semantic ecosystem of Flanders, and LDES is used for the replication and synchronization of the data towards other parties. This article gave some insights how a CMS of Axiell can be extended with an LDES using two components. This publication strategy can be generalized to other JSON APIs with search functionality. Also, the versioned objects allow knowledge to be inferred that is not contained in a single source and addresses topics, such as historiography. With the LDES publication paradigm, others can more easily integrate the data within their advanced query services. For example, the

---

[21] https://github.com/Informatievlaanderen/ldes2service.
[22] https://github.com/osoc21/ldes2service/tree/ldes-graphdb-connector.
[23] https://gitlab.com/inuits/dams.
[24] https://github.com/TREEcg/substring_fragmenter.
[25] An autocompletion demo can be found here: https://tree.linkeddatafragments. org/demo/autocompletion/?datasets[]=https://treecg.github.io/demo_data/vtmk. ttl,https://oliviervd.github.io/substrings_coghent/agents/root.ttl.

City of Ghent already had a subject page and SPARQL endpoint service running and now also supports an integrated view for cultural heritage data. Compared to sensor data, cultural heritage objects update slowly. However, a retention policy on the side of the LDES will still be necessary in the long-term. To this end, collaboration with archives may be needed.

We also showed that an LDES collection can be fragmented using TREE for text search applications. Not only objects and thesauri from the CoGhent institutions can be retrieved with a substring query, also public sector information (Flemish registry for street names) or external thesauri (Netwerk Digitaal Erfgoed) can be queried ad hoc by integrating the data on the client-side. By adding links to external thesauri, such as AAT, ULAN, TGN, we want to generate translations of descriptive texts automatically in future work. Finally, an enriched LDES with IIIF promises to be an interesting approach to replicate and synchronize CMSs and DAMs in both ways. To conclude, we advocate for the support of LDES as a standard Linked Data service at the level of CMSs.

References

1. Van de Sompel, H., Nelson, M.L., Lagoze, C., Warner, S.: Resource harvesting within the OAI-PMH framework. D-Lib Mag. **10**(12), 2004
2. Fielding, R.T., Taylor, R.N.: Principled design of the modern web architecture. ACM Trans. Internet Technol. (TOIT) **2**(2), 115–150 (2002)
3. Haslhofer, B., et al.: ResourceSync: leveraging sitemaps for resource synchronization. In: Proceedings of the 22nd International Conference on World Wide Web, WWW 2013 Companion, pp. 11–14, New York, NY, USA, 2013. Association for Computing Machinery (2013)
4. Lassila, O., Swick, R.R.: World Wide, and Web consortium. Resource description framework (RDF) model and syntax specification (1998)
5. Verborgh, R., et al.: Triple pattern fragments: a low-cost knowledge graph interface for the web. J. Web Semant. **37–38**, 184–206 (2016)
6. Van Lancker, D., et al.: Publishing base registries as linked data event streams. In: Brambilla, M., Chbeir, R., Frasincar, F., Manolescu, I. (eds.) ICWE 2021. LNCS, vol. 12706, pp. 28–36. Springer, Cham (2021). https://doi.org/10.1007/978-3-030-74296-6_3
7. Lanthaler, M., Gütl, C.: Hydra: a vocabulary for hypermedia-driven web APIs. In: LDOW (2013)
8. Snydman, S., Sanderson, R., Cramer, T.: The international image interoperability framework (IIIF): a community & technology approach for web-based images. In: Archiving Conference, vol. 2015, pp. 16–21. Society for Imaging Science and Technology (2015)
9. Delva, H., Rojas, J.A., Vandenberghe, P.-J., Colpaert, P., Verborgh, R.: Geospatial partitioning of open transit data. In: Bielikova, M., Mikkonen, T., Pautasso, C. (eds.) ICWE 2020. LNCS, vol. 12128, pp. 305–320. Springer, Cham (2020). https://doi.org/10.1007/978-3-030-50578-3_21
10. Dedecker, R., Delva, H., Colpaert, P., Verborgh, R.: A file-based linked data fragments approach to prefix search. In: Brambilla, M., Chbeir, R., Frasincar, F., Manolescu, I. (eds.) ICWE 2021. LNCS, vol. 12706, pp. 53–67. Springer, Cham (2021). https://doi.org/10.1007/978-3-030-74296-6_5

11. CRM CIDOC: The CIDOC conceptual reference model (2003)
12. Buyle, R., et al.: OSLO: open standards for linked organizations. In: Proceedings of the International Conference on Electronic Governance and Open Society: Challenges in Eurasia, pp. 126–134 (2016)

Digitizing, Transcribing and Publishing the Handwritten Music Score Archives of Ionian Islands Philharmonic Bands

Eleftherios Kalogeros[1] , Matthew Damigos[1] , Michalis Sfakakis[1] ,
Sofia Zapounidou[1,2](✉) , Aggeliki Drakopoulou[1] , Costas Zervopoulos[3] ,
Gerasimos Martinis[4] , Christos Papatheodorou[5] , and Manolis Gergatsoulis[1]

[1] Department of Archives, Library Science and Museology, Ionian University, Corfu, Greece
{kalogero,sfakakis,l12zapo,l19drak,manolis}@ionio.gr
[2] Library and Information Centre, Aristotle University of Thessaloniki, Thessaloniki, Greece
[3] Philharmonic Society "Spyros Samaras" of Korakiana, Ano Korakiana, Corfu, Greece
[4] Department of Music Studies, Ionian University and "Mantzaros" Philharmonic Society, Corfu, Greece
teragram88@yahoo.gr
[5] Department of History and Philosophy of Science, National and Kapodistrian University of Athens, Athens, Greece
papatheodor@phs.uoa.gr

Abstract. During the long history of the philharmonic bands in the Ionian Islands, since the mid of the nineteenth century, valuable archives of handwritten music scores have been established. These archives consist of the scores of original works locally created and from adaptations of western music works of Greek and other European composers. For the long-term preservation of the archives of 7 Philharmonic Bands, the handwritten music scores were digitised and a significant amount of (the most important of) them was transcribed into MusicXML. Moreover, all these archives were integrated into, and published as a single archive. All these activities were part of the project "Preservation and Prominence of the Musical Heritage of the Region of Ionian Islands Prefecture through the management of the digital archives of the Philharmonic Orchestras of the Region." This work presents the challenges, the workflows and the system developed to achieve the objectives of the project.

Keywords: Music score archives · Linked data · MARC21 · RDA · IIIF · MusicXML · Semantic web

1 Introduction

Western music has always been favoured in the Ionian Islands, Greece, due to the influences during their Venetian, French, and British occupations. Thus, these islands have a long tradition in bands. Significant Greek composers directed such bands and created a huge collection of unique musical works, known as the Ionian Islands Music School.

© Springer Nature Switzerland AG 2022
E. Garoufallou et al. (Eds.): MTSR 2021, CCIS 1537, pp. 370–381, 2022.
https://doi.org/10.1007/978-3-030-98876-0_32

Hence, the Ionian Islands Music School is considered a music wave of symphonic works, created mainly for band instruments during the 19th century [1, 2]. Most of these works are considered Western music and include various genres, such as marches, waltzes, mazurkas, cantatas, serenades, polkas, operas, symphonies.

Today, there are dozens of bands spread in the Ionian Islands and especially in the islands of Corfu, Kefalonia, Zakynthos and Lefkada that hold valuable and large archives mainly consisting of handwritten music scores (full scores and parts). Nowadays, these scores are managed and preserved by the directors of the bands who create adaptations or reproduce them in a plethora of performances in Greece and abroad, attracting the interest of the audience as well as the musicology researchers worldwide. The project "Preservation and promotion of Music Heritage of the Ionian Islands Region through Digital Management of its Philharmonic Records" focused on 7 bands from the two islands who participated in the programme, in which, unique and of great interest scores were found. In total, the archives belonging to 7 bands were selected, 5 bands from the Corfu Island, and 2 bands from the Kefalonia Island. The bands from Corfu are 1) Philharmonic Society "Mantzaros," 2) Philharmonic Society "Omonia" of Gastouri, 3) Philharmonic Association of Skripero, 4) Philharmonic Society "Spyros Samaras" of Korakiana, 5) Philharmonic of Sinarades. The bands from Kefalonia are 1) Philharmonic School of Kefallinia, Argostoli, and 2) Philharmonic School of Palli, Lixouri. Most of the above-mentioned Philharmonic Bands were established in the 19th century and since then their main musical ensemble, their bands, perform in theatres, concerts, in parades, and significant national religious events of those islands [1]. All of them, some of which have more than 300 active members, offer essential services in the cultural development of local communities, both by offering free basic musical education to all their students, and participating in various musical events, concerts and festivals.

To meet the goals of preserving and disseminating the scores from the bands' archives, more than one scientific team collaborated for describing, for curating, digitising and partially transcribing the scores, for developing systems and processes to integrate each team's output in a coherent workflow, and for publishing the whole output in a user-friendly way. For each one of these processes, the related standards and systems have been exploited. For describing and delivering the images of the scanned scores the International Image Interoperability Framework (IIIF) standard [3] was used, while the OMEKA S [4] served the online publication of the digitised scores. Metadata was created using the Koha Integrated Library System [5], the MARC21 communication format [6], and the Resource Description and Access (RDA) rules [7]. The transcription of the scores was made using the MusicXML standard [8].

This paper reports on the workflows and challenges of the project towards the development of a one-stop portal offering access to unique musical works currently dispersed over the islands of Corfu and Kefalonia in the bands' closed archives.

2 Metadata Policy

The cataloguing of the handwritten music scores found in the archives of the selected philharmonic bands presented important challenges. Most challenges were because the bands had massively used their archives in rehearsals and live performances. On many handwritten scores there was unclear information regarding the works included on the scores. Many names were on the scores, and their exact role needed to be identified. Additionally, there were many dates to be clarified if they referred to a creation date, a score production date, or a performance date. Many scores were aggregate ones including either parts or full works that were performed at some time together, or selections of a bigger work, e.g., selections of an opera. The music study of the project [9] and the close cooperation between the cataloguing team and the musicologists solved all disambiguation and enabled the production of quality metadata.

2.1 RDA in MARC21

Regarding the cataloguing policy, the RDA rules were implemented in MARC21 using the Koha ILS software. For developing the cataloguing policy, the team consulted with the MLA "Best Practices for Music Cataloging Using RDA and MARC21" incorporated in the RDA toolkit [10], the Yale policy for music cataloguing [11], and related literature [6, 12–15]. The cornerstone of the cataloguing policy is to use controlled vocabularies, and URIs, as much as possible. Even though the cataloguing focused on the description of scores at the RDA Manifestation level, uniform titles were used for easier identification of Works and Expressions. The cataloguing team aspires that the use of controlled vocabularies, URIs, and uniform titles will enable a) the conversion of MARC21 data to RDA, b) the upload on the Omeka S software describing the scores as RDA Manifestations using the relevant RDA RDF vocabularies, and c) the representation of the full WEMI structure for each Work present in the digitised music scores.

In the Koha ILS software, a template was created to enable faster and better cataloguing. The template named "Music Scores" includes many default values to help cataloguers focus on more difficult aspects of their work. The cataloguing language used in the project has been Greek. Yet, there is no official translation of controlled vocabularies in Greek. It was decided to use the Greek translation of terms in the MARC21 fields along with each term's corresponding URI in the subfields $4 or $1 depending on the MARC21 field. This "Linky MARC" approach [16] has been adopted with URIs typically used in MARC 21 bibliographic 1XX, 3XX, 6XX, 7XX fields (Fig. 1). This decision aims to both aid Greek users in their search and retrieve tasks, and use the URIs of values providing the explicit semantics of the translated terms in Greek.

Similarly, information regarding people in the Personal Name Authorities was documented using controlled vocabularies and URIs as possible. Finding information regarding the lives of composers, performers, poets has been a difficult task because the history of the philharmonic bands of the Ionian Islands has not been thoroughly studied yet. In many cases, information was found in blogs presenting speeches that scholars gave in various local cultural events. Towards the goal of developing a repository that will provide documented information about various aspects of the history of the philharmonic bands of the Ionian islands, these blog posts, and other webpages that the cataloguing team consulted with, have been archived in the Internet Archive [17] for preservation (Fig. 2).

The description of 'Aggregate Scores' has been a challenge. The scores included in the bands' archives served rehearsal and performance purposes. Thus, many 'Aggregate Scores' exist in the archives holding the bands' repertoire. These scores fall into three

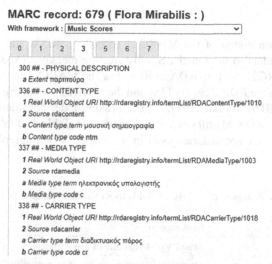

Fig. 1. Screen excerpt showing MARC21-3XX Physical description fields where translated terms from the RDA controlled vocabularies are used along with their corresponding URIS.

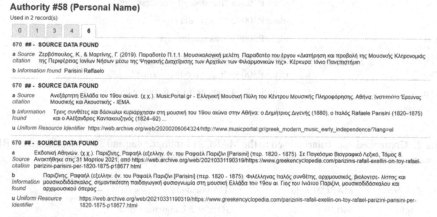

Fig. 2. Screen excerpt showing MARC21-person authority record for Parisini, Raffaele (1820–1875). The webpages providing information about this composer, have been archived in the internet archive.

categories: a) scores including more than one full musical works, b) scores including parts of more than one music works, and c) scores including parts of the same work (mostly of a symphony or an opera). 'Aggregate Scores' falling into the first two categories were described as "Aggregate Manifestations" with notes regarding the aggregated RDA Works and Expressions [10–12]. The 'Aggregate Scores' of the third category were described using uniform titles complemented with a 'Selections' form subheading, e.g., Kritikopoula. Selections.

The creation of metadata for nearly 1100 scores was completed in 6 months by a team of 6 cataloguers supervised by 2 metadata experts.

2.2 RDA in RDF

To enable i) the conversion of the MARC21 records to RDA, and ii) the upload of bibliographic metadata to the Omeka S software, the metadata experts of the project have mapped MARC21 fields to RDA in RDF. For the MARC21 to RDA mapping, the RDA alignments in the RDA Registry [18] and the MARC21 mapping to RDA elements from the original RDA Toolkit [19] have been taken under consideration. Part of the mapping related to RDA Manifestation is presented in Table 1. Table 2 below shows the selected controlled vocabularies used in the project's bibliographic and authority records.

Table 1. Mapping of MARC21 fields to RDA manifestation properties

MARC21 field	RDA property
245$a	rdam:P30134 "has title of manifestation"
245$c	rdam:P30117 "has statement of responsibility"
264$a	rdam:P30279 "has place of manifestation"
264$b	rdam:P30083 "has publisher agent"
264$c	rdam:P30278 "has date of manifestation"
337$a	rdam:P30002 "has media type"
338$a	rdam:P30001 "has carrier type"
347$a	rdam:P30018 "has file type"
347$b	rdam:P30096 "has encoding format"
856$u	rdam:P30154 "has uniform resource locator"

Table 2. Controlled vocabularies used in the MARC21 bibliographic and authority records. URIs of concepts included in these vocabularies were also used in the MARC21 records.

Type of record	MARC21 field	RDA vocabulary
Bibliographic	040 $b	ISO 639-2 Language Code
	048 $a	LC MARC Instruments and Voices Code List
	100, 700, 710 $4 $e	LC MARC Code List for Relators Scheme
	336 $a	RDA Content Type
	337 $a	RDA Media Type
	338 $a	RDA Carrier Type
	347 $b	RDA File Type
	348 $a	RDA Format of Notated Music
	382 $a	LC Medium of Performance Thesaurus for Music
	655	LC Genre/Form Terms
Authority	040 $b	ISO 639-2 Language Code
	374	LC Demographic Group Terms

3   Digital Repository of Music Score Archive

In this section, we present a repository built to provide access to several stakeholders to both the musical works and their metadata. Although the repository has been implemented to facilitate the dissemination of the handwritten historical musical archive of the Ionian philharmonic bands, it is designed towards setting up a generic repository for publishing, sharing, and accessing music works.

To create the content of the digital repository, the raw music scores are gathered and scanned, and the initial version of the digitised music files is obtained. Due to issues and errors in this version of the digitized files, such as bad-quality or corrupted figures produced during scanning, or cases where the scanned pages are misclassified, the files are further processed manually by a team of musicians. Later in this section, we present the overall architecture of the repository, along with the technologies selected and used, as well as the workflow followed for processing, managing and loading both the digital content and metadata into the repository.

3.1   Navigating Through the Content of the Repository

To describe how the repository is working, we initially analyse the main user's navigation path within the repository (a.k.a., use case). The repository aims to provide free access to all works' metadata through, mainly, a flexible search mechanism. Note that the metadata is defined per music work. Additionally, authorised users may access the works' content (in either digitized or transcribed form).

Particularly, the user can access the repository through her browser and find the music work she is looking for. To look for such a musical work, she can search the metadata of each music work. Note that the user can search several metadata fields using keywords and specify a certain metadata field she is searching on. Once a work of interest is found, the user can see all its metadata and follow the links to access its content. At most two links are provided per music work, one directing to the scanned content (digitized scores/parts, given as a structured set of image files) and one directing to the transcribed one (in MusicXML form).

For each music work, at least its digitised form is available, but not necessarily accessible to each user. Only the authorised users can access the content of a certain work. Furthermore, access privileges are defined per content form (digitized or transcribed) of each work; e.g., if a user has access to the digitised form of a certain work, she can also access all the scores/parts of this work, but not necessarily the transcribed form. The access rights of each work are defined in collaboration with the philharmonic bands.

Let us now return to the navigation path and assume that the user follows the link towards viewing the digitised content. Typically, the user is redirected to the content publishing repository. First, the user is asked to provide her credentials. If so, the authorised user accesses a content viewer, where she can view and download the content of the selected musical work. The digitised content is typically organised into scores/parts, according to the content provided for the certain work. However, once the user follows the link to access the transcribed files, she is again asked to provide her credentials to access the selected transcribed file.

3.2 Overall Architecture of the Repository

In this section, we present the overall architecture of the repository. In particular, the repository consists of the following main systems/layers: *metadata presentation and management layer, the content presentation and authentication layer, the image server,* and *the interoperability component/layer.* An overview of the repository's architectural design is illustrated in Fig. 3.

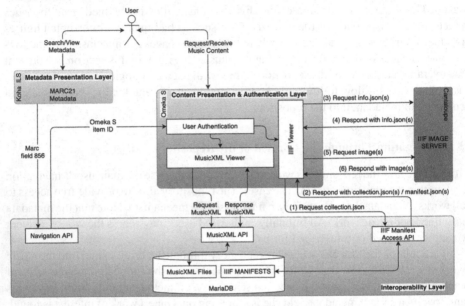

Fig. 3. Overall repository architecture

The analysis starts from the presentation layers; i.e., the systems that provide the proper user interface through which the stakeholders can access the repository's content and metadata. As displayed in Fig. 3, there are two main presentation systems in the repository, the one providing and managing the works' metadata, and the one that mainly focuses on providing access to the content. The former, the metadata presentation layer, is a system where the metadata is stored and managed. Through this system, the user can search and view the descriptive metadata of the available musical works. For each music work, there is a single record in this system containing its RDA Manifestation-level metadata. This system is built on top of the Koha ILS. As seen in Sect. 2, the metadata of each work follows the MARC 21 format.

The content presentation and authentication layer is a system used to manage the access to works' content. The user can authenticate and view works' content through certain viewers. Note here that the actual content is not stored into and managed through this system. Typically, we refer to the viewer presenting MusicXML files in a readable format, and to the viewer presenting work's digitised content. The Omeka S is used to implement this layer.

The image server is responsible for storing and providing the digitised content (scanned images) requested by the content presentation system to construct, on-the-fly, the scores requested for access. To set up this type of server, the Cantaloupe image server is used.

The *interoperability component/layer* is a system that ensures smooth coordination of the aforementioned systems. In particular, this system exposes three application programming interfaces (APIs): the navigation API, the MusicXML API, and the IIIF Manifest Access API.

The Navigation API is responsible for finding the content page in Omeka S and redirecting the user to this page, when the user asks to access the work's content by clicking on the corresponding link in Koha. To achieve this, we assign each work a unique identifier which follows a digital categorical encoding. This work identifier, also referred as work code, is stored in both work's metadata (field 856, MARC21) and Omeka S item to ensure smooth integration. Navigation API, then, uses Omeka's S REST API, and searches items according to work code. Hence, there is no need of maintaining a mapping between work entities in Koha and items in Omeka S. This type of API is mainly used towards establishing the independence of the system's record IDs.

MusicXML and IIIF Manifest Access APIs provide access to MusicXML and IIIF Manifest files, respectively. In particular, both APIs are used to deliver the requested files to the viewers. The main purpose of keeping MusicXML and IIIF Manifest files out of Omeka S is that we distinguish the presentation layer from the data layer, in that manner. Hence, setting up additional and/or alternative presentation layers on top of the same data can be achieved with minimal development effort and modifications.

The interoperability component uses an underlying storage layer which is built on MariaDB and is mainly used to store and manage operational metadata (such as data lineage, file name mappings), as well as the MusicXML and IIIF Manifest files. The transcribed scores, IIIF Manifest files and operational metadata are stored in this storage layer through a data loading process, which is described in more detail in a subsequent subsection. To manage and report this type of data, we plan to implement an administration console.

Let us now analyse the underlying process followed in order for the IIIF viewer to display the full digitised work. The viewer used for this purpose is the Universal Viewer. To better understand the communication, we initially describe the structure of the digitised music content. As previously mentioned, we use the IIIF to define the structure of the scanned content, i.e., the structure of the image files constituting the content of each work. We assume a three-level structure in the IIIF framework. Every musical work is given by a collection of IIIF manifests, where each manifest typically represents a music score or part. The manifest, then, is defined by multiple canvas consisting of a single piece of content (i.e., scanned image). Such an image shows a single page of music score. Figure 4 shows visually this structure. The structure of the image pages digitised during the preparation and loading process (see next section for more detail) is given through the IIIF Manifests.

Back to the communication between Universal Viewer, Cantaloupe, and IIIF Manifest Access API, we initially set up the URI of the collection to each work item in Omeka S. In essence, this URI represents a call to the corresponding endpoint of IIIF

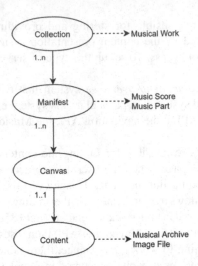

Fig. 4. IIIF structure of a music work

Manifest Access API, asking for the collection description (JSON file) of the specific work. The URI is defined in Omeka S during the creation of each item. Once the viewer receives the collection description of the requested work, it recursively asks from the IIIF Manifest Access API the manifest of each part (music score). In particular, the URIs of the manifests are included in the collection response and are used to ask from IIIF Manifest Access API the manifests' descriptions. A certain endpoint is defined and used for this purpose. Next, each manifest contains a sequence of canvases, each of which is associated with a content description (i.e., a link to a content file). Typically, such a link represents a URL of a content file stored in Cantaloupe. Hence, once the viewer receives the manifests it requests and receives the content from Cantaloupe.

3.3 Loading Process

In this section, we present the process used to prepare and load both the works' content and their metadata into the repository. In particular, we describe the steps followed to process the raw (handwritten, music scores) files that are gathered from Ionian's philharmonic bands. Figure 5 illustrates this process.

Initially, the raw music scores are gathered and scanned, i.e., the handwritten scores are digitized, in this manner, and the initial version of the digitised music files is obtained (referred as Digitized Music Files in Fig. 5). This form of digitised content might have issues and errors (such as bad-quality or corrupted figures produced during scanning, or cases where the scanned pages are misclassified) that need to be resolved to ensure high-quality and reliable content. Hence, further processing, checking and validation of the digitised files is required. This process is performed manually by field experts (i.e., a team of musicians who assess the content and perform cleaning and curation tasks).

The curated files are then categorized and organised to digitally reconstruct the original musical works and scores, e.g., gather the images referring to a certain score and

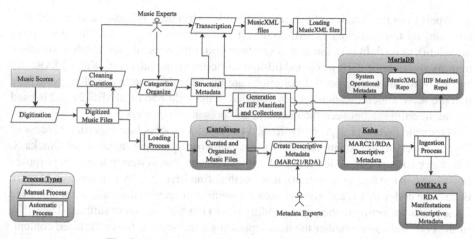

Fig. 5. Overall data management and loading process

work, put them into the correct order, and properly classify them into the file system. In this context, structural metadata is initially generated over the digitised content, defining the structure of the files, e.g., which work and part each music file belongs to, which are the music parts included in each work, which is the order of the files giving the correct music score. This process is also performed by music experts who manually provide structural metadata. The structural metadata provided is then used to automatically process the content and load it into multiple systems.

Structural metadata is initially used to organise the curated music files into the file system. Typically, for each work, a certain folder is created, which includes its music files. The file names are also harmonised. The music files following this structure are loaded into the Cantaloupe image server [20]. Furthermore, this type of metadata is used to automatically generate the IIIF manifestation and collection files, following the approach described in the previous section. The output IIIF Manifest files are then stored in the interoperability component (particularly, into MariaDB). Information about the lineage of the files (e.g., processing steps applied, mappings between original and harmonized file names) is also stored in this database, for tracking, monitoring and process management purposes (also referred as operational metadata).

The structural metadata and the curated files are also used by music and metadata experts to facilitate the creation of transcribed music files and descriptive metadata, respectively. Particularly, a predefined subset of music works is selected to be transcribed into MusicXML files. The transcription process is performed by the music experts out of the repository using proper tools (e.g., Finale, Sibelius, MuseScore). To do so, the experts gather the scores constructed by the curated files and the structural metadata, and manually create a MusicXML file for each work selected for transcription. Each MusicXML file created using this process is associated with a work code, which is mainly used to automatically load the MusicXML file into MariaDB and map it to the proper work. Typically, work code is provided as a parameter when calling MusicXML API to retrieve the requested MusicXML file.

Apart from the creation of the transcribed files, structural metadata and curated files are used by the metadata experts to describe each work (i.e., define the descriptive metadata), as well. In fact, metadata experts consider the curated files and their structure to properly describe each work, and fill-in its descriptive metadata into Koha. MARC 21 and RDA Manifestation-level descriptions are used for the score's metadata. Note here that the score's identification code is included in the field 856 of MARC 21 and is used for the interlinking between the metadata and presentation layers.

Once the metadata is properly defined in Koha, a process (see ingestion process in Fig. 5) is performed to automatically ingest the corresponding metadata in Omeka S. The work code is also added into each Omeka S item, for system integration purposes (as we saw in the previous section). It is worth noting here that, by construction of work codes, the codes that are stored in Omeka S items and refer to the same work share the same prefix (referring to the corresponding work) but have different suffixes. The suffix of the code indicates whether the item represents a transcribed file or digitised content.

In essence, the overall loading process described previously represents the process followed to load new works into the repository. In case of updating certain parts of the content and/or metadata, only the appropriate steps of this process are performed. Note also that we foresee an enhancement of the presented repository by adding a process management layer, where the different roles will be able to collaborate to add, remove, update content and metadata. Typically, such a layer will represent a collaborative environment that implements the aforementioned loading process.

4 Discussion and Conclusions

Regarding the creation of metadata by the cataloguing team, specific points must be highlighted to provide feedback to similar projects in the future. The curation of the physical archives before the digitisation is a must. If this is impossible due to the use of the physical archives, e.g., for rehearsals and live performances, then the digitised images must be curated and organised according to the music standards and the proper order of music parts.

Cataloguers need to have related literature at hand. The absence of studies regarding the history and activities of the philharmonic bands challenged the project. Thus, the music study delivered by the project's musicologists [9] and the close cooperation with them have been proved as invaluable assets. The project's "strict" cataloguing policy with the use of many controlled vocabularies and URIs was implemented easily thanks to the development of the "Music Scores" template in Koha with default values in many fields. The net result of this decision has been faster cataloguing times and high consistency of data. The "Linky MARC" approach [16] enabled the use of terms in Greek for the convenience of users eliminating at the same time any ambiguities about the identity of people (composers, adapters, etc.) or the meaning of concepts. It must be highlighted that the implementation of the "Linky MARC" approach did not burden the cataloguers in terms of effort and time.

Further research will be conducted to represent all RDA entities included in each music score. The project's metadata is consistent, URIs and uniform titles are used, thus, intriguing the full use of the RDA vocabulary to represent the RDA Works, Expressions, and Manifestations included in the music scores digitised by the project.

Acknowledgements. The publication of this paper was supported by the project: "Activities of the Laboratory On Digital Libraries and Electronic Publishing of the Department of Archives, Library Science and Museology". The research presented in the paper was supported by the European Union and Greece (Partnership Agreement for the Development Framework 2014–2020) under the Regional Operational Programme Ionian Islands 2014–2020 for the project "Preservation and Prominence of the Musical Heritage of the Region of Ionian Islands Prefecture through the management of the digital archives of the Philharmonic Orchestras of the Region".

References

1. Trikoupis, A.: Western Music in Hellenic Communities: Musicians and Institutions. National and Kapodistrian University of Athens, Athens (2015)
2. Romanou, E.: Italian musicians in Greece during the nineteenth century. Musicology, **3**, 43–55 (2003). https://dais.sanu.ac.rs/bitstream/id/20257/2602.pdf
3. International Image Interoperability Framework. https://iiif.io/
4. Omeka S. https://omeka.org/s/
5. Koha Library Software. https://koha-community.org/
6. Library of Congress: MARC standards. https://www.loc.gov/marc/
7. RDA Steering Committee: About RDA (2020). http://rda-rsc.org/content/about-rda
8. MusicXML. https://www.musicxml.com/
9. Zervopoulos, K., Martinis, G.: Deliverable 1.1. Music study (enriched and updated). Project "Preservation and Prominence of the Musical Heritage of the Region of Ionian Islands Prefecture through the management of the digital archives of the Philharmonic Orchestras of the Region (In Greek). Ionian University, Corfu (2021)
10. RDA Toolkit. https://www.rdatoolkit.org/
11. Music cataloging at Yale. https://web.library.yale.edu/cataloging/music
12. Library of Congress, Program for Cooperative Cataloging: BIBCO Standard Record (BSR) RDA Metadata Application Profile (2020). https://www.loc.gov/aba/pcc/bibco/documents/PCC-RDA-BSR.pdf
13. Strickland, A.: Cataloging Scores in RDA. In: Music in Libraries: Just the Basics Preconference Workshop, 2019 SEMLA Meeting, University of Mississippi (2019). http://semla.musiclibraryassoc.org/semla2019/presentations/preconference/Strickland_SEMLA_Preconference_Score_Cataloging_Workshop_2019.pdf
14. Gentili-Tedeschi, M.: Music presentation format: toward a cataloging babel? Cat. Classif. Q., **53**, 399–413 (2015). https://doi.org/10.1080/01639374.2014.968274
15. LC-PCC Task Group on Aggregates in Beta RDA Toolkit: Final Report. Part 1 (2020). https://www.loc.gov/aba/pcc/taskgroup/Aggregates-TG-Final-Report-Part-1.pdf
16. Wallis, R.: MARC and beyond: our three linked data choices. IFLA WLIC 2018 – Kuala Lumpur, Malaysia – Transform Libraries, Transform Societies in Session 113 - Information Technology (2018). http://library.ifla.org/id/eprint/2124
17. Internet Archive. https://archive.org/
18. RDA Registry – Alignments MARC21. http://www.rdaregistry.info/Aligns/#marc21
19. Original RDA Toolkit, MARC 21 Format for Bibliographic Data Mapped to RDA Elements. https://original.rdatoolkit.org/document.php?id=jscmap2
20. Cantaloupe. https://cantaloupe-project.github.io/

Potentials of Research Knowledge Graphs for Interlinking Participatory Archives: The Case of Distributed School Archives

Julian Hocker[1]([✉]) [iD], Christoph Schindler[1] [iD], Marc Rittberger[1] [iD], Annett Krefft[1], Marco Lorenz[2] [iD], and Joachim Scholz[2] [iD]

[1] DIPF | Leibniz Institute for Research and Information in Education, Frankfurt, Germany
{hocker,schindler,rittberger,krefft}@dipf.de
[2] Ruhr University Bochum, Bochum, Germany
marco.lorenz-z5x@uni-bochum.de, Joachim.Scholz@ruhr-uni-bochum.de

Abstract. Research knowledge graphs allow the enrichment of large amounts of data. Still, in some fields like the humanities sources are distributed in small archives not connected by the large research knowledge graphs or hubs like Wikidata. In comparison to these large research knowledge graphs, light-weight knowledge graphs allow the creation of small-scale hubs within the Linked Open Data (LOD) cloud as well as the re-usage of larger hubs like Wikidata in order to enrich one's own data. This paper describes the potentials of research knowledge graphs for interlinking archives and data hubs offering an overarching systematic overview to topic related distributed data. The potentials of the graph technology are shown in action for a concrete case in the field of history of education, focusing on school archives. Also, the research knowledge graph enables archivists and researchers to annotate and enrich the graph in order to customize it to their needs and research interests. It also facilitates processing of the heterogeneously structured data from larger hubs in order to increase coverage of the graph.

Keywords: Archive 2.0 · Digital humanities · Participatory design · Research knowledge graph

1 Introduction

While research today faces nearly infinite amounts of data, the main challenges concern overarching systematic overviews of topic related distributed silos of data and structural heterogeneity. Institutionalized archives, libraries, research data centers, open government data portals and Wikidata offer huge amounts of data, while other data remain untouched in local archives. It has therefore become important to provide a centralized overview over these decentralised data silos for relevance checking in research and an easy way of data integration and enrichment for non-archival experts.

© Springer Nature Switzerland AG 2022
E. Garoufallou et al. (Eds.): MTSR 2021, CCIS 1537, pp. 382–388, 2022.
https://doi.org/10.1007/978-3-030-98876-0_33

In order to address these research needs, the aim of this article is to describe the potentials of research graphs for an overarching systematic overview in distributed archival environments. Light-weight graph structures can solve the problem of decentralized data structures via interlinking of sources within a research graph. There are many solutions to research graphs, but few light-weight systems that focus on adjustable and participatory solutions for a concrete added value of research communities [5].

This article argues for smaller flexible graphs that are easier to maintain and easier to build up than large knowledge graphs [2] and presents a bottom-up approach allowing users to extend the graph to their needs and interconnect to several data hubs. It highlights the potentials for small archives to use the full range of capacities of a research graph in an interconnected and participatory environment.

This research knowledge graph allows to connect the worlds of archives and research in a new deeper interlinked and participatory way. Both worlds right now often work independently, lacking established platforms of common interaction [3]. Thereby, the research knowledge graph enables archivists and researchers to annotate and enrich the graph in order to fit to their needs. Additionally, it facilitates the processing of the heterogeneously structured data from larger hubs in order to increase the coverage of the graph and enrich the data. In this respect, light-weight research knowledge graphs provide several potentials to solve these issues: The creation of standards and hubs, flexible adjustment of data, easy extension of semantic structure and a common search space.

The case of school archives in the field of educational history exemplifies the potential of graph technologies. The main sources about schools range from yearly reports to exam protocols and student magazines to additional information about schooling in earlier times. Besides few sources in state archives, a big amount of these sources is archived in distributed schools in an honorary capacity. Therefore, it is time-consuming to find them and check the relevance. Sharing of the knowledge about these sources in schools is an added value for researchers and archivists.

The article is structured as follows: The following Sect. 2 gives an overview of previous work concerning knowledge graph technologies in research and their capacities for interlinking distributed data silos. Additionally, it discussions participatory approaches to archives. Section 3 provides more detailed information about the case of distributed school archives in the history of education. In Sect. 4 the potentials of research graphs for participatory and interlinked archives are outlined and exemplified in relation to the exemplified case. Section 5 discusses the outcomes and gives an outlook.

2   Related Work

Recently, the usage of knowledge graph technologies for systematized overviews or referatories has reached a new level of visibility. The following Sect. 2.1 outlines these developments. Section 2.2 discusses participatory aspects of archives, which address in more detail the user activities within the graph.

2.1   Knowledge Graphs and Their Potentials in Research

Research knowledge graphs [5] focus mainly on the connection of large amounts of data, especially in the STEM fields. For instance, a realized research knowledge graph, which focuses on life sciences, physics, and engineering [2].

Several potentials are named for research graphs, especially for scientific publications: making research more findable, automatically creating comparison tables, and also inserting one's own insights rapidly into the current ecosystem. There are also potentials to connect research artefacts like datasets and source code using identifiers like DOI. This also enables machine-interpretable semantic content [2]. Other research graphs link research data to information about grants and publications via connecting research data centers and literature information systems [1].

Still, there is the open question whether these large scale infrastructures might work for smaller research communities like in (digital) humanities and social sciences. In these disciplines, earlier approaches to large-scale infrastructure have been described as a dead-end [10]. However, there might be potentials for smaller graphs which can easily connect large hubs using Linked Open Data (LOD). Capacities of both are thus combined, that is, the flexibility and agility of small platforms as well as large amounts of structured and standardized data

One central hub that can be used to interconnect distributed data especially in social sciences and humanities is Wikidata. This crowd-sourced project collects structured data in a lot of different fields and offers a rage of research capacities in humanities [9]. Wikidata also encourages its users to link the data items to other hubs like national libraries, OpenStreetMap and Wikipedia. These potentials has been targeted as well in the context of semantic research environments [7].

2.2   Participatory Archives

Participation of archives was discussed under the term archives 2.0 [3]. This includes decentralised curation, radical user orientation, and contextualisation of records and the entire archival process. Theimer [8] broadens this definition adding among other things the usage of shared standards as well as the iterative development of archives. All of these aspects allow archives to become more user-centered and participatory.

In this context there have been several projects involving citizens and users in the archival process, e.g. publishing letters of detainees from the United States [4] or involving people who share a special cultural heritage, especially of marginalized groups [6]. To broaden participation, such archives can be framed as citizen science projects and encouraging additionally lecturers through providing Open Educational Resources (OER) [11].

3   The Case of Interlinking Distributed School Archives in Germany

The platform school archives (Schularchive)[1] was created to provide a platform for researchers to find relevant sources about schools. It collects references of different sources which are often scattered between different archives at school-level, state-level or nation-level. The project encourages voluntary school archivists to describe their material and researchers to comply with Open Science principles. With this, the location of all sources is made public which lowers the barrier to re-use these sources and re-trace the realized research. In order to allow broad participation, a wiki-based system[2] was choosen.

To grasp the community's requirements adequately, a participatory design approach was used. The project team consists not only of information scientists, but also researchers in educational history and archivists. To balance the needs of all stakeholders, two workshops with external participants were conducted in order to connect archivists, teachers and researchers. These workshops allowed them to articulate their requirements and give feedback. The platform has also been used in two lectures on the history of education. The scripts of the lectures are also provided as open educational resources (OER) in order for lecturers and teachers to reuse them. Additionally, the platform was evaluated in an information science seminar where students from history of education have been asked about their experiences with the platform.

The classes of the ontology encompasses heterogeneous sources (2072 entities), schools (1565 entities), archives (27 entities) and research literature based on these sources (332 entities). Figure 1 shows the structure of the data and their connection of the archival sources to archives and schools. The ontology uses Dublin Core for the description of the literature. Sources, archives and schools are described by own created metadata schema. General information about archives and schools like images or links to Wikipedia is directly provided by Wikidata.

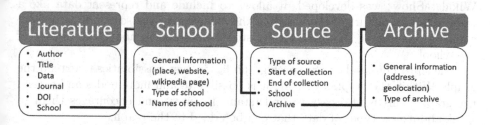

Fig. 1. Local data structure of school archive platform

---

[1] https://schularchive.bbf.dipf.de.

[2] https://www.semantic-mediawiki.org.

4 Potentials of Research Knowledge Graphs for Interlinking Participatory Archives

This chapter outlines four potentials for light-weight research graphs. The potentials are exemplified at the case study: Firstly, creating new hubs within the network of graphs; secondly, easy enrichment of data; thirdly, easy extension of semantic structure and finally, creation of a common interconnected search space within the domain.

The first potential is the simplicity of creating new hubs within the existing structure of data sources for LOD by using graph technologies. This new graph offers the possibility to create and use one's own standards, but to also connect these to existing hubs. Therefore, it is not necessary to find a common standard for everyone dealing with a certain type of data – this would be difficult concerning the different hubs and small archives dealing with data about schools. All hubs can thus retain their standards, while it is still possible to connect all the data sources by using identifiers.

In the case of school archives, there was a new ontology created tailored to the needs of the researchers within the project. It was also important to include historical information about schools, which no other ontology yet provided. The ontology also covers the research need of grasping the school structure of the federated German educational system, which underlies fundamental changes over time.[3] Using LOD allowed linking to other data hubs like Wikidata and the Integrated Authority File (Gemeinsame Normdatei) by German National Library.

A second potential of a research graph for these domains is the easy, flexible interlinking of data. Connecting local data with generally used identifiers and standards like Wikidata ID allows first a tailored connection of local data with external knowledge. A second step then can be the automatic display of external information adjusted within the own local system according to the respective user's needs.

In the school archives project, external data from Wikidata is used to enrich the information about schools. To interlink and display this data, the extension WikidataShow[4] was developed. It allows to include and represent data like a website link, a picture of the school or the inception of the school directly from wikidata, combining this with locally stored information about the history of the school.

The third potential of a research graph lies in easy possibilities to extend the graph: Within the graph structure, it is possible to add more nodes and extend the graph. This is also easy to understand for users and encourages them to think about new types of data that can be added to the graph.

In the school archives project, all users can add new data to the graph. This allows school archivists and researchers to publish metadata about their sources

---

[3] Further detailed description of all metadata can be found at https://schularchive.bbf.dipf.de/index.php/Struktur_Schularchive_Wiki.

[4] https://www.mediawiki.org/wiki/Extension:WikidataShow.

and where to find them. The flexible data structure also allowed to add new entities to the graph like school museums, which also provide relevant sources.

A fourth potential of research knowledge graphs lies in the common search space covering the complete graph. The connection to external sources is made clear by the use of identifiers, and this also allows searches across the entire graph. Thereby, the search interface is improved via external data.

In the school archives project, the research graph allows a better overview of the history of schools and provides one central search interface for all archival sources about schools in Germany. At present, these sources are distributed across schools, archives at state level or archives at national level. Connecting these sources via a research graph allows to search over all these sources and finding them easily. Via the graph, it is not necessary to import all data into our system, therefore all connected platforms can stick to their metadata models.

5 Discussion and Outlook

Light-weight research knowledge graphs are a solution to the lacking connection between distributed archival silos offering a systematic overarching overview of topic related data. While established research knowledge graphs address large infrastructures, mostly unable to meet concrete needs of smaller communities, a light-weight research knowledge graph can address such requirements easier. The potentials of these research knowledge graphs lie in the capacity to define own standards and to create of a hubs in relation to larger infrastructures like Wikidata. Thereby, the data can be adjusted flexible, the semantic structure can be extended and a common search space can be created. Here, a close connection to the Wikidata community can help. Archives should broaden their scope and also curate data from wikidata or at least support the volunteers at such platforms.

The case describes the implementation of such a light-weight research graph for school archives by offering a participatory approach. The approach worked well on the case study, but there are several limitations: One limitation concerns the bottom-up input of data: This might take a long time. The process can be sped up by importing large datasets from state archives, which was done already. This makes the sources of these archives better known to the research community. The project also exemplified that even on Wikidata, data quality gives room for improvements: not all schools in Germany do have a Wikidata page yet and a solid data curation is lacking at a large scale.

In the future, it is planned to include more archives into the platform as well as extending the scope to archives in other German-speaking countries. The case shows that researchers and archivists alike profit from contributing to an open platform. The light-weight research graph can be set up within one small field of research, in our case educational history, but still make use of larger hubs like Wikidata. A new challenge for archives is initiating, moderating, and maintaining this kind of interlinked and structured data. This structured data is likely stored in hubs like Wikidata rather than distributed archives.

Acknowledgements. The project is funded by the Leibniz Competition 2016 entitled "Abiturprüfungs-praxis und Abituraufsatz 1882 bis 1972". The authors would also like to thank DIPF for the funding.

References

1. Aryani, A., et al.: A Research Graph dataset for connecting research data repositories using RD-Switchboard. Sci. Data **5**, 180099 (2018). https://doi.org/10.1038/sdata.2018.99
2. Brack, A., Hoppe, A., Stocker, M., Auer, S., Ewerth, R.: Analysing the requirements for an open research knowledge graph: use cases, quality requirements and construction strategies. arXiv preprint arXiv:2102.06021 (2021)
3. Huvila, I.: Participatory archive: towards decentralised curation, radical user orientation, and broader contextualisation of records management. Arch. Sci. **8**(1), 15–36 (2008). https://doi.org/10.1007/s10502-008-9071-0
4. Lamont, L., et al.: The immigration dilemma; legal, ethical and practical issues in creating a living, growing archive. In: Doucet, A., Isaac, A., Golub, K., Aalberg, T., Jatowt, A. (eds.) TPDL 2019. LNCS, vol. 11799, pp. 177–184. Springer, Cham (2019). https://doi.org/10.1007/978-3-030-30760-8_16
5. Jaradeh, M.Y., et al.: Open research knowledge graph: next generation infrastructure for semantic scholarly knowledge. In: Proceedings of the 10th International Conference on Knowledge Capture, pp. 243–246 (2019). https://doi.org/10.1145/3360901.3364435
6. Liew, C. L., Goulding, A., Nichol, M.: From shoeboxes to shared spaces: participatory cultural heritage via digital platforms. Inf. Commun. Soc. 1–18 (2020). https://doi.org/10.1080/1369118X.2020.1851391
7. Schindler, C., Veja, C., Rittberger, M., Vrandečič, D.: How to teach digital library data to swim into research. In: Proceedings of the 7th International Conference on Semantic Systems, pp. 142–149 (2011). https://doi.org/10.1145/2063518.2063537
8. Theimer, K.: What is the meaning of archives 2.0?. Am. Arch. **74**(1), 58–68 (2011). https://doi.org/10.17723/aarc.74.1.h7tn4m4027407666
9. Thiery, F., Schmidt, S.C., Voß, J.: Wikidata as a research tool for data modelling and integration in the humanities: examples from the German Wikimedia fellow program free knowledge. In: SORSE - International Series of Online Research Software Events (SORSE), Virtual, Zenodo (2021). https://doi.org/10.5281/zenodo.4575128
10. Van Zundert, J.: If you build it, will we come? Large scale digital infrastructures as a dead end for digital humanities. Hist. Soc. Res./Historische Sozialforschung **37**, 165–186 (2012)
11. Veja, C., Hocker, J., Schindler, C., Kollmann, S.: Bridging citizen science and open educational resource. In: Proceedings of the 14th International Symposium on Open Collaboration, pp. 1–12 (2018). https://doi.org/10.1145/3233391.3233539

A Morpheme-Based Paradigm
for the Ontological Analysis of Modern Greek
Derivational Morphology

Nikos Vasilogamvrakis(✉) ⓘD and Michalis Sfakakis ⓘD

Department of Archives, Library Science and Museology, Ionian University, Corfu, Greece
{120vasi,sfakakis}@ionio.gr

Abstract. Morphology is the linguistic field that investigates the minimal meaningful units within words and their interactive processes. In coping with the ontological representation of Modern Greek (MG) derivational morphology the morpheme-based or lexicalist paradigm was tested due to the highly productive concatenative nature of the language. Following this, a specific domain ontological model, the MMoOn was chosen to assess MG morpheme-based morphological representation while being prepared to incorporate other formation approaches when required by the lexical data. Among others, MMoOn was chosen because of its targeted morphological character, its conceptual granularity, the covering of derivational aspects of morphology, its elasticity of embedding different inflectional language data models and its reference to previous frameworks. Accordingly, the model was appropriately extended for the MG language schema and tested towards a very productive MG derivational pattern revealing its high dynamics of representation and usability as a computed lexical inventory that semantically interlinks its entries.

Keywords: Modern Greek morphology · Linguistic linked data · MMoOn · Ontologies · Derivation

1 Introduction

One of the core areas of language analysis constitutes the grammatical structure, most commonly known as morphology, which explores the minimal semantically atoms within lexical formations [1, 34] and is regarded as a separate grammatical sector despite its admitted association with syntax [28, 33]. On the other hand, morphological - or broadly linguistic - analysis has been tremendously boosted, within informational contexts, i.e. by ontological modelling and related technologies [2, 6, 29]. The ontological representation and analysis of language morphology has proven to support multiple language analysis areas such as lexicography [6, 7] theory representation [10, 18], data extraction, text linking and information retrieval [11, 32], NLP and language annotation or various other DH applications [6] either for a given language or at a multilingual level.

In respect of derivational morphological theory in particular, the debate has been mainly expressed by two major word-formation paradigms, usually dependent on the

© Springer Nature Switzerland AG 2022
E. Garoufallou et al. (Eds.): MTSR 2021, CCIS 1537, pp. 389–400, 2022.
https://doi.org/10.1007/978-3-030-98876-0_34

specific language testbed: the morpheme-based or Item and Arrangement (IA) which goes along with the strong lexicalist hypothesis and the word-based or Item and Process (IP) which takes the word as the core morphological unit and introduces specific template rules to operate on derivational processes [1, 12, 21]. Regarding MG in particular, the analysis choice becomes particularly challenging because of its highly synthetic character, the variety and elasticity of structures and also its strong diachronic bond to Ancient Greek (AG) forms.

In view of the ontological representation of MG derivational morphology in this article we test the lexicalist, i.e. the morpheme-based approach to justify common MG derivational patterns and we show how a specific ontological model can contribute to that.

2 Setting the Framework

2.1 Morphological Context and Analysis

The debate between the strong and weak lexicalism is one that also intersects between the identification or not of morphemes as lemmatic entries or differently put as *lexical* "Item and Arrangement" (IA) and *inferential* "Item and Process" (IP) approaches [21, 31]. It has been however shown that whereas in less synthetic languages morphemic arrangement may not overtly rule word formation [1, 12, 21, 34], languages with a large volume of synthesis (e.g. Modern or Ancient Greek, German) at all areas of formation are dependent on morpheme concatenative processes [26–28, 33, 34] with the segmentation of words providing representational solutions [21] which go along with redundant analysis processes[1] [13, 20, 30, 34].

Adopting Lieber's tree analysis model [21] in Fig. 1 we deconstruct the derivational lexemic sequence of *kallierg-ó* 'cultivate' > *kalliergi-tí-s* 'cultivator' > *kalliergit-ik-ós* 'cultivating' from MG after that of *operate* > *operation* > *operational* > *operational-ize* from English. The stems *operation, operational* overlap the lexemic limits because inflection is a poor morphological process in English. By contrast MG has a rich inflectional system spreading over several inflectional affixes allocated to different paradigms, which always precede derivational [34] (thus the inverse provisional properties *precedes* ↔ *follows*). Moreover, stems[2] are a clearly discernible and indispensable structural entity and allomorphic occurrences loom large. It is thus necessary to differentiate between different morph types (stem, affix type) to have a clear and precise view of formation processes. Even in cases where strict concatenative procedures are not meant in formations and a more complex or unpredictable syntax is necessary [21], a morpheme-based approach may provide adequate explanation by representing internal morpho-phonological interactions as in Fig. 1b. This granular morph-segmented process actually unfolds the *Lexical Morphology* viewpoint as it demonstrates the lexical structure of words in derivational levels, from the less to the more productive affixes along with their morphemic alternations [14, 24, 34] (i.e. *kallierg-ó* > *kalliergi-tí-s* > *kalliergi-t-ik-ós).*

---

[1] We refer to redundancy rules of the lexicalist hypothesis.

[2] For MG morphological analysis we will use the stem entity as the minimal lexical atom because a root concept in MG cannot frequently be located or justified synchronically as roots are actually traced back in AG lexical forms [34].

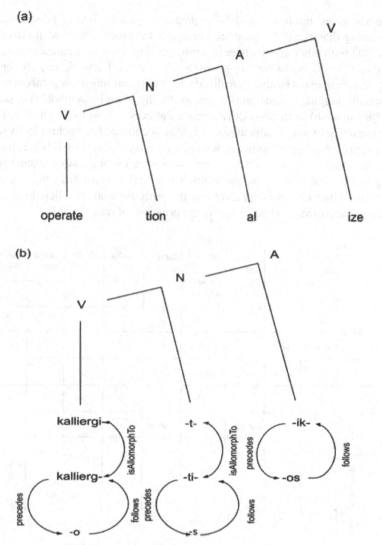

Fig. 1. Morpheme-based analysis between low- (a) and high- (b) synthetic languages

Derivational concatenative patterns are very productive in MG as we elaborate in
Fig. 2. Paradigmatically we use a series of lexical units (stems) that are combined with an
ordered alignment of candidate affixes (prefixes, suffixes) syntagmatically. A vice versa
direction (various bases are attached to an affix) is also technically possible putting the
process into the many-to-many framework. A morpheme-based approach would most
of all contribute to identifying the morphemic units of words (e.g. *xoref-tí-s* > 'dancer'
xoref-t-ik-ós 'dancing', *ek-δó-ti-s* 'publisher' > *ek-δo-t-ik-ós* 'publishing' *or* > *ek-δo-
tí-rio* 'ticket office') even when these may fall into morpho-lexical (e.g. **anti-δrás-ti-s*
'possibly someone who reacts' > *anti-δras-tí-ra-s* 'reactor' or *anti-δras-tí-rio* 'reagent')
or morpho-semantic (*pro-δó-ti-s* 'traitor' is unlikely to come from *δó-ti-s* 'donor or

someone who gives' but from *pro-δíδ-o* > *proδιδ-* ~ *proδo-* 'betray') discrepancies. It is worth noting that except for simplex stems, affixes are combined with affixal stems and as a result with other given affixes in a row, creating normative concatenative affixal strings (e.g. *-t-* + *-ik-* > *-tik-* or *-ti-* + *-rio-* > *-tirio-* etc.). These either poly- or mono-morphemic units may not be always realized within the same morphological environment due to specific language constraints as shown by the ✓ and - symbols (i.e. *pro-δíδ-o* but not *pro-xorév-o) or in cases of [✓]-marked affixes at least one formation is either possible to emerge or not broadly used or might be accounted for diachronically (*δia-δó-ti-s* 'propagator', *δo-tí-ra-s* 'someone who gives', *xoref-tí-rio*, 'possibly a locus where dancing takes place' etc.) or even an intermediary pseudo- or possible lexeme is meant for bridging a derivational lexical gap (*anti-δr-ó* 'react' > *anti-δrás-ti-s > *anti-δras-tí-ra-s*). In the latter case it is apparent that the bridging word parallels its unprefixed equivalent lexeme (*δrás-ti-s*) according to the principle of *analogy* [1].

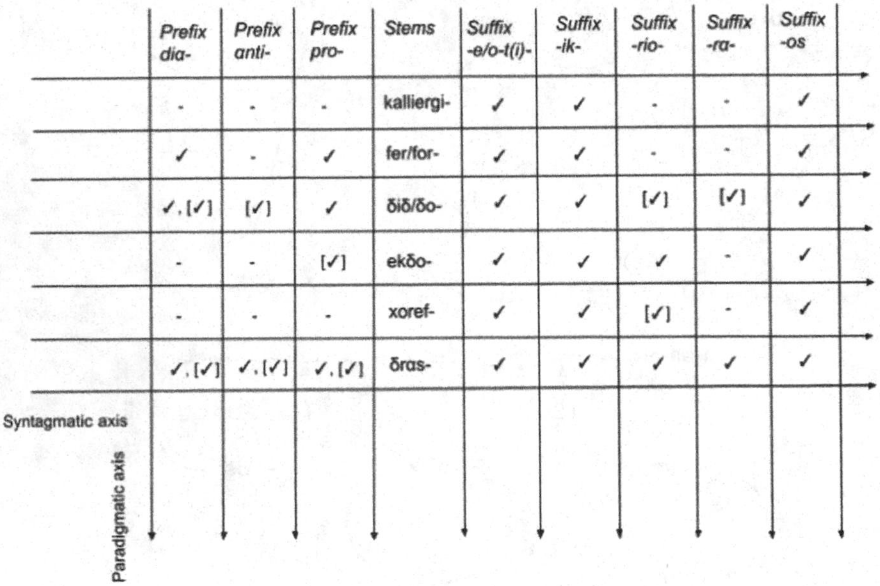

Prefix dia-	Prefix anti-	Prefix pro-	Stems	Suffix -e/o-t(i)-	Suffix -ik-	Suffix -rio-	Suffix -ra-	Suffix -os
-	-	-	kalliergi-	✓	✓	-	-	✓
✓	-	✓	fer/for-	✓	✓	-	-	✓
✓,[✓]	[✓]	✓	δiδ/δo-	✓	✓	[✓]	[✓]	✓
-	-	[✓]	ekδo-	✓	✓	✓	-	✓
-	-	-	xoref-	✓	✓	[✓]	-	✓
✓,[✓]	✓,[✓]	✓,[✓]	δras-	✓	✓	✓	✓	✓

Syntagmatic axis

Paradigmatic axis

Fig. 2. Concatenative patterns of derivatives in MG

Although the high volume of concatenative procedures in MG puts forward the *strong lexicalist hypothesis* [8, 20, 26, 30] we should bear in mind that in certain cases and within specific morphological environments other approaches or procedures may also apply [1, 12, 21, 31].

2.2 Ontological Context

The ontological representation of language in linguistic terms has been systematically explored in recent years at a more holistic level by engaged language communities (i.e. Open Linguistics Working Group) within the Semantic Web paradigm resulting in a series of initiatives and in the creation of the LLOD cloud [6]. For the domain of morphology in particular it has been recently shown that the MMoOn is the only published ontology to date that allows for the documentation of specifically morphological information both at lexical and sublexical levels [2, 15, 17].

Other established lexical or linguistic-driven ontologies such as lemon[3] and Ontolex[4] [15, 23], LexInfo[5] [3, 5], OLiA[6] [4] or GOLD[7] [10], although they handle morphological information to some extent, were not specifically designed for that [17] and are therefore not this analytical or consistent.

Lemon and its successor Ontolex, which have been authorized under the W3C Ontology-Lexica community group, although both cater for morphology representation they do so rather selectively covering most of all inflectional aspects of morphology or compound decomposition. It is interesting that *lemon* provides a separate morphology module[8] that allows to record patterns and rules for agglutinative languages but not assessed as most appropriate to be included in Ontolex-*lemon* [2, 22, 23].

OLiA [4] has rather the intention "to achieve semantic and syntactic interoperability between current linguistic annotation schemes and external terminologies through the use of a reference model" [2] and appears to have no reference to morphological units. GOLD [9] addresses morphosyntax, morphosemantics and phonetic layers with the aim for cross-lingual studies [2] but it does not define strict relationships between morphological constituents at the morph type level (e.g. a stem may also consist of another stem and an affix of derivational nature) and derivational semantics are absent. In general terms those two are more focused on harmonizing linguistic categorical labels within different markup schemes for the multitude of languages [15]. LexInfo comprises a lexical ontology widely used along with Ontolex-*lemon* focusing on morphosyntax [2] and inflectional morphology yet poor at morphological units' analysis while "lacks expressiveness in describing derivational morphology" [15].

Above all the aforementioned models fall short of a targeted morphologically-driven approach catering for more generic linguistic documentation which is questionable either in terms of successfully discerning the semantic limits between different linguistic areas (e.g. morphology and syntax) or defining common inter-linguistic entities. They are also insufficient in depicting derivational semantics or the impact of allomorphy on justifying derivational structures.

By contrast, MMoOn [15, 17, 19] (Fig. 3) "is currently the only existing comprehensive domain ontology for the linguistic area of morphological language data" [15] which:

- Systemizes both grammatical and semantic meaning associated with form at all constituent levels (root, stem, affix, word etc.).

---

[3] https://lemon-model.net/.

[4] https://www.w3.org/2016/05/ontolex/.

[5] https://lexinfo.net/.

[6] http://acoli.cs.uni-frankfurt.de/resources/olia/.

[7] http://linguistics-ontology.org/.

[8] This is separately available as the *Lemon Inflectional Agglutinative Morphology*: http://lemon-model.net/liam.

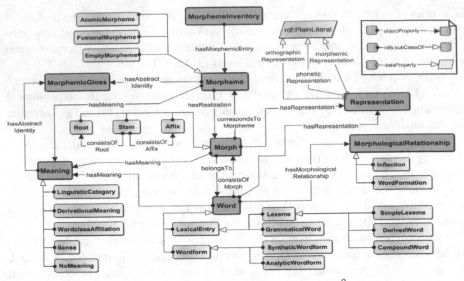

Fig. 3. The MMoOn Core model architecture[9]

- Creates separate concepts for morpheme and its realization, morph.
- Clearly discerns between different morphological aspects (Fig. 3): structure, form, meaning, representation and morphological relationship.
- Defines core language-agnostic morphological concepts and encapsulates their necessary semantics with no interference of other linguistic areas (e.g. syntax etc.) establishing specific relationships between them.
- Covers derivational morphology for the first time both at structural and semantic layer.
- Is granular enough regarding all morphological levels (inflection, derivation, composition), taking a morpheme-based, i.e. a lexicalism approach and at the same time abstract enough encouraging its extension in view of different language modelling instances and promoting the integration of multi-language inventories.
- Draws on the Semantic Web (SW) technology and its rigorous expressiveness (RDF, RDFs, OWL).
- Builds upon and refers to: a) the aforementioned models and vocabularies complying to the SW practice for reusing existing data models while discerning between the ontological and lexical layer and b) prevalent theoretical accounts adopting widely used linguistic encodings (e.g. morphemic glosses) and a familiar to linguists terminology.

The impact of MMoOn on the need for an advanced onto-morphological analysis was also recently reflected in its alignment with Ontolex-*lemon* as a Morphology Module[10] to cover aspects of derivational morphology and the systematic relations between form and meaning [15, 19]. In view of this alignment and because of its still unofficial status we have a further reason why we should choose MMoOn as Ontolex constitutes a well maintained and highly usable LOD ontology.

---

[9] Image taken from https://mmoon.org/mmoon-core-model/.

[10] MMoOn was after all initially motivated so as to cover morphological gaps in Ontolex-*lemon*.

3   Ontological Analysis

3.1   MG Schema Analysis

An important aspect of the model is that it provides specifications on the way it should be further extended, if there is such a need, so that new morphemic inventories are created. The structure of the model consists of three levels:

- The language-independent schema level representing eight classes (orange rectangles in Fig. 3) which are essentially the core skeleton of the model.
- The language-specific schema level where extensions of specified classes required by a given language analysis are allowed and
- The language-specific data level that incorporates the particular data or conceptual instances of that language.

This modular structure succeeds in combining two data levels, the ontological and the lexical, or otherwise the secondary data which are the linguistic concepts of a language and the primary data which are the lexical representations of that language. The three aforementioned levels are interconnected thus achieving the desired consistency and interoperability between different language inventories. In respect of creating new properties (object or data) the model is also flexible, acknowledging the possibility of missing semantics [17].

Considering the multilingual character of the model (i.e. MG representation) and following its extension guidelines as also done by other implementations such as the *OpenGerman*[11] project and the Hebrew morpheme inventory [16] the following choices were made:

- For identifying and referring to the language specific objects the MG namespace *ell_schema* was created, incorporating the ISO 639–3 language code.
- For the language-specific schema file English-based IRIs were adopted for defining MG ontological entities (either classes, instances or relations between them) because a MG label would not be so familiar to get across. At all events MG labels will be given along with the English ones (e.g. the MG label *Μορφή* will be assigned to the equivalent English *Morph*) as well as other descriptive characteristics as data properties.
- For the inventory data file every language lexical instance was named after the MG form adopting the more flexible *Internationalized Resource Identifiers* (IRIs) pattern which incorporates every Unicode alphabet within a URI. In this case a second assigned English translated label will be given when recording lexemes in particular to reach an inter-lingual comprehension level.

Furthermore, as shown in Fig. 4, in conforming to the MMoOn core schema structural conventions for the MG schema extension: a) equivalent MG classes as subclasses of semantically identical classes in the core schema were created (i.e. *ell_schema:Morph*

---

[11] https://github.com/MMoOn-Project/OpenGerman.

class is defined as a subclass of the core *Morph* class) and b) MG classes were appropriately assigned in the *ell_schema* hierarchy (e.g. *ell_schema:Suffix* should be a subclass of the *ell_schema:Affix*).

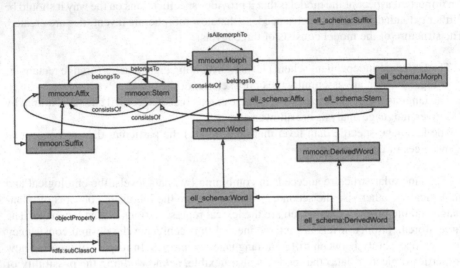

Fig. 4. Alignment of the ell_schema with the core MMoOn

In this way two objectives are met, i.e. the alignment with the core MMoOn and the independent development of the MG language schema, ensuring the MG schema consistency to the model and adhering to its multilingual and aggregating nature.

3.2 MG Onto-Lexical Analysis

In Fig. 5 we analyze ontologically the structural units participating in concatenative morphology choosing a common MG derivational pattern, i.e. *-ti-s > t-ik-os* applied to two different lexical bases: *kalliergi- (∼ kallierg-)* and *xoref- (∼ xorev-)*. We accordingly represent those in the ontology by just using the classes *mmoon:Word* and *mmoon:Morph* (and their subclasses) in binary formation structures [13, 30, 34] and leveraging the inverse *consistsOf ↔ belongsTo* object properties (OP) as follows:

- A lexeme (either simple or derived word), i.e. καλλιεργητής is analyzed into a stem (simplex or affixal), i.e. καλλιεργητη- and an inflectional affix, i.e. -ς.
- An affixal (complex) stem, i.e. καλλιεργητη- is analyzed into a stem (simplex or affixal), i.e. καλλιεργη- and a derivational affix, i.e. -τη-.

In this way morphological constituents are represented at every level of formation (cf. Lexical Morphology theory) while the same instances of affixes have the role of attaching "satellites" to lexical bases (-ικ- to καλλιεργητ- and χορευτ-, -ς to καλλιεργητη- and χορευτη- and -ος το καλλιεργητικ- and χορευτικ-). It is also significant that the OP *isAllomprhTo* allows for the interconnection of allomorphs belonging to the same morpheme and thus for a thorough justification of the derived forms (the affixal stem καλλιεργητικ- is derived from the allomorph stem καλλιεργητ- ∼ καλλιεργητη- - which in turn is analyzed into the affixal stem καλλιεργη- and the allomorph affixal instance -τ- ∼ -τη- respectively - and the affix -ικ-). In a similar way to these lexicalizations are analyzed all examples of Fig. 2.

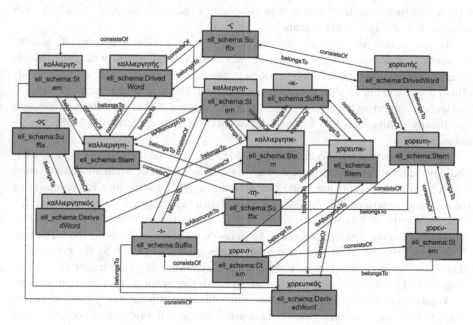

Fig. 5. MMoOn ell_schema onto-lexical analysis and representation

Although it is assumed that structures become non-transparent from one level to another according to *Lexical Morphology* [14, 24, 34] for morphological analysis reasons we can easily gain access to all levels of formation in the ontology if we select the *Stem* nodes from the path starting from a *Word* or *Stem* node and walking through using the property *consistsOf* or *belongsTo* as appropriate (i.e. by exploiting the *transitive closure* of *Word* or *Stem*). As an example, let us consider the instance of the *ell_schema:DerivedWord* χορευτής: in order to gain access to its formation the transitive closure of χορευτής (using the *consistsOf* property and selecting the *Stem* nodes) is constructed as follows: χορευτής – *consistsOf* – χορευτη – *consistsOf* – χορευ. In a similar way, the verbal stem χορευ- (*xoref*- from the verb *xorév-o*) which stands at level 1 is easily spotted at all sequential levels as in χορευ-τη- > χορευ-τή-s > χορευ-τικ- > χορευ-τικός. The same applies to the other derived stems (e.g. χορευτη-) or to affixes alone (-τη-, -ικ- etc.).

N. Vasilogamvrakis and M. Sfakakis

4 Discussion and Conclusions

So far we have tested some MG onto-derivational structures towards the morpheme-based or lexicalist paradigm applying strict concatenative formation procedures as these are very productive in the language. More specifically, we have preliminarily assessed an ontological model, MMoOn, which within the Semantic Web framework stands out as the most appropriate and fine grained among others. Except the fact that it is the only model focused solely on language morphology the recent alignment with Ontolex ensures its usability and maintenance.

To start testing MG derivational morphology we have adopted appropriate schema conventions and extended the respective MG classes in alignment with the MMoOn core according to the model specifications to ensure consistency while simultaneously allowed the schema to develop as an independent MG conceptual network. This is particularly important because in certain cases the schema is likely to introduce concepts specifically pertinent to MG morphology without necessarily having a MMoOn core counterpart.

On its assessment the model has appeared to suit well the lexicalist or Lexical Morphology theory serving simultaneously as a morphological lexicon that allocates an entry for each different morpheme while incorporating syntactic semantics for re-analyzing the resulting structures [25, 30, 34]. We have shown that morphological units are inter-linked not only in part-whole relations but also with their allomorph instances thus bridging sequential discrepancies (e.g. *kallierg-* ~ *kalliergi-* > *kalliergi-tí-s*). The high dynamics of the model in structural analysis has been also shown by the potential of identifying bridging morphemic units among different levels of formation (*xorév-o* > *xoref-* > *xoref-tí-s* > *xoreft-* > *xoreft-ik-ós*) towards the creation of lexical families sets.

What may also interestingly come up is that this approach can easily explain derived words that have no true precedents but are just dependent on bridging or possible words as in *antiδró* > **antiδrástis* > *antiδrastíras*. Of course in this case analogy plays its role (*δrástis* > **antiδrástis*) but it would be a plus point if a model stored hidden entries (i.e. no true lexical entries) that would serve as connecting rings in formation concatenative chains.

On the other hand, MG lexical structures does not necessarily depend solely on attaching affixes to lexical bases or vice versa but also on other procedures such as conversion, morpho-phonological phenomena (ablaut, synizesis etc.), reanalysis etc. [21] which is questionable whether they can be explained in the same way or other approaches should be also considered. Inasmuch as other procedures are involved in MG derivation we are due to explore them trying to describe MG derivational intricacies with the intention to extend and optimize the model when and where necessary.

It has been clear so far that an ontological approach of MG derivational morphology goes well with the morpheme-based paradigm due to the excessively synthetic and con-catenative nature of the language. On the other hand, it is also probable that our modelling will be coupled with other paradigms for covering different formation modes. We have shown that the MMoOn model fits well the lexicalist approach by appropriately extend-ing its core structural classes and testing MG indicative lexical patterns and can serve as a first-hand computed lexical tool. MMoOn was chosen because of its targeted mor-phological character, its conceptual granularity, the covering of aspects of derivational morphology, its elasticity of embedding different inflectional language data models and its reference to previous frameworks. This preliminary article is part of a PhD research on the ontological approach of MG morphology and therefore we are due to investigate more specialized issues thereof in the near future.

Acknowledgements. This research was supported by the project: "Activities of the Laboratory on Digital Libraries and Electronic Publishing of the Department of Archives, Library Science and Museology".

References

1. Booij, G.: The Grammar of Words: An Introduction to Linguistic Morphology. Oxford University Press (2012)
2. Bosque-Gil, J., et al.: Models to represent linguistic linked data. Nat. Lang. Eng. **24**(6), 811–859 (2018). https://doi.org/10.1017/S1351324918000347
3. Buitelaar, P., Cimiano, P., Haase, P., Sintek, M.: Towards linguistically grounded ontologies. In: Aroyo, L., et al. (eds.) ESWC 2009. LNCS, vol. 5554, pp. 111–125. Springer, Heidelberg (2009). https://doi.org/10.1007/978-3-642-02121-3_12
4. Chiarcos, C., Sukhareva, M.: OLiA – ontologies of linguistic annotation. SW **6**(4), 379–386 (2015). https://doi.org/10.3233/SW-140167
5. Cimiano, P., et al.: LexInfo: a declarative model for the Lexicon-ontology interface. J. Web Seman. **9**(1), 29–51 (2011). https://doi.org/10.1016/j.websem.2010.11.001
6. Cimiano, P., et al.: Linguistic Linked Data: Representation, Generation and Applications. Springe, Cham (2020). https://doi.org/10.1007/978-3-030-30225-2
7. Declerck, T. et al.: Using OntoLex-Lemon for representing and interlinking German multi-word expressions in OdeNet and MMORPH. In: Proceedings of the Joint Workshop on Multi-word Expressions and WordNet (MWE-WN 2019), pp. 22–29. Association for Computational Linguistics, Florence, Italy (2019). https://doi.org/10.18653/v1/W19-5104
8. Di Sciullo, A.M., Williams, E.: On the Definition of the Word. MIT Press, Cambridge, Mass (1987)
9. Farrar, S., Langendoen, D.: A linguistic ontology for the semantic web. Glot Int. **7**, 97–100 (2003)
10. Farrar, S., Langendoen, D.T.: An OWL-DL implementation of gold. In: Witt, A., Metzing, D. (eds.) Linguistic Modeling of Information and Markup Languages: Contributions to Language Technology, pp. 45–66 Springer, Dordrecht (2010). https://doi.org/10.1007/978-90-481-333 1-4_3
11. Ganino, G., et al.: Ontology population for open-source intelligence: a GATE-based solution. Softw.: Pract. Exp. **48**(12), 2302–2330 (2018). https://doi.org/10.1002/spe.2640
12. Haspelmath, M., Sims, A.: Understanding morphology. Routledge (2013)
13. Jackendoff, R.: Morphological and semantic regularities in the Lexicon. Linguist. Inquiry **7**, 89–150 (1975)
14. Kiparsky, P.: Lexical Morphology and Phonology (1982)
15. Klimek, B., et al.: Challenges for the representation of morphology in ontology Lexicons. In: Kosem, I., et al. (eds.) Electronic Lexicography in the 21st Century. Proceedings of the eLex 2019 Conference: Smart Lexicography, pp. 570–591 (2019). https://elex.link/elex2019/wp-content/uploads/2019/09/eLex_2019_33.pdf
16. Klimek, B., et al.: Creating linked data morphological language resources with MMoOn the hebrew morpheme inventory. Presented at the the the 10th edition of the Language Resources and Evaluation Conference, 23–28 May 2016, lovenia, Portorož (2016)

17. Klimek, B., et al.: MMoOn core - the multilingual morpheme ontology. Seman. Web **4**, 1–30 (2020). http://www.semantic-web-journal.net/system/files/swj2549.pdf
18. Klimek, B., McCrae, J.P., Lehmann, C., Chiarcos, C., Hellmann, S.: OnLiT: an ontology for linguistic terminology. In: Gracia, J., Bond, F., McCrae, J.P., Buitelaar, P., Chiarcos, C., Hellmann, S. (eds.) LDK 2017. LNCS (LNAI), vol. 10318, pp. 42–57. Springer, Cham (2017). https://doi.org/10.1007/978-3-319-59888-8_4
19. Klimek, B.: Proposing an OntoLex - MMoOn alignment: towards an interconnection of two linguistic domain models. In: LDK Workshops 2017, p. 16 (2017)
20. Lieber, R.: On the Organization of the Lexicon. MIT (1980)
21. Lieber, R.: Theoretical issues in word formation. In: Audring, J., Masini, F. (eds.) The Oxford Handbook of Morphological Theory. pp. 33–55 Oxford University Press (2018). https://doi.org/10.1093/oxfordhb/9780199668984.013.3
22. McCrae, J.P., et al.: The lemon cookbook. Technical report (2010)
23. McCrae, J.P., et al.: The OntoLex-Lemon model: development and applications. In: Kosem, I., et al. (eds.) Electronic Lexicography in the 21st century: Proceedings of eLex 2017 Conference : Lexicography from Scratch, pp. 587–597 (2017)
24. Mohanan, K.P.: The Theory of Lexical Phonology. Studies in Natural Language and Linguistic Theory. D. Reidel, Dordrecht (1986)
25. O'Neill, P.: Lexicalism, the principle of morphology-free syntax and the principle of syntax-free morphology. In: Hippisley, A., Stump, G. (eds.) The Cambridge Handbook of Morphology, pp. 237–271. Cambridge University Press, Cambridge (2016)
26. Ralli, A.: Eléments de la Morphologie du Grec Moderne: La Structure de Verbe. University of Montreal (1988)
27. Ralli, A.: IE, Hellenic: Modern Greek. Oxford University Press (2011). https://doi.org/10.1093/oxfordhb/9780199695720.013.0024
28. Ralli, A.: Morphology in Greek linguistics: a state-of-the art. J. Greek Linguist. **4**, 77–130 (2003)
29. Schalley, A.C.: Ontologies and ontological methods in linguistics. Lang. Linguist. Compass **13**(11), e12356 (2019). https://doi.org/10.1111/lnc3.12356
30. Selkirk, E.: The Syntax of Words. MIT Press, Cambridge (1982)
31. Spencer, A.: Morphology. In: The Handbook of Linguistics, pp. 211–233. Wiley (2017). https://doi.org/10.1002/9781119072256.ch11
32. Università Cattolica del Sacro Cuore: LiLa: Linking Latin. https://lila-erc.eu/. Accessed 25 May 2021
33. Ράλλη, Α.: Η μορφολογία ως αυτόνομο τμήμα της γραμματικής. In: Μόζερ, Α. (ed.) Γλώσσης Χάριν. Τόμος αφιερωμένος από τον Τομέα Γλωσσολογίας στον καθηγητή Γεώργιο Μπαμπινιώτη. pp. 141–156 Ελληνικά Γράμματα (2008)
34. Ράλλη, Α.: Μορφολογία. Εκδόσεις Πατάκη, Αθήνα (2005)

Author Index

Printed in the United States
by Baker & Taylor Publisher Services